T0180951

Communications in Computer and Information Science 1526

More information about this series at https://link.springer.com/bookseries/7899

Vladimir Jordan · Ilya Tarasov ·
Vladimir Faerman (Eds.)

High-Performance Computing Systems and Technologies in Scientific Research, Automation of Control and Production

11th International Conference, HPCST 2021
Barnaul, Russia, May 21–22, 2021
Revised Selected Papers

 Springer

Editors
Vladimir Jordan ⓘ
Altai State University
Barnaul, Russia

Ilya Tarasov ⓘ
MIREA - Russian Technological University
Moscow, Russia

Vladimir Faerman ⓘ
Tomsk State University of Control Systems
and Radioelectronics
Tomsk, Russia

ISSN 1865-0929 ISSN 1865-0937 (electronic)
Communications in Computer and Information Science
ISBN 978-3-030-94140-6 ISBN 978-3-030-94141-3 (eBook)
https://doi.org/10.1007/978-3-030-94141-3

This Springer imprint is published by the registered company Springer Nature Switzerland AG
The registered company address is: Gewerbestrasse 11, 6330 Cham, Switzerland

Preface

The 11th International Conference on High-Performance Computing Systems and Technologies in Scientific Research, Automation of Control and Production (HPCST 2021) took place at the Altai State University during May 21–22, 2021. Altai State University (AltSU) is located in the center of Barnaul city—the capital of the Altai region in the southwestern part of Siberia.

HPCST is a regular scientific meeting that has been held annually since 2011. It attracts specialists in the various fields of modern computer and information science, as well as their applications in the automation of control and production, mathematical modeling, and computer simulation of processes and phenomena in natural sciences through high-performance computing.

The goal of the conference is to present state-of-art approaches and methods for solving contemporary scientific problems and to exchange the latest research results obtained by scientists from both universities and research institutions. All the reported results are valuable contributions to the field of applied information and computer science.

Sessions of the conference are devoted to the relevant scientific topics:

- architecture and design features of the high-performance computing systems;
- digital signal processors (DSP) and their applications;
- IP-cores for field-programmable gate array (FPGA);
- technologies for distributed computing using multiprocessors;
- GRID-technologies and cloud computing and services;
- high-performance and multi-scale predictive computer simulation; and
- control automation and mechatronics.

The conference was first introduced at the international level back in 2017 since more than 100 researchers from Russia, China, Ukraine, Kazakhstan, Kyrgyzstan, Uzbekistan, and Tajikistan participated in past events. The average number of participants in a single year was about 60 for a long time.

This year, the geography of countries, cities, and research organizations expanded, with new researchers who had not previously participated in the conference attending. For example, foreign participants were added to the conference from Brazil (from far abroad), as well as from neighboring countries—Kazakhstan and Uzbekistan. New participants from Russia were representatives of state universities from such cities as Moscow, St. Petersburg, Sevastopol, Chelyabinsk, Tomsk, and Novosibirsk.

Due to the global COVID-19 pandemic, travel restrictions were still in place in Russia, so the committee decided to hold the conference in a semi-virtual format. The local audience from Barnaul, its suburbs, and surrounding cities participated in person. At the same time, nonresidents participated remotely via Zoom. Specifically for the purpose, several rooms in the AltSU main building were supplied with the equipment for videoconferencing.

The conference was attended virtually or in person by 142 scholars with 82 qualified reports. Compared to the previous conference (HPCST 2020), the total number of participants increased by 30, and the number of presented papers increased from 46 to 82. The most significant reported studies were thoroughly reviewed and included in these post-proceedings. The vast majority of the conference papers (52 papers) that were not selected by the committee for this volume were published as regular proceedings.

Only 32 full papers featuring original studies in the field of computing, mathematical simulation, and control science are included in this volume. The papers cover the following topics:

- hardware for high-performance computing and signal processing;
- information technologies and computer simulation of physical phenomena;
- computing technologies in discrete mathematics and decision making;
- information and computing technologies in automation and control science; and
- computing technologies in information security applications.

To select the best papers among those presented at the conference the following procedure was applied:

1. Session chairs prepared a shortlist of the most significant original reports, which had a clear potential to be extended to full-paper format.
2. The editorial board, comprised of the session chairs and corresponding editor, made a list of 30 items at most.
3. Authors of the selected manuscripts then were contacted and asked to extend their papers and resubmit them for review.

To promote the conference among the professional community in Russia, Kazakhstan, and Uzbekistan, the editorial board distributed dozens of personal invitations to our collaborators and reviewers to encourage these distinguished academics to contribute to the volume. Authors of all guest papers were invited to report them at the next event as keynote speakers.

Every paper without any exceptions was reviewed by at least three experts. In addition to a routine plagiarism check with iThenticate.com, we applied another check with Antiplagiat.ru. The goal was to detect and decline the papers that were already published in Russian. A single-blind review method was applied. The review criteria were as follows:

- technical content,
- originality,
- clarity,
- significance,
- presentation style, and
- ethics.

Among the 32 papers in this volume, 28 papers were selected from the 82 accepted reports. The other four papers were selected from the six manuscripts submitted by the invited authors. Therefore, the acceptance rate is a little less than 40%.

The organizing committee would like to express our sincere appreciation for the organizational support to the administration of Altai State University and the staff of the Institute of Digital Technologies, Electronics and Physics of Altai State University. Only the outstanding effort of the technical staff made the conference possible in the time of travel restrictions.

The editors would like to express their deep gratitude to the Springer editorial team for the opportunity to publish the best papers as post-proceedings and for their great work on this volume.

October 2021

Vladimir Jordan
Ilya Tarasov
Vladimir Faerman

Organization

General Chair

Vladimir Jordan   Altai State University, Russia

Program Committee Chairs

Ella Shurina   Novosibirsk State Technical University, Russia
Ilya Tarasov   Russian Technological University, Russia
Nikolay Filimonov   V.A. Trapeznikov Institute of Control Sciences, RAS, Russia

Organizing Committee

Vasiliy Belozerskih   Altai State University, Russia
Vladimir Faerman   Tomsk State University of Control Systems and Radioelectronics, Russia
Alexander Kalachev   Altai State University, Russia
Vladimir Pashnev   Altai State University, Russia
Viktor Sedalischev   Altai State University, Russia
Yana Sergeeva   Altai State University, Russia
Igor Shmakov   Altai State University, Russia
Petr Ulanov   Altai State University, Russia

Program Committee

Viktor Abanin   Biysk Technological Institute, Russia
Darya Alontseva   Serikbayev East Kazakhstan Technical University, Kazakhstan
Valeriy Avramchuk   Tomsk State University of Control Systems and Radioelectronics, Russia
Sergey Beznosyuk   Altai State University, Russia
Alexander Filimonov   MIREA - Russian Technological University, Russia
Pavel Gulyaev   Yugra State University, Russia
Ishembek Kadyrov   Kyrgyz National Agrarian University, Kyrgyzstan
Alexander Kalachev   Altai State University, Russia
Vladimir Khmelev   Polzunov Altai State Technical University, Russia

Shavkat Fazilov	Research Institute for the Development of Digital Technologies and Artificial Intelligence, Uzbekistan
Vladimir Kosarev	Khristianovich Institute of Theoretical and Applied Mechanics, SB RAS, Russia
Nomaz Mirzaev	Tashkent University of Information Technologies, Uzbekistan
Lyudmilla Kveglis	Amanzholov East Kazakhstan State University, Kazakhstan
Roman Mescheryakov	V.A. Trapeznikov Institute of Control Sciences, RAS, Russia
Aleksey Nikitin	Altai State University, Russia
Viktor Polyakov	Altai State University, Russia
Leonid Mikhailov	Al-Farabi Kazakh National University, Kazakhstan
Oleg Prikhodko	Al-Farabi Kazakh National University, Kazakhstan
Sergey Pronin	Polzunov Altai State Technical University, Russia
Alisher Saliev	Kyrgyz Technical University, Kyrgyzstan
Viktor Sedalischev	Altai State University, Russia
Vitaliy Titov	Southwest State University, Russia
Pedro Filipe do Prado	Federal University of Espirito Santo, Brazil
Aleksey Yakunin	Polzunov Altai State Technical University, Russia

External Reviewers

Olga Berestneva	Tomsk Polytechnic University, Russia
Fedor Garaschenko	Kyiv National University, Ukraine
Bruno Pissinato	Methodist University of Piracicaba, Brazil
Anatoliy Gulay	Belarus National Technical University, Belarus
Gambar Guluev	Institute of Control Systems of National Academy of Sciences of Azerbajan, Azerbajan
Semyon Kantor	Polzunov Altai State Technical University, Russia
Bibigul Koshoeva	Kyrgyz Technical University, Kyrgyzstan
Eugeniy Kostuchenko	Tomsk State University of Control Systems and Radioelectronics, Russia
Andrey Kutyshkin	Yugra State University, Russia
Elena Luneva	Tomsk Polytechnic University, Russia
Narzillo Mamatov	Research Institute for the Development of Digital Technologies and Artificial Intelligence, Uzbekistan
Oleg Stukach	Higher School of Economics – Moscow Institute of Electronics and Mathematics, Russia

Andrey Malchukov	Tomsk State University of Control Systems and Radioelectronics, Russia
Leonid Mikhaylov	Al-Farabi Kazakh National University, Kazakhstan
Sobirjon Radjabov	Research Institute for the Development of Digital Technologies and Artificial Intelligence, Uzbekistan
Evgeniy Mytsko	Tomsk Polytechnic University, Russia
Stepan Nebaba	Tomsk Polytechnic University, Russia
Normakhmad Ravshanov	Research Institute for the Development of Digital Technologies and Artificial Intelligence, Uzbekistan
Vladislav Kukartsev	Siberian Federal University, Russia
Andrey Russkov	Yandex, Russia
Vadim Tynchenko	Siberian Federal University, Russia
Rasul Mamadlyev	Tyumen Industrial University, Russia
Antonina Karlina	Moscow State University of Civil Engineering, Russia

Contents

**Information and Computing Technologies in Automation and Control
Science**

Hardware for High-Performance Computing and Signal Processing

Modeling of Processor Datapaths with VLIW Architecture at the System Level

Ilya Tarasov$^{(\boxtimes)}$ (iD), Larisa Kazantseva, and Sofia Daeva

MIREA – Russian Technological University, Vernadsky Avenue 78, 119454 Moscow, Russia
tarasov_i@mirea.ru

Abstract. The article discusses an approach to designing a datapath for a processor with a VLIW architecture. A feature of this architecture is the ability to implement an arithmetic-logic device with a complex structure, which leads to an explosive growth of possible options. The choice of the best option is complicated by conflicting requirements for the functionality and characteristics of the topological implementation of the processor. The article discusses the application of modeling at the transaction level to assess the characteristics of the processor when performing model tasks, followed by a description of the resulting solution at the RTL level. To describe the structure of the arithmetic-logical unit, a modification of the known description is proposed with the help of four parameters characterizing the number of operations, operands and latency in the datapath. The proposed modification makes it possible to describe asymmetric datapaths as part of an arithmetic-logic device with a complex structure. A consistent description of the high-level programming model and the register transfer layer allows for reduced design time and allows for joint design of hardware and support tools.

Keywords: Processor · VLSI · Computational system · Compilation · Modelling

1 Introduction

In the current situation, the development of new processor architectures seems to be a promising direction. In particular, in [1, 2] it is noted that the development of processors consistently received the main impetus from the CISC and RISC architectures, and then from multi-core and specialized architectures. The transition to multicore systems made it possible to expand the effect of Moore's empirical law on the regular doubling of processor performance, but the associated Dennard's law of scaling [3] has practically ceased to be relevant. In such situation, the improvement of technological indicators ceases to be the main direction of the evolution of processors, being replaced by an increase in the number of processor cores and their specialization.

Amdahl's Law [4] is a fundamental obstacle to unlimited performance scaling by increasing the number of processor cores. Elimination of the negative impact of this limitation cannot be carried out speculatively, since the possibility of running parallel computations depends entirely on the features of the algorithms being executed.

© Springer Nature Switzerland AG 2022
V. Jordan et al. (Eds.): HPCST 2021, CCIS 1526, pp. 3–12, 2022.
https://doi.org/10.1007/978-3-030-94141-3_1

Therefore, the design of processors that allow parallel computations at any levels of the hierarchy should be based on the analysis of the target group of algorithms.

When identifying algorithms that allow parallel computations, it becomes possible to combine two main approaches to such computations: data level parallelism and instruction level parallelism. The obvious solution is symmetric parallelism, where the individual datapaths are identical. A possible improvement could be the implementation of an asymmetric structure of the data processing path, which would take into account the peculiarities of data processing in the preferred areas of application of the developed processor. The practical steps of designing such structure imply the possibility of rapid prototyping of the datapath with verification of its main characteristics when implementing typical algorithms in the intended field of application. It is desirable to perform this verification using high-level modeling tools that are abstracted from implementation details. The use of hardware description languages at the level of register transmissions is complicated by the need for a separate development of a synthesized description of the datapath and a set of test sequences for its simulation.

2   Architectural Description of the VLIW Processor Datapath

Due to the increasing importance of joint optimization of software and hardware, the design route of the datapath must be adjusted to avoid chaotical modification of the datapath circuit. For this, formal methods of describing complex datapaths should be used. For example, in [5], a unified description of a computing node with four parameters (I, O, D, S) is considered, where.

- I is the number of instructions executed per cycle;
- O is the number of operations determined by the instruction;
- D is the number of operands (pairs of operands) related to operations;
- S is the factor of pipelining.

For SIMD architectures $D > 1$, and for MIMD (Multiple Instruction, Multiple Data) also $I > 1, D > 1$. For massive parallelism, one can additionally consider the parallelism of data processing paths at the level of an individual computational node, which allows you to apply the architectural description of the node in the form of a quartet (R, $<O>$, $<D>$, $<S>$), where:

R is the number of independently calculated results;
$<O>$ is a vector of the number of operations performed by the instruction for each of the datapaths;
$<D>$ is a vector of the number of operands (pairs of operands) for each of the datapaths;
$<S>$ is the pipelining vector for each of the datapaths.

This approach implies replacing the parameters O, D, S with vectors describing the characteristics of the corresponding data processing paths that form R outputs.

The following options for a single datapath can be considered as examples. Figure 1 shows a chain of computing devices using 2 pairs of operands and 3 operations (O = 3, D = 2). Figure 2 shows an example of a datapath using pipelining (S = 1). In this case, latency is formed in the datapath, which must be taken into account in the instrumental software or in the hardware formation of waiting cycles in the processor. If we consider the shown examples as separate outputs of the combined ALU processor, its architectural description will look like (2, <3, 3>, <2, 2>, <0, 1>). This description does not consider possible variations in the composition of computing nodes shown as ALU1, ALU2, ALU3, although their functionality may differ both within one path and for individual paths.

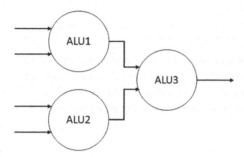

Fig. 1. Datapath with multiple operations on two data pairs.

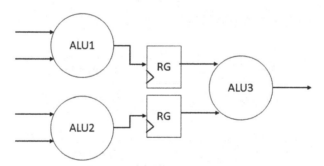

Fig. 2. Datapath with pipelining.

For a VLIW processor, the datapaths used may not be identical. For example, one or more paths can be used to organize work with memory, generating an address and data for each of the used memory access interfaces. For example, the following snippet contains operations that can be performed in parallel:

Listing 1. An example of converting pseudocode into a set of VLIW processor transactions.

```
// In C-style high-level language

  for (i = 0; i < 10; i++)  x[i] = 0;

  // In pseudo code:

          i = 0;
  loop :  x[i] = 0;
          i = i + 1;
          cmp i, 10
          jless loop

  // in VLIW:
          i = 0;
  loop :  x[i] = 0; i = i + 1; cmpjless loop
```

The actions shown in Listing 1 can be performed in an ALU, which contains three compute nodes that implement the corresponding operations in a loop. Figure 3 shows a datapath that allows the body of a loop to be executed in one clock cycle. The branch operation is not shown, since it relates to the processor control flow and not to the data processing path.

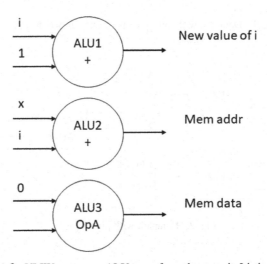

Fig. 3. VLIW processor ALU to perform the steps in Listing 1.

The considered example is a fragmentary solution to the problem, since the resulting ALU structure is essentially intended to speed up the only considered example. Repetition of this technique will lead to the receipt of ALU structures, which, possibly, will differ from that shown in Fig. 3. Therefore, it is required to consider an ALU design route that would be based on a formalized design methodology and would be suitable for creating ALUs specialized for a given corpus of model problems.

3   Design Flow for Hardware and Software Co-design

The increasing complexity of the datapath and the ability to combine combinations of operands, operations and interconnection of computational nodes open up overwhelming opportunities for building datapaths, which ultimately leads to an explosive increase in design complexity. The implementation of seemingly obvious architectures in practice can lead to negative effects.

1. Implementation of identical datapaths will lead to a proportional increase in ALU resources; however, for the algorithms being executed, it can lead to downtime situations of individual paths due to existing data dependencies.
2. Implementation of hardware support for program fragments can lead to local improvements in the quality of the code; however, such fragments may not be detected by compilers later, which will not allow the positive effect of adding computational nodes to appear.
3. The asymmetric architecture of individual paths can lead to uneven propagation delay, which will lead to limiting the processor clock frequency to the worst implemented paths. To equalize latency, pipelining should be used based on latency analysis and critical chain pipelining.

Scenarios 1 and 2 require the use of preliminary modeling of target algorithms with the construction of a tree of operations, while scenario 3 requires studying the characteristics of the topological basis. Thus, the improvement of the characteristics of a processor using the VLIW architecture in the data processing path should be based on a joint analysis of hardware and software, which also includes studies of the characteristics of hardware when implemented in a specific technological basis. Such approaches are actively used in the design of processors, including those with the VLIW architecture. For example, a multi-objective Genetic Algorithm (GA) is used [6] in an attempt to achieve complex optimality criteria that take into account both processor performance and area. An FPGA with the corresponding design route are used as a prototyping tool [7]. Approaches and special tools to creating software for processors are also noted [8, 9]. In some cases, this process is significantly complex because of using traditional approaches to compiler development [10].

The suggested datapath design flow is as follows:

1. the choice of an architecture model in space (R, <O>, <D>, <S>);
2. compilation of pseudocode for a set of model tasks, identification of the most common sequences of operations and creation of computational nodes for their single-cycle execution, checking the result using an emulator and creating processor element nodes at the level of register transfers (i.e., RTL descriptions);
3. checking the synthesizability of the resulting circuit and performing functional verification at the system level;
4. the assessment of the topological implementation in the selected technological basis.

4 Meta Description for a Cross-Compiler and Emulator

As a practical approach to design, you can suggest the use of meta-descriptions. For the same design path based on hardware description languages, it is possible to use parameterized descriptions using constants describing individual fields, but the transaction level model in general cannot use HDL parameters automatically. Therefore, a meta-description of the datapath should be used, i.e. a higher-level description that generates both information for building a cross-assembler and parameters for an HDL description of the datapath. The interaction of metadescription with other design tools is shown in Fig. 4.

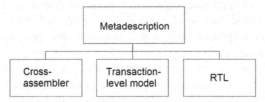

Fig. 4. Interaction of datapath metadescription, transaction level model and cross-assembler in the processor modeling route with VLIW architecture.

Listing 2 shows a cross-assembler implementation using a regular grammar. A well-known solution to this class is the Forth programming language, which uses a regular grammar in combination with a stacked computational model and concatenative compilation. This allows for the rapid development of problem-oriented languages based on it. The example in Listing 2 is implemented using a Forth virtual machine that was developed independently for Qt and Object Pascal environments.

The listing shows that the definition of the so-called. creating definitions using the CREATE DOES > construct allows you to describe assembler commands within a regular grammar (according to Chomsky's classification). This approach makes individual descriptions independent and does not require the use of mutually agreed descriptions, for example, BNF.

For the VLIW architecture, the description of commands has an important specificity - the presence of several data outputs, which in general can be independent. Therefore, to describe the VLIW within the framework of a regular grammar, one should pay attention to the independent description of the operation of the corresponding fragments of the datapath, which, in accordance with the chosen architecture (R, < O >, < D >, < S >), can have a different organization, a set of operations performed, types of operands, etc. A cross-assembler code snippet showing the node names for channels A and B is shown in Listing 3.

Listing 2. An example of a Forth cross-assembler description for a specialized processor.

```
65536 CONSTANT MAXCODE
16384 CONSTANT MAXDATA
CREATE CODE[] MAXCODE ALLOT
CREATE DATA[] MAXDATA CELLS ALLOT
0 VALUE CODE^
0 VALUE DATA^

: TC,
  CODE[] CODE^ + C!
  CODE^ 1 + TO CODE^
;

0 CONSTANT cmdNOP

: CMD CREATE , DOES> @ TC, ;
: CMD2 CREATE , DOES> cmdNOP TC, @ TC, ;

TARGET DEFINITIONS

0 CMD NOP
1 CMD NOT
2 CMD2 @
3 CMD SHL
4 CMD SHR
5 CMD SHRA
6 CMD2 INPORT
7 CMD SWAP
8 CMD DUP
9 CMD OVER
10 CMD R>
11 CMD DEPTH
12 CMD RDEPTH
13 CMD +
14 CMD -
15 CMD AND
16 CMD OR
17 CMD XOR
18 CMD =
19 CMD <
20 CMD >
21 CMD2 *
22 CMD DROP
23 CMD cmdJMP
24 CMD cmdCALL
25 CMD cmdRJMP
26 CMD >R
27 CMD !
28 CMD OUTPORT
29 CMD cmdRIF
30 CMD cmdUNTIL
31 CMD RET
```

Listing 3. A snippet of the cross-assembler description for the VLIW architecture.

```
0 CONSTANT AMUXOP0
1 CONSTANT AMUXOP1
2 CONSTANT AMUXOP2
3 CONSTANT AMUXOP3

0x00 CONSTANT BMUXOP0
0x10 CONSTANT BMUXOP1
0x20 CONSTANT BMUXOP2
0x30 CONSTANT BMUXOP3

0x000 CONSTANT ALUANOP
0x100 CONSTANT ALUA+
0x200 CONSTANT ALUA-
0x300 CONSTANT ALUA&
0x400 CONSTANT ALUA|
0x500 CONSTANT ALUA^
0x600 CONSTANT ALUA~

0x0000 CONSTANT ALUBNOP
0x1000 CONSTANT ALUB+
0x2000 CONSTANT ALUB-
0x3000 CONSTANT ALUB&
0x4000 CONSTANT ALUB|
0x5000 CONSTANT ALUB^
0x6000 CONSTANT ALUB~

: ALUA
  CMDALUA CASE
    ALUANOP OF OP1 -> ENDOF
    ALUA+ OF OP1 -> OP2 -> + ENDOF
    ALUA- OF OP1 -> OP2 -> - ENDOF
    ALUA& OF OP1 -> OP2 -> AND ENDOF
    ALUA| OF OP1 -> OP2 -> OR  ENDOF
    ALUA^ OF OP1 -> OP2 -> XOR ENDOF
    ALUA~ OF OP1 -> INVERT ENDOF
  ENDCASE
;

: ALUB
  CMDALUB CASE
    ALUBNOP OF OP1 -> ENDOF
    ALUB+ OF OP1 -> OP2 -> + ENDOF
    ALUB- OF OP1 -> OP2 -> - ENDOF
    ALUB& OF OP1 -> OP2 -> AND ENDOF
    ALUB| OF OP1 -> OP2 -> OR  ENDOF
    ALUB^ OF OP1 -> OP2 -> XOR ENDOF
    ALUB~ OF OP1 -> INVERT ENDOF
  ENDCASE
;
```

The cross-assembler description format has a similar form to the structural description of components in RTL representation. For example, the fragment OP1 $->$ OP2 $->$ $+$ explicitly corresponds to the structure of the adder, the operands of which are OP1 and OP2. This allows you to quickly move from a high-level model to an RTL representation using general metadescription data that specifies the position of the bit fields in the command and codes for individual operations.

The presented materials were used to create a control processor for a system-on-a-chip based on FPGA [11].

5 Conclusions

The proposed approach makes it possible to design a processor with the VLIW architecture, by implementing a datapath with a complex structure, focused on hardware support for operations characteristic of the target group of algorithms. This approach aims to reduce the design time by transferring some of the tests to the high-level processor description level, which will subsequently be appropriately described at the register transfer level. An approach seems promising, in which the arithmetic-logical device of the processor is an asymmetric structure of computational nodes, which allows organizing hardware support for frequently used sequences of operations characteristic of the target group of algorithms for which the developed processor is intended.

References

1. Hennessy, J.L., Patterson, D.A.: A new golden age for computer architecture: domain-specific hardware/software co-design, enhanced security, open instruction sets, and agile chip development. In: Proceedings of the 2018 ACM/IEEE 45th Annual International Symposium on Computer Architecture (ISCA), Los Angeles, CA, USA, 1–6 June 2018 (2018). https://doi. org/10.1109/ISCA.2018.00011
2. Hennessy, J.L., Patterson, D.A.: Computer Architecture: A Quantitative Approach, 6th edn. Morgan Kaufmann, Burlington (2017)
3. Dennard, R.H., Gaensslen, F., Yu, H.-N., Rideout, L., Bassous, E., LeBlanc, A.: Design of ion-implanted MOSFET's with very small physical dimensions. IEEE J. Solid State Circ. 9, 256–268 (1974). https://doi.org/10.1109/JSSC.1974.1050511
4. Amdahl, G.M.: Validity of the single processor approach to achieving large-scale computing capabilities. AFIPS Conf. Proc. 30, 483–485 (1967)
5. Jouppi, N.P., Wall, D.W.: Available instruction-level parallelism for superscalar and super-pipelined machines. ACM SIGARCH Comput. Arch. News 17(2), 272–282 (1989). https:// doi.org/10.1145/68182.68207
6. Florea, A., Vasilas, T.: Optimizing the integration area and performance of VLIW architectures by hardware/software co-design. Commun. Comput. Inf. Sci. 1341, 35–51 (2021). https://doi. org/10.1007/978-3-030-68527-0_3
7. Reddy, V., Sudhakar, A., Sivakumar, P.: Computing performance enhancement of vliw architecture using instruction level parallelism. Int. J. Innov. Sci. Res. Technol. 5, 431–435 (2020). https://doi.org/10.38124/IJISRT20SEP241
8. Mego, R., Fryza, T.: A tool for VLIW processors code optimizing. In: 13th IEEE International Conference on Computer Engineering and Systems, Cairo, Egypt, 18–19 December 2018, pp. 601–604 (2018). https://doi.org/10.1109/ICCES.2018.8639186

9. Egger, B., Ryu, S., Yoo, D., Park, I.: Apparatus and method for generating VLIW, and processor and method for processing VLIW. Patent US 8601244B2. Accessed 12 Mar 2021

10. Kessler, C.W.: Compiling for VLIW DSPs. In: Bhattacharyya, S.S., Deprettere, E.F., Leupers, R., Takala, J. (eds.) Handbook of Signal Processing Systems, pp. 979–1020. Springer, Cham (2019). https://doi.org/10.1007/978-3-319-91734-4_27

11. Tarasov, I.E., Potekhin, D.S.: Real-time kernel function synthesis for software defined radio and phase-frequency measuring digital systems. Russ. Technol. J. **6**, 41–54 (2018). https://doi.org/10.32362/2500-316X-2018-6-6-41-54. (in Russian)

Calculation of Activation Functions in FPGA-Based Neuroprocessors Using the Cordic Algorithm

Ilya Tarasov$^{(\boxtimes)}$ and Dmitry Potekhin

MIREA – Russian Technological University, Vernadsky Avenue 78, 119454 Moscow, Russia
tarasov_i@mirea.ru

Abstract. The article discusses the use of configurable IP-cores that implement the CORDIC algorithm for calculating activation functions in neuroprocessors based on FPGA and VLSI. Currently, a large number of neuron activation functions based on transcendental operations are known in the field of artificial intelligence algorithms. The elementary step of the CORDIC algorithm uses the addition/subtraction and shift operations, which are also used for the elementary step of the sequential multiplication algorithm. This makes it possible to develop a unified computational node that, in various modes of signal switching, performs either a multiplication (or multiplication with accumulation) step to calculate the output of a neuron, or a CORDIC algorithm step to calculate the activation function. Combining elementary computational nodes into a pipelined module allows you to build a VLSI accelerator for neural network computing, which can use both simple activation functions and select some elementary nodes to implement more complex activation functions by reducing the number of multiply-accumulate operations. This approach expands the capabilities of specialized accelerators when they are implemented in VLSI and when using the considered architecture in FPGA, involving logic cells for calculating transcendental functions.

Keywords: Neural network · VLSI · CORDIC · Digital signal processing

1 Introduction

The performance of hardware platforms for the implementation of neural networks has been steadily increasing in recent years. In this case, not so many general-purpose processors are used, including devices with a high degree of parallelism of operations. Among mass products, there are GPUs, involving specialized VLSI for the implementation of neural networks. The performance that may be in demand in this class of computing is currently not implemented on the basis of a single microcircuit, which leads to non-trivial architectural and technological solutions. For example, the Cerebras Wafer Scale Engine (WSE) neuroprocessor has an area of 46225 mm^2 [1]. Such processor is manufactured in a single copy on one wafer.

Currently used high-performance hardware platforms for neural networks are represented by three large classes of devices. GPUs in GPGPU mode are actively used

V. Jordan et al. (Eds.): HPCST 2021, CCIS 1526, pp. 13–20, 2022.
https://doi.org/10.1007/978-3-030-94141-3_2

in a wide class of tasks due to their widespread use in computer technology and the fundamental similarity of the tasks of constructing 3D graphics and modeling the operation of neurons. At the same time, the need to provide an efficient implementation of 3D graphics causes the possible redundancy of GPU hardware resources. Research in the field of neural network algorithms is actively considering reducing the bit depth of data, up to binary networks [2], which minimize the hardware costs of their implementation. At the same time, the GPU requires support for the fp32 format, so these devices are obviously in more difficult conditions compared to a specialized element base. In addition, GPUs have a certain hardware architecture, which may not correspond to the structure of connections of the implemented neural network.

The use of FPGAs with FPGA architecture allows partially solving the described problems. The reduction in the bit width of neurons, justified in a mathematical model, can be adequately reflected in a neural network based on FPGA, since individual components of neurons will be synthesized with a given bit width. At the same time, there is no redundancy in hardware costs. In addition, the structure of connections can be reproduced in the FPGA-based design. Reducing the number of neurons and removing connections with low weights (thinning) are actively used in FPGA-based neural networks [3, 4].

On the other hand, FPGAs themselves are devices with redundant hardware resources, since they contain switching resources, and logic cells implement combinational circuits based on truth tables, which is also redundant compared to the implementation of similar circuits based on logic gates. Therefore, along with GPU and FPGA, specialized computing devices designed for neural networks are also used [5–7]. When designing them, it is assumed that the architecture of computational elements and connections between them will be more consistent with the specifics of neural networks, which favorably distinguishes neurocomputers from GPUs. At the same time, the wider use of hardware implementation of components will be an advantage over FPGA.

2 Neuroprocessor Architecture

Specialized VLSI for the implementation of neural networks use several subsystems designed to solve problems of modeling the behavior of neurons, loading their weights, exchanging data with external sources, general control of work, etc. These tasks have significantly different parameters - the complexity of calculations, the possibility of parallelization, the required amount of memory, bandwidth of interfaces, etc. Therefore, as part of a neuroprocessor, it is necessary to use subsystems that are consistent in characteristics, which could distribute tasks in an optimal way. This is usually achieved by the combined use of general-purpose processors for solving control problems and specialized computing units, which is also typical of other areas of application that use high-performance computing [8]. For example, VLSI Celerity [9] consists of the following subsystems: 5 64-bit general-purpose RISC-V processors, a binary tunable neural network, and 496 RISC-V processor cores in a 32-bit configuration.

An example of the architecture of a neuroprocessor is shown in Fig. 1. In this figure, the main subsystems are highlighted: control processor cores of general purpose, controllers of external interfaces and the main matrix of computational elements that simulate the behavior of neurons.

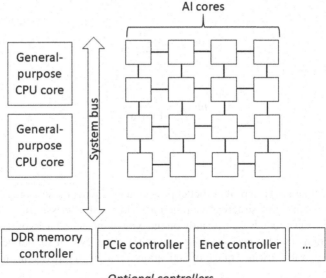

Fig. 1. General architecture of the neuroprocessor.

The well-known model of the neuron by McCulloch and Pitts uses the formula:

$$y = \varphi\left(b + \sum_{i=1}^{N} x_i \cdot k_i\right)$$

where

x is a vector of input values;
k is vector of weights of individual inputs;
b is offset;
φ is the activation function.

The presence of the activation function significantly distinguishes the neuron model from a conventional filter with constant coefficients. If you have a hardware platform that is optimized for multiply-accumulate operations, you can calculate the argument of the activation function, but the calculation of the function itself can be much more complicated. Devices such as FPGAs can combine the use of DSP hardware components to perform multiply-accumulate operations and configurable logic cells to calculate the activation function.

The used activation functions can be divided into two groups according to the use of transcendental functions for their calculation. Activation functions such as identity (f (x) = x), single step, linear rectifier, linear rectifier with leakage are easy to calculate and do not require significant hardware costs. However, many activation functions are based on transcendental computation. Examples include:

– sigmoid

$$\sigma(x) = \frac{1}{1 + e^{-x}},$$

– hyperbolic tangent

$$th(x) = \frac{e^x - e^{-x}}{e^x + e^{-x}},$$

– arctangent

$$arctg(x).$$

The listed functions can provide better performance for neural networks compared to simpler identical or stepwise activation functions. Obviously, the issue of using a specific activation function depends significantly on the type of the neural network, the structure of its connections and the used learning algorithms. However, it should be recognized that the ability to use a wider range of activation functions improves the attractiveness of the neuroprocessor.

3   CORDIC Algorithm

The calculation of transcendental functions can be implemented in various ways. With a small bit width of the argument, the tabular presentation of the result seems to be optimal from the point of view of both computational resources and execution time. Placing a table on the VLSI chip in the form of a fragment of RAM with a capacity of 2N cells allows one to implement arbitrary functions of an N-bit argument. In this case, the time for providing the result is 1 clock cycle, possibly with the addition of additional clock cycles when using long trace lines, which increases latency, but does not reduce memory bandwidth.

The tabular presentation of functions has the obvious disadvantage of rapidly increasing the required memory capacity. If 8 bits of the operand correspond to 256 memory cells, then 16 bits already require 65536 cells. Duplication of such relatively large components over the VLSI chip reduces the efficiency of using the chip area. This approach can be used to a limited extent; however, initially it provides redundancy in the hardware implementation of the neural network.

Another approach is to compute functions in real time. Since the main difficulty in the above overview is the computation of transcendental functions, efforts should be focused on ensuring their support. The known algorithm Coordinate Rotating Digital Computer (CORDIC) provides for the sequential calculation of the components of transcendental functions by rotating the vector and simultaneously tracking the angle of rotation and coordinates of the end of the vector [10].

If the vector initially had an angle α with the abscissa axis, and the coordinates of its end (x; y), then when rotating through an angle φ, the new coordinates (x'; y') will be determined by the formula:

$$x' = \cos(\alpha + \varphi) = \cos\alpha \cdot \cos\varphi - \sin\alpha \cdot \sin\varphi,$$

$$y' = \sin(\alpha + \varphi) = \sin\alpha \cdot \cos\varphi + \cos\alpha \cdot \sin\varphi.$$

The first transformation is to bracket cos φ:

$$x' = \cos \varphi \, (x \cdot 1 - y \cdot \text{tg } \varphi),$$

$$y' = \cos \varphi \, (y \cdot 1 + x \cdot \text{tg } \varphi).$$

If the rotation will be performed only through such angles for which tg φ is equal to an integer power of two (i.e. 1, 1/2, 1/4, 1/8, etc.), then the operation of multiplication $x \cdot \text{tq } \varphi$ is performed through the shift of x by 0, 1, 2, 3... positions to the right. The calculation of $y \cdot \text{tq } \varphi$ is performed in a similar way. Therefore, one step of the algorithm can be performed using shift and add/subtract operations.

If the angles of rotation φ are specified in the table, the tangents of which are equal to an integer power of two, then performing successive rotations by these angles will bring the total angle to the required value. For this it is necessary to take into account that:

$$x' = \cos(\alpha - \varphi) = \cos \alpha \cdot \cos \varphi + \sin \alpha \cdot \sin \varphi,$$

$$y' = \sin(\alpha - \varphi) = \sin \alpha \cdot \cos \varphi - \cos \alpha \cdot \sin \varphi.$$

Having a table of angles and initializing $x = 1$, $y = 0$, you can rotate the angle φ as close as possible to the desired angle $\varphi 0$ given as an argument. If after the next rotation $\varphi > \varphi_0$, then at the next iteration of the algorithm the rotation occurs by a negative angle. Thus, by the method of successive approximation, φ rushes φ_0, and its coordinates x, y represent the cosine and sine of the angle φ. hyperbolic sine and cosine sinh x, cosh x, as well as arctangent, hyperbolic arctangent and square root.

The calculation of the exponent is based on the formulas of hyperbolic functions:

$$\sinh x = \left(e^x - e^{-x}\right)/2,$$

$$\cosh x = \left(e^x + e^{-x}\right)/2.$$

Adding the left and right sides of these equations, we get:

$$\sinh x + \cosh x = e^x,$$

$$\cosh x - \sinh x = e^{-x}.$$

The computation of hyperbolic functions can be performed using the CORDIC algorithm with a corresponding optimized IP core. However, a feature of this algorithm when calculating hyperbolic functions is a limited range of possible arguments. The fact is that these functions are calculated by changing the signs in the angle rotation formulas, as a result of which the end of the vector moves along a hyperbolic curve with the equation $x^2 - y^2 = 1$. For too large values of the argument, the vector drawn at such an angle will not intersect the hyperbolic curve, and the result of successive rotations of the vector will be incorrect.

To solve this problem, the property of power functions should be used:

$$e^{a+b} = e^a \cdot e^b.$$

If the argument of the exponent is decomposed into two terms, the resulting exponent can be calculated as the product of the two components. In this case, one part of the argument can be represented in the table, and the second - obtained using the CORDIC algorithm through hyperbolic functions. The first part of the argument should be selected, for example, with a step of 0.5, i.e. set exponent values in the table for arguments 0.5, 1, 1.5, 2, etc. Since the exponent increases rapidly as the argument grows (and decreases rapidly for negative arguments), the table size will be small at 42 for a 32-bit representation.

4   Configurable Compute Module Architecture

Since the step of the CORDIC algorithm is performed using addition/subtraction and shift, based on the same resources, you can perform the basic operation of a neuron - multiply with accumulation. Thus, in order to increase the flexibility of the hardware, the computational module should be implemented on the basis of a chain of configurable computational nodes connected in a pipeline. Figure 2 shows an example of a computational node in the mode of calculating the step of the CORDIC algorithm.

Shown in Fig. 2 the node contains hardware components that directly calculate the values of x, y, φ at the next step of the algorithm. A memory block containing a table of arctangents can be generalized for several computational channels, but this is only valid for cases when the generalized channels perform computations with the same bit width of the result and start them synchronously.

The capabilities of the configurable block, which includes the addition and shift blocks, are not limited only by the calculation of the step of the CORDIC algorithm. As shown in [11], you can also perform multiplication or multiplication and accumulation using shift and addition.

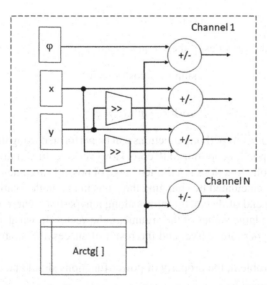

Fig. 2. Computing node in the mode of calculating the step of the CORDIC algorithm.

Thus, in the presence of appropriate multiplexers, the computing node can be both an element that calculates the sum of the products of arguments, and an element that calculates the value of the activation function.

Figure 3 shows a computational module consisting of identical chains of computational nodes, which, depending on the loaded configuration, can either compute the output of a neuron or apply an activation function to it.

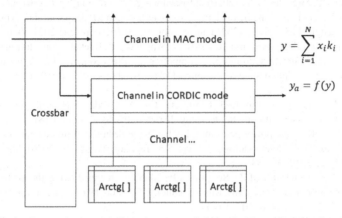

Fig. 3. Computing module based on several channels of computational nodes.

The ability to dynamically reconfigure individual elements does not impose strict requirements on the applied activation functions, up to the use of an identical function that does not change the output y. Therefore, if it is possible to use a simpler activation function, the number of nodes calculating the sum of the products will be increased.

Computing nodes shown in Fig. 3 are quite compact and can be implemented within a single clock tree. At the same time, if it is necessary to scale the VLSI, the nodes can be placed on a chip under the control of a general-purpose processor subsystem, exchanging data using input and output FIFOs.

5   Conclusions

The materials considered in the article make it possible to develop a unified computational node capable of operating both in the mode of calculating a product or sum of products, and in the mode of generating transcendental functions, which make it possible to implement a number of activation functions used in modern neural networks. The use of sequential distributed arithmetic simplifies the topological implementation of the VLSI and reduces the functional redundancy of the circuit by applying the required number of steps of sequential conversion corresponding to the width of the operand.

References

1. Woo, M.: The world's biggest computer chip. Engineering **6** (2019). https://doi.org/10.1016/j.eng.2019.11.001
2. Daokun, Z., Yin, J., Zhu, X., Zhang, C.: Search efficient binary network embedding. ACM Trans. Knowl. Discov. Data **15**, 1–27 (2021). https://doi.org/10.1145/3436892
3. Véstias, M.: Efficient design of pruned convolutional neural networks on FPGA. J. Sig. Process. Syst. **93**(5), 531–544 (2020). https://doi.org/10.1007/s11265-020-01606-2
4. Yeom, S.-K., et al.: Pruning by explaining: a novel criterion for deep neural network pruning. Pattern Recogn. **115**, 107899 (2021). https://doi.org/10.1016/j.patcog.2021.107899
5. Esser, S.K., Merolla, P., Arthur, J., Cassidy, A., Appuswamy, R. et al.: Convolutional networks for fast, energy-efficient neuromorphic computing. In: Proceedings of the National Academy of Sciences of the United States of America **113** (2016). https://doi.org/10.1073/pnas.1604850113
6. Davies, M., Srinivasa, N., Lin, T.-H., Chinya, G., Cao, Y., Choday, S.H., et al.: A neuromorphic many-core processor with on-chip learning. IEEE Micro **38**, 82–99 (2018)
7. Lee, J., Kim, K.: Low power neuromorphic hardware design and implementation based on asynchronous design methodology. J. Sens. Sci. Technol. **29**, 68–73 (2020). https://doi.org/10.5369/JSST.2019.29.1.68
8. Sorokin S.A., Benenson M.Z., Sorokin A.P.: Methods for evaluating the performance of heterogeneous computer systems. Russ. Technol. J. **5**(6), 11–19 (2017). (In Russ.) https://doi.org/10.32362/2500-316X-2017-5-6-11-1
9. Davidson, S., Xie, S., Torng, C., Al-Hawai, K., Rovinski, A., Ajayi, T., et al.: The celerity open-source 511-core RISC-V tiered accelerator fabric: fast architectures and design methodologies for fast chips. IEEE Micro **38**, 30–41 (2018). https://doi.org/10.1109/MM.2018.022071133
10. Volder, J.E.: The CORDIC computing technique. In: Proceedings of the Western Joint Computer Conference, pp. 257–261. National Joint Computer Committee, San Francisco, California, USA (1959)
11. Tarasov, I.E., Potekhin, D.S.: VLSI architecture with a configurable data processing path based on serial distributed arithmetic. J. Phys. Conf. Ser. **1565**, 012001 (2020)

Implementation of LTC2500-32 High-Resolution ADC and FPGA Interface for Photodiode Circuit Harmonic Distortions Analysis

Vadim S. Oshlakov$^{(\boxtimes)}$, Ivan G. Deyneka , Artem S. Aleynik ,
and Ilya A. Sharkov

Research Institute of Light-Guided Photonics – Russian National Research ITMO University,
Novoizmaylovskiy Avenue 34, k.3, 196191 Saint-Petersburg, Russia

Abstract. This article describes the implementation of the data exchange interface between Intel Cyclone IV FPGA and the LTC2500-32 32-bit ADC with a
sampling rate of 1 MSps for the photodiode circuit of a fiber-optic gyroscope.
Dedicated hardware features that allow the optimal implementation of the interface are considered. The fact that the interface is not directly applicable to a standard synchronous interface such as Source Synchronous or System Synchronous
complicates timing analysis. This article proposes a methodology for describing
timing constraints for this special case and provides an example of commands in
sdc (Synopsis Design Constraint) format. The result of solving the timing analysis
problem and the result of testing the input stage of the ADC using the Rohde &
Schwartz SMB100A generator are presented. The resulting spurious free dynamic
range of the ADC input stage is 90.1 dB. Results of using the LTC2500-32 ADC
for a presence of harmonics distortion in photodiode circuit are presented. The
resulting spurious free dynamic range of the photodiode circuit accounts for 70 dB.

Keywords: Timing analysis · Hardware implementation · FPGA ·
High-resolution ADC · Dynamic range

1 Introduction

At present, fiber-optic gyroscopes (FOGs) based on the Sagnac effect [1] are widely
used in ground, sea, air and space navigation systems. Therefore, there is an increasing
trend towards miniaturization of these devices and an improvement in their accuracy
and operational parameters. The advantages of FOGs include high sensitivity in a wide
range of angular velocities, a high degree of linearity of the transfer characteristic and
relatively short start-up time.

© Springer Nature Switzerland AG 2022
V. Jordan et al. (Eds.): HPCST 2021, CCIS 1526, pp. 21–29, 2022.
https://doi.org/10.1007/978-3-030-94141-3_3

Nowadays a closed-loop circuit is traditionally used to construct FOGs. One of the main components of FOGs is a multifunctional integrated optical circuit (MIOC) based on lithium niobate, which is used as a modulator, a polarizer and an optical splitter. Generally, a sawtooth waveform is used as a modulating signal, which imposes bandwidth requirements on MIOC. MIOC has a number of negative characteristics [2], which affect the accuracy and operational parameters of the FOGs. Particularly, these are the phase drift, amplitude and phase characteristics, which are unstable due to temperature and over long time intervals.

An improved algorithm for passive homodyne demodulation can be used, a sinusoidal signal is used as a modulation signal, as a result of which the requirement for the MIOC bandwidth can be reduced [3]. However, to implement this algorithm, special linearity requirements are imposed on the modulation circuit and the FOG photodiode circuit. In particular, to achieve the navigation grade FOG, the dynamic range and total harmonic distortions should be over 90 dB [4]. For verification, an algorithmic solution of the sufficient spurious free dynamic range (SFDR) is 70 dB.

Analog Devices released high-resolution successive approximation analog-to-digital converters (ADC) [5], in particular, 32-bit LTC2500-32 ADC with a sampling rate of 1 Msps is able to provide SFDR over 100 dB, which is acceptable for designing a photodiode circuit and implementing an improved homodyne demodulation algorithm. It also makes it possible to reduce the effects associated with the influence of frequency and phase responses of the MIOC on the FOG signal. To interact with such ADCs in FOGs, field programmable gate arrays (FPGAs) are used. Taking into account the high resolution and clock frequency of the ADC and FPGA interaction interface, which can reach up to 100 MHz, special constraints and technical restrictions are imposed on the interaction of the interface [6, 7] for correct data exchange. The standard and simplest technique for analyzing the ADC's input stage for harmonic distortions is to apply a sinusoidal signal with low and known harmonic distortions to the ADC's input stage and analyze the converted signal into the frequency domain. The use of such technique in the case of optoelectronic circuits is difficult due to the uncommon test equipment, which is capable to generate an optical intensity sinusoidal modulated signal with low harmonic distortions in a low-frequency range. Photodiode circuits testing is a relevant task due to the widespread use of interferometric optical sensors based on homodyne and heterodyne detection.

2   Methods

2.1   Hardware Implementation on FPGA

The LTC2500-32 is the 32-bit ADC currently available with a sampling rate of 1Msps. The ADC has built-in programmable digital filters and is capable of providing the dynamic range of 120 dB. There are 2 data output lines, SDOA with a sampling rate of 250 kSPS and SDOB – with a sampling rate of 1 MS/s. Data from the SDOB output can be received in "no latency - no delay" mode, which is required in FOG. The timing diagram for interacting with the LTC2500-32 ADC is shown in Fig. 1.

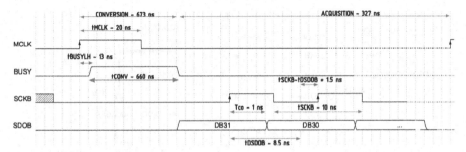

Fig. 1. LTC2500-32 ADC interface timing diagram.

The entire data exchange process can be roughly divided into 2 stages:

1. The FPGA initiates the exchange by sending a 20 ns pulse on the MCLK line, after which the ADC raises the BUSY line to the state of a logical one, until the data is converted. This process takes an interval from 600 to 660 ns.
2. After the ADC lowers the BUSY line to a logical zero, the 32-bit value of the converted sample on the SDOB line can be sequentially read by the FPGA by applying 32 signal clocks to the SCKB line with a period of 10 ns (tSCKB) and registering the sample on the rising edge.

A feature of this ADC is that the data at the SDOB output can be correctly recorded only for 2.5 ns (from the maximum available 10 ns interval). Here the data is stable for 1.5 ns until the rising edge of the SCKB line arrives (tSCKB-tDSDOB interval on 1) and 1 ns after the arrival of the rising edge of SCKB (Tco interval in Fig. 1). The reason is the clock signal frequency of 100 MHz, strict time constraints are required to correctly capture the data.

According to [8], special conditions for jitter are imposed on the signal of the beginning of conversion on the MCLK line, taking into account the sampling frequency (1 MS/s) and the ADC bit rate (32-bit). Jitter should be tens of femtoseconds, since it directly affects the conversion result and signal-to-noise ratio. To generate such a signal, it is wrong to use the input ports (pins) of the FPGA, since, even in the case of using special I/O pins for the FPGA clock signals, the jitter on them can reach hundreds of picoseconds. The optimal solution is to use an external clock signal generator in conjunction with a D-flip-flop, the data input of which is the MCLK signal from the FPGA pin (see Fig. 2). This solution provides the greatest number of effective ADC bits and the signal-to-noise ratio of the output signal.

For the hardware implementation of the data exchange interface between the FPGA and the ADC, there are many options that have their own advantages and disadvantages, the specific implementation features depend on the vendor and the FPGA series, in particular, on the availability of special architectural capabilities. In this work, we used a debug board based on Intel FPGA (Altera) Cyclone IV [9].

The entire implementation of the interface can be built on logical elements of FPGAs and this option will be universal for any FPGAs; however, many families have special blocks that allow you to save logical resources and simplify time analysis.

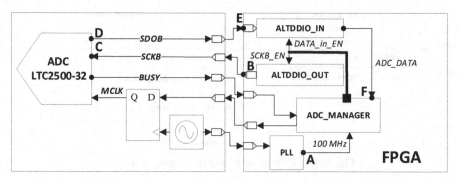

Fig. 2. Block diagram of connecting LTC2500-32 to FPGA.

The clock signal (clock) SCKB is supplied to the ADC not constantly, but is used only when reading data. Such an implementation of the interface can be justified by the fact that during the process of converting the sample, digital lines do not induce interference and do not distort the conversion result. Due to this decision, it is difficult to implement and impractical to use hardware deserializers to interact with the ADC and output of the clock signal from the phase-locked loop (PLL) directly to clock the ADC.

There are several possibilities for generating SCKB:

1. Generation of SCKB is possible by the logical conjunction of a clock from the PLL output with an external signal (through the "AND" element), while in our case it is necessary to change the state of the signal with which the clock is multiplied with a falling edge in order to avoid possible short-term impulse noise (glitches). The method will be universal for all FPGA families, but in this case it is necessary to manually localize the "AND" element and the control signal closer to the FPGA pin. The main disadvantage will be the need to output the clock signal from a specialized clock line (global / regional) to the logic, which will cause additional delay and additional clock jitter, which ultimately worsens the likelihood of converting time constraints (successfully solving the problem of static time analysis).

2. Using the specialized ALTCLKCONTROL block allows you to avoid glitches; however, the output signal, as well as in the first version, will have to be output from a specialized clock line (except for the case of special CLKout pins, but their number is very limited). The method is also not universal for all FPGA families; moreover, the amount of data blocks is small.

To read data, it is also convenient to use DDR registers ALTDDIO_IN, but the CYCLONE IV family does not have hardware registers, but if you use this IP component, then at the stage of placement and routing ALTDDIO_IN is created from logical elements and is automatically located closer to the input port. No special requirements are imposed on the generation of MCLK, this signal can be implemented using logic without additional time constraints. The data exchange interface between the ADC and FPGA is not a standard synchronous interface such as System Synchronous or Source Synchronous, and therefore, there is no generally available methodology for analyzing such interfaces.

2.2 Timing Analysis of the Interface

Timing analysis in Quartus Software for Intel FPGAs is performed in the Timing Analyzer tool. The first step in the analysis is to describe all the clocks in use. To do this, the commands are written in the SDC file for the project:

1. the command set_time_format -unit ns -decimal_places 3 - sets the time units - in this case nanoseconds (ns);
2. command create_clock -name {FPGA_CLK} - period 20.000 -waveform {0.000 10.000} [get_ports {FPGA_CLK}] - describes the input clock signal with a frequency of 50 MHz, from which the FPGA is clocked;
3. command derive_pll_clocks - automatically creates and describes clock signals for all PLL outputs;
4. command create_generated_clock -name SCKB -source [get_nets {inst4 I b2v_inst1 I ALTDDIO_OUT_component I auto_generated I dataout [0]}] - serves to describe the SCKB clock signal.

To check the correctness of the analysis, you can look at the clock signal dependency tree. In addition to describing the clock frequencies, it is necessary to take into account the signal delays and indicate to the analyzer the interval in which the data can be recorded correctly. On conductors 0.2 mm wide and 10 mm long with FR4 textolite, the estimated propagation delay is 0.007 ns/mm. For the analysis, a value of 0.01 ns was taken, as for a more pessimistic scenario.

1. The command set SCKB_delay [expr 10 * 0.01] - initialization of the SCKB_delay variable, the propagation delay of the SCKB signal on the conductor from the FPGA to the ADC (path BC in Fig. 2).
2. The command set DATA_delay [expr $ 10 * 0.01] - initialization of the DATA_delay variable, the propagation delay of the data signal from the SDOB output on the conductor (DE path in Fig. 2).

The time constraints for executing tsu/th in FPGA input flip-flops are described as follows:

1. command set usedTsu [expr $ Tco_max + $ SCKB_delay + $ DATA_delay];
2. command set usedTh [expr $ Tco_min + $ SCKB_delay + $ DATA_delay];
3. command set_input_delay –max –clock [get_clocks {SCKB}] $ usedTsu [get_ports {SDOB}];
4. command set_input_delay –min –clock [get_clocks {SCKB}] $ usedTh [get_ports {SDOB}].

The constraints take into account signal delays and worst-case ADC parameters. During the analysis, it was found that the total delay on the A-F path (Fig. 2) can exceed 10 ns (see Fig. 3), which exceeds the clock period.

As a solution, you can tell the analyzer that the data will be captured 2 clock cycles later and invert the clock signal, which will ensure that the correct data is recorded:

1. the command set_multicycle_path -setup -from [get_clocks SCKB] -to [get_clockspll_adc | altpll_component | auto_generated | pll1 | clk [0]] 2 - indicates that it is necessary to take into account the second edge of the clock when analyzing by setup, i.e. the second edge of the PLL output clock relative to SCKB;

2. command create_generated_clock -name SCKB –source [get_nets {inst4 | b2v_inst1 | ALTDDIO_OUT_component | auto_generated | dataout [0]}] -invert [get_ports {SCKB}] - indicates that the clock generated at the output of the PLL is inverted SCKB.

The result of time analysis with added commands is shown on the oscillogram in Fig. 4.

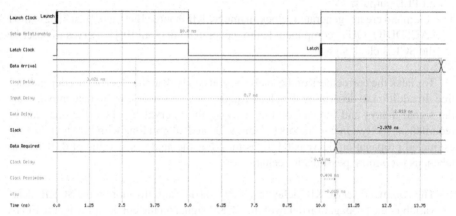

Fig. 3. Timing analysis diagram.

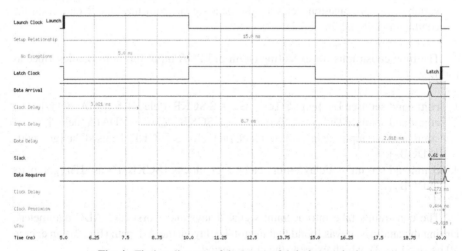

Fig. 4. Timing diagram of the successful timing analysis.

3 Results

3.1 ADC's Input Stage Harmonic Distortion Analysis

The result of ADC's input stage analysis with the implemented data exchange interface and imposed timing constraints is shown in Fig. 5. The Rohde & Schwartz SMB100A generator, designed for ADC and DAC testing, was used in order to test SFDR. A sinusoidal signal with the frequency of 50 kHz was applied to the ADC's input stage. By specification, this generator provides a sinusoidal signal with SFDR that is greater than 90 dB in a wide frequency range. The recorded signal spectrum is shown in Fig. 5, SFDR is over 90.1 dB. When an input signal frequency changed, SFDR changed by ±1 dB in the 500 kHz bandwidth.

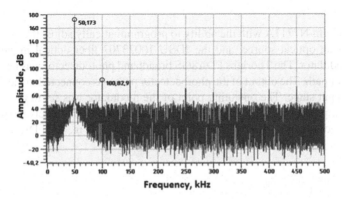

Fig. 5. Spectrum of the recorded signal obtained by Rohde & Schwarz SMB100A.

3.2 Harmonic Distortion Analysis of the Photodiode Circuit

An optical intensity of the sinusoidal modulated signal with low harmonic distortions can be considered as an equivalent of a sinusoidal electrical signal for the ADC's input stage in the case of optoelectronics circuits. Direct modulation can be used to create such a signal. As a rule, though, such current drivers are not intended for this mode and have low linearity [10]. The most convenient solution is employing electro-optical Mach-Zehnder amplitude modulators used in optical communication. These modulators are highly linear and have 50 Ω terminated RF modulation inputs to use with standard RF equipment such as the SMB100A. The linearity characteristics of a modulator, especially in a low-frequency range, are usually not indicated in the specification. Therefore, analyzing the linearity of the tract is reduced to finding the modulator and measuring its characteristics as part of the investigated photodiode circuit and ensuring the highest SFDR.

In this work, we used SFDR measuring scheme for the photodiode circuit shown in Fig. 6. The sinusoidal signal with a frequency of 50 kHz, an amplitude of 1 V and an SFDR of over 90 dB was applied to the modulator using an SMB100A generator.

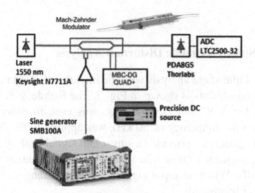

Fig. 6. Scheme for measuring SFDR of the photodiode circuit.

The Keysight N7711A with the ability to programmatically adjust the output power was used as an optical source, and the JDSU 10023707 fiber optical modulator was used as a modulator. The Thorlabs PDA8GS broadband photodetector was used as a test photodetector path. The output of the photodetector path was connected to the LTC2500-32 ADC's input stage. The operating point of the modulator was set to the quadrature point using a precision DC voltage source. The spectrum of the received signal from the photodetector using the LTC2500-32 ADC is shown in Fig. 7, SFDR accounts for 70 dB.

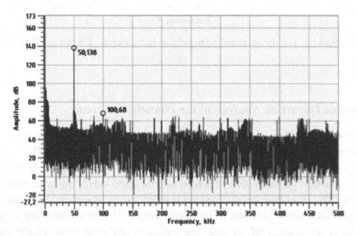

Fig. 7. Spectrum of the registered optical signal from the PDA8GS photodetector.

4   Conclusion

The input stage of the LTC2500-32 ADC provides the spurious free dynamic range exceeding 90 dB in the frequency range of 500 kHz. As a result of the experiment, an optical intensity modulated signal was obtained with SFDR equal to 70 dB. The obtained results will be useful for testing the developed FOG photodiode circuit, starting from the SFDR of 70 dB. The obtained dynamic range is sufficient for testing algorithmic solutions of homodyne demodulation in FOGs. In the future, the results obtained will make it possible to develop solutions for analyzing amplitude and phase-modulated optical signals and optoelectronic components in a low-frequency range.

1. References

1. Lefevre, H.C.: The fiber-optic gyroscope: achievement and perspective. Gyroscopy Navig. 3(4), 223–226 (2012)
2. Volkovskiy, S.A., Aleynik, A.S., Nikitenko, A.N., Smolovik, M.A., Pogorelaya, D.A.: Evaluation method for parasitic effects of the electro-optical modulator in a fiber optic gyroscope. Sci. Tech. J. Inf. Technol. Mech. Opt. 16, 780–786 (2016). https://doi.org/10.17586/2226-1494-2016-16-5-780-786
3. Nikitenko, A.N.: Razvitie metoda passivnojgo homodinnoj demodulyacii s cel'yu povysheniya tochnostnyh harakteristik volokonno-opticheskih giroskopov (Development of the method of passive homodyne demodulation in order to improve the accuracy characteristics of fiber-optic gyroscopes). Candidate Thesis, ITMO University, St. Petersburg, Russia (2016) (in Russian)
4. Kester, W.: Understand SINAD, ENOB, SNR, THD, THD+ N, and SFDR so You Don't Get Lost in the Noise Floor. Tutorial MT-003, Rev. A., 10/08, WK. Analog Devices (2009)
5. Butler, P.: Antialiasing filtering considerations for high precision SAR analog-to-digital converters. Analog Dialogue 52(3), 54–59 (2018)
6. Harris, D.M., Harris, S.L.: Hardware description languages. In: Digital Design and Computer Architecture, pp.167–230. Morgan Kaufmann, Waltham, MA, USA (2007). https://doi.org/10.1016/b978-012370497-9/50005-6
7. Golshan, K.: Design constraints. The Art of Timing Closure. Springer, Cham, pp. 77–85 (2020). https://doi.org/10.1007/978-3-030-49636-4_3
8. Lai, Y.: Aperture Time, Aperture Jitter, Aperture Delay Time. In: Proceedings of 9th International Meeting on Information Display, IMID 2009, 12–16 October 2009, Ilsan, Seoul, Korea, pp. 1069–1072 (2009)
9. Krill, B., Ahmad, A., Amira, A., Rabah, H.: An efficient FPGA-based dynamic partial reconfiguration design flow and environment for image and signal processing IP cores. Signal Process. Image Commun. 25(5), 377–387 (2010)
10. Gordon, G.S.D., Crisp, M.J., Penty, R.V., White, I.H.: High-order distortion in directly modulated semiconductor lasers in high-loss analog optical links with large RF dynamic range. J. Light. Technol. 29, 3577–3586 (2011). https://doi.org/10.1109/JLT.2011.2172773

Hardware and Software Suite
for Electrocardiograph Testing

Sergei A. Ostanin[1,2] 🆔, Denis Yu. Kozlov[2](✉) 🆔, and Maksim A. Drobyshev[2]

[1] LLC «Altai Geophysical Plant», Kalinin Avenue 15, Building 7, 656002 Barnaul, Russia
[2] Altai State University, Lenin Avenue 61, 656049 Barnaul, Russia

Abstract. Standard-compliant testing of manufactured high-technology products is one of the most important production steps necessary for quality assurance. This paper considers the development of a hardware and software suite for portable electrocardiograph testing for compliance with the international standard IEC 60601-2-25: 2011. The software and hardware suite for electrocardiograph testing described here consists of an Arduino Mega 2560 board, a digital-to-analog converter, conditioning amplifiers, and a computer with the LabVIEW15 visual programming environment installed. The generator program is written in the Arduino C language. To establish compliance of frequency response of electrocardiograph with the standard, 4 types of waveforms were generated with different frequencies, which were selected from the standard-compliant band (21 frequency values in total). In the course of the work, portable electrocardiographs from various manufacturers were tested. The paper demonstrates that the hardware and software suite developed on the basis of microprocessor equipment and virtual instrument allows one to achieve cost-effective testing of portable electrocardiographs.

Keywords: Virtual instruments · Test automation · Portable electrocardiographs · Telemedicine · Frequency response · Microcontrollers

1 Introduction

Recently, the Russian government has been paying great attention to the development of the country's healthcare system. Despite this, Universal Health Coverage for Russia was 62–69% in 2015 according to the report of the World Health Organization [1]. As in many developed nations, cardiovascular diseases and cancer are the most common causes of premature deaths. In terms of the premature deaths number due to cardiovascular diseases, Russia ranked second among the countries of Eurasia in 2015 [2]. It is a matter of fact that the reduction in the number of premature deaths can be achieved by increasing the availability of cardiological services. The problem of increasing the availability of services can be solved with minimal costs by using intelligent medical informational systems and technical means of telemedicine, which provide remote acquisition of biomedical information, its automated processing and analysis, in every medical institution in Russia. These measures will increase the productivity of healthcare professionals without increasing the labour intensity.

V. Jordan et al. (Eds.): HPCST 2021, CCIS 1526, pp. 30–42, 2022.
https://doi.org/10.1007/978-3-030-94141-3_4

2 Problem Description

The number of available devices that can record and analyze the electrical signals emitted by the cardiac conduction system is on the rise. However, as noted in the review [3], the published biomedical literature on their diagnostic accuracy, reproducibility or usefulness is scant. Despite the presence of a large number of foreign and domestic electrocardiographs on the medical appliance market, the availability level of electrocardiogram registration services is significantly lower than the availability level of blood pressure registration services. This can be explained by the fact that almost every family has an inexpensive and high-quality automatic tonometer, but there are no electrocardiographs of the same price category on the market. Meanwhile, the effectiveness of using even single-channel mobile electrocardiographs for detecting QTc interval prolongation and predicting potentially life-threatening arrhythmias has been proven [4]. It is worth mentioning that in the current era of the COVID-19 pandemic, the disease itself and several drugs used to treat it were associated with a prolongation of the QTc interval. Mobile electrocardiographs (ECG) are used for remote identification of patients at risk of developing drug-induced syndrome of prolonged QTc and sudden cardiac death. They help to make recommendations for urgent drug therapy [5].

Development and manufacturing of inexpensive and high-quality instruments for remote acquisition of data on the cardiovascular system status is a highly topical issue. To provide the Russian healthcare system with low-cost devices for remote acquisition of electrocardiograms, the Altai Geophysical Plant (AGPP) LLC has developed a series of pocket-sized portable electrocardiographs. The series includes single-channel, three-channel, and six-channel electrocardiographs. They allow one to record electrocardiograms in one, seven and twelve leads. The electrocardiographs are intended for personal use, for use in medical treatment and educational facilities. It is a known fact that the cost of a serial product contains the costs of marketing, development, preparation for manufacturing, and testing. Therefore, low retail cost of the final product can be ensured if each stage of product creation is carried out with minimal costs (maximum economic efficiency).

Testing of electrocardiographs in the manufacturing process is a routine procedure, but it requires the use of the labor of a tester (inspector) of high qualification and payment rate. Developers of medical appliances pay great attention to the automation of the testing process. Most of their efforts are aimed at creating of special generators - simulators of the electrocardiographic signal. So, in the article [6], models of electrocardiographic, blood pressure and ballistocardiographic signals are generated by a microcontroller, which makes it easy to control the output signal parameters. The device was developed and used for educational purposes, especially for biomedical engineering. The article [7] describes a biomedical signal generator using an Arduino Mega 2560 R3 microcontroller. It is shown that the circuit is able to generate ECG waveforms by sending binary signals to its PWM output and low-pass filter. The study [8] reports on a plug-in board for a Raspberry-Pi microcomputer (more expensive than the Arduino Mega 2560 R3 microcontroller) for reproducing multi-channel original electrocardiograms. To generate single-channel ECG signals, the authors of [9] used ATmega32 or ATmega16 microcontrollers. The authors of the article [10] proposed a dynamic model based on three coupled ordinary differential equations, which is capable to generate electrocardiogram signals. It is shown that the equations can model the dispersion of the QT interval and the modulation of the R-peak amplitude. These differential equations can be programmed in the microcontroller of the ECG signal generator. An inexpensive open-source ECG simulator, including both MATLAB software for signal generation and a dedicated circuit board for signal output via a commercial sound card, is described in the article [11]. An original ECG signal generator was created on the basis of a discretized reaction-diffusion system to obtain a set of three nonlinear oscillators [12]. The mathematical model of the generator reproduces electrocardiograms from healthy hearts and from patients suffering from rhythm disorders. The diagram of an electronic device based on the model is given. Despite the numerous publications, a few generators are suitable for testing electrocardiographs for compliance with the requirements of the IEC 60601–2-25:2011 standard [13]. Unfortunately, the articles describing the technology of automation of the electrocardiograph testing process contain only structural diagrams.

3   Technical Solution

In order to minimize costs and reduce the duration of testing, an automated hardware and software suite was created to check electrocardiographs for compliance with the main requirements of the international standard IEC 60601-2-25:2011 [9]. The functional diagram of the hardware and software automated system is shown in Fig. 1.

The automated hardware and software system for portable electrocardiograph testing consists of a waveform generator (positions 1 and 2 in Fig. 1), an electrocardiograph under test (3), and a laptop (4). The generator contains the program code for generating test signals, the laptop contains the visual programming environment LabVIEW15 for analysing test signals.

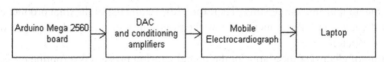

Fig. 1. Functional diagram of the automated testing system for portable electrocardiographs

The characteristics of analog waveforms for testing are defined in the international standard IEC 60601–2-25:2011. They come from the output of the digital programmable generator to the inputs of the electrocardiograph under test. The digital signal from the USB output of the electrocardiograph is sent to the USB input of the laptop, which performs the analysis with a virtual instrument made in the LabVIEW15 environment.

In the medical appliance market there already are waveform generators for electrocardiograph testing. However, if we want to minimize the cost of testing, we have to automate the process of generator control (changing the frequency, amplitude, waveform according to a certain algorithm). Currently available industrial waveform generators for electrocardiograph testing do not have the automation control feature without the use of an external device.

3.1 Test System Design

The waveform generator developed for testing purposes includes an Arduino Mega 2560 board based on the ATmega2560 microcontroller, a digital-to-analog converter based on the R-2R resistive matrix, and conditioning amplifiers. The controller allows automating the process of generating testing signals and controlling their parameters in accordance with various algorithms. The choice of the Arduino Mega 2560 is conditioned by the low cost of the generator developing, as well as the possibility to use the software with other controllers, which are several times cheaper than the ATmega2560 microcontroller.

In accordance with the requirements of the international standard IEC 60601-2-25:2011, the generator provides four types of waveform.

1. To test the electrocardiograph for the mutual influence of channels, a triangle waveform with a frequency of 30 Hz and an amplitude of 25 V is used;
2. To test the electrocardiograph for compliance with the international standard in terms of frequency response, short sinusoidal signals with an amplitude of 1 mV and a frequency from 0.1 Hz to 200 Hz are used;
3. To determine the pulse response of the electrocardiograph, a signal in the form of a pulse with a duration of 100 ms, a period of 1 s, and an amplitude of 3 mV is used;
4. To test the electrocardiograph for linearity and dynamic range, sequences of sinusoidal signal bundles were used. They had a frequency of 40 Hz, peak-to-peak amplitude of 10 mV, and follow each other with a period of 0.5 s. The constant component of the bundles varies within the effective width of the electrocardiogram.

The analog part of the generator along with the conditioning amplifier for the electrocardiograph testing for compliance with the international standard in terms of frequency response is shown in Fig. 2. The digital code of the test signal from the outputs of the Arduino Mega 2560 board (ports PA0-PA7 of the ATmega2560 microcontroller, pins 22–29 of the Arduino Mega 2560 board) is sent to the R-2R matrix, which consists of resistors R1, R3, R7, R8, R11-R14, R17-R22, R28, R29. From the output of the matrix, the analog test signal is sent to an adjustable voltage divider (resistors R4, R9), which sets the peak-to-peak amplitude of the test sinusoidal signal at the output of the operational amplifier UA1 (LM358AN). A voltage divider (resistors R6, R10) is connected to the output of the amplifier to reduce the span of the test signal to a value of 1 mV. The generator signal is sent to the inputs of the electrocardiograph under test from the "Gen" output.

A particular algorithm, which controls the test signal generator, is selected using the R15 potentiometer, whose voltage is supplied to one of the analog inputs of the Arduino Mega 2560 (port PF1 of the ATmega2560 microcontroller, pin 55 "A1" of the Arduino Mega 2560 board). The microcontroller program detects the voltage at the PF1 input and proceeds to the execution of that particular generator's operating algorithm which corresponds to a certain voltage range where the voltage value fall within.

LEDs X1-X4 are used to indicate a particular active algorithm of the test signal generator. LED X5 is reserved for an opportunity to indicate the activity of a new algorithm. The microcontroller operates the LEDs via PC3-PC7 ports (pins 34–30 of the Arduino Mega 2560 board).

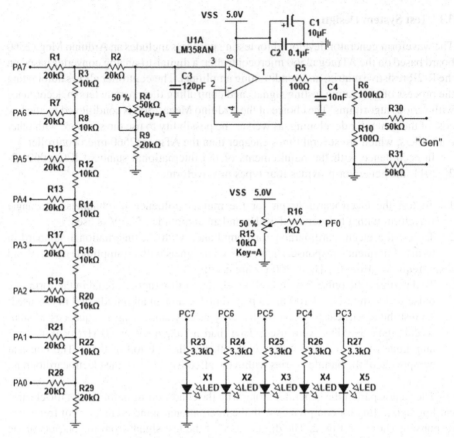

Fig. 2. Schematic circuit diagram of the analog part of the test signal generator.

3.2 Test Signal Generator Software

The test signal generator program code is written in Arduino C (a kind of the C++ language with the Wiring framework) [13]. It provides the selection of the waveform type, generation and display of the waveform.

To program a triangular waveform with a frequency of 30 Hz, the linear increase of the cycle number "i" is used:

```
void setup()
{
// Program 1 "Triangle"
//Setport/pinmode
DDRA = 0xFF;                // all outputs PINS 0-7
// Generate the date of a tr function
   for(int i=0;i<255;i++){
   tr[i]=i;                 // ascending part
      }
    for(int i=0;i<255;i++){
   tr1[i]=255-i;            // falling part
      }
```

The generated arrays tr1[i] and tr1[i] are output to the microcontroller port "A":

```
// Program 1 "Triangle"
void tr_Function(int freq){
    for (int i=0; i<255; i++){
    PORTA =  tr[i];          // ascending part
    delayMicroseconds(freq);
      }
}
void tr1_Function(int freq){
    for (int i=0; i<255; i++){
    PORTA =  tr1[i];         // falling part
    delayMicroseconds(freq);
      }
}
```

The main code is used for programming short sinusoidal signals with different amplitudes and frequencies from 0.1 Hz to 200 Hz:

```
// Program 2 "FRF"
//Setport/pinmode
DDRA = 0xFF;                // all outputs PINS 0-7
// Generate the date of a sine function
  float x,y;
  for(int i=0;i<255;i++){
    x=(float)i;
    y=sin((x/255)*2*PI);
     sine[i]=int(y*128)+127;
    sine_05[i]=int(y*64)+127;
    sine_025[i]=int(y*32)+127;
      }
```

The generated arrays sine [i], sine_05[i] and sine_025 [i] contain sinusoidal signals of different amplitudes and they are output to microcontroller port "A":

```
Program 2 "FRF"
void Sine_Function(int freq){
    for (int i=0; i<255; i++){
    PORTA = sine[i];
    delayMicroseconds(freq);
    }
}
void Sine05_Function(int freq){
    for (int i=0; i<255; i++){
    PORTA = sine_05[i];
    delayMicroseconds(freq);
    }
}
void Sine025_Function(int freq){
    for (int i=0; i<255; i++){
    PORTA = sine_025[i];
    delayMicroseconds(freq);
    }
}
```

To indicate the activity of a particular test signal generator algorithm, logic levels controlling the LEDs X1-X4 are applied to the PC3-PC7 ports of the controller (pin30-pin34):

```
if (prog>200 && prog<400)
 {
//Program 2 "FRF"
digitalWrite(30, LOW);
digitalWrite(31, HIGH);
digitalWrite(32, LOW);
digitalWrite(33, LOW);
digitalWrite(34, LOW);
```

The frequency of the sinusoidal signals is set by the "freq" constant:

```
// Run the sine function with the "frequency" (freq) pa-
rameter for 12 seconds
//(t = 12000 ms)
 t = millis();
if (t < 12000) { freq = 20; //        frequency =   182 Hz
      Sine05_Function(freq);
            }
if (t > 12000 && t < 14000){freq =25; //frequency =158 Hz
      Sine05_Function(freq);
```

For other frequency values, the code has a similar form:

```
if(t > 70000 && t < 90000){freq = 7730;//frequency = 0.5 Hz
      Sine_Function(freq);
           }
if(t > 90000 && t < 110000){freq = 16090;//frequency = 0.25 Hz
      Sine_Function(freq);
            }
  }
```

To program a pulse waveform with a duration of 100 ms and a period of 1 s, the following code is used:

```
// Program 3 "Impulse"
//initialize digital pin «led_builtin» as an output.
   pinMode(LED, OUTPUT);
   pinMode(LED_ind, OUTPUT);
...
if (prog>400 && prog<600)
 {
// Program 3 "Impulse"
   digitalWrite(LED, HIGH);  // turn the LED on (HIGH is
the voltage level)
   delay(100);    // wait for a second
   digitalWrite(LED, LOW);   // turn the LED off by making
the voltage LOW
   delay(1000);   // wait for a second
 }
```

In this case, the "LED" digital output is used as a source of the pulsed analog signal.

To program the signal in the form of a sequence of sinusoidal signal bundles with a frequency of 40 Hz, a period of 0.5 s and a varying constant component, the main code is used:

```
// Program 4 "DynamicRange"
// Generate the date of a sine function
  for(int i=0;i<255;i++){
    x=(float)i;
    y=sin((x/255)*2*PI);
    sine__05[i]=int(y*64)+63;
     sine__05_1[i]=int(y*64)+95;
      sine__05_2[i]=int(y*64)+127;
       sine__05_3[i]=int(y*64)+159;
        sine__05_4[i]=int(y*64)+191;
      }
   }
```

3.3 Test Signal Analysis Software

The test signal analysis program (virtual instrument) is installed on a laptop, to which the tested electrocardiographs are connected via USB port.

Let us consider the operation principle of the program for analyzing the signal by the example of the most complicated type of waveform, intended for testing the compliance of electrocardiograph in terms of its frequency response with the international standard. The standard specifies the following requirements for the frequency response of the electrocardiograph:

- when the frequency of the sinusoidal signal is from 0.67 to 40 Hz, the relative output amplitude of the response should not be more than $\pm 10\%$ (relating to the sinusoidal signal with a frequency of 10 Hz);
- when the frequency of the sinusoidal signal is from 40 to 100 Hz, the relative output amplitude of the response should be in the range of $+10\%$–30%;
- when the frequency of the sinusoidal signal is from 100 to 150 Hz, the relative output amplitude of the response should be in the range of $+10\%$–30%;
- when the frequency of the sinusoidal signal is from 150 to 500 Hz, the relative output amplitude of the response should be in the range of $+10\%$–100%.

The generator, which sequentially generates short sinusoidal signals with an amplitude of 1 mV and a frequency from 0.1 Hz to 200 Hz (21 frequency values in total), is connected to the input of the electrocardiograph. The digital electrocardiogram is sent to the laptop via the USB port. The electrocardiograph is designed in such a way that when it is connected to the USB port, it is treated by the computer's operating system as an external sound card. Therefore, the program, which automatically plots the amplitude-frequency response (Fig. 3), uses a virtual sub-instrument (hereinafter "subVI") for recording a microphone signal ("Acquire Sound") to read the electrocardiograph signal.

Next, the beginning of the signal is removed by the "Extract Portion of Signal Express VI" subVI to eliminate transients. Then the signal is centered by subtracting the average value, which is calculated by the "Statistics Express VI" subVI. The result of centering is shown in Fig. 4.

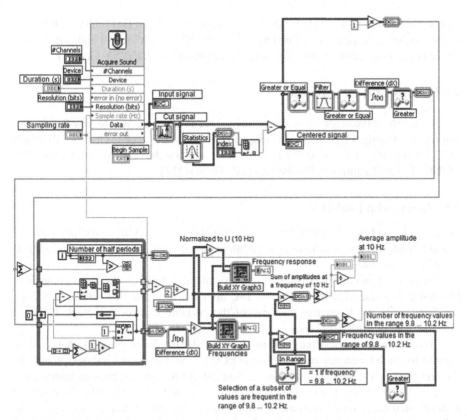

Fig. 3. Block diagram of the virtual instrument for automatic measurement of the electrocardiograph's frequency response

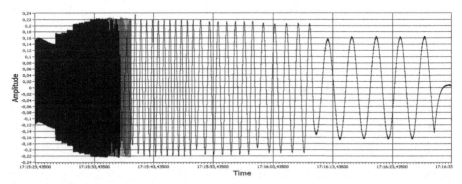

Fig. 4. The signal from the test signal generator at the output of the electrocardiograph after centering

The calculation of the current frequency value is performed outside the loop structure by the subVIs "Difference 2 (dX)" and "Divide Function". The values of the centered signal amplitudes at all frequencies are normalized to the amplitude of the centered signal at a frequency of 10 Hz by the "Normalization by U(10 Hz)" subVI. The graph of the frequency response is formed by the "Build XY Graph" subVI and is displayed on the two-coordinate indicator "Frequency response ECG-1.1"("XY Graph").

4   Results and Discussion

As an example of the output from the automated hardware and software suite for electro-cardiograph testing, Fig. 5 shows the frequency response of portable electrocardiograph ECG-1.1 manufactured by AGP LLC (Barnaul) and portable electrocardiograph ECG DONGLE manufactured by Nordavind, JSC (Dubna) [14].

4.1   Testing with LabVIEW

In the graph (see Fig. 5, generated by LabVIEW15) the acceptability range for frequency and amplitude values, as required by the international standard IEC 60601-2-25:2011, is limited by rectangles.

The figure shows that the frequency response of the portable electrocardiograph ECG DONGLE manufactured by Nordavind JSC does not meet the IEC 60601-2-25:2011 standard, while the frequency response of the portable electrocardiograph ECG-1.1 manufactured by AGP LLC does.

Considering the shape of the graph in the 40–150 Hz band we can assume that possible reasons for such frequency response of the ECG DONGLE electrocardiograph may be the presence of a constantly switched-on band-stop filter that suppresses interference from the 50 Hz mains, as well as faults in the design of the low-pass filter. The second assumption is based on the increase of the transmission factor at frequencies close to the upper value of the bandwidth (see Fig. 5), that is typical of different types of filters, for example, of an active Sallen-Key second order filter.

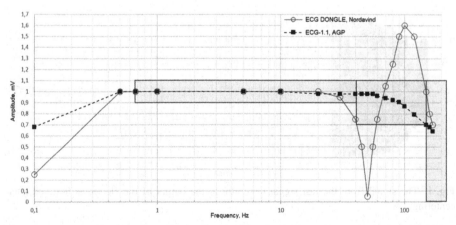

Fig. 5. The frequency responses of the portable electrocardiograph ECG-1.1 produced by AGP LLC (Barnaul) and the amplitude-frequency characteristics of the mobile electrocardiograph ECG-1.1 manufactured by AGP LLC, Barnaul and the mobile electrocardiograph ECG DONGLE manufactured by Nordavind, Dubna.

The generation of each amplitude-frequency response graph was carried out within 66 s. It took about two minutes to compare the responses of two mobile electrocardiographs and to compare their characteristics quantitatively.

4.2 Discussion

The described software and hardware suite for electrocardiograph testing has a number of competitive advantages. It combines the simplicity of design, which is provided by a cheap Arduino-compatible microcontroller, and the ability to perform all the tests provided for by the IEC 60601-2-25:2011 standard. While most of the works are devoted to test generators, the proposed suite is a measuring system that combines an easily reprogrammable waveform generator, a cheap and efficient digital-to-analog converter (DAC) and an intelligent signal analyzer. The implementation of DAC without pulse-width modulation made it possible to avoid pulse noise and the need to design low-pass filters. Using a powerful visual programming environment allowed to increase the signal-to-noise ratio of the analyzed signals using a package of statistical virtual instruments.

5 Conclusions

The automated hardware and software suite has been developed and created for testing low-cost portable electrocardiographs for compliance with the requirements of Russian and international standards. It was made using the ATmega2560 microcontroller, the Arduino C language, and the laptop with the LabVIEW15 visual programming environment installed. In the LabVIEW15 environment, the virtual instrument for automatic analysis and display of analysis results has been created. In particular, it automatically plots the frequency response of the mobile electrocardiograph. Experimental evaluation of the automated suite performance shows that the duration of automatic recording of a single frequency response is 70 ± 5 s. The implementation of the automated hardware and software suite for electrocardiograph testing allows one to check at least 300 products in a shift, which is 10 times higher than the performance of testing without automation.

The increase in productivity will undoubtedly lead to a reduction in the cost of production of electrocardiographs and a decrease in their retail value. It will make them available to even more people in need. Thus, the implementation of the proposed technical solution will increase the ECG service availability. Mass availability of the electrocardiogram registration and distribution procedure will provide an opportunity for early diagnosis of cardiovascular diseases, reducing premature mortality rates.

Since the testing process ends with the generation of measurement protocols, in order to further improve testing performance and reduce costs, it is important to additionally automate the generation of test protocols in a convenient format. Since the test results are often used by many people, it would be useful to automate the process of the protocol allocation on a network resource (local or global network).

References

1. World Health Organization: Tracking universal health coverage: 2017 global monitoring report, https://www.who.int/healthinfo/universal_health_coverage/report/2017/en/, last accessed 19 March 2021
2. World Health Organization: World health statistics 2017: monitoring health for the SDGs, sustainable development goals, https://apps.who.int/iris/handle/10665/255336, last accessed 19 March 2021
3. Bansal, A., Joshi, R.: Portable out-of-hospital electrocardiography: A review of currenttechnologies. J Arrhythmia **34**, 129–138 (2018). https://doi.org/10.1002/joa3.12035138
4. Marín, O., Garcia, A., Munoz, O., Castellanos, R., Caceres, E., Santacruz, D.: Portable single-lead electrocardiogram device is accurate for QTc evaluation in hospitalized patients, Heart Rhythm O2, **2**(4), 382–387 (2021). https://doi.org/10.1016/j.hroo.2021.06.005
5. Hoehns, J., Witry, M., Oelmann, M., Frerichs, R., Greemwood, J., Nichols, R.: Community pharmacist use of mobile ECG to inform drug therapy decision making for patients receiving QTc prolonging medications. Clinical Pharmacy Research Report. Journal of the American College of Clinical Pharmacy (2021). https://doi.org/10.1002/jac5.1435
6. Stork, M.: Simulation of ECG, blood pressure and ballistocardiographic signals. Analog Integr. Circ. Sig. Process **108**(1), 111–117 (2021). https://doi.org/10.1007/s10470-021-01830-1
7. Yener, S.C., Mutlu, R.: A microcontroller-based ECG signal generator design utilizing microcontroller PWM output and experimental ECG data. In: Proceedings of 2018 Electric Electronics, Computer Science, Biomedical Engineerings' Meeting (EBBT), April 2018, Istanbul, Turkey. https://doi.org/10.1109/EBBT.2018.8391465
8. Haber, T., Striebel, P., Melichercik, J., Ismer, B.: Plug-in circuit board for the Raspberry-Pi microcomputer to reproduce multi-channel original electrocardiograms. Current Directions in Biomedical Engineering **5**(1), 561–564 (2019)
9. Shirzadfar, H., Khanahmadi, M.: Design and development of ECG simulator and microcontroller based displayer. J. Biosens. Bioelectron. **9**, 256 (2018). https://doi.org/10.4172/2155-6210.1000256
10. McSharry, P. E., Clifford, G. D., Tarassenko, L. Smith, L.A.: A dynamical model for generating synthetic electrocardiogram signals. IEEE Transactions on Biomedical Engineering **50**(3), 289–294. https://doi.org/10.1109/TBME.2003.808805
11. Edelmann, J-C, Mair, D, Ziesel, D., Burtscher, M. Ussmueller, T.: An ECG simulator with a novel ECG profile for physiological signals. Journal of Medical Engineering & Technology, **42**(7), 501–509 (2018). https://doi.org/10.1080/03091902.2019.1576788
12. Quiroz-Juárez, M.A., Jiménez-Ramírez, O., Vázquez-Medina, R., Brena-Medina, J., Aragon, J.L., Barrio, R.A.: Generation of ECG signals from a reaction-diffusion model spatially discretized. Sci. Rep. **9**, 19000 (2019). https://doi.org/10.1038/s41598-019-55448-5
13. International Electrotechnical Commission: Medical electrical equipment - Part 2–25: Particular requirements for the basic safety and essential performance of electrocardiographs. TC 62/SC 62D. IEC 60601-2-25, Geneva (2011)

Digital Device for the Computer Stabilometry Based on the Microcontroller ATmega328

Ravil Utemesov$^{(\boxtimes)}$ ⓘ and Elena Shimko ⓘ

AltSU – Altai State University, Lenin Avenue 61, 656049 Barnaul, Russia

Abstract. The article is devoted to the development of a digital measuring and computing complex for stabilometric studies based on the ATmega328 microcontroller on the Arduino Uno R3 board. The block diagram of the developed device is given. The analysis of the electronic components of the device and the main design, technological, technical, and operational characteristics of the stabilometric platform is carried out. A physical model and an algorithm for calculating the main stabilometric indicators are presented. Trial measurements and calculations have shown that the designed installation fully meets the technical requirements for devices for stabilometry. The device allows you to register and calculate the spatial and time characteristics of the movement of patients.

Keywords: ATmega328 · Computer stabilometry · Stabilometric platform · Strain gauge · Analog-to-digital converter

1 Introduction

The global trend of our time is the digitalization of all spheres of the activity. The medical industry is no exception. Therefore, the most important component of the training of technical specialists in the medical industry (medical physicists) is the creation of a modern digitalized physical workshop [1]. The students should learn not only the physical basics of various medical methods, but also modern approaches to the creation and operation of digital medical equipment. In addition, the study of the device and the principle of operation of the digital medical devices during laboratory work provides the formation of a system of practical skills in the use of modern technologies to solve a wide range of the tasks in the field of operation and design of the digital medical equipment and the apparatuses.

Among the methods that have found wide and effective application, as well as being able to answer the main questions that arise in posturologists, is the stabilometry [2]. The stabilometry is a method for diagnosing humans balance disorders. The essence of the method of computer stabilometry is to consider the biomechanical parameters of a person in the process of adopting and maintaining a vertical pose in a standing or sitting position. The importance of stabilometry for medicine is associated with the convenience of using the method and its effectiveness. With the help of stabilography, it is possible to assess the functional state of a person, diagnose motor disorders, perform the rehabilitation process, and predict the results of a treatment [3].

© Springer Nature Switzerland AG 2022
V. Jordan et al. (Eds.): HPCST 2021, CCIS 1526, pp. 43–54, 2022.
https://doi.org/10.1007/978-3-030-94141-3_5

The stabilometric studies are carried out using stabilometric platforms. A stabilometric platform is a fixed, flat surface on which there are sensors at the edges that measure the force applied to them. This platform is designed to determine the position of the patient's pressure center and its deviation from the equilibrium position [4].

There are several main types of the stabilometric platforms: hydraulic, pneumatic and electromechanical. The device with hydraulic control includes several hydraulic drives in which a special liquid is poured to actuate it, the stabilometer itself works on the principle of a hydraulic lever. The pneumatic stabilometers consist of a pneumatic drive system and a control and registration unit.

The electromechanical stabilometers are a square platform, on the edges of which there are force sensors (usually 4 of them). When the patient stands on the center of the platform, the force applied by the patient acts on the strain gauge. The sensor readings are transmitted to the computer as a digital signal. The software processes them and plots them in real time.

The factory stable platforms do not allow you to study your hardware device and software. This is their huge disadvantage in the training of technical specialists in the medical industry. Therefore, for use in the educational process, there was a need to develop the author's stabilometric platform. The device under development must meet the following requirements: simplicity of design, compactness, visibility and accessibility of hardware and software parts, ease of use, intuitive interface, long operating time, and ease of possible repair and modernization of the device, low cost of device [1].

2 Hardware of the Stabilometric Device

The electromechanical stabilometers have a simpler and more visual design in comparison with hydraulic and pneumatic devices. The platforms of this type are the easiest to manufacture. In addition, they have found the greatest application in medical practice. Therefore, the stabilometric platform of the electromechanical type was taken as the basis of the developed device. The block diagram of the developed stabilometric platform is shown in Fig. 1.

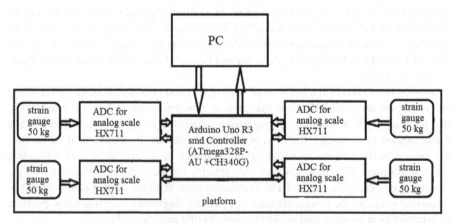

Fig. 1. The block diagram of the stabilometric platform.

2.1 Microcontroller

The ATmega328 microcontroller on the Arduino Uno R3 board was chosen as the electronic basis of the device (Fig. 2a). Arduino Uno R3 specifications are shown in the Table. The board length is 68.6 mm; the board width – 53.4 mm and weight – 25 g.

This hardware platform has the necessary number of digital and analog inputs and outputs, a built-in ADC and DAC, a C++ is like programming language, which makes it possible to transfer the project to another controller without significant correction of the program code [5].

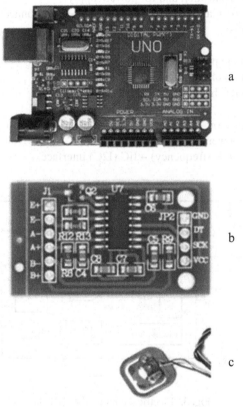

Fig. 2. a - Arduino Uno R3 controller (ATmega328), b - ADC NX711, c - The strain gauge of 50 kg

The Arduino Uno R3 controller is the most popular device on the ATmega328 chip and is the most affordable device. This board is one of the most successful choices for working with the Arduino environment. It has optimal dimensions (not too large, like the Mega and not so small as the Nano), in connection with the mass release of this controller, it will not be difficult to buy it and all sorts of clones, so a lot of libraries and sketches are written for it [3].

2.2 Analog-To-Digital Converter

The NX711 board was chosen as the analog-to-digital converter (ADC) (Fig. 2b, 3).

The NX711-24-bit ADC is used as an ADC for the strain gauge, scales, and Arduino and can be used in simple projects on microcontrollers where it is necessary to accurately take readings from strain gauge [6]. Practical applicationis creating household scales, measuring force on servos in 3D printers.

To work, you need to connect the HX711 ADC to the strain gauge (according to the bridge scheme), to the Arduino controller (or other control microprocessor device) and supply power. The HX711 ADC has two connectors for connection to the strain gauge, for connection to the controller, and for power supply:

The first connector, marked on the board J1, is used for connecting the strain gauge. Contact designation is:

- E+, E− (strain gauge power supply);
- A−, A+ (channel A) channel gain 124 or 64;
- B−, B+ (channel B) channel gain 32.

The second connector, indicated on the JP2 board, is used to connect to the controller and to supply power. Contact designation: VCC (supply voltage), GND (common contact), DT (data), SCK (frequency) – IIC (I2C) interface.

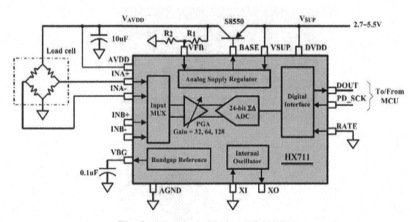

Fig. 3. Electrical circuit ADC HX711.

Channel A can be programmed for a gain of 64 or 128 (depending on the batch). Channel B has a fixed gain of 32.

The power supply to the HX711 ADC board can be carried out both from the Arduino controller (another microprocessor control device), and from an external power source. The characteristics of NX711 are as follows. The chip - HX711; CPU bit rate of 24-bit; the channel gain of 32, 64 or 128 (depending on the channel); the measurement speed: 10 measurements per second (Hz) or 80 measurements per second (Hz); the supply voltage: 2.6–5.5 V; differential input voltage: ±40 mV; the dimensions: 38 × 21 × 10 mm.

2.3 Force Sensor

As a force sensor in the developed installation, a strain gauge of 50 kg is used (Fig. 2c). In the design of the stabilometric platform, four sensors are used. Due to this it is possible to conduct examinations of patients with a body weight of up to 200 kg.

The 50 kg strain gauge is a strain-resistive sensor designed to create scales, pressure sensors, or end sensors based on it [7]. It should be noted that the stabilometric platform and the balance have almost the same hardware and mechanical design. The main difference is in the software processing of the received digital data.

At the heart of its design, the sensor has thin-film resistors that change their resistance when deformed. These resistors form a half-bridge, which must either be supplemented with resistors to a full bridge, or connected together with another sensor or sensors, after which this bundle can be connected directly to the ADC. The sensor is made of aluminum, has the shape of a square, in the center of which is a protruding part with a strain gauge. Its characteristics: the power supply voltage is 5 V; the operating temperature range: − 10 … +50 °C; the maximum measured weight is 50 kg; the complex error is 0.2%; the device dimensions: 34 × 34 mm.

In the developed stabilometric platform, two resistors of 10 kOhm each are used to create the Wheatstone bridge.

2.4 Stabilometric Platform

As the mechanical basis of the device, a square platform with dimensions of 70 × 70 × 2 cm is used (see Fig. 4).

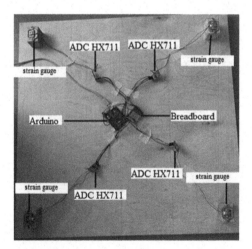

Fig. 4. The stabilometric platform, bottom view.

At the corners of the platform there are legs measuring 5 × 3 × 4 cm. The legs serve as the basis for mounting the strain gauge. Also on the lower side of the platform, the entire hardware part of the device is mounted (Arduino Uno R3 microcontroller (ATmega328) and NX711 ADC). A separate ADC is used to take readings from each sensor. All four ADCs are connected to the microcontroller. Additionally, a breadboard is used to supply power to the ADC. To reduce the influence of electromagnetic interference during the installation of the device, shielded wires are used. This design provides visibility and easy access to any electronic component of the stabilometric platform. The unit allows measurements to be made at a frequency of 1 Hz. The connection to the computer is made via a standard USB interface. The microchips are powered via a USB cable and digital data is exchanged between the microcontroller and the computer.

3   Instruments for Stabilometric Indicators Calculations

3.1   Software

Software development for the interaction of a microcontroller and a personal computer was carried out in the Arduino IDE environment in a C++ is like programming language. It is the use of C++ of this language that makes this project flexible for use on the basis of other microcontrollers, with minor edits in the code. To take into account the features of the NX711 board, third-party libraries written for this ADC were used. For example, Excel builds graphs online and outputs zeros if there is a load weighing less than 1 kg on the platform. It is also possible to stop and resume reading from the sensors. The sensors themselves do not require additional calibration and configuration and are fully ready for operation after connecting the device to a computer.

The sensor readings are displayed in a real-time MS Excel spreadsheet. For this purpose, the PLX-DAQv2 macro was used (Fig. 5).

Fig. 5. PLX-DAQv2 macro running with excel.

Data output in Excel provides visibility of the measurement process and the ability to quickly analyze data and plot graphs.

The measurement algorithm is reduced to the following steps:

- Connect the Arduino to a personal computer,
- Launch the Arduino IDE app,
- Uploading a sketch,
- Launch the port monitor,
- The patient stands on the platform,
- Get the values from the sensors,
- Perform calculations and build graphs.

3.2 Physical Model

A simple static stabilometric test (the Romberg test) was used as a test measurement [4]. To obtain correct results, the patient must stand on a stabilometric platform according to the method:

- the patient should stand on straight legs;
- his body should not be bent;
- the patient is looking straight ahead, the head is not tilted, the arms hang in a free position;
- the patient is strongly discouraged from making any movements during the procedure.
- to reduce the psychoemotional component of the measurement error, it is necessary to position the computer screen in such a way that it does not fall into the field of view of the patient [8].

To understand the methodology of further calculations, let us turn to the physical model of the stabilometric platform (see Fig. 6).

First of all, it is necessary to calculate the coordinates of the patient's pressure center [9]. This is necessary for constructing a statokinesiogram and for further calculations. Let us write down a system of equilibrium equations:

$$G - P_1 + P_2 + P_3 + P_4 = 0, \ G \cdot Y_C - P_2 \cdot y_2 - P_3 \cdot y_3 = 0,$$
$$G \cdot X_C - P_3 \cdot x_3 - P_4 \cdot x_4 = 0.$$

From where we express the coordinates of the pressure center:

$$X_C = \frac{P_3 \cdot x_3 + P_4 \cdot x_4}{G},$$

$$Y_C = \frac{P_2 \cdot y_2 + P_3 \cdot y_3}{G},$$

$$G = P_1 + P_2 + P_3 + P_4,$$

where G is the patient's gravity (the patient's weight); $P_{1,\ldots,4}$ – pressure forces on the sensors (reaction forces of the sensors); $x_{1,\ldots,4}$, $y_{1,\ldots,4}$ – sensor coordinates (distances between sensors); X_C and Y_C – coordinates of the patient's pressure center [10].

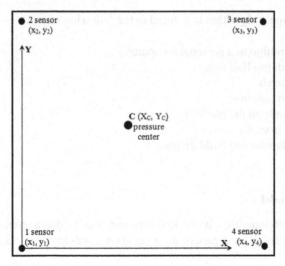

Fig. 6. The physical model of the stabilometric platform.

3.3 Method of Calculating the Stabilometric Indicators

Over time, the position of the pressure center will move in the plane of the support. The method of stabilometry consists in considering the characteristics of this movement. The algorithm for further calculations of the main stabilometric indicators is schematically shown in Fig. 7.

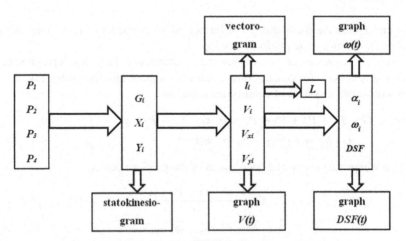

Fig. 7. Scheme for calculating the main stabilometric indicators.

First, the coordinates of the pressure center at the current time X_i, Y_i are calculated. A statokinesiogram is constructed based on these values. Next, the distances between the positions of the pressure center at the current and previous time points l_i and the total length of the statokinesiogram L are calculated.

Next, the vector characteristics are calculated [11, 12]. The modulus of the average velocity of the center of pressure in the interval between the two measurements V_i. The graph V(t) is plotted. The projections of the average velocity on the coordinate axes V_{xi}, V_{yi} are also calculated. A vectorogram is constructed, i.e., a statokinesiogram in the phase space of velocity projections.

Knowing the projections of the average velocity on the coordinate axis, you can calculate the direction of the average velocity vector (the angle α_i) at the current time. After that, you can calculate the average angular velocity ω_i of the rotation of the vector V_i in the time interval between the two dimensions and plot $\omega(t)$.

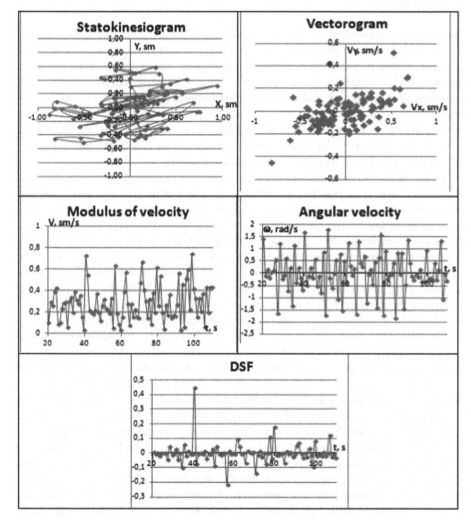

Fig. 8. Example of graphs of stabilometric characteristics.

As a result, the dynamic stabilization factor (DSF) is calculated. The DSF is the area of an elliptic sector on a vector graph that sweeps the average velocity vector over the time interval between the two dimensions.

All calculations are performed using a simple finite-difference method. Stabilometric studies of 10 subjects were conducted and the necessary graphs were constructed. The total deviation of the weight on the stabilometric platform from the standard scales was on average 2.5%. For each subject, 100 measurements were taken from the stabilometric platform. Examples of the obtained graphs are shown in Fig. 8.

4   Conclusions

The digital stabilometric device based on the ATmega328 microcontroller on the Arduino Uno R3 board has been developed and created. The device is created according to the classical scheme of an electromechanical stabilometer and fully meets the technical requirements for devices for stabilometry [13]. The developed device and software allow registering and calculating scalar and vector stabilometric indicators. The test results obtained are in good agreement with the literature data [2, 4, 8, 14], which confirms the operability of the created software and hardware complex. Thus, the developed stabilometric platform is fully ready for implementation in the educational process during the training of technical specialists in the medical industry.

At the same time, the developed device has a number of distinctive features. The first distinctive feature is the possibility of smooth adjustment of the measurement frequency from 0 to 20 Hz. The vast majority of factory stabilometers operate at a fixed frequency. Some models allow measurements to be carried out at various preset frequencies, that is, the measurement frequency is adjusted discretely, and not continuously. The possibility of continuous frequency adjustment allows us to investigate, for example, which of the stabilometric parameters are frequency-dependent and which are not. It should be recognized that with a maximum measurement frequency of 20 Hz, the time-frequency analysis of the obtained data is not sufficiently effective [15]. Therefore, in the future, it is planned to modernize the device in order to increase the measurement frequency to at least 50 Hz [16]. Such modernization will allow the device to be used not only in the educational process, but also for solving research tasks.

The second distinctive feature is the ability to easily and quickly change the relative position of the force sensors and their number. For example, using three force sensors instead of four will allow you to use a stabilometric platform not only on a perfectly flat horizontal surface (as you know, three points are always in the same plane). However, the possibility of using three sensors instead of four requires additional research.

The third distinctive feature of the developed device is a completely open program code. On the one hand, this allows you to upgrade the hardware of the device without significantly changing the program code. On the other hand, it allows you to upgrade the program code for calculating any parameters of stabilometric signals. At the moment, more than 50 stabilometric parameters are known. However, the reliability and significance of many of these parameters is controversial among researchers [3, 8, 17]. In addition, most of the stabilometric parameters are poorly related to physical models of maintaining human equilibrium [2, 9]. Thus, at present, there are a large number of research problems in the field of stabilometric research, the solution of which requires not only conducting experiments, but also modern computational methods for processing measurement results.

References

1. Nizamova, E.I., Garnaeva, G.I., Nefediev, L.A., Mingazov, R.R.: Application of modern physical laboratory equipment for professional competence formation of practice-oriented teachers in physics. J. Adv. Res. Dyn. Control Syst. **11**(8), 1889–1897 (2019)
2. Ruhe, A., Fejer, R., Walker, B.: The test–retest reliability of centre of pressure measures in bipedal static task conditions – a systematic review of the literature. Gait Posture **32**(4), 436–445 (2010). https://doi.org/10.1016/j.gaitpost.2010.09.012
3. Tamburella, F., Scivoletto, G., Iosa, M., Molinary, M.: Reliability, validity, and effectiveness of center of pressure parameters in assessing stabilometric platform in subjects with incomplete spinal cord injury: a serial cross-sectional study. J NeuroEng. Rehabil. **11**, 86 (2014). https://doi.org/10.1186/1743-0003-11-86
4. Takada, H., Ono, R., Nakane, K., Kinoshita, F., Nakayama, M.: Stabilometry. In: Takada, H., Yokoyama, K. (eds.) Bio-information for Hygiene. CTEHPM, pp. 93–111. Springer, Singapore (2021). https://doi.org/10.1007/978-981-15-2160-7_9
5. Cameron, N.: Arduino Applied. Apress, Berkeley (2019). https://doi.org/10.1007/978-1-4842-3960-5
6. Dunbar, N.: ATmega328P hardware: ADC and USART. In: Arduino Software Internals. Apress, Berkeley (2020). https://doi.org/10.1007/978-1-4842-5790-6_9
7. Makarov, D.: Strain gauge: operating principle, device, types, connection diagrams (Tenzo-datchik: princip raboty, ustrojstvo, tipy, skhemy podklyucheniya). https://www.asutpp.ru/ten zodatchik.html. Accessed 24 May 2021 (in Russian)
8. Grohovsky, S.S., Kubryak, O.V.: Metrological assurance of stabilometric study. Biomed. Eng. **48**(4), 196–199 (2014). https://doi.org/10.1007/s10527-014-9451-0
9. Kruchinin, P.A.: Mechanical models of stabilometry. Russ. J. Biomech. **18**(2), 158–166 (2014)
10. Lafond, D., Duarte, M., Prince, F.: Comparison of three methods to estimate the center of mass during balance assessment. J. Biomech. **37**(9), 1421–1426 (2004). https://doi.org/10.1016/S0021-9290(03)00251-3
11. Usachev, V.I., Artemov, V.G., Kononov, A.F.: A method for assessing the functional state of a person (Sposob ocenki funkcionalnogo sostoyaniya cheloveka). Patent RU2380035C1, issued 27 Jan 2009 (in Russian)
12. Grokhovskii, S.S., Kubryak, O.V.: A Method for integral assessment of the effectiveness of posture regulation in humans. Biomed. Eng. **52**(2), 138–141 (2018). https://doi.org/10.1007/s10527-018-9799-7
13. Sliva, S.S.: Domestic computer stabilography: engineering standards, functional capabilities, and fields of application. Biomed. Eng. **39**, 31–34 (2005). https://doi.org/10.1007/s10527-005-0037-8
14. Stergiou, N., Decker, L.M.: Human movement variability, nonlinear dynamics, and pathology: is there a connection? Hum. Mov. Sci. **30**(5), 869–888 (2011). https://doi.org/10.1016/j.humov.2011.06.002

15. Aljawarneh, S., Anguera, A., Atwood, J.W., Lara, J.A., Lizcano, D.: Particularities of data mining in medicine: lessons learned from patient medical time series data analysis. EURASIP J. Wirel. Commun. Netw. **2019**(1), 1–29 (2019). https://doi.org/10.1186/s13638-019-1582-2
16. Safi, K., et al.: Automatic analysis of human posture equilibrium using empirical mode decomposition. SIViP **11**(6), 1081–1088 (2017). https://doi.org/10.1007/s11760-017-1061-3
17. Chiari, L., Rocchi, L., Cappello, A.: Stabilometric parameters are affected by anthropometry and foot placement. Clin. Biomech. **17**(9), 666–677 (2002). https://doi.org/10.1016/S0268-0033(02)00107-9

Real-Time Correlation Processing of Vibroacoustic Signals on Single Board Raspberry Pi Computers with HiFiBerry Cards

Vladimir Faerman[1]([✉]) [iD], Valeriy Avramchuk[1] [iD], Kiril Voevodin[1] [iD],
and Mikhail Shvetsov[2] [iD]

[1] Tomsk State University of Control Systems and Radioelectronics,
40 Lenina Avenue, Tomsk 634050, Russia
fva@fb.tusur.ru
[2] Tomsk Polytechnic University, 30 Lenina Avenue, Tomsk 634050, Russia

Abstract. The paper discusses the implementation of a time-frequency correlation algorithm for time delay estimation (TDE) on Raspberry Pi single-board computers. The implemented correlation algorithm is based on Fourier transform with the frequency sweep. In the paper, we analyzed the task of real-time acquisition and processing of acoustic signals with the Raspberry Pi computers. Then we modified the algorithm of computation of time frequency-correlation function to be applicable in real-time and implemented it as a C++ object. To increase the performance, we implemented GPU acceleration using GPU_FFT and Vulkan FFT libraries. The first library is a firmware that utilizes VideoCore IV on Raspberry Pi 3B+. Vulkan FFT library was implemented as an alternative compatible with VideoCore VI on Raspberry 4B. To estimate the efficiency of applying the graphical cores to we conducted a set of experiments. Those experiments were designed to measure the reduction in processing time after accelerating the most time computationally operation of inverse Fourier transform with the GPU. According to the results, we have concluded that GPU acceleration is efficient and makes possible the real-time processing of acoustic signals even of Raspberry Pi 3B+. The GPU acceleration proved to be the most crucial when large Fourier transform window size and the significant number of frequency bands are used.

Keywords: Correlation analysis · Time delay estimation · FFTW · Vulkan FFT · Raspberry Pi · GPU_FFT

1 Introduction

Nowadays the advances in digital technology are characterized by the spreading of accessible and portable computing devices. The use of such devices gives a start to the new technology direction specializing in the designing of devices that are supposed to be distributed in the environment but interconnected within the telecommunication network [1].

V. Jordan et al. (Eds.): HPCST 2021, CCIS 1526, pp. 55–71, 2022.
https://doi.org/10.1007/978-3-030-94141-3_6

Single-board computers have become an important element in sensor networks. They have a number of features that make them an efficient solution to use in the Internet of Things (IoT) applications. Unlike microcontrollers, single-board computers have a hardware configuration corresponding to a full-fledged computer. They have their own RAM and GPU, and also provide wide support of different peripheral devices [2]. Modern single-board computers have natively built-in adapters for the numerous standards of wireless telecommunications and work under the operating system control. These advantages make system configuration based on single-board computers much easier than when using microcontrollers or boards based on them. At the same time, in contrast to personal computers, single-board solutions have significantly smaller dimensions and relatively low power consumption.

The article proposes a solution based on single-board Raspberry Pi computers designed for the time delay estimation (TDE) for two vibroacoustic signals acquired simultaneously through two audio channels. Signal processing is carried out in real-time in accordance with the generalized correlation method [3] with frequency sweep [4]. Such functionality is sufficient to create a leak noise correlator [5]. The signal processing algorithm is described in Sect. 2. Hardware and software are discussed in Sect. 3. Section 4 is devoted to the evaluation of the correlator's performance. The applicability of the device in a sensor network for monitoring pipeline systems is addressed in the conclusion.

2   Practical Correlation Analysis

Signal processing in this application is carried out to estimate the time difference of arrival (TDOA) between the instances of the signal received by two distributed sensors. This problem is the classical passive TDE scenario [6], and various methods can be applied to solve it [7–10]. Correlation analysis is the signature method for its solution [3, 10, 11]. The statement of the problem and the algorithm analysis are given in this section.

Let the source S emits the signal $s_0(t)$ which is received by two sensors A and B laying at a distance from each other. When the pipeline leak detection application is considered, the source and both sensors are located along a line. The signals $s_A(t)$ и $s_B(t)$ are [10]

$$s_A(t) = k_A \cdot s_0(t - \tau_A) + n_A(t),$$
$$s_B(t) = k_B \cdot s_0(t - \tau_B) + n_B(t), \tag{1}$$

where k_A, k_B are attenuation coefficients ($0 \leq k_{A,B} \leq 1$); τ_A, τ_B are positive delays introduced by the lag of $s_0(t)$ propagation; $n_A(t)$, $n_B(t)$ are additive random noises. The problem is in the estimation of time delay value T

$$T = \tau_B - \tau_A. \tag{2}$$

A common practice is to use the following expression measure T [9]

$$\overline{T} = \arg\max[r_{AB}(\tau)], \tag{3}$$

where $\overline{T}$ is the measured time delay; $r_{AB}(\tau)$ is an estimate of the cross-correlation function of the signals $s_A(t)$ and $s_B(t)$. Obtaining an estimate for $r_{AB}(\tau)$ is a complex problem which is going to be discussed below.

2.1   Short Time Fourier Transform

Signal processing in modern systems is carried out mainly in the digital form. The signals $s_A(t)$ and $s_B(t)$ are sampled with a frequency f_d in such a way that

$$s_A(t_l) = s_A(l \cdot \Delta), \quad s_B(t_l) = s_B(l \cdot \Delta), \quad l \cdot \Delta < L, \tag{4}$$

where $\Delta = 1/f_d$ is a sampling interval; L is the time period when signals are recorded. The time series $s_A(t_l)$ and $s_B(t_l)$ are used to obtain estimates of the instantaneous signal spectrums $S_A(f_k)$ and $S_B(f_k)$ by applying windowed discrete Fourier transform (DFT) [3]

$$S_A^{(q)}(f_k) = \mathrm{DFT}\big[s_A(b_q + t_i) \cdot w(t_i)\big], \quad S_B^{(q)}(f_k) = \mathrm{DFT}\big[s_B(b_q + t_i) \cdot w(t_i)\big], \tag{5}$$

where $i = 0, 1, ..., N - 1$; N is the integer size of the time window; $w(t_i)$ is time-domian window function; $b_q = q \cdot N \cdot \Delta$ is the first tick to which the window is applied. Hereinafter, it is considered that the condition $b_q + (N - 1) \cdot \Delta < L$ is satisfied. Window functions $w(t_i)$ go with various frequency response characteristics [11], and the choice of one or another option is usually depend on the spectral characteristics of the signals and on the goal of spectral analysis. In the simplest case, the rectangular window function $w(t_i)$ can be equal to 1 ($w_0(t_i) = 1, i = 0, 1, ..., N - 1$).

To implement DFT in (5), it is a good choice to use efficient fast Fourier transform algorithms (FFT) [12]. So, to meet the requirements for FFT, let us assume that $N = 2^n$, where n is a positive integer. In addition, considering that all possible values of $s_A(t)$ and $s_B(t)$ are real, we will also assume that in $S_A(f_k)$ and $S_B(f_k)$ spectrums there are $(N/2 + 1)$ values. In this case, all frequency samples values except the first and the last are complex-valued.

Instantaneous spectrums are used to estimate the spectrum characteristics of the signals.

2.2   Obtaining Spectral Characteristics

Spectral characteristics like the cross-spectrum of the $S_{AB}(f_k)$ signals, as well as the spectral power densities $S_{AA}(f_k)$, $S_{BB}(f_k)$ of each of the signals, are of great practical importance in TDE. The instances of these spectral characteristics can be obtained by the following formulas [15]

$$S_{AB}^{(q)}(f_k) = S_A^{(q)}{}^*(f_k) \cdot S_B^{(q)}(f_k), \quad k = 0, 1, ..., N/2; \tag{6}$$

$$S_{AA}^{(q)}(f_k) = S_A^{(q)}{}^*(f_k) \cdot S_A^{(q)}(f_k), \quad S_{BB}^{(q)}(f_k) = S_B^{(q)}{}^*(f_k) \cdot S_B^{(q)}(f_k), \quad k = 0, 1, ..., N/2. \tag{7}$$

Averaging over multiple windows is used to obtain the best estimates of the spectral characteristics taking into account the presence of noises $n_A(t)$, $n_B(t)$ in (1) [13]

$$S_{AB}(f_k, Q) = \frac{1}{Q} \sum_{q=0}^{Q-1} S_{AB}^{(q)}(f_k), \quad k = 0, 1, ..., N/2 \tag{8}$$

$$S_{AA}(f_k, Q) = \frac{1}{Q} \sum_{q=0}^{Q-1} S_{AA}^{(q)}(f_k), \quad S_{BB}(f_k, Q) = \frac{1}{Q} \sum_{q=0}^{Q-1} S_{BB}^{(q)}(f_k), \tag{9}$$

where Q is the number of obtained instantaneous spectra estimates ($Q \cdot N \cdot \Delta \leq L$). When processing data in real-time, it is convenient instead of (8) and (9) to use the corresponding recurrence formulas ($k = 0, 1, ..., N / 2$)

$$S_{AB}(f_k, Q) = \frac{1}{Q} \cdot \left[(Q-1) \cdot S_{AB}(f_k, Q) + S_{AB}^{(q)}(f_k) \right], \tag{10}$$

$$S_{AA}(f_k, Q) = \frac{1}{Q} \cdot \left[(Q-1) \cdot S_{AA}(f_k, Q) + S_{AA}^{(q)}(f_k) \right], \tag{11}$$

$$S_{BB}(f_k, Q) = \frac{1}{Q} \cdot \left[(Q-1) \cdot S_{BB}(f_k, Q) + S_{BB}^{(q)}(f_k) \right]. \tag{12}$$

2.3 Weighting in Frequency-Domain

The cross-spectrum estimate $S_{AB}(f_k, Q)$ can be multiplied by the frequency weighting function $\psi(f_k, Q)$ to compensate for signal distortions due to additive noises. This TDE technique is called the generalized correlation method [3].

$$S_{AB}^{\psi}(f_k, Q) = S_{AB}(f_k, Q) \cdot \psi(f_k, Q), \quad k = 0, 1, ..., N/2. \tag{13}$$

Here the superscript ψ indicates the type of the used weighting function and will be omitted in further discourse.

The specific forms of the frequency weighting functions $\psi(f_k)$ are various and is chosen depending on the application [3, 14]. Nevertheless, the spectral estimates (10)–(12) are always sufficient to obtain ψ regardless it's form

$$\psi(f_k, Q) = F\left(S_{AB}(f_k, Q), S_{AA}(f_k, Q), S_{BB}(f_k, Q) \right), \quad k = 0, 1, ..., N/2. \tag{14}$$

It should be noted that all values of $\psi(f_k)$ are always real-valued. In the simplest case, the frequency weighting function can be equal to 1 ($\psi_0(f_k) = 1, k = 0, 1, ..., N / 2$).

2.4 Frequency Sweep

An approach was originally proposed in [4] for determining the correlation on a set of M non-overlapping frequency intervals. The usefulness of this approach is obvious in cases when the signal $s_0(t)$ is located in a narrow frequency band, and the additive noises $n_A(t)$, $n_B(t)$ are wideband on the contrary. In this case, band-pass filtering enhances the signal-to-noise ratio in one of the intervals.

To apply this method, it is sufficient to use the formula below ($m = 0, 1,..., M$-1) instead of (13)

$$S_{AB}^{m}(f_k, Q) = \begin{cases} S_{AB}(f_k, Q) \cdot \psi(f_k, Q), & \left\lfloor \frac{m \cdot (N+2)}{2M} \right\rfloor \leq k < \left\lfloor \frac{(m+1) \cdot (N+2)}{2M} \right\rfloor, \\ 0, \text{ else} \end{cases} \tag{15}$$

The frequency sweep is not used at $M = 1$, and (15) downgrades to (13).

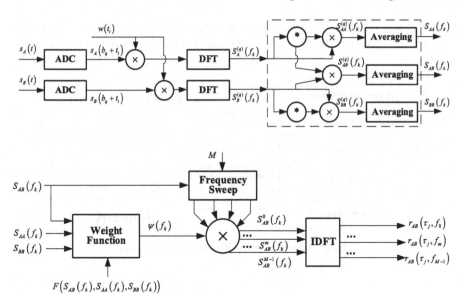

Fig. 1. Scheme of generalized correlation method with the frequency sweep.

2.5 Inverse Fourier Transform

After applying of (15), each of the M sub-spectrums undergoes an inverse DFT [4]

$$r_{AB}(\tau_j, f_m, Q) = \mathrm{DFT}^{-1}\left[S_{AB}^m(f_k, Q)\right], \ m = 0, \ 1, \ ..., M - 1. \tag{16}$$

Here the Q indicates the amount of processed data and is not essential in further considerations. Each of the M obtained correlation functions $r_{AB}(\tau_j, f_m)$ contains N real-valued points and indicates the correlation of the signals $s_A(t)$ и $s_B(t)$ in the frequency interval (f_m, f_{m+1}).

TDE can be performed in accordance with (3), however, the dependence on frequency should be considered as well.

It should be noted that no attention was paid to postprocessing the results of (16). Such issues as normalization of the correlation function, the shift of its argument, as well as overlapping while segmentation are not discussed. However, the described stages are shown in the diagram in Fig. 1.

3 Hardware and Software

Modern single-board computers of the Raspberry Pi series were used in this research. The advantages of these devices are their availability, manufacturer comprehensive support, and a wide range of supported peripheral devices. HiFiBerry sound cards were used as signal receiving devices. The hardware diagram is shown in Fig. 2.

The algorithm described in Sect. 2 is realized mainly in the C++ language. For efficient utilization of sound cards, a special RtAudio library was used [15]. This library provides a convenient C++ API functioning over the ALSA module. Various specialized libraries for performing DFT were used to ensure high efficiency of computations in the course of the signal processing. They are discussed in the corresponding subsection.

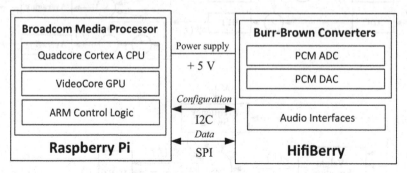

Fig. 2. Hardware composition of the used devices.

3.1 Single Board Computers

Single-board computers Raspberry Pi 3B+ [16] and Raspberry Pi 4B [17] were used in the study. These devices have a similar purpose and comparable hardware capabilities, however, there are some significant differences. The key difference between those two computers is GPU. The VC 4 graphics core was part of the SoC BCM 2835 which Raspberry Pi B computers have been equipped with since the end of 2012 [18]. There were no significant differences in graphics processors until the release of the Raspberry Pi 4 which had a new sixth-generation core VC 6. This became a significant change since a dedicated firmware for FFT calculations using GPU was developed for VC 4 [18]. Unfortunately, this solution is not compatible with the new VC 6.

3.2 HiFiBerry DAC + ADC

High-quality sound cards designed specifically for Raspberry Pi computers are used as devices for receiving vibroacoustic signals. Connecting devices to computers is carried out according to the HAT principle (hardware attached on top). No additional power is required.

During the research two different sound cards HiFiBerry DAC + ADC [19] and HiFiBerry DAC + ADC Pro [20] were used. Both devices support audio recording and playback at all standard frequencies up to 192 kHz with a coding depth of up to 24 bits. Audio interfaces are identical for both boards and are represented by a pair of RCA output connectors and a stereo input line with a minijack. The advantages of the solutions are the ultra-low level of internal noises and the ability to amplify the input signal [19, 20].

The Pro version has a number of advantages over its analog [20]. Firstly, it is the absence of jitter even in full-duplex mode. Secondly, there is no hardware anti-aliasing filter that allows getting clearer sound in hi-fi audio systems. Thirdly, there is an advanced software-configurable amplifier for input and output signals. On the basic revision of the bord, the amplifier had only three possible amplification factors, and to choose one of those, user must put the jumper in the corresponding position.

3.3 Libraries for FFT

The signal processing procedure is based on DFT. The complete processing of a single segment of data requires 2 forward and M inverse DFTs. Effective transforms implementation is a key factor for the effective algorithm's implementation. It was stated earlier that computers have both CPU and GPU that can be used to perform DFT. The efficiency of using one or another processing unit is determined by the volume of the input data. The optimal GPU vs CPU choice for each computer and the operating mode is the subject of research.

The conventional standard for computing DFT on the CPU is the FFTW library [21]. We used FFTW v. 3.3.8 and applied the functions that perform real-to-complex transform with aligned data. Such an approach has turned to be the most effective in the preliminary research.

We used the firmware library GPU_FFT v. 3.0 [18] to compute the DFT on the GPU of the Raspberry Pi 3B+. It is an efficient and convenient solution designed and optimized for the VC 4 architecture. This library supports complex-to-complex direct transform of aligned data. To make it efficiently work with real-valued data we followed the recommendations in [12] and introduced some modifications discussed in the following subsection.

Since GPU_FFT is not supported by the new VC 6, the VkFFT library [22] was chosen as an alternative. The solution is based on the cross-platform low-level API for graphics and computational applications named Vulkan [26]. The interface is developed by Khronos company. Vulkan support for Raspberry Pi 4 computers was announced and at the time of the study was only roughly confirmed [23]. Despite the fact that the library offers a wide range of functions, the direct complex-to-complex transformation was the only one actually used. The data preprocessing was carried out in the same way as when using GPU_FFT.

3.4 Computation Schemes for GPU

Libraries that perform calculation FFT on GPU, as a rule, are focused on executing a certain number B of complex-to-complex transforms in a single call of the function. Direct use of complex-to-complex transformations for real data is redundant. In this regard, the data is preliminarily reorganized in order to increase the efficiency of their processing in the future. The data preprocessing is based on the guides in [12]. The operations applied prior to the direct DFT are trivial so the algorithm of preprocessing prior to the inverse DFT is described below.

In [12] the scheme for calculating the inverse FFT for two real sequences through one FFT for a complex sequence of the same length is proposed. The main point of the scheme is the following.

At first, from two sequences $S^m{}_{AB}(f_k)$ and $S^{m+1}{}_{AB}(f_k)$, having $(N/2+1)$ complex-valued points, a sequence $S^{m,\,m+1}{}_{AB}(f_k)$ containing N complex-valued points is formed. For this, the following transitions are carried out for the real.

$$
\begin{cases}
\mathrm{Re}\left[S_{AB}^{m,m+1}(f_k)\right] = 0, \ 1 \leq k < \left\lfloor \frac{m \cdot (N+2)}{2M} \right\rfloor; \\[4pt]
\mathrm{Re}\left[S_{AB}^{m,m+1}(f_k)\right] = \mathrm{Re}\left[S_{AB}^{m}(f_k)\right] - \mathrm{Im}\left[S_{AB}^{m+1}(f_k)\right], \ \left\lfloor \frac{m \cdot (N+2)}{2M} \right\rfloor \leq k < \left\lfloor \frac{(m+1) \cdot (N+2)}{2M} \right\rfloor; \\[4pt]
\mathrm{Re}\left[S_{AB}^{m,m+1}(f_{N-k})\right] = \mathrm{Re}\left[S_{AB}^{0}(f_k)\right] + \mathrm{Im}\left[S_{AB}^{m+1}(f_k)\right], \ \left\lfloor \frac{m \cdot (N+2)}{2M} \right\rfloor \leq k < \left\lfloor \frac{(m+1) \cdot (N+2)}{2M} \right\rfloor; \\[4pt]
\mathrm{Re}\left[S_{AB}^{m,m+1}(f_k)\right] = 0, \ \left\lfloor \frac{m \cdot (N+2)}{2M} \right\rfloor \leq k \leq N/2 - 1;
\end{cases}
$$

and imaginary components $S^{m,\,m+1}{}_{AB}(f_k)$

$$
\begin{cases}
\mathrm{Im}\left[S_{AB}^{m,m+1}(f_k)\right] = 0, \ 1 \leq k < \left\lfloor \frac{m \cdot (N+2)}{2M} \right\rfloor; \\[4pt]
\mathrm{Im}\left[S_{AB}^{m,m+1}(f_k)\right] = -\mathrm{Im}\left[S_{AB}^{m}(f_k)\right] - \mathrm{Re}\left[S_{AB}^{m+1}(f_k)\right], \ \left\lfloor \frac{m \cdot (N+2)}{2M} \right\rfloor \leq k < \left\lfloor \frac{(m+1) \cdot (N+2)}{2M} \right\rfloor; \\[4pt]
\mathrm{Im}\left[S_{AB}^{m,m+1}(f_{N-k})\right] = \mathrm{Im}\left[S_{AB}^{m}(f_k)\right] - \mathrm{Re}\left[S_{AB}^{m+1}(f_k)\right], \ \left\lfloor \frac{m \cdot (N+2)}{2M} \right\rfloor \leq k < \left\lfloor \frac{(m+1) \cdot (N+2)}{2M} \right\rfloor; \\[4pt]
\mathrm{Im}\left[S_{AB}^{m,m+1}(f_k)\right] = 0, \ \left\lfloor \frac{m \cdot (N+2)}{2M} \right\rfloor \leq k \leq N/2 - 1.
\end{cases}
$$

The first and the second harmonic components should be segregated and considered

$$
\begin{cases}
S_{AB}^{m,m+1}(f_0) = \mathrm{Re}\left[S_{AB}^{m}(f_0)\right] - i \cdot \mathrm{Re}\left[S_{AB}^{m+1}(f_0)\right], \ m = 0; \\[4pt]
S_{AB}^{m,m+1}(f_0) = 0, \ m > 0,
\end{cases}
$$

$$
\begin{cases}
S_{AB}^{m,m+1}(f_{N/2}) = \mathrm{Re}\left[S_{AB}^{m}(f_{N/2})\right] - i \cdot \mathrm{Re}\left[S_{AB}^{m+1}(f_{N/2})\right], \ m = M - 1; \\[4pt]
S_{AB}^{m,m+1}(f_{N/2}) = 0, \ m < M - 1.
\end{cases}
$$

The above-mentioned operation is performed for M original sequences in cases when M is even or for $M+1$ sequences when M is odd. In this case m takes values from 0 to $M/2-1$ or to $(M-1)/2$ respectively. Any available sequence can be used as the auxiliary one in the latter case.

The forward DFT is calculated at the next step for all obtained complex sequences $S^{m,\,m+1}{}_{AB}(f_k)$

$$
x_{AB}^{m,m+1}(\tau_j) = \mathrm{DFT}\left[S_{AB}^{m,m+1}(f_k)\right].
$$

Finally, the sequences $r_{AB}(\tau_j, f_0)$ and $r_{AB}(\tau_j, f_1)$ are derived from the intermediate results

$$
r_{AB}(\tau_j, f_m) = \mathrm{Re}\left[x_{AB}^{m,m+1}(\tau_j)\right], \ j = 0, 1, ..., N - 1;
$$

$$
r_{AB}(\tau_j, f_{m+1}) = -\mathrm{Im}\left[x_{AB}^{m,m+1}(\tau_j)\right], \ j = 0, 1, ..., N - 1.
$$

The result corresponding to the auxiliary sequence if M is odd is discarded.

The described algorithm is shown in Fig. 3. The advantage of this approach is that the complex-to-complex DFT can be executed with massively parallel computations on GPU. Potential and actual computational benefits will be assessed further in Sects. 4.1 and 4.3.

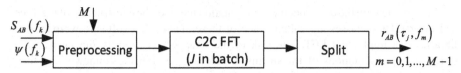

Fig. 3. Scheme of IFFT implementation on GPU.

3.5 Correlation Class

The software solution used in the study was based on the class the diagram of which is shown in Fig. 4.

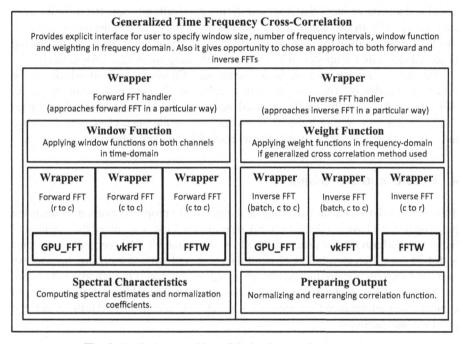

Fig. 4. Logical composition of the implemented primary class.

The constructor of the main class demands parameters such as.

- the size N of data segment for which FFT is applied;
- type of time-domain window function $w(t)$;
- type of frequency weighting function $\psi = F(S_{AA}(f_k), S_{BB}(f_k), S_{AB}(f_k))$;
- the number M of intervals in the frequency sweep of the correlation function;
- implementation of FFT used to compute forward and inverse DFT.

Complying with the user-specified computation method, the constructors of the direct and inverse DFT classes are called. Each of these classes is a software wrapper over libraries that implement FFT. The task of the wrappers is to unify the interfaces to different implementations of transforms. In addition, within the framework of these classes, the time-domain, and frequency-domain weighting functions are applied, as well as some other manipulations described in Sect. 2.

Constructors of auxiliary classes allocate the required memory and create plans for transforms according to their type and implementation. Further transforms are executed out in accordance with previously created plans which ensures that the data in memory is aligned.

Each of the auxiliary classes has one main method *Execute*, which is supplied with input data. Before executing the transform the input data is placed in the memory area associated with the created plan. After transforms, the results are copied from the memory area associated with the plan to the position of the pointer given to the method's input. The *Execute* methods of the forward and reverse FFT classes implement data processing in accordance with the upper and lower parts of the diagram in Fig. 1 respectively.

The main class has two methods *Update* and *Conclude*, each of which can be called independently. The *Update* method calls the *Execute* method of the direct FFT class, processes the newly received data, and modifies the spectral estimates $S_{AA}(f_k)$, $S_{BB}(f_k)$, $S_{AB}(f_k)$ stored in the instance of the main class. The *Conclude* method calls the *Execute* method of the inverse FFT class and forms up $r_{AB}(\tau_j, f_m)$.

4 Results and Discussion

This section is devoted to the performance analyses of the proposed solution. To study the performance, we have conducted several experiments. First, we studied the potential of increasing performance by using a GPU. To measure that we made several experiments with FFT for different volumes of input data with and without batching. Second, we measured the time required to execute each significant step in the proposed algorithm for time-frequency analysis. Finally, we conducted several additional experiments to compare the performance time with and without GPU acceleration. All the results are provided and discussed.

4.1 Evaluating the Potential

To estimate the potential increase in performance with the GPU acceleration we designed the simple test described further. To ensure that GPU is utilized efficiently it is required to process as much data at once as possible. We measured the time required to execute B complex-to-complex FFT of 2^n points and calculated the acceleration achieved by using the batching technique. All values in the table are obtained with averaging over 100 replications. Some results are in Table 1.

Table 1. FFT on GPU with and without batching (Raspberry Pi 3B+).

N	B	No batching, sec	With batching, sec	Acceleration, %
2^{10}	10	0.001801	0.001604	112.28
	20	0.002423	0.002064	117.39
	50	0.003727	0.000982	379.53
	100	0.006548	0.001022	640.70
2^{12}	10	0.003871	0.001225	316.00
	20	0.006578	0.001447	454.59
	50	0.013933	0.001072	1299.72
	100	0.026663	0.000737	3617.78
2^{15}	10	0.000804	0.000701	114.69
	20	0.001141	0.007901	144.43
	50	0.002033	0.001179	172.43
	100	0.004548	0.004200	108.28

According to data in Table 1 using batching when possible is advantageous for increasing the performance. There is a threshold value of the volume of input data, and after reaching it the GPU performance increases drastically. So, batching allows fully utilizing video core to make a frequency sweep of correlation function even for smaller N. To utilize it in the project we implemented the batching on the stage of executing inverse FFT as it is shown in Fig. 3.

4.2 Studying the Performance

To get full and consistent data on the performance we tested the implemented code for processing sound recorded in real-time. We divided all the pipelined computations of a single segment of input data into several stages:

1. acquiring and preprocessing data from the soundcard prior to execution of FFT;
2. execution of the forward FFT;
3. updating of the cross-spectrum estimate using instantaneous cross-spectrum and preprocessing it prior to execution of inverse FFT;
4. execution of the inverse FFT;
5. postprocessing the results.

Then we measured time instances for every stage for various window sizes (N) and numbers of frequency intervals (M). It should be noted, that in the course of the experiment we discovered that accelerating forward FFT with GPU does not make sense for practical values of N. So, for the forward FFT the CPU was used all the time. All values in the figures below are obtained with averaging over 100 replications.

Figures 5 and 6 show the processing time distribution over all five stages for various N and M. Figures 7 and 8 show the execution times for the inverse FFT with frequency sweep for various N and M with the postprocessing time included.

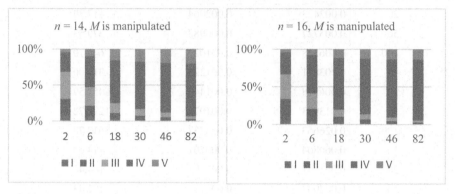

Fig. 5. Time distributions over all stages of computations (CPU is used for inverse FFT).

By studying Fig. 5 we concluded that the most computationally intensive part of the algorithm is the inverse transform. It requires the more time the more bands in frequency sweep we distinguish. At the same time, for higher values of N, the relative contribution of this computational stage to the total time increases.

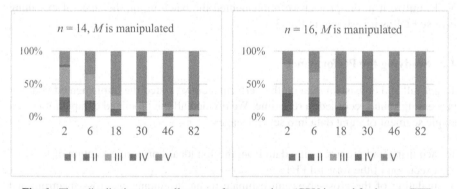

Fig. 6. Time distributions over all stages of computations (GPU is used for inverse FFT).

Figure 6 indicates that the postprocessing stage is the most time-consuming one. Therefore, GPU acceleration greatly decreases time of inverse transform making it literally insensible. It should be noted, that postprocessing stage for CPU is less time consuming, cause FFTW has natural real-valued output. In the contrary, both GPU_FFT and Vulkan FFT provide complex-valued outputs, that should be split to two real-valued sequences.

As one can see in Fig. 7 the processing time is proportional to the number M of frequency bands in the sweep. Despite the fact, that inverse FFT is much faster with GPU acceleration, additional complexity in the postprocessing stage almost nullifies this advantage for $N \leq 2^{13}$. Figure 7 shows that for $N = 2^{13}$ GPU and CPU demonstrates comparable performance for practical values of M.

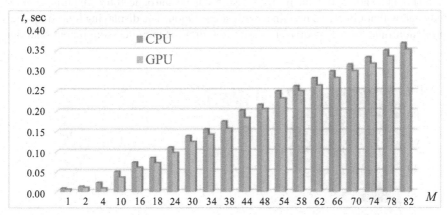

Fig. 7. Performance time of inverse FFT and output postprocessing ($N = 2^{14}$).

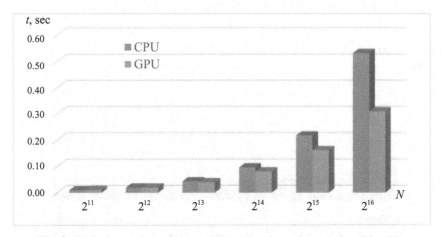

Fig. 8. Performance time of inverse FFT and output postprocessing ($M = 20$).

According to Fig. 8, the processing time demonstrates a nonlinear increase for CPU and about a linear increase for GPU. The former fact is due to the computational complexity of FFT that is considered to be $N \cdot \log(2, N)$. However, as far as GPU time of the execution of FFT is not essential, the total processing time is determined by the postprocessing stage. The completion time of this stage is proportional to both N and M and so far doubles in every next bar.

4.3 Estimating the Effect of GPU Acceleration

To estimate the effect of GPU acceleration on the performance we calculated the acceleration coefficients for the experimental data. The acceleration in the course of the execution of full routine is shown in Fig. 9a. The acceleration of the entire procedure without the postprocessing shown in Fig. 9b.

It should be noted, that the postprocessing stage is introduced for the purpose of the study and will not likely be used in a hardware solution. The displaying time-frequency correlation function will require its own algorithm for preprocessing output data that

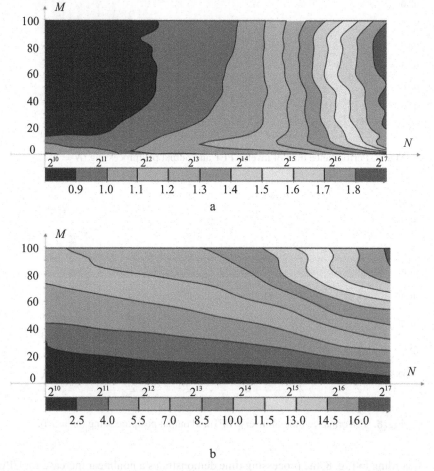

Fig. 9. Level map diagrams of performance acceleration: a – total performance time of all five stages of the algorithm; b – performance time of the algorithm without the last postprocessing stage. The acceleration is calculated as a rate by which computation time decreases when GPU is used for reverse FFT. All results time measurements are acquired after averaging over 100 replications.

could be applied directly to the output of inverse FFT. That could make the postprocessing advantage of using CPU for inverse FFT insignificant.

In Fig. 9a we can see that the CPU demonstrates slightly better performance for relatively small N. For some reason the CPU has a worse performance for small values of M also. For larger N GPU acceleration introduces a significant increase in the performance, despite the inefficiency of postprocessing the output data. The advantage of GPU is not increasing with the increase of M. Figure 9b shows that if postprocessing is not the case the GPU is universally better. The acceleration in the latter case is increasing with the increase of N and M.

5   Conclusion

The article describes the time-frequency real-time correlator implementations based on the Raspberry Pi single-board computers. The complex analysis of the correlation method is performed in the second section of the manuscript. The core operations of the processing algorithm are forward and inverse DFT. Despite the efficient FFT algorithms that could be applied, those operations are still can be considered computationally intensive for real-time processing on single-board computes. It should be noted that computation of time-frequency correlation function requires multiple inverse FFTs.

To deal with this problem we proposed the modified algorithms of computing the time-frequency correlation function introduced in [4]. The key features of the modification are the recursive scheme of updating the cross-spectrum estimate when the new segment of the input data is acquired and the new computational scheme for inverse FFT. Both introduced modifications proved to be essential during the computational experiment. To implement the modified algorithm, we developed a C++ object that integrates a few well-known FFT libraries. We used FFTW v 3.3.8 to execute FFT on CPU, GPU_FFT to execute FFT on GPU of Raspberry Pi 3B+, and Vulkan FFT to execute FFT on GPU of Raspberry Pi 4B.

To estimate the effect of GPU acceleration on performance we conducted a series of computational experiments. During the experiments, we processed the data acquired from the sound card in real-time with various computational parameters with GPU acceleration enabled and without it.

According to the results, we have concluded that GPU acceleration is efficient and makes possible the real-time processing of vibroacoustic signals both for Raspberry Pi 3B+ and for Raspberry Pi 4B. Due to the suboptimal utilization of Vulkan FFT library in our solution, the former shows more consistent performance. Therefore, the GPU acceleration proved to be the most crucial when large Fourier transform window size and a significant number of frequency bands are used.

The device was tested in a leak detection system with a virtual pipe rig [24] and proved its functionality. The hardware supports sampling of vibroacoustic signals at frequencies up to 192 kHz. At a sampling rate of 44.1 kHz, both implementations are capable of real-time computations with such settings as $N < 2^{18}$ and $M < 100$. However, the workflow proves to be unstable when $N \times M > 2^{20}$ due to size limitations of buffer shared between CPU and GPU. The latter is applied to both implementations.

References

1. Bell, C.: Sensor Networks with Arduino and Raspberry Pi. Apress, New York (2013)
2. Almeida, F.C.L., Brennan, M.J., Joseph, P.F., Gao, Y., Paschoalini, A.T.: The effects of resonances on time delay estimation for water leak detection in plastic pipes. J. Sound Vib. **420**, 315–329 (2018). https://doi.org/10.1016/j.jsv.2017.06.025
3. Knapp, C.N., Carter, G.C.: The generalized correlation method for estimation of time delay. IEEE Trans. Acoust. **24**, 320–327 (1976). https://doi.org/10.1109/TASSP.1976.1162830
4. Avramchuk, V., Goncharov, V.: Time-frequency correlation method for improving the accuracy in detecting leaks in pipelines. Adv. Mater. Res. **650**, 443–446 (2013). https://doi.org/10.4028/www.scientific.net/AMR.650.443
5. Glentis, G.O., Angelopoulos, K.: Leakage detection using leak noise correlation techniques - overview and implementation aspects. In: ACM International Conference Proceeding Series (2019). https://doi.org/10.1145/3368640.3368646
6. Faerman, V., Avramchuk, V.: Comparative study of basic time domain time-delay estimators for locating leaks in pipelines. Int. J. Networked Distrib. Comput. **8**, 49–57 (2020). https://doi.org/10.2991/ijndc.k.200129.001
7. Ma, Y., Gao, Y., Cui, X., Brennan, M.J., Almeida, F.C.L., Yang, J.: Adaptive phase transform method for pipeline leakage detection. Sensors **19** (2019). https://doi.org/10.3390/s19020310
8. Gao, Y., Brennan, M.J.Ã., Joseph, P.F.: On the effects of reflections on time delay estimation for leak detection in buried plastic water pipes. J. Sound Vib. **325**, 649–663 (2009). https://doi.org/10.1016/j.jsv.2009.03.037
9. Carter, C.C., Knapp, C.N.: Time delay estimation. In: ICASSP, IEEE International Conference on Acoustics, Speech and Signal Processing – Proceedings, pp. 357–360. IEEE (1976). https://doi.org/10.1109/ICASSP.1976.1169979
10. Björklund, S.: A Survey and Comparison of Time-Delay Estimation Methods in Linear Systems. Linkopings Universitet, Linkoping (2003)
11. Basir, M.S.S.M., Yusof, K.H., Faisal, B., Shahadan, N.H.: Optimised window selection for harmonic signal detection using short time fourier transform. In: AIP Conference Proceedings, vol. 2306 (2020). https://doi.org/10.1063/5.0032397
12. Matusiak, R.: Implementing Fast Fourier Transform algorithms of real-valued sequences with the TMS320 DSP platform (2001)
13. Carter, G.C.: Coherence and time delay estimation. Proc. IEEE. **75**, 236–255 (1987). https://doi.org/10.1109/PROC.1987.13723
14. Gao, Y.Ã., Brennan, M.J., Joseph, P.F.: A comparison of time delay estimators for the detection of leak noise signals in plastic water distribution pipes. J. Sound Vib. **292**, 552–570 (2006). https://doi.org/10.1016/j.jsv.2005.08.014
15. Scavone, G.: RT Audio 5.10. http://www.music.mcgill.ca/~gary/rtaudio/. Accessed 12 Mar 2021
16. Raspberry Foundation: Raspberry Pi 3 Model B+. https://static.raspberrypi.org/files/product-briefs/Raspberry-Pi-Model-Bplus-Product-Brief.pdf. Accessed 19 Mar 2021
17. Raspberry Foundation: Raspberry Pi 4 Computer. https://datasheets.raspberrypi.org/rpi4/raspberry-pi-4-product-brief.pdf. Accessed 19 Mar 2021
18. Holmes, A.: GPU_FFT library v. 3.0. http://www.aholme.co.uk/GPU_FFT/Main.htm. Accessed 12 Feb 2021
19. Datasheet for HifiBerry DAC+ADC. https://www.hifiberry.com/docs/hardware/using-dynamic-microphones-with-the-dac-adc/. Accessed 12 Feb 2021
20. Datasheet for HiFiBerry DAC+ ADC Pro. https://www.hifiberry.com/docs/data-sheets/datasheet-dac-adc-pro/
21. FFTW library v. 3.3.8. http://www.fftw.org/. Accessed 12 Feb 2021

22. Tolmachev, D.: VkFFT GPU-accelerated FFT library. https://github.com/DTolm/VkFFT. Accessed 19 Mar 2021
23. Upton, E.: Vulkan update: we're conformant! https://www.raspberrypi.org/blog/vulkan-upd ate-were-conformant/
24. Faerman, V., Tsavnin, A.: Concept and implementation of the laboratory test bench for simulating the case of leak detection with the use of leak-noise correlator. In: AIP Conference Proceedings, vol. 2195 (2019). https://doi.org/10.1063/1.5140106

Processing of a Spectral Electromyogram by the Method of Wavelet Analysis Using the Modified Morlet Function

Dmitry Potekhin[1]([⊠]) [ID] and Yuliya Grishanovich[2]

[1] MIREA –Russian Technological University, 78 Vernadsky Ave., Moscow 119454, Russia
msyst@msyst.ru
[2] KGTA named after V.A. Degtyarev — Russian Technological Academy,
19 Mayakovskaya str., Kovrov 601910, Russia

Abstract. Spectral electromyography (EMG), which supplements classical electromyography (EMG), is one of the diagnostic techniques of the physical health of a person. Different spectral analysis techniques are suitable for carrying out EMG; Fourier transform and wavelet analysis are the basic ones. Fourier transform has one serious drawback, i.e. meaningful measurements are misleading due to the Gibbs phenomenon. According to the authors, the best solution is the Morlet wavelet function, which also has drawbacks. Firstly, compensation for the Gibbs effect is incomplete. Secondly, the basic view of the Morlet wavelet function prevents changing the properties of functions for different applications. Thirdly, it requires significant computing resources (millions of multiply-accumulate operations per second). The article is devoted to the ways of solution of these problems using myosignal processing as an example.

Keywords: Hardware generation · Convolutional functions · Morlet wavelet · Spectral analysis · Electromyogram

1 Introduction

Wavelet transform is one of the methods popular in various disciplines, such as telecommunications, computer graphics, biology, astrophysics and medicine. Due to its good adaptability to the analysis of non-stationary signals it has become a powerful alternative to the Fourier transform in some medical applications [1]. Since many medical signals are non-stationary, wavelet analysis techniques are applied to recognize and detect key diagnostic signs [2].

Spectral electromyography is a further step in the development of the surface electromyography technology based on extra processing of the classical myographic signal by a complex of modern mathematical algorithms [3]. This technology makes it possible to extract additional useful information about the processes in the muscular system [4].

2 Morlet Wavelet Function

One of the problems concerned with the processing of the signals of different nature is that their direct analysis is difficult due to the complexity of the original signals. For example, it is impossible to determine the set of characteristics that uniquely characterize the state of muscles of different people due to the sensitivity of the parameters of myosignals to the place and method of fixing the sensors, physiological characteristics of people, such as different resistance of human skin, different levels of electrical signals, etc. [5].

2.1 Description of the Morlet Function

It is necessary to develop signal analysis techniques that have minimum sensitivity to the place and method of fixing the sensors, physiological characteristics of people, such as different resistance of human skin, different levels of electrical signals, etc. These parameters will adapt to the changing characteristics of the signal and noise. One of such techniques is the integral method of vector diagram restoration in digital data processing systems [6].

Wavelet functions denoted as $\psi(\tau)$ form a set of functions that satisfies the following conditions:

– Finite amplitude, i.e.

$$\psi(\tau) = 0, \tau \to \infty \text{ and } \tau \to -\infty; \tag{1}$$

– zero mean or

$$\int\limits_{-\infty}^{+\infty} \psi(\tau)d\tau = 0. \tag{2}$$

The possibility of solving various problems depends on the type of basic functions (wavelet functions). The choice of the wavelet function for the analysis of a specific signal is a rather difficult task. The correctness of its solution to a large extent affects the accuracy of the results obtained and the possibility of their use in subsequent calculations. Due to the fact that no significant restrictions are imposed on the form of the wavelet function there are various classes of wavelet functions with specific properties [7]. The choice of a specific wavelet function or its synthesis is a mandatory step in the development of a digital analysis method for a specific signal.

The wavelet transform consists in calculating an integral of the form:

$$W_f(t, a) = \frac{1}{a} \int\limits_{\tau_1}^{\tau_2} \psi\left(\frac{\tau - t}{a}\right) \cdot X(\tau)d\tau, \tag{3}$$

where is the time; a is the scale of the wavelet function; $\psi(\tau)$ is the wavelet function; $X(\tau)$ is the signal under investigation; τ_1 and τ_2 are the integration boundaries, which are usually chosen to be the same in absolute value, i.e. $-\tau_1 = \tau_2 = \tau_b$.

Thus, for continuous wavelet analysis it is necessary to use a function that combines the properties of the sine-cosine Fourier series and the Gaussian function. In the theory of wavelet analysis, the Morlet wavelet function is used for this purpose; its classical form is (4):

$$\psi(x) = (\cos 5x + j \cdot \sin 5x) \cdot e^{-\frac{x^2}{2}}, \tag{4}$$

and the wavelet transform has the form (5):

$$W_f(t, a) = \frac{1}{a} \int\limits_{-4\pi}^{+4\pi} \psi\left(\frac{x-t}{a}\right) \cdot f(x)dx. \tag{5}$$

The classical Morlet wavelet function has at least two significant drawbacks [6], i.e.

- real (cosine) part of the wavelet function is not equal to zero and it results in the occurrence of the Gibbs phenomenon though less significantly than when using Fourier transform;
- classical representation of expressions (4) and (5) does not allow changing the properties of the Morlet wavelet function for different applications.

2.2 Modification of the Morlet Function

The drawbacks of the Morlet wavelet function described by expression (4), which are specified in the previous section, can be eliminated by modifying it to the form:

$$\psi(\tau) = (\cos 2\pi f_0\tau + j \cdot \sin 2\pi f_0\tau) \cdot e^{-\frac{(2\pi f_0\tau)^2}{k}}, \tag{6}$$

where f_0 is the center frequency; k is the attenuation constant.

In this case in expression (6) the interpretation of the integration boundaries, classically specified in radians, and the scale a is changed. In a modified form the integration boundaries are expressed in time units, and the coefficient a has the meaning of a scale factor.

When the property of commutativity of convolution is used, considering (6) we can rewrite expression (5):

$$W_f(t, a) = \frac{1}{a} \int\limits_{-\tau_{\lim}}^{\tau_{\lim}} (\cos 2\pi f_0\tau + j \cdot \sin 2\pi f_0\tau) \cdot e^{-\frac{(2\pi f_0\tau)^2}{k}} \cdot X(t-\tau) \cdot d\tau. \tag{7}$$

Expression (7) describes the modified wavelet transform using the Morlet function, which has integration boundaries expressed in the number of half-periods x of the signal under analysis:

$$\pm \tau_{\lim} = \pm x \cdot T = \pm x \cdot \frac{1}{f}, \tag{8}$$

where f and T are the frequency and the period of the signal respectively.

The match of classic and modified boundaries - $\pm 4\pi$ means that the wavelet function takes 4 half periods [6].

The optimal coefficient k is determined empirically for different integration limits of the modified Morlet wavelet function:

$$k = 3.7895 + 6.4582 \cdot x. \tag{9}$$

Practical experience of using the modified Morlet wavelet function for the analysis of nonstationary signals allows us to recommend the integration limits $\pm 5.5\pi$ for calculations with an error of no more than 0.1%. Integration limits $\pm 1.5\pi$ lead to a larger error due to the occurrence of the Gibbs phenomenon, and the limits $\pm 7.5\pi$ and $\pm 9.5\pi$ significantly increase computational costs.

An interesting fact is that at the integration limits $\pm 1.5\pi$ the real part of the modified Morlet wavelet becomes identical to the wavelet function known as the "Mexican Hat".

The Morlet wavelet function modified in the way described above turns out to be insensitive to the occurrence of a constant component in the signal.

One of the differences between the wavelet transform and the Fourier transform is the dependence of the wavelet function window width on frequency (the analysis window width is constant in the number of signal periods). Expression (7) contains a scale factor a, which is proportional to the signal period. The scale factor compensates the change in the power of the wavelet function at different integration boundaries.

The scale factor a does not depend on the signal phase; therefore, to simplify calculations we can take the test signal which is complex-conjugate to expression (7):

$$X(\tau) = A(\cos 2\pi f \tau - j \sin 2\pi f \tau). \tag{10}$$

Let us substitute test signal (10) into expression (7) and get:

$$W_f(t, a) = \frac{A}{a} \int_{-\tau_{\lim}}^{\tau_{\lim}} \left[(\cos 2\pi f \tau)^2 + (\sin 2\pi f \tau)^2 \right] \cdot e^{-\frac{(2\pi f \tau)^2}{k}} d\tau = \frac{A}{a} \int_{-\tau_{\lim}}^{\tau_{\lim}} e^{-\frac{(2\pi f \tau)^2}{k}} d\tau. \tag{11}$$

The normalization condition is $W_f(t,a) = 1$, where $A = 1$, taking this value into account we find the actual scale factor from (11):

$$a = \int_{-\tau_{\lim}}^{\tau_{\lim}} e^{-\frac{(2\pi f \tau)^2}{k}} d\tau. \tag{12}$$

In real conditions $W_f(t,a) \neq 1$ even if $A = 1$; therefore the signal amplitude is found in the expression:

$$A = \frac{\sqrt{(ReW)^2 + (ImW)^2}}{a}. \tag{13}$$

The phase shift is found with the expression:

$$tg\phi = \frac{ImW}{ReW}. \tag{14}$$

Since expression (14) contains the ratio of the imaginary and real parts of the wavelet transform, the normalization factor does not affect the phase shift since it is the same for both real and imaginary parts of the wavelet transform by the Morlet function.

The spectrum of the Morlet wavelet function $W(t)$ corresponds to the spectrum of the Fourier transform with the Laplace-Gauss window function:

$$W(f) = \sqrt{\frac{k}{2} \frac{1}{2\pi f_0}} \cdot e^{-\frac{k}{4} \cdot \frac{(f-f_0)^2}{f_0^2}} \tag{15}$$

where f_0 is the central frequency of the wavelet function.

Figure 1 shows the spectrum of the wavelet function which corresponds to the Gaussian function.

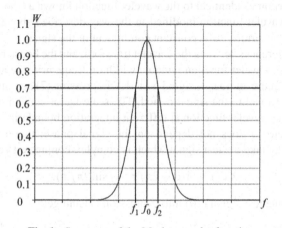

Fig. 1. Spectrum of the Morlet wavelet function.

The quality factor of the function is determined by the expression:

$$Q = \frac{f_0}{\Delta f}, \tag{16}$$

where $\Delta f = f_2 - f_1$ is the bandwidth at level:

$$W_{f_1} = W_{f_2} = \frac{\sqrt{2}}{2} W_{f_0}$$

that corresponds to half the power. Respectively, f_1 and f_2 are threshold frequencies. To find the quality factor, it is necessary to determine the frequency interval Δf (Fig. 1), which is $\Delta f = 2(f_2 - f_1)$ due to the symmetry of the Gaussian function.

$$\frac{W(f_0)}{W(f_2)} = e^{-\frac{k}{4} \cdot \frac{(f_0-f_0)^2}{f_0^2}} \cdot e^{\frac{k}{4} \cdot \frac{(f_2-f_0)^2}{f_0^2}} = \sqrt{2}. \tag{17}$$

The first exponent will be zero. To find the bandwidth of the filter let us take the natural logarithm of the right and left sides of expression (17), after transformation we will obtain the expression for the bandwidth:

$$\Delta f = 2(f_2 - f_0) = 2f_0 \sqrt{\frac{2\ln 2}{k}}. \tag{18}$$

Transforming (18) in accordance with (16), we determine the Q-factor of the Morlet wavelet function:

$$Q = \frac{\sqrt{k}}{2\sqrt{2\ln 2}}. \tag{19}$$

As can be seen from expression (19), the Q-factor of the Morlet wavelet function is determined only by its damping coefficient.

Considering the dependence of the damping coefficient on the integration boundary (9) and expression (18), the dependence of Q-factor on the integration boundaries is plotted as shown in Fig. 2.

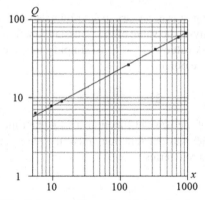

Fig. 2. The dependence of the Q-factor on the optimal integration boundaries expressed in signal periods.

The dependence is given in logarithmic coordinates and its empirical value is represented by expression (20):

$$\ln Q = 0.9650 + 0.4724 \cdot \ln x. \tag{20}$$

As in the case of Fourier transform, the transition from an ideal form of signal representation to a digital one introduces additional errors. The amplitude-quantized signal requires the refinement of the scale factor [9].

The damping coefficient of the wavelet function is related to its duration, i.e. depends on the size of the window. It is necessary that the window function decay strictly at the integration boundary (Fig. 3, c). If the window function decays before reaching the boundaries of integration (Fig. 3, b), then some of the coefficients of the digital filter will be equal to 0. These coefficients will not have any effect on the convolution result, but computing resources will be used. Thus, the order of the digital filter will be unnecessarily high. If the window function decays beyond the integration boundaries (Fig. 3, a), then the leakage effect will be observed due to the presence of discontinuities at the ends of the time series, leading to an increase in the Gibbs phenomenon [10].

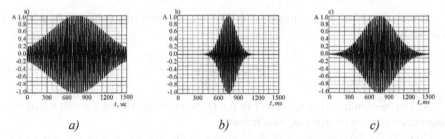

a)   b)   c)

Fig. 3. The influence of the attenuation coefficient on the envelope of the Morlet wavelet function: a) attenuates beyond the window boundaries, b) attenuates before reaching the boundaries, c) attenuates strictly at the boundaries

Based on the foregoing, it is necessary to determine at what distance from the center of the function under analysis the value of the Gaussian function (18) will become equal to one if in the center this value is $2^n - 1$. To simplify the calculations we neglect the value -1, and from (15) we obtain:

$$2^n \cdot e^{-\frac{(2\pi f_0 \tau_{lim})^2}{k}} = 1, \tag{21}$$

where n is the capacity of the wavelet function; τ_{lim} is the time interval corresponding to half the duration of the wavelet function since the whole wavelet function fits the boundaries $\pm \tau_{lim}$. In discrete terms:

$$2\tau_{lim} = N \cdot \frac{1}{f_{adc}},$$

f_{adc} is ADC frequency, N is the number of points of the wavelet function, which in its turn is equal to:

$$N = \frac{f_{adc}}{f_0} \cdot x,$$

N is the number of points per signal period, x is the number of periods in the half of the function under analysis. We substitute the integral boundaries in (22) and express the damping coefficient k:

$$k = \frac{\pi^2 \cdot x^2}{n \cdot \ln 2}. \tag{22}$$

The number of points of the wavelet function N, based on its symmetry, should be odd. But for calculations the value N should not be rounded to an integer since after rounding, the result of the wavelet analysis will be quantized.

Substituting the value of the attenuation coefficient k found from expression (22) into the expression for the Q-factor of the wavelet function (19), we obtain:

$$Q = \frac{\pi}{2 \cdot \sqrt{2n} \cdot ln2} x. \tag{23}$$

Thus, formula (23) expresses the analytical relationship of the integration boundaries taken in the number of half-periods and the quality factor of a non-recursive integer digital filter synthesized using the Morlet wavelet function.

Using formulas (23) and (16) it is possible to express the dependence of the integration boundaries on the bandwidth and on the quality factor:

$$x = \frac{1}{Q} \cdot \frac{2 \cdot \sqrt{2n} \cdot ln2}{\pi} = \frac{\Delta f}{f_0} \cdot \frac{2 \cdot \sqrt{2n} \cdot ln2}{\pi}. \tag{24}$$

Figure 4 shows a graph where the dependence of the Q-factor on the integration boundaries (Fig. 2) is superimposed on the empirical dependence of the Q-factor on the integration boundaries. The integration boundaries provide optimal filling of the integration window calculated for a different capacity of the wavelet function according to (24).

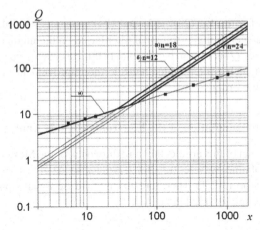

Fig. 4. Dependence of the Q-factor on integration boundaries.

The practice of using the wavelet transform shows that for small integration boundaries (before the intersection of the graphs) it is necessary to use the empirical dependence (Fig. 8 a), and after the intersection it is necessary to use the dependences for the capacity being used (Fig. 4 b), c) and d)).

Figure 5 shows the frequency response of various functions, curves a), b), c) and d) the Morlet wavelet function with the integration boundaries $\pm 3.5\pi$; $\pm 5.5\pi$; $\pm 13.5\pi$; $\pm 53.5\pi$ respectively. For all curves the number of sample points per signal period is:

$$\frac{f_d}{f_0} = 50. \tag{25}$$

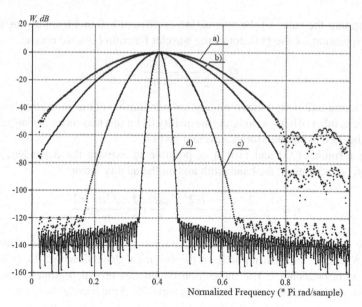

Fig. 5. Frequency response of the Morlet wavelet function.

Thus, the use of formulas (22), (23) and (24) makes it possible to calculate the coefficients of an integer digital orthogonal filter based on the modified Morlet wavelet function with the given Q-factor and bandwidth. In this case, there are no zero coefficients at the boundaries of such a filter, which leads to the improvement in the quality factor in the unchanged filter order.

2.3   Hardware Implementation of the Electromyosignals Analysis

As stated in the abstract of this article, the third drawback of the Morlet wavelet function, as well as for most of other wavelet functions, is the absence of fast transforms similar to the fast Fourier transform (FFT). Therefore, to calculate the signals spectrum, significant computing resources are required [11].

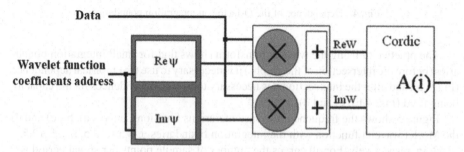

Fig. 6. Block diagram of one wavelet transform module performing linear convolution.

The wavelet transform with the modified Morlet function is complex; therefore, two filters with a different set of coefficients are required to carry out the calculation at one frequency, the output of which will be the real and imaginary parts, which are then used to determine the amplitude (see Fig. 6). It is necessary to carry out a wavelet transform at different frequencies to construct the signals spectrum. These calculations require hundreds of billions of MAC operations per second (multiply-accumulate operations).

Such computational performance can be realized on FPGAs (programmable logic integrated circuits), which can have thousands of MAC operations and are capable of performing spectral analysis with the required resolution [12].

3   Morlet Wavelet Function for Electromyogram Analysis

In order to get more information during the processing and analyzing electromyosignals, an original method of mathematical synthesis and technical implementation of a hardware generator of convolutional functions based on the Morlet wavelet function was applied. Realization of this method is based on the intensive use of the hardware components of high-performance programmable logic integrated circuits (FPGA) [13].

3.1   Experimental Setup and Results

The EMG signal recorded in the classical way is passed through a set of wavelet filters specially adapted for solving this problem [12]. The result of the wavelet transform is the signal power spectrum which characterizes the distribution of the total signal power over frequencies regardless of phase oscillations.

The sum of the powers over the entire frequency range shows the total power of the recorded EMG signal and characterizes the power developed by the muscle at the moment of signal registration. This parameter can be used to estimate the amount of energy expended by the muscle to maintain the current state (tension), i.e. it is a quantitative characteristic of the process of involvement of motor units.

The frequency distribution of power is a qualitative characteristic of the state of the muscle, and, in the general case, it depends on the type of muscle tension at the moment of signal registration. In real life, muscle tension is a combination of several types of tension of various intensity, and the recorded EMG signal is a kind of the mixture of signals of "pure" types of tension.

In order to demonstrate the capabilities of spectral myography, an experiment was conducted with people of different ages and different levels of fitness (Fig. 7, 8, 9). The spectra were summed up in series of 12.5 s during 100 s. As the result, series of 8 summed spectra were obtained.

Comparative analysis shows that at the moment of the same load the spectra have a high degree of similarity.

The total power obtained by spectral myography shows the direct value of the potential difference that makes it possible to determine the state (the degree of tension) of the muscular system at any time regardless of the initial position.

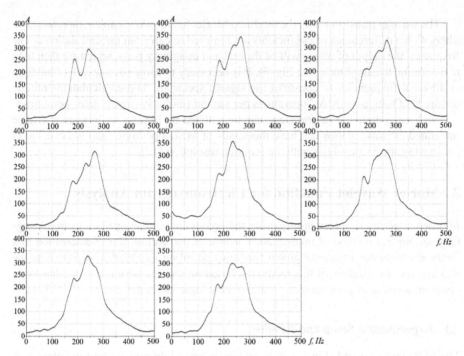

Fig. 7. 49-year-old male. Static load is 5 kg. Signal from the biceps.

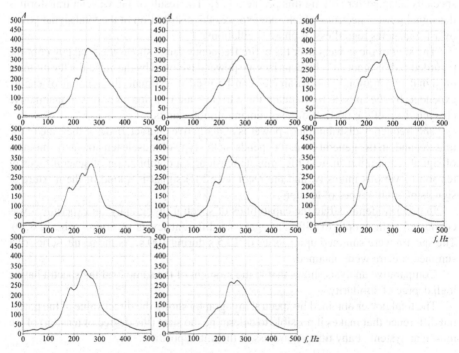

Fig. 8. 26-year-old male. Static load is 5 kg. Signal from the biceps.

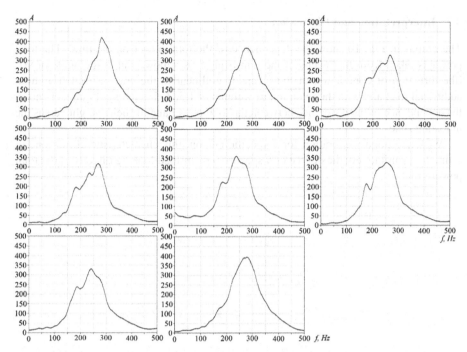

Fig. 9. 69-year-old male, master of sport. Static load is 5 kg. Signal from the biceps.

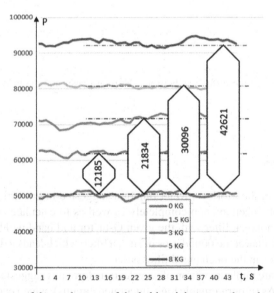

Fig. 10. Dependence of the total power of the held weight versus the unloaded state on time.

3.2 Interpretation and Discussion

The graphs in Fig. 10 show the dependence of the total power on the time. The total power is taken from the biceps of the arm bent at the elbow joint at the angle of 90° (the direction of contraction of the biceps is collinear to the gravity vector) without additional load and with the retention of weights of 1.5, 3, 5 and 8 kg. Figure 11 shows the dependence of the difference between the total power and the held weight versus the unloaded state.

With additional calibration for a specific person, this characteristic allows one to estimate quantitatively the degree of a specific type of load looking directly at the total power graph.

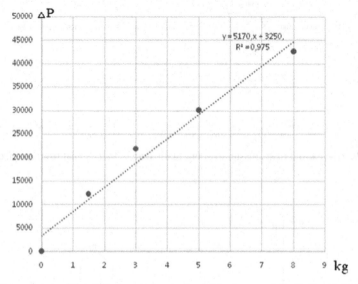

Fig. 11. Dependence of the difference between the total power and the held weight versus the unloaded state.

4   Conclusions

The modification of the Morlet wavelet function suggested in this article allows one to eliminate the Gibbs phenomenon completely as well as to calculate coefficients of an integer digital orthogonal filter with the given Q-factor and band width. Besides, there are no zero coefficients at the boundaries of such a filter, which leads to the improvement in the quality factor in the unchanged filter order.

For the hardware implementation of wavelet transform it is suggested to perform calculations on FPGAs (programmable logic integrated circuits), which can have thousands of MAC operations and are capable of performing spectral analysis with the required resolution.

The application of the original method of mathematical synthesis and technical implementation of the hardware computation of the wavelet transform by the modified Morlet function for processing electromyosignals allows obtaining new information about the state of a person's muscles, that is not available when classical methods of spectral analysis are used.

References

1. Ifeachor, E.C., Jervis, B.W.: Digital Signal Processing: A Practical Approach. 2nd ed. Pearson, London, UK (2004)
2. Denisenko, A.N., Isakov, V.N.: Application of various methods of recovery of continuous signals by their discrete values (Primenenie razlichnyh metodov vosstanovleniya nepreryvnyh signalov po ih diskretnym znacheniyam). Radiotekhnia **10**, 16–20 (2001). (in Russian)
3. Sanchez, B., Martinsen, O., Freeborn, T., Furse, C.: Electrical impedance myography: a critical review and outlook. Clin. Neurophysiol. **132**(7), 152–1753 (2020). https://doi.org/10.1016/j.clinph.2020.11.014
4. Kusche, R., Ryschka, M.: Multi-frequency impedance myography: the phase X effect. IEEE Sens. J. **21**(3), 3791–3798 (2020). https://doi.org/10.1109/JSEN.2020.3022899
5. Englehart, K., Hudgins, B., Parker, P.A.: A Wavelet based continuous classification scheme for multi-function myoelectric control. IEEE Trans. Biomed. Eng. **48**, 302–311 (2001)
6. Antoniou, A.: Digital Filters: Analysis and Design. McGraw-Hill, New York, NY, US (1979)
7. Pathak, R.S.: The Wavelet Transform. Atlantis Press, Amsterdam, Netherland (2009)
8. Walter, G.C.: Wavelets and generalized functions. In: Chui, C. (ed.) Wavelets- A Tutorial Theory and Applications. Academic Press, New York, NY, USA (1992)
9. Potekhin, D.S., Tarasov, I.E., Teterin, E.P.: Influence of coefficients and limits of integration of the Morlet wavelet function on the accuracy of the results of the analysis of harmonic signals with non-stationary parameters (Vliyaniye koeffitsiyentov i predelov integrirovaniy na veyvlet-funktsii Morle na tochnost' rezul'tatov analiza garmonicheskikh signalov s nestatsionarnymi parametrami). Scientific Instrumentation **12**(1), 90–95 (2002)
10. Grishanovich, Y.V., Potekhin, D.S.: Processing of the EGG orthogonal band-pass filter with the subsequent transfer in the phase plane. J. Phys. Conf. Ser. **1333**, 032025 (2019)
11. Potekhin, D.S., Tarasov, I.E.: Development of Digital Signal Processing Systems Based on FPGA (Razrabotka System Tsifrovoy Obrabotki Signalov na Baze PLIS). Gorjachaja linija telekom, Moscow, Russia (2017)
12. Isakov V.N., Timoshenko P.I.: Local interpolation and approximation in tasks of heuristic synthesis of digital filter. Russ. Technol. J. **6**(4), 42–64 (2018). https://doi.org/10.32362/2500-316X-2018-6-4-42-64
13. Andrianova, E., Sovietov, P., Tarasov, I.: Hardware acceleration of statistical data processing based on FPGAs in corporate information systems. In: 2nd International Conference on Control Systems, Mathematical Modeling, Automation and Energy Efficiency (SUMMA), 11–13 November 2020, Lipetsk, Russia, pp. 669–671 (2020). https://doi.org/10.1109/SUMMA50634.2020.9280689

Two-Stage Method of Speech Denoising by Long Short-Term Memory Neural Network

Rauf Nasretdinov⬛, Ilya Ilyashenko⬛, and Andrey Lependin$^{(\boxtimes)}$⬛

AltSU – Altai State University, Lenin Avenue 61, 656049 Barnaul, Russia

Abstract. This work is devoted to the development of a method for cleaning single-channel speech audio signals from additive noise. The main feature of the method is the application of a two-stage neural network. At the first stage, wideband processing of the input noisy signal is carried out, which allows the effective estimation of noise with a sophisticated spectral structure. The second stage of signal processing is a two-component neural network over the result of matrix representations that reveals the quasi-stationary characteristics of the clean and noise signal components in separate overlapping narrow frequency bands. The use of two components of noisy signals, which estimate complex masks of the clean and noise parts, makes it possible to improve useful information extraction about the formant structure of speech and effectively clean the input signal from noises of various nature. All of this together made it possible to develop a new method of speech enhancement, surpassing the best existing solutions in most quality metrics.

Keywords: Signal processing · Speech enhancement · Noise masking · Recurrent neural networks · Long short-term memory

1 Introduction

Automatic speech processing is used in many areas of information technology. We talk on the phone, check our actions at the bank, our speech is processed by recognition systems when we use voice interfaces. In many cases, the audio signal received by our devices is distorted with all kinds of noise. The human brain can efficiently reconstruct a clear and understandable message from an audible noisy audio stream. But this is not always the case with computer systems. Developing effective noise reduction algorithms is very important to automate speech processing.

Classical approaches to noise suppression in single-channel speech [1, 2] include spectral-subtractive algorithms, Wiener filtering, statistical-model-based methods, sub-space algorithms, and noise-estimation methods. These approaches are not robust enough in noisy environments, especially when the additive noise is wideband or speech-like. Therefore, for real applications, we need more intelligent and complex methods.

Over the past few years, the development of deep learning techniques has allowed to view speech enhancement as a supervised learning task, in which clean and noisy speech samples used as training examples. Modern deep neural networks for speech processing

© Springer Nature Switzerland AG 2022
V. Jordan et al. (Eds.): HPCST 2021, CCIS 1526, pp. 86–97, 2022.
https://doi.org/10.1007/978-3-030-94141-3_8

can operate in the time domain or in the frequency domain. For example, a raw noisy signal could be directly transformed to its clean version, using a deep neural network of Wavenet [3] type. Some methods use spectral representation by means of discrete wavelet decomposition [4] or discrete cosine transform [5].

However, the most common neural network methods of speech enhancement use the Fourier spectrum of the signal as input and calculate the spectrum of the cleaned signal spectrum directly [6] or the corresponding mask, which is applied to the spectrum of the noisy signal [7]. Noise masking techniques have evolved over time. Early works used binary [8] or real masks [9]. They determined the spectral amplitudes ratio of the clean and noisy speech. However, the lack of the ability to adjust the phase of the resulting signal resulted in a low perceived quality of the cleaned speech, albeit with a relatively high intelligibility. Therefore, recently two-channel complex ratio masks are actively used [10].

Another important feature of modern speech enhancement methods is the use of multicomponent neural networks with some kind of learnable interaction between individual components. It is possible to divide the problem of speech enhancement into processing the entire operating frequency band (full-band component) and individual frequency bands (narrowband component) [11]. This approach made it possible to capture the global wideband context of the speech signal. At the same time, it remains possible to estimate stationary behavior in individual frequency bands and take into account the low variability of stable local patterns in the spectrum. In another multicomponent approach, the neural network is divided into interacting parts, restoring the amplitude and phase of the cleaned signal [12]. The interaction mechanism made it possible to suppress the noise component of the signal more effectively.

2 Proposed Method

2.1 Two-Stage Neural Network Model

In this work, we propose a new deep neural network model that estimates two-channel complex masks to recover clean speech from a noisy spectrogram. The input data for the model are represented by complex Fourier transform coefficients. For the input noisy signal $\widehat{X}(t, f)$, the additive noise model was used:

$$\widehat{X}(t, f) = \widehat{S}(t, f) + \widehat{N}(t, f), \tag{1}$$

where t is discrete time, f is discrete frequency, $\widehat{S}(t, f)$ and $\widehat{N}(t, f)$ correspond to time-frequency representations of clean and noisy signals, respectively. In this work, the possible influences of reverberation effects or other multiplicative mechanisms were not taken into account.

The vectors of real amplitudes $\widehat{X}_t = \left[\left| \widehat{X}(t, 0) \right|, \left| \widehat{X}(t, 1) \right|, \ldots, \left| \widehat{X}(t, F - 1) \right| \right]^T$, calculated over the entire frequency range for a time window with index t were sequentially fed to the input of the neural network (Fig. 1). This sequence was processed in two stages, which conceptually coincides with the ideas of works [11]. At the first stage, the signal was processed in the entire operating frequency range (full-band processing in the G_{full} block). This allowed the neural network model to efficiently find global spectral patterns in the signal, which are responsible for the informative and noise components.

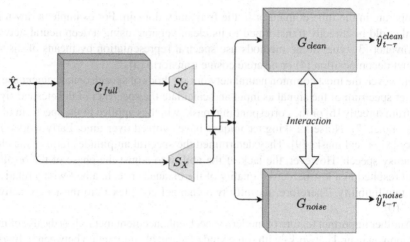

Fig. 1. General scheme of the two-stage speech enhancement method.

2.2 Full-Band Processing Block

The G_{full} transform block (see Fig. 2) is a two-layer LSTM with 512 hidden units. The vectors of amplitudes were normalized before feeding to the G_{full} block. Normalization was provided by dividing by the average value of the vector. The output values of the recurrent network were fed to a fully connected layer with ReLU.

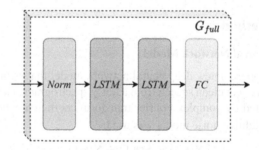

Fig. 2. Full-band block architecture.

Full-band block transformed signal representation was the same size as an input vector $\hat{X}_t$:

$$G_{full}\left(\hat{X}_t\right) = [g(0), g(1), \ldots, g(F-1)]^T. \tag{2}$$

It was divided into overlapping frequency bands with a width of $2n_G + 1$ samples with central frequencies f using the S_G transformation:

$$S_G\left(G_{full}\left(\hat{X}_t\right)\right) = [g(f - n_G), \ldots, g(f), \ldots, g(f + n_G)]^T. \tag{3}$$

For boundary bands, which indexes were out of range $0 \leq f \leq F - 1$, continued cyclically values were used. A similar transformation S_X with the width parameter n_S was applied to the input vectors $\widehat{X}_t$:

$$S_X\left(\widehat{X}_t\right) = \left[\left|\widehat{X}(t, f - n_S)\right|, \ldots, \left|\widehat{X}(t, f)\right|, \ldots, \left|\widehat{X}(t, f + n_S)\right|\right]^T. \qquad (4)$$

The concatenations (symbol "|" in Fig. 1) of $S_G\left(G_{full}\left(\widehat{X}_t\right)\right) S_X\left(\widehat{X}_t\right)$ representations of the separate signal frequencies were combined into matrices of size $F \times (2n_G + 2n_S + 2)$.

2.3   Narrowband Processing Blocks

At the second stage, the obtained matrix representation of individual spectral bands was processes. It made it possible to take into account the effects associated with the voice formants stationarity behavior, and ensured effective identification of the quasi-stationary noise component. The G_{clean} and G_{noise} blocks estimated complex two-channel masks to calculate the spectral representations of the cleaned signal $\hat{y}_{t-\tau}^{clean}$ and the additive noise component $\hat{y}_{t-\tau}^{noise}$, respectively. The mask was estimated with delay: not for the time window with index t, but for an earlier window with index $t - \tau$.

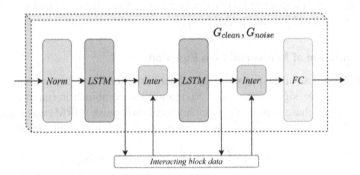

Fig. 3. Block of narrowband processing.

The second stage blocks architecture was developed to give the possibility of information exchange between them (Fig. 3). Like G_{full}, they used normalization and two recurrent LSTM layers with 384 hidden units. Normalization, in contrast to the first stage, was performed by dividing the representation coefficients of each narrowband by the average of the corresponding narrowband. The output fully connected layer contained only a linear transformation with trained weights, without a nonlinear activation function, since there was no need to limit the range of the mask's output coefficients.

The key feature of the second stage was the interaction of the G_{clean} and G_{noise} blocks: the outputs of each of the internal LSTM layer in one block were mixed with the outputs in the second block and vice versa. This interaction had a set of trainable parameters. The information exchange between the blocks allowed the neural network to suppress unwanted noise in the signal, and at the same time to more efficiently restore the emerging gaps in the speech spectrum.

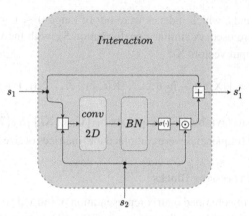

Fig. 4. Interaction module.

Mixing the outputs of the LSTM layers was carried out by interaction blocks. Their structure is shown in Fig. 4. The output of the recurrent layer of the first block s_1 was concatenated with the output of a similar layer of the second block s_2. Then this was fed to the two-dimensional convolution layer with batch normalization. From resulting representation, the multiplicative mask was produced via the sigmoidal function. The mask was multiplied by s_2 and added to s_1.

2.4 Computation of Masks and Loss Function

The learning process of the proposed neural network model was carried out on a set of signal triplets: clean signal S(t), noise N(t), and their combination (input noisy signal X(t)). For each of these triplets, the complex ideal ratio mask (cIRM) was calculated in advance [10]. First, the ideal mask for restoring clear speech was calculated:

$$\tilde{y}^{\text{clean}} = \left(\hat{X}_r\hat{S}_r + \hat{X}_i\hat{S}_i\right)\Big/\left(\hat{X}_r^2 + \hat{X}_i^2\right) + j\left(\hat{X}_r\hat{S}_i - \hat{X}_i\hat{S}_r\right)\Big/\left(\hat{X}_r^2 + \hat{X}_i^2\right), \qquad (5)$$

where the indices r and i denote the real and imaginary components of the Fourier transform of the signal S(t) and the noise N(t), j denotes the imaginary unit. The ideal mask for extraction of the additive noise $\overset{\sim\text{noise}}{y}$ was calculated in a similar way. Then, to improve model convergence, compressed cIRM masks were calculated [10]:

$$(\text{cIRM}(\tilde{y}))_x = K \cdot \left(1 - e^{-C\cdot\tilde{y}_x}\right)\Big/\left(1 + e^{-C\cdot\tilde{y}_x}\right), \qquad (6)$$

where x means r or i - real or imaginary components of the ideal mask $\tilde{y}$. Compression parameters according to [10, 11] took the values K = 10 and C = 0.1.

The loss function included two terms. All terms use a mean-square-error (MSE) loss. The first term is a loss over noise masks $\hat{y}^{\text{noise}}$ with its pre-calculated compressed ideal masks and the second – over the clean signal mask $\hat{y}^{\text{clean}}$:

$$\mathcal{L} = \text{MSE}\left(\hat{y}^{\text{clean}}, \text{cIRM}\left(\overset{\sim\text{clean}}{y}\right)\right) + \text{MSE}\left(\hat{y}^{\text{noise}}, \text{cIRM}\left(\overset{\sim\text{noise}}{y}\right)\right). \qquad (7)$$

3 Experiments

3.1 Datasets Description and Training Setup

The proposed model was trained and tested on the DNS Challenge 2020 dataset [13]. It consisted of a set of clean voice audio recordings and noise samples. The clean recordings in this dataset were selected from English-speaking open corpus of audiobooks Librivox. The selection criterion was the quality according to the mean opinion score (MOS) [14]. Recordings from the first quartile of the distribution of this metric were selected, which corresponded to the range of values $4.3 \leq \text{MOS} \leq 5$. The final clean audio set included 500 h of voice recordings by 2150 speakers. Noise samples were selected from the Audioset, Freesound and DEMAND datasets. Due to the imbalance of these sets, which was expressed in the fact that some classes of noise were represented by a small number of samples, only those classes of noise that were represented by at least 500 different samples were selected in the final dataset. The resulting dataset contained 150 classes of noise audio recordings, presented in more than 65000 samples, each 10 s long.

Noisy samples were generated according to the standard methodology used in the DNS Challenge [13]. At each step, a clean voice recording and a set of noise recordings were selected at random. Further, the noise recordings were concatenated and cropped to be the same length as the clean recordings. Then the noise recordings were scaled in amplitude so that the signal-to-noise ratio of the sum of the clean and noise components were equal to a randomly selected value taken from a uniform distribution over the interval from 0 dB to 40 dB. No artificial reverberation was applied. The test subset of the DNS Challenge 2020 dataset consisted of 150 synthetic noisy signals without reverberation with a signal-to-noise ratio distributed over the interval from 0 to 20 dB.

The proposed model was implemented in Python using the PyTorch library. The training was carried out on two GPU Nvidia GeForce 1080Ti. An Adam optimizer with a learning rate of 10^{-3} was used.

All audio samples were split into 32 ms time windows with 16 ms overlap. To calculate the time-frequency bin representation $\widehat{X}(t, f)$, an STFT transform with a Hann window was used. All training samples were cropped to a duration of 3 s. Each sample contained $T = 192$ time windows with $F = 257$ frequency-scale representations each. The value of τ was 2 frames, which corresponded to a 32 ms delay in predicting masks coefficients. The values of the width parameters of the transformations S_G and S_X were $n_G = 1$ and $n_S = 15$ respectively. The size of the intermediate matrix representations after the first full band block was $F \times (2n_G + 2n_S + 2) = 257 \times 34$.

3.2 Experimental Results

For the speech enhancement method quality evaluation, it is necessary to be strict in the choice of the appropriate metrics. The nontriviality of the problem of choosing metrics is due to the fact that two levels of evaluation should be distinguished. The first is related to the "technical" quality - measuring the signal-to-noise ratio, evaluating the nonlinear distortion coefficients. In most works of recent years (for example, in [15–19]), such characteristics are not used, since they poorly correlate with the quality of the reconstructed speech actually perceived by the listener.

The second level of evaluation, "perceptual", is precisely based on the human quality perception of the cleaned signal. The "naturalness" or, on the contrary, presence of weak but clearly noticeable distortions as "metallicity" becomes significant. Such human-perceived distortions are not associated with high noise levels, but with the ear's high sensitivity to distortion in certain frequency ranges and to phase imbalances in the audio signal. The ideal perceptual quality metric is the MOS (mean opinion score) metric [14], which is speech enhancement system quality rated by human experts. However, the widespread use of these estimates is associated with high time and often monetary costs. That is why most often in modern works [11, 16, 19], approximate automatic estimates of the quality of enhanced speech are used.

In this work, the following speech quality evaluation metrics were used (see Table 1):

- Perceptual Evaluation of Speech Quality (PESQ) [20] is an automatic speech quality score that simulates a MOS quality metrics on a continuous scale of −0.5 to 4.5 (higher is better). There are two types of PESQ metrics: narrowband NB-PESQ for signals with a sampling rate of 8 kHz, and wideband WB-PESQ for signals with a sampling rate of 16 kHz.
- Scale-Invariant Signal Distortion Rate (SI-SDR) [21] is a modification of the signal-to-noise ratio robust to rescaling of speech signals.
- Short-Time Objective Intelligibility Measure (STOI) [22] is a metric for the automatic assessment of speech intelligibility, expressed in percentage.

Table 1. The quality of speech enhancement methods on the DNS challenge test set.

Method	Parameters, $\times 10^6$	Delay, ms	WB-PESQ	NB-PESQ	SI-SDR	STOI
Noisy			1.582	2.454	9.071	91.52
NSNet [23]	5.1	0	2.145	2.873	15.613	94.47
Conv-TasNet [19]	5.08	33	2.73			
DCCRN-E [24]	3.7	37.5		3.266		
PoCoNet [16]	50		2.748			
FullSubNet [11]	5.6	32	2.777	3.305	17.29	**96.11**
Our method	7.5	32	**2.832**	**3.338**	**17.58**	96.05

Table shows the comparisons with state-of-the-art methods on DNS Challenge dataset. Methods was compared using the above metrics, as well as the specific characteristics of this methods - the number of neural network parameters and the delay in calculating the next frame mask. The delay is critical when applying the method in real time applications. The top line in Table, labeled Noisy, shows the DNS Challenge test set quality metrics values of noisy signals before enhancement.

Table shows that the proposed model, in comparison with the alternative approaches, shows low latency in mask estimation, and has a comparable number of parameters. The proposed model generally outperforms all of the alternative approaches (the best values are bold).

3.3 Discussion

It is also necessary to discuss changes in the spectral structure of the enhanced speech signals after the operation of the proposed method. Figure 5 and Fig. 6 show a comparison of the results obtained on two representative samples of noisy signals. The comparison was carried out with the closest method in terms of quality [11]. In Fig. 5, we see comparison on example with wideband noise of bird trills with a wide frequency range from 2 kHz to about 7–8 kHz. Figure 6 shows the results on sample with speech-like noise that is, on the contrary, concentrated mainly in the frequency range of up to 2 kHz.

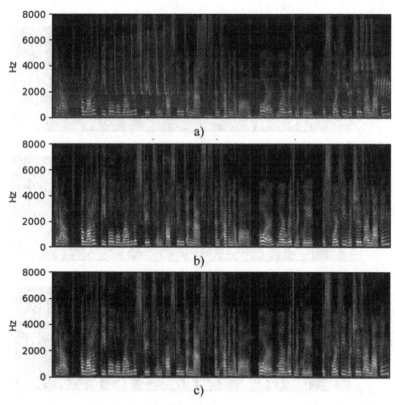

Fig. 5. An example with wideband noise (bird trills): a) noisy signal; b) result of method [11]; c) result of the proposed method.

The noise additive spectrum is seen in the first half of the signal in Fig. 5a as narrow vertical stripes. These noises are clearly distinguishable by the human ear. Figure 5b shows the result of denoising by the method [11]. It is seen that the residual high-frequency noise components are quite distinguishable against the background of the enhanced spectrum. The noise volume has become lower, but it is still well heard. On the other hand, the method proposed in this work practically eliminates this type of noise from the enhanced signal (Fig. 5c), which gives a significant increase in the subjective speech quality.

In the second example (Fig. 6a), the frequency range of the clean speech signal and the added noise practically coincide. The noise contribution is represented by more powerful and longer formant stripes, which fall both to the sections with the speaker's speech and to pauses. In this case, both methods give satisfactory results. However, Fig. 6b shows residual noise in pauses and on a part of the speech signal (from the first quarter to half of its duration). On the enhanced signal from Fig. 6c, these distortions are practically suppressed, which is confirmed by listening.

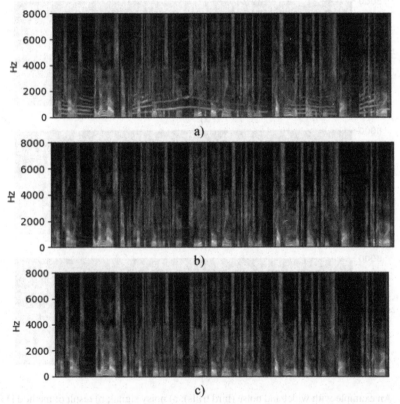

Fig. 6. An example with speech-like noise («crying baby»): a) noisy signal; b) the result of method [11]; c) the result of the proposed method.

Speech enhancement quality gain of the proposed method in general and in the above examples can be associated with the following main architecture features:

1. The presence of the full-band processing block that allows one to track noise distortions affecting areas with a width comparable to the entire operating frequency range. The use of recurrent layers with long short-term memory in this block makes it possible for the neural network to memorize in the internal state of the layer information about quasi-stationary patterns of speech part in the signal and filter out abrupt changes in a wide frequency range as in Fig. 5.
2. The second stage blocks process information from both narrow spectral bands of the input signal (due to the S_X transformation) and the embedding of the first stage (after the S_G transformation). This made it possible to more accurately predict the behavior of the noise and useful signals in these frequency bands. The interaction between the G_{clean} and G_{noise} blocks led to more efficient separation of corresponding signals, by introducing a kind of «contrast» into the predicted complex masks. In particular, this made it possible to more effectively separate speech-like noises from speech.

4 Conclusion

In this paper, we propose a new method for single-channel speech enhancement. This method was designed to integrate advantages of interacting noise and speech estimation blocks with global and local spectral processing technique. It has relatively small amount of neural network parameters and low delay in mask estimation. The proposed noise reduction method was compared with state-of-the-art methods on DNS Challenge test dataset. It outperforms these methods on most metrics. It introduces weak distortions in the phase characteristics of the signal, and is suitable for a wide class of practical applications.

References

1. Loizou, P.C.: Speech Enhancement: Theory and Practice. CRC Press, Boca Raton (2007)
2. Stahl, V., Fischer, A., Bippus, R.: Quantile based noise estimation for spectral subtraction and Wiener filtering. In: Proceedings of the 2000 IEEE International Conference on Acoustics, Speech, and Signal Processing, Istanbul, 5–9 June 2000, vol. 3, pp. 1875–1878 (2000)
3. Oord, A.V.D., Dieleman, S., Zen, H., Simonyan, K., Vinyals, O., Graves, A., et al: WaveNet: a generative model for raw audio. Preprint at https://arxiv.org/abs/1609.03499 (2016)
4. Lependin, A.A., Ilyashenko, I.D., Nasretdinov, R.S.: Use of trainable wavelet transform with adaptive threshold filtering for noise reduction of speech signals. J. Phys. Conf. Ser. **1615**(1), 012005 (2020)
5. Li, Q., Gao, F., Guan, H., Ma, K.: Real-time monaural speech enhancement with short-time discrete cosine transform. Preprint at https://arxiv.org/abs/2102.04629 (2021)
6. Tan, K., Wang, D.A.: Convolutional recurrent neural network for real-time speech enhancement: In: Proceedings of the Interspeech 2018, Hyderabad, India, 2–6 September 2018, pp. 3229–3233 (2018)

7. Xia, S., Li, H., Zhang, X.: Using optimal ratio mask as training target for supervised speech separation. In: 2017 Asia-Pacific Signal and Information Processing Association Annual Summit and Conference (APSIPA ASC), Kuala Lumpur, 12–15 December 2017, pp. 163–166 (2017)
8. Hu, G., Wang, D.: Monaural speech segregation based on pitch tracking and amplitude modulation. IEEE Trans. Neural Netw. 15(5), 1135–1150 (2004)
9. Wang, Y., Narayanan, A., Wang, D.: On training targets for supervised speech separation. IEEE/ACM Trans. Audio Speech Lang. Process. 22(12), 1849–1858 (2014)
10. Williamson, D.S., Wang, Y., Wang, D.: Complex ratio masking for monaural speech separation. IEEE/ACM Trans. Audio Speech Lang. Process. 24(3), 483–492 (2016)
11. Hao, X., Su, X., Horaud, R, Li, X.: FullSubNet: a full-band and sub-band fusion model for real-time single-channel speech enhancement. In: IEEE International Conference on Acoustics, Speech, and Signal Processing (ICASSP), Toronto, Canada, 6–11 June 2021, pp. 6633–6637 (2021)
12. Yin D., Luo C., Xiong, Z., Zeng W.: PHASEN: a phase-and-harmonics-aware speech enhancement network. In: AAAI Conference on Artificial Intelligence, AAAI-20, New York, NY, USA, 7–12 February 2020, pp. 9458–9465 (2020)
13. Reddy, C., Beyrami, E., Dubey, H.: Deep noise suppression challenge: datasets, subjective testing framework, and challenge results. In: Proceedings of the INTERSPEECH 2020, Shanghai, 25–29 October 2020, China, pp. 2492–2496 (2020)
14. International Telecommunication Union: ITU-T P.808 Subjective evaluation of speech quality with a crowdsourcing approach (2018)
15. Li, X., Horaud, R.: Online monaural speech enhancement using delayed subband LSTM. Preprint at https://arxiv.org/abs/2005.05037 (2020)
16. Umut, I., Giri, R., Phansalkar, N., Valin, J.-M., Helwani, K., Krishnaswamy, A.: PoCoNet: better speech enhancement with frequency-positional embeddings, semi-supervised conversational data, and biased loss. In: Proceedings of the INTERSPEECH 2020, Shanghai, 25–29 October 2020, pp. 2487–2491 (2020)
17. Valin, J.-M., Isik, U., Phansalkar, N., Giri, R., Helwani, K., Krishnaswamy, A.: A perceptually-motivated approach for low-complexity, real-time enhancement of fullband speech. In: Proceedings of the INTERSPEECH 2020, Shanghai, 25–29 October 2020, pp. 2482–2486 (2020)
18. Xu, R., Wu, R., Ishiwaka, Y., Vondrick, C., Zheng, C.: Listening to sounds of silence for speech denoising. In: Conference on Neural Information Processing Systems, NeurIPS 2020, Vancouver, Canada, 6–12 December 2020, pp. 9633–9648 (2020)
19. Luo, Y., Mesgarani, N.: Conv-TasNet: surpassing ideal time-frequency magnitude masking for speech separation. IEEE/ACM Trans. Audio Speech Lang. Process. 27(8), 1256–1266 (2019)
20. Rix, A.W., Beerends, J.G., Hollier, M.P., Hekstra, A.P.: Perceptual evaluation of speech quality (PESQ) – a new method for speech quality assessment of telephone networks and codecs. In: Proceedings of the IEEE International Conference on Acoustics, Speech, and Signal Processing, Salt Lake City, UT, USA, 7–11 May 2001, pp. 749–752 (2001)
21. Roux, J.L., Wisdom, S., Erdogan, H., Hershey, J.R.: SDR – half-baked or well done? In: IEEE International Conference on Acoustics, Speech and Signal Processing, Brighton, UK, 12–17 May 2019, pp. 626–630 (2019)
22. Taal, C.H., Hendriks, R.C., Heusdens, R., Jensen, J.: A short-time objective intelligibility measure for time-frequency weighted noisy speech. In: IEEE International Conference on Acoustics, Speech and Signal Processing, Dallas, TX, USA, 15–19 March 2010, pp. 4214–4217 (2010)

23. Xia, Y., Braun, S., Reddy, C.K.A., Dubey, H., Cutler, R., Tashev, I.: Weighted speech distortion losses for neural network-based real-time speech enhancement. In: IEEE International Conference on Acoustics, Speech and Signal Processing (ICASSP), Barcelona, Spain, 4–8 May 2020, pp. 871–875 (2020)
24. Hu, Y., et al.: DCCRN: deep complex convolution recurrent network for phase-aware speech enhancement. In: Proceedings of the INTERSPEECH 2020, Shanghai, China, 25–29 October 2020, pp. 2472–2476 (2020)

**Information Technologies and Computer
Simulation of Physical Phenomena**

Method for Intermetallide Spatial 3D-Distribution Recognition in the Cubic Ni@Al "Core-shell" Nanoparticle Based on Computer MD-Simulation of SHS

Vladimir Jordan[1,2(✉)] and Igor Shmakov[1]

[1] Altai State University, 61 Lenin Avenue, Barnaul 656049, Russia
jordan@phys.asu.ru
[2] Khristianovich Institute of Theoretical and Applied Mechanics, SB RAS,
4/1 Institutskaya Street, Novosibirsk 630090, Russia

Abstract. The paper presents the results of computational experiments (CEs) on computer MD-simulation of "self-propagating high-temperature synthesis (SHS)" in a cubic Ni@Al "core-shell" nanoparticle. In the center of the cubic nanoparticle $25 \times 25 \times 25$ nm in size, there is the spherical core with the diameter of 25 nm, containing Ni atoms, and in the shell surrounding the core, Al atoms. By heating the flat layer with dimensions of $10 \times 25 \times 25$ nm to 1200 K, SHS ignition was initiated. Based on the results of CEs carried out using the LAMMPS software package, the analysis of SHS microkinetics was carried out using the calculated one-dimensional distributions of the averaged values of the temperature and matter density (temperature and matter density profiles). One-dimensional profiles of temperature and matter density were obtained by "integral" averaging in layers with dimensions of $4 \times 25 \times 25$ nm. In addition, the authors have developed and software implemented the new method for recognizing the spatial 3D-distributions of synthesized intermetallides in the volume of a nanoparticle using pre-calculated sets of 3D-distributions of the matter density. In contrast to one-dimensional matter density profiles, the new method proposed by the authors makes it possible to effectively recognize the structure of formation and transformations of intermetallic phases at the "core-shell" interface of a nanoparticle in a given time interval. On the basis of the performed CEs, a sufficiently high efficiency of this recognition method and its advantage in comparison with the methods of similar analysis implemented in the well-known OVITO software package have been shown. In other words, the authors have created a sufficiently effective software toolkit for studying the microkinetics of SHS in nano- and micro-sized binary atomic systems (for example, Ni-Al, Ti-Al, etc.), and, in particular, for studying the process of structure and phase formation at the interface boundaries of such heterogeneous systems in a given time interval.

Keywords: SHS · Molecular dynamics method · Crystal cell · Temperature and matter density profiles · Parallel computing · LAMMPS and OVITO packages

© Springer Nature Switzerland AG 2022
V. Jordan et al. (Eds.): HPCST 2021, CCIS 1526, pp. 101–120, 2022.
https://doi.org/10.1007/978-3-030-94141-3_9

1 Introduction

The object of research in this article is "self-propagating high-temperature synthesis (SHS)" as one of the methods for obtaining new materials with programmable functional properties. In binary systems, for example, Ni-Al or Ti-Al, as a result of a strong exothermic chemical reaction in a heated localized thin layer due to the contact of many pairs of different metal particles (particles of Ni and Al, or Ti and Al), intense heat release occurs (otherwise speaking, combustion). In the process of heat transfer, after a certain time of "thermochemical induction", ignition occurs in the next layer of the powder mixture of particles. Thus, when the SHS combustion wave passes through the binary powder mixture, stable intermetallic compounds (phases) are formed in the so-called "aftercombustion" zone. For example, for the Ni-Al system, such phases are the following: Ni_3Al, $NiAl$, Ni_2Al_3 and $NiAl_3$. The initiation of the "ignition" of the SHS combustion wave on the surface of the powder mixture can be caused, for example, by a short-term heat pulse from an electric coil.

The subject of research in such systems is the micro- and macrokinetics of the structure and phase formation of intermetallic phases (intermetallides). Nickel and titanium aluminides, characterized by high corrosion resistance at high temperatures, are widely used in modern mechanical engineering, for example, in aircraft engines, turbines and combustion sections of engines and other equipment.

The molecular dynamics simulation method (MD-simulation) using high-performance supercomputers and software packages in a parallel computing configuration, such as LAMMPS, OVITO [1, 2] and others [3], makes it possible to effectively study the microkinetics of the nucleation and transformations of intermetallides at the interfaces and blocks in nano- and micro-sized layered [4–7], layered-block (checkerboard-like) [8] and other various atomic structures. For example, one type of

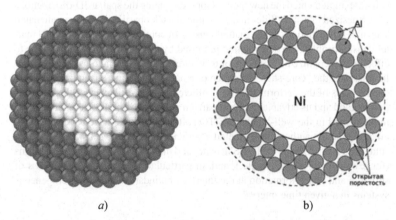

a)   *b)*

Fig. 1. The cross sections snapshots of spherical particles: *a* – the cross section snapshot of spherical Ni@Al "core-shell " nanoparticle [9]; b – the cross section snapshot of spherical "mesocell" [10, 12].

layer (block) may be composed of Ni atoms and the other of Al atoms. Of great interest are nanoscale atomic structures such as spherical Ni@Al "core-shell" nanoparticles (Fig. 1a) [9].

In such a nanoparticle the atomic structure of the spherical "core" consists of crystalline cells of Ni atoms, and crystalline cells of Al atoms are located in the spherical shell surrounding the core (see Fig. 1a). Such structures can be: Al@Ni, Ti@Al and Al@Ti with different ratios of atomic concentrations in the core and shell.

The study of phase transformations in nanoparticles is of independent interest, since the kinetics of changes in the structural-phase properties in the nanoscale subsystem affects and, often, forms the structural properties and elementary processes in the meso- and macroscale systems of the reacting medium.

When studying the macrokinetics of SHS in powder mixtures by computer simulation methods, a model structure of a particle in the form of a "core-shell" is also used, which is called a "mesocell" [10–12], since its size is at the level of the "mesoscale" of the heterogeneity of the mixture of particles (from tens to one hundred and more microns). The core of the "mesocell" may contain a large particle (Fig. 1b), for example, Ni with a radius of about 30 μm, and the shell of the "mesocell" - a compacted mixture of Al particles with a radius of 8 to 12 μm [10, 12].

For binary systems of "gasless combustion", this simulation approach turns out to be effective, since the initial medium with a chaotic distribution of "mesocells" over the reaction volume in the process of SH-synthesis largely retains its spatial structure, and diffusion layers of intermetallides are to a greater extent nucleated and developed inside mesocells at the interface between the core and the shell [11]. In other words, we can talk about some similarity of properties and features in the processes of structural-phase transformations occurring at different levels of the scale of heterogeneity, namely, in nano- and mesocells.

Carrying out physical experiments in the study of the SHS process requires a significant investment of time, as well as finance and material resources. Based on the application of computer simulation methods using high-performance supercomputers and software packages in a parallel computing configuration, the number of computational experiments (CEs) can be carried out significantly more compared to physical experiments [1]. Thus, such studies can be very effective in terms of scientific novelty and practical significance.

This paper examines the Ni@Al "core-shell" nanoparticle with a spherical core of Ni atoms, and the addition to the spherical core of the shell with Al atoms forms an "outer" form of nanoparticle in the cubic form (see Fig. 2). MD-simulation is carried out on the basis of using the LAMMPS package in the configuration of parallel computations, the OVITO package and software created by the authors of the paper. In the LAMMPS package, the EAM-potential (in embedded atom model) is chosen as the interatomic interaction potential [13].

2 Methodology for MD-Simulation of SHS in Cubic Ni@Al "Core-shell" Nanoparticles

Using a perspective view, Fig. 2 shows a schematic representation of a cubic Ni@Al core-shell nanoparticle. In reality, using the LAMMPS package, an atomic structure was created (built), in the center of which there is a spherical core with crystalline cells of Ni atoms, and the surrounding shell contains crystal cells of Al atoms. The diameter of the Ni-core coincides with the cube size (edge) of 25 nm. Due to the discreteness and crystallinity of the atomic structure of the nucleus, several Ni atoms appear at the centers of all six faces of the cube. Therefore, in Fig. 2 (fragments a, b), in the centers of six faces, there are similar circles of small diameter, around which ring-shaped "halos" are visible - these are Ni atoms located as close as possible to the cube faces, nevertheless, located on a spherical surface of the core of the nanoparticle.

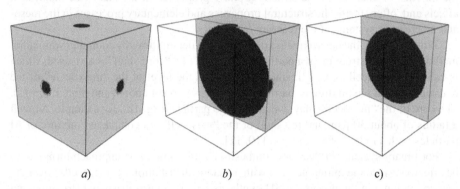

a)   b)   c)

Fig. 2. Schematic perspective image of cubic Ni@Al "core-shell" nanoparticle: a – full nanoparticle; b – a half volume of a nanoparticle; c – a quarter volume of a nanoparticle.

In a nanoparticle (Fig. 2a), the total number of atoms is 1200584. Of these, the number of Ni atoms is 747560, and the number of Al atoms is 453024. In the Ni-core, using the LAMMPS package, an atomic structure with unit cells of the fcc type is realized (parameter $a = 0.3524$ nm), and the shell has an atomic structure with cells of Al atoms also of the fcc type (parameter $a = 0.405$ nm) [13]. The stoichiometric ratio of the components is determined by the ratio of the number of Ni atoms to the number of Al atoms, namely, $N_{Ni}/N_{Al} = 1.65$. In other words, the relative fraction of Ni atoms is $n = 0.6061$ (60.61%), and the fraction of Al atoms is 0.3939 (39.39%). Analyzing the equilibrium state diagram of the Ni-Al system [14], we can say that, taking into account the ratio $N_{Ni}/N_{Al} = 1.65$, upon completion of the SHS reaction in a cubic Ni@Al "core-shell" nanoparticle, almost one intermetallic NiAl phase is expected to form (dominance over others phases).

2.1 Stages of MD-Simulation of SHS in a Cubic Ni@Al "Core-shell" Nanoparticle

At the first stage of MD-simulation of SHS, the computational experiment (CE) begins with uniform heating of the studied nanoparticle (Fig. 2a) for 0.4 ns at temperatures from 600 to 800 K. As a result, the atomic structure of the nanoparticle "relaxes" with fixed thermodynamic parameters: $N = 1200584$ – the number of all atoms in the structure, $P = 1$ Bar – external pressure, temperature $T = 800$ K (NPT-ensemble). At this stage of simulation, for the nanoparticle, periodic boundary conditions were established in 3 dimensions, which are retained at the next stage for 0.1 ns.

At the second stage, for 0.1 ns, linear heating from 800 to 1200 K was carried out in the cube part with dimensions of 10 x 25 x 25 nm, which is enclosed between the flat face YZ (with coordinate X = 0) and a secant parallel plane with coordinate X = 10 nm. That is, the fraction of 0.4 of the cube volume warmed up, which is slightly less (by 0.1) of the fraction of 0.5 of the cube volume (see Fig. 2b). With this heating in the $10 \times 25 \times 25$ nm layer, the conditions of the NVT-ensemble (V is the volume of the heating zone) were observed, and in the remaining part of the volume (from 10 to 25 nm along the X coordinate), the conditions of the NVE-ensemble (E is the total energy of all atoms of this part volume).

At the third stage (0.5 ns from the beginning of the CE) in cubic Ni@Al "core-shell" nanoparticle, "free" boundary conditions were fixed along the X-direction, and periodic conditions were maintained along the Y- and Z-directions. As a result, the SHS process was initiated in the initial part of the nanoparticle volume (within 10 nm along the X coordinate) with the propagation of the combustion wave along the X-direction. It should be noted that periodic conditions in the Y- and Z-directions return the atoms that emerged from the nanoparticle beyond any face (out of 4 possible) into the nanoparticle again from the side of the opposite parallel face. This behavior of atoms in a nanoparticle is equivalent to a situation when instead of one nanoparticle, a two-dimensional parallel to the YZ plane lattice of identical cubic Ni@Al "core-shell" nanoparticles, infinitely repeated in the Y- and Z-directions, is investigated.

The results of SHS-simulation in a nanoparticle using the LAMMPS package and the EAM potential of 2009 [13] are shown in Figs. 3 and 4, which show sets of temperature and matter density profiles (along the X-axis) corresponding to different points in time. For this, the volume of a cubic nanoparticle was divided by vertical cuts into layers transverse to the X-direction with dimensions of 4 x 25 x 25 nm (layers with a thickness of 4 nm), in each of which the "averaged" values of the temperature and matter density were calculated. In this way, "one-dimensional" distributions of the averaged values of temperature and matter density along the X-direction were obtained. Averaging in these layers was carried out by the "integral" method. The averaged temperature in each layer was calculated using the total value of the kinetic energies of all atoms in this layer and the Boltzmann constant k_B. The average density of the substance in each layer was calculated as the sum of the masses of all atoms in this layer, divided by the volume of the layer.

In this case, the "averaged" values of temperature and matter density in all graphs of Figs. 3 and 4 are "tied" to the centers of these layers with X-coordinates corresponding to the values of 2, 6, 10, 14, 18 and 22 nm. Similar profiles of temperature and matter density are given in [4–6, 8] when studying the microkinetics of layered and layered-block atomic systems.

2.2 Analysis of SHS Microkinetics in a Cubic Ni@Al "Core-shell" Nanoparticle Based on the Calculated Temperature and Matter Density Profiles

As can be seen from Fig. 3, in the time interval from 0.5 ns (from the start of the SHS process) to 1 ns, the heat wave has already reached the final face of the nanoparticle. In this case, the temperature in the entire volume of the nanoparticle has practically leveled off (about 1060 K), but the process of the exothermic chemical reaction of SHS continues in the entire volume of the nanoparticle. According to the method of MD-simulation of the SHS process, heat exchange with the external environment (with vacuum) does not occur due to the "closed nature" of the thermodynamic system, therefore, the released thermal energy accumulates in it with a further increase of temperature. Temperature profiles in the time interval from 1 ns to 5 ns confirm this fact (see Fig. 3).

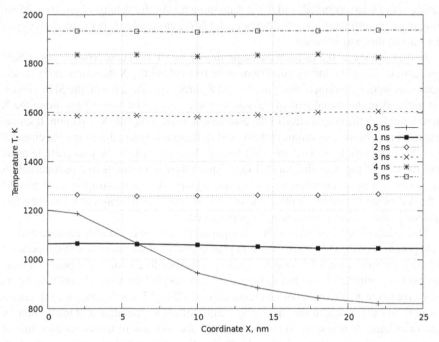

Fig. 3. The set of temperature profiles as functional dependences of the combustion temperature on the X-coordinate for successive times of the combustion wave propagation.

By the time instant 5 ns, the temperature rises to the melting point of the NiAl phase (about 1911 K) and then slightly exceeds it. According to the equilibrium phase diagram of the Ni-Al system [14], at such temperatures, the Ni-Al system contains the following components: the NiAl phase and the metals Ni and Al in the liquid states. In the temperature range from 1911 to 1950 K, the matter densities of these components have values [15], which are lower than the density values at room temperature (about 300 K). For the NiAl phase, the matter density is close to 4.7 g/cm^3, the Ni matter density is about 7.8 g/cm^3, and the Al matter density is about 2.2 g/cm^3. Taking into account the ratio of the concentrations of these components, the expected value of the matter density of the component mixture in the nanoparticle bulk should be in the range 5.6–5.8 g/cm^3, which confirms the matter density profile for 5 ns (see Fig. 4).

Analyzing Fig. 4, a sharp underestimation of the matter density value after the X = 22 nm coordinate can be noted (for different times from 0.5 to 5 ns, the matter density is in the range from 2.2 to 3.2 g/cm^3). The underestimation is largely explained by the presence of "voids" in the outer layers. In other words, faces with coordinates X = 0 nm and X = 25 nm, taking into account the "free" boundary conditions acting along the X-axis, become not flat. Therefore, a barrel-like shape distortion effect is observed and voids appear in the outer flat layers.

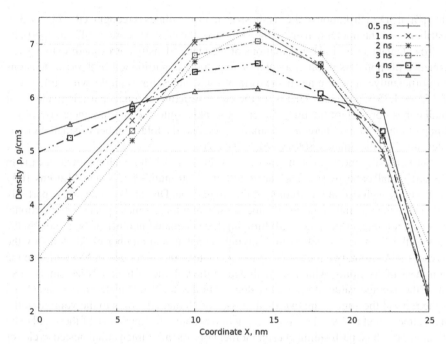

Fig. 4. The set of matter density profiles as functional dependences of the matter density on the X-coordinate for successive times of the combustion wave propagation.

In the first layer (from X = 0 to X = 4 nm), there were few voids, and the underestimation of the density turned out to be small. That is, it would be more correct to perform for all graphs (see Fig. 4) "extrapolation" to the coordinate of 25 nm of all linear sections determined in the interval from the point X = 18 nm to X = 22 nm. In this case, for a time of 5 ns and for the X = 25 nm coordinate, the matter density value would be at the expected level of about 5.7 g/cm^3.

In the next section of the paper, instead of one-dimensional profiles of "integrally" averaged temperatures and matter densities, the authors propose algorithms for estimating 3D-temperature and matter density distributions in cubic Ni@Al "core-shell" nanoparticles. In addition, on the basis of the calculated 3D-distributions of temperature and matter density, a method is proposed for recognizing the spatial 3D-distributions of intermetallides in a nanoparticle bulk.

3 Description of the Method for Recognizing the Spatial 3D-Distribution of Intermetallides in a Ni@Al "Core-shell" Nanoparticle

The spatial 3D-distribution of the synthesized intermetallides is recognized using the 3D-distribution of the matter density in the volume of the Ni@Al "core-shell" nanoparticle.

To calculate a set of 3D-distributions of the matter density corresponding to a given sequence of moments in time, a cubic nanoparticle is partitioned in three dimensions into sufficiently small volumes in the form of small cubes, for example, with dimensions of $1.25 \times 1.25 \times 1.25$ nm. That is, in the cubic structure of a nanoparticle made up of small cubes, for each of the three dimensions, taking into account the linear size of the nanoparticle of 25 nm, there are 20 small cubes, and the total number of small cubes is determined by the number $8000 = 20 \times 20 \times 20$.

Further, using the algorithm described in Subsect. 3.1, for each moment of time in each such small cube, two numbers are determined - the number of Ni and Al atoms, fully and partially included in the volume of the small cube. Due to the some atoms partially included in the volume of the small cube, these two numbers may appear with fractional parts (i.e. not integer numbers). Multiplying the calculated number of Ni atoms by the mass of the Ni atom, as well as multiplying the calculated number of Al atoms by the mass of the Al atom, two total masses are calculated - the total mass of Ni atoms and the total mass of Al atoms, which are included in the volume of the analyzed small cube. Then, the average value of the matter density in the analyzed small cube is calculated as the ratio of the sum of the two total masses of Ni and Al atoms to the volume of the small cube (equal to 1.953125 nm^3, taking into account the linear size of the small cube of 1.25 nm). Thus, performing at each moment of time a 3-dimensional nested cycle for enumerating all small cubes in a cubic partition of a nanoparticle, the averaged values of the matter density in all 8000 small cubes in the form of a 3-dimensional array are determined.

A set of 3D-distributions of temperature in the volume of the nanoparticle (for all 8000 small cubes) at successive times is determined in a similar way. Below, in Subsect. 3.1, an informal description of the algorithm for calculating the matter density in each small cube of a cubic partition of a nanoparticle is considered in a brief form. In Subsect. 3.2, on the basis of the computed set of 3D-distributions of the matter density in the volume of a cubic nanoparticle, we consider an algorithm for recognizing the presence in each small cube of some intermetallic phase or a mixture of phases synthesized at successive times.

3.1 Algorithm for Calculating the 3D-Distribution of Matter Density in a Cubic Ni@Al "Core-shell" Nanoparticle

When the simulation of the SHS process is completed, the LAMMPS package saves to an external disk an array of data describing various parameters of all atoms of the nanoparticle, including coordinates, velocities and types of atoms (Ni- and Al-types).

The algorithm starts by running an external loop with an index variable l, which reads data on coordinates and types of atoms from a disk file. Inside the outer cycle, using an additional 3-dimensional nested cycle along three dimensions of the cubic partition of a nanoparticle, the conditions for the location of the l-th atom inside a small cube are checked, or the location of this atom by its parts simultaneously in several adjacent small cubes (possibly in 2, or in 4, or in 8).

In the first case, the l-th atom is entirely located in one small cubic, for example, with number n. For this small cube, 3 pairs of parallel flat faces, bounding the small cube by 6 faces, correspond to 3 pairs of equations: $\{X = X_{1,n},\ X = X_{2,n}\}, \{Y = Y_{1,n},\ Y = Y_{2,n}\}$ and $\{Z = Z_{1,n},\ Z = Z_{2,n}\}$. Then the condition for the location of the l-th atom inside the n-th small cube corresponds to the conditions for all three coordinates of the center of the atom $(X_l,\ Y_l,\ Z_l)$ to belong to the corresponding segments: $X_l \in [X_{1,n} + R_l;\ X_{2,n} - R_l]$, $Y_l \in [Y_{1,n} + R_l;\ Y_{2,n} - R_l]$ and $Z_l \in [Z_{1,n} + R_l;\ Z_{2,n} - R_l]$, where R_l is the radius of the l-th atom (either R_{Ni}, or R_{Al}). Then one of the 2 counters corresponding to a specific type of the l-th atom (either Ni-type or Al-type) and corresponding to the n-th small cube increases by 1. That is, two one-dimensional arrays of counters can be reserved in the program, each of which has 8000 elements, or two 3-dimensional arrays of counters with the same dimension of $20 \times 20 \times 20$ elements.

The following other cases of the arrangement of the l-th atom simultaneously in several adjacent small cubes are possible.

1. If the l-th atom is cut by only one common face of 2 adjacent small cubes, then the volume of the atom of radius R_l is divided into two parts. If one of the 3 coordinates of the center of the l-th atom coincides with the corresponding coordinate defining the equation of the common face of 2 adjacent small cubes, then both parts of the volume (and mass) of the atom during dissection are equal to each other. In this case, for each of these 2 adjacent small cubes, both counters of the number of atoms corresponding to the type of atom increase by 0.5 fractions, respectively. In another case, the counter of the "number of atoms" corresponding to the type of atom and the number of the small cube inside which the center of the atom is located is added a larger value of the fraction of the volume of the dissected atom, and a smaller fraction of the volume is added to the counter of the 2nd adjacent small cube.

Consider two adjacent small cubes numbered $(n\text{-}1)$ and n, for which the common flat face separating the l-th atom is determined, for example, by an equation $X = X_{2,n-1} = X_{1,n}$. In addition, suppose that the center of the l-th atom is inside the cube with number $(n\text{-}1)$, i.e. $X_{2,n-1} - R_l < X_l < X_{2,n-1}$ or $X_{1,n} - R_l < X_l < X_{1,n}$. Then a smaller fraction of the volume of the dissected l-th atom will be determined by the ratio of the volume of the ball segment $V_{b.s.} = \pi h^2 (R_l - h/3)$ to the volume of the sphere $V_b = (4/3)\pi R_l^3$, where h is the height of the ball segment. Therefore, a smaller fraction of the volume of the dissected atom added to the counter of the n-th small cube (corresponding to the type of the l-th atom) is determined by the expression $k_{small} = 0.75 \cdot \overline{h}^2 \cdot (1 - \overline{h}/3)$, and a larger fraction $k_{larger} = 1 - k_{small}$ is added to the counter of the $(n\text{-}1)$-th small cube, also corresponding to the type of the l-th atom. In the sum, both parts give the correct value 1. The height of the ball segment h is determined as $h = X_l + R_l - X_{1,n}$, and its normalized value is equal to $\overline{h} = h/R_l$.

2. Consider the case when the l-th atom is cut simultaneously by 2 mutually perpendicular faces of the n-th small cube, i.e. the common edge of 2 faces of the n-th small cube

passes through the volume of the l-th atom. This edge is a common edge of simultaneously 4 adjacent small cubes with numbers n_1, n_2, n_3 и n_4, and, therefore, the l-th atom
is simultaneously distributed by its parts over these 4 adjacent small cubes. Suppose, for
example, $n_4 = n$ and the center of the l-th atom is inside the n_1-th small cube and the three
coordinates of the center of the atom do not fall into three intervals, which are determined
by 3 pairs of equations for the faces of the n-th small cube. Then, having determined two
normalized heights $\overline{h}_1$ and $\overline{h}_2$ of ball segments cut off by the 2 above mentioned mutually
perpendicular faces of the n-th small cube, we can calculate the relative values of 2 vol-
umes of ball segments: $k_{s,1} = 0.75 \cdot \overline{h}_1^2 \cdot (1 - \overline{h}_1/3)$ and $k_{s,2} = 0.75 \cdot \overline{h}_2^2 \cdot (1 - \overline{h}_2/3)$. Thus,
4 parts of the volume of the l-th atom added to the corresponding counters of 4 adjacent
small cubes are determined as follows. For small cubes with numbers n_1 and $n_4 = n$,
the following expressions are true: $k_{n_1} = (1 - k_{s,1}) \cdot (1 - k_{s,2})$, $k_{n_4} = k_n = k_{s,1} \cdot k_{s,2}$.
A pair of products $(1 - k_{s,1}) \cdot k_{s,2}$ and $k_{s,1} \cdot (1 - k_{s,2})$ determines the fractions for the
small cubes n_2 and n_3 (depending on the location of these small cubes in relation to the
coordinates of the center of the l-th atom). The sum of all the shares of the 4 small cubes
is also 1.

3. The last case, when the l-th atom is cut simultaneously by 3 mutually perpendicular
faces of the n-th small cube, i.e. the volume of the l-th atom is penetrated by 3 edges
intersecting at one of the vertices of the n-th small cube. In this case, the l-th atom with
its parts is simultaneously located in 8 adjacent small cubes, and the common vertex of
the 3 dividing faces of the small cube is inside the volume of the atom. Summarizing
the provisions considered in the previous cases, having determined the three normalized
heights $\overline{h}_1$, $\overline{h}_2$ and $\overline{h}_3$ of ball segments cut off by the 3 above-mentioned mutually
perpendicular faces of the n-th small cube, we can calculate the relative values of the 3
volumes of ball segments: $k_{s,1} = 0.75 \cdot \overline{h}_1^2 \cdot (1 - \overline{h}_1/3)$, $k_{s,2} = 0.75 \cdot \overline{h}_2^2 \cdot (1 - \overline{h}_2/3)$
and $k_{s,3} = 0.75 \cdot \overline{h}_3^2 \cdot (1 - \overline{h}_3/3)$. For 8 adjacent small cubes, the volume fractions of the
l-th atom added to the corresponding counters of 8 adjacent small cubes are determined
by the following products: $(1 - k_{s,1}) \cdot (1 - k_{s,2}) \cdot (1 - k_{s,3})$, $k_{s,1} \cdot (1 - k_{s,2}) \cdot (1 - k_{s,3})$,
$(1 - k_{s,1}) \cdot k_{s,2} \cdot (1 - k_{s,3})$, $(1 - k_{s,1}) \cdot (1 - k_{s,2}) \cdot k_{s,3}$, $(1 - k_{s,1}) \cdot k_{s,2} \cdot k_{s,3}$, $k_{s,1} \cdot (1 - k_{s,2}) \cdot k_{s,3}$,
$k_{s,1} \cdot k_{s,2} \cdot (1 - k_{s,3})$, $k_{s,1} \cdot k_{s,2} \cdot k_{s,3}$. Their sum is 1. The assignment of each of the 8
products to the corresponding counter of one or another small cube is associated with
checking the conditions for the location of these small cubes in relation to the coordinates
of the l-th atom center.

Thus, after completing the execution of all the cycles of the above-stated algorithm,
for each small cube of the nanoparticle, 2 counters of the "number of atoms" (Ni-type
and Al-type) are calculated. Then, in additional cycles for each small cube, counters of
2 types are multiplied by the corresponding masses of Ni and Al atoms (as mentioned
above) and, summing up among themselves, determine the value of the total mass of
atoms in each small cube. In the same cycles for each small cube, the division of its total
mass of atoms by the value of its volume determines its matter density.

In addition, the data on the velocity components of the l-th atom make it possible to
calculate its kinetic energy and, if necessary, also distribute the corresponding fractions
of the atom's energy over adjacent small cubes (or the energy is completely assigned to
one small cube in which the atom is located).

Thus, the result of performing all these cycles is the computed 3D-distributions of the matter density and temperature in the volume of cubic Ni@Al "core-shell" nanoparticle (two three-dimensional arrays) at a certain point in time from a given sequence. That is, performing the above algorithm (with a time step) in an additional cycle, two sets of 3D-distributions (of matter density and temperature) corresponding to different points in time are formed with storage on an external disk.

3.2 Algorithm for Recognizing the Spatial 3D-Distribution of Intermetallides in a Cubic Ni@Al "Core-shell" Nanoparticle

In addition to the calculated sets of 3D-distributions of matter density and temperature in nanoparticle volume (see Subsect. 3.1), the considered recognition algorithm uses analytical dependences of the matter densities of Ni and Al components, as well as their intermetallic phases, on temperature. In [15] experimental data of matter density values depending on temperature are given, on the basis of which the authors generalized the analytical dependences of matter densities on temperature $\rho_{lS}(T)$ and $\rho_{lL}(T)$, where l is the phase serial number (from 1 to 6), the indices S and L denote the states of the phases, respectively, " solid"and" liquid"(see Table 1).

Table 1. Analytical dependences of matter densities for Ni, Al and intermetallic phases of the Ni-Al system (in solid and liquid states): $T_0 = 300$ K, $T_{max} = 2000$ K.

Phases	In solid state: $T_0 \leq T < T_{melt, l}$	In liquid state: $T_{melt, l} \leq T < T_{max}$
1. Ni	$\rho_{1S}(T) = 8.91 - 4.286 \cdot 10^{-4}(T - 300)$	$\rho_{1L}(T) = 7.824 - 6.894 \cdot 10^{-4}(T - 1728)$
2. Ni$_3$Al	$\rho_{2S}(T) = 7.52 - 8.0 \cdot 10^{-4}(T - 300)$	$\rho_{2L}(T) = 6.4296 - 8.0 \cdot 10^{-4}(T - 1658)$
3. NiAl	$\rho(T) = 6.02 - 8.0 \cdot 10^{-4}(T - 300)$	$\rho(T) = 4.65384 - 1.92 \cdot 10^{-3}(T - 1911)$
4. Ni$_2$Al$_3$	$\rho(T) = 4.76 - 1.718 \cdot 10^{-4}(T - 300)$	$\rho(T) = 4.5654 - 1.758 \cdot 10^{-4}(T - 1406)$
5. NiAl$_3$	$\rho(T) = 3.96 - 2.418 \cdot 10^{-4}(T - 300)$	$\rho(T) = 3.74 - 7.6 \cdot 10^{-4}(T - 1127)$
6. Al	$\rho(T) = 2.699 - 3.736 \cdot 10^{-7}(T - 300)^2$	$\rho(T) = 2.368 - 2.667 \cdot 10^{-4}(T - 933.6)$

In the table, the values of the coefficients in the formulas are given with rounding, since the error of the experimental values turns out to be at least 5% [15]. In the table, in parentheses of formulas, the values of the melting temperatures of the phases (with a minus sign) are indicated: $T_{melt, 1} = T_{melt, Ni} = 1728$ K, $T_{melt, 2} = T_{melt, Ni_3Al} = 1658$ K, $T_{melt, 3} = T_{melt, NiAl} = 1911$ K, $T_{melt, 4} = T_{melt, Ni_2Al_3} = 1406$ K, $T_{melt, 5} = T_{melt, NiAl_3} = 1127$ K, $T_{melt, 6} = T_{melt, Al} = 933.6$ K.

The algorithm for recognizing the spatial 3D-distribution of intermetallic phases in the nanoparticle volume is reduced to the following informal description.

1. Two sets of 3D-arrays are used as input data. The 1st set of 3D-arrays is a set of 3D-distributions of matter density values over all small cubes of a nanoparticle, and the 2nd set of 3D-arrays is a set of 3D-distributions of temperature values over all small cubes. The equal number of 3D-arrays in each set is M. Parameter M is the number of points in time specified by the user of the program for analyzing the dynamics of changes

in matter density and temperature in small cubes at times t_m, where m is the iteration number of the outer cycle and $m = 1, 2, \ldots., M$.

2. An additional 3-dimensional cycle nested in the outer cycle with a change in the index m corresponds to three spatial dimensions of the (i, j, k)-cubic partition of the nanoparticle. The nested 3D-cycle for each small cube with a number n_{ijk} compares its density value, taken from the 3D-distribution of matter density (from 3-dimensional matter density array), with the matter density values $\overline{\rho}_{n_{ijk}}(t_m)$ calculated using tabular formulas for those phases with numbers l for which inequalities $T_0 \leq T < T_{melt,l}$ and/or $T_{melt,l} \leq T < T_{max}$ are true. In calculations according to the tabular formulas for the analyzed small cube, the corresponding temperature value T is used, taken from the 3D-array of temperatures corresponding to the moment in time t_m. The comparison criterion is formulated according to the conditional operator:

a) if during the comparison process for the analyzed small cube its matter density value $\overline{\rho}_{n_{ijk}}(t_m)$ in modulus in a relative sense differs from the calculated density value $\rho_{lS}(T)$ (or $\rho_{lL}(T)$) for any l-th phase by no more than a small value γ specified by the user (for example, it is reasonable to determine the value γ from 0.03 to 0.1 or as a percentage - from 3 to 10%), i.e. when inequality $\left|\overline{\rho}_{n_{ijk}}(t_m) - \rho_{lS}(T)\right|/\rho_{lS}(T) \leq \gamma$ or $\left|\overline{\rho}_{n_{ijk}}(t_m) - \rho_{lL}(T)\right|/\rho_{lL}(T) \leq \gamma$ is fulfilled, then it is considered that the analyzed small cube is filled with the l-th phase, otherwise step b) of the algorithm is executed;

b) taking into account the fulfillment of inequality $T_0 \leq T < T_{melt,l}$ or $T_{melt,l} \leq T < T_{max}$, then either inequality $(1 + \gamma) \cdot \rho_{(l+1)S}(T) < \overline{\rho}_{n_{ijk}}(t_m) < (1 - \gamma) \cdot \rho_{lS}(T)$ or inequality $(1 + \gamma) \cdot \rho_{(l+1)L}(T) < \overline{\rho}_{n_{ijk}}(t_m) < (1 - \gamma) \cdot \rho_{lL}(T)$ must be verified.

If case a) fails, but case b) is satisfied, then the decision is made that the small cube with the number n_{ijk} is filled with a mixture of two phases with numbers l and $l + 1$. Case b) must be satisfied only for one value of l, since all graphical dependences in the entire temperature range are "absolutely separable" by intervals (with an increase in the serial number of phase l, the matter density graphs shift down).

Note 1: if the condition $(1 + \gamma) \cdot \rho_{1S}(T) < \overline{\rho}_{n_{ijk}}(t_m)$ (or condition $(1 + \gamma) \cdot \rho_{1L}(T) < \overline{\rho}_{n_{ijk}}(t_m)$) is met, then it is assumed that the analyzed small cube with the number n_{ijk} is filled with the first phase (nickel).

Note 2: if the condition $\overline{\rho}_{n_{ijk}}(t_m) < (1 - \gamma) \cdot \rho_{6S}(T)$ (or condition $\overline{\rho}_{n_{ijk}}(t_m) < (1 - \gamma) \cdot \rho_{6L}(T)$) is met, then it is assumed that the volume of the analyzed small cube is not completely filled (this is possible for small cubes located on the outer boundary of the nanoparticle, where the aluminum layer is located).

4   Results and Discussion

The authors have implemented a program for the recognition method of spatial 3D-distributions of intermetallides in the nanoparticle volume and a program for their visualization. The 3D-representation of such a 3D-distribution of intermetallides in the nanoparticle volume (in our case, $20 \times 20 \times 20 = 8000$ small cubes with their sizes of $1.25 \times 1.25 \times 1.25$ nm) is visualized for ease of analysis by a set of 2D-lattices perpendicular to the X-direction. The number of 2D-lattices in the set is 20.

Each N_x- numbered 2D-lattice (20×20 small cubes) parallel to the YZ plane contains 400 small cubes. Figs. 5, 6, 7, 8 and 9 show 2D-lattices of 20×20 small squares (in other words, "maps" of phase distribution) corresponding to N_x – numbered 2D-lattices of small cubes and for different times τ (for example, $\tau = 0.5$, 1.1, 2.3 and 3.6 ns). The small squares on the phase distribution maps are marked with different color shades and numbers of intermetallic phases, incl. small squares with "double" numbers for phase mixtures. Let us explain the interpretation of the numbers: 0 – incompletely filled small cube with low density (less than Al density); 1 – Ni; 2 – Ni_3Al; 3 – NiAl; 4 – Ni_2Al_3; 5 – $NiAl_3$; 6 – Al. For example, in Fig. 5b, a small square with a double number "1; 2" indicates a mixture of Ni and Ni_3Al phases.

On the example of the central transverse layer with the serial number $N_x = 10$, it can be seen (Fig. 5a) that at the beginning of the SHS process ($\tau = 0.5$ ns) all intermetallides are generated at the interface between the Ni-core and the Al-shell, but Al still predominates at the periphery. Then (Fig. 5b) by the time $\tau = 1.1$ ns the combustion temperature T, equal to 1065 K (Fig. 3), still does not exceed the melting point of the 5-th phase ($T_{melt, 5} = 1127$ K), therefore, the thickness of the spherical layer of the 5-th phase ($NiAl_3$) increases and the amount of Al decreases (Fig. 5b).

Using the method of interpolating graphs in Fig. 3, for a time $\tau = 2.3$ ns, the combustion temperature can be estimated as 1360 K, which is higher than $T_{melt, 5} = 1127$ K. Consequently, the 5-th phase ($NiAl_3$) has entered the stage of decomposition, and the 4-th phase (Ni_2Al_3) increases in thickness (see Fig. 6 and 7), since the combustion temperature of 1360 K is lower than the melting point of the Ni_2Al_3 phase ($T_{melt, 4} = 1406$ K). Figure 7 shows a layer with the serial number $N_x = 15$, which is separated from the opposite face by a quarter of the size of a cubic nanoparticle and cuts off a ball segment at the Ni-core.

Subsequently ($2.3 < \tau < 3.6$ ns), the combustion temperature increases (Fig. 3), exceeding $T_{melt, 4} = 1406$ K. As a result, the 4-th phase (Ni_2Al_3) also begins to decay, and the 5-th phase ($NiAl_3$) completely decays by the time $\tau = 3.6$ ns. During this time, the layers of the 2nd phase (Ni_3Al) and, to a greater extent, the 3rd phase (NiAl) grow in thickness (see Figs. 8 and 9). However, by the time $\tau = 3.6$ ns, the combustion temperature, close to 1700 K (Fig. 3), also exceeds the melting point of the 2nd phase ($T_{melt, 2} = 1658$ K). Therefore, the 2nd phase (Ni_3Al) also begins to decompose, and the temperature conditions satisfy only one third phase (NiAl phase). Figure 9 confirms the dominance of the NiAl phase (in accordance with the stoichiometry of the Ni and Al reagents in the investigated nanoparticle).

It is necessary to explain the visualization results obtained by the OVITO program [2] and displayed in Figs. 6(a, b) and 7(a, b). In the center of each of the Figs. 6a and 6b, a Ni-core is clearly distinguished, the geometric shapes and sizes of which are similar to the shape and size of the Ni-core shown in Fig. 6c (1st phase). Similarly, we can note the similarity of the shapes and sizes of Ni-cores in the corresponding fragments of Fig. 7. Distribution of intermetallic phases with numbers 2, 3, 4, 5 in the form of spherical layers (or other structures) according to Figs. 6(a, b) and 7(a, b) is practically impossible to establish. However, we note the following.

Analyzing the distributions of Ni and Al atoms, shown in Figs. 6a and 7a, it can be noted that with distance along the radial directions from the Ni core to the periphery, the concentration of Ni atoms gradually decreases synchronously with an increase in the concentration of Al atoms. Such a regularity of changes in the concentrations of Ni and

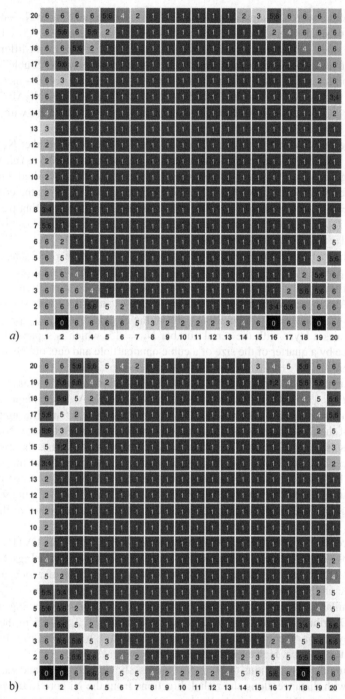

Fig. 5. Phase distribution maps: a) $N_X = 10$, $\tau = 0.5$ ns; b) $N_X = 10$, $\tau = 1.1$ ns. (Color figure online)

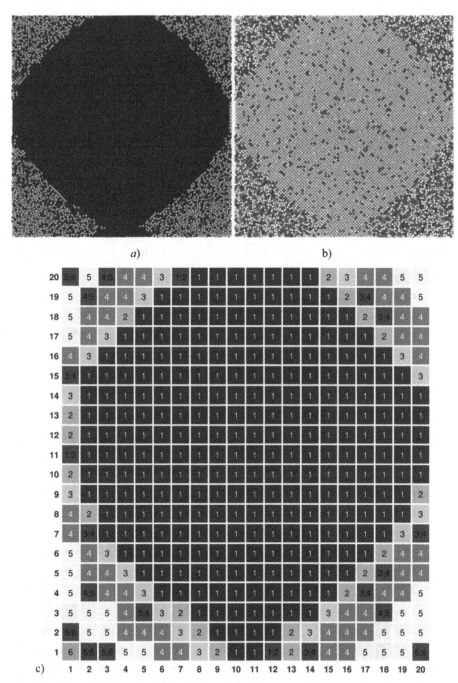

Fig. 6. Different distributions in a layer ($N_X = 10$, $\tau = 2.3$ ns): a) distribution of atoms Ni and Al; b) distribution of types of crystal cells: green dots - fcc, blue dots - bcc, red dots - hcp, yellow dots - ico type; white dots - "other" type; c) phase distribution map. (Color figure online)

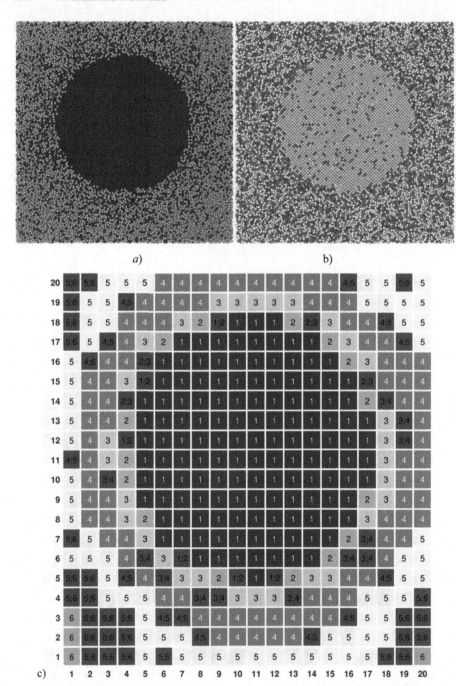

Fig. 7. Different distributions in a layer ($N_X = 15$, $\tau = 2.3$ ns): a) distribution of atoms Ni and Al; b) distribution of types of crystal cells: green dots - fcc, blue dots – bcc, red dots – hcp, yellow dots – ico type; white dots – "other" type; c) phase distribution map. (Color figure online)

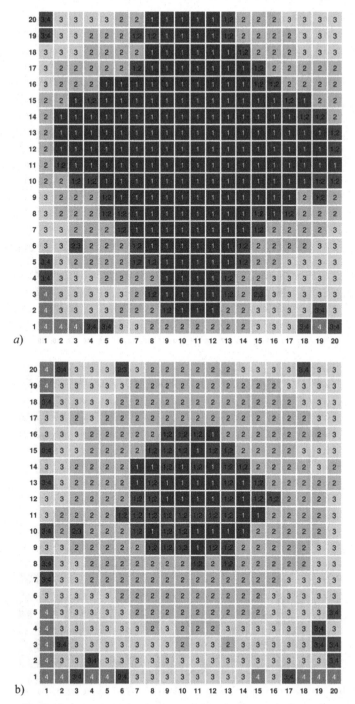

Fig. 8. Phase distribution maps: a) $N_x = 10$, $\tau = 3.6$ ns; b) $N_x = 15$, $\tau = 3.6$ ns. (Color figure online)

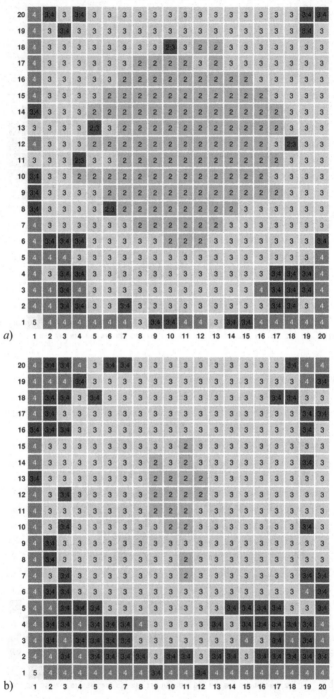

Fig. 9. Phase distribution maps: a) $N_x = 17$, $\tau = 3.6$ ns; b) $N_x = 19$, $\tau = 3.6$ ns. (Color figure online)

Al atoms outside the Ni-cores corresponds (in a qualitative sense) to the sequence of the arrangement of spherical layers of intermetallic phases shown in the maps of Figs. 6c and 7c. That is, phases with a predominance of the number of Ni atoms over the number of Al atoms in their respective chemical formulas are located closer to the Ni-core, and phases in which in the chemical formulas the number of Al atoms dominates over the number of Ni atoms are found on the periphery of the maps.

Figures 6b and 7b show the distributions of types of crystal structures (fcc, bcc, hcp, ico, etc.) obtained using Ackland-Jones analysis (in other words, Bond-angle analysis), implemented in the composition OVITO package [16]. In the case of repainting the colors in grayscale in the Figs. 6b and 7b, green and yellow are converted to light gray, blue and red to dark gray. Analysis of Figs. 6b and 7b shows that it is practically impossible to distinguish any one or several regions in which an accumulation of structures of the same type would be observed. Therefore, Ackland-Jones analysis is not efficient enough to recognize the spatial 3D-distribution of intermetallic phases in the volume of the cubic Ni@Al "core-shell" nanoparticle.

5 Conclusion

Using the LAMMPS software package, computational experiments (CEs) were carried out for MD-simulation of the SH-synthesis of intermetallic phases in a cubic Ni@Al "core-shell" nanoparticle (Fig. 2) with dimensions of $25 \times 25 \times 25$ nm. At the first stage of MD-simulation for 0.4 ns, the nanoparticle was uniformly heated throughout its volume at temperatures from 600 to 800 K. Then, by rapid heating (within 0.1 ns) from 800 to 1200 K, SHS was initiated in a layer with dimensions of $10 \times 25 \times 25$ nm, which is enclosed between the flat face YZ (with the $X = 0$ coordinate) and the secant parallel plane with the $X = 10$ nm coordinate. Based on the CEs results, an analysis of SHS microkinetics was carried out using the calculated one-dimensional distributions of the averaged values of temperature and matter density along the X-direction (sets of temperature and matter density profiles, see Figs. 3 and 4), obtained by "integral" averaging along the Y- and Z-directions in layers with dimensions of $4 \times 25 \times 25$ nm. One-dimensional profiles of the integrally averaged matter density do not allow one to effectively recognize in time the spatial structure of the formation and transformations of intermetallic phases at the core-shell interface of the nanoparticle.

Therefore, the authors have implemented a program for the method of recognizing the spatial 3D-distributions of synthesized intermetallides in the volume of a nanoparticle using pre-calculated sets of 3D-distributions of the matter density. On the basis of the performed CEs, a sufficiently high efficiency of this method of recognition of intermetallic compounds in the volume of a nanoparticle was shown (Figs. 5, 6, 7, 8 and 9), as well as its advantage in comparison with the methods of similar analysis, implemented in the widely proven OVITO software package.

Summing up, we can say that the authors have created a fairly effective software toolkit for studying the SHS microkinetics in nano- and micro-sized binary atomic systems (for example, Ni-Al, Ti-Al and etc.) and, in particular, for studying the process of structure and phase formation at the interfaces of such heterogeneous systems in a given time interval.

References

1. Plimpton, S.: Fast parallel algorithms for short-range molecular dynamics. J Comp. Phys. **117**, 1–19 (1995)
2. Stukowski, A.: Visualization and analysis of atomistic simulation data with OVITO – the Open Visualization Tool. Model. Simul. Mater. Sci. Eng. **18**, 015012 (2010)
3. Nelson, M., et al.: NAMD: a parallel object-oriented molecular dynamics program. Int. J. Supercomput. Appl. High-Perf. Comput. **10**, 251–268 (1996)
4. Turlo, V., Politano, O., Baras, F.: Microstructure evolution and self-propagating reactions in Ni-Al nanofoils: an atomic-scale description. J. Alloys Compd. **708**, 989–998 (2017)
5. Baras, F., Politano, O.: Epitaxial growth of the intermetallic compound NiAl on low-index Ni surfaces in Ni/Al reactive multilayer nanofoils. Acta Mater. **148**, 133–146 (2018)
6. Shmakov, I.A., Jordan, V.I., Savicheva, T.M.: Molecular-dynamic simulation of SHS in nanoscale layered Ti-32.89wt%Al composition using parallel computing. High-Perf. Comput. Syst. Technol. **3**(1), 77–81 (2019). (in Russian)
7. Rogachev, A.S., et al.: Combustion in reactive multilayer Ni/Al nanofoils: experiments and molecular dynamic simulation. Combust. Flame **166**, 158–169 (2016)
8. Jordan, V., Shmakov, I.: Thermal and microstructural analysis of intermetallide synthesis in the Ni-Al layered-block atomic structure based on the computer-aided simulation of SHS. Commun. Comput. Inf. Sci. **1304**, 43–61 (2020)
9. Ozdemir Kart, S., Kart, H.H., Cagin, T.: Atomic-scale insights into structural and thermodynamic stability of spherical Al@Ni and Ni@Al core–shell nanoparticles. J. Nanopart. Res. **22**(6), 1–19 (2020). https://doi.org/10.1007/s11051-020-04862-2
10. Kovalev, O.B., Belyaev, V.V.: Mathematical modelling of metallochemical reactions in a two-species reacting disperse mixture. J Comb. Explos. Shock Waves **49**(5), 563–574 (2013). (in Russian)
11. Rogachev, A.S., Mukas'yan, A.S.: Combustion for the synthesis of materials: an introduction to structural macrokinetics. Fizmatlit, Moscow (2012). (in Russian)
12. Jordan, V.I., Shmakov, I.A., Grigorevskaya, A.A.: 3D computer-aided simulation of SHS macrokinetics in the Ni-Al porous medium with the closest packing of "mesocells". J. Phys. Conf. Ser. **1745**, Article ID 012062 (2021).https://iopscience.iop.org/article/10.1088/1742-6596/1745/1/012062/pdf
13. Purja, P.G.P., Mishin, Y.: Development of an interatomic potential for the Ni-Al system. Phil. Mag. **89**(34–36), 3245–3267 (2009)
14. Kovalev, O.B., Neronov, V.A.: Metallochemical analysis of the reaction in a mixture of Nickel and Aluminum powders. J Comb. Explos. Shock Waves **40**(2), 172–179 (2004). (in Russian)
15. Plevachuk, Y., Egry, I., Brillo, J., Holland-Moritz, D., Kaban, I.: Density and atomic volume in liquid Al–Fe and Al–Ni binary alloys Int. J. Mat. Res. (formerly Z. Metallkd.) **98**(2), 107–111 (2007). (in Russian)
16. Ackland, G.J., Jones, A.P.: Applications of local crystal structure measures in experiment and simulation. Phys. Rev. B. **73**(5), 054104 (2006)

Ab Initio Computer Modeling
of a Diamond-Like 5–7 Bilayer

Vladimir Greshnyakov[(✉)] [iD] and Evgeny Belenkov [iD]

Chelyabinsk State University, Bratiev Kashirinykh Street 129, 454001 Chelyabinsk, Russia
greshnyakov@csu.ru

Abstract. An ab initio investigation of the atomic structure, thermostability, electronic characteristics and methods obtaining a novel layer diamond-like nanostructure is carried out by using the Quantum ESPRESSO software package, which supports MPI parallelization of computations. The density functional perturbation theory method is used for the computations. This diamond-like bilayer can be obtained by polymerization of two defect 5–7 graphene layers at a pressure exceeding 12 GPa. The diamond-like 5–7 bilayer has a centered rectangular unit cell with the following parameters: $a = 0.8261$, $b = 0.6483$ nm, and $Z = 32$ atoms. The calculated surface density of the novel bilayer is 1.192 mg/m^2, which is 60% higher than the corresponding density of ordinary hexagonal graphene. The bilayer structure contains pentagonal and heptagonal prismatic units, the maximum diameter of which is 0.1983 nm. The diamond-like 5–7 bilayer should be stable up to 300K, but its corrugation occurs at temperatures above 200K. This bilayer is a semiconductor with a straight bandgap of 2.89 eV. The experimental identification of the 5–7 bilayer is possible using the calculated Raman spectrum.

Keywords: Graphene · Diamond-like bilayer · Modeling · Parallel computing · Molecular dynamics calculations · Phase transitions

1 Introduction

Graphene is a layered structural type of carbon consisting of three-coordinated carbon atoms. Graphene has unique physicochemical properties; therefore, materials based on it are widely used in the manufacture of ultrasensitive molecular sensors, electrodes in supercapacitors, nanoelectronic devices, and molecular sieves [1–5]. In addition, graphene layers can be used in another area of materials science as a raw material for the synthesis of high-strength diamond-like compounds at high pressures [6, 7]. As a rule, diamond-like compounds with structures of the diamond polytypes and its polymorphic varieties are formed during the synthesis process [7–9]. However, the layered diamond-like nanostructures proposed in [10, 11] have not yet been obtained until now. These nanostructures could find practical application in the production of high-strength structural materials and devices for semiconductor micro- and nanoelectronics. As a result of ab initio calculations performed in [12], it was found that the proposed diamond-like layers could be synthesized under strong compression of two graphene layers (bilayer

© Springer Nature Switzerland AG 2022
V. Jordan et al. (Eds.): HPCST 2021, CCIS 1526, pp. 121–130, 2022.
https://doi.org/10.1007/978-3-030-94141-3_10

graphene), and the pressure of the phase transition of the bilayer graphene into the diamond-like layer can be significantly reduced by using defective graphene layers as precursors.

Any study of the possibilities of the diamond-like layer formation and the search for conditions under which they can stably exist can be most effectively performed using ab initio methods of theoretical calculations based on the density functional theory. Such methods of computer modeling make it possible to carry out studies of new hypothetical compounds with the lowest computational costs. The scope of the research and the calculation speed cannot be increased without the use of parallel computing. This is especially important for systems containing a large number of atoms, since the calculation time increases in proportion to the number of atoms in the third or fourth power. In this regard, the packages of quantum mechanical calculations adapted for parallel computations in multiprocessor systems should be used in modeling the structure and formation processes of diamond-like bilayers.

Therefore, first-principles investigations of thermal stability, structure formation, and electronic properties of a novel layered diamond polymorph obtained on the basis of bilayer defective 5–7 graphene are carried out in this work using high-performance computing systems.

2   Calculation Methods

In this work, the structural characteristics and properties of carbon compounds were calculated using the Quantum ESPRESSO software package within the framework of the density functional perturbation theory (DFPT) method [13]. In the DFPT method, the generalized gradient approximation (GGA) was used [14]. The norm-preserving pseudopotential was used to take into account the influence of ionic cores of carbon atoms [15]. Calculations of the structure and properties of the diamond and layer diamond-like nanostructure were carried out for k-point grids $16 \times 16 \times 16$ and $20 \times 20 \times 1$, respectively. The wave functions are expanded over a truncated basis set of plane waves. The cutoff energy is 60 Ry. Geometrical optimization of the diamond-like structures under consideration was carried out until the magnitude of the forces acting on the atom and the stress becomes less than 10^{-2} eV/nm and 100 MPa, respectively. The thermal treatment of the layer diamond-like nanostructure is simulated in the scope of the molecular dynamics method. The simulation involved the use of an orthorhombic supercell consisting of one hundred twenty-eight atoms and a $6 \times 6 \times 1$ k-point grid with a time step of 1 fs. The study of the phase transition process of the bilayer graphene into the diamond-like layer are carried out according to the method described in [12]. The Raman spectrum of these carbon diamond-like compounds is calculated by the method from [16]. To reduce the time of quantum mechanical computation, parallelization using the Message Passing Interface (MPI) technology is applied. The advantage of using the message passing mechanism is to ensure complete independence of applications written using MPI from the architecture of a multiprocessor system without any significant performance loss. The performed test calculations for the cubic diamond, carried out on a sixteen-core processor, showed that the computation time using the parallel version of the Quantum ESPRESSO software package was reduced by about 90% compared to the computation time for the serial version of this software.

3 Results and Discussion

3.1 Crystalline Structure

The model preparation of any layered type of diamond belonging to the structural group $[2D_c, 4]$ is possible on the basis of layered graphene-like precursors from the structural group $[2D_c, 3]$ [10]. Graphene layers consisting of Stone-Wales defects are chosen as these precursors (Fig. 1a). The formation of the diamond-like layer structure occurs only in the process of cross-linking the bilayer 5–7 graphene (the point symmetry group is *mmm*). The structure of the diamond-like layer obtained in the course of geometric optimization of the cross-linked bilayer 5–7 graphene is shown in Fig. 1b.

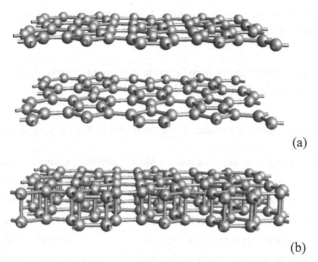

(a)

(b)

Fig. 1. Geometrically optimized structures of the graphene 5–7 bilayer (a) and diamond-like 5–7 bilayer (b).

The diamond-like 5–7 bilayer has a two-dimensional centered orthorhombic (rectangular) unit cell with parameters $a = 0.8261$ nm and $b = 0.6483$ nm, which contains thirty-two carbon atoms (Fig. 2). The crystal lattice of this bilayer belongs to the layer symmetry group *cmmm* (no. 47). The calculated atomic positions in the unit cell are listed in Table 1. The bilayer thickness varies from 0.1582 to 0.1607 nm. The atoms in the structure of this bilayer are in three crystallographically nonequivalent four-coordinated states (Fig. 2). The calculated surface density of the 5–7 bilayer is 1.192 mg/m^2. This value is 57% higher than the experimental density value of ordinary hexagonal graphene (L$_6$) [6] and 3.1% lower than the calculated density value of the diamond-like DL$_6$ bilayer [12]. The diamond-like bilayer contains units in the form of pentagonal and heptagonal prisms, the maximum diameter of which is 0.1983 nm.

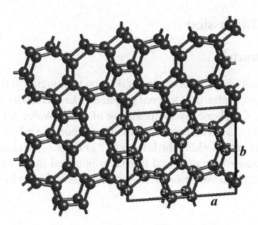

Fig. 2. Rectangular unit cell of the diamond-like 5–7 bilayer (equivalent crystallographic atomic positions are marked with numbers).

The bilayer structure contains nine different interatomic bonds, the lengths of which vary from 0.1538 to 0.1627 nm (Table 2).

Table 1. Atomic coordinates in the diamond-like 5–7 bilayer unit cell.

Atomic number	x, nm	y, nm	z, nm	Atomic number	x, nm	y, nm	z, nm
1	0.6963	0.1774	0.0001	17	0.4130	0.2446	0.0000
2	0.2831	0.5015	0.0001	18	0.0000	0.5686	0.0000
3	0.6963	0.1774	0.1608	19	0.4130	0.2446	0.1609
4	0.2831	0.5015	0.1608	20	0.0000	0.5686	0.1610
5	0.2831	0.1467	0.0001	21	0.4899	0.0000	0.0013
6	0.6963	0.4709	0.0001	22	0.0769	0.3241	0.0014
7	0.2831	0.1467	0.1608	23	0.4899	0.0000	0.1596
8	0.6963	0.4709	0.1608	24	0.0769	0.3241	0.1596
9	0.3362	0.0000	0.0013	25	0.1297	0.1774	0.0001
10	0.7492	0.3241	0.0014	26	0.5430	0.5015	0.0001
11	0.3362	0.0000	0.1596	27	0.1297	0.1774	0.1608
12	0.7492	0.3241	0.1596	28	0.5430	0.5015	0.1608
13	0.0000	0.0797	0.0000	29	0.5430	0.1467	0.0001
14	0.4130	0.4037	0.0000	30	0.1297	0.4709	0.0001
15	0.0000	0.0797	0.1610	31	0.5430	0.1467	0.1608
16	0.4130	0.4037	0.1609	32	0.1297	0.4709	0.1608

The average value of the interatomic bond length is 0.1588 nm. The carbon-carbon bond length values in the 5–7 bilayer differ from the experimental bond length value for cubic diamond (L_{diam} = 0.154 nm [6]) by 0.1–5.6%.

The number of different bond angles in the structure of the diamond-like 5–7 bilayer is thirteen (Table 3). The bond angle values vary from 89.56 to 140.4° and differ from the diamond angle (β_{diam} = 109.5°) by 0.3–28%. We also calculated the average deformation parameters of the 5–7 bilayer, which characterize the stress of the diamond-like structure relative to the cubic diamond structure, using the following formulas:

$$\overline{Str} = \frac{1}{N_c} \sum_{\kappa=1}^{N_p} n_\kappa Str_\kappa = \frac{1}{N_c} \sum_{\kappa=1}^{N_p} n_\kappa \sum_{\mu=1}^{4} \left| L_\mu^\kappa - L_{diam} \right|,$$

$$\overline{Def} = \frac{1}{N_c} \sum_{\kappa=1}^{N_p} n_\kappa Def_\kappa = \frac{1}{N_c} \sum_{\kappa=1}^{N_p} n_\kappa \sum_{\mu=1}^{3} \sum_{\nu=\mu+1}^{4} \left| \beta_{\mu\nu}^\kappa - \beta_{diam} \right|,$$

where N_c is the number of atoms in the unit cell; κ is the number of crystallographic positions; μ and ν are the numbers of different interatomic bonds; N_p is the number of different crystallographic positions; n_κ is the number of equivalent atomic positions. The computations showed that the parameters $\overline{Str}$ and $\overline{Def}$ were 0.013 nm and 94.1°, respectively. These values are larger than the values of the corresponding parameters for the DL_6 bilayer formed from ordinary bilayer graphene [12]. Consequently, the novel bilayer can be attributed to highly stressed diamond-like nanostructures in comparison with cubic diamond and diamond-like phases [7].

Table 2. Interatomic bond lengths (L) in the diamond and diamond-like 5–7 bilayer (κ determines the number of the nonequivalent atomic position; n_κ determines the number of atoms in the i-crystallographic position).

Phase	κ	n_κ	L_1, nm	L_2, nm	L_3, nm	L_4, nm
Diamond	1	8	0.1558	0.1558	0.1558	0.1558
5–7 bilayer	1	8	0.1609	0.1591	0.1627	0.1627
	2	8	0.1582	0.1538	0.1560	0.1560
	3	16	0.1607	0.1627	0.1560	0.1564

Table 3. Angles between carbon-carbon bonds (β) in the diamond and diamond-like 5–7 bilayer.

Phase	κ	β_{12}, °	β_{13}, °	β_{14}, °	β_{23}, °	β_{24}, °	β_{34}, °
Diamond	1	109.47	109.47	109.47	109.47	109.47	109.47
5–7 bilayer	1	90.00	89.95	89.95	126.97	126.97	106.05
	2	90.00	90.45	90.45	109.80	109.80	140.38
	3	90.05	89.56	90.01	107.06	131.72	121.21

3.2 Thermal Stability

The calculations of the total energy (E_{total}) of the diamond-like 5–7 bilayer and cubic diamond showed that E_{total} of this bilayer is greater than the calculated total energy magnitudes for the 3C diamond and diamond-like DL_6 bilayer by 0.10 and 0.01 Ry/atom, respectively. In addition, the obtained magnitude of the difference total energy exceeds the corresponding energy magnitudes of the *LA, TA, TB, SA, CA,* and *CB* phases of sp^3-hybridized carbon atoms studied using the same ab initio method in [7]. Therefore, it is necessary to investigate the thermodynamic stability the novel orthorhombic 5–7 bilayer. The crystal lattice annealing is simulated using the molecular dynamics method for the following temperatures: 200, 220, 240, 260, 280, and 300K. Figure 3a shows a plot of the total energy versus the heat treatment time of the studied bilayer at 240K. The 5–7 bilayer supercell after annealing is shown in Fig. 3b and Fig. 3c. It was found that, during annealing for 7 ps, the bilayer was slightly corrugated and was not collapsed, which indicates the stability of the orthorhombic diamond-like 5–7 bilayer at temperatures up to 300K.

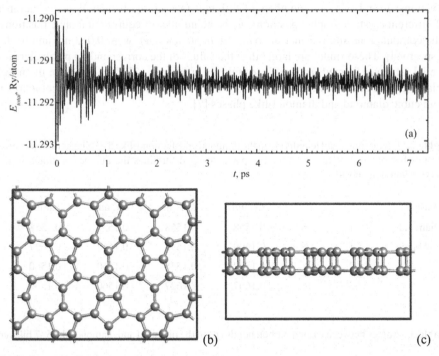

Fig. 3. Dependency graph of the total energy (E_{total}) on the time of heat treatment (t) of the diamond-like 5–7 bilayer at 240K (a). Projections of the diamond-like 5–7 bilayer structure on the XY (b) and XZ (c) planes after the simulated annealing process.

3.3 Electronic Properties

The diamond-like 5–7 bilayer electronic properties are studied when calculating the band structure and spectrum of electronic states in the Brillouin zone of a simple orthorhombic unit cell containing thirty-two carbon atoms. A detailed analysis of the band structure of the 5–7 bilayer in the intervals between five high symmetry points (G, X, S, Y, and Z) in the Brillouin zone showed that the largest value of the straight bandgap was observed at the S-point and was equal to 3.68 eV (Fig. 4). The smallest value of the straight bandgap is observed in the GY interval and is equal to 2.89 eV. This value is 51% less than the calculated value corresponding to the 3C diamond polytype [7]. The calculated spectrum of electronic states is shown in Fig. 5. It is found that the smallest difference between the electronic energies of the completely occupied valence band and the unoccupied conduction band is 2.67 eV. Therefore, the novel bilayer must have semiconducting properties.

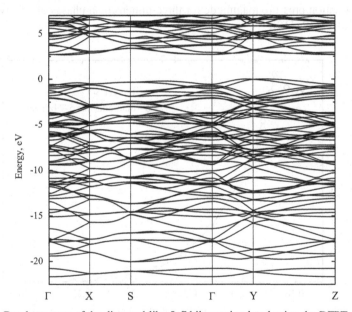

Fig. 4. Band structure of the diamond-like 5–7 bilayer simulated using the DFPT method.

3.4 Synthesis Pathway

Further, the possibility of obtaining the diamond-like 5–7 bilayer is investigated. The most probable method for the synthesis of this bilayer is strong static compression of a graphite-like material [6, 17, 18]. It is found that the 5–7 bilayer can be formed by compressing the bilayer defective 5–7 graphene along an axis perpendicular to the graphene planes. Figure 6 shows the dependence of the relative total energy on the interlayer distance, which characterizes the structural transformation of the bilayer graphene into the

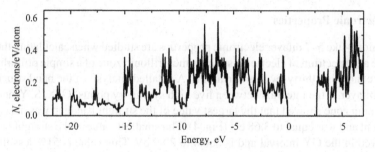

Fig. 5. Electron density of states of the 5–7 bilayer simulated using the DFPT method.

diamond-like bilayer. The phase transition occurs if the graphene layers approach each other at a distance of 0.1729 nm, when the pressure on the layers begins to exceed 12 GPa. The magnitude of the pressure at which the 5–7 bilayer formation occurs is smaller than the formation pressure magnitude for three-dimensional phases of sp^3-hybridized atoms by 28–59 GPa [19].

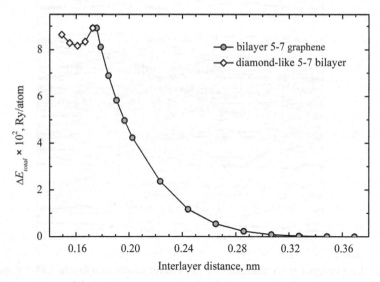

Fig. 6. Dependence of the relative total energy (ΔE_{total}) versus the interlayer distance for the first-order phase transition «bilayer 5–7 graphene → diamond-like 5–7 bilayer».

3.5   Raman Spectrum

At the final stage of the study, the Raman spectrum of the novel 5–7 bilayer is calculated for the possibility of its detection in synthesized carbon nanomaterials. The Raman spectrum of the cubic diamond is also calculated (Fig. 7). This spectrum contains one vibrational mode at 1340 cm^{-1}, which is in good agreement with the experimental value

(1332 cm^{-1}) [6]. The diamond-like 5–7 bilayer Raman spectrum is shown in Fig. 7. The calculations are shown that the vibrational spectrum of the bilayer is characterized by four high-intensity maxima located at 967, 1085, 1179, and 1199 cm^{-1}, which correspond to in-plane and out-off-plane atomic vibrations in the 5–7 bilayer. The calculated Raman spectrum of the 5–7 bilayer differs significantly from the theoretically calculated spectrum of diamond and experimental spectra of graphite and carbon nanotubes [6, 20]. Therefore, its identification in carbon materials should not cause difficulties.

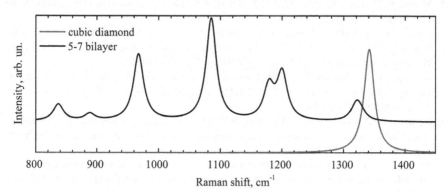

Fig. 7. Calculated Raman spectra of the cubic diamond and diamond-like 5–7 bilayer.

4   Conclusions

The use of parallel computations within the framework of ab initio calculations made it possible to efficiently predict the atomic structure, electronic characteristics, and thermodynamic stability for a novel diamond-like bilayer obtained on the basis of defect 5–7 graphene layers. As a result of the density functional perturbation theory method calculations, it is established that the diamond-like 5–7 bilayer with a centered rectangular crystal lattice can be obtained by polymerization of the bilayer defective 5–7 graphene under pressure of 12 GPa and is stable up to 300K. The structure of the diamond-like bilayer contains only pentagonal and heptagonal prismatic blocks with the maximum diameter of 0.1983 nm. The surface density of the novel bilayer is 1.192 mg/m^2. The diamond-like 5–7 bilayer should be a semiconductor, since the minimum straight bandgap energy is 2.89 eV. The theoretical Raman spectrum of the 5–7 bilayer, containing several of the most intense vibrational modes in the range from 960 to 1200 cm^{-1}, can be used for its experimental identification.

Acknowledgements. The research was funded by RFBR and Chelyabinsk Region, project number 20-43-740015. Greshnyakov V.A. thanks the Young Scientist Support Fund of the Chelyabinsk State University for partial financial support of this study.

References

1. Novoselov, K.S., Falko, V.I., Colombo, L., Gellert, P.R., Schwab, M.G., Kim, K.: A roadmap for graphene. Nature **490**, 192–200 (2012)
2. Ivanovskii, A.L.: Graphene-based and graphene-like materials. Russ. Chem. Rev. **81**(7), 571–605 (2012)
3. Tiwari, S.K., Kumar, V., Huczko, A., Oraon, R., De Adhikari, A., Nayak, G.C.: Magical allotropes of carbon: prospects and applications. Crit. Rev. Solid State **41**, 1–61 (2016)
4. Stoller, M.D., Park, S., Zhu, Y., An, J., Ruoff, R.S.: Graphene-based ultracapacitors. Nano Lett. **8**(10), 3498–3502 (2008)
5. Celasco, E., et al. (Eds.): Handbook of graphene. Scrivener Publishing LLC, Salem (2019)
6. Pierson, H.O.: Handbook of Carbon, Graphite, Diamond, and Fullerenes: Properties, Processing and Applications. Noyes, Park Ridge, IL, USA (1993)
7. Belenkov, E.A., Greshnyakov, V.A.: Structure, properties, and possible mechanisms of formation of diamond-like phases. Phys. Solid State **58**(10), 2145–2154 (2016). https://doi.org/10.1134/S1063783416100073
8. Rysaeva, L.K., Baimova, J.A., Dmitriev, S.V., Lisovenko, D.S., Gorodtsov, V.A., Rudskoy, A.I.: Elastic properties of diamond-like phases based on carbon nanotubes. Diamond Relat. Mater. **97**, 107411 (2019)
9. Rysaeva, L.K., Lisovenko, D.S., Gorodtsov, V.A., Baimova, J.A.: Stability, elastic properties and deformation behavior of graphene-based diamond-like phases. Comput. Mater. Sci. **172**, 109355 (2020)
10. Belenkov, E.A., Greshnyakov, V.A.: Classification schemes of carbon phases and nanostructures. New Carbon Mater. **28**(4), 273–283 (2013)
11. Ohno, K., Satoh, H., Iwamoto, T., Tokoyama, H., Yamakado, H.: Exploration of carbon allotropes with four-membered ring structures on quantum chemical potential energy surfaces. J. Comput. Chem. **40**(1), 14–28 (2019)
12. Greshnyakov, V.A., Belenkov, E.A.: Theoretical study of the stability and formation methods of layer diamond-like nanostructures. Lett. Mater. **10**(4), 457–462 (2020)
13. Giannozzi, P., Andreussi, O., Brumme, T., Bunau, O., Buongiorno Nardelli, M., Calandra, M., et al.: Advanced capabilities for materials modelling with quantum ESPRESSO. J. Phys. Condens. Matter **29**(46), 465901 (2017)
14. Perdew, J.P., Burke, K., Ernzerhof, M.: Generalized gradient approximation made simple. Phys. Rev. Lett **77**(18), 3865–3868 (1996)
15. Troullier, N., Martins, J.L.: Efficient pseudopotentials for plane-wave calculations. Phys. Rev. B **43**(3), 1993–2006 (1991)
16. Lazzeri, M., Mauri, F.: First-principles calculation of vibrational Raman spectra in large systems: signature of small rings in crystalline SiO_2. Phys. Rev. Lett. **90**(3), 036401 (2003)
17. Baimova, J.A., Rysaeva, L.K.: Deformation behavior of three-dimensional carbon structures under hydrostatic compression. J. Struct. Chem. **59**(4), 884–890 (2018)
18. Geng, P., Branicio, P.S.: Atomistic insights on the pressure-induced multi-layer graphene to diamond-like structure transformation. Carbon **175**, 243–253 (2021)
19. Belenkov, E.A., Greshnyakov, V.A.: Modeling of phase transitions of graphites to diamond-like phases. Phys. Solid State **60**(7), 1294–1302 (2018)
20. Jorio, A., Saito, R.: Raman spectroscopy for carbon nanotube applications. J. Appl. Phys. **129**, 021102 (2021)

Mathematical Simulation of Coupled Elastic Deformation and Fluid Dynamics in Heterogeneous Media

Ella P. Shurina[1,2] , Natalya B. Itkina[2,3] , Anastasia Yu. Kutishcheva[1,2] ,
and Sergey I. Markov[1,2(✉)]

[1] Trofimuk Institute of Petroleum Geology and Geophysics, SB RAS, Koptug Avenue 3,
630090 Novosibirsk, Russia
www.sim91@list.ru
[2] Novosibirsk State Technical University, Karl Marx Avenue 20, 630073 Novosibirsk, Russia
[3] Institute of Computational Technologies, SB RAS, Academician M.A. Lavrentiev Avenue 6,
630090 Novosibirsk, Russia

Abstract. Mathematical simulation of deformation processes occurring in fluid-saturated media requires solving multiphysical problems. We consider a multiphysical problem as a system of differential equations with special conjugation conditions for the physical fields on the interfragmentary surfaces. The interfragmentary contact surface between solid and liquid phases is a 1-connected contact surface. Explicit discretization of the interfragmentary contact surfaces leads to an increase in the degrees of freedom. To treat the problem, we propose a hierarchical splitting of physical processes. At the macro-level, the process of elastic deformation is simulated, taking into account the pressure on the inner surface of fluid-saturated pores. At the micro-level, to determine the fluid pressure inside the pores, the Navier-Stokes equations are numerically solved with the external mechanical loading. For coupling the physical fields, we use the matching conditions for the normal components of the stress tensor on the interfragmentary surfaces. Mathematical simulation of the coupled processes of elastic deformation and fluid dynamics is a resource-intensive procedure. In addition, a computational scheme has to take into account the specifics of the multiphysical problem. We propose modified computational schemes of multiscale non-conforming finite element methods. To discretize the mathematical model of the elastic deformation process, we apply a heterogeneous multiscale finite element method with polyhedral supports (macroelements). To discretize the Navier-Stokes equations, the non-conforming discontinuous Galerkin method with the tetrahedral supports (microelements) is used. This strategy makes it possible to apply a parallel algorithm to solve the elastic deformation and fluid dynamics problems under the assumption of the hydrophobicity of macroelements surfaces. In computational experiments, we deal with idealized models of heterogeneous natural media. The developed computational schemes make it possible to accelerate the solution of problems more than five times.

Keywords: Elastic deformation · Fluid-saturated media · Mathematical modelling · Multiscale non-conforming finite element methods

© Springer Nature Switzerland AG 2022
V. Jordan et al. (Eds.): HPCST 2021, CCIS 1526, pp. 131–147, 2022.
https://doi.org/10.1007/978-3-030-94141-3_11

1 Introduction

To study mechanical and transport properties of reservoir rocks, for planning and carrying out hydraulic fracturing, mathematical simulation of the elastic deformation processes in heterogeneous fluid-saturated media is applied. In the paper, we consider the mathematical simulation of the elastic deformation of a heterogeneous medium saturated by a viscous fluid. There are two principles for constructing mathematical models in the poroelasticity theory.

In the context of the averaging theory, the macroscale Biot models belong to the group of variational models. In the Biot models, the volume concentration of the liquid phase is assumed to be known. The applicability of the Biot models is limited by a lot of the physical parameters that are selected experimentally [1].

The continual mathematical models of the elastic deformation of fluid-saturated media are built using the conservation laws. There are two main troubles with discretization techniques for the mathematical models. The first problem deals with the conjugation conditions for physical fields on the interfragmentary surfaces "solid-liquid". As a rule, the conjugation conditions are determined by the specifics of the multiphysics problem being solved [2]. The second problem is the choice of a suitable computational scheme to discretize the mathematical models. Geomechanical problems are multiphysical and multiscale problems. The splitting of physical processes and the need to take into account all structural micro-inclusions lead to the proliferation of the degrees of freedom and an increase in the cost of computational resources [3].

To solve the first problem, we consider the isothermal linear process of elastic deformation in the fluid-saturated medium without destruction of the rock skeleton. Then, at the pore-scale level, the process of fluid dynamics is described by the Navier-Stokes equations for an incompressible fluid (microscale model). At the rock skeleton scale level, geomechanical processes are described by the elastic deformation problem of a solid (macroscale model). The conjugation conditions for the physical processes are formulated by concerning the elasticity tensor on the interfragmentary surfaces "solid-liquid".

To treat the second problem, multiscale finite element approximations of the selected mathematical models are used [3]. Today, to discretize the linear poroelasticity problem, computational schemes of the multiscale generalized finite element method (GMsFEM) [4–6], heterogeneous finite element method (FE-HMM) [7–9], virtual finite element method (VFEM) [10, 11], extended multiscale finite element method (XMsFEM) [12, 13] and their numerous modifications in conformal and non-conforming ideology [14, 15] are used.

In the paper, to discretize the mathematical model of the elastic deformation process, we apply a heterogeneous multiscale finite element method with polyhedral supports (macroelements). To discretize the hydrodynamics model, the non-conforming discontinuous Galerkin method with the tetrahedral supports (microelements) is used. This strategy makes it possible to apply a parallel algorithm for solving the elastic deformation problem, as well as the fluid dynamics problem under the assumption of non-seepage of the fluid through the surface of macroelements.

2   Problem Statement

We consider an idealized model of a fractured porous medium. There are fluid-saturated inclusions of various shapes in the medium matrix. In the paper, a pore is a closed-boundary 3D object. If the inclusion has multiscale sizes, then this object is a crack. We will simulate the incompressible fluid flow in the inclusions, taking into account external mechanical effects on the medium matrix. In computational experiments, the inclusions contain oil.

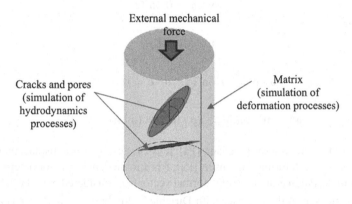

Fig. 1. Structure of the rock sample.

The sample has a cylindrical shape (see Fig. 1). Its physical properties correspond to the physical properties of dry sandstone. Volumetric inhomogeneities and their clusters contain oil. Tables 1 and 2 show the physical characteristics.

Table 1. Elastic properties of the sample.

Medium	Modulus of elasticity, MPa	Thermal conductivity, [W/(m•K)]	Poisson's ratio
Oil	1273	1.6	0.5
Sandstone	18000	0.13	0.3

Table 2. Hydrodynamic properties of the sample.

Medium	Viscosity, Pa•sec	Density, kg/m^3	Permeability, 10^{-6} m^2
Sandstone	–	1800–2100	0.5–0.9
Oil	0.095	800	–

3 Methods

3.1 Mathematical Model of the Elastic Deformation

A sample of heterogeneous media $\Omega \subset R^3$ consists of a matrix Ω_0 and inclusions Ω_k.

If there is no external loading and the influence of internal forces, such as gravity, is insignificant, the elastic deformation process of a solid Ω obeys the generalized Hooke's law. The mathematical model is described by the following boundary value problem:

$$-\nabla \cdot \sigma = 0 \text{ in } \Omega, \tag{1}$$

$$\mathbf{u} = 0 \text{ on } \Gamma_D, \tag{2}$$

$$\sigma \cdot \mathbf{n} = -\mathbf{f} \text{ on } \Gamma_N^f, \ \sigma \cdot \mathbf{n} = 0 \text{ on } \Gamma_N^0, \tag{3}$$

$$\mathbf{u}^+ = \mathbf{u}^- \text{ on } \Gamma_{in}, \ (\sigma \cdot \mathbf{n})^+ = (\sigma \cdot \mathbf{n})^- \text{ on } \Gamma_{in}, \tag{4}$$

where $\sigma_q = \mathbf{D} : \nabla_s \mathbf{u}_q$ is a stress tensor, [Pa]; $\mathbf{u} = (u_x, u_y, u_z)^T$ is a displacement vector, [m]; $\mathbf{D}$ is an elastic deformation tensor, [Pa]; $\mathbf{f}$ is a force density vector determining the external action, [Pa]; $\mathbf{n}$ is an outer unit normal vector to a considered boundary; $\Gamma_D \subset \partial\Omega$ is a bottom surface of the cylinder with Dirichlet's conditions; $\Gamma_N^f \subset \partial\Omega$ is the upper surface of the cylinder that is acted upon by the density force vector $\mathbf{f}$; $\Gamma_N^0 \subset \partial\Omega$ is the free surface of the cylinder with Neumann's zero conditions; $\Gamma_{in} = \Omega_0 \cap \left(\bigcup\limits_{i=1}^{m} \Omega_m \right) \subset \partial\Omega$ is matrix and inclusion boundaries inside the medium Ω, $\Gamma_{in} \cup \Gamma_D \cup \Gamma_N = \partial\Omega$.

The pressure on the pore surface Γ_{in} is calculated as the normal component of the stress tensor σ in the points $\mathbf{x} \in \Gamma_{in}$:

$$p(\mathbf{x}) = \sigma(\mathbf{x}) \cdot \mathbf{n}_{in} \cdot \mathbf{n}_{in} \tag{5}$$

where $\mathbf{n}_{in}$ is a unit normal vector to the surface Γ_{in}.

Since the pore boundaries are assumed to be impermeable to the fluid and taking into account the pressure on the inner surface of the pores, we obtain the boundary value problem (1)–(4) as:

$$-\nabla \cdot \sigma = 0 \text{ in } \Omega_0, \tag{6}$$

$$\mathbf{u} = 0 \text{ on } \Gamma_D, \tag{7}$$

$$\sigma \cdot \mathbf{n} = -\mathbf{f} \text{ on } \Gamma_N^f, \ \sigma \cdot \mathbf{n} = -\mathbf{p} \text{ on } \Gamma_{in}, \ \sigma \cdot \mathbf{n} = 0 \text{ on } \Gamma_N^0 \tag{8}$$

where $\Gamma_{in} \subset \partial\Omega_0$ is a pore surface inside Ω_0, $\mathbf{p}$ is fluid pressure, $\mathbf{n}$ is an outer normal vector.

As a result of solving the problem (6)–(8), we obtain the displacement vector field and pressure on the pore surface.

3.2 Mathematical Model of the Incompressible Fluid Flow

The Navier-Stokes equations describe the isothermal hydrodynamics processes inside fluid-saturated pores:

$$\rho\frac{\partial \mathbf{v}}{\partial t} + \rho\mathbf{v}\cdot\nabla\mathbf{v} + \nabla p = \rho\mathbf{g} + \nabla\cdot\mu\left(\nabla\mathbf{v} + (\nabla\mathbf{v})^T\right)\text{in }\Omega_i, \ i = 1\ldots m, \tag{9}$$

$$\nabla\cdot\mathbf{v} = 0 \text{ in }\Omega_i, \ \ i = 1\ldots m, \tag{10}$$

where $\mathbf{v}$ is a velocity [m/sec], μ is dynamic viscosity [Pa·sec], ρ is density [kg/m^3], p is pressure [Pa], $\mathbf{g}$ is a constant gravitational vector [m/sec^2].

The initial fluid velocity is zero:

$$\mathbf{v}|_{t=0} = \mathbf{0}. \tag{11}$$

On the pore surface $\partial\Omega_i$, $i = 1\ldots m$, the stress tensor normal component is determined as:

$$\sigma\cdot\mathbf{n}|_{\partial\Omega_i} = \mu\left(\nabla\mathbf{v} + (\nabla\mathbf{v})^T\right)\cdot\mathbf{n} - (p\,\mathbf{I})\cdot\mathbf{n}\Big|_{\partial\Omega_i} = \mathbf{t}, \tag{12}$$

where $\mathbf{n}$ is a normal vector.

The problems (9)–(12) can be solved in parallel if the liquid does not flow through the medium matrix.

3.3 Variational Formulation of the FE-HMM

We define the functional spaces:

$$\mathbf{H}(\text{grad}, \Omega) = \left\{\mathbf{u}|\mathbf{u}\in\mathbf{L}^2(\Omega), \nabla\mathbf{u}\in\left[\mathbf{L}^2(\Omega)\right]^3\right\}, \tag{13}$$

$$\mathbf{H}_0(\text{grad}, \Omega) = \{\mathbf{u}|\mathbf{u}\in\mathbf{H}(\text{grad}, \Omega): \ \mathbf{u} = \mathbf{0} \text{ on } \partial\Omega\}, \tag{14}$$

Let T^H be the polyhedral irregular mesh as the top level of the mesh hierarchy. This mesh is built in the entire modelling area Ω excluding internal inclusion borders $\Gamma_N^{\mathbf{p}}$. We determine the discrete Hilbert subspace as $\mathbf{V}^{HMM}\left(T^H\right)\subset\mathbf{H}(\text{grad}, \Omega)$ [9]. The subspace contains finite nonpolynomial multiscale shape functions $\boldsymbol{\psi}_i^{HMM}(\mathbf{x}) = \left(\psi_x^i(\mathbf{x}), \ \psi_y^i(\mathbf{x}), \ \psi_z^i(\mathbf{x})\right)^T, i = \overline{1, N^H}$. The number of functions in $\mathbf{V}^{HMM}\left(T^H\right)$ is equal to the number of degrees of freedom in T^H.

In FE-HMM, a microelement contains four connected components $K = \left\{K^H, \mathbf{V}_K^{HMM}, P, \Lambda\right\}$, where K^H is a geometric polyhedral finite element, P is subspace of the degrees of freedom (the subspace size equals the number of vertexes in T^H), $\mathbf{V}_K^{HMM}$ is subspace of nonpolynomial multiscale shape functions associated with P and based on the linear Lagrange functions, Λ is a numerical integration formula used in K^H:

$$\int_{K^H} g(\mathbf{x})dK^H = \sum_{l=1}^{n_l}\omega_l g(\mathbf{x}_l), \tag{15}$$

where ω_l is integration formula weights, $\mathbf{x}_l$ is integration formula points.

Now we can determine the discrete Hilbert subspace in the form $\mathbf{V}^{HMM}\left(T^H\right) =$ span$\left\{\boldsymbol{\psi}_i^{HMM}(\mathbf{x}),\ \forall i = \overline{1, N^H}\right\}$. The variational formulation for the elastic deformation problem is stated to find $\mathbf{u}^H(\mathbf{x}) \in \mathbf{V}^{HMM}\left(T^H\right) + \mathbf{u}_0\left(\Gamma_D^0\right)$ that $\forall \mathbf{v}^H \in \mathbf{V}^{HMM}\left(T^H\right)$:

$$\int_\Omega \nabla \mathbf{u}^H(\mathbf{x}) : \mathbf{D}(\mathbf{x}) : \nabla \mathbf{v}^H(\mathbf{x})d\Omega = \int_{\Gamma_N^f} \mathbf{f} \cdot \mathbf{v}^H(\mathbf{x})d\Gamma + \int_{\Gamma_N^p} \mathbf{p} \cdot \mathbf{v}^H(\mathbf{x})d\Gamma. \quad (16)$$

The discrete analogue of the variational formulation can be written as:

$$\mathbf{A}^{global}\mathbf{u} = \mathbf{b}^{global}, \quad (17)$$

where $\mathbf{A}^{global}$ is a global matrix of SLAE obtained by assembling the local matrices. $\mathbf{A}^{k,\,local}, \forall K \in T^H$:

$$\mathbf{A}_{i,j}^{K,local} = \int_{K^H} \nabla \boldsymbol{\psi}_i^{HMM}(\mathbf{x}) : \mathbf{D}(\mathbf{x}) : \nabla \boldsymbol{\psi}_j^{HMM}(\mathbf{x})dK^H$$

$$= \sum_{l=1}^{n_l} \omega_l \nabla \tilde{\boldsymbol{\psi}}_i^{HMM}(\mathbf{x}_l) : \mathbf{D}^H : \nabla \tilde{\boldsymbol{\psi}}_j^{HMM}(\mathbf{x}_l), \quad (18)$$

where $\mathbf{D}^H$ is a homogenized elastic tensor defined in the macroelement K, $\tilde{\boldsymbol{\psi}}_i^{HMM}(\mathbf{x}_l)$ is a multiscale shape function.

3.4 Local Homogenization

Unlike other multiscale methods, the FE-HMM can significantly reduce the cost of computational resources [9, 16]. The values of the multiscale shape functions are sampled only near the points of the numerical integration formula for calculating local stiffness matrices (18). Thus, it is possible to calculate multiscale shape functions only in some neighborhoods of integration points (15). The choice of the integration points depends on the location of inhomogeneities inside the macroelement.

Let $I(\mathbf{x}_l) \subset K^H$ be neighborhoods near each numerical integration point $\mathbf{x}_l$. Neighborhoods can overlap each other. In the general case, the union of neighborhoods is not equal to the macroelement. In the neighborhoods $I(\mathbf{x}_l)$, we define adaptive irregular simple micropartitions $T_K^{l,h}(I(\mathbf{x}_l))$. The micropartitions take into account all microscale features in the area Ω, where the finite element is a triplet $k = \{k^h, f, p\}$. In the triplet, k^h is a tetrahedron, p is a subspace of the degrees of freedom, f is a subspace of the second order functions associated with p. In the tetrahedral meshes $T_K^{l,h}$, $l = \overline{1, n_l}$, the subspaces $\mathbf{V}_K^{l,h}\left(T_K^{l,h}\right) = \text{span}\left\{\boldsymbol{\varphi}_i(\mathbf{x}),\ i = \overline{1, N^{l,h}}\right\}$ were built with the vector shape functions $\boldsymbol{\varphi}_i(\mathbf{x}) = \left(\varphi_x^i(\mathbf{x}), \varphi_y^i(\mathbf{x}), \varphi_z^i(\mathbf{x})\right)^T$. We note that we apply the Lagrange quadratic finite basis functions on tetrahedral for constructing the vector shape functions.

In the neighborhood $I(\mathbf{x}_l)$, the multiscale shape function can be expressed by the linear combination of the basis shape functions as:

$$\psi_i^{HMM}(\mathbf{x}) = \sum_{j=1}^{N^{l,h}} \mathbf{q}_j^i \varphi_j(\mathbf{x}),$$

where $\mathbf{q}_j^i = (q_x, q_y, q_z)^T$ are coefficients associated with the vector functions $\varphi_j(\mathbf{x})$ in the linear combination.

Since the FE-HMM requires the multiscale shape functions only near the integration points (i.e., local approximations), we formulate the system of reduced subproblems:

$$\nabla \cdot \left(\mathbf{D}(\mathbf{x}) : \nabla \psi_i^{HMM}(\mathbf{x}) \right) = \nabla \cdot \left(\mathbf{D}^H : \nabla \psi_i^{FEM}(\mathbf{x}) \right) \text{ in } I(\mathbf{x}_l), \ l = \overline{1, n_l},$$

$$\psi_i^{HMM}(\mathbf{x}) = \gamma_i^{face}(\mathbf{x}) \text{ on } \partial I(\mathbf{x}_l) \in \mathbf{R}^2,$$

where $\psi_i^{FEM}(\mathbf{x})$ is the second order function determined in the macroelement K^H. The function $\psi_i^{FEM}(\mathbf{x})$ equals 1 in the i-th vertex of the polyhedron K^H, and $\psi_i^{FEM}(\mathbf{x})$ equals 0 in all other vertexes. Let $\gamma_i^{face}(\mathbf{x})$ be a function associated with the i-th face in the area $I(\mathbf{x}_l)$. The face basis function is built by solving the 2D problem:

$$\nabla \cdot \left(\mathbf{D}(\mathbf{x}) : \nabla \gamma_i^{face}(\mathbf{x}) \right) = 0 \text{ on } \partial I(\mathbf{x}_l) \in \mathbf{R}^2, \ l = \overline{1, n_l},$$

$$\gamma_i^{face}(\mathbf{x}) = \gamma_i^{edge}(\mathbf{x}) \text{ on } \partial I(\mathbf{x}_l) \in \mathbf{R}^1,$$

where $\gamma_i^{edge}(\mathbf{x})$ is a function associated with the i-th edge in the area $I(\mathbf{x}_l)$. The edge basis function is built by solving the 1D problem:

$$\nabla \cdot \left(\mathbf{D}(\mathbf{x}) : \nabla \gamma_i^{edge}(\mathbf{x}) \right) = 0 \text{ on } \partial I(\mathbf{x}_l) \in \mathbf{R}^1, \ l = \overline{1, n_l},$$

$$\gamma_i^{edge}(\mathbf{x}) = \psi_i^{FEM}(\mathbf{x}) \text{ in } \partial I(\mathbf{x}_l) \in \mathbf{R}^0.$$

Taking into account the constructed local approximations and formulas of the numerical integration in the $K \in T^H(\Omega)$, we can obtain the local matrix as:

$$\mathbf{A}_{i,j}^{K,local} = \int_{K^H} \nabla \psi_i^{HMM}(\mathbf{x}) : \mathbf{D}(\mathbf{x}) : \nabla \psi_j^{HMM}(\mathbf{x}) dK^H$$

$$= \sum_{l=1}^{n_l} \frac{\omega_l}{|I(\mathbf{x}_l)|} \sum_{k \in T_K^{l,h}} \int_k \nabla \psi_i^{HMM}(\mathbf{x}) : \mathbf{D}(\mathbf{x}) : \psi_j^{HMM}(\mathbf{x}) dk,$$

where $|I(\mathbf{x}_l)|$ is the volume of the area $I(\mathbf{x}_l)$.

Thus, the FE-HMM performs the implicit local homogenization during the construction of the local stiffness matrices at the macro-level.

3.5 Discontinuous Galerkin Method for the Hydrodynamic Problem

Let $\Xi_h(\Omega) = \bigcup_k \Omega_k$ be a disjointed set union, $\Gamma = \bigcup_k \partial\Omega_k$ is a union of all boundaries, $\Gamma_0 = \Gamma \backslash \partial\Omega$ is a union of inner boundaries, $T(\Gamma) = \prod_{\Omega_k \in \Xi_h(\Omega)} L^2(\partial\Omega_k)$ is trace space. In the $\Xi_h(\Omega)$, we define the discrete functional spaces:

$$P^h = \left\{ p | p \in L^2(\Omega) : p \in \Im_m(K) \forall K \in \Xi_h(\Omega) \right\}, \tag{19}$$

$$V^h = \left\{ v | v \in \mathbf{H}(\text{div}, \Omega) : v \in [\Im_m(K)]^3 \forall K \in \Xi_h(\Omega) \right\}, \tag{20}$$

where $\Im_m(K)$ is the m-degree polynomials space.

We need introduce averages {.} and jumps [.] to determine the trace of functions on the interfragmentary surface. For functions $\mathbf{v} \in [T(\Gamma)]^3$ and $p \in T(\Gamma)$ on the outer boundary $\partial\Omega$, the operators have the forms:

$$[p]|_{\partial\Omega} = p\mathbf{n}, \quad \{p\}|_{\partial\Omega} = p, \quad [\mathbf{v}]|_{\partial\Omega} = \mathbf{v} \cdot \mathbf{n}, \quad \underline{[\mathbf{v}]}\big|_{\partial\Omega} = \mathbf{v} \otimes \mathbf{n}, \quad \{\mathbf{v}\}|_{\partial\Omega} = \mathbf{v}, \tag{21}$$

on the boundary $\Gamma_0 = \partial\Omega_k \cap \partial\Omega_n$ these operators are computed as:

$$\underline{[\mathbf{v}]}\big|_{\Gamma_0} = \mathbf{v}_k \otimes \mathbf{n}_k + \mathbf{v}_n \otimes \mathbf{n}_n, \quad [\mathbf{v}]|_{\Gamma_0} = \mathbf{v}_k \cdot \mathbf{n}_k + \mathbf{v}_n \cdot \mathbf{n}_n, \quad \{\mathbf{v}\}|_{\Gamma_0} = (\mathbf{v}_k + \mathbf{v}_n)/2,$$

$$[p]|_{\Gamma_0} = p_k \mathbf{n}_k + p_n \mathbf{n}_n, \quad \{p\}|_{\Gamma_0} = (p_k + p_n)/2. \tag{22}$$

The variational formulation is based on the IP-DG discretization for the Navier-Stokes problem to find $\mathbf{v}^h \in V^h \times [0, T]$, $p^h \in P^h \times [0, T]$, $\forall \mathbf{w}^h \in V^h$ and $q^h \in P^h$:

$$a\left(\mathbf{w}^h, \mathbf{v}^h\right) + c\left(\mathbf{v}^h; \mathbf{w}^h, \mathbf{v}^h\right) + b_1\left(\mathbf{w}^h, p^h\right) = \left(\mathbf{w}^h, \mathbf{F}\right),$$
$$b_2\left(\mathbf{v}^h, q^h\right) + d\left(q^h, p^h\right) = 0, \tag{23}$$

$$a\left(\mathbf{w}^h, \mathbf{v}^h\right) = \int_\Omega \rho \mathbf{v}_t^h \cdot \mathbf{w}^h d\Omega + \int_\Omega \mu(\nabla \mathbf{v}^h + \nabla^T \mathbf{v}^h) : \nabla \mathbf{w}^h d\Omega$$
$$- \int_{\Gamma_0 \cup \partial\Omega} \left\{\mu\left(\nabla \mathbf{v}^h + (\nabla \mathbf{v}^h)^T\right)\right\} : \underline{[\mathbf{w}^h]} + \left\{\mu\left(\nabla \mathbf{w}^h + (\nabla \mathbf{w}^h)^T\right)\right\} : \underline{[\mathbf{v}^h]} - \tau^{DG}\underline{[\mathbf{v}^h]} : \underline{[\mathbf{w}^h]} dS,$$

$$b_1\left(\mathbf{v}^h, q^h\right) = -\int_\Omega \nabla \cdot \mathbf{v}^h q^h d\Omega + \int_\Gamma \{q^h\}[\mathbf{v}^h] dS,$$

$$c\left(\mathbf{a}; \mathbf{w}^h, \mathbf{v}^h\right) = -\int_\Omega \rho \nabla \mathbf{w}^h \cdot \mathbf{a} \cdot \mathbf{v}^h d\Omega + \int_\Gamma \rho\left(\underline{[\mathbf{w}^h]} \cdot \mathbf{a}\right) \cdot \left(\underline{[\mathbf{v}^h]} \cdot \mathbf{n}\right) dS,$$

$$b_2\left(\mathbf{v}^h, q^h\right) = \int_\Omega \rho \nabla \cdot \mathbf{v}^h q^h d\Omega + \int_\Gamma \rho\{q^h\}[\mathbf{v}^h] dS,$$

$$\left(\mathbf{w}^h, \mathbf{F}\right) = \int_\Omega \rho \mathbf{g} \cdot \mathbf{w}^h d\Omega + \int_{\Gamma_2} \mathbf{t} \cdot \mathbf{w}^h dS,$$

$$d\left(q^h, p^h\right) = \tau^{DG} \int_{\Gamma_0} \left[q^h\right] \cdot \left[p^h\right] dS.$$

The LBB-condition (or inf-sup condition) determines the uniqueness of the solution to the hydrodynamic problem:

$$\inf_{p^h \in P^h} \sup_{v^h \in V^h} \frac{\left(\nabla \cdot v^h, p^h\right)_{L_2(\Omega)}}{\left\|p^h\right\|_{L_2(\Omega)} \left\|v^h\right\|_{[H^1(\Omega)]^3}} \geq \alpha > 0, \; \alpha\text{-const.} \tag{24}$$

Condition (24) is satisfied when using matched pairs of finite elements to approximate the velocity and pressure fields (Crouzeix-Raviar, Taylor-Hood, etc.) or by using stabilized and non-conforming finite element methods.

We use the second-order basis of the $\mathbf{H}$(div)-space to approximate the velocity. To approximate the pressure, the first-order hierarchical basis of the $H^1(\Omega)$-space is applied. The discrete analogue of the variational formulation (23) has a block structure, which makes it possible to use a multilevel solver with a physical block preconditioner to solve SLAE.

3.6 Solving Discrete Analogues for the Hydrodynamic Problem

We consider the Helmholtz expansion of the velocity vector $\mathbf{v} = \mathbf{v}_0 + \nabla p$, where $\mathbf{v}_0 \in \mathbf{H}_0(\text{div}, \Omega) \mathbf{v}_0 \in \mathbf{H}_0(\text{div}, \Omega), p \in H^1(\Omega)$.

The projection methods use physical splitting (see Table 3) and contain two stages. At the first stage, to approximate the dissipative and convective terms, computational schemes of the discontinuous Galerkin method are applied. At the second stage, the pressure and divergence constraint are integrated in time explicitly.

Table 3. Physical splitting algorithm.

Physical splitting
1: $\mathbf{v}^0$ – initial velocity;
2: **for** $k = 0, 1, \ldots$ **do**
3: find $\mathbf{v}_0^{k+1}$ from $\begin{cases} \rho\left(\dfrac{\mathbf{v}_0^{k+1} - \mathbf{v}^k}{\Delta t} + \left(\mathbf{v}^k \cdot \nabla\right)\mathbf{v}_0^{k+1}\right) = \nabla \cdot \mu\left(\nabla \mathbf{v}_0^{k+1} + \left(\nabla \mathbf{v}_0^{k+1}\right)^T\right) + \rho\mathbf{g}, \\ \mathbf{v}_0^{k+1}\big|_{\partial\Omega} = \mathbf{v}_D, \end{cases}$
4: find $\mathbf{v}^{k+1}$ and p^{k+1} from $\rho\dfrac{\mathbf{v}^{k+1} - \mathbf{v}_0^{k+1}}{\Delta t} + \nabla p^{k+1} = 0, \nabla \cdot \mathbf{v}^{k+1} = 0, \; \mathbf{n} \cdot \mathbf{v}^{k+1} = \mathbf{n} \cdot \mathbf{v}_D,$ $\mathbf{v}^{k+1} = \Re\mathbf{v}_0^{k+1}, \; \Delta t\nabla p^{k+1} = \left(\mathbf{I} - \Re\right)\mathbf{v}_0^{k+1},$ where $\Re$ is the orthogonal projection operator,
5: **end for.**

At steps 3 and 4, the operators of the equations are not self-adjoint. It is expedient to solve the equations using the discontinuous Galerkin method. We have the block structure:

$$\begin{pmatrix} \mathbf{M}/\Delta t & \mathbf{P} \\ \mathbf{P}^T & 0 \end{pmatrix} \begin{pmatrix} \mathbf{v}^{k+1} \\ p^{k+1} \end{pmatrix} = \begin{pmatrix} \mathbf{M}\mathbf{v}_0^{k+1}/\Delta t \\ 0 \end{pmatrix},$$

where $\mathbf{P}$ is a divergence constraint matrix, $\mathbf{M}$ is a mass matrix. $\mathbf{M}$ is a positive definite and not degenerate matrix, then:

$$\left(\mathbf{P}^T\mathbf{M}^{-1}\mathbf{P}\right)p^{k+1} = \frac{1}{\Delta t}\mathbf{P}^T\mathbf{v}_0^{k+1},$$

$$\mathbf{M}\mathbf{v}^{k+1} = \mathbf{M}\mathbf{v}_0^{k+1} - \Delta t\mathbf{P}p^{k+1}.$$

The Courant–Friedrichs–Lewy (CFL) condition determines the stability of the projection methods:

$$\Delta t \le Cd^k,$$

where C is a real number, d is a finite element diameter, k is an order of used basis functions.

Computing the inverse mass matrix $\mathbf{M}$ is not a resource-intensive problem, since the basis of the $\mathbf{H}(\text{div})$-space is constructed using the Legendre polynomials that provide the diagonal form of the mass matrix.

Algebraic splitting (see Table 4) deals with the block matrix of the special form:

$$\begin{pmatrix} \mathbf{B} & \mathbf{P} \\ \mathbf{P}^T & 0 \end{pmatrix} \begin{pmatrix} \mathbf{v}^{k+1} \\ p^{k+1} \end{pmatrix} = \begin{pmatrix} \mathbf{F} \\ 0 \end{pmatrix},$$

where $\mathbf{B} = 1/\Delta t\,\mathbf{M} + \mathbf{A} + \mathbf{C}$, $\mathbf{M}$ is a mass matrix, $\mathbf{A}$ is a stiffness matrix, $\mathbf{C}$ is a convective matrix, $\mathbf{P}$ is a divergence constraint matrix.

In the matrix form, this system is rewritten as:

$$\left(\mathbf{P}^T\mathbf{B}^{-1}\mathbf{P}\right)p^{k+1} = \mathbf{P}^T\mathbf{B}^{-1}\mathbf{F},$$

$$\mathbf{B}\mathbf{v}^{k+1} = \mathbf{F} - \mathbf{P}p^{k+1},$$

$$\mathbf{B}^{-1} = \Delta t\left(\mathbf{I} + \Delta t\mathbf{M}^{-1}(\mathbf{K} + \mathbf{C})\right)^{-1}\mathbf{M}^{-1}.$$

There is an incomplete LU-decomposition for the block matrix:

$$\begin{pmatrix} \mathbf{B} & \mathbf{P} \\ \mathbf{P}^T & 0 \end{pmatrix} \approx \underbrace{\begin{pmatrix} \mathbf{B} & 0 \\ \mathbf{P}^T & -\mathbf{P}^T\mathbf{B}^{-1}\mathbf{P} \end{pmatrix}}_{L} \underbrace{\begin{pmatrix} \mathbf{I} & \mathbf{B}^{-1}\mathbf{P} \\ 0 & \mathbf{I} \end{pmatrix}}_{U} = \begin{pmatrix} \mathbf{B} & \mathbf{B}\mathbf{H}_2\mathbf{P} \\ \mathbf{P}^T & \mathbf{P}^T(\mathbf{H}_2 - \mathbf{H}_1)\mathbf{P} \end{pmatrix},$$

where $\mathbf{H}_1$ is a lower block approximation of $\mathbf{B}^{-1}$, $\mathbf{H}_2$ is an upper block approximation of $\mathbf{B}^{-1}$.

To fulfill the mass conservation law, it is necessary to choose $\mathbf{H}_1 = \mathbf{H}_2 = \mathbf{H}$, and in the first approximation $\mathbf{H} \approx 1/\Delta t\,\mathbf{M}^{-1}$.

When $\mathbf{H}_1 = \mathbf{H}_2$, the algorithms for physical and algebraic splitting coincide. Each stage $\mathbf{B}\mathbf{v}_0^{k+1} = \mathbf{F}$ is implemented using algebraic multilevel methods. For the smoothing procedure, iterations of the block Jacobi method are applied.

Table 4. Algebraic splitting algorithm.

Algebraic splitting	
1: Let $\mathbf{v}^0$ be an initial velocity;	
2: **for** $k := 0, 2, 3 \ldots$ **do**	
3: find $\mathbf{v}_0^{k+1}$ from $\mathbf{B}\mathbf{v}_0^{k+1} = \mathbf{F}$, find p_0^{k+1} from $\mathbf{P}^T\mathbf{v}_0^{k+1} - \mathbf{P}^T\mathbf{H}_1\mathbf{P}p_0^{k+1} = 0$,	L-step
4: $\mathbf{I}\,p^{k+1} = p_0^{k+1}$, find $\mathbf{v}^{k+1}$ from $\mathbf{v}^{k+1} + \mathbf{H}_2\mathbf{P}p^{k+1} = \mathbf{v}_0^{k+1}$,	U-step
5: **end for.**	

4   Results

The developed software allows performing the numerical simulation in media containing both the micro-inclusions and macro-subobjects (large cracks or pores). To analyze the stress-strain state of heterogeneous media, we consider media with single internal inclusions filled with fluid: samples with pores, elliptical cracks, and cluster structures.

For analyzing the scalability and efficiency of the developed software, the mathematical simulation of elastic deformation and fluid dynamics in samples containing microcracks is carried out.

During the computational tests, the sample is a sandstone cylinder (its diameter is 30 mm, height is 100 mm). The microinclusions are saturated with fluid (oil). Tables 1 and 2 present the physical characteristics.

4.1   Samples Containing Single Inclusions

Figure 2 shows the samples containing single inclusions. To solve the simulation problem, depending on the sample, we use the finite element meshes containing from 100 to 400 cells.

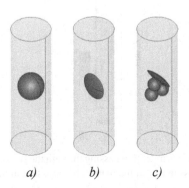

a)   *b)*   *c)*

Fig. 2. Samples with single inclusions: a – cylinder with a pore (radius is 10 mm), b – cylinder with a crack (size is $20 \times 20 \times 4$ mm), c – cylinder containing a cluster of three pores (radius is 5 mm) and crack (size is $20 \times 20 \times 4$ mm).

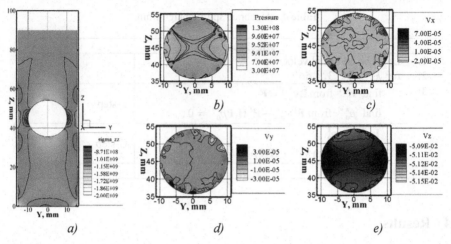

Fig. 3. Distributions of the fields in section passing through the sample center, containing a pore: *a* – zz-component of the stress tensor in the matrix; *b* – pressure in the pore; *c, d, e* – flow velocity in the pore.

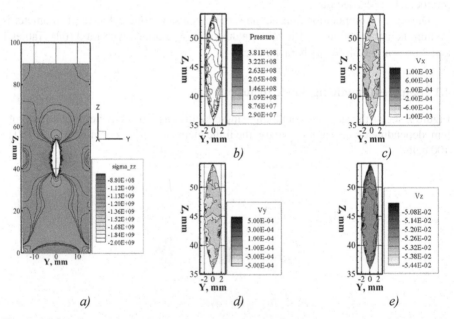

Fig. 4. Distributions of the fields in section passing through the sample center, containing a crack: a – zz-component of the stress tensor in the matrix; b – pressure in the crack; c-e – flow velocity in the crack.

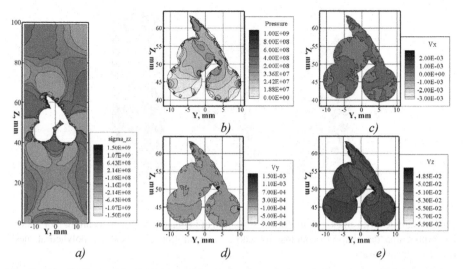

Fig. 5. Distributions of the fields in section passing through the sample center, containing a cluster structure: a – zz-component of the stress tensor in the matrix; b – pressure in the inclusions; c-e – flow velocity in the inclusions.

Figures 3, 4 and 5 present the distributions of stress fields in the matrix, hydrodynamic pressure, and velocity distributions in the fluid-saturated inclusions in sections passing through the centers of samples.

Figure 3 and Fig. 4 show the symmetry of stress fields. The symmetry of fields depends on the geometry of the samples and the physics experiment conditions. Symmetry errors are associated with the features of used unstructured finite element meshes, as well as with the numerical errors. However, the computational experiments make it possible to analyze the applicability of these methods for mathematical modelling of the elastic deformation processes of heterogeneous media.

4.2   Samples with Inclusions Distributed Randomly

We consider two distribution laws of inclusions in samples. In the first case, inclusions are distributed according to the uniform law in the volume (see Fig. 6.a). In the second case, the exponential distribution law with a coefficient of 1 is used (see Fig. 6.b). The inclusions are ellipsoids with diameters of 4 mm, 3 mm, and 1 mm. The volumetric concentration of inclusions varies from 0% (homogeneous sample) to ~2%. The physical properties of the fluid (oil) and matrix (sandstone) are presented in Tables 1 and 2.

The macroelement mesh is the same in all tests and contains 109 polyhedra (see Fig. 6.c). Using this mesh leads to 1620 degrees of freedom in the discrete variational formulation at the macrolevel (18). The microelement mesh is built for each sample individually. The mesh contains 59427 to 394398 tetrahedra in aggregate for all macroelements.

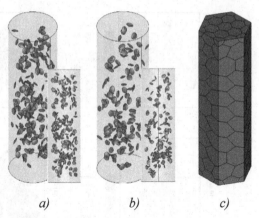

a)   *b)*   *c)*

Fig. 6. Samples with cracks: a - uniform distribution of inclusions with a concentration of 1.85%, b - exponential distribution of inclusions with a concentration of 1.34%, c - polyhedral mesh (macroelement mesh).

Figure 7 presents the results of solving the problem in the sample with inclusions distributed uniformly in the matrix. The bottom sample surface is rigidly fixed, the upper surface moves downward on 0.01 mm (the sample is compressed). Figure 7.a presents the obtained distribution of the z-component of the displacement vector. The dark lines are the boundaries of macroelements.

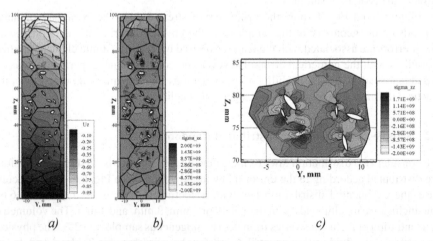

a)   *b)*   *c)*

Fig. 7. Distributions of the fields in section passing through the sample center: a – z-component of the displacement vector in the matrix; b – zz-component of the stress tensor in the matrix; c – zz-component of the stress tensor in the matrix inside the macroelement.

To evaluate the efficiency and scalability, we run the software on a personal computer using AMD Ryzen 7 2700X Eight-Core Processor (3.70 GHz). The scaling was done by applying OpenMP with dynamic load balancing [17]. The results of time measurements are shown in Table 3.

Table 5. Time to solve the problem in seconds.

Sample	Inclusion number	Total tetrahedral number at the micro-level	1 thread	2 threads	4 threads	8 threads
Homogeneous sample	0	59427	112.554	73.777	51.59231	39.38344
Inclusions distributed uniformly	35	85491	244.853	144.299	86.40659	57.60439
	70	116316	316.512	183.654	108.671	65.27125
	250	243024	2051.785	1064.02	575.1459	326.7875
	500	394398	9157.737	5235.984	3212.26	2046.026
Inclusions distributed exponentially	35	72576	162.244	90.046	50.58764	31.03536
	70	99663	291.002	178.081	113.4274	84.6473
	250	204144	2538.067	1472.759	892.5812	568.5231
	500	352140	10504.67	6956.732	5077.906	4095.086

We can see an increase in efficiency with an increase in the number of inclusions. The high efficiency is found in the tests with 250 inclusions for both distribution options. The acceleration coefficient equals 1.76–1.92 for the uniform distribution and 1.57–1.72 for the exponential distribution of inclusions. In the tests with a small number of inclusions, scaling is the least efficient. In this case, the prevalence of time spent on operations outside of parallel blocks (Table 5).

There is an increase in time for solving the problems in samples with inclusions distributed exponentially with inclusions distributed uniformly, where a smaller number of tetrahedra in the finite element meshes is used. In the first case, a lot of inclusions are contained in a smaller number of the macroelements since the inhomogeneities are concentrated in the bottom part of the sample. The macroscale polyhedral mesh remains uniform. Thus, there are macroelements with subproblems of the great dimension in the samples with inclusions distributed uniformly. It is necessary to construct the adaptive macroelement meshes, taking into account the assumed localization of inhomogeneities.

5   Conclusion

The computational schemes of the multiscale non-conforming finite element methods for solving the multiphysical problem of the elastic deformation of fluid-saturated media have been developed and implemented.

We proposed a hierarchical splitting of physical processes using the multiscale approach. The multiscale approach made it possible to construct an effective parallel algorithm for the multiscale mathematical simulation of the elastic deformation problem in heterogeneous media under external mechanical load.

As a property of the multiscale methods, algorithmic parallelism provides the scalability of developed software using two or more computing processors. The acceleration, closest to linear acceleration, was obtained for samples with a large number of inclusions distributed uniformly. The nonuniform distribution of inclusions in the sample increases the requirements for the quality of the macroelement mesh. For example, the local mesh adaptation is required in subdomains with a high concentration of inhomogeneities.

Acknowledgments. The research was supported by RSF Project No. 20-71-00134 (hydrodynamics problem), Project No. MK-3230.2022.1.5 (elastic deformation problem).

References

1. Carcione, J.: Wave Fields in Real Media: Wave Propagation in Anisotropic, Anelastic, Porous and Electromagnetic Media, 3rd edn. Elsevier, Amsterdam (2015)
2. Feng, X., Ge, Z., Li, Y.: Multiphysics finite element methods for a poroelasticity model. J. Num. Anal. **38**(1), 1–39 (2014)
3. Fu, S., Altmann, R., Chung, E., Maier, R., Peterseim, D., Pun, S.-M.: Computational multiscale methods for linear poroelasticity with high contrast. J. Comput. Phys. **395**(1), 1–14 (2018)
4. Brown, D., Vasilyeva, M.: A generalized multiscale finite element method for poroelasticity problems I: linear problems. J. Comput. Appl. Math. **294**, 372–388 (2016)
5. Chung, E.T., Efendiev, Y., Fu, S.: Generalized multiscale finite element method for elasticity equations. GEM – Int. J. Geomath. **5**(2), 225–254 (2014)
6. Tyrylgin, A., et al.: Generalized multiscale finite element method for the poroelasticity problem in multicontinuum media. J. Comput. Appl. Math. **374**, 112783 (2020)
7. Fumagalli, A., Scotti, A.: A mathematical model for thermal single-phase flow and reactive transport in fractured porous media. Numer. Anal. **434**(2), 110205 (2021)
8. Janicke, R., Quintal, B., Steeb, H.: Numerical homogenization of mesoscopic loss in poroelastic media. Eur. J. Mech. A Solids **49**, 382–395 (2015)
9. Abdulle, A., Grote, M.J., Jecker, O.: Finite element heterogeneous multiscale method for elastic waves in heterogeneous media. Comput. Meth. Appl. Mech. Eng. **335**, 1–23 (2018)
10. Caceres, E., Gatica, G., Sequeira, F.: A mixed virtual element method for a pseudostress-based formulation of linear elasticity. Appl. Numer. Math. **135**, 423–442 (2019)
11. Wriggers, P., Hudobivnik, B., Aldakheel, F.: A virtual element formulation for general element shapes. Comput. Mech. **66**(4), 963–977 (2020). https://doi.org/10.1007/s00466-020-01891-5
12. Teng, Z.H., Sun, F., Wu, S.C., Zhang, Z.B., Chen, T., Liao, D.M.: An adaptively refined XFEM with virtual node polygonal elements for dynamic crack problems. Comput. Mech. **62**(5), 1087–1106 (2018)
13. Zhang, H.W., Liu, Y., Zhang, S., Tao, J., Wu, J.K., Chen, B.S.: Extended multiscale finite element method: its basis and applications for mechanical analysis of heterogeneous materials. Comput. Mech. **53**(4), 659–685 (2013)
14. Liu, R., Wheeler, M., Dawson, C., Dean, R.: On a coupled discontinuous/ continuous Galerkin framework and an adaptive penalty scheme for poroelasticity problems. Comput. Meth. Appl. Mech. Eng. **198**, 3499–3510 (2009)

15. Eyck, A., Celiker, F., Lew, A.: Adaptive stabilization of discontinuous Galerkin methods for nonlinear elasticity, analytical estimates. Comput. Meth. Appl. Mech. Eng. **197**, 2989–3000 (2008)
16. Eidel, B., Fischer, A.: The heterogeneous multiscale finite element method for the homogenization of linear elastic solids and a comparison with the FE^2 method. Comput. Meth. Appl. Mech. Eng. **329**, 332–368 (2018)
17. Guo, X., Lange, M., Gorman, G., Mitchell, L., Weiland, M.: Developing a scalable hybrid MPI/OpenMP unstructured finite element model. Comput. Fluids **110**, 227–234 (2014)

Numerical Modeling of Electric and Magnetic Fields Induced by External Source in Frequency Domain

Nadezhda Shtabel[1,2]([⊠]) [iD] and Daria Dobroliubova[1] [iD]

[1] Trofimuk Institute of Petroleum Geology and Geophysics of Siberian Branch
Russian Academy of Sciences, Koptuyg Avenue 3, 630090 Novosibirsk, Russia
orlovskayanv@ipgg.sbras.ru

[2] Novosibirsk State Technical University, K. Marks Avenue 20, 630073 Novosibirsk, Russia

Abstract. To study effective electromagnetic properties of the heterogeneous media, it is important to know both electric and magnetic field distributions. In this paper, we consider the harmonic electromagnetic field induced by an external current source in the heterogeneous media. We propose an approach that couples the electric field and the magnetic field via special boundary conditions for the magnetic field strength, which act as a source of the magnetic field. Discretization of the mathematical model is performed by the vector finite element method in a space with partial continuity H (curl). Electric and magnetic fields are calculated on the same unstructured tetrahedral mesh. We analyze the behavior of the magnetic field obtained by means of our approach at the interfaces separating the media and contrasting conductive or magnetic inclusions.

Keywords: Electric field · Magnetic field · External source · Vector finite element method · OpenMP

1 Introduction

Electromagnetic sounding methods are widely used to study native and artificial media in geophysics (well logging [1], CSEM [2], non-destructive retrieval of the rock samples properties [3, 4]); material science (composites [5, 6] and metamaterials [7, 8]); biophysical applications [9]. Since most of these media are characterized by a complex internal structure with numerous interfaces, modern numerical methods for modeling physical phenomena in such media employ homogenization techniques [10, 11]. In the most general case, macroscopic electromagnetic properties of a heterogeneous medium are anisotropic and may be frequency- or time-dependent. Their numerical homogenization requires knowledge of the distribution of both electric and magnetic fields [12].

The relationship between the electric and magnetic components of the electromagnetic field is described by Maxwell's system of equations. In the time domain, the electric field strength $\mathbf{E}$ and the magnetic field strength $\mathbf{H}$ can be obtained as a result of solving the system of first-order differential equations [13]. The electric field strength $\mathbf{E}$ and the

© Springer Nature Switzerland AG 2022
V. Jordan et al. (Eds.): HPCST 2021, CCIS 1526, pp. 148–158, 2022.
https://doi.org/10.1007/978-3-030-94141-3_12

magnetic induction **B**, or, alternatively, the electric displacement **D** and the magnetic field strength **H** are taken as the primary unknowns. The discretization of such models with finite-difference or finite-element methods often requires using staggered grids (FDTD) [14] or dual meshes (FEM) [15]. For the finite element method, it raises the question of dual, as well as primary, mesh quality, and may lead to a conditionally stable computational scheme, hence, restricting the time-step.

In the frequency domain, a second-order wave equation (vector Helmholtz equation) is commonly formulated in terms of the electric or magnetic field strength [12, 16]. The magnetic field strength is related to the electric field strength by Faraday's law and can be calculated by taking the curl. Therefore, to sufficiently accurately compute the magnetic field strength, one needs to use higher-order computational schemes.

The second-order wave equation in the quasi-static frequency domain can also be formulated in terms of magnetic vector potential **A** and scalar electric potential φ [17, 18]. The magnetic induction **B**, in this case, is determined by taking the curl of the magnetic vector potential, and the electric field strength **E** is related to the gradient of the scalar electric potential φ and the change in the magnetic vector potential in time.

We propose an approach to modeling the electromagnetic field excited by an external source in a heterogeneous medium. The approach is based on the sequential solution of the vector Helmholtz equation for the electric field **E** excited by an external source and then the vector Helmholtz equation for the magnetic field strength **H**. For the 'magnetic' problem, special boundary conditions that ensure the coupling of the fields are imposed. The paper considers several test examples of the electromagnetic field in samples with contrasting microinclusions, demonstrating that the proposed approach allows one to obtain a more complete picture of the magnetic field **H,** compared to the calculation via Faraday's law. Since both problems are computationally costly, we make use of the parallelization on CPU cores and analyze its efficiency.

2 Problem Description

Let us consider a sample of the heterogeneous medium exposed to an external harmonic electric field induced by a closed current source. In this paper, we focus on calculating both the electric and magnetic fields induced by the same source, considering the microstructure of the medium. Let Ω be the computational domain. We denote its lateral surface by Γ_e. The top and bottom faces of the sample are denoted by Γ_m (Fig. 1).

In the frequency domain, the electric field induced by the nonhomogeneous Dirichlet boundary conditions is a solution to the following boundary-value problem:

$$\mathrm{curl}\mu^{-1}\mathrm{curl}\mathbf{E} - \left(\varepsilon\omega^2 - i\omega\sigma\right)\mathbf{E} = 0 \tag{1}$$

$$\mathbf{E} \times \mathbf{n}|_{\Gamma_e} = \mathbf{E}_g, \qquad \mu^{-1}\,\mathrm{curl}\mathbf{E} \times \mathbf{n}\Big|_{\Gamma_m} = 0, \tag{2}$$

where **E** is the electric field [V/m], ε – dielectric permittivity [F/m], μ – magnetic permeability [H/m], σ – electrical conductivity [S/m], ω – angular frequency [Hz]; **E$_g$** is a known electric field prescribed at the lateral surface of the sample.

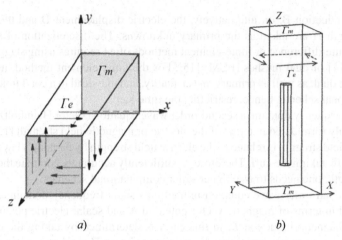

Fig. 1. Examples of the computational domain: (a) – homogeneous sample; (b) – sample with cylindrical inclusion.

The magnetic field **H** [A/m] in the frequency domain is governed by the following second-order equation:

$$\text{curl}\varepsilon^{-1}\text{curl}\mathbf{H} + i\omega\varepsilon^{-1}\sigma\mu\mathbf{H} - \omega^2\mu\mathbf{H} = 0, \tag{3}$$

$$\mathbf{H} \times \mathbf{n}|_{\Gamma_m} = 0, \qquad (i\omega\varepsilon + \sigma)^{-1}\text{curl}\mathbf{H} \times \mathbf{n}\Big|_{\Gamma_e} = \mathbf{H}_g \tag{4}$$

where **Hg** is the magnetic field equivalent to the source of the electric field.

We use the vector finite element method to solve the problems (1)–(2) and (3)–(4). Let us introduce the space **H**(*curl*, Ω) [19] of the functions with tangential continuity:

$$\mathbf{H}(curl, \Omega) = \Big\{\mathbf{u} \in \mathbf{L}^2 : \text{curl}\mathbf{u} \in \mathbf{L}^2\Big\},$$

$$\mathbf{H}_0(curl, \Omega) = \{\mathbf{u} \in \mathbf{H}(curl, \Omega) : \mathbf{n} \times \mathbf{u} = 0\}.$$

For Eqs. (1)–(2) and (3)–(4) the following variational statements can be formulated:
Find **E** ∈ **H**(*curl*, Ω) × **E**g *such that* ∀**v** ∈ **H**0(*curl*, Ω)

$$\int_\Omega \mu^{-1}\text{curl}\mathbf{E} \cdot \text{curl}\mathbf{v}dV - \int_\Omega \Big(\varepsilon\omega^2 - i\omega\sigma\Big)\mathbf{E} \cdot \mathbf{v}dV = 0. \tag{5}$$

Find **H** ∈ **H**(*curl*, Ω) *such that* ∀**N** ∈ **H**0(*curl*, Ω)

$$\int_\Omega \varepsilon^{-1}\text{curl}\mathbf{H} \cdot \text{curl}\mathbf{N}dV + \int_\Omega \Big(i\omega\varepsilon^{-1}\mu\sigma - \mu\omega^2\Big)\mathbf{H} \cdot \mathbf{N}dV = -\int_{\Gamma_e} \varepsilon^{-1}(\text{curl}\mathbf{H} \times \mathbf{n}) \cdot \mathbf{N}dS \tag{6}$$

The integral over the Γ_e boundary in (6) contains the curl of the magnetic field strength, the tangential component of which is prescribed at the boundary according to

(4). However, the field $\mathbf{H_g}$ is not known explicitly. To define the integral over the Γ_e boundary, we make use of Maxwell-Ampere law:

$$\mathrm{curl}\mathbf{H} = i\omega\varepsilon\mathbf{E} + \sigma\mathbf{E}.$$

The electric field $\mathbf{E}$ calculated from (1) satisfies Maxwell's equations, therefore the boundary integral in (6) can be rewritten as follows:

$$\int_{\Gamma_e} \varepsilon^{-1}(\mathrm{curl}\mathbf{H} \times \mathbf{n}) \cdot \mathbf{N}dS = \int_{\Gamma_e} \varepsilon^{-1}((i\omega\varepsilon + \sigma\mathbf{E}) \times \mathbf{n}) \cdot \mathbf{N}dS$$
$$= \int_{\Gamma_e} \left(\left(i\omega + \varepsilon^{-1}\sigma\right)\mathbf{E}_{FE} \times \mathbf{n}\right) \cdot \mathbf{N}dS \tag{7}$$

where $\mathbf{E}_{FE}$ is a finite element solution of (5).

Now we have boundary conditions (7) connecting the magnetic and electric fields from an external source. The closed current on the lateral surface, represented by the Dirichlet conditions, acts as a source of the electric field. The magnetic field is excited by the Neumann conditions (7) at the same surface. The value of this boundary condition is determined by the calculated electric field induced by an external source. Thus, we couple variational problems (5) and (6) for electric and magnetic fields, respectively, through the boundary conditions defined in a special way. The sequential solution of problems (5) and (6) yields the electric and magnetic fields induced by the same external source.

To approximate the fields $\mathbf{E}$ and $\mathbf{H}$ in space, we choose Nedelec's vector edge functions [19]:

$$\mathbf{E} = \sum_{i=1}^{N_e} \alpha_i \mathbf{W}_i, \qquad \mathbf{H} = \sum_{j=1}^{N_e} \beta_j \mathbf{W}_j, \tag{8}$$

where α_i, β_j are the expansion weights, $\mathbf{W}_i$, $\mathbf{W}_j$ are curl-conforming basis functions from $W^h \subset H_0\ (curl,\ \Omega)$, N_e – number of degrees-of-freedom.

By substituting expansions (8) into (5) and (6), respectively, we get the following linear systems:

$$\mu^{-1}A\alpha - \left(\varepsilon\omega^2 + i\sigma\omega\right)B\alpha = 0, \tag{9}$$

$$\varepsilon^{-1}A\beta + \left(i\omega\varepsilon^{-1}\mu\sigma - \mu\omega^2\right)B\beta + C\alpha_{FE} = 0, \tag{10}$$

where

$$A_{ij} = \int_{\Omega} \mathrm{curl}\mathbf{W}_i \cdot \mathrm{curl}\mathbf{W}_j dV, \tag{11}$$

$$B_{ij} = \int_{\Omega} \mathbf{W}_i \cdot \mathbf{W}_j dV, \tag{12}$$

$$C_{ij} = \int_{\Gamma_e} \left(\left(i\omega + \varepsilon^{-1}\sigma\right)\mathbf{W}_i \times \mathbf{n}\right) \cdot \mathbf{W}_j dS \tag{13}$$

α_{FE} – expansion weights of $\mathbf{E}_{FE}$.

3 Numerical Results for Homogeneous Sample

First, we check that the magnetic field obtained using the proposed approach agrees with the magnetic field generated by an external electric source. According to Faraday's law, the magnetic field in the frequency domain can easily be calculated from the electric field as follows:

$$\mathbf{H} = i(\omega\mu)^{-1}\text{curl}\mathbf{E}. \tag{14}$$

The electric field, calculated from (9), can be used to get the distribution of the magnetic field in a homogeneous medium. By comparing the magnetic field strengths obtained from (14) to the solution of the problem (10), we can check the correctness of the proposed approach.

Let us consider a homogeneous sample of $0.05 \times 0.05 \times 0.15$ m in size. On the lateral surface, we prescribe a closed electric field with an amplitude of 1 V/m. On the top and bottom surfaces, we prescribe the PMC conditions for the magnetic field.

The media is nonmagnetic, with the following characteristics: $\varepsilon = \varepsilon_0$, $\mu = \mu_0$, $\sigma = 10^{-3}$ S/m. Throughout the section, we consider the frequency of 100 MHz.

A source closed around the lateral surface forms a so-called TE-wave in the sample. It is characterized by two components of the electric field (Ex, Ey) and one component of the magnetic field Hz. Let us compare the component Hz of the magnetic field strength calculated using Eqs. (10) and (14). Figure 2 shows the distribution of the imaginary part of the Hz components over the line $Y = 0.025$ m, $Z = 0.075$ m. Here and below, *Hz_from_E* on the graph legend denotes the field calculated in accordance with (14); *Hz* denotes the field obtained as a result of solving the problem (10). In Fig. 2, the distribution of the Hz component of the magnetic field strength calculated using the proposed approach is constant inside the sample. The Hz component calculated from the electric field according to Faraday's law oscillates near the boundaries. This can be explained by the computational error for both the electric field and the curl of the electric field near the boundary. However, the discrepancy between the curves near the boundaries of the sample is insignificant (less than 2%).

4 Numerical Results for Two Subdomains

Once we made sure the proposed approach gives the correct magnetic field induced by a closed current, we can now consider a sample with the horizontal interface ($Z = 0.0075$ m) separating contrasting subregions with the following electrophysical characteristics:

- Case 1: contrasting magnetic permeability, $\mu_1 = \mu_0$, $\mu_2 = 10\mu_0$, $\varepsilon_1 = \varepsilon_2 = \varepsilon_0$, $\sigma_1 = \sigma_2 = 10^{-3}$ S/m.
- Case 2: contrasting electrical conductivity, $\sigma_1 = 10^{-2}$ S/m, $\sigma_2 = 10^{-3}$ S/m, $\varepsilon_1 = \varepsilon_2 = \varepsilon_0$, $\mu_1 = \mu_2 = \mu_0$.

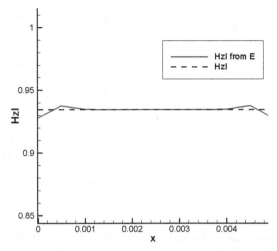

Fig. 2. Imaginary part of the Hz component of the magnetic field strength H over the line Y = 0.0028 m, Z = 0.0075 m.

Figure 3 shows the Hz component of the magnetic field strength plotted over a line normal to the interface between the subdomains. It is known that the normal component of the magnetic field undergoes a jump at the interface between materials with different magnetic properties. For a sample considered, it is the Hz field component that is discontinuous. The ratio of normal components of the magnetic field above and below the boundary is the same as the ratio of the magnetic permeabilities of the materials: $H^2_z/H^1_z = \mu_2/\mu_1$. In Fig. 3a, the magnetic field calculated by solving the linear system (10) and magnetic field obtained according to Faraday's law coincide and change values by a factor of 10 when crossing the boundary between subdomains, which is physically correct.

In the case of contrasting electric properties, the magnetic field obtained as a solution of (10) behaves differently from the magnetic field calculated via (14). The magnetic permeability of both materials is the same. However, the change in electrical conductivity induces surface current at the interface. The magnetic field obtained by solving the problem (10) captures the contrast of electrical conductivity (Fig. 3b).

The magnetic field calculated according to Faraday's law is undisturbed at the interface (Fig. 3b). Indeed, such a field is obtained by taking the curl of the electric field containing only two components (Ex, Ey), which are tangential to the interface separating the media. It means that they do not undergo a jump when passing from one conductive medium to another. Accordingly, the curl of such a field has no jumps either.

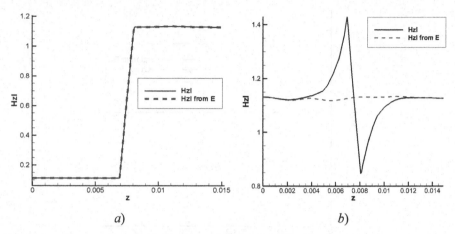

a)   *b)*

Fig. 3. Imaginary component of Hz over the line X = 0.0025 m, Y = 0.0025 m (*a*) – Case 1 (μ_1 = 10μ_2); (*b*) – Case 2 (σ_1 = 10σ_2).

5   Numerical Results for Sample with Localized Inclusion

A cylindrical vertical inclusion is located in a brick sample. The diameter of the cylinder is 0.2 m and its height is 0.15 m. The sample 0.1 × 0.1 × 0.3 m in size is shown in Fig. 1b. Once again, we consider two cases:

- Case 1: magnetic cylinder in a non-magnetic media, $\mu_1 = \mu_0$, $\mu_2 = 10\mu_0$, $\varepsilon_1 = \varepsilon_2 = \varepsilon_0$, $\sigma_1 = \sigma_2 = 10^{-3}$ S/m.
- Case 2: conductive non-magnetic cylinder in a non-magnetic media $\sigma_1 = 10^{-2}$ S/m, $\sigma_2 = 10^{-3}$ S/m, $\varepsilon_1 = \varepsilon_2 = \varepsilon_0$, $\mu_1 = \mu_2 = \mu_0$.

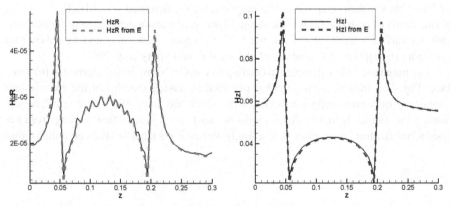

Fig. 4. Real (to the left) and imaginary (to the right) components of Hz over the line X = 0.05 m, Y = 0.05 m in the object with magnetic inclusion.

As expected, the magnetic field in the sample containing the magnetic cylinder is the same for both calculation methods (Fig. 4). The magnetic field resulting from solving the problem (10) is in good agreement with the magnetic field obtained according to Faraday's law (14). The non-magnetic conductive cylinder turns out to be 'invisible' to the magnetic field obtained in accordance with (14). Contrasting, the distribution of the magnetic field calculated as a solution to the problem (10) highlights the contours of the cylinder (Fig. 5).

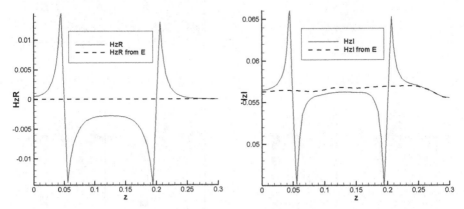

Fig. 5. Real (to the left) and imaginary (to the right) components of Hz over the line X = 0.05 m, Y = 0.05 m in the object with conductive inclusion.

6   Numerical Results for Sample with Microinclusions

Finally, we consider a sample $0.1 \times 0.1 \times 0.3$ m in size containing randomly oriented thin plates $0.01 \times 0.01 \times 0.01$ m in size and cylinders 0.02 m high and 0.01 m in diameter. The distribution of microinclusions in the sample is shown in Fig. 6a. The sample material (matrix) is non-magnetic. The plates concentrated in the upper part of the sample have greater magnetic permeability than the matrix does ($\mu_1 = \mu_0$, $\mu_2 = 10\mu_0$, $\varepsilon_1 = \varepsilon_2 = \varepsilon_0$, $\sigma_1 = \sigma_2 = 10^{-3}$ S/m). Cylinders are concentrated in the lower half of the sample, with their electrical conductivity contrasting to the electrical conductivity of the matrix ($\sigma_1 = 10^{-2}$ S/m, $\sigma_2 = 10^{-3}$ S/m, $\varepsilon_1 = \varepsilon_2 = \varepsilon_0$, $\mu_1 = \mu_2 = \mu_0$.).

Figure 6 shows the real components of the magnetic field in the cross-section of the sample (X = 0.05 m). The left picture corresponds to the solution yielded by Faraday's law (14), the right picture shows the magnetic field obtained using the proposed approach. We see a similar field pattern in the upper part of the figures, corresponding to the area with magnetic inclusions. The contours of the magnetic plates in the cross-section X = 0.05 m can be identified in the field pattern of all components of the magnetic field. In the lower part of the sample containing conductive cylinders, the magnetic field obtained according to Faraday's law (14) is uniform, despite the presence of arbitrarily oriented conductive inclusions. Hence, conductive inclusions can only be identified using the magnetic field obtained by solving the boundary value problem (10).

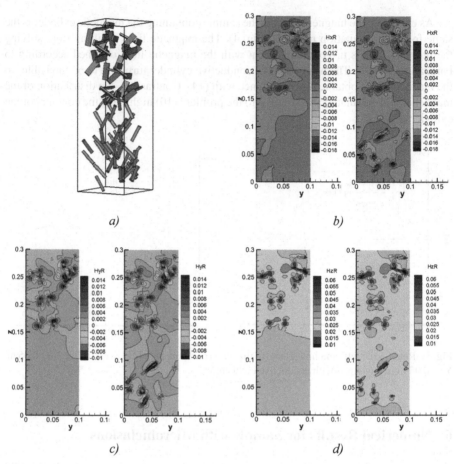

Fig. 6. Results for the sample with microinclusions: (a) – Sample with magnetic and conductive inclusions; (b)–(d) – real components of the magnetic field strength **H** obtained by Faraday's law (to the left) and the proposed approach (to the right), cross-section X = 0.05 m.

7 Computational Cost

The vector finite element approximation of wave Eqs. (1)–(4) involves solving a linear system with a sparse matrix. The dimensions of such linear systems may vary from tens of thousands to millions, depending on the internal structure of the computational domain and the fineness of the mesh partition. The iterative solution process requires significant computational resources, such as memory for storing the data and the time required for the iterative solver to reach the desired accuracy. Computational cost can be reduced by using parallel computing, for example, on CPU cores. To solve the linear systems (9) and (10), we use the BiCGstab iterative solver with residual refinement. The most frequently performed operation at each iteration of the solver is matrix-vector multiplication. To reduce the computational time, we use the OpenMP technology for the matrix-vector multiplications in a sparse row format. We measure the time of solving the problems

(9) and (10) for the matrices with the dimension of 1629183 entries, which stems from discretizing the sample with microinclusions (Fig. 6). The calculations were carried out on the AMD EPYC 74022.8 GHz 24 cores/48 threads processor. Table 1 shows the computational time for problems (9) and (10) for a varying number of computational threads on the processor.

Table 1. Computational times for problems (9) and (10) for varying number of CPU threads.

Problem	Threads				
	1	2	4	8	16
Electric problem	21.171 min	15.489 min	14.959 min	13.767 min	11.993 min
Magnetic problem	10.55 h	9.71 h	6.87 h	6.39 h	6.75 h

Using parallelization on CPU cores is the most simple parallel computation technique. As the results of test calculations show, even such a procedure leads to a significant reduction in the solution time for the same number of solver iterations. However, it is evident that the solver we used for the magnetic problem turned out to be inefficient, and the convergence process is very slow. To further reduce the cost of solving the magnetic problem, a more efficient solver or preconditioner is required.

8   Conclusion

In this paper, we proposed an approach to modeling the electric and magnetic fields from a single external source that allows one to obtain an electromagnetic field in variables **E** and **H** using the same finite element mesh. As demonstrated by the numerical experiments, the magnetic field obtained as a result of solving the joint problem identifies both subregions with contrasting electric and magnetic properties, while the magnetic field obtained from the electric field using Faraday's law only reacts to the contrasting magnetic subregions.

Our approach requires solving two second-order wave equations for the electric and magnetic fields. Since these equations have different coefficients and different boundary conditions, the spectral properties of the resulting finite element matrices are also essentially different. The computational cost of solving the magnetic problem with iterative methods greatly exceeds the computational cost of the electric problem, as a high condition number of the 'magnetic' matrix results in stagnation and slow convergence. While it is obvious that efficient preconditioning is needed, making use of the parallel matrix-vector operations may provide some relief. In particular, it reduced the computational time by almost a half for the magnetic problem, although, the effect declines with the increase in the number of CPU cores, which might be due to the load imbalance.

Since solving both electric and magnetic problems is computationally costly, in the objects with contrasting magnetic properties only it is overall preferable to solve the electric problem and to compute the magnetic field using Faraday's law.

Acknowledgments. The research was supported by Project No. FWZZ-2022-0025, Project No. FWZZ-2022-0030.

References

1. Mondol, N.H.: Well logging: principles, applications and uncertainties. In: Bjørlykke, K. (ed.) Petroleum Geoscience. Springer, Heidelberg (2015). https://doi.org/10.1007/978-3-642-34132-8_16
2. Ziolkowski, A., Slob, E.: Introduction to Controlled-Source Electromagnetic Methods: Detecting Subsurface Fluids. Cambridge University Press, Cambridge (2019)
3. North, L., Best, A.I., Sothcott, J., MacGregor, L.: Laboratory determination of the full electrical resistivity tensor of heterogeneous carbonate rocks at elevated pressures. Geophys. Prospect. **61**(2), 458–470 (2013). Rock Physics for Reservoir Exploration, Characterization and Monitoring
4. Yu, M., Wu, D., Chen, Y., Wang, H., Chen, J.: Electromagnetic rock properties' characterization and modeling using 3D micro-CT rock images. J. Electromagn. Waves Appl. **34**(8), 1073–1089 (2020)
5. Aladadi, Y.T., Alkanhal, M.A.S.: Classification and characterization of electromagnetic materials. Sci. Rep. **10**(1), 1–11 (2020). https://doi.org/10.1038/s41598-020-68298-3
6. Ouchetto, O., Zouhdi, S., Bossavit, A., Griso, G., Miara, B.: Modeling of 3-D periodic multiphase composites by homogenization. IEEE Trans. Microw. Theor. Tech. **54**(6), 2615–2619 (2006)
7. Zhang, F., Kang, L., Zhao, Q., Zhou, J., Lippens, D.: Magnetic and electric coupling effects of dielectric metamaterial. New J. Phys. **14**(3), 033031 (2012)
8. Wang, H., Yang, W., Huang, Y.: An adaptive edge finite element method for the Maxwell's equations in metamaterials. Electron. Res. Arch. **28**(2), 961 (2020)
9. Wallis, T., Kabos, P.: Nanoscale electromagnetic measurements for life science applications. In: Measurement Techniques for Radio Frequency Nanoelectronics. The Cambridge RF and Microwave Engineering Series, pp. 251–278. Cambridge University Press, Cambridge (2017)
10. Ouchetto, O., Essakhi, B.: Frequency domain homogenization of Maxwell equations in complex media. Int. J. Eng. Math. Model. **2**(1), 1–15 (2015)
11. Gallistl, D., Henning, P., Verfürth, B.: Numerical homogenization of H (curl)-problems. SIAM J. Numer. Anal. **56**(3), 1570–1596 (2018)
12. Shurina, E.P., Epov, M.I., Shtabel, N.V., Mikhaylova, E.I.: The calculation of the effective tensor coefficient of the medium for the objects with microinclusions. Engineering **6**(3), 101–112 (2014)
13. Rajamohan, S.: A streamline upwind/Petrov-Galerkin FEM based time-accurate solution of 3D time-domain Maxwell's equations for dispersive materials. Ph.D. dissertation. University of Tennessee at Chattanooga, Chattanooga, Tennessee (2014)
14. Sheu, T.W.H., Wang, Y.C., Li, J.H.: Development of a 3D staggered FDTD scheme for solving Maxwell's equations in Drude medium. Comput. Math. Appl. **71**(6), 1198–1226 (2016)
15. Kim, J.: Finite element time domain techniques for Maxwell's equations based on differential forms. Ph.D. dissertation. Ohio State University, Columbus, Ohio (2011)
16. Ernst, O.G., Gander, M.J.: Why it is difficult to solve Helmholtz problems with classical iterative methods. In: Graham, I., Hou, T., Lakkis, O., Scheichl, R. (eds.) Numerical Analysis of Multiscale Problems. Lecture Notes in Computational Science and Engineering, vol. 83. Springer, Heidelberg (2012). https://doi.org/10.1007/978-3-642-22061-6_10
17. Bello, M., Liu, J., Guo, R.: Three-dimensional wide-band electromagnetic forward modelling using potential technique. Appl. Sci. **9**(7), 1328 (2019)
18. Niyonzima, I., Sabariego, R., Dular, P., Jacques, K., Geuzaine, C.: Multiscale finite element modeling of nonlinear magnetoquasistatic problems using magnetic induction conforming formulations. Multiscale Model. Simul. **16**(1), 300–326 (2018)
19. Nédélec, J.-C.: Mixed finite elements in R3. Numer. Math. **3**, 315–341 (1980). https://doi.org/10.1007/BF01396415

Computing Technologies in Discrete Mathematics and Decision Making

Improving the Heterogeneous Computing Node Performance of the Desktop Grid When Searching for Orthogonal Diagonal Latin Squares

Alexander M. Albertian[1] , Ilya I. Kurochkin[2(✉)] , and Eduard I. Vatutin[3]

[1] Federal Research Center "Computer Science and Control", Russian Academy of Sciences,
Vavilova Street 44, Building 2, 119333 Moscow, Russia
admin@isa.ru
[2] Institute for Information Transmission Problems, Russian Academy of Sciences,
Bolshoy Karetny lane 19, Building 1, 127051 Moscow, Russia
[3] Southwest State University, 50 Let Oktyabrya Street 94, 305040 Kursk, Russia

Abstract. The main goal of the work was aimed to create a parallel application using a multithreaded execution model, which will allow the most complete and efficient use of all available computing resources. At the same time, the main attention was paid to the issues of maximizing the performance of the multithreaded computing part of the application and more efficient use of available hardware. During the development process, the effectiveness of various methods of software and algorithmic optimization was evaluated, taking into account the features of the functioning of a highly loaded multithreaded application, designed to run on systems with a large number of parallel computing threads. The problem of loading all available computing resources at the moment was solved, including the dynamic distribution of the involved CPU cores/threads and the computing accelerators, installed in the system.

Keywords: Distributed computing system · Desktop grid system · Desktop grid · Performance enhancement · Xeon Phi · Latin squares

1 Introduction

Desktop grid systems are the types of distributed computing systems [1]. Desktop grid has become quite widespread due to their ability to scale [2]. So, some of them consist of tens and hundreds of thousands of computing nodes. The features of grid systems include: the autonomy of calculations on individual computing nodes, the heterogeneity of computing nodes, as well as the unreliability of nodes and data transmission channels [1]. All this significantly narrows the range of problems that can be solved quite efficiently using systems of this type. Problems of the "bag of tasks" type are completely suitable for solving using desktop grid systems [3, 4], since they involve dividing the initial computational problem into many small autonomous subtasks. Problems of this

© Springer Nature Switzerland AG 2022
V. Jordan et al. (Eds.): HPCST 2021, CCIS 1526, pp. 161–173, 2022.
https://doi.org/10.1007/978-3-030-94141-3_13

type include of network simulation and machine learning, SAT [5] and combinatorial problems.

In accordance with the distributed computing paradigm, a computing application is launched asynchronously at each node of the desktop grid. In contrast to specialized computing systems, such as computing clusters, the desktop grid uses completely different computing nodes in terms of performance and configuration, which were not initially optimized for long-term calculations with a high load on the CPU and other system components.

Simultaneous (or time-spaced) use of desktop grid nodes for solving other tasks, including those not related to high-performance computing [1], as well as the need to comply with energy consumption restrictions, imposes additional requirements for flexible configuration of resource consumption in the computing process.

The instability and different bandwidths of data transmission channels between individual computing nodes in the desktop grid limit the possibility of load balancing by redistributing tasks between nodes.

In most cases, it is impossible to modernize individual computing nodes of the desktop grid, for example, by replacing the CPU, increasing the amount of RAM or installing specialized computing accelerators.

To provide computational experiments on a grid system, it was necessary to create a portable multithreaded application for personal computers. The Intel 64 (x86-64) platform was chosen as the main target architecture for application optimization (application is also POSIX and Win32 compatible). The selected platform provides the possibility of using computing accelerators installed in the system with the Intel Many Integrated Core (MIC) architecture – Intel Xeon Phi generation x100, codenamed Knights Corner (KNC) [6]. The application is compatible with a wide range of different computing systems and architectures.

2   Methods for Improving the Performance

2.1   Computational Problem

The computational problem of construction of a list of canonical forms (CF) of orthogonal diagonal Latin squares (ODLS) of order 10 was chosen. They form a set of combinatorial structures—graphs from diagonal Latin squares (DLS) on the orthogonality binary relation. Some of them may include a triple of pairwise ODLS also known as mutually orthogonal Latin squares (MOLS) that is an open mathematical problem for order 10 [7, 8]. The processing of the DLS is performed according to the scheme "Square generator → Processor → Post-processor". One of the known sources of squares is used as a generator of initial squares (general-type DLS, symmetric DLS, generalized-symmetric DLS, partially generalized-symmetric DLS). The canonizer [9] was used as a processor (Latin squares canonization procedure provides getting diagonal Latin squares from given Latin square combined with checking squares for orthogonal mates). First of all, a set of transversals [10] of the analyzed square is constructed. Then a pair of symmetrically placed transversals among them is selected. After that, permutation of rows and columns of the square is performed in order to set the selected pair of transversals on the diagonals. Then constructing the corresponding binary matrices [11] and searching for covers using the dancing links algorithm (DLX) were performed [12]. Using the canonizer in the specified problem of constructing a collection of ODLS CFs of order 10 allows increasing the efficient processing rate of squares from 1000–2000 DLS/s – for implementing the classical Euler-Parker method to 8000 DLS/s – for single-threaded CPU-oriented implementation. The postprocessor is used for the new ODLS CFs based on existing CFs collection with low computational time [13]. The DLS generators provide the pace from 500 thousands DLS/s (recurrent software implementations) to 6 millions DLS/s (specialized software implementations based on nested loops and bit arithmetic [14]). The postprocessor is executed only for the found CF ODLS (for DLS of the order of 10 – one ODLS per 30 millions of DLS without orthogonal mates (bachelors)) and it does not significantly increase the total processing time. Thus, the total processing time is limited by the canonizer working, which makes it relevant to attempt high-level software optimization of its operation in combination with parallelization of computationally hard procedures within them.

2.2 Software Implementation for Multicore Computing Devices

One of the problems of using a desktop grid is to increase the efficiency of calculations. As a result, it is necessary to optimize the computational application for more complete usage of the available resources of a heterogeneous computing node of the desktop grid.

The most widespread Intel 64 (x86-64) was chosen as the main target architecture, with the possibility of using computing accelerators installed in the system with the Intel Many Integrated Core (MIC) architecture – Intel Xeon Phi of the x100 generation, codenamed Knights Corner (KNC), connected via the PCIe bus [6].

The main goals for optimizing the computing application were:

- Improving the efficiency of the application when working on modern multi-processor (multi-core) architectures.
- Implementing the portable source code of the application to ensure execution in various operating environments. For example, on Xeon Phi coprocessors the base environment is Linux-compatible, despite the fact that the main application can run under Microsoft Windows.
- Maximizing the full use of the capabilities of the Xeon Phi accelerators installed in the system.
- Reducing the total calculation time and the load on the system as a whole.

In order to ensure the portability of the application, the C++ language was used during development without the use of non-standard libraries and language extensions, excluding support for Xeon Phi coprocessors and some additional features of compilers and architectures, when they are detected. Thus, the capabilities of the C++ 11 standard (ISO/IEC 14882:2011) were used to implement multithreaded work and synchronization of threads. Various system-independent and portable components have been implemented. They are adapted for the target platform and provide error and exception handling, precise calculating of the time intervals, working with various localizations, consistent with I/O streams, re-capture of interrupt and control commands. The part of the application intended for execution on Xeon Phi coprocessors starts automatically in the offload mode when accelerators are available for using. The ability to utilize the available resources of a specific computing system can be flexibly configured when the application is launched to process each subsequent input data block.

Software products from Intel Parallel Studio XE 2017 were used as the main development tools. They provide working with Intel Xeon Phi x100 processors, as well as an extensive list of tools for solving optimization, debugging and maintenance problems for high-performance parallel applications for all supported architectures.

First of all, the initial single threaded version of the application was profiled. The performance of the program as a whole as well as its individual fragments was investigated and an assessment of the impact of their execution time on the final total calculation time was performed. The main goal of this is to find "hot spots" – the sections of code that take the most time to complete. The available capabilities of the development tools used to optimize the resulting code to get a significant gain in computing time without drastic changes in the source code of the application, for example, using interprocedural optimization options (IPO) together with optimization during linking (LTO) that allows reducing the total calculation time by 10–15%. In addition, the programming language tools such as C++ exception handling have a significant impact on performance.

The impact of data alignment in memory also was evaluated. Different organizations of data structures (containers) aimed to the features of cache memory and prefetching mechanisms, branch prediction, data links over the PCIe bus (for Xeon Phi), various implementations of thread synchronization methods and objects used by operating systems, such as kernel address space isolation, were implemented.

At the same time, the possibility of improving performance by using additional hardware capabilities of the computers (for example, support for extended SIMD large instruction sets, especially for Xeon Phi coprocessors with 512-bit SIMD (KNC SIMD)) was investigated.

To ensure the efficient operation of a parallel computing application using a multithreaded execution model, specialized data structures and containers with low-level optimization of the most significant operations were implemented. They guaranteed the necessary alignment of elements and minimized the number of operations for allocating and reallocating allocated memory blocks. In addition, they made it possible to simplify the process of copying data between the main system and Xeon Phi coprocessors. This significantly reduced the additional time and resources spent on creating a stream for processing the next portion of input data and minimized the number of calls to system and library functions, including memory allocation functions, during its further working.

Measures were taken to ensure the most complete use of the available computing resources of the heterogeneous desktop grid node in automatic mode. As a result, additional load balancing algorithms between the Xeon Phi accelerators and the CPU were developed.

2.3   Improving the Performance of a Parallel Computing Application

One of the problems of the applied computational algorithm is a significant spread in the processing time of each individual unit of the input data stream. For example, for the set of Latin squares (LS) the time spent on processing some elements is different and polynomially depends on the number of transversals [14]. At the same time, the number of input data that require long processing is relatively small, and the total computing time spent on them, on the contrary, is large (Fig. 1).

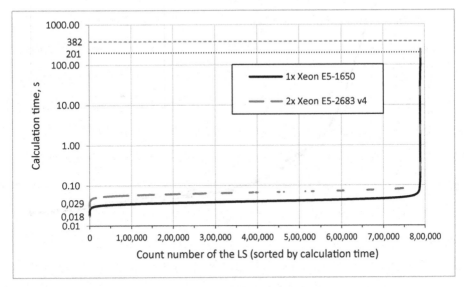

Fig. 1. The calculation time of the DLS depending on the input data.

In the process of computing, the input sequence of data is divided into portions that are transmitted for processing to each of the computing threads. Each next piece of data is a queue of tasks that are sequentially processed by this computing thread. In order to optimize the use of computing resources, the influence of the size of the portion of processed data (task queue) for each of the computing threads on the total computing time was studied (Fig. 2).

For short queues, the overhead costs associated with the process of starting and completing each new thread, synchronizing threads, and transmitting service information begin to have a significant impact. At the same time, in this case the load of computing devices is not optimal, and the total calculation time increases. However, the final calculation time for queues containing elements that require long-term processing is minimal due to each of these elements is processed by a separate computing thread.

With the increased length of the task queue, a minimum of overhead costs is required for input data that can be processed in a short time. But data that requires long processing is unevenly distributed over long queues of tasks and leads to a significant increase in the total calculation time.

The choice of the optimal length of the task queue, in addition to the relative complexity of each unit of the input data sequence, is significantly influenced by the efficient performance of a particular computer when executing a single thread-taking into account all the performed algorithmic and software optimizations, the use of available SIMD instructions, etc.

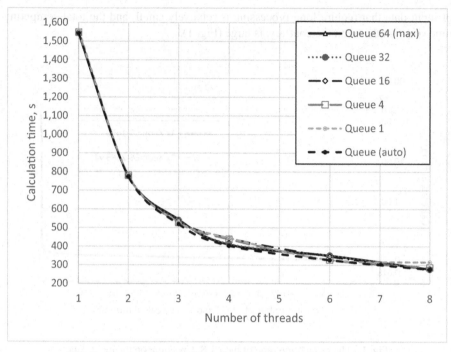

Fig. 2. The dependence of the calculation time on the queue length.

To minimize the average calculation time, during the calculations, the processing time of each element of the input data stream is analyzed and the corresponding change in the size (length) of the task queue for the calculated streams is performed. In the proposed method of dynamic selection of the length of the task outlines, the final result is also influenced by the number of calculators available at a particular time. Since one of the key factors influencing the choice of the queue length is the average calculation time of the input data unit for the last analyzed time period.

As a result of the application of the proposed method, it was possible to significantly improve the average total calculation time of each individual block of input data, as well as to make the total calculation time for various heterogeneous computing nodes of the desktop grid more predictable.

2.4 Features of Xeon Phi Usage

Intel Xeon Phi generation x100 computing accelerators (coprocessors) are expansion cards installed in the main system as an additional device connected via the PCIe x16 interface [6]. Each accelerator includes one multi-core computing device compatible with the Intel 64 instruction system (x86-64) and 8 or more GB of local RAM of the GDDR5 standard. At the same time, the number of cores connected by a bidirectional ring bus is at least 50 and is usually 60 or 61, depending on the accelerator model.

Unlike most modern CPUs, the Intel Xeon Phi x100 architecture supports only sequential execution of instructions in order (in-order execution) and does not use dynamic execution of instructions (out of order execution, abbr. OoO), which includes such performance improvement methods as speculative instruction execution, branch prediction, data flow analysis, etc. In fact, each Intel Xeon Phi x100 computing core is a deeply modified dual-core processor with the Intel Pentium (P5) architecture, which was introduced to the public back in the early 1990s, but with some extensions:

- modern 22 nm process technology;
- clock frequency from 1 GHz and higher;
- 64-bit Intel 64 instruction set;
- 512 KB of local L2 cache;
- support for specialized 512-bit SIMD instructions – KNC SIMD;
- 4 computing threads per core (Simultaneous Multithreading – SMT) [15].

Using SMT with 4 threads per core gives 240 or more hardware threads per accelerator and to a certain extent allows elimination of the delays associated with the outdated architecture with sequential execution of instructions. At the same time, using an application for Intel Xeon Phi at least two threads per core is almost always beneficial in terms of increasing performance. For the application under consideration, a certain performance gain is also observed when using all the hardware threads provided by the accelerator on all available cores.

Based on the stated characteristics, it can be seen that the single-threaded performance of the accelerator is relatively low, especially when it is impossible to use SIMD instructions, and the amount of simultaneously processed data is also limited by the amount of RAM. At the same time, the low single-threaded performance of the coprocessor is compensated by a large number of hardware computing threads, as well as a full set of instructions, which distinguishes it from various GPGPU (General-Purpose computing on Graphics Processing Units, non-specialized computing on graphics processors) and other specialized computers. This fact is especially convenient and important when solving combinatorial problems like this, containing a large number of conditional branches, subroutine calls when implementing recurrent algorithms, irregular memory access patterns, etc. The volume of processed data in this case is limited and is not a determining factor.

As a result, the final average performance of one Intel Xeon Phi coprocessor, taking into account the use of all available hardware threads, when solving the presented problem is quite comparable to the performance of fairly modern Intel Xeon server CPUs (Table 3).

This application supports automatic unloading (Offload mode) on all Intel Xeon Phi accelerators available in the system. At the same time, you can control the number of accelerators used, the number of computational threads for each accelerator, the size of the block of input data transmitted for processing, etc.

2.5 Load Balancing Method

To minimize this dependence, a load balancing method was proposed between processors, as well as between coprocessors and CPUs. The essence of the balancing method is to change the size of the upload block (task queue) for the coprocessor. The method consists of several stages:

Stage 1: the maximum size of the processed block (task queue) for the accelerator is determined using formula:

$$S_i = mN_i,$$

where i is the serial number of the coprocessor, S is expressed in the number of Latin squares in the input data block, m is the specified size factor of the upload queue, by default equal to 40, and N_i is the number of computing threads used. By default, N_i is taken equal to the number of threads returned by the operating environment of this device minus 4, since the Intel Manycore Platform Software Stack (Intel MPSS) operating environment reserves one core (4 threads) for system needs.

Stage 2: during the calculations, the total average performance for each of the coprocessors and CPUs is constantly evaluated.

Stage 3: the size of the unloading block changes depending on the number of remaining LS, in proportion to the previously obtained data – on the performance of a particular computer in the complex.

At the initial stage of calculations, in the absence of statistics, the performance of the coprocessor is considered proportional to the maximum block size of this S_i device and depends on the number of physical threads.

To prevent the reduction of the block size below a reasonable limit, which becomes possible when using this algorithm and prohibiting calculations on the central processor of the system (when calculating only on processors and the number of accelerators used is more than one), the block size is limited from below by the number of computing threads of the N_i coprocessor.

The new block size is calculated for each subsequent unloading, starting from the moment when the number of remaining LS for processing becomes no more than the predicted total productivity of the heterogeneous computing complex.

3   Results

3.1   Load Balancing Method for a Heterogeneous Node

The initial optimized version of the heterogeneous application showed strong deviations in the total calculation time, depending on the specified coefficient m and various input data (Table 1).

Table 1. Dependence of the calculation time (s) on the coefficient m without balancing.

Coeff. m	1x Xeon Phi 7120P	2x Xeon Phi 7120P	2x Xeon Phi 7120P and 2x Xeon E5-2683 v4	2x Xeon E5-2683 v4	1x Xeon Phi 5110P	2x Xeon Phi 5110P	2x Xeon Phi 5110P and 1x Xeon E5-2696 v2	1x Xeon E5-2696 v2
20	131.3	69.9	37.6	59.2	159.5	84.4	56.9	106.5
25	129.4	65.3	35.4		158.7	80.9	52.9	
30	130.5	65.8	38.1		159.1	80.6	48.8	
35	125.3	67.8	36.4		151.0	82.2	55.5	
40	127.3	66.4	33.5		152.7	78.3	60.6	
45	126.2	69.9	38.7		153.6	85.0	48.6	
50	125.5	63.7	41.2		152.4	76.6	48.9	
55	127.3	69.1	45.5		154.9	82.9	58.0	
60	126.7	75.1	48.9		152.7	89.3	58.5	
80	123.8	64.8	32.5		148.6	77.0	62.1	
100	123.7	82.5	40.5		149.2	98.0	47.6	
Best	**123.7**	**63.7**	**32.5**	**59.2**	**148.6**	**76.6**	**47.6**	**106.5**

The obtained results showed a strong dependence of the total calculation time on the amount of data in the last block of unloading, the presence of LS in it that need long-term processing, as well as on the difference in the size of the final data blocks for several calculators in the heterogeneous computing node of the desktop grid. This dependence is a consequence of the fact that the average processing time of one LS by a coprocessor is more than an order of magnitude higher than the processing time when using a CPU (for example, Intel Xeon of previous generations – Ivy Bridge EP and Broadwell).

As a result of using balancing, almost identical results of the total time spent on calculations were obtained for different sizes of the upload queue (Table 2) (Fig. 3).

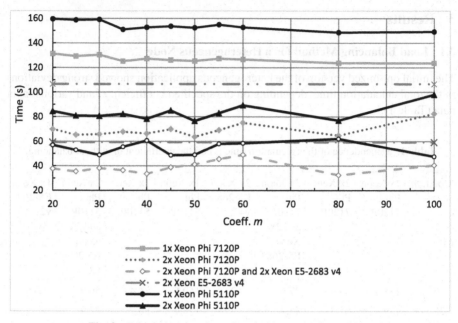

Fig. 3. Calculation time in various hardware configurations.

Table 2. Calculation time (s) during using the described balancing algorithm.

Coeff. m	1x Xeon Phi 7120P	2x Xeon Phi 7120P	2x Xeon Phi 7120P and 2x Xeon E5-2683 v4	2x Xeon E5-2683 v4	1x Xeon Phi 5110P	2x Xeon Phi 5110P	2x Xeon Phi 5110P and 1x Xeon E5-2696 v2	1x Xeon E5-2696 v2
20	131.3	68.4	34.0	60.6	158.6	82.8	51.6	106.5
30	131.0	68.4	32.4				49.4	
40	127.0	67.5	33.2		151.7	80.9	48.7	
50	125.6	67.3	33.3				47.2	
60	126.5	66.9	33.6		151.7	80.4	48.9	

When setting too large values of m (more than 60), due to the relatively small amount of test input data (72238 LS), the results of the algorithm practically do not differ from each other. For small values of m = 20, the overhead costs for uploading data to coprocessors, as well as for creating new service threads, increase. This is somewhat more noticeable in the case of using Intel Xeon Phi 5110P coprocessors (especially one coprocessor), since in addition to their lower clock frequency, in the test computing complex they are connected to the main system via the PCIe 2.0 x8 bus, and not x16, as in the case of Intel Xeon Phi 7120P (Fig. 4).

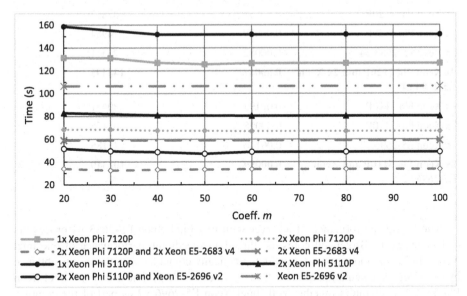

Fig. 4. Calculation time after applying the load balancing method.

The results of the performance measurement showed sufficient efficiency of the selected load balancing algorithm when performing calculations in a heterogeneous computing environment consisting of central processes and Xeon Phi accelerators, as well as sufficient stability of the total calculation time for various input data, when choosing reasonable sizes of the unloading queue.

3.2 Performance Improvement for a Heterogeneous Node

According to the results of the performance assessment, it can be seen that the overall performance of a heterogeneous computing complex depends almost linearly on the number and performance of computers used in its composition (Tables 1 and 2). At the same time, the actual performance of a particular calculator depends on the number of physical threads provided by it.

Thus, the average performance of one Intel Xeon Phi 5110P accelerator (8 GB, 1.053 GHz, 60 in-order cores, 236 threads) is only about a quarter less than that of the Intel Xeon E5-2696 v2 CPU (3.2 GHz, 12 Ivy Bridge EP cores, 24 threads), and the performance of Intel Xeon Phi 7120P (16 Gb, 1.238 GHz, 61 in-order cores, 240 threads) is almost identical to it (Table 3). The values of the LS average processing time (s) and performance (Latin squares per minute) in the table are normalized taking into account the number of used computing threads.

Table 3. Estimation of the average performance (LS /min) of various devices

Configuration	LS average processing time, s	Performance, LS/min
1x Xeon Phi 7120P	0.00158	37863
2x Xeon Phi 7120P	0.00079	74984
2x Xeon E5-2683 v4	0.00082	73511
2x Xeon Phi 7120P and 2x Xeon E5-2683 v4	**0.00041**	**148495**
1x Xeon Phi 5110P	0.00197	30451
2x Xeon Phi 5110P	0.00098	61155
1x Xeon E5-2696 v2	0.00146	41185
2x Xeon Phi 5110P and Xeon E5-2696 v2	**0.00059**	**102340**

The overall performance of a server with two Intel Xeon E5-2683 v4 processors (2.1 GHz, 2x 16 Broadwell cores, 64 threads) exceeds the performance of one Intel Xeon Phi 7120P about two times, which practically coincides with the results obtained by sampling the calculation time for these devices (Table 2). The use of two Intel Xeon Phi 5110P accelerators together with Intel Xeon E5-2696 v2 as part of the complex allows increasing the average performance more than twice, and the use of two Intel Xeon Phi 7120P together with two Intel Xeon E5-2683 v4 – approximately twice.

4 Conclusion

The conducted studies of the performance of various multiprocessor systems in solving this combinatorial computational problem have shown the possibility of successful application for the calculation of relatively low-performance devices with an outdated basic architecture, if they provide a sufficient number of computing blocks for parallel multithreaded calculations. When using the proposed load balancing method, the total operating time of the DLS canonizer practically ceases to depend on the size of the task queue for MIC architecture coprocessors.

Acknowledgements. This work was funded by RFBR according to research projects No. 19-07-00834 and No. 18-29-03264.

References

1. Mengistu, T.M., Che, D.: Survey and taxonomy of volunteer computing. ACM Comput. Surv. **52**(3), 1–35 (2019). https://doi.org/10.1145/3320073
2. Anderson, D.P.: BOINC: a platform for volunteer computing. J. Grid Comput. **18**(1), 99–122 (2019)

3. Cirne, W., Brasileiro, F., Sauvé, J.P., Andrade, N., Paranhos, D., Santos-neto, E., et al.: Grid computing for bag of tasks applications. In: Proceedings of the 3rd IFIP Conference on E-Commerce, E-Business and E-Government (2003)
4. Anglano, C., Brevik, J., Canonico, M., Nurmi, D., Wolski, R.: Fault-aware scheduling for bag-of-tasks applications on desktop grids. In: 2006 7th IEEE/ACM International Conference on Grid Computing, pp 56–63. IEEE (2006)
5. Posypkin, M., Semenov, A., Zaikin, O.: Using BOINC desktop grid to solve large scale SAT problems. Comput. Sci. **13**(1), 25 (2012)
6. Intel Xeon Phi Coprocessor System Software Developers Guide, pp 160–164. Intel Corporation (2014)
7. Colbourn, C.J., Dinitz, J.H.: Handbook of Combinatorial Designs, 2nd edn., pp. 821–1016. Chapman and Hall/CRC, New-York (2006)
8. Keedwell A.D., Dénes J.: Latin Squares and their Applications, pp. 325–438. Elsevier (2015). https://doi.org/10.1016/C2014-0-03412-0
9. Brown, J.W., Cherry, F., Most, L., Most, M., Parker, E.T., Wallis, W.D.: Completion of the spectrum of orthogonal diagonal Latin squares. Lect. Notes Pure Appl. Math. **139**, 43–49 (1992). https://doi.org/10.1201/9780203719916
10. McKay, B.D., McLeod, J.C., Wanless, I.M.: The number of transversals in a Latin square. Des. Codes Cryptogr. **40**, 269–284 (2006)
11. Vatutin, E., Nikitina, N., Belyshev, A., Manzyuk, M.: On polynomial reduction of problems based on diagonal Latin squares to the exact cover problem. In: Proceedings of the Second International Conference Information, Computation, and Control Systems for Distributed Environments, ICCS-DE 2020. CEUR Workshop Proceedings, vol. 2638, pp 289–297. Technical University of Aachen, Germany (2020). https://doi.org/10.47350/ICCS-DE.2020.26
12. Knuth, D.E.: The Art of Computer Programming. Combinatorial Algorithms, Part 1, vol. 4A. Pearson Education, India (2011)
13. Vatutin, E., Belyshev, A., Nikitina, N., Manzuk, M.: Evaluation of efficiency of using simple transformations when searching for orthogonal diagonal Latin squares of order 10. In: Jordan, V., Filimonov, N., Tarasov, I., Faerman, V. (eds.) HPCST 2020. CCIS, vol. 1304, pp. 127–146. Springer, Cham (2020). https://doi.org/10.1007/978-3-030-66895-2_9
14. Kochemazov, S., Zaikin, O., Vatutin, E., Belyshev, A.: Enumerating diagonal Latin squares of order up to 9. J. Integer Sequences **23**(1), 1–21 (2020). Article 20.1.2
15. Jeffers, J. Reinders, J.: Intel Xeon Phi Processor High Performance Programming, pp 243–383. Morgan Kaufmann (2013)

Visual Metamodeling with Verification Based on Surrogate Modeling for Adaptive Computing

Alexander A. Lobanov[1]([✉]) [iD], Aleksey N. Alpatov[1] [iD], and Irina P. Torshina[2] [iD]

[1] MIREA – Russian Technological University, Vernadsky Avenue 78, 119454 Moscow, Russia
aa.lobanoff@ya.ru

[2] Moscow State University of Geodesy and Cartography, Gorokhovsky pereulok 4,
105064 Moscow, Russia

Abstract. The issue of creating a methodology for designing computing systems for space probes is discussed in this paper. According to the authors, it is the modern paradigm of metamodeling that makes it possible to reduce labor costs when creating software and hardware systems for deep space scientific missions. The paper proposes a semantic approach, based on metamodeling. The approach makes a conceptually new low-level metamodel by combining two well-known IDEF0 graphic symbols and a flowchart notation. This solution makes it possible to practically eliminate the disadvantages inherent in each of the methodologies separately. A new methodology and rules for its application based on the semantic element have been obtained. An example of a metamodel is presented. The proposed approach allows designing and simulating the operation of on-board computing systems of a space probe. We assume that this virtually eliminates the shortcomings of the initial models. In our opinion, this will also reduce labor costs in the design of various on-board computing systems, increasing the quality and unambiguity of work. The ideology of metamodeling has a peculiarity. The created model can fully comply with the rules, but not provide the required parameters. Surrogate modeling can be the solution to the problem. An iterative process to achieve the required metamodel parameters is proposed.

Keywords: Metamodeling · Metamodel · Space probe · Surrogate modeling · MOF · Iterative process

1 Introduction

Modern onboard systems of automatic spacecrafts (SC) for the study of small bodies of the solar system (MTSS) are unique software and hardware systems. According to onboard systems, it includes disparate hardware and software elements that operate independently of each other in accordance with separate sequencing diagrams. This approach creates problems. Unique technical solutions in the design and implementation require huge funding. However, the predicted increasing of a number of deep space missions demands reducing the resource costs. The main idea of this article is to unify the process using metamodeling. Metamodeling will make it possible to create unified systems operating in a single key [1–6]. On the one hand, this will reduce costs, and on the other hand, it will increase the quality of the on-board of computing systems.

© Springer Nature Switzerland AG 2022
V. Jordan et al. (Eds.): HPCST 2021, CCIS 1526, pp. 174–185, 2022.
https://doi.org/10.1007/978-3-030-94141-3_14

2 Modeling the Space Probe's Systems

2.1 Creating Onboard Computing Systems

In this case, we assume that previously independent elements/subsystems could be combined into a single on-board computing system. The advantage of this approach is the possibility of mutual monitoring of elements/subsystems. It also helps us to build a fault-tolerant onboard computing system. This approach makes it possible to adapt the operation of onboard subsystems depending on the specific tasks of a particular mission. We gain an opportunity to create unified onboard hardware and software computing systems that can be adapted to the specific research tasks of the space mission. That produces a possibility to reduce costs and increase the number of deep space exploration missions.

The proposed approach is very sensitive to the choice of an adequate instrument. To solve this problem, a methodology for designing, modeling and developing complexes that meet the previously stated conditions is required. In the author's opinion, the modern concept of metamodeling is the most appropriate tool for solving this problem. Currently, a large number of frameworks have been developed, for example, GOPRR, MOF, ORM/NIAM, etc.

The OMG (Object Management Group) consortium proposed the MOF (Meta Object Facility) standard in 1996. The standard was intended to reduce the cost and accelerate the production of ready-made software [7, 8]. The MOF standard is represented by a set of informal descriptions of the metamodel specification, its semantics and display rules. The MOF standard is aimed primarily at creating more complex modeling systems on its basis, since the metamodel that is part of it is a subset of the UML set, and the MOF model itself, in fact, under certain assumptions, can be reduced to a UML class diagram, but this does not in the least mean their direct correspondence. Consequently, the use of the MOF standard for solving the problem formulated in this work will make it possible to create a full-fledged system for modeling complex systems.

According to the MOF standard, there are 4 levels of metamodels [9]:

- the M0 layer is the instance implementation mechanism (real data layer). This layer is intended to describe and understand the subject area;
- the M1 layer describes the elements and subsystems as functional models;
- the M2 layer combines the models from the M1 layer into a complete system using a set of graphic notations;
- the M3 layer is represented by the so-called meta-metamodel, which fully corresponds to itself and allows one to describe the metamodel of the M2 layer level.

Based on the MOF standard, it defines a set of models and metamodels, characterized by a large number of parameters. The parameters provide flexibility in the modeling process and improve the quality of the final metamodel. The key feature of the MOF standard is a strict hierarchy, which allows us to determine the full correspondence of the underlying model element to the corresponding element of the higher level in the specified hierarchy.

The infrastructure of metamodeling systems is based on the MOF standard. The main purpose is to match the working metamodel and the MOF model. The elements of the models must be common. The unified modeling language UML is, in fact, an M2 level metamodel that allows us to define a complete MOF object. We should notice that the MOF standard does not imply only UML for using the M2 level.

The UML language has a number of advantages for the purposes mentioned above. In particular, the ability to interpret diagrams into a program code is very important. The property of interpretation is valuable in the design and reengineering of software systems. On the other hand, there are a number of disadvantages. UML is difficult to study and design. The UML does not support the implementation of the hardware component of the system. It is known that, to solve this problem, the SysML language was created and is being developed, which, however, is as difficult to learn as it is in the case of UML.

Unlike the UML, the SADT methodology (IDEF notation) is simple to study and use. It can be used for a general design. However, IDEF also has drawbacks. In particular, it is difficult to design the operation of software tools, especially in terms of low-level algorithms.

The Flowchart diagrams on the contrary to IDEF0 were created to describe low-level algorithms. It is easy to create the detailed low-level algorithms of the operation using the Flowchart diagrams. Unlike the IDEF the Flowchart diagrams don't represent the general abstract information of the system. At the same time, the Flowchart diagrams have a possibility of interpreting the programming code. The analysis carried out by the authors shows that the most preferable would be a metamodel based on the combination of IDEF0 and Flowchart diagrams [10, 11]. The combination of these two notations compensates for mutual disadvantages while maintaining cognitive simplicity. The created bilingual metamodel must satisfy several important requirements at once.

The structure of the new modeling language should be hierarchical and allow the possibility of decomposition to describe individual functions and elements of the computing system in detail. This is important when solving complex problems, when the design of on-board computing systems, in particular of individual subsystems, can be performed in parallel by different commands, each of which can work only with the required level of decomposition, without using a common scheme.

The metamodeling language (notation) should support the semiautomatic or even automatic execution of the development/reengineering of the programming code to create software for computing systems. This requirement reduces labor costs due to partial or complete automation of the procedure.

The methodology should support the creation of not only models of software systems, but also the hardware component, as well as special equipment and space probe subsystems.

This article proposes a metamodel (semantic) solution that allows you to combine the IDEF0 designation and a block diagram for designing and modeling the architecture of onboard computing systems for a deep space exploration spacecraft.

2.2   Application of the Joint Model of Semantic Objects

The task of creating a specific metamodel essentially boils down to creating an "M2" metamodel based on the "M1A" and "M1B" models. The M1A model is the IDEF0 notation and the M1B model is a block diagram. The purpose of this work is to create a semantic element for the transition/unification of the "M1A" and "M1B" models, as well as the semantics of using such element for organizing the rules for the transition, transformation and use of IDEF and the block diagram designations in one model. It is necessary to automate the processes of the design or reengineering of the on-board computing system software.

This article proposes a single element that can act as an element for combining nota- tions. It can also be used as an independent element describing functional transformations performed by the subsystems of the designed computing system (Fig. 1).

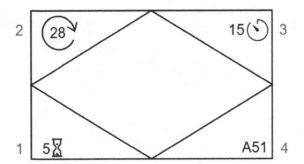

Fig. 1. The suggested semantic block for combining the notations.

The proposed semantic element contains an embedded rhombus indicating further decomposition of the algorithm in the form of a flowchart.

Element 1 – "Labor intensity" shows the labor intensity of performing the function in standard reduced labor costs, for example, standard days.

Element 2 – the "Cycle" is used if the block is decomposed according to a cyclic algorithm and indicates:

1. a number of iterations (Fig. 2). In this case, the number of iterations will be 28;
2. the implementation of the condition in the body of the cycle (Fig. 3).

Fig. 2. Semantic element indicating the number of iterations in the body of the loop.

Fig. 3. Symbol denoting a previously prepared cycle.

Element 3 – "Timer" shows the duration of the task in predefined units of measure (days, hours, seconds, etc.).

Element 4 - this is a unique identification number for a block as in the case of the standard IDEF0 notation.

The proposed semantic element should be used to create the M2 metamodel. The element combines abstract SADT models and M1 level algorithmic flowchart models. Accordingly, the M1 level models are based on the M0 level models (Fig. 4).

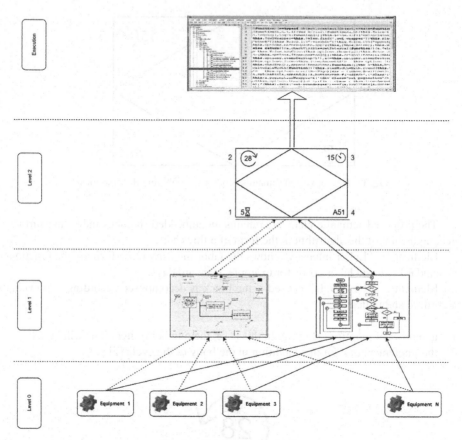

Fig. 4. Model usage hierarchy.

Let us consider the possibility of using the developed semantic element on the example of a laser altimetry subsystem as part of a multifunctional onboard guidance and landing system for a space probe (Fig. 5).

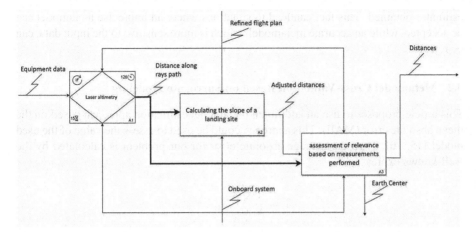

Fig. 5. An example of using the developed semantic element.

Figure 5 shows that the procedure "Measurement of distances to the underlying surface" will be active until the specified conditions are met. In this case, the conditions are as follows: the period of operation of this unit is 15 measurements within 120 min.

3   Cross-Validating of the Metamodel

The developed mechanism of the joint model of semantic objects to implement a meta-modeling of complex computing systems is proposed. A preliminary assessment and validation of models are a main feature of the metamodel-oriented approach. Scientific papers discussed a large number of approaches to solving the problem of the valida-tion of a metamodel. One of the most common approaches to validating a metamodel is the cross-validation mechanism [12, 13]. In this approach the K pairs of input and output data (x, y) should be decomposed onto the f subsets of the initial set S (X, Y) = S0 (X0, Y0), S1 (X1, Y1),…, Sf {Xf, Yf}.

3.1   Peculiarities of Classic Cross-Validation Approach

This procedure is necessary in order to separate the selected subset from the initial set each time during the iterative run of the metamodel for the next step of the metamodel run. The extracted subset allows calculating the resulting metamodel error and quantifying the developed metamodel. In the task of validating the metamodel, this approach is reduced to the formation of a training sample for performing analysis and a test sample, on which the correctness and accuracy of the performed analysis are checked [14]. Cross-validation provides an estimation of the metamodel using averaged model suitability evaluation. That allows one to test the generality of the model under operational conditions that is equal to testing the model on real data sets.

The task of building a metamodeling system requires not only cross-validation mech-anisms, but also a large number of initial parameters. A constant control over the input dataset is demanded. The existing verification methods have insufficient accuracy of the estimates obtained. This fact can lead to situations where an imprecise metamodel can be accepted, while an accurate metamodel, which is more sensitive to the input data, can be rejected.

3.2 Metamodel Cross-Validation Based on Surrogate Modeling

This article proposes to use an additional metamodel estimation approach based on the mean absolute error (MAE). This approach could be used to assess the value of the used model [15, 16]. Then the average absolute error for our problem is calculated by the well-known expression:

$$T = \frac{1}{N} \sum_{n=1}^{N} |y_i - x_i|$$

where N – a number of the points of the model validation; y_i – an obtained value; x_i – a predicted value for the obtained value (fitted model).

In fact, the cross-validation method involves dividing an existing set of inputs into N subsets of $\Phi_1, \Phi_2, ..., \Phi_n$. In this case, the model $\hat{Y}^{(-n)}$ in the interval [1, N] is approximated based on the $\bigcup_{i \neq n} \Phi_n$ dataset. And the model validation is done based on the Φ_n dataset.

For the selected model quality criteria, based on the cumulative mean absolute error (MAE) and cross-validation criteria, the model accuracy is calculated using the following formula:

$$\Psi_N = \frac{1}{N} \sum_{n=1}^{N} \frac{1}{S/N} \sum_{i \in \Phi_n} T(y_i, \hat{Y}^{(-n)}(x_i))$$

where N – a size of the dataset; T – the selected quality criteria (in this case, the criteria is MAE); $\hat{Y}^{(-n)}$ – a model for estimation.

A feature of the proposed approach is the applying of the cross-validation method in conjunction with the statistical method of time series analysis. The cross-validation method improves the quality of the metamodel assessment. In this case, a suitable approach is required. The required approach should provide both an estimate of the proximity of the metamodel to fitness function and the ranking of data points at the sample points. Practically more accurate estimates can be obtained using adaptive approaches. Adaptive approaches are based on iterative refinement of the metamodel based on new data sets obtained during the previous step of the optimization and evaluation of the optimization performed. The methodology for choosing an initial model for surrogate modeling is given in [17]. Thus, the authors of the study have shown that the method of Gaussian processes is the most preferable for this problem.

"Classic" schemes of metamodels validation emerged as a result of the design of the experiment. The schemes are based on the fact that any error in the model has a strong impact on the confirmation or the rejection of the hypothesis. The widespread use of these methods is associated, first of all, with the simplicity of their implementation and practical usage. Systematic errors are a significant drawback of the described schemes. Such errors often arise due to a large class of deviations from a given model. The "classical" approach, in most cases, supposes the use of an approximating function of the appropriate type, the selection of which allows one to reduce the model error. In the paper [18] it is shown that an increase in the sample size of the initial data gives more information about the model, but under certain conditions, a further increase in the sample size does not greatly affect the accuracy of the approximation.

4 Results

4.1 Algorithm of the Metamodeling Framework

An iterative modeling is proposed to implement the presented metamodel. The proposed approach is based on the use of surrogate approximations in the global metamodel optimization. This article suggests using Kendall tau rank correlation coefficient for the bias-corrected validation method. The Kendall correlation coefficient, according to the authors' opinion, is the optimal choice for improving the metamodel validation mechanism based on the combined mean absolute error (MAE) and cross-validation criteria.

Kendall's τ coefficient of two-dimensional random variables (X, Y) is defined as the difference between variants of matching pairs $(X1, Y1)$ and variants of mismatched pairs $(X2, Y2)$ [19]. Let $\lambda = \lambda_1, \lambda_2, \lambda_3, ..., \lambda_n$ be a countable set of ranking items. If we denote by ω and υ two different orders λ and by $Z(\omega, \upsilon)$, in this case the total number of adjacent transpositions is $Z(\omega, \upsilon) \to min$. Thus, the general form of Kendall's τ coefficient could be presented as follows:

$$\tau = 1 - \frac{2 \cdot Z(\omega, \upsilon)}{\frac{1}{2}n(n-1)}$$

where n is the sample size.

Kendall rank correlation coefficient (KRCC) is defined in the range of values from $-$1 to 1. The advantage of KRCC is its independence from the distribution law of random variables. These facts make the usage of KRCC for validation of the metamodel very useful.

The metamodel validation mechanism suggested in this article could be presented by the following sequence of steps:

1. Formation of the initial sample of points of the model validation with dimension N, as well as the vector of observed values Y and the vector of values of the fitted metamodel X.
2. Calculation of the absolute error (MAE) based on the obtained mean values.
3. Reconfiguring the metamodel to the required MAE level.
4. Normalization of the sample objects in increasing (decreasing) order by criteria x. Assignment of the appropriate rank. Formation of the final sample.
5. Normalization of the sample objects in the increasing (decreasing) order by criteria y. Assignment of the appropriate rank. Formation of the final sample.
6. Comparison of the obtained rank sequences with each other, considering that there is a direct rank correlation for the same and opposite ranks.
7. Calculation of Kendall rank correlation coefficient.

8. Determination of the level of significance of the coefficient. The hypothesis that the GCR is equal to zero is used to test the significance level of the coefficient [17]. Selective KRCC is calculated by the formula:

$$T_{kp} = C_{kp}\sqrt{\frac{2(2n+5)}{9n(n-1)}}$$

where n is the size of the general sample and C_{kp} - the value of the argument of the Laplace function (tabular data).
9. Testing the null hypothesis H_0. If the null hypothesis is rejected ($|\tau| > T_{kp}$), then, respectively, the values of t and T are strongly correlated, and the values of the corresponding features of the samples X and Y are not correlated. If $|\tau| > T_{kp}$, then we can assume that the opposite hypothesis is confirmed and the values of the sample's features are fully correlated.
10. Correlation level control. The presence of metamodel anomalies can be considered established if, at the given MAE values, the correlation values are below the set threshold.

4.2 Functional Model of the Metamodeling Framework

In general, the mechanism of an iterative metamodeling system is shown in Fig. 6.

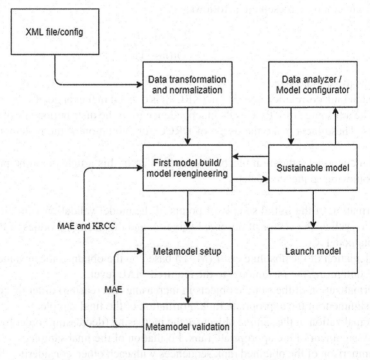

Fig. 6. The mechanism of an iterative metamodeling system.

The main purpose of the metamodeling in practice is to improve the accuracy of the metamodel on a global scale and to ensure reasonable costs for its development and use. A distinctive feature of the proposed approach is the ability to improve the quality of the metamodel assessment by using the cross-validation method in combination with statistical methods for time series analysis. In practice, it is useful to apply the approaches that provide not only estimates of the metamodel proximity to the fitness function, but also a way of the data points ranking, especially at certain points of the sample. It is possible to provide accurate results of the metamodeling process by using new adaptive approaches. The adaptability of the proposed approach is based on a step-by-step refinement of the metamodel using new datasets. The metamodel is constantly being optimized in the process of refinement. Each optimization step is evaluated. The described technique is based on a Gaussian process. This choice is not accidental. The process of selecting an initial surrogate model for adaptive surrogate modeling is discussed in [17]. It is shown that the Gaussian process is the most preferable for this class of problems.

5   Conclusion

The approach to solve the problems of creating special onboard computing systems for the guidance and landing the space probes in a completely autonomous mode is proposed. The suggested technique can be applied to the design and development of other computing and information systems [20].

According to the authors, the development of onboard computing systems using metamodeling could be useful in the design of a whole class of spacecrafts for deep space exploration. It provides the possibility to change the programming code quickly according to the modifications in graphic models. This will allow us to adjust the computing subsystems of the space probe according to tasks of the current mission with minimal costs. The main advantage of the proposed approach is the combination of the two notations. Each of the notations has worked well enough in practice. The combined use of these notations allows us to compensate for the disadvantages of each approach taken separately. In addition, it becomes possible to interpret each of the methodologies in the programming code. The original techniques did not possess this property. The proposed metamodel will allow the mission team not only to modify, but also to create computing subsystems of the space probe in a short time. This makes it possible to adapt the space probe's computing system to the specifics of the tasks of a unique space mission with the help of reasonable labor costs. It is important to note that the structure of the combined notation remains clear and simple. This makes it possible to use the proposed approach for modeling complex hardware and software systems for various purposes.

For the elaboration of the process of metamodeling of complex onboard computing systems, it is additionally proposed to implement a mechanism based on the method of interpreted surrogate models. The main purpose of using a surrogate model in this task is to bring the characteristics of the selected base model as close as possible to the customer's requirements [21]. Parameters such as forecasting quality, classification, etc., must meet all requirements. At the same time, the methodology should ensure the interpretability of the created model. This is necessary for a better understanding of the decisions made on the basis of the model. This is most important for the practical use of basic characteristics such as forecast accuracy and classification. Without this, the accuracy of the model is not always sufficient for practical tasks. Ensuring the interpretability of the model will make it possible to detect systematic errors in solving practical problems. The mean absolute error (MAE) and cross-validation method is proposed as a measure of the estimate obtained during an iterative run. The MAE method is a set of criteria. The proposed solution could be used as a basis for creating a framework.

References

1. Paramonov, P.P., Zharinov, I.O.: Integrated airborne computing systems: a review of the current state and analysis of development prospects in aircraft instrument engineering (Principy postroenija otraslevoj sistemy avtomatizirovannogo proektirovani). Sci. Tech. J. Inf. Technol. Mech. Opt. **2**(82), 1–17 (2013). (in Russian)
2. Branets, V.N., Clubb, J., Knutov, A.S., Mikrin, E.A., Chertok, B.E., Sherrill, J.: Development of computer systems supported by artificial intelligence elements applied to spacecraft control systems. Izvestija Rossijskoj Akademii Nauk. Teorija i Sistemy Upravlenija **4**, 146–149 (2004). (in Russian)
3. Krat, N.M., Savin, A.A., Sharygin, G.S.: Test equipment for autonomous navigation system of space vehicles. Proc. TUSUR Univ. **1**(31), 28–32 (2014). (in Russian)
4. Dodonov, A.R.: The principles of organizing on-board computing systems of automatic spacecraft (Principy organizacii bortovyh vychislitel'nyh kompleksov avtomaticheskih kosmicheskih apparatov). Dostizheniya Nauki i Obrazovaniya **8**(30), 41–45 (2018). (in Russian)
5. Kulumani, S., Takami, K., Lee, T.: Geometric control for autonomous landing on asteroid Itokawa using visual localization. arXiv preprint on Systems and Control (2017). https://arxiv.org/abs/1708.09435v2. Accessed 4 Apr 2021
6. Belinskaya, E.V.: The history and prospects of using vision systems to control the process of landing on planets and small bodies of the solar system (Istorija i perspektivy ispol'zovanija sistem tehnicheskogo zrenija dlja upravlenija processom posadki na planety i malye tela solnechnoj sistemy). Mekhanika, Upravlenie i Informatika **1**, 268–278 (2009). (in Russian)
7. Miotto, E., Vardanega, T.: On the integration of domain-specific and scientific body of knowledge in model driven engineering. In: Proceedings of Workshop on the Definition, Evaluation and Exploitation of Modelling and Computing Standards for Real-Time Embedded Systems, STANDRTS 2009 (2009). http://citeseerx.ist.psu.edu/viewdoc/summary?doi=10.1.1.372.3058. Accessed 1 Apr 2021
8. Standards Development Organization: About the meta, object facility specification version 2.5.1. https://www.omg.org/spec/MOF/. Accessed 2 Apr 2021
9. Zimmermann, A., Schmidt, R., Sandkuhl, K., Jugel, D., Bogner, J., Möhring, M.: Evolution of enterprise architecture for digital transformation. In: Proceedings of the IEEE 22nd International Enterprise Distributed Object Computing Workshop (EDOCW), Stockholm, Sweden, 16–19 October 2018, pp. 87–96 (2018). https://doi.org/10.1109/EDOCW.2018.00023
10. Lobanov, A., Strogankova, N., Bolbakov, R.: Meta-modeling of space probe on-board computing complexes. In: Jordan, V., Filimonov, N., Tarasov, I., Faerman, V. (eds.) HPCST 2020. CCIS, vol. 1304, pp. 14–28. Springer, Cham (2020). https://doi.org/10.1007/978-3-030-66895-2_2
11. Torshina, I.P., Lobanov, A.A., Kuzubov, N.A., Nahabenko, A.M., Olefir, M.V.: Computer vision system as part of the spacecraft guidance and landing onboard complex (Sistema komp'yuternogo zreniya v sostave bortovogo kompleksa navedeniya i posadki KLA). Nat. Tech. Sci. **6**(144), 143–146 (2020). (in Russian)

12. Bischl, B., Mersmann, O., Trautmann, H., Weihs, C.: Resampling methods for meta-model validation with recommendations for evolutionary computation. Evol. Comput. **20**(2), 249–275 (2012)
13. Meckesheimer, M., Barton, R.R., Simpson, T.W., Booker, A.J.: Computationally inexpensive metamodel assessment strategies. In: Proceedings of International Design Engineering Technical Conferences and Computers and Information in Engineering Conference, pp. 191–201. American Society of Mechanical Engineers (2001). https://doi.org/10.1115/DETC2001/DAC-21028
14. Karagiannis, D., Moser, C., Mostashari, A.: Compliance evaluation featuring heat maps (CE-HM): a meta-modeling-based approach. In: Ralyté, J., Franch, X., Brinkkemper, S., Wrycza, S. (eds.) CAiSE 2012. LNCS, vol. 7328, pp. 414–428. Springer, Heidelberg (2012). https://doi.org/10.1007/978-3-642-31095-9_27
15. Barbashova, E.V., Gaydamakina, I.V.: Forecasting in short time series: methodological and methodical aspects. Bull. Agrarian Sci. **2**(83), 84–98 (2020). (in Russian)
16. Chuchueva, E.: Basic estimates of time series prediction accuracy (Osnovnye ocenki tochnosti prognozirovanija vremennyh rjadov). (in Russian). https://www.mbureau.ru/blog/osnovnye-ocenki-tochnosti-prognozirovaniya-vremennyh-ryadov. Accessed 1 Apr 2021
17. Wang, C., Duan, Q., Gong, W., Ye, A., Di, Z., Miao, C.: An evaluation of adaptive surrogate modeling based optimization with two benchmark problems. Environ. Model. Softw. **60**, 167–179 (2020)
18. Kitagawa, T., Nybom, M., Stuhler, J. Measurement error and rank correlations. Working paper CWP28/18. ESRC Research Centre, Swindon, UK. https://www.ifs.org.uk/uploads/CWP281 818.pdf. Accessed 12 Apr 2021
19. Akoglu, H.: User's guide to correlation coefficients. Turk. J. Emerg. Med. **18**(3), 91–93 (2018)
20. Kudzh, S.A., Tsvetkov, V.Y.: Trinitarian systems. Russ. Technol. J. **7**(6), 151–167 (2019). (in Russian). https://doi.org/10.32362/2500-316X-2019-7-6-151-167
21. Alpatov, A.N., Lobanov, A.A., Lobanova, J.S.: Testing and Debugging Software (Testirovanie i Otladka Programmnogo Obespechenija). Mezhregional'nyj centr innovacionnyh tehnologij v obrazovanii, Kirov (2021). (in Russian). https://doi.org/10.52376/978-5-907419-18-6

Recognition Algorithms Based on the Selection of 2D Representative Pseudo-objects

Olimjon N. Mirzaev[1] , Sobirjon S. Radjabov[1] , Gulmira R. Mirzaeva[2] ,
Kuvvat T. Usmanov[3] , and Nomaz M. Mirzaev[2(✉)]

[1] Research Institute for the Development of Digital Technologies and Artificial Intelligence,
17A, Buz-2, Mirzo Ulugbek, 100125 Tashkent, Republic of Uzbekistan
[2] Tashkent University of Information Technologies named after Muhammad al-Khwarizmi, 108,
Amir Temur Avenue, 100200 Tashkent, Republic of Uzbekistan
[3] Tashkent Institute of Architecture and Civil Engineering, 13 Navoi Avenue, 100011 Tashkent,
Republic of Uzbekistan

Abstract. Building of a recognition algorithms (RA) based on the selection of representative pseudo-objects and providing a solution to the problem of recognition of objects represented in a big-dimensionality feature space (BDFS) are described in this article. The proposed approach is based on the formation of a set of 2D basic pseudo-objects and the determination of a suitable set of 2D proximity functions (PF) when designing an extreme RA. The article contains a parametric description of the proposed RA. It is presented in the form of sequence of computational procedures. And the main ones are procedures for determining: the functions of differences among objects in a 2D subspace of representative features (TSRF); groups of interconnectedness pseudo-objects (GIPO) in the same subspace; a set of basic pseudo-objects; functions of differences between the basic pseudo-object in a TSRF. There are also groups of interconnectedness and basic PF; the integral recognizing operator with respect to basic PF. The results of a comparative analysis of the proposed and known RA are presented. The main conclusion is that the implementation of the approach proposed in this paper makes it possible to switch from the original BDFS to the space of representative features (RF), the dimension of which is significantly lower.

Keywords: Recognition algorithms · Representative feature · 2D pseudo-objects · Proximity function · Basic proximity functions

1 Introduction

A detailed study of the literature, in particular [1–5], shows that pattern recognition (PR) issues are one of the main issues for specialists in computer science and applied mathematics. The reason for this is that lately the PR methods and algorithms are increasingly used in various fields of science and technology.

Currently, a number of recognition algorithms (RA) models have been developed and deeply studied [1, 4]. These include the following RA models:

© Springer Nature Switzerland AG 2022
V. Jordan et al. (Eds.): HPCST 2021, CCIS 1526, pp. 186–196, 2022.
https://doi.org/10.1007/978-3-030-94141-3_15

- models based on discriminant functions [1, 6–10];
- models developed on the basis of mathematical statistics [8, 11–14];
- models based on the potential principle [8, 15–18];
- models developed on the basis of mathematical logic [19–24];
- models based on evaluation [1, 4, 25–28].

It is shown in [29] that these AR models were developed mainly for solving such PR problems, in the space of independent features (or the relationship between them is weak). Also, in real life there are often applied PR-tasks associated with the classification of objects described in BDFS. Under these conditions, when solving such problems, the assumption of the independence of features is not always true [29–32]. The study of available publications on PR, as well as the accumulated experience in solving a number of applied and model problems, shows that in conditions of violation of this assumption, many known RAs do not work correctly [29]. This circumstance indicates the relevance of the issues of modifying the existing and developing new AR models designed to solve the problems of object recognition presented in the BDFS.

The purpose of this work is the development of AR models based on 2D PF and providing a solution to the problems of object recognition presented in the BDFS.

To solve such problems, an approach is proposed, the key point of which is the formation of groups of interconnectedness elements in each pair of RF and the selection of representative pseudo-objects.

The concepts and designations used in this article are taken from works [1, 4, 5, 27, 28, 29].

2 Basic Concepts and Notation

Consider the case when, given a set $\mathbb{M}$ of admissible objects, in the n-dimensional feature space $\mathbb{X}$. Each admissible object $\mathfrak{D}$ ($\mathfrak{D} \in \mathbb{M}$) in the space $\mathbb{X}$ corresponds to an n-dimensional numerical characteristic (n- dimensional description vector) of the object $\mathfrak{J}(\mathfrak{D})$, where $\mathfrak{J}(\mathfrak{D}) = (\mathfrak{o}_1, .., \mathfrak{o}_u, .., \mathfrak{o}_n)$[1, 4]. Supposed that the set $\mathbb{M}$ consists of $\hbar$ disjoint subsets (classes) $C_1, .., C_j, .., C_\hbar$:

$$\mathbb{M} = \bigcup_{j=1}^{\hbar} C_j, \qquad C_i \cap C_j \neq \emptyset, \ i \neq j, \ i, j \in \{1, ..., \hbar\}. \tag{1}$$

The partition (1) is not completely defined, but only some initial information $\mathbb{I}_0$ about the subsets $C_1, .., C_j, .., C_\hbar$ is given. For clarify the concept of initial information, select m objects from the set of possible objects $\mathbb{M}$ and denote by $\tilde{\mathfrak{D}}^m$:

$$\tilde{\mathfrak{D}}^m = \{\mathfrak{D}_1, ..., \mathfrak{D}_u, ..., \mathfrak{D}_m\}.$$

Let us introduce the following notations:

$$\tilde{C}_j = \tilde{\mathfrak{D}}^m \cap C_j, \quad \tilde{D}_j = \tilde{\mathfrak{D}}^m / \tilde{C}_j.$$

In this case, the initial information can be described in the form of some set $\mathbb{I}_0$, elements of which are the pairs $< \mathfrak{D}_i, \mathfrak{i}(\mathfrak{D}_i) > \ (\forall \mathfrak{D}_i \in \mathbb{M}, i = \overline{1, m})$::

$$\mathbb{I}_0 = \{< \mathfrak{D}_1, \mathfrak{i}(\mathfrak{D}_1) >, ..., < \mathfrak{D}_i, \mathfrak{i}(\mathfrak{D}_i) >, ..., < \mathfrak{D}_m, \mathfrak{i}(\mathfrak{D}_m) >\},$$

$$\mathfrak{i}(\mathfrak{D}_i) = (\xi_{i1}, ..., \xi_{ij}, ..., \xi_{i\hbar}),$$

$$\tag{2}$$

where $\mathfrak{O}_i$ is an admissible object, and $\mathfrak{i}(\mathfrak{O}_i)$ is the information vector of the object $\mathfrak{O}_i$.
Every element of the information vector $\mathfrak{i}(\mathfrak{O}_i)$ is given in the form:

$$\xi_{ij} = \begin{cases} 1, \text{if } \mathfrak{O}_i \in \tilde{C}_j; \\ 0, \text{if } \mathfrak{O}_i \notin \tilde{C}_j. \end{cases}$$

3 Statement of the Problem

Let us consider the problem of PR in the standard setting [1, 26]. Let the set of objects $\tilde{\mathfrak{S}}^q \left(\tilde{\mathfrak{S}}^q = \left\{ \mathfrak{O}_1', \ldots, \mathfrak{O}_i', \ldots, \mathfrak{O}_q' \right\}, \tilde{\mathfrak{S}}^q \subset \mathbb{M} \right)$, described in the space of features $\mathbb{X}$. The problem is to develope such a modek of RA $\mathfrak{A}$, which, using the initial information $\mathbb{I}_0$ calculates the values of the predicate $P_j \left(\mathfrak{O}_i' \right) \left(P_j(\mathfrak{O}_i') = "\mathfrak{O}_i' \in C_j" \right)$ for all objects $\tilde{\mathfrak{S}}^q$:

$$\mathfrak{A}(\mathbb{I}_0, \tilde{\mathfrak{S}}^q) = \left\| \beta_{ij} \right\|_{m \times \hbar}, \beta_{ij} = P_j(\mathfrak{O}_i').$$

$$\beta_{ij} = \begin{cases} 1, \text{if the object } \mathfrak{O}_i' \text{ belongs to the class } C_j; \\ 0, \text{if the object } \mathfrak{O}_i' \text{ does not belong to the class } C_j; \\ \Delta, \text{if the model has not computed the values of the predicate } P_j(\mathfrak{O}_i'). \end{cases}$$

4 Method of Solution

The article proposes an approach based on the choice of a set of representative pseudo-objects in each RF pair when constructing the RA model. The essence of the proposed RA model is based on the formation of a proximity function in 2D subspaces of the RF. Let us consider an arbitrary admissible object $\mathfrak{O}$ ($\mathfrak{O} \in \mathbb{M}$) given in an n-dimensional feature space $\mathbb{X}$. Let $\tilde{\omega}\mathfrak{O}$ mean that the object $\mathfrak{O}$ is described in the n-dimensional feature space. Moreover, to each n-dimensional space there corresponds an n-dimensional Boolean vector $\tilde{\omega}(\tilde{\omega} = (\omega_1, \ldots, \omega_i, \ldots, \omega_n), \mathfrak{d} = \tilde{\omega}_B)$, the components of which take on values 1 or 0 depending on whether or not the corresponding features are included in the description of some $\tilde{\omega}$-part of the object $\mathfrak{O}$. Thus, $\tilde{\omega}\mathfrak{O}$ is not an object, but consists of its $\tilde{\omega}$-part. Next, let us call $\tilde{\omega}$-parts of the object as a pseudo-object.

Defining the proposed RA model includes the following main stages.

1. Formation of groups of tightly coupled features. A set of n' ($n' < n$) "indepen-dent" groups of tightly coupled features (TCF) are formed. Issues related to the formation of TCFs are considered in more detail in [31, 32].

2. Selection of a set of RF. One representative from each TCF is determined, which is a typical element of its group of features. As a result, n' RF is determined, which is isolated by an n-dimensional Boolean vector $\mathbb{r}$ ($\mathbb{r} = (r_1, .., r_i, .., r_n), n' = \| \mathbb{r} \|_B$),, where $r_i = 1$, if the feature x_i is an RF, or $r_i = 0$ otherwise. The issues of RF isolation are considered in works [31–33].

The generated RF space is denoted by $\mathbb{X}' \left(\dim\left(\mathbb{X}' \right) = n' \right)$.

3. Determination of the diversity function in the TSRF. The diversity function (DF), which characterizes the remoteness of the objects $\mathfrak{O}_u$ and $\mathfrak{O}$ in the TSRF, is given. Let in the space $\mathbb{X}'$ a set $\mathfrak{C}$, consisting of n elements, that is $\mathfrak{C} = (\mathcal{D}_1, \ldots, \mathcal{D}_\tau, \ldots, \mathcal{D}_n)$, be given. And each $\mathfrak{C}$ element forms a 2D RF subspace: $\mathcal{D}_\tau = (x_{\tau_1}, x_{\tau_2}), x_{\tau_1}, x_{\tau_2} \in \mathbb{X}')$. Then the difference between the objects $\mathfrak{O}_u$ and $\mathfrak{O}$ in the subspace $\mathcal{D}_\tau$ is determined as follows [8]:

$$d_\tau(\mathfrak{O}_u, \mathfrak{O}) = \sum_{i=1}^{2} \gamma_{\tau_i}(a_{u,\tau_i} - a_{\tau_i})^2, \tag{3}$$

where $\gamma_{\tau_i}, \gamma_{\tau_2}$ are the parameters of the algorithm, which we denote by $\widetilde{\gamma_\tau} = (\gamma_{\tau_1}, \gamma_{\tau_2})$.

4. Selection of GIPO in the TSRF. m' "independent" GIPO $\mathbb{V}_A$ are determined on the basis of pairwise comparison of these objects in order to assess their proximity in the 2D RF subspace. After the implementation of this stage, disjoint m' groups are separated out:

$$\mathbb{V}_A = \{\mathfrak{V}_1, \ldots, \mathfrak{V}_q, \ldots, \mathfrak{V}_{m'}\}; \tag{4}$$

In doing so, GIPOs (4) are formed using the function (3).

5. Determination of basic pseudo-objects in the TSRF. A set of basic pseudo-objects E_q^τ, which are typical representatives of each GIPO in the TSRF, is determined. The components of the basic pseudo-object E_q^τ in each group of interconnectedness objects can be calculated as the average values for all elements of the group $\mathfrak{V}_q\left(q = \overline{1, m'}\right)$:

$$b_{qi}^\tau = \frac{1}{|\mathfrak{V}_q|} \sum_{a_{ui} \in \mathfrak{V}_q} a_{ui}, \; i = \overline{1, 2}. \tag{5}$$

As a result, we obtain m' basic pseudo-objects for each set of 2D RF subspace:

$$\mathbb{E}^\tau = \left\{E_1^\tau, \ldots, E_q^\tau, \ldots, E_{m'}^\tau\right\}.$$

Each of them is specified as a 2D vector, i.e., $E_q^\tau = \left(b_{qi_1}^\tau, b_{qi_2}^\tau\right)$.

6. Determination of the diversity function $d\left(E_q^\tau, \mathfrak{O}\right)$ between the basic pseudo-object E_q^τ and the object $\mathfrak{O}$ in the TSRF. At this stage, the DF is determined between the base pseudo-object E_q^τ and the object $\mathfrak{O}$ in the TSRF. The difference between them is determined by the formula (3):

$$d_\tau\left(E_q^\tau, \mathfrak{O}\right) = \sum_{i=1}^{2} \varrho_{\tau_i} \rho\left(b_{q,\tau_i}, a_{\tau_i}\right), \tag{6}$$

where $\rho\left(b_{q,\tau_i}, a_{\tau_i}\right)$ is the estimate of the difference between the base pseudo-object E_q^τ and the object $\mathfrak{O}$, calculated from x_{τ_i}; ϱ_{τ_i} is a parameter of the algorithm $\left(\widetilde{\varrho_\tau} = (\varrho_{\tau_i}, \varrho_{\tau_i})\right)$.

7. Specifying the proximity function $\mathfrak{H}(E_q^\tau, \mathfrak{O})$ *between the* E_q^τ *and the* $\mathfrak{O}$ *in the TSRF.* At this stage, based on the radial functions, the PF between the pseudo-object E_q^τ and the object $\mathfrak{O}$ in the TSRF is determined, for example, in the following form [15]:

$$\mathfrak{H}_\tau\left(E_q^\tau, \mathfrak{O}\right) = 1/\left(1 + \xi_\tau d_\tau\left(E_q^\tau, \mathfrak{O}\right)\right). \tag{7}$$

We obtain $\mathfrak{n}$ PFs. Each PF given in the form (7) is determined by the parameter ξ_τ.

8. Selection of groups of interconnectedness PF. At this stage, the systems $\mathfrak{W}_A$ of 'independent' groups of PF are specified. Let each proximity function $\mathfrak{H}_u$ correspond to a numerical matrix:

$$\mathfrak{H}_\tau\left(\mathbb{E}_2, \tilde{\mathfrak{O}}^m\right) = \|\mathfrak{h}_{ij}^{(\tau)}\|_{m \times m'}.$$

Let us consider the PF set $\{\mathfrak{H}_1, \ldots, \mathfrak{H}_n\}$. Let us introduce the function $\eta(\mathfrak{H}_u, \mathfrak{H}_v)$, which characterizes the strength of the pairwise connection between the numerical matrices $\|\mathfrak{h}_{ij}^{(u)}\|_{m \times m'}$ and $\|\mathfrak{h}_{ij}^{(v)}\|_{m \times m'}$. Let $\mathcal{W}_q$ $(q = \overline{1, \mathfrak{n}'})$ be a group of interconnectedness PF. The measure of proximity $\mathfrak{K}(\mathcal{W}_p, \mathcal{W}_q)$ between the groups $\mathcal{W}_p$ and $\mathcal{W}_q$ can be specified in different ways, for example:

$$\mathfrak{K}(\mathcal{W}_p, \mathcal{W}_q) = \frac{1}{N_p \cdot N_q} \sum_{\mathfrak{H}_i \in \mathcal{W}_p} \sum_{\mathfrak{H}_i \in \mathcal{W}_q} \eta\left(\mathfrak{H}_i, \mathfrak{H}_j\right), \tag{8}$$

where N_p, N_q is the number of elements included, respectively, in the sets $\mathcal{W}_p, \mathcal{W}_q$; $\eta(\mathfrak{H}_i, \mathfrak{H}_j)$ is a function that characterizes the assessment of the pairwise relationship between $\mathfrak{H}_i$ and $\mathfrak{H}_j$.

We obtain $\mathfrak{n}'$ groups of DF in each TSRF.

9. Determination of basic PF in each group of interconnectedness PF. At this stage, basic PFs are selected and the set $\mathfrak{B}$, consisting of $\mathfrak{n}'$ basic PFs, is formed. The choice of basic PF is based on the removal $N_p - 1$ $\left(p = \overline{1, \mathfrak{n}'}\right)$ PFs, giving almost the same results when evaluating the membership, from the selected group of basic PFs $\mathcal{W}_p$. Moreover, each allocated PF should be a typical representative of the selected group of tightly coupled PFs. We obtain $\mathfrak{n}'$ PFs, which is much less than the initial one, i.e., $\mathfrak{n}' < \mathfrak{n}$.

10. Synthesis of an integral recognition operator based on basic PF. At this stage, the integral recognition operator B is determined by the selected basic PFs:

$$B\left(\mathcal{C}_j, \mathfrak{O}\right) = \sum_{u=1}^{\mathfrak{n}'} \mathcal{v}_u \mathfrak{H}_u\left(\mathcal{C}_j, \mathfrak{O}\right), \tag{9}$$

where $\mathcal{v}_u$ is the parameter of the integral recognition operator B; $\mathfrak{n}'$ is the number of basic PF.

11. Decision rule. The decision is made element by element [1, 4], i.e.

$$\beta_{ij} = C\left(B\left(\mathcal{C}_j, S\right)\right) = \begin{cases} 0, & \text{if } B\left(\mathcal{C}_j, \mathfrak{O}\right) < c_1, \\ 1, & \text{if } B\left(\mathcal{C}_j, \mathfrak{O}\right) > c_2, \\ \Delta, & \text{if } c_1 \leq B\left(\mathcal{C}_j, \mathfrak{O}\right) \leq c_2 \end{cases}$$

where c_1, c_2 – are algorithm parameters.

Thus, we have defined the AR model $\mathfrak{A}(\tilde{\pi}, \mathfrak{O})$, based on a two-dimensional PF of the intensional type. Any AR from the model $\mathfrak{A}(\tilde{\pi}, \mathfrak{O})$ is one-to-one in the parameter space $\tilde{\pi}$:

$$\tilde{\pi} = \left(n', \mathbb{r}, \{\tilde{\gamma}_\tau\}, m', \{\mathfrak{E}_q\}, \{\tilde{\varrho}_\tau\}, \{\xi_\tau\}, n', \{\mathfrak{H}_u\}, \{\nu_u\}, c_1, c_2\right).$$

The search for the best RA within the framework of the considered model is carried out in the parameter space $\tilde{\pi}$ [34, 35].

5 Experiments and Results

In order to conduct experimental studies on the assessment of the considered RA model, functional diagrams of the created software complex and the corresponding procedures were developed. The software for these procedures is developed in the C++ programming language using the OpenCV library.

An experimental study of the performance of the proposed RA model was carried out when solving a number of problems. The following were chosen as the tested RA models: 1) the classical RA model based on potential functions ($\mathfrak{A}_1$-models) [15]; 2) the proposed model ($\mathfrak{A}_2$-models). The selection of the $\mathfrak{A}_1$-model for comparison is explained by the fact that $\mathfrak{A}_1$ and $\mathfrak{A}_2$ belong to the same category of RA models.

When solving the problems under consideration (see Sects. 5.1 and 5.2), the comparative analysis of the above-mentioned RA models based on three indicators was carried out: recognition accuracy of objects in the control sample (in%); the time spent by the algorithm for training (in seconds); the time spent by the algorithm to recognize objects in the control sample (in seconds).

Let the initial sample T, consisting of m objects $\{\mathfrak{O}_1, \ldots, \mathfrak{O}_u, \ldots, \mathfrak{O}_m\}$, be given. To calculate the quality assessment by the accuracy of the tested models of recognition operators, the set T ($T = \{\mathfrak{O}_1, \ldots, \mathfrak{O}_u, \ldots, \mathfrak{O}_m\}$) is divided into two parts – V_t and V_c ($T = V_t \cup V_c$, V_t – the training sample, V_c – the control sample). To exclude a successful (or unsuccessful) partition of the set T into two parts, let us use the cross-validation method [36], the essence of which is as follows. The initial sample of objects T is divided by random selection into 10 subsets. As a result, we obtain the sets $\mathbb{T}$:

$$\mathbb{T} = \{\mathcal{T}_1, \ldots, \mathcal{T}_u, \ldots, \mathcal{T}_{10}\}.$$

In this case, the elements of $\mathbb{T}$ are required to meet the following simple conditions (at $u, v \in \{1, \ldots 10\}$):

1. $\mathcal{T}_u \cap \mathcal{T}_v = \emptyset, u \neq v$;
2. $|\mathcal{T}_1| = \cdots = |\mathcal{T}_u| = \cdots = |\mathcal{T}_{10}|$;
3. $|\mathcal{T}_1 \cap C_j| \approx \ldots \approx |\mathcal{T}_u \cap C_j| \approx \ldots \approx |\mathcal{T}_{10} \cap C_j|$;
4. $|\mathcal{T}_u| = \sum_{j=1}^{l} |\mathcal{T}_u \cap C_j|$.

The cross-validation process for these subsets consists of the following cyclically performed steps ($\mathfrak{v} = 0; \mathfrak{u} = 1$):

– the condition of completion of the process of forming the set $\mathbb{T}$. If ($\mathfrak{v} < \mathfrak{h}$), then the following actions are performed: a) initial data is generated for the given distributions. The initial sample consists of m implementations (for objects of each class, m_j implementations). In this case, the number of features is equal to n. The number of groups of strongly connected features - n'; b) the original sample is split into $\mathfrak{h}$ random subsets of objects. As a result, we get $\mathfrak{h}$ subsets of objects;
– choose ($\mathfrak{h} - 0.1\mathfrak{h}$) from $\mathfrak{h}$ blocks as V_t and on this sample AR are trained with the given parameters;
– the trained RA is compared with (V_c). As a result of the implementation of this stage, the RA accuracy is estimated at V_c;
– the condition $\mathfrak{u} \leq \mathfrak{h}$ checked; if it is true, then $\mathfrak{u} := \mathfrak{u} + 1$ and go to step 5; otherwise, go to step 1;
– from V_t one subset is selected as V_c. In this case, the subset used as V_c is fixed accordingly, and it does not participate in the procedure for selecting candidates when forming the next sample of control objects. one subset is selected from the training samples as a control sample. In this case, the subset used as a control sample is fixed accordingly, and it does not participate in the procedure for selecting candidates when forming the next sample of control objects.

5.1 Model Problem

The main characteristics of the initial data generated for the model problem in this experiment are as follows: the size of the original sample $m = 1000$, the number of classes $\mathit{k} = 2$, the number of features $n = 500$, the strongly coupled features groups $n' = 6$, the amount of training and control sample, respectively $|V_t| = 900$, $|V_c| = 100$.

The model problem was solved using the RA models $\mathfrak{A}_1$ and $\mathfrak{A}_2$. Accuracy of recognition in the training for $\mathfrak{A}_1$ is 96,8%, for $\mathfrak{A}_2$ is 97,5%. The results of solving the problem under consideration with the use of these RAs in the verification process are 82.7% and 94.6%, respectively (see Table 1).

Table 1. The results of the considered models

RA models	Time, s		Recognition accuracy, %
	Training	Recognition	
$\mathfrak{A}_1$-model	1.3869	0.00083	82.7
$\mathfrak{A}_2$-model	4.1218	0.00027	94.6

Analysis of the results shows that the proposed $\mathfrak{A}_2$ improves the accuracy of recognition described in the space of interrelated features (more than 10% higher than $\mathfrak{A}_1$). This is due to the fact that in the $\mathfrak{A}_2$ model, in contrast to the $\mathfrak{A}_1$, a number of procedures are used to improve the recognition accuracy, for example, the determination of representative representatives of each class; selecting representative and preferred combinations of features. Thus, the CV-dimension of the developed algorithm is much less than the same indicator of the original recognition algorithm. Consequently, the accuracy of the proposed RA should be higher (on the control sample with the same size of the training sample), which was shown by the results of this experimental study.

5.2 Practical Tasks

With the development of information technology capabilities, systems with the ability to recognize a person using biometric characteristics are widely spread [37–40]. This is due to the fact that the introduction of biometric recognition (BR) methods based on unique biological characteristics that uniquely identify each person is relatively inexpensive and convenient. In addition, the use of BRs for solving various applied problems is constantly expanding [37].

Among BRs, a special place is occupied by recognition systems based on images of auricles. The advantages of such BRs are unobtrusiveness, inactivity and relatively low cost [37].

In this task, the initial sample T included 500 images of the auricles (250 images of the left and right auricles). The number of classes is five. Each class included 50 pairs of auricle images of one person. The images of the auricle were described by 147 features. Table 2 shows the results of solving this problem.

Table 2. The results of the proposed models for the recognition problem from the images of the auricle

RA models	Time, s		Recognition accuracy, %
	Training	Recognition	
$\mathfrak{A}_1$-model	0.23155	0.00230	83.07
$\mathfrak{A}_2$-model	0.82436	0.00019	97.84

The calculation results show that when using the $\mathfrak{A}_2$ model it allows to improve the recognition accuracy than RA $\mathfrak{A}_1$.

Also, the results of the experiment showed the high accuracy of the developed model when solving recognition problems from the images of the auricle.

The time spent on training the proposed model is more than the time spent on training RA $\mathfrak{A}_1$. It should be noted that the time spent by the RA $\mathfrak{A}_2$ model on recognizing objects from the control sample is less than the same indicator for the RA $\mathfrak{A}_1$ model.

Considering the results of the experimental study, we can say that the proposed RA model more accurately solves the PR problem under conditions when the size of the training sample and the dimension of the feature space are large enough.

6   Conclusions

A new approach based on formation of a set of 2D basic pseudo-objects within the training set is proposed. The implementation of the proposed approach makes it possible to move from the BDFS to the RF space, which has a lower dimension. Based on this approach, an RA model was developed taking into account the structure of the original data. The essence of the proposed model is to identify independent groups of interrelated features and the corresponding set of RF. A distinctive feature of this RA model is the determination of the preferred PF when constructing a base of 2D functions.

The proposed new approach allows: expanding models of recognition operators based on potential functions; improving the recognition accuracy of objects described in BDFS; increasing the area of application of the RA model based on potential functions when solving applied problems.

The results of experiment showed that the proposed RA model (see Sect. 4) improves accuracy and significantly reduces the number of computational operations in the process of recognizing an unknown object specified in the BDFS. At the same time, the time spent on training the model increased. This circumstance is explained by the fact that rather complex optimization procedures are used to train it than to train the traditional RA model.

In the process of solving considered in Sect. 5, it was determined that the stages of the formation of groups of "independent" features, namely, the issues of determining the number of these groups, isolating basic PFs and constructing an integral recognizing operator based on basic PFs, are most important in determining the extreme RA within the proposed model. Therefore, it is necessary to continue research towards the development of algorithms that refine these parameters of the RA model.

References

1. Zhuravlev, Y.: An algebraic approach to recognition or classifications problems. Pattern Recogn. Image Anal. **8**(1), 59–100 (1998)
2. Homenda, W., Pedrycz, W.: Pattern Recognition: A Quality of Data Perspective. Wiley, New York (2018)
3. Beyere, M., Richter, M., Nagel, M.: Pattern Recognition: Introduction, Features, Classifiers and Principles. De Gruyter Oldenbourg, Boston (2018)
4. Zhuravlev, Y.I.: Selected Scientific Works. (Izbrannye Nauchnye Trudy). Magister, Moscow (1998). (in Russian)
5. Kamilov, M., Fazilov, S., Mirzaeva, G., Gulyamova, D., Mirzaev, N.: Building a model of recognizing operators based on the definition of basic reference objects. J. Phys. Conf. Ser. **1441**(1), 012142 (2020). https://doi.org/10.1088/1742-6596/1441/1/012142
6. McLachlan, G.J.: Discriminant Analysis and Statistical Pattern Recognition. Wiley, New York (2004)
7. Zhuravlev, Y.I., Dyusembaev, A.E.: A neural network construction for recognition problems with standard information on the basis of a model of algorithms with piecewise linear surfaces and parameters. Rep. Acad. Sci. **488**(1), 11–15 (2019). (in Russian). (Zhuravlev Yu.V. I., Dyusembaev A.E. Postroenie nejroseti dlya zadach raspoznavaniya so standartnoj informaciej na osnove modeli algoritmov s kusochno-linejnymi poverhnostyami i parametrami. Doklady Akademii Nauk). https://doi.org/10.31857/S0869-5652488111-15
8. Tou, J., Gonzalez, R.: Pattern Recognition Principles. Addison-Wesley, Boston (1974)
9. Li, Y., Liu, B., Yu, Y., Li, H., Sun, J., Cui, J.: 3E-LDA: three enhancements to linear discriminant analysis. ACM Trans. Knowl. Disc. Data **15**(4), 1–20 (2021). https://doi.org/10.1145/3442347

10. Li, C.-N., Shao, Y.-H., Yin, W., Liu, M.-Z.: Robust and sparse linear discriminant analysis via an alternating direction method of multipliers. IEEE Trans. Neural Netw. Learn. Syst. **31**(3), 915–926 (2020). https://doi.org/10.1109/TNNLS.2019.2910991
11. Duda, R., Hart, P., Stork, D.: Pattern Classification. Wiley, New York (2001)
12. Webb, A.R., Copsey, K.D.: Statistical Pattern Recognition. Wiley, New York (2011)
13. Jain, A.K., Duin, P.W., Mao, J.: Statistical pattern recognition: a review. IEEE Trans. Pattern Anal. Mach. Intell. **22**(1), 4–37 (2000). https://doi.org/10.1109/34.824819
14. Merkov, A.B.: Pattern Recognition: An Introduction to Statistical Learning Methods (Raspoznavanie Obrazov: Vvedenie v Metody Statisticheskogo Obuchenija). URSS, Moscow (2019). (in Russian)
15. Ayzerman, M.A., Braverman, E.M., Rozonoer, L.I.: Method of Potential Functions in the Theory of Machine Learning (Metod potencialnyh funkcij v teorii mashinnogo obucheniya). Nauka, Moscow (1970).(in Russian)
16. Dubrovin, V.I., Koretsky, N.K., Subbotin, S.A.: Modified method of potential functions. Complex systems and processes (Modificirovannyj metod potencialnyh funkcij. Slozhnye sistemy i processy), vol. 1, pp. 12–19 (2002). (in Russian)
17. Oliveri, P.: Potential function methods: efficient probabilistic approaches to model complex data distributions. SAGE J. **28**(4), 14–15 (2017). https://doi.org/10.1177/0960336017703253
18. Sulewski, P.: Potential function method approach to pattern recognition applications. In: Environment, Technology, Resources. Proceedings of the 11th International Scientific and Practical Conference, Rezekne, Latvia, pp. 30–35 (2017). https://doi.org/10.17770/10.17770/etr2017vol2.2512
19. Kudryavtsev, V.B., Andreev, A.E., Hasanov, E.E.: Test Recognition Theory (Teoriya raspoznavaniya testov). Fizmatlit, Moscow (2007).(in Russian)
20. Lbov, G.S., Startseva, N.G.: Logical Decision Functions and Questions of Statistical Stability of Decisions (Logicheskie reshayushie funkcii i voprosy statisticheskoj ustojchivosti reshenij). IM SB RAS, Novosibirsk (1999).(in Russian)
21. Djukova, E.V., Masliakov, G.O., Prokofyev, P.A.: Logical classification of partially ordered data. In: Kuznetsov, S.O., Panov, A.I. (eds.) RCAI 2019. CCIS, vol. 1093, pp. 115–126. Springer, Cham (2019). https://doi.org/10.1007/978-3-030-30763-9_10
22. Fazilov, Sh., Khamdamov, R., Mirzaeva, G., Gulyamova, D., Mirzaev, N.: Models of recognition algorithms based on linear threshold functions. J. Phys. Conf. Ser. **1441**(1), 012138 (2020). https://doi.org/10.1088/1742-6596/1441/1/012138
23. Povhan, I.F.: Logical recognition tree construction on the basis of a step-to-step elementary attribute selection. Radio Electron. Comput. Sci. Control **2**, 95–105 (2020). https://doi.org/10.15588/1607-3274-2020-2-10
24. Povhan, I.: Logical classification trees in recognition problems. Informatyka, Automatyka, Pomiary w Gospodarce i Ochronie Środowiska **10**(2), 12–15 (2020). https://doi.org/10.35784/iapgos.927
25. Ignat'ev, O.A.: Construction of a correct combination of estimation algorithms adjusted using the cross validation technique. Comput. Math. Math. Phys. **55**(12), 2094–2099 (2015)
26. Nishanov, A.K., Djurayev, G.P., Khasanova, M.A.: Improved algorithms for calculating evaluations in processing medical data. COMPUSOFT Int. J. Adv. Comput. Technol. **8**(6), 3158–3165 (2019)
27. Zhuravlev, Y.I., Ryazanov V.V., Senko O.V.: "Recognition". Mathematical methods. Software system. Practical applications (Raspoznavaniye. Matematicheskiye metody. Programmnaya sistema. Prakticheskoye primeneniye), Fazis, Moscow (2006). (in Russian)
28. Kamilov, M.M., Fazilov, S.K., Mirzaev, N.M., Radjabov S.S.: Algorithm of calculation of estimates in condition of features' correlations. In: 3rd International Conference on Problems of Cybernetics and Informatics, PCI 2010, Baku, Azerbaijan, pp. 278–281. ANAS (2010)

29. Kamilov, M.M., Fazilov, S.K., Mirzaev, N.M., Radjabov S.S.: Models of recognition algorithms based on the assessment of the interconnectedness of features (Modeli algoritmov raspoznavaniya na osnove otsenki vzaimosvyazannosti priznakov). Science and Technology, Tashkent (2020). (in Russian)
30. Lantz, B.: Machine Learning with R: Expert Techniques for Predictive Modeling. Packt Publishing, Birmingham (2019)
31. Fazilov, S.K., Mirzaev, N.M., Mirzaeva, G.R., Tashmetov, S.E.: Construction of recognition algorithms based on the two-dimensional functions. In: Santosh, K.C., Hegadi, R.S. (eds.) RTIP2R 2018. CCIS, vol. 1035, pp. 474–483. Springer, Singapore (2019). https://doi.org/10. 1007/978-981-13-9181-1_42
32. Fazilov, S., Mirzaev, N., Mirzaeva, G.: Modified recognition algorithms based on the construction of models of elementary transformations. Procedia Comput. Sci. **150**, 671–678 (2019). https://doi.org/10.1016/j.procs.2019.02.037
33. Fazilov, S.K., Lutfullaev, R.A, Mirzaev, N.M., Mukhamadiev, A.S.: Statistical approach to building a model of recognition operators under conditions of high dimensionality of a feature space. J. Phys. Conf. Ser. **1333**, 032017 (2019). https://doi.org/10.1088/1742-6596/1333/3/ 032017
34. Fazilov, S., Mirzaev, N., Radjabov, S., Mirzaev, O.: Determining of parameters in the construction of recognition operators in conditions of features correlations. CEUR Workshop Proc. **2098**, 10 (2018)
35. Fazilov, S., Mirzaev, N., Radjabov, S., Mirzaeva, G.: Determination of representative features when building an extreme recognition algorithm. J. Phys. Conf. Ser. **1260**, 102003 (2019). https://doi.org/10.1088/1742-6596/1260/10/102003
36. Braga-Neto, U.M., Dougherty, E.R.: Error Estimation for Pattern Recognition. Springer, New York (2016)
37. Fazilov S., Mirzaev O., Saliev E., Khaydarova M., Ibragimova S., Mirzaev N.: Model of recognition algorithms for objects specified as images. In: Proceedings of the 9th International Conference Advanced Computer Information Technologies, ACIT 2019, Ceske Budejovice, Czech Republic, 5–7 June 2019 (2019). https://doi.org/10.1109/ACITT.2019.8779943
38. Bolle, R.M., Connell, J.H., Pankanti, S., Ratha, N.K., Senior, A.W.: Guide to Biometrics. Springer, New York (2004). https://doi.org/10.1007/978-1-4757-4036-3
39. Benzaoui, A., Kheider, A., Boukrouche, A.: Ear description and recognition using ELBP and wavelets. In: International Conference on Applied Research in Computer Science and Engineering, Beirut, Lebanon, pp. 1–6. IEEE (2015). https://doi.org/10.1109/ARCSE.2015. 7338146
40. Pflug, A., Busch, C.: Ear biometrics: a survey of detection, feature extraction and recognition methods. IET Biometrics J. **1**(2), 114–129 (2012). https://doi.org/10.1049/iet-bmt.2011.0003

Applied Interval Analysis of Big Data Using Linear Programming Methods

Nikolay Oskorbin$^{(\boxtimes)}$

Altai State University, Lenin Avenue 61, 656049 Barnaul, Russia

Abstract. The article describes the problems of mathematical modeling of processes using an experimental database and a knowledge base. This research relates to multidimensional dependency building. It uses regression analysis and machine learning techniques within the framework of probability theory and mathematical statistics. A large observation table often cannot be processed on a single computer. The analysis of such data requires parallel computations and in this article it is carried out by the method of interval mathematics, which allows performing such computations. The analysis of linear dependences on parameters is reduced to solving systems of interval linear algebraic equations. Among the approaches to systems study known in the literature, an approach was chosen that takes into account the so-called "single set of solutions". This method provides a guaranteed estimate of the required dependencies and allows the use of linear programming in some cases. Using this method, interval forecasts of the output variable of the modeled process are calculated. Interval estimates of the parameters of the studied dependence were also obtained. Two methods of sequential and parallel analysis of a large database are proposed, using methods for solving large-scale linear programming problems. The optimality of the algorithms is substantiated using the well-known technique of removing constraints in optimization problems of large dimension. The research was carried out on model processes and on real data of statistics of road traffic accidents in England.

Keywords: Big data · Applied interval analysis · Linear programming · Guaranteed estimation of parameters of linear dependencies

1 Introduction

In recent years, Big Data Analysis Methods have been significantly developed in connection with new opportunities for collecting, storing, transmitting situational information and the use of artificial intelligence technology to support decision-making based on them [1]. In practice, the analysis of large data tables requires the use of parallelization schemes in computational algorithms. The use of special high-performance computing systems and cloud technologies for solving complex problems is becoming effective.

Big data is characterized by a large number of observations and the lack of the necessary structure for representing factors and output variables. Therefore, the analysis of these data sets is carried out in two stages. The first stage is associated with solving

© Springer Nature Switzerland AG 2022
V. Jordan et al. (Eds.): HPCST 2021, CCIS 1526, pp. 197–209, 2022.
https://doi.org/10.1007/978-3-030-94141-3_16

various problems of structuring the information flow of data: identifying essential factors; digital coding of qualitative assessments of factors; transformation of descriptive characteristics of factors in natural language; data coding in order to obtain a digital table of input and output variables of the modeled process.

At the second stage, a study of causal relationships, assessing the adequacy and performance of the obtained empirical model is carried out. Among the methods of the second stage, both classical probability-theoretic methods [2–6] and relatively new ones, in particular, applied interval analysis [7–9] are used.

Currently, regression analysis based on the least squares method is traditionally used for big data analysis. Methodological approaches to this analysis are presented in [2, 3]. In [4, 5], the use of high-performance computing systems for solving problems of regression analysis of big data is considered.

The initial idea and the first applications of the interval approach to data analysis are presented in [7] to estimate the parameters of the linear dependence of the output variable, measured with interval error, on n input variables accurately measured in each of the N tests. The processing of the experimental data table of the model was carried out by solving special linear programming (LP) problems.

The development of this approach in science and practice has been associated in recent decades with the use of interval approximation of experimental data [8–11]. New methods of interval mathematics had a significant impact on the formation of interval data analysis [12, 13]. Interval data analysis in a number of applications is more efficient in comparison with known methods and has significant development potential, including for solving big data processing problems.

In the general case, the problem of constructing linear dependences with respect to parameters with interval measurement errors of all variables is reduced to solving interval systems of linear algebraic equations. Among the set of solutions for interval systems of linear algebraic equations known in the literature [12, 13], one set of solutions is selected that provides a guaranteed estimate of the desired dependencies. For the purposes of this work, it is useful to be able to solve mathematical problems by methods of mathematical programming. These methods can also be used to solve high-dimensionality optimization problems [14, 15].

The research is carried out in the following order:

– the theoretical foundations of applied interval analysis in the modeling of linear processes are considered;
– methods of sequential analysis of a large database of experimental data in one computer and parallel data analysis in high-performance computing systems are proposed;
– computer modeling of algorithms for big data analysis is carried out;
– the last section analyzes the real data of road traffic accidents statistics in England for the period of 2005–2017.

Using the considered approach in the analysis of big data, interval estimates of the output variable of the modeled process are obtained for given values of the input variables and interval estimates of the parameters of the studied dependence. Two algorithms are proposed for the implementation of the method using sequential reading of database rows and parallel computer calculations.

The optimality of the calculations is substantiated using the method of relaxation of constraints when solving optimization problems of large dimensions [14, 15]. Computer modeling of the proposed algorithms for analyzing big data has been carried out in order to study the possibility of their use in practice and to assess the errors of their limited implementations. The study was carried out on model processes under the conditions of the feasibility of the assumptions of interval data analysis and on real data, the source and description of which are presented in [16, 17].

2 Methods and Data

2.1 Optimization Methods in Interval Data Analysis

Mathematical models of processes are represented as a scalar function, the input and output variables of which are generally measured for each of N observations with interval errors. It is assumed that the systematic components of errors in measuring variables are equal to zero. This general case of analyzing such a database with all observation errors will be discussed later.

Further, we assume that the variables $x = (x_1, \ldots, x_n)$ are measured exactly (without measurement errors), and the measured value of the output variable is the interval:

$$Y_j = \left[y_j^H, y_j^V \right]; \ y_j^H = y_j^M - \varepsilon_j^0; \ y_j^V = y_j^M + \varepsilon_j^0; \ j = 1, \ldots, N. \tag{1}$$

Here y_j^M is the measurement of the output variable in the j-th observation; ε_j^0 – estimate of the maximum value of the modulus of the interval measurement error.

Then the unknown values of the true coefficients of the linear model:

$$y = a_1 x_1 + \ldots + a_n x_n \tag{2}$$

satisfy the system of N two-sided inequalities:

$$y_j^H \leq a_1 x_{1j} + \ldots + a_n x_{nj} \leq y_j^V; \ j = 1, \ldots, N. \tag{3}$$

Let M denote the set of values of the vector $a = (a_1, \ldots, a_n)$, which satisfy the system of inequalities (3). In the literature, this set is called the "set of uncertainty" or "information set" [12, 13].

The goals and results of data analysis are considered complete when the set M is not empty, bounded and allows obtaining process estimates with a given accuracy.

In the case of an empty set M, the information of the knowledge bases and databases is inconsistent and requires their correction. The case when the set M is not bounded indicates that there is insufficient information for analysis and it is required to expand the composition of databases or knowledge.

Let us consider the main applied problems that are solved when modeling processes.

1. *The problem of forecasting the output variable at a given point of the factor space* $x^P = (x_1^P, \ldots, x_n^P)$. The interval estimate $[y^H(x^P), y^V(x^P)]$ is obtained by solving two LP problems:

$$y^H(x^P) = \min_{a \in M}\left(a_1 x_1^P + \ldots + a_n x_n^P\right); \quad y^V(x^P) = \max_{a \in M}\left(a_1 x_1^P + \ldots + a_n x_n^P\right). \quad (4)$$

2. *Interval estimation of the parameters of the sought dependence.* In applied interval analysis, the set of true values of the vector a is specified by the information set, but for its visualization in practice, the hyper-rectangle approximation is traditionally used. This representation can be considered as independent interval estimates of the components of the vector a. To calculate them, it is enough to solve $2n$ linear programming problems. For example, the guaranteed estimate of the coefficient a_1 belongs to the interval $[a_1^H, a_1^V]$:

$$a_1^H = \min_{a \in M} a_1; \quad a_1^V = \max_{a \in M} a_1. \quad (5)$$

3. *The projection of the point a^P onto the set M.* The point a^P belongs to the set M if and only if δ is equal to zero, where δ is the solution to the following quadratic programming problem:

$$\delta = \min_{a \in M}\left\| a^P - a \right\|. \quad (6)$$

In practice, problem 3 is solved to study the properties of the information set and to test the feasibility of the initial assumptions of applied interval data analysis, including for assessing the significance of the selected input variables.

4. *Point estimation of parameters of linear models (method of the center of uncertainty).* In some cases, it is required to check the feasibility of the initial assumptions (for example, in the case when M is an empty set) or to obtain point estimates of the model parameters. One of the ways to solve this problem is associated with the "expansion" or with the "contraction" of the set M. Let us set the information set M (k) by the following system of inequalities:

$$y_j^H - k\varepsilon_j^0 \leq a_1 x_{1j} + \cdots + a_n x_{nj} \leq y_j^H + k\varepsilon_j^0; \quad j = 1, \ldots, N; \quad k > 0. \quad (7)$$

The system of inequalities (7) coincides with (3) for $k = 1$. This parameter is called the coefficient of expansion $(k > 1)$ or contraction $(k < 1)$. The next minimum problem is called the problem of finding the center of uncertainty:

$$k^* = \min_{a \in M(k)} k. \quad (8)$$

As the practice of solving problem (8) on real and model data shows, the minimum is reached at a single point, which can be considered as a point estimate of the parameters of the modeled process. The k^* value is an indicator of the fulfillment of the initial assumptions of interval data analysis. Thus, the indices of active observations for $k^* > 1$ allocate a portion of the database observations, among which gross errors in data recording or underestimated errors in measuring variables are possible. Such information can be used to adjust the database and knowledge base.

5. *The task of eliminating insignificant factors of the modeled process.* One of the ways to solve this problem in applied interval analysis is based on the use of interval estimation of the model coefficients according to (5). If the zero value of the investigated parameter belongs to the found interval, then the corresponding input variable can be considered insignificant and the factor space can be reduced. In practice, there are other methods for solving this problem using, for example, the results of the analysis of complete and reduced databases.

It should be noted that the considered mathematical formulations of data analysis problems do not change in the general case of the presence of measurement errors for all variables. The changes concern systems of inequalities (3) and (7), which define an information set as a set of solutions to interval systems of linear algebraic equations.

We will consider these differences below in computer modeling of algorithms for analyzing big data.

2.2 Algorithms for Interval Analysis of Big Data

It is required that the computational process provides an optimal solution to one of the LP problems given above.

Let us introduce the following notation:

- $J = \{1, \ldots, N\}$ – indexes of records of the complete database;
- J_l – partition of the set J – indices of the l-th piece of data; $l = 1, \ldots, m;$ m is the number of chunks allocated when splitting big data;
- I_l – a set of observation indices that are active when analyzing the l-th chunk of data;
- M_l – information set when analyzing the l-th piece of data;
- I_0 – indices of observations that are heuristically allocated at the initial stage of calculations from the totality of all observations and provide non-emptiness and boundedness of the corresponding information set.

If it is not possible to single out such observations from the entire database, then the set of data is incomplete or inconsistent and, therefore, needs to be corrected. In particular, such a situation can arise for n > N or for an insufficient number of different points of the factor space. Further, we assume that such a situation does not arise when analyzing the data and the set I_0 selects n linearly independent constraints of the LP problem being solved ($|I_0| = $ n).

Let us write the algorithm for sequential processing of a large base in the following form.

1. *Step 0.* Let us define a partition of the set J into subsets $J_1, \ldots, J_m$, select the data analysis problem and the objective function of the corresponding LP problem. We put $\mu = 0$.
2. *Step 1.* We form the set I_0 and set $l = 1$.
3. *Step 2.* Let us solve the analysis problem for observations with indices $J_l \cup I_{l-1}$, which define the set M_l. If this set is empty, then the calculations are stopped with the issuance of the corresponding message.

4. *Step 3.* Selecting the indices of active constraints in the LP problem solved at step 2. If $I_l \neq I_{l-1}$, then we set $\mu = 1$. Further, we *put* $l = l + 1$. If $l \leq m$ go to step 2.
5. *Step 4.* If $\mu = 1$, we put $I_0 = I_k$; $l = 1$, go to step 2. Otherwise, we analyze the results of solving the LP problem and the information set of the database, which coincides with the set M_m.

The possibilities of implementing this computational algorithm are determined by the acceptable dimension of the LP problem for the selected computer in step 2.

Let us consider an algorithm for parallel processing of big data, which is a variant of hierarchical algorithms for solving large-scale problems, similar to the algorithms in [18]. The task of the Center is to form the set I_0 and its sequential refinement until the condition of optimality of the solution of the selected LP problem is satisfied for the entire large database. We will present the algorithm according to a similar scheme given above.

1. *Step 0 - Task of the Center.* We define the partition of the set J into subsets $J_1, \ldots, J_m$, select the data analysis problem and the objective function of the corresponding LP problem.
2. *Step 1 - Task of the Center.* We form the set I_0 and transfer the corresponding rows of the observation matrix to the data exchange buffer.
3. *Step 2 - Task of the Computers.* We solve in each computer l the analysis problem for observations with indices $J_l \cup I_0$, which determine the set M_l; $l = 1, \ldots, m$. If there is a computer for which this set is empty, then the calculations are stopped with the issuance of the corresponding message. Next, we select the index sets I_l of active constraints, and transfer the corresponding rows of the observation matrix to the data exchange buffer.
4. *Step 3 - Task of the Center.* We compare the index sets I_0 and I_l; $l = 1, \ldots, m$. If there is a computer l for which $I_l \neq I_0$, then using all active observations we form a new set I_0 and go with it to step 1. Otherwise, we analyze the results of processing the entire database, the composition of which is represented by the set I_0.

Specific implementations of the described computational algorithm are determined by the nature of the big data and the software of the used computing system. It should be noted that at step 3 of the algorithm, the Center can refine the composition of active constraints by solving the LP problem with constraints that correspond to the index sets I_0 and I_1; $l = 1, \ldots, m$. In the case when the LP problem turns out to be a problem of large dimension, the Center can use the first algorithm for sequential data processing.

In addition, it should be emphasized that in the considered algorithms there are no requirements for the number of observations when partitioning a large database into chunks.

3   Results and Discussion

3.1   Computer Modeling of Interval Analysis of Big Data

This section discusses the implementation of distributed computing, taking into account the limited capabilities of the selected software and hardware tools. Computer modeling of big data analysis processes is carried out in the Excel environment using the "Search for a solution" tool. The maximum size of the database for the number of model variables is determined by the capabilities of this tool.

We take into account (in our case of computer modeling) that in order to check the optimality of the calculations, it is necessary to find a solution to the LP problem for the entire database, and its dimension in the number of variables should not be more than 200, and in the number of main constraints – more than 100.

Let us consider the mathematical problems of computational experiments for interval data analysis in the general case of the presence of observation errors for all variables. These tasks relate to obtaining estimates of the information set. This section uses the notation accepted in the literature on the theory of interval systems of linear algebraic observations and the traditional notation of linear algebra and LP.

Interval systems of linear algebraic observations in matrix form are written by an interval (N × n) matrix of coefficients and an interval (N × 1) vector of the right-hand side in the following form:

$$Ax = B. \tag{9}$$

Elements of matrices A and B are interval estimates of the measurement results of input and output variables in N observations and are conventionally represented by inequalities: $A^H \leq A \leq A^V; B^H \leq B \leq B^V$.

The values of the vector $x \in R^n$ in (9) correspond to the estimates of the parameters of the linear dependence, and the combined set of solutions Ξ_{uni} corresponds to the set of uncertainty described above. In work [13], it is argued that "computing for the combined set of solutions of external coordinate-wise estimates with any given absolute or relative accuracy is an NP-hard problem".

the particular case of positive components of the solution to interval systems of linear algebraic observations, a single set of solutions is given by a system of linear inequalities, which we write in the following form:

$$\Xi_{uni} = \left\{ x \in R^n_+ : A^V x \geq B^H; A^H x \leq B^V \right\}. \tag{10}$$

Let us write down LP problems for the interval estimation of the value of the output variable b at a given point $a_p \in R^n$ of the factor space:

$$b^H(a_p) = \min_{x \in \Xi_{uni}} a_p x; \quad b^V(a_p) = \max_{x \in \Xi_{uni}} a_p x \tag{11}$$

Thus, LP problems in the selected version of applied interval data analysis have n variables, and the number of constraints is equal to twice the number of observations of the analyzed portion of the data base.

Let us move on to the computer implementation of computational algorithms. In general, the number m and the size of the data portions must satisfy the inequality $2(n + N/m) < D$, where D is the maximum number of constraints in the LP problem allowed by the optimization software package.

In our case ($D = 100$), n = 20 was chosen for the main variant of the experimental base, and the admissible 50 observations were cut into 5 portions. Note that the minimum number of portions in our case can be three, for example, with the number of observations 17, 17, 16, respectively. In computational experiments, other variants of the size of the observation tables were also investigated, including much larger (50 × 20), for linear processes of different parameters.

In all variants, the observation table was filled in the selected intervals for the input variables and for measurement errors with uniform pseudo-random numbers by the Excel function RAND(). The values of the output variable for the given parameters of the linear dependence were modeled with an interval error. For the basic version of the database, the intervals for the input variables were equal to [5, 100], for their errors – [−1, 1], for the observation error of the output variable – [−2, 2]. The value of the dependency coefficients for all variables was 10.

Computational experiments were carried out in one Excel workbook and the program scheme for the two computational algorithms was chosen the same: some of the sheets were occupied by the database generators, then one of the LP problem (10), the Center problem (step 1) and 5 computer tasks (step 2). The differences between the algorithms for sequential and parallel analysis of data pieces consisted in different transmission schemes for the index set I_0 formed and adjusted by the Center for observations, which determine the matrix of the basic variables of the LP problem.

For the main version of the database with its repeated updates, it is shown that the proposed computational technologies make it possible to obtain an optimal solution to the LP problem when analyzing big data. All other things being equal, parallel analysis is more preferable in terms of the number of LP subproblems for obtaining an exact solution.

The number of LP problems solved at Step 2 of the algorithms essentially depends on the initial set I_0 of the entire LP problem. The corresponding matrix of constraints, in addition to the absence of linearly dependent rows, must be well conditioned. In this case, it is shown that, on average, for m solved LP problems at step 2, it is possible to obtain the optimal or close to it value of the desired estimate. According to the experience of solving large LP problems [8, 9], in practice, one should expect a fast approximation (in 1, 2 runs) in the vicinity of the optimal estimate and slow motion to its exact value.

In computer modeling, the features of the application of linear programming methods to identify variables, the influence of which on the output variable of the process is absent or not significant, are considered. To solve this problem of data analysis, the hypothesis of the belonging of the zero value of the investigated coefficient to its interval estimation was tested by solving the LP problems (5).

In this case, you can use the solution of nonlinear programming problems (6) for the selected set of variables. The composition of variables for checking their significance is obtained by the method of the center of uncertainty by solving problem (8), a version of which in our case is reduced to two criterial nonlinear programming problem.

It should be noted that the efficiency of solving the problem of big data analysis in practice could be increased by modifying the parallelization schemes in the proposed algorithms, using additional methods of organizing the computational process and using high-performance computing systems.

3.2   Analysis of Road Accidents in England

The study is conducted using large baseline data of road traffic accidents (RTA) throughout England for 2005–2017. Sources from the Internet and a description of the accident data are presented in [16, 17]. The general database, including its main variables and records of the factors of each accident, obtained from the Internet, takes hundreds of megabytes and requires universal software for processing.

In our case, a sample of the records of road accidents with fatal outcomes was made. The total number of such accidents registered in the database is 26370, including 17010 on rural roads. For the analysis, data on accidents on rural roads in the county of Cornwall in the south-west of England were selected. This data was converted and processed in the MS Excel environment in three stages.

At the first stage of the transformation of records, some of the variables were excluded during the formation of the working database, including a number of fields were excluded. These are, for example, road class for 2-road accident participant, highway number for 2-road accident participant, highway number for 1 road accident participant, traffic control method, geographic Cartesian coordinates, speed limit level, weather conditions, astronomical time of an accident, etc.

These exceptions are caused, firstly, by the fact that for some road accidents there are no complete data sets for the excluded items, and, secondly, we considered them insignificant in our estimates. In particular, weather conditions are related to the condition of the road surface (dry, wet), and the time of the accident is associated with the level of illumination (darkness, daylight).

The next stage of data analysis is converting the table into numerical formats in accordance with the requirements of applying formula (2). It is necessary to highlight the time period in the description of the causes of the accident. This time period is the number of the month, starting from January 2005 to December 2017. Summing up the number of accidents for each month, we obtain for analysis a data table for 13 years, the number of rows of which is 156. Thus, the resulting database for processing in MS Excel is large and exceeds the capabilities of the "Search for a solution" tool.

The last transformation of the data table is associated with the decision to take into account the time factor by encoding from 1 to 156 and take into account the quarter number of each record as an input variable. In the considered case, a mathematical model similar to (2) takes the following form:

$$y = a_0 + a_1 t_1 + K_1 d_1(t) + \ldots + K_4 d_4(t) + Prd_{Pr}(t) + Cvd_{Cv}(t) + Cpd_{Cp}(t). \quad (12)$$

In the mathematical model (12), the following variables are identified: a_0, a_1–free term of the regression equation and the coefficient of the time trend of the number of accidents in the selected area; t – month number; $K_i d_i(t)$ – contribution to the number of road accidents from the conditions of quarter i, i = 1, …, 4; $Prd_{Pr}(t)$, $Cvd_{Cv}(t)$, $Cpd_{Cp}(t)$–contributions, respectively, of holidays, illumination and road conditions to the level of road accidents in the month t, t = 1, …, 156.

Data analysis was carried out using the algorithms proposed in this work. The obtained estimates of the coefficients of the model (12) make it possible to solve applied problems of forecasting a selected class of accidents in the study area and assessing the influence of individual factors on their occurrence.

Below is a Table of the causal analysis of road accidents in the designated area by quarters 2017.

The base number of road accidents in each quarter was determined taking into account the quantitative variables in the model (12) and the base (zero) values of the qualitative risk factors. The contributions of qualitative factors are highlighted in separate lines: road accidents on holidays and at night (Table 1).

Table 1. The results of the quarterly analysis of the factors of road traffic accidents for 2017.

Characteristics of road accident conditions in 2017	Pr	Cv	Cp	The fact of the accident	Accident assessment
Base number of road accident per quarter 1	–	Daylight	3		2.27
Increase in road accidents on rest days	1	Daylight	Dry		0.45
Increase in road accidents with Darkness or lights lit	–	1	Dry		0.27
Total for quarter 1 in 2017				**4**	**2.99**
Base number of road accident per quarter 2	–	Daylight	5		3.57
Increase in road accidents on rest days	3	Daylight	Dry		1.36
Increase in road accidents with Darkness or lights lit	–	2	Dry		0.53
Total for quarter 2 in 2017				**6**	**5.46**
Base number of road accident per quarter 3	–	Daylight	5		3.79
Increase in road accidents on rest days	3	Daylight	Dry		1.36
Increase in road accidents with Darkness or lights lit	–	5	Dry		1.33
Total for quarter 3 in 2017				**6**	**6.48**

(continued)

Table 1. (*continued*)

Characteristics of road accident conditions in 2017	Pr	Cv	Cp	The fact of the accident	Accident assessment
Base number of road accident per quarter 4	–	Daylight	2		3.40
Increase in road accidents on rest days	3	Daylight	Dry		1.36
Increase in road accidents with Darkness or lights lit	–	1	Dry		0.27
Total for quarter 4 in 2017				**5**	**5.03**

The quality of analytical research can be assessed by the following indicator. The actual number of road accidents in 2017 in the allocated area is 21. An explanation of the causes of road accidents in this area is given – 19.96, i.e. the analysis error was 4.94%.

4 Discussion

The main result of this article is to substantiate the possibility of using applied interval analysis for big data. The main idea of the work is based on the fact that the mathematical problems of this analysis (estimating the parameters of the required dependence, identifying and eliminating outliers of observation results, interval forecasting of the resulting variable's values, etc.) can be solved by optimization methods. This property is distinguished by the interval approach and the regression analysis based on the method of least squares. In particular, simple schemes for separating data blocks and using average results (as in [2]) do not work in interval analysis. However, optimization methods of large dimensions become effective for interval analysis of big data [14, 15].

In Sect. 2 of the article, using the example of linear processes, applied problems of interval analysis are systematized and the universality of the application of optimization methods for their solution is shown. This conclusion is also valid in the general case of modeling nonlinear processes. In the methodological section, two implementations of the method of relaxation of constraints are proposed [15] in the general case of measurement errors for all variables, which are directly generalized for the case of analysis of nonlinear processes. These studies have elements of scientific novelty.

Section 3 presents new results of the study of interval analysis of big data of model and real processes. On specific examples of big data analysis in the Excel environment, the organization of distributed computing is considered, an estimate of the final convergence rate is given, and empirical estimates of the error of linear calculations are obtained. It is shown that in practice the number of rows of the observation matrix is not limited, and the number of columns (the number of factors) is determined by the capabilities of the computer program for solving optimization problems. The ways of reducing the factor space of the modeled process are investigated. On the example of the analysis of big data of road traffic accidents (RTA) in England, all stages of interval data analysis are considered, including the tasks of structuring the information flow of data in order to obtain a digital table of input and output variables of the modeled process. Thus, the results of the work can be used for interval analysis of big data of similar applications.

5 Conclusions

The article proposes using an interval approach to solve the problem of big data analysis, in which LP methods are used in the study of dependences linear in parameters. Two methods of sequential reading of constraints and parallel computer computations are proposed for solving LP problems of large dimension. The optimality of the calculations is substantiated using the well-known technique of relaxation of constraints when solving optimization problems of large dimensions.

Computational experiments have shown the possibility of using applied interval analysis in practice. The research was carried out for model processes and for real data.

References

1. Müller, A., Guido, S.: Introduction to Machine Learning with Python: A Guide for Data Scientists. O'Reilly Media, Newton (2016)
2. Fan, T.-H., Lin, D.K.J., Cheng, K.-F.: Regression analysis for massive datasets. Data Knowl. Eng. **61**(3), 554–562 (2007). https://doi.org/10.1016/j.datak.2006.06.017
3. Adjout, M.R., Boufares, F.A.: Massively parallel processing for the multiple linear regression. In: Proceedings of International IEEE Conference on Signal-Image Technologies and Internet-Based System, Marrakech, Morocco, 27–27 November 2014, pp. 666–671 (2015). https://doi.org/10.1109/SITIS.2014.26
4. Frank, A., Fabregat-Traver, D., Bientinesi, P.: Large-scale linear regression: development of high-performance routines. Appl. Math. Comput. **275**, 411–421 (2016). https://doi.org/10.1016/j.amc.2015.11.078
5. Khine, K.L.L., Nyunt, T.T.S.: Predictive big data analytics using multiple linear regression model. In: Zin, T.T., Lin, J.-W. (eds.) ICBDL 2018. AISC, vol. 744, pp. 9–19. Springer, Singapore (2019). https://doi.org/10.1007/978-981-13-0869-7_2
6. Wang, K., Li, S.: Robust distributed modal regression for massive data. Comput. Stat. Data Anal. **160**, 107225 (2021). https://doi.org/10.1016/j.csda.2021.107225
7. Kantorovič, L.V.: Towards novel approaches to computational methods and the processing of observed phenomena (O nekotoryh novyh podhodah k vychislitel'nym metodam i obrabotke nabljudenij). Sib. Math. J. **3**, 701–709 (1962). (in Russian)
8. Milanese, M., Norton, J., Piet-Lahanier, H., Walter, E. (eds.): Bounding Approaches to System Identification. Plenum Press, New York (1996). https://doi.org/10.1007/978-1-4757-9545-5
9. Jaulin, L., Kieffer, M., Didrit, O., Walter, É.: Applied Interval Analysis. Springer, London (2001). https://doi.org/10.1007/978-1-4471-0249-6
10. Zhilin, S.I.: On fitting empirical data under interval error. Reliable Comput. **11**, 433–442 (2005). https://doi.org/10.1007/s11155-005-0050-3
11. Gutowski, M.W.: Interval experimental data fitting. In: Liu, J.P. (ed.) Focus on Numerical Analysis, pp. 27–70. Nova Science, New York (2006). https://doi.org/10.13140/2.1.5156.3520

12. Shary, S.P.: Maximum consistency method for data fitting under interval uncertainty. J. Global Optim. **66**(1), 111–126 (2015). https://doi.org/10.1007/s10898-015-0340-1
13. Shary, S.P.: Weak and strong compatibility in data fitting problems under interval uncertainty. Adv. Data Sci. Adapt. Anal. **12**(1), 2050002 (2020). https://doi.org/10.1142/S2424922X205 00023
14. Lasdon, L.S.: Optimization Theory of Large Systems. Collier-Macmillan, London (1970)
15. Geoffrion, A.: Reducing concave programs with some linear constraints. SIAM J. Appl. Math. **15**, 653–664 (1967)
16. Tsiaras, T.: UK road safety: traffic accidents and vehicles, detailed dataset of road accidents and involved vehicles in the UK (2005–2017) by Kaggle, ver. 3. https://www.kaggle.com/tsi aras/uk-road-safety-accidents-and-vehicles. Accessed 12 Feb 2021
17. UK Department for Transport: Road Safety Data. https://data.gov.uk/dataset/cb7ae6f0-4be6-4935-9277-47e5ce24a1 1f/road-safety-data. Accessed 12 Feb 2021
18. Oskorbin, N.M.: Computational technologies for the synthesis of decentralized control systems for multistage technological processes. J. Phys. Conf. Ser. **1615**, 012020 (2020). https://doi.org/10.1088/1742-6596/1615/1/012020

Parallel Computing in Problems of Classification of Teenagers Based on Analysis of Digital Traces

Vera Zhuravleva(✉) ⓘ, Anastasiya Manicheva ⓘ, and Denis Kozlov ⓘ

Altai State University, Lenin Avenue 61, 656049 Barnaul, Russia
vvzhuravleva@mc.asu.ru

Abstract. This paper considers a model for classifying high school students by digital traces obtained from the VKontakte social network. The classification is based on the belonging of social network users to communities, the number of which is about hundreds of thousands, which leads to the emergence of big data in the process of analysis. The problem of working with big data is solved by parallelizing computations. The classification model was developed with the aim of recovering information from digital traces of users of social networks. On the basis of the trained model, the identification of users of the VKontakte social network was carried out by place of residence (village or city of the Altai Territory) and age (9 or 11 grade) among teenagers with incomplete information on the grade and place of study in the digital traces. The best prediction accuracy for the trained model was of the order of 0.9. In the future, it is planned to build an extended classification model by including in the data sample of users of social networks of other age groups and to develop a support system for making managerial decisions for the university's admissions campaign.

Keywords: Digital trace · Social media · Gradient boosting · Machine learning · Hyperparameter optimization · Parallel computing · Big data analysis

1 Introduction

Using digital traces of the social networks users in various studies has gained a great popularity due to the development of big data analytics methods. The user data analysis and their interpretation in order to improve information impact are used in diverse studies: political, marketing, and others. For example, the article [1] describes the results of an analysis of the language and personality of Facebook volunteer users in the study of psychosocial processes and finding new connections. In [2], the results of marketing research show the existence of psychologically significant connections between the personalities of users, their preferences on websites, and the functions of the Facebook profile. The aim of the article [3] is to study and model the behavior of social network users based on personality indicators encrypted in Facebook profiles and actions, and a set of functions extracted from Facebook data. In [4], the development of smart recommendation systems for the social network Twitter is considered based on an approach that combines sentiment analysis and classification of tweets into various categories to

V. Jordan et al. (Eds.): HPCST 2021, CCIS 1526, pp. 210–220, 2022.
https://doi.org/10.1007/978-3-030-94141-3_17

highlight the topic that interests users. Articles [5] and [6] cover the experience of Tomsk State University in the search for promising applicants from social networks using big data analysis methods and modeling the educational profile of a student through digital traces on social networks. In [7] describes the application of machine learning methods in the career guidance of social network users and substantiates the importance of social networks in psychological research. Article [8] is devoted to assessing the capabilities of a social network to identify the psychological qualities and interests of high school students that are important for determining giftedness based on machine learning methods. In [9], the sentiment analysis of social media data is used to evaluate the quality of large-scale group decision-making, and then to dynamically determine the influence of experts from the statistical perspective. In [10], the relationship between the psychometric indicators of a user, which are poorly formalized, and his digital traces on social networking sites have been studied in order to create a digital twin of the user in social networks.

Within the framework of the big data analytics application, this article considers the digital traces of prospective university students on the VKontakte social media platform to identify the aptness signs in schoolchildren and to make a prediction model for their future field of study in order to invite them to join the recommended training program.

When processing the data from social networks, we face the problem of the incomplete information provided by the users (no indication of residency, age, educational institution, enrollment/graduation year, etc.). The users with such gaps stay under the radar, which results in a significant decrease in the number of prospective students.

The introduction of a unified state exam and the possibility to submit application documents to several universities (i.a. in the remote mode) boosted the competition among the universities for applicants with a high level of training and motivation. In this regard, regional universities faced the problem of retaining graduates of secondary and secondary vocational education institutions in the region and recruiting them to study in certain programs. This problem is especially acute for the natural sciences, engineering, physics and mathematics, where a significant increase in state-financed openings is planned in the upcoming years. These tasks can be solved by working with school leavers and vocational institution graduates, as well as by organizing early career counseling. Schoolchildren of non-graduation classes are involved in educational and career counseling activities of the university; highly motivated students are identified among them; their further guidance is provided.

Correspondingly, the purpose of the project was determined as the application of artificial intelligence technologies in developing support systems for management decision making during the university admission campaign. The project highlights a number of objectives related to the analysis of the teenagers' (residing in Altai Krai) digital traces on the VKontakte social network.

In particular, this article considers the following project objective: designing the algorithm to recover information in the digital trace of a social networks user and applying it to identify the groups of teenagers whose digital traces hold incomplete information. In the future, it is planned to use the results of the project to develop a marketing strategy of the university when building a plan for career counseling and recruiting activities.

The research presented in the article follows the works [11–13] dealing with the topic of classification and identification of social networks users by digital traces.

2 Data and Methods

2.1 Data Acquisition

Within the scope of the study, we collected the data on the VKontakte social network users living in Altai Krai that is actual for February 2020. Part of this data was analyzed in articles [11, 12].

Users were selected in the age range from 14 to 18 years old. It corresponds to the age of high school students: the 9th grade chooses further education at school or admission to vocational education, the 11th grade chooses between admission to vocational education and universities or refusal of further education.

The total number of the spotted users aged 14–18 was about 33 thousand. This comprises approximately 27% of the region's population of the corresponding age. In the resulting sample, the teenagers living in urban areas are most massively represented, which corresponds to the natural distribution by the place of residence.

In total, about 35% of the bulk data set comprised the users whose profiles contained partial information on the educational institution and the grade, or did not have such information at all. Another 10% of the sample could be attributed to "noise". Most of the sample lacks accurate information on the place of study and enrollment/graduation years, which leads to the problem of identifying schoolchildren groups by the grade and the place of residence (grades 9 and 11, village and city).

Data pre-processing revealed the following problem in tagging: the groups of 11th- and 9th-graders have cross cuts by age. Therefore, it was decided not to consider the group of 10th-grade teenagers separately, since the overlap in age and interests with Grades 9 and 11 is essential and the accuracy of their identification will be low.

As a result, we identified about 42% of all the spotted users (about 14 thousand teenagers) whose profiles contained the information allowing us to classify them into one of four groups: Group 1 – 9th grade, city; Group 2 – 9th grade, village; Group 3 – 11th grade, city; Group 4 – 11th grade, village. These data were used to compile a training and test samples, which were used in the model for classifying users by digital traces.

2.2 Data Processing Tools

By authors, the Python programming language was used for designing the algorithm to recover information in the digital trace of a social network's user. The following python libraries were mainly used: Pandas, NumPy, CatBoost, Matplotlib.

When building a classification model, the CatBoost machine learning method developed by Yandex for the Python language is used [14]. This method is based on gradient boosting of decision trees. The essence of boosting is to train each subsequent model and to reduce possible further errors, while using the data on the errors in the previous model [15, 16]. The CatBoost method was chosen for the reason that it allows classifying categorical data and setting classification hyperparameters.

One of the key stages in the development of a model for classifying social networks users by digital traces is compiling a matrix of the users' affiliation to various communities (in fact, the membership matrix can be classified as categorical). The filling of the matrix is based on the application of the data binarization function included in the programming language library. The use of this function becomes impossible in this study due to the very large order of the matrix, which depends on the number of communities and users. Namely, the number of communities reaches hundreds of thousands, while the number of users totals tens of thousands.

3 Parallel Computing Technologies in Big Data Analytics

The term "parallel", as applied to solving complex tasks, replaces the words "independent", "simultaneous" and indicates that parts of a complex task are performed independently of one another [17]. Parallel computing theory covers the issues related to creating parallelism resources in problem solving processes and ensuring its efficient implementation. The goal of any parallelism is to improve the efficiency of the computer work at various levels:

- at the level of tasks;
- at the level of data;
- at the level of algorithms;
- at the level of instructions;
- at the level of bits.

Parallel algorithms do not always demonstrate a higher degree of efficiency than sequential algorithms. Nevertheless, there are a great number of sample problems, the solution of which is significantly improved through the use of parallel computations [17].

With regard to the tasks of big data mining, we face the problems associated with great time as well as RAM expenditures. One of the ways to solve these problems is the use of parallel computing at different stages of data processing and analysis. Work [18] analyzes the efficiency of parallel computing application for processing large data arrays in various computing systems. In work [19], parallel computations are used to process data originated from different sources, then the outputs of each parallel are merged at subsequent stages using an aggregation mechanism. Work [20] considers parallel programming as one of the ways to improve the efficiency of training. Work [21] reveals various problems arising while storing and processing big data, and considers the available tools, technologies and algorithms, including parallel computing, for solving these problems. Work [22] studies the architecture of systems that includes parallel processing algorithms, which allows increasing the efficiency of the big data flow analysis.

In this study, the authors used the parallelism techniques at the levels of tasks and algorithms.

Parallelization of computations at the task level belongs to the parallel programming paradigm and involves breaking the task into subtasks – multithreading. This approach involves [17]:

- identification of the computations, whose implementation can be carried out parallelly, in the program;

- subsequent distribution of data by CPU local storage modules;
- subsequent coordination of computational parallelism and data distribution.

This article considers parallelism at the level of algorithms, which involves replacing sequential algorithms of some computations with the parallel ones. First of all, this concerns search and sorting algorithms.

The classification of the social network users by digital traces, based on the construction of a binary matrix of the users' affiliation/non-affiliation to specific communities, requires both a lot of time and RAM. Therefore, to reduce the order of the binary matrix, communities with few subscribers were excluded from consideration.

The filling of the binary matrix was carried out by means of parallel processing of the data stored in various files.

The algorithm scheme including parallelized steps is presented in Fig. 1.

The algorithm steps for classifying users by digital traces are defined as follows:

1. **Step 1**. Origination and pre-processing of the files containing the data with a specific group mark (with the known affiliation to the grade and residency: Group 1 – 9th grade, city; Group 2 – 9th grade, village; Group 3 – 11th grade, city; Group 4 – 11th grade, village).

   The application of parallelization of the data origination and pre-processing process made it possible to reduce the algorithm execution time.This resulted in obtaining the data files, whose number corresponds to the number of the specified groups ($N = 4$).

2. **Step 2.** Determination of the list of unique communities that characterize each group.

   In this step, the files of each group were processed parallely and independently of one another in order to identify unique communities, i.e. compiling a list of non-duplicate community identifiers.

3. **Step 3.** Determination of the unique communities' list common to all groups.

   In this step, the information obtained in the previous step is combined with the removal of duplicate identifiers.To reduce the order of the binary matrix constructed in Step 4, the communities, for which the number of subscribed users from the considered sample is less than 10, were excluded from the unique communities list.

4. **Step 4.** Data binarization.

   It this step, a binary matrix, whose values characterize the presence or absence (1/0) of the subscription to a unique community was filled. The matrix was filled parallely for the users of different groups.

5. **Step 5.** Creation of a common file with group marks and a common file with binary data.

   This step merges the information obtained in Steps 3 and 4.

6. **Step 6.** Partition of the data (obtained in Step 5) into training and test samples in a 3:1 ratio for the implementation while building and training a model of user classification by digital traces.

7. **Step 7.** Setting the model hyperparameters: the number of iterations, class weights, the tree depth.

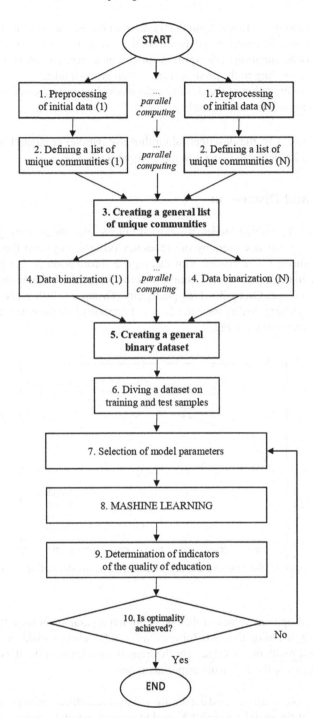

Fig. 1. The classification scheme of social network users by digital traces with parallel computations.

8. **Step 8.** Training the model from the training set by the CatBoost method.
9. **Step 9.** Prediction based on the data from the test sample of the user group marks.
10. **Step 10.** Determination of the training quality indicators (accuracy, completeness, f1-score) according to the predicted and actual group marks.
11. **Step 11.** Optimization of the classification model hyperparameters for the purpose of obtaining the best model quality.

Steps 1–2 and 4 of the described algorithm use parallel computations, with each parallel process implemented on a separate computing device.

4   Results and Discussion

On the basis of the trained model, we carried out the identification by groups of the VKontakte social network users by the residency (village, city) and the age (9th and 11th grades) among the teenagers with incomplete information on the grade and the place of study in the digital trace. Group 1 was the 9th grade, living in the city; Group 2 – 9th grade, village; Group 3 – 11th grade, city; Group 4 – 11th grade, village. The changes in the learning quality indicator f1-score depending on the number of iterations for four groups are shown in Fig. 2.

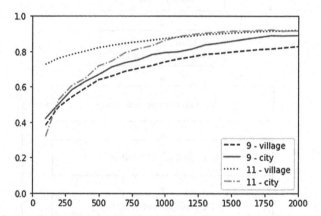

Fig. 2. The changes in the learning quality indicator f1-score depending on the number of iterations.

The selected optimal values of the algorithm hyperparameters were the following: max_depth = 2; learning_rate = 0.7; iterations = 2000; class_weights = [1,3,2,3]. As a result, the best prediction accuracy for the trained model was of the 0.9 order.

It is worth noting the following important points.

1. The authors previously carried out the algorithm of identification by groups of adolescent users of the social network VKontakte without parallel computing technology. At the same time, the available computational capabilities limited the volume of the

training sample. Consequently, the prediction accuracy for the trained model previously had a value of the order of 0.6–0.7. In the studies of other authors, for example [8], it is indicated that the problems of classifying users of social networks by digital footprints are solved using sequential calculations. Currently, no sources have been found indicating the use of parallel computing in classification tasks similar to that described in this article. On the one hand, this is due to the use of a limited amount of data in solving problems, on the other hand, to the availability of suitable computing power for researchers.

2. At step 4 of the identification algorithm, the list of unique communities did not include those communities for which the number of subscribed users from the training sample was less than 10. This additional requirement significantly reduced the dimension of the binary matrix of membership (users to social network communities), which was important to save working memory and did not lead to significant loss of information. The works of Feshchenko [8] and other authors noted the need to reduce the dimension of the data by excluding communities, which include several dozen users from the training sample. In that works, the large value of this restriction made it possible to more strongly limit the size of the community's binary membership matrix and perform computations without using parallel computations. However, the loss of information did not allow detecting some features of the structure of the studied data and reduced the quality of the trained model. This point is important when analyzing social media data for regions with a small number of adolescents. In addition, the "soft" restriction used in this study made it possible to more clearly divide users of social networks not only by age but also by type of residence.

3. The use of the CatBoost method in the data identification algorithm of social networks is also an important point and leads to a significant increase in prediction accuracy. For the problem considered here, the increase in accuracy was from 10% to 20% compared to the classification methods K-Nearest Neighbors, Support Vector Machines, Random Forest (provided that the technology of parallelization of computations is used).

Thus, the efficiency of using the technology of parallelization of computations in classification problems is undeniable and is associated with the possibility of training models on big data using "limited" computational capabilities.

5   Conclusions

The main result of this study is to increase the algorithm's efficiency for identifying users of social networks through the use of parallel computing technology at the stage of forming a binary matrix of community membership.

The authors also note that previously only the problem of classifying users of social networks by age was considered, and no sources were found that indicated the classification by age and type of residence at the same time. Such a comprehensive solution will allow for a more targeted formulation of strategies for events aimed at potential applicants of Altai State University. The constructed classification model can become the basis for developing a management decision support system in the recruiting activities of a university, and then its introduction into the university's information system in the form of, for example, a web service.

One of the problems that arose during the study and associated with the limited available computing power was solved by modifying the identification algorithm. The second problem associated with the presence of "noise" in the data is unavoidable. Nevertheless, the efficiency of the identification algorithm can be improved by increasing the training sample.

A significant increase in the amount of data in the future (due to the expansion of the study area and the age range of users, and the collection of user data over time) can be complicated. The reason for this is the presence of the original "closed" profiles and the possible transition of a large number of user profiles from "open" to "closed" status.

In the future, it is planned to expand and enrich the database of the target audience within the framework of career guidance and recruiting activities, namely: search in the VKontakte social network for digital traces of adolescents studying in grades 7–11 and secondary vocational education; additional training of the developed model, as well as the construction of an extended classification model; development and subsequent correction of the marketing strategy of the university (as a tool for managing the admission campaign) based on the results obtained.

Combining such a tool with monitoring the educational achievements of adolescents (for example, taking into account the results of participation in various Olympiads and conferences) can serve to create a comprehensive model for identifying factors that affect the educational achievements of a student.

The purpose of further research may be to develop a model for predicting the educational achievements of students based on the analysis of digital footprint data as a tool for finding talents and the development of a system of tutoring in universities and secondary educational institutions.

Acknowledgements. The authors express their sincere gratitude to:
– the head of the laboratory of computer teaching aids of Tomsk State University Feshchenko A.V. for help in collecting data, methodological assistance, and discussions,
– an anonymous reviewer for attention and valuable comments on this article.
The work was carried out as part of the implementation of the Program for the Support of Scientific and Pedagogical Workers of the Altai State University, the project "Development of tools for managing the admission campaign and the educational process of the university using artificial intelligence technologies through the analysis of digital traces of schoolchildren and students."

References

1. Schwartz, H.A., Eichstaedt, J.C., Kern, M.L., Dziurzynski, L., Ramones, S.M., Agrawal, M., et al: Personality, gender, and age in the language of social media: the open-vocabulary approach. PloS ONE **8**(9), e73791 (2013). https://doi.org/10.1371/journal.pone.0073791
2. Kosinski, M., Bachrach, Y., Kohli, P., Stillwell, D., Graepel, T.: Manifestations of user personality in website choice and behaviour on online social networks. Mach. Learn. **95**(3), 357–380 (2013). https://doi.org/10.1007/s10994-013-5415-y

3. Markovikj, D., Gievska, S., Kosinski M., Stillwell, D.: Mining Facebook data for predictive personality modeling. In: ICWSM, vol. 7(2), pp. 23–26 (2021)
4. Mangal, N., Niyogi, R., Milani, A.: Analysis of users' interest based on tweets. In: Gervasi, O., et al. (eds.) ICCSA 2016. LNCS, vol. 9790, pp. 12–23. Springer, Cham (2016). https://doi.org/10.1007/978-3-319-42092-9_2
5. Feshchenko, A., Goiko, V., Stepanenko, A.: Recruiting university entrants via social networks. In: Proceedings 9th International Conference on Education and New Learning Technologies EDULEARN17, 3–5 July 2017, Barcelona, Spain, pp. 6077–6082 (2017)
6. Feshenko, A.V., Gojko, V.L., Matsuta, V.V., Stepanenko, A.A., Kiselev, P.B.: Modelling of an educational profile of a student by analyzing public user data from social networks. In: Proceedings 12th International Technology, Education and Development Conference INTED2018, 5–7 March 2018, Valencia, pp. 640–646 (2018)
7. Kiselev, P., Matsuta, V., Feshchenko, A., Bogdanovskaia, I.M., Kosheleva, A.N., Kosheleva, A.: Career guidance based on machine learning: social networks in professional identity construction. Procedia Comput. Sci. **169**, 158–163 (2020)
8. Matcuta, V.V., Kiselev, P.B., Feshchenko, A.V., Gojko, V.L.: A study of the potential of social networks to identify gifted high school students. Psihologiya i Psihotekhnika **4**, 104–121 (2017) (in Russian). Doi: https://doi.org/10.7256/2454-0722.2017.4.24931
9. Wan, Q., Xu, X., Zhuang, J., Pan, B.: A sentiment analysis-based expert weight determination method for large-scale group decision-making driven by social media data. Expert Syst. Appl. **185**, 115629 (2021). Doi: https://doi.org/10.1016/j.eswa.2021.115629
10. Deevaa, I.: Computational personality prediction based on digital footprint of a social media user. Procedia Comput. Sci. **156**, 185–193 (2019). https://doi.org/10.1016/j.procs.2019.08.194
11. Zhuravleva, V.V., Manicheva, A.S., Feschenko, A.V., and Berestov, A.V.: Study of the distinguishability of digital traces in various groups of schoolchildren in the Altai Territory. High-Perfomance Comput. Syst. Technol. **4**(1), 121–125 (2020). (in Russian)
12. Zhuravleva, V.V., Manicheva, A.S., Feshchenko, A.V., Berestov, A.V.: Optimization of the algorithm for identifying digital traces of schoolchildren in the Altai Territory. J. Phys. Conf. Ser. **1615** (2020). https://doi.org/10.1088/1742-6596/1615/1/012013
13. Zhuravleva, V.V., Manicheva, A.S., Feschenko, A.V., Zhuravlev, E.V., Zhurenkov, O.V., Kozlov, D.Yu.: Examples of the use of machine learning for the development of management tools for the admission campaign and the educational process of the university. In: Proceedings of the International Conference on Advanced Learning Technologies EdCrunch-Tomsk, 2–4 December 2020, Tomsk, pp. 112–114 (2021). (in Russian)
14. Yandex: CatBoost library source code. https://github.com/catboost. Accessed 26 Aug 2021
15. Kaftannikov, I.L., Parasich, A.V.: Decision tree's features of application in classification problems. Bulletin of the South Ural State University Series "Computer Technologies, Automatic Control, Radioelectronics", **15**(3), 26–32 (2015). (in Russian). https://doi.org/10.14529/ctcr150304
16. Prokhorenkova, L., Gusev, G., Vorobev, A., Dorogush, A.V., Gulin, A.: CatBoost: unbiased boosting with categorical features. Adv. Neural. Inf. Process. Syst. **31**, 6638–6648 (2018)
17. Volosova, A.V.: Parallel methods and algorithms (Parallel'nye metody i algoritmy). MADI, Moscow (2020). (in Russian)
18. Rygovskiy, I.A.: Analysis of the effectiveness of methods for processing large data arrays using computer systems. Problemy informatiki **2**, 54–58 (2004). (in Russian)
19. Gupta, G., Katarya, R.: Research on understanding the effect of deep learning on user preferences. Arabian J. Sci. Eng. **46**(4), 3247–3286 (2020). https://doi.org/10.1007/s13369-020-05112-2

20. Guerrero-Higueras, A.M., Sanchez-Gonzalez, L., Conde-González, M.A., Castejón-Limas, M.: Facilitating the learning process in parallel computing by using instant messaging. J. Supercomput. **77**, 3899–3913 (2021). Doi: https://doi.org/10.1007/s11227-020-03416-6

21. Desarkar, A., Das, A.: Big-data analytics, machine learning algorithms and scalable/parallel/distributed algorithms. In: Bhatt, C., Dey, N., Ashour, A.S. (eds.) Internet of Things and Big Data Technologies for Next Generation Healthcare. SBD, vol. 23, pp. 159–197. Springer, Cham (2017). https://doi.org/10.1007/978-3-319-49736-5_8

22. Ahmad, A., Paul, A., Din, S., Rathore, M.M., Choi, G.S., Jeon, G.: Multilevel data processing using parallel algorithms for analyzing big data in high-performance computing. Int. J. Parallel Prog. **46**(3), 508–527 (2017). https://doi.org/10.1007/s10766-017-0498-x

Identification of Key Players in a Social Media Based on the Kendall-Wei Ranking

Alexander A. Yefremov[1]([⊠]) [iD] and Elena E. Luneva[2]

[1] Tomsk Polytechnic University, Lenin Avenue 30, 634050 Tomsk, Russia
alexyefremov@tpu.ru
[2] Tomsk State University of Control Systems and Radioelectronics,
Lenin Avenue 40, 634050 Tomsk, Russia

Abstract. The paper concerns studying the effectiveness of Kendall-Wei ranking procedure applied to the problem of identification of opinion leaders in social media. In order to achieve this, authors conducted both model data and real data experiments, using the original technique of constructing social graphs, and compared the sets of key players, obtained by the popular methods as well as by the procedure under consideration. The comparison results demonstrate that in some instances Kendall-Wei ranking procedure outperforms other methods of ranking nodes in a social graph, which plays a significant part in solving the problem of detecting major actors in social networks.

Keywords: Social graph · Key players · Distance-based methods · Ranking · Rank correlation

1 Introduction

It is impossible to picture the modern world without social networks with the number of their users increasing every year. Moreover, each user could join, and usually does, several social media platforms. Such a level of personal engagement in the process of virtual communication, combined with a modern man's habit of getting news from social media, attracts a lot of attention of advertisers, opinion research companies and government institutions.

Social network data analysis allows researchers to solve a broad spectrum of problems such as product/service demand forecasting [1] and public opinion monitoring [2]. In order to increase the scope of the analysis, it is necessary to determine a set of social network users, regarded as opinion leaders in a certain subject domain. In [3] such problem is referred to as Key Players Problem/Positive or KPP-Pos. It is generally agreed that the primary approach to solving KPP-Pos involves graph theory's distance-based methods, which take into account distances between vertices in a social graph [3–6]. Among such methods the entropy model, introduced by Shetty and Adlibi in [7], and Borgatti's measure, suggested in [3], is considered the most powerful.

It should be noted that aforementioned distance-based methods allow obtaining the desired results, provided that a social graph is unweighted and/or undirected. The

© Springer Nature Switzerland AG 2022
V. Jordan et al. (Eds.): HPCST 2021, CCIS 1526, pp. 221–237, 2022.
https://doi.org/10.1007/978-3-030-94141-3_18

representation of an actual group of social network users with models based on such graphs considerably reduces their adequacy, since they do not account for an additional information on user relationship.

This paper proposes the approach to the identification of the set of influential users based on Kendall-Wei ranking procedure (KWR), introduced by Wei in [8] and elaborated further by Kendall [9]. Since this technique was intended primarily for tournament analysis, it is commonly applied in the field of sport statistics [10].

The main objective of this paper is to demonstrate the applicability of KWR to the problem of identification of the most influential social network users considered as subject matter experts (SME). To achieve that we perform model and real data experiments and a comparative study of KWR with procedures based on the Entropy model and Borgatti's measure.

2   Kendall-Wei Ranking Procedure

Ranking players of a round-robin tournament is a well-known problem in the graph theory [11–13]. Its solution implies constructing a complete directed graph with n vertices, where n indicates the number of players. An arc directed from the vertex i to the vertex j indicates the i-th player's win over the j-th player. In such a case, the corresponding element a_{ij} of the tournament's adjacency matrix $\mathbf{A}$ equals one; otherwise $a_{ij} = 0$.

The sum of the elements in the i-th row

$$s_i^{\langle 1 \rangle} = \sum_{j=1}^{n} a_{ij}$$

coincides with the number of i-th player's wins within the tournament and, therefore, is the measure of his strength. The vector $\mathbf{S}^{\langle 1 \rangle}$ composed of the elements $s_i^{\langle 1 \rangle}$ can be referred to as a first-order strength vector.

When all entries of the vector $\mathbf{S}^{\langle 1 \rangle}$ are different, the ranking of the players is trivial. However, this problem could be rather challenging, provided that some players have an equal number of wins [14, 15].

The procedure of Kendall-Wei ranking involves iterative calculation of players' k-th order strengths with the following formula:

$$\mathbf{S}^{\langle k \rangle} = \mathbf{A} \cdot \mathbf{S}^{\langle k-1 \rangle},$$

where $k \geqslant 2$ is the iteration index, $\mathbf{A}$ is the adjacency matrix and $\mathbf{S}^{\langle j \rangle}$ is the j-th order strength vector. The iterative procedure continues until there are no ties in the ranking or the ranks remain unchanged for a predefined number of iterations.

The absolute values of k-th order strengths are often replaced with relative strengths σ_i defined as follows:

$$\sigma_i = \lim_{k \to \infty} \frac{s_i^{\langle k \rangle}}{\sum_{j=1}^{n} s_j^{\langle k \rangle}}.$$

As demonstrated in [16, 17], the vector $\boldsymbol{\sigma}$, comprised of elements σ_i, asymptotically converges to the normalized eigenvector of $\mathbf{A}$ corresponding to the spectral radius of the graph, i.e. to the largest absolute value of the adjacency matrix's eigenvalues [18]. Therefore, the KWR procedure could be reduced to the problem of computing eigenvalues and eigenvectors of a matrix.

Berge in [19] stated that this approach can be applied not only for tournaments but also for any directed graph and, in particular, for social graphs [20–22].

We define a social graph as $G = (V, E)$, where $V = \{v_i\}$ is a nonempty set of vertices and $E = \{e_{ij}\}$, $E \subseteq V^2$ is a set of arcs with $e_{ij} = (v_i, v_j)$ designating an arc directed from the vertex v_i to v_j $(i, j = 1, 2, ..., n)$. If G is weighted, the definition should be supplemented with a weight function $w: E \rightarrow (0, 1]$, which assigns weights $w_{ij} = w(e_{ij})$ to each directed arc e_{ij}.

In order to identify SME in a social network, we should construct a social graph $G = (V, E, w)$ where w_{ij} corresponds to the j-th user's level of interest in messages of the i-th user, as specified in [22]. Consequently, the weight matrix $\mathbf{W} = w(\mathbf{A})$ should be used instead of the adjacency matrix when performing the KWR procedure.

3 Experiments

3.1 Design of Model Experiment

Among the variety of approaches toward the identification of the most influential users (key players) of a social network, the distance-based methods, founded on evaluation of graph entropy and Borgatti's measure, are universally acclaimed. Specifically, the entropy model combines information theory with statistical techniques in order to obtain event-based graph entropy, while so-called distance-weighted reach, defined in [3], allows a set of key players to be identified. The application of these methods implies sequential reduction of vertices and edges in a graph, followed by recalculation of respective numerical values, thus resulting in a relatively high algorithmic complexity. The detailed description of these methods is provided in [23].

The objective of this study is to ascertain that the ability of the KWR procedure to identify the set of key players in a social graph is on par with those of other well-renowned methods. In order to achieve this goal, we suggest a comparison of rankings for the vertices of various kinds of graphs. Obviously, the main mathematical tools for such a task are Spearman's and Kendall's rank correlation coefficients.

In order to compare the rankings obtained by the KWR procedure with the ones by above-mentioned methods, we have generated a random unweighted 100-tournament T (a tournament with 100 vertices) and an unweighted directed graph G_1 with the same number of vertices. For the latter graph the probability that there is an arc directed from the vertex i to the vertex j was set at the value of $p = 0.075$, which yielded a weakly connected sparse graph with 762 arcs.

Lastly, each directed arc of G_1 was attributed with a random weight, drawn from beta distribution, defined by the following probability density function (pdf):

$$f(x) = \frac{x^{\alpha-1}(1-x)^{\beta-1}}{\int\limits_0^1 t^{\alpha-1}(1-t)^{\beta-1}dt}, \ x \in (0, \ 1).$$

To generate weights, the shape parameters α and β of beta distribution were set at $\alpha = \beta = 4$, which results in a pdf shown in Fig. 1.

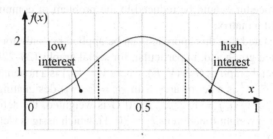

Fig. 1. Probability density function of beta distribution with $\alpha = \beta = 4$.

The weight w_{ij} of a directed arc a_{ij} represents j-th user's interest in i-th user's messages, with higher values of w_{ij} corresponding to the higher level of interest. This allowed us to obtain a weighted graph, G_2 which was also subjected to the comparative study.

It is worth mentioning that KWR offers the opportunity to account for loops in a graph, yet they do not affect the result of the ranking, provided that their weights are identical ($w_{ii} = w_{jj}$). When ranking players of a round-robin tournament with KWR, a loop w_{ii} could indicate a tie in a virtual game of the i-th player with himself. However, a loop in a social graph means that a certain user influenced his own opinion while reacting to his own messages. The absurdity of this assumption is obvious; therefore, loops were not allowed in the graphs generated for the experiment.

In order to conduct the experiment, we have developed a web application, using the C# and ASP.NET framework. The application allows generating random graphs (including directed and weighted ones) and implementing the key players' identification algorithms, covered in the study. Additionally, the Accord.NET framework library was used to implement numerical liner algebra algorithms for eigenvalues and eigenvectors computation. Considering this, the KWR algorithm is comprised of the following straightforward steps [10, 19]:

1. obtaining the vector **VL** of eigenvalues for a $n \times n$ weight matrix **W**:

$$VL \leftarrow eigenvalue(W);$$

2. finding the eigenvalue V_{max} with the maximal absolute magnitude:

$$V_{max} \leftarrow max(|VL_i|), \quad i \in 1..n;$$

3. obtaining the eigenvector **VC**, corresponding to V_{max}:

$$VC \leftarrow eigenvector(W, V_{max});$$

4. calculating the sum VC_{sum} of elements in **VC**:

$$VC_{sum} \leftarrow \sum VC_i, \quad i \in 1..n;$$

5. dividing the vector **VC** by VC_{sum} to obtain the vector σ of vertices' relative powers, expressed as numbers in an interval $[0, 1]$:

$$\sigma \leftarrow \frac{\mathbf{VC}}{VC_{sum}}.$$

Then, the vertices v_i of a graph should be ranked according to the corresponding values of.

Let us denote by **X** and **Y** the vectors, which contain the ranks x_i and y_i, calculated by two different methods for the i-th vertex of a certain graph G with n vertices ($i = 1, 2, ..., n$). Then, Spearman's rank correlation coefficient (or Spearman's rho) ρ, which measures the degree of correspondence between these two rankings, is obtained as:

$$\rho = 1 - \frac{6}{n(n^2 - 1)} \sum_{i=1}^{n} d_i^2, \tag{1}$$

where $d_i = x_i - y_i$ is the difference between ranks.

However, Eq. 1 is only applicable if all ranks are represented by distinct integers, i.e. there are no tied ranks produced by either of the ranking methods. If this is not the case, each member of a tied group is assigned with a midrank, and Eq. 1 must be modified as follows:

$$\rho = \frac{n(n^2 - 1) - 6\sum_{i=1}^{n} d_i^2 - \frac{1}{2}\left\{ \sum_{j=1}^{g} \left[t_j \left(t_j^2 - 1 \right) \right] + \sum_{k=1}^{h} \left[u_k \left(u_k^2 - 1 \right) \right] \right\}}{\left\{ \left[n(n^2 - 1) - \sum_{j=1}^{g} \left[t_j \left(t_j^2 - 1 \right) \right] \right] \left[n(n^2 - 1) - \sum_{k=1}^{h} \left[u_k \left(u_k^2 - 1 \right) \right] \right] \right\}^{1/2}}. \tag{2}$$

Here g and h denote the number of tied groups in rankings **X** and **Y**, respectively; t_j is the size of j-th tied group in **X**, and u_k is the size of k-th tied group in **Y**.

To check whether the obtained result is statistically significant, we need to perform the two-tailed test for independence, assuming the null hypothesis H_0: "rankings are independent". In order to do that, we should calculate the z-score as specified by [24]:

$$z = \rho\sqrt{n - 1}, \tag{3}$$

where ρ is obtained by Eq. 1 or Eq. 2, and n is a sample size. The null hypothesis is rejected when $z \geqslant z_c$. With the two-tailed test, the critical value z_c for the significance level α is equal to the quantile $z_{1-\alpha/2}$ of the standard normal distribution.

The reasoning behind the hypothesis testing with Kendall's rank correlation coefficient is quite similar. If there are no ties presented in the rankings, the coefficient, often referred to as Kendall's τ_a, is obtained by:

$$\tau_a = \frac{2(C - D)}{n(n - 1)}, \tag{4}$$

where C and D are the numbers of concordant and discordant pairs in the rankings [25].

Kendall's τ_b coefficient provides adjustment for ties and is defined as:

$$\tau_b = \frac{2(C - D)}{\left\{ \left[n(n-1) - \sum_{j=1}^{g} [t_j(t_j - 1)] \right] \left[n(n-1) - \sum_{k=1}^{h} [u_k(u_k - 1)] \right] \right\}^{1/2}}, \tag{5}$$

with the same notations as that in Eq. 2.

Statistical significance of the result is also determined by comparing the z-score, obtained in this case, as:

$$z = \frac{3\tau \sqrt{n(n-1)}}{\sqrt{2(2n+5)}}, \tag{6}$$

with the critical value z_c. The value of τ for Eq. 6 is obtained from Eq. 4 or Eq. 5.

3.2 Design of the Real Data Experiment

To estimate the feasibility of Kendall-Wei ranking for identification of key players in a real social network, authors acquired the data from Twitter marked with certain hashtag. Twitter was chosen as a social network for the study due to its popularity for expressing opinions in various subject areas, as well as convenient API interface and short maximum length of text messages, which could be relevant for the future studies as brief messages could increase the reliability of identification results.

At the first step of the experiment, the data on certain subject area were gathered using specified keyword or hashtag. The authors had chosen #westworld to collect opinions on the TV series of the same name. The data had been collected on June 25, 2018, the day of season 2 finale. Prior to the analysis, messages that were not commented or retweeted were excluded from consideration. As a result, 1022 unique messages (tweets) were selected, authored by 714 unique users.

Next, based on the collected data, the weighted social graph $G_{WW} = (V, E, w)$ was built according to the principles stated in Sect. 2. However, as opposed to the model experiments, the weights of directed arcs in G_{WW} were obtained by the interest function, generalized as follows:

$$w(a_{ij}) = f(r_{ij}, c_{ij}, m_{ij}, x_{ij}), \tag{7}$$

where $w(a_{ij})$ is the weight of an arc a_{ij} directed from the node i to the node j; r_{ij}, c_{ij}, m_{ij} and x_{ij} are, respectively, the numbers of reposts, comments, mentions and reposts with comments made by the j-th user with regard to the i-th user's posts. Therefore, the function $f(r_{ij}, c_{ij}, m_{ij}, x_{ij})$ reflects the measure of the j-th user's aggregate interest in the i-th user's messages. The exact analytic form of the interest function could be obtained with the analytic hierarchy process (AHP) as specified by [26].

According to AHP, we define the interest function as:

$$f(r_{ij}, c_{ij}, m_{ij}, x_{ij}) = a_r r_{ij} + a_c c_{ij} + a_m m_{ij} + a_x x_{ij}, \tag{8}$$

where a_r, a_c, a_m, a_x are the coefficients, indicating the significance (weight) of activity criteria of social network users. In order to evaluate these weights, each criterion should be assigned with the significance value, ranging from 1 to 9. Table 1 lists the proposed significance values which were used to build the pairwise comparison matrix and, subsequently, to calculate the criteria weight vector containing coefficients a_r, a_c, a_m, a_x, also presented in Table 1.

As a result of AHP the analytic form of Eq. 8 is as follows:

$$f\left(r_{ij}, c_{ij}, m_{ij}, x_{ij}\right) = 0.291r_{ij} + 0.208c_{ij} + 0.125m_{ij} + 0.375x_{ij}. \tag{9}$$

The weights obtained by Eq. 9 were subjected to min-max normalization and assigned to the directed arcs of the social graph G_{WW}.

Table 1. Data obtained by AHP.

User activity criterion	Significance value	Weight of criterion
Number of reposts – r	7	0.291
Number of comments – c	5	0.208
Number of mentions – m	3	0.125
Number of reposts with comments – x	9	0.375

The histogram depicted in Fig. 2 demonstrates that the weights in the real data social graph do not follow beta distribution shown in Fig. 1. This can be explained by the fact that data for the experiment were collected during the limited time span due to the restrictions of Twitter's Standard API.

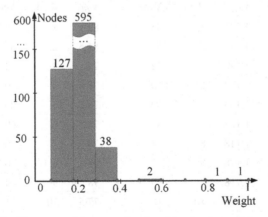

Fig. 2. The histogram of the normalized weights for the social graph G_{WW}.

Finally, the procedures of Kendall-Wei ranking and Borgatti's ranking were performed based on the obtained weight matrix of the social graph.

Similar to the model experiments with random data, the feasibility of Kendall-Wei ranking for the identification of key players in the real social graph should be tested with Spearman's rank correlation coefficient and Kendall's τ_b coefficient to determine whether the obtained results are statistically significant.

3.3 Results and Discussion

The vertices of the analyzed graphs were ranked in a descending order of their strengths obtained by the method of graph entropy (GE), Borgatti's measure (BG) and KWR procedure (KW). The results are presented in Tables 2, 3, 4 and 5 which specify 10 most influential vertices, according to these ranking procedures, along with their ranks and the numerical values of respective measures (V_{GE}, V_{BG} and V_{KW}). Please, note that the values of V_{KW} are expressed in percent as a matter of convenience.

For the sake of brevity, we have not listed rankings for all 100 vertices of the graphs under study, since for KPP-Pos problem it is sufficient to identify only top-ranked users. Naturally, the rank correlation coefficients, contained in Table 4, have been calculated for the entire graphs.

Table 2 demonstrates perfect agreement of the ranking results obtained by GE and BG for the 100-tournament T. In fact, these methods produce identical results for any unweighted tournament, thus confirming the same fundamental principle behind the distance-based methods. The results acquired by KWR differs slightly, although all three methods allowed us to identify the same unordered set of 10 most influential users.

Table 2. Top-ranked vertices of T according to different ranking methods.

Graph entropy			Borgatti's measure			Kendall-wei Ranking		
Rank	Vertex ID	V_{GE}	Rank	Vertex ID	V_{BG}	Rank	Vertex ID	V_{KW}
1	35	1.237	1	35	82	1	35	1.317
2	54	1.222	2	54	81.5	2	54	1.295
3	72	1.148	3	72	79	3	72	1.192
5	50	1.133	5	50	78.5	4	50	1.177
5	69	1.133	5	69	78.5	5	86	1.162
5	86	1.133	5	86	78.5	6	69	1.153
8	44	1.118	8	44	78	7	70	1.149
8	51	1.118	8	51	78	8	10	1.148
8	70	1.118	8	70	78	9	44	1.144
10	10	1.102	10	10	77.5	10	51	1.142

Figure 3 demonstrates almost complete linearity between the rankings obtained by BG and KW. The coordinates of each point in this plot are the ranks of a certain vertex. Distinguishable horizontal stripes of the datapoints indicate large number of tied groups in Borgatti's ranking. Since GE has produced the same result for the tournament as BG, the plot for the KW-GE pair is identical to Fig. 3.

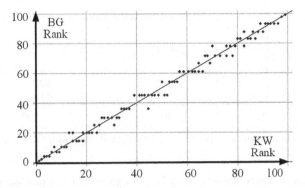

Fig. 3. Rank-rank plot for the vertices of the tournament using KW and BG methods.

Unlike tournaments, the unweighted directed graph G1 is quite sparse, which is more feasible for modelling actual social graphs. Table 3 contains 10 top-ranked vertices of G_1 found by different methods. Similar to the tournament, both GE and BG have identified the same unordered set of vertices, though their individual ranks might be different. The list of top 10 vertices, pinpointed by KWR procedure, contains only one vertex not presented in the sets of key players, specified by distance-based methods.

Table 3. Top-ranked vertices of G_1 according to different ranking methods.

Graph entropy			Borgatti's measure			Kendall-wei ranking		
Rank	Vertex ID	V_{GE}	Rank	Vertex ID	V_{BG}	Rank	Vertex ID	V_{KW}
1	65	1.699	1	65	52.833	1	65	1.953
2.5	69	1.613	2	29	52	2	69	1.796
2.5	98	1.613	3	69	51.333	3	29	1.757
4.5	29	1.526	4	98	51.25	4	98	1.709
4.5	42	1.526	5.5	42	50.667	5	73	1.673
7.5	3	1.436	5.5	73	50.667	6	34	1.602
7.5	34	1.436	7.5	3	50	7	42	1.592
7.5	73	1.436	7.5	34	50	8	72	1.535
7.5	93	1.436	9	72	49.667	9	83	1.483
10	72	1.344	10	93	49.5	10	3	1.478

Figures 4 and 5 show the rank comparison results for the KW-GE and KW-BG pairs, respectively. While demonstrating noticeable linearity, the plots are quite different.

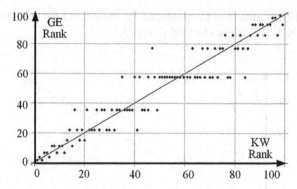

Fig. 4. Rank-rank plot for the vertices of the unweighted graph using KW and GE methods.

The prominent horizontal stripes in Fig. 4 signify that GE ranking have arranged most of the vertices into several tied groups. This feature can be useful when clustering users of a social network, though it complicates solving KPP-Pos. Figure 5 illustrates a general agreement between BG and KW methods in identifying the most and the least influential vertices in the social graph with considerable discrepancies in ranks for the middle-ranked ones.

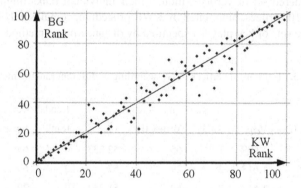

Fig. 5. Rank-rank plot for the vertices of the unweighted graph using KW and BG methods.

Table 4 contains rankings for the weighted directed graph G2.

Table 4. Top-ranked vertices of G_2 according to different ranking methods

Graph entropy			Borgatti's measure			Kendall-wei ranking		
Rank	Vertex ID	V_{GE}	Rank	Vertex ID	V_{BG}	Rank	Vertex ID	V_{KW}
1	65	1.702	1	65	28.948	1	65	2.059
2	98	1.671	2	73	28.874	2	73	1.889
3	42	1.623	3	94	28.373	3	29	1.887
4	69	1.595	4	29	28.359	4	34	1.755
5	29	1.549	5	42	28.031	5	69	1.74
6	93	1.543	6	93	27.844	6	94	1.703
7	34	1.533	7	34	27.743	7	98	1.669
8	73	1.526	8	69	27.557	8	42	1.657
9	3	1.52	9	98	27.415	9	93	1.604
10	26	1.37	10	22	27.076	10	3	1.509

As previously mentioned, weights of directed arrows in a social graph reflect interest of users in another users' messages. Hence, such graphs are even more appropriate for the social network modeling since they provide additional information on relations between its members. The data in Table 4 shows a high level of agreement between the results, obtained by all three methods. At least eight out of top 10 vertices, identified by either method, are also listed in other rankings.

The plots in Figs. 6 and 7 are quite similar. Even though the differences between ranks, obtained by KWR procedure and distance-based methods, are more conspicuous than in the previous case, these plots demonstrate an unmistakable linear tendency.

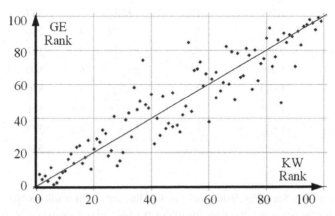

Fig. 6. Rank-rank plot for the vertices of the weighted graph using KW and GE methods.

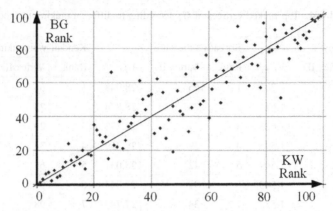

Fig. 7. Rank-rank plot for the vertices of the weighted graph using KW and BG methods.

The data in Table 5 shows a high level of the agreement between the results, obtained by all three methods. However, IE and BG methods demonstrate greater pairwise similarity in comparison with the IE-KW or BG-KW results. The authors propose that the KWR procedure allows the identification of hidden experts in a social network who could be undervalued by IE and BG methods.

Table 5. Top-ranked vertices of G_{WW} according to different ranking methods.

Graph entropy			Borgatti's measure			Kendall-wei ranking		
Rank	Vertex ID	V_{GE}	Rank	Vertex ID	V_{BG}	Rank	Vertex ID	V_{KW}
1	4	3.939	1	15	217.96	1	133	4.766
2	151	2.987	2	16	182.91	2	471	2.975
3	15	2.304	3	133	143.106	3	550	2.939
4	128	2.229	4	4	124.24	4	235	2.938
5	133	2.043	5	12	91.81	5	281	2.187
6	152	1.995	6	151	83.61	6	560	1.985
7	213	1.914	7	281	80.128	7	570	1.981
8	1	1.668	8	120	60.968	8.5	541	1.98
9	252	1.659	9	128	57.32	8.5	577	1.98
10	2	1.597	10	541	56.423	10	561	1.979

The plots in Fig. 8 and Fig. 9 demonstrate less linearity in the rank comparison results, as expected for the real-data. Even so, the majority of key players were correctly identified by all methods (bottom left part of the plots). However, there is some discrepancy between ranks of moderately influential users; more specifically, for several users their ranks, obtained by distance-based methods and KWR, differ substantially.

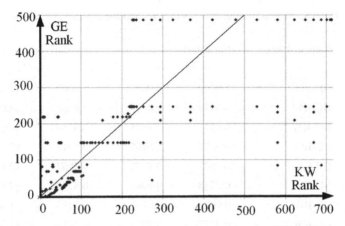

Fig. 8. Rank-rank plot for vertices of the real-data graph using KW and GE methods.

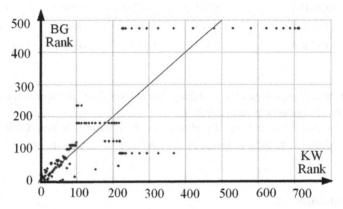

Fig. 9. Rank-rank plot for vertices of the real-data graph using KW and BG methods.

Another noticeable feature is that both plots contain prominent series of dots, forming horizontal lines, representing a large number of users having tied ranks according to GE or BG methods. It should be noted that ranking nodes of the social graph with KWR yields less tied-ranked groups, implying a better capability of KWR to differentiate users by their ranks.

In order to estimate the relevance of KW ranks and to confirm statistical significance of the obtained results, we have calculated the values of Spearman's and Kendall's rank correlation coefficients for each pair of ranking methods and performed two-tailed independence tests with the significance level $\alpha = 0.01$ (see Table 6).

The numerical values of the correlation coefficients and z-scores, presented in Table 6, have been obtained using PTC Mathcad software according to Eqs. 1–6.

Since the critical z-value for the significance level $\alpha = 0.01$ is $z_c = 2.5758$, z-scores z_S and z_K for both correlation coefficients are considerably greater than z_c. Therefore, we

Table 6. The rank correlation coefficients and corresponding z-scores.

Graph	Rank pairings	Spearman		Kendall	
		ρ	z_S	τ	z_K
T	GE-BG	1.0000	9.9499	1.0000	14.0839
	GE-KW	0.9942	9.8925	0.9554	14.0839
	BG-KW	0.9942	9.8925	0.9554	14.0839
G_1	GE-BG	0.9677	9.6285	0.8917	13.1456
	GE-KW	0.9523	9.4750	0.8557	12.6147
	BG-KW	0.9748	9.6988	0.8790	12.9586
G_2	GE-BG	0.9075	9.0291	0.7487	11.0373
	GE-KW	0.9272	9.2251	0.7731	11.3971
	BG-KW	0.9273	9.2267	0.7804	11.5038
G_{WW}	GE-BG	0.9265	24.7398	0.8469	33.8598
	GE-KW	0.7819	20.8794	0.6605	24.4097
	BG-KW	0.8179	21.8402	0.6881	27.5111

must reject the null hypothesis H_0: "rankings are independent" in favor of the alternative H_1: "there is a relation between rankings".

Within the context of the stated problem, it is highly unlikely that KWR have accidentally yielded results akin to those by the methods of graph entropy and Borgatti's measure.

4   Conclusions

When solving the problem of identification of opinion leaders, one may have to deal with a social graph, constructing as a result of data sampling in a particular subject area, that tally roughly 300 to 2000 nodes. Such relatively small amount of data obtained from social media provides sufficiently representative sample for assessing the sentiments of a certain audience with regard to the opinion of its leaders. Most social graphs, constructed by the authors from data searches on popular topics, demonstrate the features inherent to the class of scale-free networks [27]. Specifically, they have a small number of nodes with a high degree of connectivity, and, at the same time, a large number of small degree nodes. However, other characteristics of obtained graphs, such as an average shortest path, clustering coefficient, number of segments, graph diameter, etc. may vary significantly.

Another difficulty of KPP-Pos class problems, including the problem under consideration, resides in the fact that the problem-solving effectiveness depends largely on the appropriate choice of data analysis method, which can be complicated due to a significant variation of graph characteristics. To overcome this obstacle, one can transit from the graph structure towards the vector representation of each node by means of the graph embedding techniques, such as semi-supervised deep learning [28–30]. By doing so, the data, contained within the graph structure, can be transformed into a low-dimensional space, which makes it suitable for further processing with machine learning methods. Furthermore, since similar nodes in a social graph have similar spatial coordinates, it is possible to identify opinion leaders using cluster analysis. However, neural network-based graph embedding requires analyzed data to be at least partially labeled. Besides, some of the graph-to-vector transformation methods acquire a model by training a neural network on a particular graph, which make it unsuitable for any other graph. It should be noted that GraphSAGE algorithm [30, 31] does allow constructing a computational graph of a neural network for a specific class of social graphs. Even so, this stipulates a large training data set, and thereby makes the method efficient only when social media as a whole (e.g. Pinterest, YouTube, etc.) is considered as a social graph.

Authors believe that Kendall-Wei ranking, applied together with other efficient methods of subject matter expert identification, provides the versatile tool for a vector representation of graph nodes and allows applying further the machine learning methods, including data clustering. Therefore, such combination of methods should enhance the reliability of the results by exploiting the advantages of all the approaches involved as well as provide additional information on importance of social network users. For example, if a ranking method assigns high rank to a vertex not included at the top of other rankings, it could indicate the presence of a "hidden" opinion leader. If, in contrast, a vertex is ranked highly by several methods, it should solidify its position as a key player.

Summarizing the results of the study, it has been proven that the Kendall-Wei ranking procedure successfully solves KPP-Pos, demonstrating similar outcome in comparison with distance-based methods. Furthermore, since it is based on the well-known algorithm of eigenvalues computation, the software implementation of KWR is quite simple. In addition, it is worth noting that ranks of vertices in social graphs are less likely to be tied, when obtained by KWR. However, further studies are needed to compare the results of KWR and other methods in a case of disjointed graphs, or when data on the network structure is imperfect. Experiment analysis on data, selected from social networks for different subject areas, and study of the correlation between the obtained results and the users' level of interest should provide an additional outcome and better understanding of merits and flaws of the KWR procedure.

References

1. Dalal, M.K., Zaveri, M.A.: Opinion mining from online user reviews using fuzzy linguistic hedges. Appl. Comput. Intell. Soft Comput. **2014**, 735942 (2014). https://doi.org/10.1155/2014/735942
2. Bollen, J., Mao, H.N., Zeng, X.J.: Twitter mood predicts the stock market. J. Comput. Sci. **2**(1), 1–8 (2011). https://doi.org/10.1016/j.jocs.2010.12.007
3. Borgatti, S.P.: Identifying sets of key players in a social network. Comput. Math. Organ. Theory **12**(1), 21–34 (2006). https://doi.org/10.1007/s10588-006-7084-x
4. Diestel, R.: Graph Theory, 2nd edn. Springer, New York (2000). https://doi.org/10.1007/978-3-662-53622-3_12
5. Huang, B., Yu, G., Karimi, H.R.: The finding and dynamic detection of opinion leaders in social network. Math. Probl. Eng. **2014**, 328407 (2014). https://doi.org/10.1155/2014/328407

6. Ortiz-Arroyo, D.: Discovering sets of key players in social networks. In: Abraham, A., Hassanien, A.-E., Snáặel, V. (eds.) Computational Social Network Analysis. CCN, pp. 27–47. Springer, London (2010). https://doi.org/10.1007/978-1-84882-229-0_2

7. Shetty, J., Adibi, J.: Discovering important nodes through graph entropy the case of Enron email database. In: Proceedings of the 3rd International Workshop on Link Discovery (LinkKDD '05), pp. 74–81. ACM, New York (2005). https://doi.org/10.1145/1134271.1134282

8. Wei, T.-H.: The Algebraic Foundations of Ranking Theory. Ph.D. thesis, University of Cambridge, UK (1952)

9. Kendall, M.G.: Further contributions to the theory of paired comparisons. Biometrics 11(1), 43–62 (1955). https://doi.org/10.2307/3001479

10. Burk Jr., J.L.: Eigenspaces of tournament matrices. Ph.D. thesis, Washington State University, WA, USA (2012)

11. Boldi, P., Vigna, S.: Axioms for centrality. Internet Math. 10(3–4), 222–262 (2014). https://doi.org/10.1080/15427951.2013.865686

12. Gross, J.L., Yellen, J., Zhang, P. (eds.): Handbook of Graph Theory, 2nd edn. CRC Press, Boca Raton (2014)

13. Ray, S.S.: Graph Theory with Algorithms and its Applications. Springer India, New Dehli (2013). https://doi.org/10.1007/978-81-322-0750-4

14. Swamy, M.N.S., Thulasiraman, K.: Graphs, Networks, and Algorithms. Wiley, New York (1980)

15. Tutte, W.T.: Graph Theory. Addison-Wesley, Menlo Park (1984)

16. Harary, F.: Graph Theory. Addison-Wesley, Reading (1969)

17. Keener, J.P.: The Perron-Frobenius theorem and the ranking of football teams. SIAM Rev. 35(1), 80–93 (1993). https://doi.org/10.1137/1035004

18. Cvetković, D., Rowlinson, P., Simić, S.: Eigenspaces of Graphs. Cambridge University Press, Cambridge (1997). https://doi.org/10.1017/CBO9781139086547

19. Berge, C.: The Theory of Graphs and its Applications. Methuen, London (1962)

20. Kadushin, C.: Understanding Social Networks: Theories, Concepts, and Findings. Oxford University Press, Oxford (2012)

21. Lapenok, M.V., Patrusheva, O.M.: Identification of the user in various social networks by means of analysis of user social relationships and profile attributes (Identifikaciya polzovatelya v razlichnyh socialnyh setyah po sredstvam analiza socialnyh svyazej polzovate-lya i atributov profilya). Educ. Technol. Soc. 19(3), 584–594 (2016). (in Russian)

22. Veremyev, A., Prokopyev, O., Pasiliao, E.: Critical nodes for distance-based connectivity and related problems in graphs. Networks 66(3), 170–195 (2015). https://doi.org/10.1002/net.21622

23. Luneva, E.E., Yefremov, A.A., Kochegurova, E.A., Banokin, P.I., Zamyatina, V.S.: The comparison of identification methods of social network users regarded as subject-matter experts. Sistemy upravleniya i informacionnye tekhnologii. 70(4), 63–68 (2017). (in Russian)

24. Gibbons, J.D., Chakraborti, S.: Nonparametric Statistical Inference, 4th edn. Marcel Dekker, New York (2003)

25. Hollander, M., Wolfe, D.A.: Nonparametric Statistical Methods, 2nd edn. Wiley, New York (1999)

26. Saaty, T.L., Vargas, L.G.: Models, Methods, Concepts & Applications of the Analytic Hierarchy Process, Springer Science+Business Media, New York (2001)

27. Barabási, A.-L., Albert, R., Jeong, H.: Scale-free characteristics of random networks: the topology of the world-wide web. Phys. A 281(1), 69–77 (2000). https://doi.org/10.1016/S0378-4371(00)00018-2

28. Perozzi, B., Al-Rfou, R., Skiena, S.: DeepWalk: Online learning of social representations. In: Proceedings of the ACM SIGKDD International Conference on Knowledge Discovery and Data Mining, pp. 701–710. ACM, New York (2014). https://doi.org/10.1145/2623330.2623732

29. Grover, A., Leskovec, J.: Node2vec: scalable feature learning for networks. In: Proceedings of ACM SIGKDD International Conference on Knowledge Discovery and Data Mining, pp. 855–864. ACM, New York (2016). https://doi.org/10.1145/2939672.2939754

30. Hamilton, W.L., Ying, R., Leskovec, J.: Inductive representation learning on large graphs. In: Proceedings of 31st Annual Conference on Neural Information Processing Systems (NIPS 2017), pp. 1025–1035. ACM, New York (2017)

31. Ying, R., He R., Chen K., Eksombatchai P., Hamilton W.L., Leskovec Y.: Graph convolutional neural networks for web-scale recommender systems. In: Proceedings of the ACM SIGKDD International Conference on Knowledge Discovery and Data Mining, pp. 974–983. ACM, New York (2018). https://doi.org/10.1145/3219819.3219890

Using Time Series and New Information Technologies for Forecasting Sugarcane Production Indicators

Bruno Pissinato[1] , Carlos Eduardo de Freitas Vian[2] , Tatiana Bobrovskaya[3](✉) ,
Caroline Caetano da Silva[1], and Alex Guimarães Pereira[4]

[1] UNIMEP – Methodist University of Piracicaba, Highway Açúcar, KM 156, 13.423-170,
Piracicaba, Brazil
bruno.pissinato@unimep.br
[2] USP/ESALQ – Luiz de Queiroz College of Agriculture, University of Sao Paulo,
235 Avenue Pádua Dias, Agronomia, Piracicaba 13418-900, Brazil
cefvian@usp.br
[3] AltSU – Altai State University, Lenin Avenue, 61, 656049 Barnaul, Russia
[4] DBCU – Don Bosco Catholic University, 6000, Tamandaré Avenue, Jardim Seminário,
Campo Grande, Brazil
alex.pereira37@etec.sp.gov.br

Abstract. Sustainable development of the agricultural sector is an important role
in assuring the national security of any state. The article reveals the possibilities
of using the R program code for statistical processing and visualization of analysis results. The characteristics of the ARIMA model for forecasting agricultural
production are described in this article. An ARIMA model selection algorithm
is presented for a specific time series that describes the sugarcane production in
one state of the Federative Republic of Brazil. Data processing and visualization
of the main stages of the construction of the ARIMA model are coded in the
R language. The directions and advantages of the new information technologies
used in agriculture within the framework of the paradigm of the fourth industrial
revolution are shown in this article. The results of the study show that the forecast
using the ARIMA model can be successfully applied to time series that describe
agricultural production. The conclusions and results of this study can be used to
develop sustainable agricultural practices.

Keywords: Time series · ARIMA model · R language · Fourth industrial
revolution · Sugar cane production · Brazil

1 Introduction

The need to solve problems related to the cost of values in the future, based on retroactive
data, is typical of any economic sector. Agricultural production is becoming a guarantor
of food security while also being globally updated. Digital agribusiness is a characteristic
feature of the global economy in the framework of the fourth industrial revolution taking

© Springer Nature Switzerland AG 2022
V. Jordan et al. (Eds.): HPCST 2021, CCIS 1526, pp. 238–248, 2022.
https://doi.org/10.1007/978-3-030-94141-3_19

place today. Moreover, it is crucially important to use modern tools and methods of forecasting as the main indicator, as it characterizes agriculture development.

This study aims to investigate the state of the sugar cane industry in the state of São Paulo using the ARIMA model as a common method of time series forecasting. The toolkit was chosen for research considering: a) its sufficient flexibility, b) ample opportunities to describe a variety of time series characteristics. Based on the results obtained, other applications of new information technologies in sugarcane production are presented, including their possibilities within the framework of the paradigm of the fourth industrial revolution.

The statistical data processing and visualization of the analysis results were performed using the R software. The data basis of this research is from the municipal agricultural research, *Instituto de Geografia e Estatística do Brasil*, and the sugarcane harvest bulletin from *Companhia Nacional de Abastecimento (CONAB)*, including the authors' projections. The information about sugarcane production is presented in tons for the period from 1980 to 2020. The observation frequency is annual.

2 Problem Description

The dynamics of global demand for food and energy is increasing the pressure on commodities sectors, causing interest in production projections. Considering Brazil in this perspective, sugarcane production has an important role, because it allows the production of a wide range of products: from sugar to electricity and bioethanol. During the 1970s oil crisis, considering sugarcane as an alternative energy source, the Brazilian government established the "Programa Nacional do Proálcool" (Proálcool) to increase industrial alcohol fuel production. This brought together research centers, universities, factories, distilleries, and sugarcane plantations [1].

This agro-industrial complex organization, matching the agricultural production and the industrial processing, requires accuracy of information along the entire production chain. Figure 1 shows a sizeable increase in sugarcane production, with some stability during the last periods. However, it is not clear whether production will decrease, increase, or maintain a stable level in the future. To better predict this, an R software was used based on packages which include this traditional methods in time series analysis: Box and Jenkins [2] method, Box, Jenkins and Reinsel [3]. This classic approach combines theory and empirical evidence interacting with the researcher. Discussions about seasonality, unit roots, linearity, and trends are presented by Hamilton [4], Chatfield [5], and Enders [6].

According to the classic methodology of Box-Jenkins, the specified algorithm for the ARIMA model (p, d, q) follows the steps below:

1. Recognizing the model includes choosing the template that best corresponds to the process under study, in other words, firstly parameter d is determined, secondly – parameters p and q are determined. In this case, using the logarithm, built of stationary series, from this we determined the order of integration for the d parameter. The ARIMA parameters (p, q) are adjusted to the time series received using autocorrelation functions (ACF) and partial autocorrelation function (PACF).

2. Estimating the model, as long as we know the parameters (p, d, q). At the same time, the seasonality factor is also assessed by the Kruskal-Wallis.
3. The test of the model built for residues includes an analysis of the basic prerequisites for the application of regression analysis methods; use of unitary root tests Dickey-Fuller, ADF; diagnosis of the model from the point of view of its adequacy through tests of normality of residues, the autocorrelation of residues, and constant variances of random residues.
4. Using the template to predict the development indicators from the sugarcane industry. Figure 1 shows the dynamic sugarcane production in tons since 1980 and clearly demonstrates the variability that increases with time, which requires logarithms.

3 Time Series Analysis with Linear Regression in R

3.1 Time Series Application for Sugar Cane

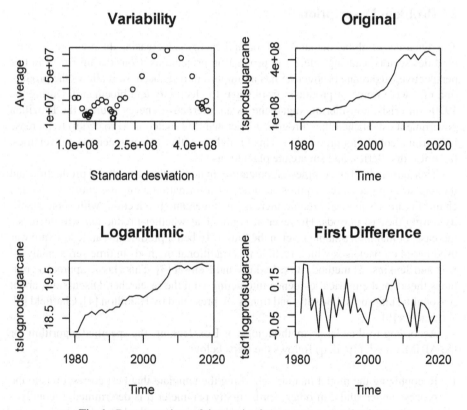

Fig. 1. Representations of time series from sugarcane production.

Figure 1 shows that the variability of the series increases over time for the original series. This behavior reveals the need or the best adequacy of the logarithmic transformation for the continuity of the analysis. When performing the logarithmic transformation, the coefficient of variation from the original time series 0.51 decreases to 0.02, reinforcing the potential decline of variability in this process.

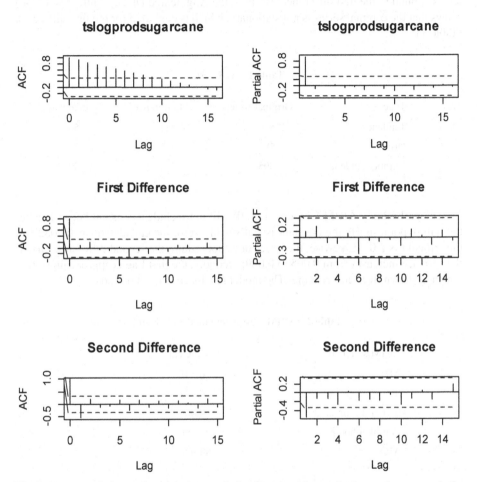

Fig. 2. Autocorrelation and partial autocorrelation functions. Legend: tslogprodsucarcane is the logarithm of the original sugarcane production dataset time series.

The Kruskal-Wallis test was used to verify the series seasonality. At the same time, the evidence of seasonality was rejected, because the value of the parameter p was 0.4699. The next step was the presentation of the autocorrelations and partial autocorrelations of sugarcane production (Fig. 2).

Observing the partial original series autocorrelation, it was concluded that the model AR (1) is necessary, considering the value of the first lag. The behavior of the original series autocorrelation function and the rapid decrease in the second phase show the

MA (0) process. As stated by Morettin, Toloi [7], the general aspect of autocorrelation suggests an ARIMA model preliminary 1, 1, 0. Based on these results, model root tests are performed. Stationarity tests are part of the necessity for the treatment of time series. The Dickey-Fuller test shows a p-value of 0.2778 for the logarithmic series, which means that the null hypothesis of series stationarity is rejected. This fact is not verified when the test is applied to the first difference. Besides, the Augmented Dickey-Fuller test (ADF) shows that the original series is not stationary, which is corrected for the first difference (Table 1).

Table 1. ADF test.

Test	Type	Original series	1ª Difference	Critical value
ADF	Tendency	−2.590	−4.921	−3.450
	Drift	−2.585	−4.947	−2.890
	Without tendency	−0.095	−3.572	−1.950

The preliminary ARIMA model (1, 1, 0) will not include a constant because under the null hypothesis H_0 the constant is statistically zero, the calculated t is 0.4082 and the critical t is 2.02. Likewise, the series does not require the second difference: firstly, the variance increases from 0.005 to 0.009; secondly, the first Lag is approaching − 0.5, which is shown over differencing. The model results are shown in Table 2.

Table 2. ARIMA estimated model (1, 1, 0).

ARIMA (1,1,0)	Coefficients
AR1	0.348
S.e.	0.147
Sigma^2 estimated	0.006
Log likelihood	43.980
AIC	−83.970

For the estimated process variable AR1, the p-value is 0.018. This rejects the H_0 of nullity of the coefficient, which is a significant factor. The diagnosis of the model is identified in Fig. 3.

3.2 Results and Analysis

Production stability with small deviations is a strong trend with the possibility of increasing or decreasing: the light gray area with 95% of probability and the dark gray area with a confidence interval of 80%. The Ljung-Box test assumes a null hypothesis of H_0

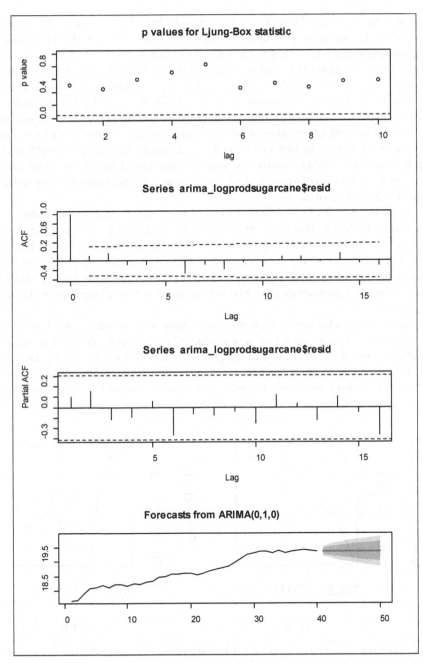

Fig. 3. Diagnosis of the estimated model ARIMA (1, 1, 0). Legend: Series arima_logprodsugarca$resid and Series arima_logprodsugarcane$resid are the autocorrelation (ACF) and partial autocorrelation (PACF) of residues. The authors used the functions auto.arima and compara_sarima, which identified the model automatically. The result was a model ARIMA (0, 1, 0), strengthening production stability. However, it was discarded due to the significance of the coefficient AR (1). (Color figure online)

of white noise for waste. There is no rejection of the hypothesis, as the analysis shows the value of the parameter p being bigger than $\alpha = 0.05$ relative to the model and in Fig. 3 there is stability according to the white noise hypothesis.

The autocorrelation (ACF) and partial autocorrelation (PACF) of residues represent a relatively satisfactory control for model Lags below the confidence interval (the dashed lines). In the production, the forecast for future periods shows a blue line and possible variations in the colored area. Preliminary stability is observed in sugarcane production. The evidence of production stabilization is climatic and financial, but with factors, such as the large-scale introduction of mechanized sugarcane harvesting. Harvesting this crop by mechanized means results in damage to the stem, reducing the useful life of the plantations from 5 to 2 years, and the burnt straw from the traditional crop reduces phytopathological problems [8].

The justification used for the introduction of mechanized sugarcane harvesting was associated with the fact that the manual harvesting involved the burning of the plantation and later cutting the plants by hand. Many discussions have been raised about the environmental and social impacts of this traditional form of harvesting. Mechanized harvesting has an advantage in this context, in that it does not burn the sugarcane plantation, thus releasing less greenhouse gas emissions, in addition to resulting improvements in air quality.

Figure 4 shows changes in mechanized harvesting of sugar cane in the State of São Paulo and the corresponding behavior of productivity. There is a substantial increase in the introduction of mechanization in the period from 2008 to 2011. During the same period, productivity begins to decline and then stabilize at a new level below previous periods. It is worth mentioning the occurrence of some climatic problems that contributed to the decline in sugarcane production in the period.

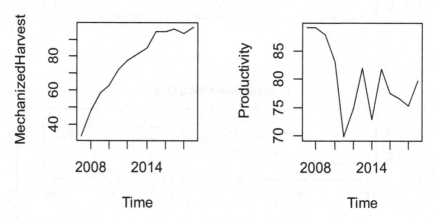

Fig. 4. Evolution of harvest mechanization (%) and productivity, tons per hectare between 2007 and 2019.

To better understand the recent period of sugarcane production between 2010 and 2019, the Zivot and Andrews Structural Break Test (1992) and the Wilcoxon Sign Post

Test were performed. The Structural Break Test in Fig. 5 shows the presence of a break-point for the year 2006. For the intercept modality, we see a new level where production began to stabilize. The same test when done in the "trend" modality does not indicate a break. This can be explained by the production levels continuing to rise until 2014, yet also with of periods of decline, especially after this year.

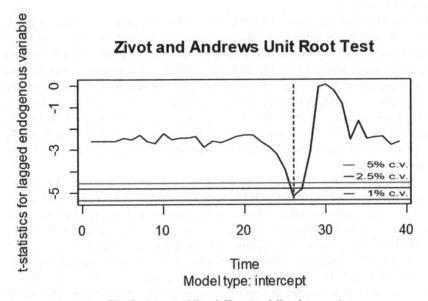

Fig. 5. Structural Break Test (modality: intercept).

The last decade is demonstrated within the Wilcoxon Sign Post Test, comparing the production media between 2010–2014 and 2015–2019. The p-value found was 0.3125, which means that the null hypothesis has no differences between periods and is not rejected, reinforcing the forecast at work.

3.3 Prospects and Discussion

The fourth industrial revolution meant that not only econometric methods, but also artificial intelligence, have an important role in organizing sugarcane production. In this area of information technology associated with development and usage in agriculture, there are tools, such as drones, RFID (Radio-Frequency Identification) technology, integrated control systems, connected mobile devices, etc. These technologies allow recognition, information gathering, and even control of the different phases of agricultural creation.

Artificial intelligence is an exceptional territory for data analysis through algorithms that determine procedures suitable for cultural treatments in plantations. These include enhancement of water system, application of pesticides and herbicides, improvement of form for planting processes, and monitoring of sugar cane agriculture [9]. Machine-learning algorithms include used programming languages, given the type of information, the capacity to naturally assess and enhance measures, and in the case of sugarcane, despite the great development of new technologies, the use of drones is relatively limited [10].

In addition to the R programming language, other technologies allow working with planting data, climatic conditions, pest and soil conditions, etc., such as Phyton and Seaborn, drawing on ideas, such as Machine Learning, Deep Learning, Cyber Physical System, and so on [11].

The RFID (Radio Frequency Identification) technology is a radio frequency data capture system that uses smart tags. Simultaneously, the design utilizes a microchip to store data that is used by sensors. Information is transmitted off the control framework through high-speed wireless [12, 13]. The use of RFID technology in agricultural and industrial equipment in the sugar and alcohol sector, interconnected to management systems applied to mobile devices, are tools that enable real monitoring of each process, as in field information, logistics, and industrial processes in this sector [13, 14]. An interesting case described by Wang et al. [14] studying a farm in Australia shows the need for automated water system frameworks, for the reconciliation of it with online web instruments.

While dissecting the information, at every moment in the question of decision-making, what should be cultivated is clearly seen. This leads to greater gains in the entire process, as it generates: reduction of losses of raw material and final product during the processes; the agility of operations; improvement in data reliability; promote the correct use of production equipment; thus minimizing costs, and leading to an increase in profits and product quality concerning productions developed using only mechanical processes. Li Biqing, Miao, and Shiyong [15] claim that RFID is essential because it can integrate climate data, Co2, plant height, and growth with other new technologies. This reality creates a potential for new applications, as stated by Leon et al. [16], who used artificial Neural Networks for the treatment of sugarcane effluents. Additionally, Pivoto et al. [17], when investigating the state of these informational technologies in Brazil, reports the emergence of the combination between the sugarcane harvests and the data industry.

4 Conclusions

The use of time series models is one of the modern methods of forecasting economic indicators, including agriculture. This study allowed the construction of an ARIMA model for a specific time series describing the production of sugarcane. The use of this model has several features in contrast to an estimate based on other models (multiple regression, etc.). The content generation process for this model is first a specification of the ARIMA model (p, d, q) according to the properties of the time series, and second – the estimation of the parameters equation model, as well as the variance of the residuals using statistical methods. The correct specification of the model largely determines the properties of the regression coefficient estimates.

The authors show the capabilities of the R software to process statistical data and view the results of the analysis. The functions auto.arima e compara sarima in R, which simulates probabilistic models, resulted in the ARIMA model 0, 1, 0, which means that production is preserved in future periods. However, a computational model was chosen: a) autocorrelation in the model identification process, b) the peculiarities of sugarcane cultivation in plantations. The estimated ARIMA model 1, 1, 0 shows the forecast that sugar cane production will continue in the state of São Paulo into future periods. The effects of using mechanized harvesting suggest a decrease in productivity, which did suffer a reduction in the recent period, which in general terms explains the maintenance of the productive situation. The general conclusion: the ARIMA modeling process can be successfully applied in time series that describe the production of other agricultural products. The study also identifies machine-learning areas in technology that are fundamentally changing approaches to sugarcane production.

References

1. Vian, C.E.F., Baricelo, L.G.: Sugar cane evolution in São Paulo State: perspectives (Evolução da Cana-de-Açúcar no Estado de São Paulo: Desafios e Perspectivas). In: 57th SOBER Congress, Ilhéus, BA, Brazil, 21–25 July 2019 (2019). https://www.researchgate.net/publication/336262557_evolucao_da_cana-de/acucar_no_estado_de_sao_paulo_desafios_e_perspectivas.pdf. Accessed 06 May 2021. (in Portuguese)
2. Box, G.E.P., Jenkins, G.M.: Time Series Analysis: Forecasting and Control, 2nd edn. Holden-Day, San Francisco (1976)
3. Box, G.E.P., Jenkins, G.M., Reinsel, G.: Time Series Analysis: Forecasting and Control, 3rd edn. Prentice Hall, Englewood Cliffs (1994)
4. Hamilton, J.D.: Time Series Analysis, pp. 43–117. Princeton University Press, Princeton (1994)
5. Chatfield, C.: Time-Series Forecasting, 1st edn., pp. 44–73. Chapman & Hall/CRC, New York (2000)
6. Enders, W.: Applied Econometric Time Series, 4th edn., pp. 44–255. Wiley, New York (2014)
7. Morettin, P.A., Toloi, C.M.C.: Time Series Analysis (Análise de Séries Temporais), 2nd edn. Edgar Blucher, Sao Paulo (2006). (in Portuguese)
8. Baccarin, J.G.: Environmental, social and economic effects of recent technological changes in sugarcane in the state of Sao Paulo Brazil (Efeitos Ambientais, Sociais E Econômicos De Mudanças Tecnológicas Recentes Na Cana-De-Açúcar No Estado De São Paulo, Brasil). J. Geogr. Work **20**(3), 141–173 (2019). (in Portuguese)
9. Tanha, T., Shah, M.: Implementation of artificial intelligence in agriculture for optimization of irrigation and application of pesticides and herbicides. Artif. Intell. Agric. **4**, 58–73 (2020). https://doi.org/10.1016/j.aiia.2020.04.002
10. Maldaner, L.F., Molin, J.P.: Predicting the sugarcane yield in real-time by harvester engine parameters and machine learning approaches. Comput. Eletron. Agric. **181**, 105945 (2021). https://doi.org/10.1016/j.compag.2020.105945
11. Raykumar, M., et al.: Artificial intelligence and agriculture 5.0. Int. J. Recent Technol. Eng. (IJRTE) **8**(2), 1870–1877 (2019)
12. Valente, F.J., Colenci, N.A.: Internet of things in advanced manufacturing: case of the production of sugarcane seedlings (Internet das Coisas na Manufatura Avançada: Caso da Produção de Mudas de Cana de Açúcar). In: Proceedings of 37th Meeting of Production Engineering, Joinville, SC, Brazil, 10–13 October 2017. http://www.abepro.org.br/biblioteca/TN_STO_238_379_32741.pdf. Accessed 02 May 2021. (in Portuguese)
13. Silva, R.F., Kawano, B.R., Mare, R.M., Cugnasca, C.E.: Refined sugar traceability in the domestic market: elaboration of a model using RFID technologies and wireless sensor networks (Rastreabilidade de açúcar refinado no mercado interno: elaboração de ummodelo utilizando as tecnologias de RFID e redes de sensores sem fio). In: 10th Brazilian Congress of

Agro Informatics – XSBIAGRO, 21–23 October 2015. http://eventos.uepg.br/sbiagro/2015/anais/SBIAgro2015/pdf_resumos/10/10_roberto_fray_da_silva_111.pdf. Accessed 02 May 2021

14. Wang, E., et al.: Development of a closed-loop irrigation system for sugarcane farms using the internet of things. Comput. Eletron. Agric. **172**, 105376 (2020). https://doi.org/10.1016/j.compag.2020.105376

15. Li, B., Ling, Y., Tian, M., Shiyong, Z.: Design and implementation of sugarcane growth monitoring system based on RFID and ZigBee. Int. J. Online Eng. (IJOE) **14**(3) (2018). https://doi.org/10.3991/ijoe.v14i03.8413

16. Leon, V.B., Negreiros, B.A.F., Brusamarello, C.Z., Petrolli, G., Domenico, M., Souza, F.B.: Artificial neural network for prediction of color adsorption from an industrial textile effluent using modified sugarcane bagasse: characterization, kinetics and isotherm studies. Environ. Nanotechnol. Monit. Manag. **14**(12), 100387 (2020). https://doi.org/10.1016/j.enmm.2020.100387

17. Pivoto, D., Barliam, B., Waquil, P.D., Foguesatto, C.R.: Factors influencing the adoption of smart farming by Brazilian grain farms. Int. Food Agribusiness Manag. Rev. **22**(4), 571–588 (2019). https://doi.org/10.22434/IFAMR2018.0086

Software and Methodology for the Design of System Dynamics Models Based on the Situation-Activity Approach

Aleksey Sorokin$^{(\boxtimes)}$ [ID], Elena Brazhnikova, and Liliya Zheleznyak

MIREA – Russian Technological University, Vernadsky Avenue 78, 119454 Moscow, Russia
sorokin_a@mirea.ru

Abstract. An original approach to the system dynamics models' design as a projection of situation-activity analysis, expanding the possibilities of predictive-analytical research, is proposed for consideration. System dynamics models in this aspect are applied to human reasoning with the reference to the specific objects of activity. This makes it possible to establish the specified criteria for assessing the state and trajectory of the development of the system being modeled. This article proves the hypothesis that methods of knowledge representation in situational, expert and system dynamics models are similar. At the same time, the conceptual structures of situation-activity analysis incorporate the tools inherent in the system dynamics language. Conceptual structures are the core of the design of system dynamics models in notations: levels and flows. The result of the situation-activity design is a model represented in a conceptual language of knowledge representation, where the basic element is the act of doing. The conceptual structures of activity acts can be used to build production rules for the expert system. However, it is possible to extract partial representations from the conceptual structures of activity acts: process plans and regularities. On the aggregate of these plans, a graphical image for building system dynamics models is implemented. The knowledge of the fact that constructing conceptual structures is very challenging sparked off different searches for the best way to deal with this problem. Eventually the best solution has become a software toolkit "Designer + Solver + Interpreter which allows one to visualize conceptual structures, implement knowledge bases for expert and system dynamics models, as well as to conduct research on completeness and adequacy of the model.

Keywords: System dynamics model · Conceptual structure · Situation-activity approach

1 Introduction

Each and every one activity that is a part of a dynamically complex environment has a number of properties such as activity and the freedom to choose its state. In addition to the freedom of choice, the elements of activity (acts) have their own requirements for the product, i.e. the choice of state is made purposefully. This creates a situation where the

© Springer Nature Switzerland AG 2022
V. Jordan et al. (Eds.): HPCST 2021, CCIS 1526, pp. 249–262, 2022.
https://doi.org/10.1007/978-3-030-94141-3_20

controlled objects seek to select their states that are the best in terms of their preferences for given values of the control actions. The control actions, in turn, depend on the states of the controlled objects. These conditions create uncertainty in the dynamics of the process due to the complexity of the environment. This inevitably leads to a simplified perception of reality and the manager gets emotional while solving a problem [1, 2].

It is known that problematic situations in decision-making are resolved by the following algorithm: if it is impossible to identify certain patterns in a system object behavior, then a hypothesis of its behavior is put forward. On its basis, simulation models are created. They help to investigate possible solutions.

Simulation models are subdivided into several types: system dynamics model, discrete-event model, and agent-based model. System dynamics models operate with time-continuous processes (states), while the discrete-event model and the agent-based model operate with discrete states. Transitions from one state to another in discrete modeling are considered instantaneous. Meanwhile, the important part of these two types of processes is that they can be presented in real systems, for example, the model of the development of an infectious disease. The appearance of a group of infected people in an agglomeration is considered as a discrete event, and the dynamics of the epidemic's development is described by a set of differential equations, i.e. is continuous [3, 4].

The discrete event model is constructed from standard functional blocks, defined by the average level of abstraction and implemented on the methodology of the structural approach SADT (structured analysis and design technique) or IDEF0 (ICAM Definition). Agent modeling supports all levels of abstraction and is defined by the Unified Modeling Language (UML) state and activity diagrams.

There is a direction in imitation modeling that maintains a high level of abstraction – system dynamics. In dynamic modeling, processes occurring in the real world are represented in terms of levels, the flows between these levels and the information determining the magnitude of these flows. The formal basis for this type of modeling is the flow rate equations that use the concept of dynamic processes in the state space. An important concept in establishing the structure of system dynamics is the idea that all changes are caused by "feedback loops". Therefore, specialists in the field of simulation modeling have developed a toolkit for cause-effect diagrams taking into account the feedback effect. This graphical representation is essentially a mental map reflecting the relation between the individual elements of the system, as between cause and effect. The connection can be positive, when a change in the cause causes a similar change in the effect, and negative – a change in the cause entails the opposite change in the effect. Therefore, the success of the model directly depends on the correct understanding of the role of cause-and-effect relationships, which are difficult to determine without conceptual research [5].

It must be noted that the methods of knowledge representation in situational and expert systems are similar [6, 7]. At the same time, simulation models are actively used in situational modeling, therefore, a situational design language should include some tools inherent in modeling languages [8].

2 Materials and Methods

The methodology for constructing system dynamics models includes qualitative and quantitative stages. The qualitative stage examines the structure of the problem and the way one element of the system depends on another. At the quantitative stage, in the course of a computer simulation, the researcher determines how correct his model is and tests his hypotheses about the system behavior.

The basic construct of the qualitative stage is the representation of the process under study in the form of a diagram consisting of positive loops (a change in the cause causes a similar change in the effect) and negative feedback (a change in the cause causes the opposite change in the effect). The polarity of the bond is indicated by the "+" or "–" sign next to the corresponding arrow (see Fig. 1).

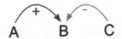

Fig. 1. Communication polarity designation.

At the same time, two serially connected negative links ultimately form a positive link. Causal relationships can form closed unidirectional loops, that is, positive or negative feedback loops. For example, in loop 1 of positive feedback (the polarity of the loop is indicated by a "+" in brackets within the loop), a growth in X results in a reduction in Y which results in an increase in Z, since the Y → Z relationship is negative, and an increase in Z causes a further increase X (see Fig. 2). In circuit 2, an increase in A causes a decrease in B. A decrease in B causes a decrease in C, since they are positively linked, in which a decrease in cause B entails a similar change in effect C [5].

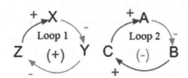

Fig. 2. Positive and negative feedback loops.

The following rules for determining the polarity of the feedback loops can be defined [3]:

- if the contour includes an even number of negative cause-and-effect relationships or there are none at all in it, this is a positive feedback loop;
- if the contour includes an odd number of negative cause-and-effect relationships, this is called a negative feedback loop.

At the same time, the polarity of the cause-and-effect relationship between the two elements of the contour is determined by the reaction of the effect element to a change in the cause element, regardless of their connections with other elements. When constructing a model of a dynamic environment, a number of difficulties arise in using the feedback method:

- in complex systems, there can be several feedback loops of parameters, both positive and negative, and the causes for changes in the system states can be far from the effects, both in time and in space. Obviously, identifying such effects in a long chain of cause-and-effect relationships is impossible;
- understanding of the intuitive processes during constructing a feedback diagram is an important and non-trivial task. As a rule, only those dependencies between cause and effect are determined that are obvious, understandable and clear;
- correction of feedbacks, if they inadequately reflect reality, is an equally important task. The change in the mental models of a group of decision-makers appears to be even more complicated task.

On the basis of the diagram of cause-effect relationships of the modeled system, a diagram of flows and levels is built. It determines the quantitative stage of building a system dynamics model. Quantitative stage in its basic structure consists of four essential elements: information and material flows, decision function and level (see Fig. 3).

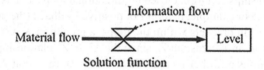

Fig. 3. Basic structure of the quantitative stage.

The levels are represented by quantitative indicators of the object under study and characterize the emerging accumulations within the system. They represent the values of the variables at the moment that they have as a result of accumulation due to the difference between the incoming and outgoing flows. The content of the levels can be of any nature [3].

The material flow, flowing into or out of the level, determines the change in the level. Thus, the value at each moment of time is characterized by a level described by the finite-difference Eq. (1) [5]:

$$X(t + h) = X(t) + (h \times V(t)) \tag{1}$$

Where h is change (increment) of time, t is model time, simulation step; $X(t)$, $X(t + h)$ is a level value at time points; $V(t)$ is a rate (pace) of level change, i.e. the magnitude of its change per unit of time.

$$V(t) = Vs(t) - Vd(t) \tag{2}$$

$Vs(t)$ is an incoming stream (source); $Vd(t)$ is an outflow (drain).

In addition, a distinction is made between information flows, which helps to make a decision on control actions, i.e. the value of the flow rate is determined for the next time interval. Thus, a decision function is defined, which is a formulation of a behavior line that determines how the available information about the levels leads to the choice of solutions related to the values of the current rates. The rate change law is set by functional dependence (3) [5]:

$$V(t) = F(p_1(t), p_2(t), \ldots, p_k(t)) \tag{3}$$

F is an arbitrary function of k arguments; $p_i(t)$ is model parameters, the values of which are known at the moment t.

In fact, the graphical structure is expressed by three types of system dynamics model, which form the level equations by graphical representation (see Fig. 4).

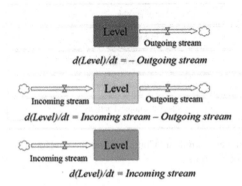

Fig. 4. Basic graphical structures of system dynamics.

Decision functions are pace Eqs. (1), which, unlike level equations (Fig. 4), are not so obvious and simple. In fact, the rate equations reflect an understanding of the factors that determine the actions that will be performed immediately at the next moment in time. Interaction in the system dynamics model occurs with the subsequent impact of paces on levels, which then, in turn, affect paces at later time intervals.

However, you cannot be guided only by the degree of direct influence considered by the parameter on the solution. It is necessary to take into account the ratio of the information flow, as well as the temporal characteristics – the delay, which characterizes the transformation process, as a result of which, based on the given rate of the incoming flow, the rate of the flow at the output is established (4):

$$Vd(t) = X(t + h)/P_{DEL} \tag{4}$$

P_{DEL} is a delay parameter representing the average time it takes to overcome the lag.

Running the system dynamics model provides, at best, obtaining reliable results at one point in the solution search space. However, the study of the environment requires the implementation of a series of experiments, the emergence of new branches of solutions as a result of bifurcation occurring due to the loss of stability of the standard state. Then it becomes necessary to choose an optimal solution from a set of possible situations, which is conditioned by certain criteria and given constraints.

3 Proposed Solution

According to the methodology of the situation-activity approach, it is necessary to identify the activities that exist in a complex dynamic environment. There can be a different number of activities in the environment that exist in the cycles of reproduction. These cycles divide activity into particular images which are acts of activity and spheres. Thus, as a result of decomposition, a hierarchical structure of a dynamically complex environment is formed [9]. This defines the reality boundary of the chosen subject area. For example, let us imagine a dynamically complex environment "Countering the development of infectious diseases" where there are many activities (see Fig. 5).

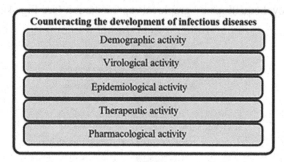

Fig. 5. Complex dynamic environment "Counteracting the development of infectious diseases" and the activities of prisoners in it.

3.1 Conceptual Structure

Thus, possibility to separate an activity from other realities by constructing its structure and to logically move from any element of this structure to another element exists. In this case, any units of activity can be distinguished; however, the elementary unit will be the act of activity [10, 11]. According to the synthesis of activity and situation analysis, let us present a conceptual scheme of the act of activity "Development of an infectious process" in virological activity (Fig. 6).

A conceptual model of a dynamically complex environment must be represented by different acts of activity, consisting of a set of conceptual structures of unit solutions. Then, from the conceptual structure of the act of activity "Development of the infectious process", the conceptual structures of unit solutions are distinguished: actions "Fall ill" and "Recover". In these conceptual structures of single solutions, the properties of the action components "Infection Equation" and "Recovery Equation" are not defined. These action components provide means for calculating the number of susceptible/infected/recovered people. We can define them in another indirect act of activity "Determine Infection Function", which consists of two unit solutions "Calculate Infection Equation" and "Calculate Recovery Equation".

From the conceptual structures of the acts of activity, four different contents of the act of activity stand out: the functional structure plan, the process plan, the context plan

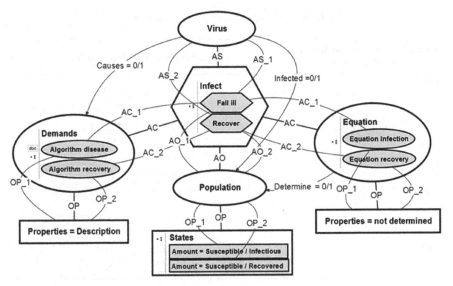

Fig. 6. Conceptual structure of the development of the infectious process.

and the analytical regularities plan. These plans are united into a coherent whole by a single structure in which they are expressed. Consequently, there is no contradiction between the plans - they not only complement each other, but can also be applied in parallel or in sequence to a certain extent. The description of these plans merits separate articles [5, 6]. Therefore, in this paper we will focus in more detail on the description of the process plan and the regularities for the system dynamics model.

The process plan of the act of activity is determined by the process as a set of actions (in a single solution, only an action), the object of the act of activity, its states – the source materials and products, the means of achieving the goal and their properties [6]. Based on the structure of the process plan, it can be assumed that it is similar to the basic structure of the quantitative stage, i.e. a diagram of flows and levels (see Table 1).

According to Table 1 the level is visualized as an object of action, which is defined by one of the quantitative states: product or the source material. The flow is interpreted by continuous activity, which is performed by an action that moves the content between the levels. If we use a hydrodynamic metaphor, the decision can be imaged as the function is a valve that controls the flow (defined as a means (tool) of the act of activity).

3.2   Regularities Plan

The plan of regularities is defined by gathering manifested properties of conceptual structured objects, which are described by a certain attitude and a ratio. Thus, regularities of transformation of initial material are fixed into a product (see Fig. 7).

During building of a plan for the regularities of a single solution, the following rules must be considered:

Table 1. Comparison of graphic notations.

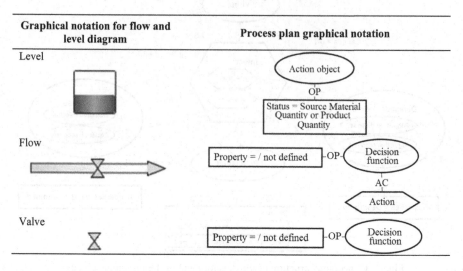

Graphical notation for flow and level diagram	Process plan graphical notation

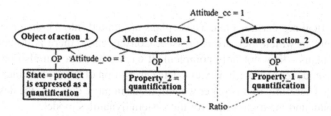

Fig. 7. Plan of regularities.

- the state of the action object (product) is associated with the solution, and the means of action - with the internal parameters of the equation.
- the relations in the regularities plan are unidirectional and singular, i.e., one relationship can come or go from one element.
- the relation between the object and the means of action and the relation between the means are presented by dependency relations and are conditioned by the types "enhances" or "delays", the relation by the type "determines" is shown as an equal sign.

ratios are associations of dependency relations, which are defined by the following types "more on", "less by" , "more in" and "less in". Ratios associations, in turn, can be mapped as arithmetic operations (see Table 2).

Table 2. Association rules.

IF	THEN	
	IF	THEN
Relation type	Ratio type	Type of arithmetic operation
enhances	more on	Addition
	more in	multiplication
delays	less by	subtraction
	less in	division

3.3 Graphical Notations

Based on the regularities plan, various analytic views can be defined, including decision functions (flow rates) for system dynamics models. When modelling the activity "Development of an infectious process", a synthesis of the process plan and the analytical regularities plan is used according to its structure. As a result, we get a structure identical to the flow and level diagram when constructing models of system dynamics (see Fig. 8 and Fig. 9).

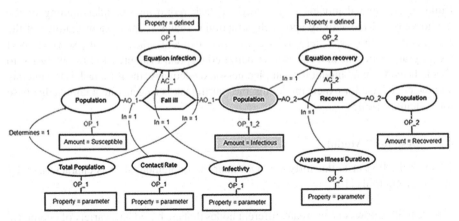

Fig. 8. Graphic notation based on the situational-activity approach.

According to the graphical notation, the population of the agglomeration undergoes several stages of transformation: *Susceptible → Infectious → Recovered*. This transformation in field of action analysis is finalized as a source material → product. Applying this concept and the corresponding software, the remaining activities are modeled (Fig. 5). The number of pools and flows enlarges correspondingly. Alike the pools already described before, the model should include population - the population of the simulated area; nosusceptible - people not susceptible, for whatever reason, to the disease. It must also include prophylaxis - the number of people covered by preventive

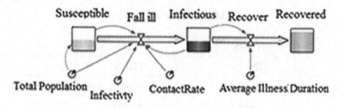

Fig. 9. Graphic notation based on the flow and level diagram.

measures; exposed - people with the disease who are in the incubation period; infectiousT - number of patients covered by therapeutic measures; final - people who died from complications. There are flows among the levels that can be arranged according to the acts of activity included in the environment of the escalation of an infectious disease. An epidemic model with a PS2E2I2RF-type phenomenology is implemented, which takes into account disease control measures [12].

Concept plans are essentially a knowledge base for designing knowledge-based systems. Accordingly, the task of separating such knowledge from the conceptual structure of the act of activity can be solved at the program level.

4 Results and Discussion

Building conceptual models is a non-trivial task requiring an understanding of the methodology of the activity approach, situational analysis, and system features of the subject area. In this case, there are tasks that can be quickly and efficiently solved only at the program level. The first task is to visualize conceptual structures; the second task is to check the conceptual model for completeness and adequacy; the third task is to generate a knowledge base for expert modeling; the fourth task is to generate a knowledge base for system dynamics.

4.1 "Designer" Module

To solve the first task, the software "Designer" is implemented. It is characterized by the following tools [10]:

– node tool – allows one to create different nodes that are based on a variety of geometric primitives (ellipse, rectangle, and irregular hexagon);
– link tool – allows creating various links, relationships, and ratio between the vertices of conceptual structures (geometric primitives) based on Bezier curves;
– text tool – allows one to change the textual content of elements of conceptual structures;
– zoom tool - allows zooming in on the node in question to a full-screen view to examine its contents in detail.

It is possible to customize the image parameters for shapes, lines and text, and to provide storage for conceptual structures. The conceptual structures depicted in the "Designer" software are represented as an XML (eXtensible Markup Language) document that is represented as a node tree. This allows any element of the conceptual structure to be accessed. Consequently, it is possible to modify and manipulate their content at the software level.

4.2 "Solver" Module

The second and third tasks are handled by the "Solver" software, which is developed in the framework of situational analysis and supports the following set of functions [8]:

- creation, storage, modification, integrity testing, influence of user knowledge bases of production type;
- organization and some optimization of direct logical inference;
- generation of reports with text descriptions of knowledge bases and results of analysis of problem situations.

The performance of these functions results from interaction of the basic parts of the integration module and "Solver" software management:

- block of knowledge formalization (problem condition editor + object editor + object relations editor + rule base editor + situation model editor + knowledge base viewer);
- block of access to a situation model (problem situation model + current situation model + target situation model + knowledge base model);
- block of organization and carrying out logical inference (editor of rules management + module of carrying out direct logical inference + situation analyzer).

Thus, in "Solver" software, "Designer" software has an XML file which is read; the selection of the needed fragments takes turn, and then building of a primary logical structure that describes conceptual schemas as marked oriented graphs is complete. The user is notified, if any syntax errors are detected in the conceptual structures.

The knowledge base is also checked for completeness and adequacy. All sets of facts are divided into the following groups [10]:

- facts describing the initial (or problematic) situation;
- facts describing the target situation;
- facts not included in the initial or target situation are not considered.

The beginning of analysis of a set of conceptual structures of unit solutions for adequacy requires establishing the values of the facts of the problem and target situation. If needed situation is reached by means of logical inference, the fact about the adequacy and completeness of the generated recommendations for the relevant knowledge base is established on the basis of the content of the generated text report. Completeness and adequacy of a conceptual model of a dynamically complex environment are surveyed by exploring the logical conclusions on situations and on activity acts. Completeness is verified against classes of situations. The knowledge base considered incomplete or the rule management strategy is misconfigured if the logical inference is interrupted because the rules cannot be applied to the initial situation. Adequacy checking depends on logical inference by class of activity acts. The resulting inference report must be consistent with the logic of the activity act process being modelled. If incompleteness or inadequacy is found, the knowledge base should be refined, or other rule management strategies should be attempted.

The knowledge base is implemented in a text file that specifies [8]:

- basic elements of the conceptual model;
- rule name <Subject Action Object>;
- the content of the rule in the form of the following construct: IF <Conditions before the action>, THEN PERFORM THE ACTION <Conditions after the action>.

Rules of the production describe the prerequisites that the objects' states involved in the action must satisfy, and the rules for changing the state of the objects at the end of the corresponding action. An expert system is implemented based on the rules.

4.3 "Interpretator" Module

The development of "Interpretator" software is based on the concept of streaming reading. It consists in representing an XML document as a stream of markers and allows you to create recursive descend parsers. This means that it is possible to split the XML parsing code into different classes. Thus, the structure of the tree is read and its objects are classified by relations (AS, AO, AC, OP (see Fig. 6)). After analyzing the XML document and forming the initial data set, the object search function is called. The execution of these actions leads to the structuring of the data required for the search of intersections and the selection of the necessary planning representations. Based on the found intersections, the necessary conceptual plan reports are output in a text file.

Based on this algorithm, four modules of the "Interpretator" program are developed. They are divided into two blocks: dynamic (functions and processes) and static (context and regularities) representations of the structure of the act of activity. Regarding the plans, a number of assertions are put forward:

- The functional plan allows designing discrete-event models.
- The process plan allows developing flow and level diagrams for system dynamics models.
- The regularities plan allows the design of analytical models in the form of simple mathematical equations.
- A context plan allows developing various models based on cognitive ideas.

Accordingly, within the framework of this report, we will consider the plans of processes and regularities regarding program recommendations for the development of models of system dynamics. In this article, the main elements of the process knowledge base are:

- level – [Object_N Quantity: = <Property of object before action>] and [Object_N Quantity: = <Property of object after action>];
- flow – [Action_N].

The identified intersections in the text file of the process plan are indicated and recommendations on its construction are proposed in the design of the following construct: Level 1 <Object N Number: = 'Properties of object N before action N' = Thread <Action N> = Level 1 <Object N Quantity: = 'Property of object N after action N'.

In the article, the main elements of the knowledge base of the regularities plan are:

- equation – [Object_N];
- parameter – [Object_N Property_N after action_N];
- mathematical sign – [Ratio];
- equal sign - [Relationship <Defines>].

The text file of the regularities plan proposes recommendations for its construction in the model of the following construct: Equation <Object N> Equality sign <Ratio 'Defines'> Parameter < Object 1Property of means 1 after action 1> Mathematical sign <Ratio> Parameter <Object 2 Property of means 2 after action 2>, etc.

Thus, an intelligent add-on for designing system dynamics models is implemented. It is represented by a knowledge showcase in the software package. The use of the software package is conditioned by the algorithm "Designer + Solver + Interpretator":

– once the acts of action have been defined, their conceptual unit solution structures are implemented in "Designer" software and defined as a holistic conceptual decision-making model;
– holistic conceptual model of decision-making is checked for completeness and adequacy in "Solver" software. If necessary, a knowledge base report is generated in the form of product rules;
– after confirming the completeness and adequacy of the model in the "Interpretator" software reports on knowledge bases of conceptual plans are generated. Synthesis of knowledge bases corresponds to defined models and systems.

5   Conclusions

The practice of using systems and their synergetic combinations shows that nowadays, in its theoretical basis, there is no methodology and conceptual structure uniting situational, imitation, expert approaches to modeling information systems. There is not an integral knowledge model and a unified graphic description language for modeling in the field of information systems development; knowledge base representation software for information systems design [13].

These circumstances indicate the existence of a problem in the area of decision support, which consists in the absence of a unified conceptual structure of informed solutions concerning the management of complex systems and software extraction of different knowledge from the conceptual model for the design of information systems. The method and software toolkit proposed in this article provides an effective solution to these problems. Thus, the application of situation-action analysis to the study of dynamically complex environments is a type of simulation and is very relevant to the form of expert systems. Therefore, the establishment of the structure of an object is largely identical with its knowledge as such. All other aspects are very imitative and determined by its structural organization. Like so, the structural characteristic of any object is central to its disclosure. Thus, conceptual structures are considered as a kind of a "substrate" on the basis of which different kinds of intellectual-information systems can be built.

The authors propose several directions for using and developing situation-activity analysis: as a language for understanding processes in a dynamically complex environment; as a language for modelling intelligent information systems; as an instrumental tool implemented in the software package "Designer + Solver + Interpretator".

References

1. Brehmer, B.: Dynamic decision making: Human control of complex systems. Acta Physiol. (Oxf) **81**(3), 211–241 (1992)
2. Andrianova, E.G., Golovin, S.A., Zykov, S.V., Lesko, S.A., Chukalina, E.R.: Review of modern models and methods of analysis of time series of dynamics of processes in social, economic and socio-technical systems (Obzor sovremennyh modelej i metodov analiza vremennyh ryadov dinamiki processov v social'nyh, ekonomicheskih i sociotekhnicheskih sistemah (). Rossijskij tekhnologicheskij zhurnal) Russian Technol. J. **8**(4), 7–45 (2020)
3. Forrester, J.W.: Information sources for modeling the national economy. J. Am. Stat. Assoc. **75**(371), 555–574 (1980)
4. Rodrigues da Silva, A.: Model-driven engineering: a survey supported by the unified conceptual model. Comput. Lang. Syst. Struct. **43**, 139–155 (2015)
5. Sterman J.D.: All models are wrong: reflections on becoming a systems scientist. J.W. Forrester Prize Lecture. System Dynamics Review **18**(4), 501–531 (2002)
6. Chen, D.-Y., Zhao, H., Zhang, X.: Semantic mapping methods between expert view and ontology view. J. Softw **31**(9), 2855–2882 (2020)
7. Sorokin, A.B., Brazhnikova, E.V., Zheleznyak, L.M.: Designing a knowledge base for expert systems based on the conceptual structure of an act of activity (Proektirovanie bazy znanij dlya ekspertnyh sistem na osnove konceptual'noj struktury akta deyatel'nosti). In: X International Conference on High-Performance Computing Systems and Technologies in Scientific Research, Automation of Control and Production, vol. 4, iss. 1, pp. 190–196, 15–16 May 2020, Barnaul, Russia (2020)
8. Sorokin, A.B., Brazhnikova, E.V., Zheleznyak, L.M.: Designing a knowledge base for the development of intelligent models based on the conceptual structure of activity act. Journal of Physics: Conference Series **1615**, 012023 (2020). Doi: https://doi.org/10.1088/1742-6596/1615/1/012023
9. Gonzalez, C.: Learning to make decisions in dynamic environments: effects of time constraints and cognitive abilities. Hum. Factors **46**(3), 449–460 (2004)
10. Sorokin, A.B., Smoljaninova, V.A.: Conceptual design of expert systems of support of decision (Konceptual'noe proektirovanie ekspertnyh sistem podderzhki prinyatiya reshenij). Informacionnye tekhnologii **23**(9), 634–641 (2017)
11. Ganter, B., Obiedkov S.: Conceptual Exploration. Springer (2016)
12. Nakamura, G.M., Cardoso, G.C., Martinez, A.S.: Improved susceptible–infectious–susceptible epidemic equations based on uncertainties and autocorrelation functions. Royal Soc. Open Sci. **7**(2), 191504 (2020)
13. Tan, R.P., Zhang, W.D., Chen, S.Q., Yang, L.H.: Emergency decision-making method based on case-based reasoning in heterogeneous information environment. Control Decis. **35**(8), 1966–1976 (2020)

Information and Computing Technologies in Automation and Control Science

Architecture of an Intelligent Network Pyrometer for Building Information-Measuring and Mechatronic Systems

Alexey Dolmatov$^{(\boxtimes)}$ [iD], Pavel Gulyaev [iD], and Irina Milyukova [iD]

Ugra State University, Chekhova Street 16, Khanty-Mansiysk 628011, Russia
adolmatov@bk.ru

Abstract. The work is devoted to the creation of an autonomous device based on an embedded computing platform that supports the network organization of information-measuring and mechatronic complexes. On the basis of a three-level information model of a specialized pyrometer, it is shown that endowing the device with intellectual capabilities reduces the messaging traffic within the complex, and the use of modern network technologies makes it possible to build complex information and control systems. The features of intelligent network devices and their interaction protocols are demonstrated by the example of an experimental complex for the study of structural phase transitions in materials. The development of the intelligent network pyrometer is based on the LR1-T digital spectrometer and the nVidia Jetson Nano embedded system. With the help of software, remote control of the device was realized, its web interface was built and the inference of a neural network trained on the results of pyrometric studies of phase transformations in thin films was organized. For streaming processing of spectral data, the CUDA cores of the GPU processor are used.

Keywords: Controller · Embedded systems · Mechatronic · Artificial intelligence · Network · Pyrometer

1 Introduction

The evolution of measuring instruments has led to the separation of functional blocks for analog signal conversion and digital data processing. The digital processing unit migrated from the device to the computer, where, as the methods of data analysis developed, its software structuring took place [1]. Within the framework of the concept of a virtual device, it became necessary to create and improve hardware-software interfaces as a means of communication for individual blocks of a measuring device [2]. On the one hand, the standardization of interfaces made it possible to use a high-performance data processing center for scaling homogeneous measuring instruments (implementation of multichannel devices) and creation of heterogeneous information devices (implementation of complex measurements and joint analysis of signals of different nature) [3]. On the other hand, the internal interfaces of the device limited its resolution and required constant work to increase their bandwidth.

© Springer Nature Switzerland AG 2022
V. Jordan et al. (Eds.): HPCST 2021, CCIS 1526, pp. 265–274, 2022.
https://doi.org/10.1007/978-3-030-94141-3_21

Currently, the solution to the urgent problem of internal interfaces has become possible on the basis of embedded microcontroller systems [4, 5]. They connect the data collection and processing units, analyzing information in real time by means of parallel computing [6]. Such a synthesis of previously separated functional blocks makes it possible to abandon a number of intermediate interfaces and localize the heavy traffic of primitive signals inside the smart device. This opens up the possibility of using network technologies for the implementation of information systems with a qualitatively new content of the processed data.

2 Intelligent Networked Device Concept

The modern level of integration of mechanical, electrical and information units in information-measuring and mechatronic systems makes it possible to create intelligent devices that specialize in performing a specific task. This gives a significant synergistic effect in the mutual adaptation of sensors, data processing methods, control signals and execution means inside an autonomous device - a module.

Complex robotic and mechatronic complexes are built from several modules, which requires the coordination of the actions of individual members in such a community. Therefore, each module must support protocols for neighborhood, clock synchronization, event messaging, and providing other modules with their own raw data mining results.

During operation, the information-measuring or mechatronic module can be used in different complexes. The module collects data only within the community that is currently active. However, analysis of previously collected information can be performed at any time after receiving it. Therefore, the module must have the ability to simultaneously exchange information with all communities in which it has ever participated. To optimize information exchange, digital twins of the intelligent module can be placed in the global network. Therefore, the module must support the virtualization protocol and data synchronization with redundant servers.

Figure 1 shows an experimental complex that implements the concept described above and consists of four autonomous devices: a high-temperature heating reactor (RHTH), a 3D positioning system, a pyrometer for monitoring structural phase transitions in materials and an intelligent thermal imaging system. Each smart module has a unique identifier: GUID. The interaction of the modules of the experimental complex is carried out only through network communications and message exchange. Any module can initiate the creation of a community. The community is a logical scheme for the interaction of intelligent modules and is built for a limited period of time, during which prospective members should not enter other information-measuring and mechatronic complexes. The physical organization of the intelligent modules in the complex lies with the user who will operate it. During the community creation process, the initiating module uses the Neighborhood Procedure, which determines the community GUID and multicast IP address for the other modules, and also assigns to each of them a program of actions associated with sets of incoming and outgoing messages.

Incoming messages are used by the modules to synchronize the steps of their individual program, and outgoing messages are used to initiate the actions of neighbors in

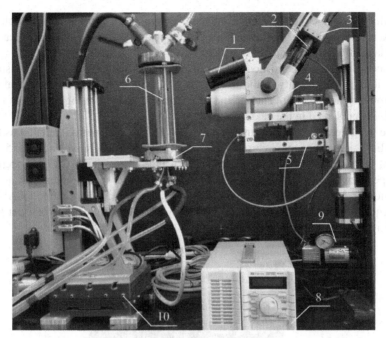

Fig. 1. Experimental complex based on information-measuring and mechatronic modules: 1 - optical channel of the spectral module; 2 - bandpass filters in the optical channels of the thermal imaging system; 3 - digital camera Photonfocus MV1-D1024E-CL; 4 - stereomicroscope Altami CM0655; 5 - ASEQ LR1-T spectrometer; 6 - sample of metal foil; 7 - RHTH; 8 - PSH-2035 current source; 9 - vacuum pump VP-215; 10 - 3D positioning system.

the experimental complex. In the course of the community's work, each module of the complex saves information specific to it in its own database. However, when identifying data in the database, the GUIDs of neighbors and communities, transmitted in messages, are used, as well as the time stamps of its own real-time clock. The synchronization of the clocks of the modules in the complex is carried out using the NTP or PTP protocol. The choice of the protocol depends on the requirement for the clock error in the experiment. Identification of records in the databases of intelligent modules allows an external entity to restore the logical structure of the community's work and combine all the information obtained by the experimental complex for its own analysis and processing.

In the complex in Fig. 1 RHTH is designed for heating film materials with electric current in a vacuum or inert medium. The source in the module is the PSH-2035 programmable power supply, which is controlled on the basis of the Arduino Yun Rev 2 microcontroller with the Linino operating system. On the SD card of the microcontroller, the module database is deployed, containing information about the programmed and actual power modes of the RHTH in the experiment.

The 3D positioning module has an original design and a control unit, in which the power supply and stepper motor drivers obey the signals of the Raspberry Pi 4B microcontroller (8 GB) with the Raspberry Pi OS operating system. The module database allows you to set the movement of the working body along the desired trajectory and save information about the dynamics of its movement. In the experimental complex, the module is responsible for positioning the prototype and keeping its sighting area in the focal plane of the thermal imaging system.

A specialized pyrometric module is used in the experimental complex to measure the temperature and emissivity of the sample, as well as to determine the structural phase transitions in the material. The internal organization and operating principles of this module are presented in the next paragraph of this article.

The intelligent thermal imaging system uses two digital cameras Photonfocus MV1-D1024E-CL, recording monochrome images of the prototype at wavelengths of 525 and 725 nm with a half-width of the passband of 40 nm. The Altami CM0655 stereomicroscope allows you to control the area of the object under investigation with a spatial resolution of 2.5 μm. Video recording is performed by the microEnable IV-AD4-CL data acquisition board, and its processing, analysis and storage are carried out by the high-performance embedded system Jetson AGX Xavier (Fig. 2).

Fig. 2. Data collection and processing tools for intelligent thermal imaging systems based on Jetson AGX Xavier and microEnable IV-AD4-CL

The latter runs under the Linux Ubuntu operating system and implements several functions in the experimental complex:

- interacting with the positioning system, it determines the optimal working distance to the object of photography;
- it performs registration of images of the area of the prototype observed at the given coordinates of the working body of the positioning system;
- it performs stitching of images of areas of the prototype at a fixed power of the RHTH source, based on the data of the positioning system;
- using the data of a specialized pyrometer with which it has a common sighting area, it identifies the structural-phase state of homogeneous zones in stitched images.

The result of the work of the intelligent thermal imaging module is the time series of images of structural-phase zones and temperature distributions on the sample surface. This information is stored in the module database deployed on the Jetson AGX Xavier embedded system SSD. It is available upon request to other members of the experimental complex and to external subjects.

3   Pyrometer for Monitoring Structural Phase Transitions

The pyrometric module consists of two functional blocks linked by a USB 2.0 interface (Fig. 3). The measuring unit is an LR1-T digital spectrometer (Aseq, Canada) operating in the range from 200 to 1100 nm with a dispersion of 0.24 nm. The nVidia Jetson Nano microcomputer running the Linux Ubuntu operating system was chosen as the data processing unit. NVidia Jetson Nano hardware includes ARM Cortex A57 with 4 cores (1600 MHz), Maxwell GPU with 128 CUDA cores, LPDDR4 - 4 GB, 4 × USB 3.0, GigabitEthernet, SD (128 GB), DP1.2, M.2 key E for connecting a wireless network interface module.

The optical channel of the pyrometric module consists of a Computar MLH-10× objective and an optical fiber. They transmit the thermal radiation of the observed object in the visible range of the spectrum to the input of the device. At the maximum performance of the CCD sensor, the traffic of the recorded data of the spectrometer is 4 Mbit/s. Their processing in the nVidia Jetson Nano is performed programmatically based on a three-tier information model.

At the first level, the additive and multiplicative correction of the digital signal is carried out using the corrections determined at the stage of calibration of the pyrometric module by the spectrum of an absolutely black body and stored in the database on the SD-card of the microcomputer:

$$S_i^* = k_i \cdot s_i^o - \delta_i, \quad \overline{i = 1, N}, \tag{1}$$

where S_i^{0}, S_i^{*} - respectively registered and corrected signal of the i-th element of the linear CCD sensor; δ_i, k_i – additive and multiplicative correction at the wavelength λ_i; N = 3648 – the number of elements of the linear CCD sensor.

At the second level, the signal S_i^{*} is used to determine conditional temperatures and calculate an estimate of the spectral emissivity of the observed object. The brightness temperature T_{bi} at the wavelength λ_i is found according to the table of correspondence of sets:

$$\{s_i^*\} \leftrightarrow \{T_{b_i}\}, \tag{2}$$

obtained at the stage of temperature calibration of the pyrometric module and stored in the database on the SD-card of the microcomputer. The spectral temperature at the wavelength λ_i is determined by the formula:

$$T_{s_i} = -\left(\frac{dy}{dx}\right)_{x_i}^{-1}, \tag{3}$$

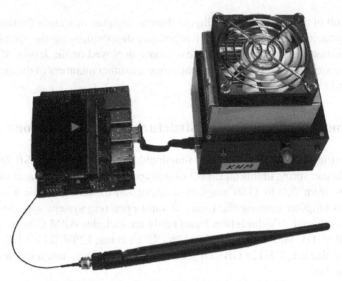

Fig. 3. Elements of an intelligent network pyrometer.

where $x_i = C/\lambda_i$, $y_i = ln(S_i^* \bullet \lambda^4)$, $C = 14388 \ \mu m \bullet K$. Evaluation of the spectral emissivity of the observed object – the brightness-spectral radiation coefficient (BSRC) at the wavelength λ_i, is calculated by the formula:

$$\varepsilon_{s_i} = \exp\left(\frac{C}{\lambda_i}\left(\frac{1}{T_{s_i}} - \frac{1}{T_{b_i}}\right)\right) \qquad (4)$$

In work [7] it is shown that BSRC is related to the spectral emissivity of the material at the wavelength of measurement of conditional temperatures λ_i by the formula:

$$\frac{\varepsilon_{s_i}}{\varepsilon_{o_i}} = \exp\left(\lambda_i \cdot \left(\frac{d(\ln \varepsilon_o)}{d\lambda}\right)_{\lambda_i}\right) \qquad (5)$$

When the material matches the gray body model, its BSRC and spectral emissivity are equal. For many real materials, it is possible to choose such λ_i that:

$$\left|1 - \varepsilon_{s_i}/\varepsilon_{o_i}\right| \cdot 100 < 5\% \qquad (6)$$

For example, for tungsten heated to 1400–2600 K, condition (6) is satisfied in the spectral range from 300 to 400 nm. The BSRC method has a high temperature sensitivity ($\sim d\varepsilon/dT$) and temporal resolution ($\sim d\varepsilon/d\tau$), and also allows the use of a non-contact and non-destructive approach to measure the optical properties of a material associated with its macro- and microstructure.

The signal processing at the third level of the information model is based on experimental works [7, 8], in which it was shown that during phase transitions of the first order, the dependence of the spectral emissivity of the material on temperature undergoes a jump, and during phase transitions of the second order, a break can be found on it, where the first derivative changes abruptly. And during phase transitions of the second order, it is possible find a break where the first derivative changes abruptly. For example, in experiments with molybdenum foil, a sample in an argon atmosphere was heated by an electric current, successively passing through a number of states in which stationary temperature and BSRC distributions ($\lambda = 725$ nm) were observed on its surface. The measurements were carried out in several zones with a diameter of 100 μm on the longitudinal axis of the sample. As a result, it was revealed that a jump in BSRC in different zones corresponds to a unique power of heat release in the sample, but the same temperature level, equal to the boiling point of MoO_3 (Fig. 4).

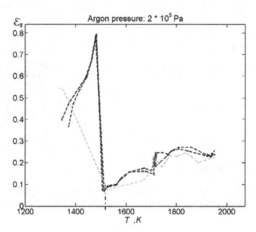

Fig. 4. Behavior of the BSRC of a molybdenum sample in zones with a displacement of 0, 5, 10 mm.

Similar results were obtained in experiments with tungsten and tantalum film materials [8]. In addition to the ability of BSRC to detect phase transitions, experiments on tantalum samples revealed additional features of this method. It turned out to be sensitive to isothermal combustion and changes in the phase composition in the surface layer of the object. The following example demonstrates this. By analyzing the phase diagrams (*Ta-O* and *Ta-C*), studies of the microstructure and microelement composition of the phases of frozen samples, it was possible to identify phase transitions, to construct a probable mechanism for changing the concentration of impurity atoms on the surface of a tantalum foil and the sequence of phase states change (Fig. 5).

According to the proposed interpretation of the experimental results, T_0 corresponds to the saturation temperature of the surface layer of the sample with O and C impurity atoms. At T_1, the α-$Ta + \alpha$-Ta_2O_5 eutectic melts, which makes it possible to dissolve impurity atoms in it and the onset of isothermal combustion with the formation of gaseous carbon oxides that leave the sample. Combustion isotherm is indicated by the narrowness of the zone of the new phase on the frozen sample and the invariability of the spectral temperature, which depends on the shape of the thermal radiation spectrum. In this case, the activation of chemical sources in the surface layer of the sample, in addition to the Joule heat release, leads to a sharp increase in the spectral radiation flux

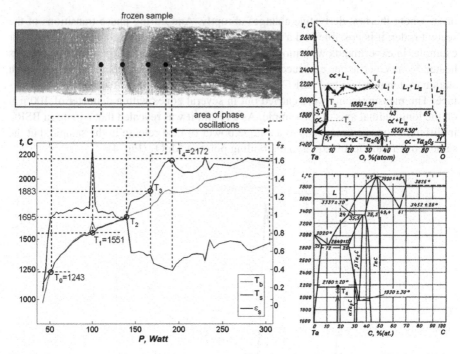

Fig. 5. Determination of characteristic temperatures of structural phase transitions and construction of probable concentration curves of impurity atoms on the surface of tantalum samples.

density, which is detected by the method of brightness pyrometry. Of course, a point ε_s cannot be an estimate of the spectral emissivity of the material (in the classical sense), but this feature allows using BSRC to detect a temporary release or absorption of heat in chemical reactions localized in structural defects of the material.

Revealing of structural phase transitions and their characteristic temperatures in materials during heating or cooling is possible due to the dependence of BSRC on time. To do this, one should analyze the full set of BSRC values obtained over the entire observation period of the object, or use a sliding window approach that allows one to determine phase changes over a limited time interval. The authors used a convolution neural network to recognize events associated with a change in the structure of the material of the observed object [9]. Its training was carried out on the basis of experimental data presented in works. The neural network structure and learning outcomes are stored in a database on an nVidia Jetson Nano embedded system SD card.

In general, the implementation of spectrometer signal processing methods based on a three-level information model on the microcomputer of the pyrometric module required the deployment of information services: DBMS MySQL, Python, Tensorflow, Apache, PHP. To speed up the processing of the spectral data stream and neural network inference, the cores of the CUDA GPU module with a performance of 472 GFLOPS are used. The website of the pyrometric module contains tools for developing client software in C++, C#, Matlab with a description of the object-oriented interface. In addition, using the Web interface, interactive interaction of the pyrometric module and the user is possible. This includes setting the exposure duration in the range from 10 μs to 10 s, selecting the spectral range from 200 to 1100 nm, setting the speed of registration of spectra (up to 500 sps), viewing spectral data. There is also analysis of the dynamics of conditional temperatures and BSRC, determination of the temperature of probable phase transitions based on built-in AI tools, loading software for developing client applications and services.

4 Conclusion

Localization of computing facilities inside the device and endowing it with the capabilities of intelligent processing of primary data allow solving the problem of interface bandwidth. In particular, this approach makes it possible to organize information-measuring and mechatronic complexes based on network technologies. Thus, the traffic of the primary data of the spectrometer of the pyrometric module is 4 Mbit/s. However, at the second level of its information model, when determining the temperature and BSRC at a single wavelength, traffic is reduced by 3 orders of magnitude. Intelligent analysis at the third level of the device information model reduces traffic by another 1–2 orders of magnitude. This makes it possible to transfer the processed data to other intelligent network devices of the experimental complex via FastEthernet and WiFi interfaces in a time of about 10 μs, and to organize fast feedback channels in information and control systems.

Modern microcontrollers and embedded computing facilities based on them have sufficient performance for processing multidimensional digital signals and make it possible to implement the concept of networked smart devices and complexes. A wide range of microcomputers in terms of power allows you to optimize the choice of an embedded computing platform for building stand-alone devices with varying data processing complexity.

Acknowledgements. This work was supported by the Russian Foundation for Basic Research (Project No. 18-47-860018).

References

1. Vento, J.A.: Application of LabVIEW in higher education laboratories. In: Proceedings Frontiers in Education Conference, pp. 444–447 (1988). https://doi.org/10.1109/FIE.1988. 35023
2. Cai, J., Ran, F., Xu, M., Zhen, L.: Design of low-power 10 bit 40 MS/s pipelined ADC converter. J. Huazhong Univ. Sci. Technol. **38**(1), 61–64 (2010)
3. Chernysheva, N.S., Ionov, A.B.: Application of a multichannel radiation thermometer for increase in adequacy of non-contact temperature measurement results. In: Proceeding of the International Conference of Young Specialists on Micro/Nanotechnologies and Electron Devices (EDM 2015), 29 June–3 July 2015, Erlagol, Russia, pp. 334–336 (2015)
4. Ganssle, J.: The Art of Designing Embedded Systems. Butterworth-Heinemann, Oxford, UK (2000)

5. Ammar, A., Fredj, H.B., Souani, C.: Accurate realtime motion estimation using optical flow on an embedded system. Electronics **10**(17), 2164 (2021)
6. nVidia: Embedded Systems for Next Generation Autonomous Machines. https://www.nvidia.com/ru-ru/autonomous-machines/embedded-systems. Accessed 15 June 2021
7. Dolmatov, A.V., Milyukova, I.V., Aliev, A.E.: Estimation of the spectral degree of black of materials by means of optical pyrometry. Vysokoproizvoditel'nye vychislitel'nye sistemy i tekhnologii **2**(1), 147–155 (2018) (in Russian)
8. Dolmatov, A.V., Milyukova, I.V., Gulyaev, P.Y.: Investigation of structure formation in thin films by means of optical pyrometry. J. Phys. Conf. Ser. **1281**(1), 012010 (2019)
9. Haykin, S.: Neural Networks and Learning Machines, 3rd edn. Prentice Hall, Hoboken, NJ, USA (2009)

Implementation of a Network-Centric Production Storage System in Distributed High-Performance Computing Systems

Anna Bashlykova[1,2(✉)] 🆔

[1] MIREA – Russian Technological University, Vernadsky Avenue 78, 119454 Moscow, Russia
bashlykova@mirea.ru
[2] V.A. Kotelnikov Institute of Radio Engineering and Electronics of the Russian Academy of Sciences, Mokhovaya Street 11-7, 125009 Moscow, Russia

Abstract. The main components of a network production data storage system in distributed high-performance computing systems are defined. A hybrid method of organizing a data storage network is considered. A feature of distributed data storage is the semantic distribution of data blocks. The interoperability of local data storage (LDS) and data export utilities is to transform the low-level organization of LDS data. When organizing a resource center, LDS plays the role of a DBMS, and the data export utility serves to organize data in a form suitable for processing by the main storage module. Thus, the interoperability of local data stores and data export utilities implies the formalization of DBMS (LDS) data for their subsequent processing. The data of interaction of the storage system when accessing computing clusters is reduced to the form of a JSON file, divided into "entities", "actions" and "links".

Keywords: High-performance environment · Distributed computing environment · Information management systems (IMS) · Distributed data storage · Network-centric production system

1 Introduction

In recent years, due to the rapid development of network technologies, the development of highly reliable data storage technologies has become increasingly important. The increase of the volume of processed data and high-speed remote access to it require the tools and methods for managing the load of servers and communication channels.

The analysis of the main ways, tasks, and methods of forming a unified information space of the digital economy in Russia shows the demand to develop and implement distributed data storage systems.

Being integrated, distributed data storage becomes fundamental in industry and economy.

Digital platforms are created on the basis of the information management systems integration (IMS). Consequently, the task was set to build the architecture of high-performance industrial computing systems.

© Springer Nature Switzerland AG 2022
V. Jordan et al. (Eds.): HPCST 2021, CCIS 1526, pp. 275–286, 2022.
https://doi.org/10.1007/978-3-030-94141-3_22

The concept of "distribution" implies the dispersion of various subsystems in space, their proximity to the sources of information resources and considerable attention to the mechanisms of information exchange and control [1]. The consequence of distribution is limited independence, reflecting the increasing importance of each individual storage subsystem in solving a common problem. The distribution of data storage subsystems makes it difficult to use a common control center, fully responsible for all decisions made and transferring control actions to all subsystems.

To organize access to a critical segment of a distributed high-performance computing system, it is necessary to provide redundancy. Grid computing focuses on integrating existing resources with their hardware, OS, local resource management, and security infrastructure.

Basic factors of the critical segment of a distributed high-performance computing system are as follows:

- critical segment services;
- critical segment redundancy;
- critical segment segmentation;
- interoperability;
- failure handling.

The interoperability of distributed data storage system modules with computing clusters is determined by indicators of the availability of remote connection to databases, as well as communication protocols.

The availability of reference information which describes the formats is important for organizing the data used in the interaction of systems developers management.

2 Problem Statement

Let us consider a hybrid method for implementing a network-centric production storage system in distributed high-performance computing systems.

When choosing an architecture, the choice can lead to a hybrid method of building a storage network (storage) with the organization of network access to the SrCD via a LAN using SAN with NAS technology.

2.1 Network-Centric Production Storage System

One of the directions of the development of interoperability is the organization of mechanisms for interaction with SCADA systems and web services. Distributed data storage subsystems with computing clusters are primarily used in research activities to study the potential of artificial intelligence.

The development of computer technology, technologies for creating software, forms and methods of storing and disseminating information has determined the widespread implementation of I&C systems in the management systems of enterprises, organizations and individual processes. Often storage systems are used to host big data (the information about this - BSI BS ISO/IEC 20546-2019 Information technology. Big data. Overview and vocabulary).

Security is important when transmitting and storing data. The higher the cost of information loss and/or the higher the stamp of information, the more comprehensive measures to protect it must be taken.

The list of terms for the above documents can be supplemented from GOST R ISO 7498-2-99 "Information technology (IT). Interconnection of open systems. Basic reference model. Part 2. Information Security Architecture".

A high-performance environment is a software and hardware complex that allows solving problems of high-performance computing of completely different types using different computing environments [2]. Among the main components of the aircraft, four groups can be distinguished: supercomputers, clusters, GRID and clouds.

Among the consumers of the Armed Forces systems, four categories can be distinguished: scientific research, business, government, and military affairs.

A production system (PrS) is a set of production, management and business processes for the safe production of work. The efficiency of the PrS is determined by the capabilities of management and interaction of enterprise resources with the least losses, development and self-learning [1].

The reasons for the main conflicts in the management of production systems are:

- sharing of resources;
- unity of goals and the difference in tasks;
- poor communication system [1].

The concept of "distribution" implies the dispersion of various subsystems in space, their proximity to the sources of information resources and considerable attention to the mechanisms of information exchange and control [1]. The consequence of distribution is limited independence, reflecting the increasing importance of each individual storage subsystem in solving a common problem. The distribution of data storage subsystems makes it difficult to use a common control center, fully responsible for all decisions made and transferring control actions to all subsystems. Thus, each storage subsystem becomes more independent in its decision making. Self-organization of system components determines the basic principles of subsystem functioning, methods of their interaction (interoperability) [3, 4, 8]. These methods and principles should contribute to the self-organization of the system as a whole to improve its suitability for solving the assigned tasks.

The main possibilities of using mechanisms for ensuring interoperability in network-centric production systems for storing distributed data are:

- increasing the volume of stored data;
- increasing the degree of data organization and, as a consequence, the speed of their processing;
- using artificial intelligence as a storage of a dataset after preprocessing;
- use of the subject area with a sufficient number of participants as a reference dataset in the interoperability process.

Overcoming the barriers of interoperability between the user and various subsystems of the production data storage system in distributed high-performance computing systems is possible when determining:

- the main components and architecture of the network production system;
- interoperability of distributed data storage subsystems of the information and production system when processing computing clusters;
- compatibility of local data stores of distributed data storage subsystems;
- quantitative calculation of the interoperability of subsystems of distributed data storage of an information production system (with frequency).

The network-centric approach is an approach based on modern communication systems that allow one in real time to receive and transmit a large amount of information to various consumers, including distributed systems [5]. The main mechanisms for creating network-centric systems include standards for mobile Internet IEEE 802.11 (Wi-Fi), IEEE 802.16 (Wireless MAN - WiMAX) and mobile communications - GPRS. The need to use both technologies is due to the fact that each of them has a number of features that provide them with advantages depending on the nature of the problem being solved. The results of a detailed study are presented in works [3–5].

2.2 Information Management System for the System

The peculiarity of the management of network-centric production systems lies in the possibility of placing decentralized intelligence and control at all levels of receiving and processing information. The network-centric environment provides for the collective distribution, storage and processing of information. The creation of a network-centric environment involves the deployment of a powerful information infrastructure [7]. This infrastructure is able to provide:

- high-performance processing of information in real time;
- a single information space for information exchange of all elements of the network-centric control system;
- efficiency of management of interaction and interoperability of the enterprise

Functional tasks are solved at the level of integration platforms.
All modern integration platforms include:

- enterprise Service Bus (ESB);
- message queue system (message broker);
- application within the enterprise (Enterprise Application Integration (EAI));
- Web Services support (within SOA);
- automation and management of business processes (Business Process Automation (BPA), Business Process Management (BPM);
- interaction with business partners (Business To Business (B2B)).

The Center for Analytical Competencies is a structural unit that determines the methodology for working with data, measures for the development of analytics tools, the introduction of effective decision support tools and changing the logic of the company's processes.

The distributed data storage system (DSS) consists of:

- software;
- specialized equipment systems;
- workstations (PC);
- computing complex.

The general architecture diagram of a network-centric production distributed data storage system is shown in Fig. 1.

Distributed storage and data processing systems and networks have flexibility in resource management, scalability and manageability.

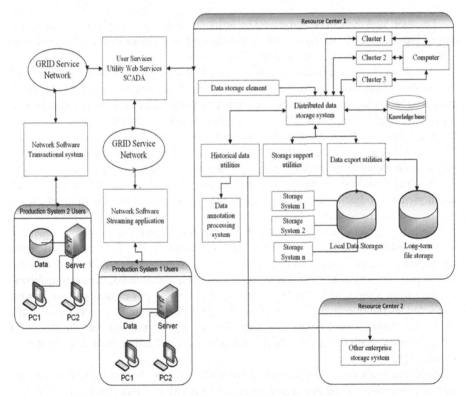

Fig. 1. Network-centric distributed architecture of production storage

In Fig. 1, SCADA (Supervisory Control And Data Acquisition) is understood as a software package designed to develop or provide real-time operation of systems for collecting, processing, displaying and archiving information about a monitoring or control object [6].

SCADA systems in the interaction and interoperability of enterprises solve the following tasks:

- maintaining a real-time database with technological information;
- data exchange with "devices for communication with the object" (i.e. with industrial controllers and I/O cards) in real time via drivers;
- semantic and organizational interoperability management;
- preparation and generation of reports on the progress of the technological process;
- implementation of network interaction between SCADA PCs;
- providing communication with external applications (DBMS, spreadsheets, word processors, etc.);
- emergency signaling and management of alarm messages [8].

Decision-making can be automated by artificial intelligence implemented in a computing cluster of a PC; the dataset of such a cluster is a distributed data storage system, a data source for preprocessing is a SCADA system.

A web service is a software system identified by a unique web address (URL) with standardized interfaces, as well as an HTML site document displayed by the user's browser. During the implementation, a technical task was written and the client and server parts were implemented. The client part of the system was executed in the Javascript language using the ExtJS framework version 6.2.

Access to the server part in the client part is carried out through the implementation of specialized classes of the framework - models and storages (see Fig. 2).

According to the developed system architecture (see Fig. 1), the system components are implemented. Each component is represented by an interconnected group of classes that extend the framework's classes.

So, for example, when a task is executed in parallel, it is necessary to create a queue of executed tasks as the data is processed. It is also necessary to provide for the prioritization of the processing process depending on the capacity of each device in the cluster. In this case, when a priority task arises, it is necessary to implement a mechanism for transferring the task from a more powerful PC in the cluster to a less powerful one. This is what characterizes the interoperability of parallel cluster interaction. It is necessary that the PC in the cluster should be able to determine the type of the task and the degree of its completion. With this approach, the transactionality of actions within the system is excluded [4, 5].

With the sequential organization of workstations in a cluster, the task of parsing and preprocessing can be performed on each computational node separately. With this approach, there is no need to create a task queue. It is enough to determine the priority of the process and assign the task to the corresponding PC cluster. Let us give an example with the processing of various production reports of SCADA systems (a certain number of reports). When sequentially processing the data of each report, it is assigned the PC of the computing cluster to perform parsing, preprocessing or processing operations. In

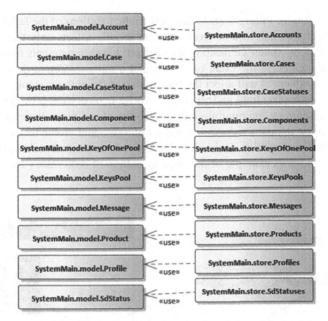

Fig. 2. Simple class model for front-end models and data stores.

the case of parallel, the report is divided into fragments and sent for processing and so on for each report of the system. At the same time, the training sample of each cluster node during sequential processing has greater accuracy (since the artificial intelligence was trained on a specific dataset), while the parallel organization of the cluster increases universality.

The main and most important goals in ensuring the security of the operation of storage networks and network storage can be identified as ensuring availability and ensuring fault tolerance.

High availability clusters typically use all available methods to make individual systems and the shared infrastructure as reliable as possible. These methods usually include:

- disk mirroring (or redundant arrays of independent disks-RAID);
- redundant network connections;
- backup connections to a storage area network (SAN);
- redundant power inputs in different circuits.

A storage network that uses redundancy consists of a fault-tolerant system of two similar SAN networks. A redundant SAN configuration provides two independent paths for each device connected to the SAN.

A critical segment of a computing system forms a fault domain - an area of the network that is affected by failures in the operation of a critical device or network service.

The impact on the failure domain depends on the functions of the failed device. For example, a faulty switch in a network segment usually affects only the hosts in that segment. And if the router connecting the segment to other segments fails, the impact will be much greater. In the event of a failure of a more important device, such as a server, the consequences will affect the functioning of the entire system.

The use of redundant links and reliable enterprise-class devices provides redundancy for the critical segment and minimizes the possibility of computer disruption. Reducing the size of failure domains reduces the impact of individual problems on the company as a whole. It also simplifies troubleshooting and reduces downtime for all users.

Figure 3 shows an example of the implementation of redundancy through channel redundancy.

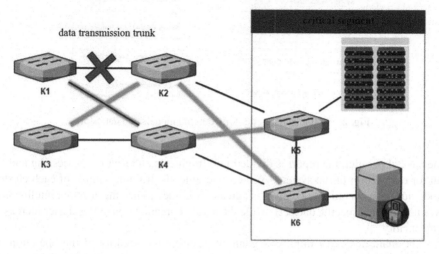

Fig. 3. An example of using redundancy of critical segments in distributed computing systems. (Color figure online)

In Fig. 3, the devices of the critical segment are shown on the right; the data line is on the left. Green lines indicate redundant links between switches K1−K6 and provide redundancy and interoperability.

3   Evaluating the Interoperability

A quantitative assessment of interoperability is based on the assumption that interoperability in a distributed system or system of systems (SoS - System of Systems) is determined by the potential ability of each of the components to exchange or use the information obtained as a result of the exchange. And there is also [the way the element effects the resulting indicator] the effect of this element on the resulting indicator, which is taken into account by the weighting factors [1].

Improving the achievement of interoperability should be seen in close connection with the following characteristics:

- functionality;
- productivity;
- reliability;
- scalability;
- security (the higher the security requirements, the more difficult it is to ensure interoperability).

Having assessed the interoperability index for each of the system components using a suitable reference model, one can quantify the interoperability of the system or the system of systems as a whole.

To obtain quantitative estimates of interoperability, we introduce a number of variables and functions:

- X is the name of a variable capable, for definiteness, of taking values in the range from 0 to 100;
- T(X) is term-set X, i.e. the totality of its linguistic meanings;
- U is a universal set;
- G is a syntactic rule generating terms of the set T(X);
- M is a semantic rule that assigns to each linguistic value X the value of a fuzzy variable M(X), which denotes a fuzzy subset of the set U [1].

The term-set T(X) can be represented as a qualitative scale, ranging from the meaning "Low" to "High". It has been shown in scientific works that in expert evaluation of the characteristics of open systems and software products, good results are obtained with the number of terms from three to five, while the differences between the extreme cases are relatively small.

If necessary, the construction of membership functions (MF) for each indicator can be performed using one of the well-known methods, for example, the method of paired comparisons, based on expert or interval estimates, using a parametric approach, etc.

First of all, the interoperability index of each element affects the interoperability index of the entire system with a certain weight (j), the formula for finding the quantitative value of interoperability:

$$I = f(I_{el1}^{j1}, \ I_{el2}^{j2}, \ \ldots, \ I_{eln}^{jn}). \tag{1}$$

To calculate the interoperability of each element of the distributed data storage system, it is necessary to calculate a set of indicators, each of which has a certain weight (k). Here is a formula for calculating the interoperability of a separate element of the system, depending on its indicators:

$$I_{eli} = f(X_{i1}^{k1}, \ X_{i1}^{k1}, \ \ldots, X_{i1}^{k1}). \tag{2}$$

The rules of fuzzy inference are in the formation of a fuzzy base of rules for assessing the "interoperability" indicator. These rules are in the table where an element of the term set of linguistic values of the interoperability indicator is assigned to each set of indicators of individual elements of the system (see Table 1):

Table 1. Fragment of a fuzzy rule base for assessing the interoperability indicator.

If	Then
X1 = L and X2 = BA and … and Xk = L X1 = L and X2 = BA and … and Xk = A X1 = L and X2 = A and … and Xk = BA	Iel1 = L
X1 = A and X2 = A and … and Xk = H X1 = A and X2 = H and … and Xk = H X1 = AA and X2 = A and … and Xk = H	Iel1 = H

Where: L – "Low", BA – "Below average", A – "Average", AA – "Above average", H – "High".

To obtain an estimate of the interoperability of a system, rules must be aggregated at each level of the hierarchy against the corresponding rule base. This requires performing an intersection operation (logical minimum, AND - $\otimes$) on each row of the rule base and a concatenation operation (logical maximum, OR - $\oplus$) corresponding to one judgment (one term). An example of such calculation using a fuzzy rule base from Table 1 for the term "H" of the first element of the system is given below:

$$\mu^H(I_{el1}) = \mu^H(X_1) \otimes \mu^{HC}(X_2) \otimes \ldots \otimes \mu^H(X_k) \oplus \mu^H(X_1) \otimes \mu^{HC}(X_2) \otimes \\ \ldots \otimes \mu HXk \oplus \mu HX1 \otimes \mu HCX2 \otimes \ldots \otimes \mu HXk \tag{3}$$

where μ is the degree of membership of the indicator of the corresponding term [1].

If the indicators have different importance and weights are attributed to them, then they are inserted into the above operations as powers of the values of each of the indicators. The weights themselves can be determined based on the procedure of paired comparison of indicators [9]. First, a matrix of importance of indicators of each element is formed, the elements of which are found from the table of importance and satisfy the following conditions: $b_{ii} = 1$; $b_{ij} = 1/b_{ji}$. Then w is found which is the eigenvector of the importance matrix corresponding to the maximum eigenvalue. The sought values of the coefficients α_i are obtained by multiplying the elements w by n to satisfy the condition $\alpha_i = nw_i$ [10].

Let us apply this scoring mechanism to evaluate a distributed data storage system with a computational cluster. As it has been mentioned earlier, a distributed data storage system consists of a distributed data store, a compute cluster, and a user client (cluster task scheduler). So, the interoperability of the distributed data storage system can be calculated by the formula:

$$I_{DDSS} = f\left(I_{storage}^{j1}, I_{comp.cluster}^{j2}, I_{client}^{jn}\right). \tag{4}$$

The interoperability of modules of a distributed data storage system with computing clusters is determined by indicators of the availability of remote connection to databases by communication protocols, the availability of reference information describing the formats and organization of data used in the process of interaction and interaction of organizations of system developers. The weight of the indicator that determines the availability of reference information describing the formats is extremely important and a coefficient of 0.6 is assigned to it. The organization of interaction between system developers is of greater priority than the availability of the ability to remotely connect to databases with communication protocols, since the availability of remote connection is described by standards and does not need additional consideration [1].

Thus, these indicators are assigned values 0.25 and 0.15, respectively. So, for each element of the system:

$$I_{eli} = f(0.6semantic.int_i + 0.25org.int_i + 0.15tech.int_i). \tag{5}$$

Weights are defined in terms of their significance, where 1 is the maximum value. Indicators are calculated on a term scale from low to high. Next, term estimates are reduced to a single term indicator. If the estimates contain values "average" and below, the indicator is reduced to the value "low", in other cases - "high" or "average" with a coefficient of closeness to the value on a quantitative scale (0.7L or 0.3A or 0.2BH). As a result of assessing the interoperability of the distributed data storage system with computing clusters, we obtain:

$$I_{DDSS} = 3(0.6semantic.int_i + 0.25org.int_i + 0.15tech.int_i). \tag{6}$$

Further calculation of interoperability depends on the choice of specific software solutions and implementations.

4 Conclusions

The infrastructure of systems and networks of distributed storage and data processing should provide:

- multiple access;
- delivery of the requested data;
- detection and reservation of information resources;
- linking custom applications and resources.

SCADA is a system for monitoring the production process of an enterprise in real time. The system integrates subsystems for interaction with industrial controllers and input-output boards for reading bar codes, GPS trackers. The prospects for the development of SCADA systems are the use of distributed data storage subsystems with computing clusters. The use of an interoperable solution for combining these systems enables monitoring streaming data from production cameras to record audio files from PCs workstations, to investigate and process data from users' input interfaces. This approach will enable us to control the production process.

Decision-making can be automated by artificial intelligence implemented in a computing cluster of a PC, the dataset of such cluster is a distributed data storage system; a data source for pre-processing is SCADA system.

The interoperability of modules of a distributed data storage system with computing clusters is determined by indicators of availability of the ability to remotely connect to databases by means of communication protocols, the availability of reference information describing the formats and data organization used in the process of interaction and interaction of organizations of system developers.

A hybrid method for the implementation of a network-centric production storage system in distributed [efficient] high-performance computing systems is considered.

The quantitative assessment of interoperability is based on the assumption that interoperability in a distributed system or system of systems is determined by a potential ability of each of the components to exchange information or use information [1].

Server clustering can be indispensable when the maintenance of the highest fault tolerance is required. Servers can be decompensated across global networks to provide the necessary distance between the servers. However, these servers can connect to the local SAN similarly, and the local SAN can contain additional clusters.

Acknowledgements. This work has been prepared within a framework of the State Assignment with the support of the Russian Foundation for Basic Research (project No. 119-07-00774).

References

1. Bashlykova, A.A.: Distributed Data Storages (Khraneniye Raspredelennykh Dannykh). MIREA, Moscow, Russia, pp. 60–72 (2021) (In Russia)
2. Shklar, L., Rosen, R.: Web Application Architecture: Principles, Protocols and Practices, pp. 46–52. Wiley, Chichester, UK (2009)
3. Rosstandart: Information technologies. Industrial automation systems and integration. Interoperability. Basic principles (Informacionnye tehnologii. Sistemy promyshlennoj avtomatizacii i ih integracija. Interoperabel'nost'. Osnovnye polozhenija). Russian state standard GOST R 55062-2012. Standartinform, Moscow (2018) (in Russian)
4. Bashlykova, A.A., Zatsarinny, A.A., Kamenshchikov, A.A., Kozlov, S.V., Oleynikov, A.Y., Chusov, I.I.: Interoperability as a scientific-methodological and normative basis for seamless integration of information and telecommunications systems (Interoperabel'nost' kak nauchno-metodicheskaya i normativnaya osnova besshovnoy integratsii informatsionno-telekommunikatsionnykh system). Syst. Means Inform. **28**(4), 61–72 (2018) (In Russian). http://cplire.ru:8080/6251/1/Zacarin_Olein_2018.pdf
5. Bashlykova, A.A., Kozlov, S.V., Makarenko, S.I., Oleynikov, À.Y., Fomin, I.A.: An approach to ensuring interoperability in network-centric control systems (Podkhod k obespecheniyu interoperabel'nosti v setetsentricheskikh sistemakh upravleniya). J. Radio Electron. **6**, 116 (2020) (In Russian). http://jre.cplire.ru/jre/jun20/13/text.pdf
6. Basok, B.M., Zakharov, V.N., Frenkel S.L.: Iterative approach to increasing quality of programs testing. Russian Technol. J. **5**(4) 3–12 (2017) (in Russian)
7. Bashlykova, A.A.: Design and standardization of information, information-computing and telecommunication systems (Proyektirovaniye i standartizatsiya informatsionnykh, informatsionno-vychislitel'nykh i telekommunikatsionnykh sistem). MIREA, Moscow, Russia (2021) (In Russian). http://catalog.inforeg.ru/Inet/GetEzineByID/331815
8. Pfandzelter, T., Hasenburg, J., Bermbach, D.: From zero to fog: Efficient engineering of fog-based Internet of Things applications. Softw. Pract. Experience **51**, 1798–1821 (2020). https://doi.org/10.1002/spe.3003
9. Tomashevskaya, V.S., Yakovlev, D.A.: Research of unstructured data interpretation problems. Russian Technol. J. **9**(1), 7–17 (2021) (in Russian)
10. Petushkov, G.V.: Evaluation and reliability prediction for highly reliable software and hardware systems: the case of data processing centers. Russian Technol. J. **8**(1), 21–26 (2020) (in Russian)

Internet of Things for Reducing Commercial Losses from Incorrect Activities of Personnel

Elena Andrianova⬚, Gayk Gabrielyan, and Irina Isaeva(✉)

MIREA – Russian Technological University, Vernadsky Avenue 78, 119454 Moscow, Russia

Abstract. Examples of using the Internet of Things in ERP systems to reduce commercial losses from incorrect activities of personnel are considered. The classification of business processes to reduce commercial losses from incorrect activities of personnel using the Internet of Things is given. Methods are proposed: exclusion of the human factor in the implementation of business processes using the Internet of Things, human factor management and a combination of both methods. It is noted that the risks associated with incorrect actions of the personnel are recognized as the main risks in the company's activities. The proposed classification of business processes in terms of reducing commercial losses from incorrect activities of personnel on the basis of the Internet of Things makes it possible to determine business processes that require control of incorrect actions of personnel. The application of the developed methods based on the Internet of Things for each selected category of business processes provides an opportunity to minimize potential losses.

Keywords: Internet of Things · ERP · Incorrect activities of personnel · Business processes · Human factor engineering

1 Introduction

The most popular approach to modeling a corporation's work is the process approach. The company's activities are considered to be a set of related procedures - business processes. Implementation of business processes ensures the continuous functioning of the technological cycle of the company.

Recent studies and reviews on the digital transformation of companies' activities primarily focus on business management and strategic company management. The human factor is a key factor influencing the digital transformation of a company as a whole and the digital transformation of an individual business process. The human factor is a weak link in business process management because of its instability, unpredictability and illogical behavior in various situations. The recent COVID-19 pandemic has accelerated business digitalization trends while increasing the importance of staff resilience to adapt to rapidly changing work environments and widespread technological incidents. The impact of human factors is often negative, though not intentional.

There are various lines of research devoted to finding ways to reduce the probability of the negative impact of the human factor.

V. Jordan et al. (Eds.): HPCST 2021, CCIS 1526, pp. 287–296, 2022.
https://doi.org/10.1007/978-3-030-94141-3_23

The article [1] suggests a conceptual model structuring the search for human factor risks in companies doing business in an international environment in the context of globalization and digitalization. The authors investigate the impact of current trends in the era of digitalization and globalization on company activities. A two-level model linking the main sources of risks (technological advances, governmental and legal issues, cultural changes) with risks arising from the human factor (work performance, work skills and competencies, work ethics and discipline, work patterns, environment and tools) is proposed. The authors provided a framework for identifying the sources of risks associated with the work environment and suggested human resource management options in view of this context.

The article [2] is devoted to the possibilities of estimating the implicit elements of the human factor's influence on the efficiency of the company's business processes performance. These factors involve unconscious competence, creativity and intuitive prognosis. The provided factors, according to the authors, are crucial in the transition to digital business and require the evolution of managerial behavior and attitude to human capital. The data obtained by the authors from the interviews of management personnel were complemented by a documentary analysis of descriptions of internal processes for the implementation of digital accounting tools, including human resource management applied to remote work during the pandemic. The results revealed a synergistic effect arising from the transition from team-based business process management to a trust-based increase in the personal responsibility of the business process performer.

The authors of the article [3] extend traditional approaches to the organization of the safe operation of the company. They suggest that people's personal tendencies should be taken into account in order to reduce the number of errors, events and incidents by improving the quality of the interaction between employees and improving the organizational culture of business process safety. The authors analyzed and verified more than half a million testimonies of how people behaved in critical production situations. The general conclusion of the article [3] is that the transfer of experience in behavior in critical situations allows companies to reduce the number of errors and incidents in critical or high-risk tasks. Also taking into account the personal elements of personnel contributes to the creation of more effective and user-friendly behavior instructions for personnel in critical situations.

The article [4] considers the communication between people and critical systems, as well as human capabilities to recognize and prognosticate the risk of an emergency situation. It has been noted that psychological well-being is a critical factor in the successful outcome of personnel actions. Psychological well-being is defined as a low level of fatigue, stress and distractibility, as well as a high level of resilience, positively influencing the coherence of personnel actions, critical thinking and decision making in work groups and critical systems. The authors of the article [4] suggest that addressing only technical or mechanical controls without considering human behavior limits efforts to secure processes and reduce serious incidents. They propose a system of resilience that takes into account several inter- and intrapersonal factors that contribute to the psychological and emotional well-being of personnel. These psychological processes are related to documented safety influences, including situational awareness and decision-making. The purpose of this research is to find out how biases and distracted thinking (lack of attentiveness) are addressed in the decision-making process in the energy industry to improve mental well-being and human performance. Examples of critical situations and their resolution by business unit managers are described, taking into account the psychological features of human behavior. Preventive measures to reduce personnel distractions are described.

The article [5] discusses the issues of ensuring the effectiveness of monitoring to obtain correct estimates of the parameters of manifestations of critical technogenic production processes. The organizational structure of the monitoring system with a reasonable time and address measurement mode, taking into account the main features and stages of the formation of controlled technogenic processes, is given. The organizational structure of the monitoring system with a reasonable time and address measurement mode, taking into account the main features and stages of the formation of controlled technogenic processes, is given. The requirements for ensuring the appropriate qualifications of personnel for the correct interpretation of the obtained results of monitoring measurements are also indicated. The correspondence of the estimates obtained with the real state is the basis for making informed decisions on a set of measures to ensure technosphere safety.

The rapid development of new digital technologies (artificial intelligence, robotics, cloud computing and the Internet of Things), radically transforms not only business models, but also the workplace of company personnel. The article [6] is devoted to assessing the impact of digital business transformation on the workplace of the company's staff and on the change in the types of skills, competencies and thinking of the staff. The results of the study [6] are integrated into a three-level structure. At the individual level, five main factors related to the effective digital transformation of staff activities are proposed: technology adoption; perception and attitude towards technological change; skills and training; sustainability and adaptability in the workplace; and work-related well-being. At the team level, three factors necessary for digital transformation are identified: team communication and collaboration; workplace relationships and team definition; and team adaptability and resilience. At the organizational level, three factors for digital transformation are identified: leadership, human resources and organizational culture. The results of the study confirm that taking into account the highlighted factors is important when planning and starting digital transformation as a basis for the company's business processes re-engineering.

To ensure effective management of the implementation of business processes ERP system is used - a set of technical and software tools that implement the ideas and methods to automate all business processes of the business system. A promising way to support and control the actions of company personnel is to use the Internet of Things technology at the lower level of the ERP system. The Internet of Things is a global network of computers, sensors and actuators that communicate with each other using the Internet Protocol. Control over the collection of information from sensors and control over the validity of manually entered data allow for increased trust and control over the execution of the company's business processes.

A traditional area of the application of the Internet of Things technology is to provide safety engineering in the implementation of business processes to support the technological cycle of the company. For example, the article [7] describes the use of the FireNot system to prevent and notify fire incidents. FireNot is a cloud system of the Internet of Things. It uses sensors to detect a fire and alert the user via the Internet. FireNot is supported and controlled by means of a simple Android app. The FireNot system is designed to provide an extensible platform for additional daily monitoring tasks and resilience against most cyber attacks. The article [8] describes a decision support system based on the location of personnel locations within a company's internal premises. Determining the exact location of personnel in real time allows us to manage the work of personnel quickly. Bluetooth Low Energy devices are used to track the location of each employee in the premises.

The aim of this work is to build and develop methods of using the Internet of Things to reduce commercial losses from incorrect actions of staff.

2 Methods

The influence of the human factor can lead to both positive and negative impacts on the results of the enterprise. In most cases, the negative impact that occurs as a result of human error is not the goal of the person who made the error. The person performs incorrect or illogical actions, treating them as correct and logical.

Possible reasons for the negative manifestation of the human factor [9]:

- lack of information in decision makers;
- insufficient level of psychological training for the tasks to be solved;
- lack of interest in the results of work;
- influence of external factors that cause stress state;
- lack of confidence in the success of the actions taken.

Currently, it is impossible to remove the person from all business processes, so it seems appropriate to introduce control over his actions and decisions at all stages of the business process. The technology of the Internet of Things can be used for this. The information collected by the Internet of Things sensors is a valuable asset. It provides insight into the subject or process that is used in software products to provide intelligence. One of the most critical requirements is the quality of the information.

The ERP system provides the collection, processing and storage of information necessary to manage the company. Accordingly, in the structure of ERP systems there are three control levels: strategic, tactical, operational [10].

At the strategic level, global tasks are solved – the company's goals are defined, and management assesses how to achieve them.

At the tactical level, medium-term tasks are solved, the achieved results are evaluated and a further action plan is determined.

At the operational level, short-term tasks and transactions are solved.

Figure 1 shows the use of the Internet of Things technology for the tactical and operational levels of management. The strategic level of company management requires the use of artificial intelligence systems and is not considered in this context.

Other modern IT technologies, such as virtual or augmented reality, can also be used to reduce the influence of the human factor [11]. From our point of view, the most

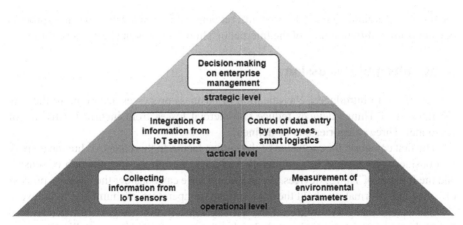

Fig. 1. Directions for the application of the Internet of Things technology at management levels of ERP systems.

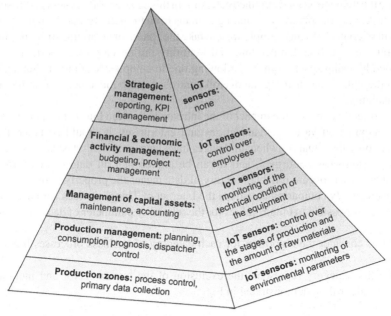

Fig. 2. Options for using the Internet of Things devices in the context of the functional architecture of the ERP system.

effective solutions are based on the Internet of Things technology, which provides not only removable information (RFID tags, sensors, controllers), but also interaction with the production environment, partially or completely replacing human functions. The Internet of Things devices can interact with the physical environment in the same way that personnel do. Introducing the Internet of Things devices into business processes modifies existing business processes and creates entirely new ones. At different levels of the functional architecture of ERP systems, reflecting different levels of business process decomposition, different uses of the Internet of Things devices can be proposed (Fig. 2).

3 Results and Discussion

It is proposed to introduce a classification of business processes according to the way the Internet of Things devices reduce commercial losses from incorrect activities of personnel. Three categories can be defined:

The first category: the exclusion of the human factor. In this category, human activity in a business process can be completely excluded through the introduction of sensors and the Internet of Things devices. As an example, we can consider the business process of collecting information about the environment: temperature, air humidity, light levels.

The second category: control of the human factor. In this category of business processes, human activity cannot be excluded, but can be controlled by an intelligent system that uses the Internet of Things technology. For example, this could include the use of a smart helmet as a measure to control compliance with safety rules at work.

The third category: the combined category. In this category of business processes, part of the tasks may be solved by excluding humans from the activity, part by introducing an element of control. As an example we can take the sphere of smart logistics - monitoring of parameters such as temperature and humidity during cargo transportation can be provided by using special sensors, allowing one to completely eliminate human input, and at the same time ensuring the overall control of cargo movement left in the human responsibility.

To correctly consider the impact of the introduction of the Internet of Things devices in the activities of various organizations and enterprises, it should be noted that we consider only the situation when all devices have been previously tested. The accuracy of their readings is confirmed, and it can be argued that all data received from the implemented sensors are reliable. Validity of data means the property of data to have no hidden errors. By comparing data from the Internet of Things devices with data entered by users, it is possible to obtain values for the reliability parameter of data received from users.

Let us consider the algorithm for each category of business processes highlighted above.

The first category represents the exclusion of the human factor and includes the following algorithm, demonstrated in Fig. 3.

1. The end user initially sets the parameters - normal values, which are stored on a special device – an anomaly detector – and monitored by it.
2. The values of the measured physical parameters, which are taken into account in the business process, instead of the employee who entered the data into the EIS, are now delivered there by the Internet of Things sensors. The data from the sensors goes to the server.
3. From the server, which aggregates the data from the sensors, the raw data is sent to the anomaly detector. It compares the obtained values with the user parameters and returns the processed and cleaned data to the server (it is possible to add special tags or another way to alert if the data goes beyond the user-defined parameters).

4. From the server, the data is transferred to the data storage, from where it is received by the ERP system and outputs, to the end user for decision-making and monitoring the situation based on the collected data.

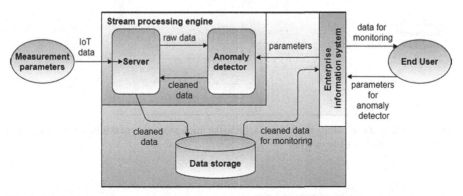

Fig. 3. Method of excluding the human factor in the implementation of business processes using the Internet of Things technologies.

The second category is human factor control, and it includes the following algorithm of actions, demonstrated in Fig. 4.

1. The end user initially sets the parameters - normal values, which are stored on a special device – an anomaly detector – and monitored by it.
2. The value of the measured physical parameters, which are required by the business process, is entered by the employee. The supporting parameters, which are not directly involved in the activity of the business process, but allow evaluating the employee's work, are transmitted from the sensors of the Internet of Things. All the data goes to the server.
3. From the server, the raw data from both the user and the sensors is sent to the anomaly detector. It combines the data, compares the obtained values with the user parameters and returns the cleaned and combined data to the server (special tags can be added or another way to alert if the data goes beyond the user-defined parameters).
4. From the server, the data is transferred to the data storage, from where it is received by the ERP system and outputs, to the end user for decision-making, employee control and monitoring the situation based on the collected data.

The third category is a combination of exclusion and control, and it includes the following algorithm, demonstrated in Fig. 5.

1. The end user initially sets the parameters - normal values, which are stored on a special device – an anomaly detector – and monitored by it.
2. The values of the measured physical parameters that are required by the business process are partly entered by the employee and partly taken from the Internet of Things sensors. All of the data goes to the server.

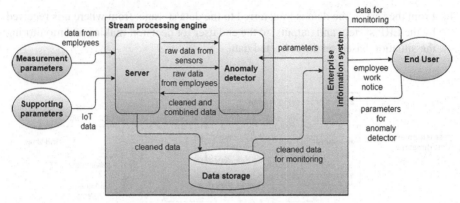

Fig. 4. Method of controlling the human factor in the implementation of business processes using the Internet of Things technologies.

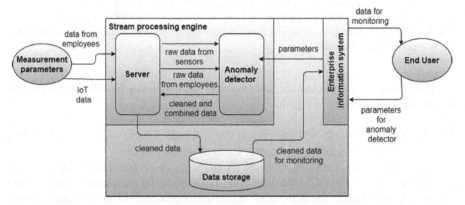

Fig. 5. Combined method for reducing the human factor in the implementation of business processes using the Internet of Things technologies.

3. From the server, the raw data from both the user and the sensors is sent to the anomaly detector. It combines the data, compares the obtained values with the user parameters and returns the cleaned and combined data to the server (special tags can be added or another way to alert if the data goes beyond the user-defined parameters).

4. From the server, the data is transferred to the data storage, from where it is received by the ERP system and outputs to the end user for decision-making and monitoring the situation based on the collected data.

In the case of the second and third methods, when the user input is involved, the data is aggregated on the server, and the resulting data is considered by the information system as valid and participate in further business processes.

Data received from users should be pre-processed and validated. For this purpose data from sensors are collected, partially duplicating the data received from users.

In order to have an array of values for the processing of data from users to be evaluated objectively, it is necessary to accumulate the values that are collected after the installation of the Internet of Things devices in advance, before the complete and final integration of the system.

Based on the collected array, after the launch of the integrated system, when receiving data from users and from sensors of the Internet of Things, 3 options of available actions can be considered:

The first option is that the information received from the user does not contradict the information from the sensors and can be marked in the information system as confirmed.

The second option: in case of inconsistency of the information received from the user, this information will not be used in the ERP system and is marked as erroneous.

In the third option, it is impossible to unambiguously trust the information from the user, it is necessary to check the array of previously collected values to assess the possibility of such situation.

One option for using, whether the data received from a user is confirmed or erroneous, could be the introduction of a user reliability factor into the system, increase in the control of employees by company management and optimization of workforce resources.

4   Conclusions

It is known that the risks associated with incorrect activities of personnel are the main risks in the company's activities. There are many organizational ways to reduce or avoid the consequences of these risks. For example, it is trust management aimed at increasing the responsibility of personnel for their actions. Trust management reduces the costs associated with the need for oversight and promotes the growth of positive communication links between staff. However, trust management does not guarantee the absence of incorrect personnel actions, which is critical when performing some business processes.

The proposed options for using Internet of Things devices in the context of the functional architecture of the ERP system guarantee either the absence of incorrect activities of personnel, or minimization of losses from incorrect activities of personnel.

The considered classification of business processes according to the method of reducing commercial losses from incorrect activities of personnel based on the Internet of Things makes it possible to determine the processes where the use of technical control of personnel actions will be effective.

The developed methods for excluding the human factor in the implementation of business processes using the Internet of Things, human factor management, or a combination of both methods ensure the regular implementation of the business process by the personnel. The application of the developed methods based on the Internet of Things for each selected category of business processes allows minimizing potential losses.

References

1. Morabito, R., Cozzolino, V., Ding, A.Y., Beijar, N., Ott, J.: Consolidate IoT edge computing with lightweight virtualization. IEEE Netw. **32**(1), 102–111 (2018)

2. Hamm, A., Willner, A., Schieferdecker, I.: Edge computing: a comprehensive survey of current initiatives and a roadmap for a sustainable edge computing development. In: Proceeding of WI2020, pp. 694–709. GITO Verlag, Potsdam, Germany (2020). https://doi.org/10.30844/wi2020g1-hamm

3. Pfandzelter, T., Hasenburg, J., Bermbach, D.: From zero to fog: efficient engineering of fog-based IoT applications. In: Mobile Cloud Computing Research Group Technische Universit at Berlin & Einstein Center Digital Future (2020)

4. Pfandzelter, T., Bermbach, D.: IoT data processing in the fog: Functions, streams, or batch processing? In: Proceeding of EEE International Conference on Fog Computing (ICFC), 24–26 June 2019, Prague, Czech Republic, pp. 201–206 (2019)

5. Mikhailov, V.M.: The effectiveness of monitoring as a necessary condition for the adoption of correct decisions on the security of technosphere. Russian Technol. J. 8(2), 23–32 (2020) (in Russian). https://doi.org/10.32362/2500-316X-2020-8-2-23-32

6. Darwish, T.S.J., Bakar, K.A.: Fog based intelligent transportation big data analytics in the Internet of vehicles environment: motivations, architecture, challenges, and critical issues. IEEE Access 6, 15679–15701 (2018)

7. Sassani, B.A., Jamil, N., Villapol, M., Abbas, M., Tirumala, S.S.: FireNot – an IoT based fire alerting system: design and implementation. J. Ambient Intell. Smart Environ. 12(6), 475–489 (2020). https://doi.org/10.3233/AIS-200579

8. Álvarez-Díaz, N., Caballero-Gil, P.: Decision support system based on indoor location for personnel management. Remote Sens. 13(2), 248 (2021). https://doi.org/10.3390/rs13020248

9. Brusakova, I.A., Mamina, R.I.: Specifics of the human factor in the conditions of digital enterprise (Specifika chelovecheskogo faktora v uslovijah cifrovogo predprijatija). In: Proceedings of XVII Russian Scientific and Practical Conference on Planning and Teaching Engineering Staff for the Industrial and Economic Complex of the Region, 14–15 November 2018, St. Petersburg, Russia, pp. 169–171 (2018)

10. Dantes, G.R., Hasibuan, Z.A.: Strategical and tactical impact on ERP implementation: case study on ERP implementation in Indonesia. In: Proceedings of the 15th IBIMA Conference on Knowledge Management and Innovation: A Business Competitive Edge Perspective, November 2010, Cairo, Egypt, pp. 1198–1207 (2010)

11. Zuev, A.S., Makushchenko, M.A., Ivanov, M.E., Merkulov, E.S.: Extended reality technology – a new component in industrial engineering and production systems. Russian Technol. J. 8(4), 46–65 (2020) (in Russian). https://doi.org/10.32362/2500-316X-2020-8-4-46-65

Method of Constructing the Assigned Trajectory of a Multi-link Manipulator Based on the "Programming by Demonstration" Approach

Vadim Kramar$^{(\boxtimes)}$ (iD), Vasiliy Alchakov (iD), and Aleksey Kabanov (iD)

Sevastopol State University, Universitetskaya Street 33, 299053 Sevastopol, Russia

Abstract. The article discusses an approach to the construction of control of an anthropomorphic (multi-link) manipulator of a robotic complex, based on applying the "Programming by Demonstration" approach. The proposed approach is based on the developed methodology for constructing a knowledge base based on the data obtained from the sensors of the copying suit as a result of training the robotic complex by the operator. The structure of the knowledge base and the data processing mechanism for filling it are given. An example of a procedure for averaging data obtained from a copying suit as a result of "training" a manipulator of a robotic complex is given. An approach to constructing the trajectory of a manipulator based on data from a knowledge base, based on the use of ideas of terminal control, is considered. In addition to the precise execution of the manipulator movements, the approach proposed in the article ensures the fulfillment of the initial and final conditions imposed on the manipulator movement. The proposed method allows organizing the control of manipulators of a robotic complex without building or using a complex and often not always accurate mathematical model. The developed technique was tested on the SAR-401 anthropomorphic robot.

Keywords: Supervised learning · Multi-link manipulator · Complex robotic system · Knowledge base

1 Introduction

The widespread use of robots and robotic systems is a steady trend in modern industry. It can be argued that the use of multi-link (anthropomorphic) manipulators of complex robotics systems (CRS) with a large number of degrees of freedom will expand, for example, for underwater operations. Such manipulators will significantly improve the accuracy of manipulation operations, approaching the repetition of a person's hand movement.

In connection with the need to increase the share of automation when performing work with anthropomorphic manipulators in remote and hazardous environments, it is necessary to solve the problem of end-effector automatic orientation (manipulation) of

© Springer Nature Switzerland AG 2022
V. Jordan et al. (Eds.): HPCST 2021, CCIS 1526, pp. 297–313, 2022.
https://doi.org/10.1007/978-3-030-94141-3_24

the multi-link manipulator. Modern robots can build a program of their actions, taking into account the external environment. They can also store an extensive array of received information but also partially process it. This allows performing complex manipulative operations in adverse environmental conditions using intelligent technologies.

One example of robots with anthropomorphic manipulators is the complex robotics system SAR-401 [1], which can be used as a prototype in underwater and space CRS development.

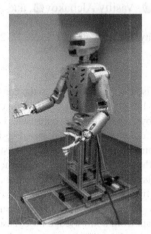

Fig. 1. The SAR-401 robot.

Currently, there are well-known and generally accepted approaches to the construction of control of anthropomorphic manipulators with kinematic redundancy, such as the approach based on the solution of complex systems of nonlinear differential and finite-difference equations of large dimension [2] and the approach based on the application of the Denavit-Hartenberg method [3]. The "Programming by Demonstration" approach is actively being developed for the CRS control construction [4, 5]. The "Supervised learning" approach consists of teaching the robot to perform various operations based on the «teacher» action results.

The "Programming by Demonstration" approach for building control of complex robotic systems is promising since mathematical models of functionally complex CRS do not take into account many factors. These are various nonlinearities arising due to saturation of engines, due to the influence of friction, due to wear and tear of equipment, as well as environmental influences, for CRS operating in a complex environment. In addition, in some cases, the mathematical model of the CRS may not be known. It should also be noted that the application of classical approaches requires significant simplifications. Otherwise, the multi-linking nature of the manipulator requires taking into account a large number of parameters, which in turn will lead to a large number of calculations that do not allow real-time control.

The "Programming by Demonstration" approach eliminates the above disadvantages, making it promising for constructing control for an anthropomorphic manipulator, especially considering its possible functioning in conditions of uncertainty.

The article discusses the construction of control based on the "Programming by Demonstration" approach of the CRS with multi-link manipulators by building a knowledge base and processing the knowledge base data in real-time. This includes using terminal control approaches to construct the trajectory of the manipulator movement, satisfying the initial and final conditions. Section 2 describes a methodology "Supervised learning" technique. Section 3 describes the method of constructing a knowledge base for controlling the movement of the CRS and the generalized structure of the CRS control system based on the application of the knowledge base. Section 4 describes the algorithm for generating the assigned motion based on the data received from the copying suit.

2 Materials and Methods

An anthropomorphic-type copying suit (Fig. 2) is associated with the CRS SAR-401 (Fig. 1) and a workstation with preinstalled specialized software required for the implementation of the "Programming by Demonstration" approach.

Fig. 2. The copying suit.

Application of the "Programming by Demonstration" approach to constructing a control provides the anthropomorphic manipulator CRS with a generated vector of the desired output values y_i, for the corresponding input vectors x_i, $i \in \{1, 2, \ldots, n\}$. The task is to form the mapping $\hat{y} = f(x)$, where $\hat{y}$ is the predicted result that minimizes the error for a given training set:

$$E = \sum \|\hat{y} - f(x)\|. \tag{1}$$

The methodology of "teaching" the control system of the CRS is based on building a connection between the sensors of the copying suit and the corresponding engines of the

CRS manipulator. As a result – the construction of a knowledge base contains processed information that facilitates the organization of the manipulator movement, for example, the values of the generalized coordinates of the manipulator that change in time.

The mapping of the sensor readings to the required rotation angles is non-trivial and non-identical since the space of the input state is large and the unknown objective function is non-linear. Such mapping is called a "2m-to-n" mapping and has the following form (Fig. 3) [6]:

$$
\begin{bmatrix} b_1 \\ t_1 \\ b_2 \\ t_2 \\ \dots \\ b_m \\ t_m \end{bmatrix} \Rightarrow \begin{matrix} Learning \\ Algorithm \end{matrix} \Rightarrow \begin{bmatrix} \theta_1 \\ \theta_2 \\ \theta_3 \\ \theta_4 \\ \dots \\ \theta_n \end{bmatrix}
$$

Fig. 3. "2m-to-n" mapping.

Here b_m and t_m are the angles of bending and twisting, respectively, for each of the m sensors, and θ_n is the angle of rotation for each of the n joints of the manipulator. In practice, not all copy sensor values can be used. It should also be noted that the same sensors would give different values for "teachers" with various anthropomorphic indicators. Also, we note that since the robot's knowledge is not static, it is necessary to maintain regular data updates.

3   Results

The software for the "Programming by Demonstration" approach has a client-server structure. On the client's side, the user can choose between various options: collect data for the training phase, train and test the training algorithms, or control the robot manipulator in real-time using a trained system. The server part is a shared database for storing and accumulating new data on typical trajectories of the CRS manipulator.

The copy suit (Fig. 2) is a set of sensors, each of which corresponds to one of the CRS manipulator and gripper system actuators. Each sensor of the suit is equipped with an individual analog-to-digital converter (ADC). The signals from the ADC, in turn, form data packets, which are transmitted to the control programs and the server database. Then these signals are sent to the CRS actuators. As a result, the sensors of the copying suit form data packets, which are transmitted to the control programs and the server database, after which they are broadcast to the CRS actuators.

As a result, the trajectory of movement of the manipulator, which is a time series, is formed. It is also called "virtual trajectory" [7]. This virtual trajectory is the basis for building a knowledge base about typical movements and modes of operation of the CRS, which, in turn, is the core of the CRS control system [6].

The client-server software solution for implementing the proposed approach "Programming by Demonstration" implies the presence of a centralized control server with a knowledge base and a set of client programs for interaction between the hardware parts of the copying suit and the CRS. The client program of the copying suit is the main agenda of the software for network packets coming from the IP address 127.0.0.1 and port 10003 via the UDP protocol. It registers the digitized signals from the copying suit sensors in the knowledge base. Next, it records the digitized signals from the suit sensors in the knowledge base. The client program for CRS control selects specific control programs from the database server and sends information frames of control commands to the CRS via the TCP protocol (connection is made to IP address 127.0.0.1, port number 10099). Simultaneous operation of the copying suit client program and the CRS client program is not provided.

The data package from the copying suit is an array of bytes, the structure of which is determined in the program settings file and may vary depending on the task being solved and the design of the CRS. The package is divided into three parts. The first part of the package is responsible for the current timestamp, which corresponds to the registered sensor signal, followed by a text label – the sensor ID and the third part – the corresponding numerical value – the registered sensor signal.

The peculiarity of the sensors is that the numerical values corresponding to the rotation angles of the CRS control devices come from sensors in the "Raw Data" format. For the convenience of storing and subsequent processing of information, these numerical sequences are transformed into values corresponding to the actual angle of rotation of the control motors. The coefficients responsible for converting raw data into actual values are contained in a particular configuration XML – file.

The calculation of the value of the registered signal from the sensor copying suit is performed using the ratio:

$$realDataValue = (rawDataValue + offset) \times K, \qquad (2)$$

where the scaler K and *offset* coefficients are the attributes that are used to convert the "Raw Data" format to the actual values of the rotation angles of the actuators.

An example of recording a configuration file for the elbow joint of the anthropomorphic manipulator (attribute name = "L.ElbowR") has the form:

```
<jointname="L.ElbowR" scaler="0.094">
<raw index="258" type="_int16" offset="-1770" />
</joint>
```

Here the scaling factor – "scaler" = 0.094. The coefficient "offset" = –1770. The beginning of the information packet corresponding to this sensor starts with 258 bytes of the information frame and takes 2 bytes (following the data type for this sensor signal).

As mentioned above, the CRS software package includes a client program that communicates with the copying suit and allows you to register "Raw Data" streams from the sensors and recalculate the "Raw Data" into actual values of the rotation angles in real-time. Collected from sensors and converted information is logged as external files and is also used to populate data tables on the database server. The use of various formats and structures for the presentation of data is allowed. In particular, the ability to save the collected data as CSV-files is supported. Figure 4 is an example of such a file with data obtained using the client application.

	A	O	P	Q	R	S	T
1	Time	R.ShoulderF	R.ShoulderS	R.ElbowR	R.Elbow	R.WristR	R.WristS
2	100	-1,008	-6,776	-11,938	0,8	34,684	1,598
3	200	-1,008	-6,864	-12,032	0,8	34,626	1,786
4	300	-1,071	-6,952	-12,22	0,8	34,626	1,598
5	400	-1,071	-6,952	-12,22	0,8	34,626	1,692
6	500	-1,071	-7,04	-12,502	0,8	34,626	1,692
7	600	-1,071	-7,04	-12,408	0,8	34,568	1,598
8	700	-1,386	-7,216	-13,536	0,08	34,568	0,752
9	800	-2,016	-7,656	-16,45	-4,58	34,51	-2,538
10	900	-2,646	-8,448	-13,442	-12,86	34,22	-3,854
11	1000	-3,528	-9,856	-10,058	-22,48	34,162	-5,358

Fig. 4. Presentation of data from sensors in the form of a CSV – file.

The specified format is quite convenient for analysis and preliminary processing of results, particularly for visualization, which is necessary for preliminary analysis of the collected data for the presence of outliers or erroneously collected data.

When implementing the "Programming by Demonstration" approach, we are dealing with many data. Consequently, by adding information about new typical movements of the CRS manipulator, the knowledge base will grow. For the information storing in the knowledge base, the MS SQL Server database can be used [8]. The database consists of a set of tables for various purposes. Some tables are used to describe the configuration of the CRS – reference tables; another part describes the reference movement for various typical operations. An example of the lookup table structure is shown in Fig. 5.

VADESKTOP.SAR - db...AR - dbo.tblJoints ⇌ ✕		
Column Name	Data Type	Allow Nulls
⚷ ID	int	☐
JointName	varchar(50)	☐
JointCode	tinyint	☐
▶		☐

Fig. 5. TblJoint reference table structure.

The knowledge base table tblJoint is used to store the names of the nodes and their corresponding numeric codes. The ID field is used as a unique primary key and is automatically generated. The JointName field is intended to store the text names of the manipulator nodes (Table 1), and the JointCode field is intended to store the corresponding numeric code. The need to use numeric codes instead of textual naming of nodes is due to the need to save space in the data tables and the speed of accessing these tables and retrieving the necessary data.

Table 1. Manipulator node names.

Name	Description
R.ShoulderF or L.ShoulderF	The shoulder forward movement
R.ShoulderS or L.ShoulderS	The side shoulder movement
R.Elbow or L.Elbow	The elbow fold
R.ElbowR or L.ElbowR	The elbow rotation
R.WristF or L.WristF	The wrist forward movement

Another look-up table is designed to store information about typical control programs stored in the knowledge base. The table format is shown in Fig. 6.

VADESKTOP.SAR - d...ogramsDescription		
Column Name	Data Type	Allow Nulls
ID	int	☐
ProgramName	varchar(50)	☑
ProgramDescription	varchar(MAX)	☑
ProgramCode	smallint	☑
ProgramTypeCode	smallint	☑
		☐

Fig. 6. TblProgramsDescription lookup table structure.

The tblProgramsDescription table is intended for storing information about the existing standard reference programs for the movement of the CRS. The table structure contains a unique ID field used as the unique primary key. ProgramName is a string value used for the short name of the program, this value coincides with the name of the table in which the corresponding motion program is stored. ProgramDescription is a detailed description of the reference motion program (used by the CRS operator). ProgramCode is a unique numeric code corresponding to the driving program. ProgramTypeCode is a numeric code used to group motion programs by type (for example, manipulator positioning programs, object capture programs, reset programs, etc.).

Programs of typically assigned movements are stored in tables with the same structure, but with different names of typical movements, which, in turn, are stored in the tblProgramsDescription table. An example of the structure of one of these tables is shown in Fig. 7.

VADESKTOP.SAR - db....tblProgramInitial ⊓ ✕		
Column Name	Data Type	Allow Nulls
🔑 ID	int	☐
TimeSpan	int	☑
JointCode	smallint	☑
JointValue	float	☑
▶		☐

Fig. 7. The structure of the table of the typically assigned motion tblProgramInitial, intended for transferring the CRS to the initial state for performing the operation.

The ID field is a unique field. It is generated automatically and acts as a primary key. The TimeSpan field is an integer value characterizing the time interval relative to the beginning of the motion program execution, upon the occurrence of which a control signal is sent to the control node, the code of which is stored in the JointCode field, the value of which is stored in the JointValue field.

Thus, in the tables of typically assigned movements, the codes of the control nodes are stored and not the text labels corresponding to them. This approach speeds up the process of searching tables and simplifies the structuring of data. The program responsible for executing a typically assigned motion accesses the corresponding data table, grouping control signals by the TimeSpan field, and forms a temporary table of the motion program in RAM. After that, the execution timer starts, and commands begin to flow to the CRS.

In the case of a polynomial representation of the assigned trajectory of movement, data tables, having the format shown in Fig. 8, are used.

VADESKTOP.SAR - d...bo.tblProgramCoef ⊓ ✕		
Column Name	Data Type	Allow Nulls
▶🔑 ID	int	☐
ProgramID	int	☐
TimeSpan	int	☑
CoefVector	nvarchar(MAX)	☐
		☐

Fig. 8. The structure of the table for storing the coefficients of the assigned trajectory of movement for various modes of operation of the CRS.

In many scenarios, robot-learning algorithms deal with large amounts of data from the imaging suit's sensors. Based on the learning outcomes, the control algorithms of the RTK should be efficient in terms of computations without sacrificing the training accuracy [9]. Therefore, when teaching RTK to specific movement programs with a

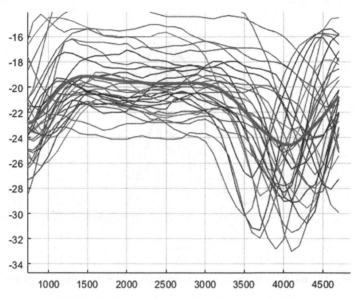

Fig. 9. Training program data and averaging result.

teacher, the same movement program is repeated a certain number of times (in most cases, about 20–30 times) by the teacher. At the same time, it is assumed that when executing a typical program, "operator-teacher" performs the same action with a particular error, i.e., the signals from the sensors of the copying suit vary within a specific range. Thus, it becomes necessary to perform a preliminary procedure for averaging the obtained data sets before using the collected data to build control programs on their basis. So, for example, the learning outcomes of one of the designated movement programs and the averaging result have the form shown in Fig. 9.

The averaging procedure is carried out using the standard Matlab function "mean" [10]. An example of averaging is:

$$R\_WristS = mean(R\_WristS\_Data).$$

However, not all typical assigned trajectories can be averaged in this way. For example, this approach is not applicable for some signals recorded or reproduced with a time-shifted master suit, as shown in Fig. 10.

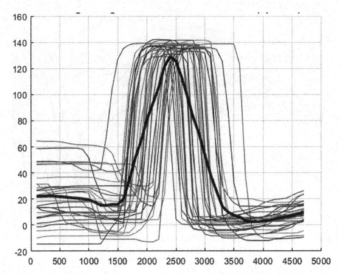

Fig. 10. Incorrect averaging of experimental data of the training program.

Characteristics of this type must be pre-centered on the timeline. Such centering is performed using a specially developed algorithm, shown in Fig. 11.

Applying the averaging operation for centered data, we get the dependence, shown in Fig. 12.

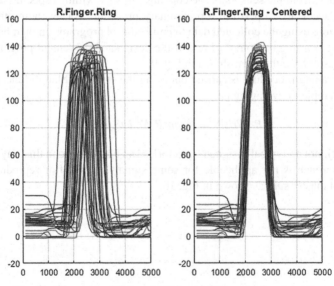

Fig. 11. The result of the work of the timeline centering algorithm.

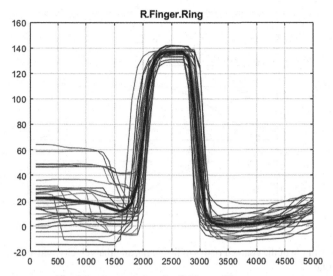

Fig. 12. Average data for R.Finger.Ring sensor.

4   Discussion

4.1   Algorithm for Generating the Assigned Motion

We consider a fragment of a set of data reflecting the dependence of the angle of rotation of the CRS manipulator in relative coordinates (Fig. 13). The data contains a solution to achieve the control goal and match the trajectory of the manipulator to the learning path. Based on the data received from the copying suit, dependencies can be obtained that reflect the dynamics of changes in control parameters over time, which will help to solve the task of the "trajectory of the manipulator", mentioned above.

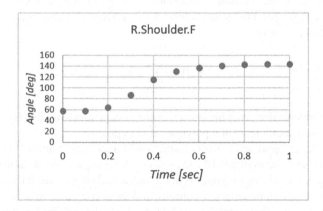

Fig. 13. Experimental data for node R.Shoulder.F.

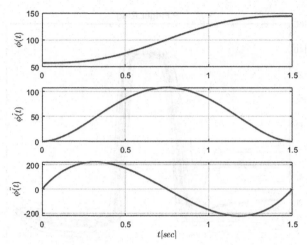

Fig. 14. An example of the characteristics of the angle, angular velocity, and angular acceleration of the manipulator.

As shown in Fig. 14, the time series is characterized by the initial and final state at time instants $t_0 = 0$ s and $t_f = 1$ s. The initial value of the rotation angle is $\varphi_0 = 57.436$ deg, and the final value is $\varphi_t = 144.088$ deg. We require that the angular velocity and angular acceleration of the controlled parameter at the initial and final moments be equal to zero: $\dot{\varphi}_0 = \dot{\varphi}_f = 0$, $\ddot{\varphi}_0 = \ddot{\varphi}_f = 0$.

The last requirement is typical of the operation of the manipulator. An example of the characteristics of the angle, angular velocity, and angular acceleration of the manipulator is shown in Fig. 14.

The problem is solved by finding, according to the values from the knowledge base, a polynomial that describes the change in the angle of rotation of the manipulator in time in such a way that the values of the polynomial at the initial and final moments completely coincide with the given boundary conditions $X_0 = [\varphi_0 \; \dot{\varphi}_0 \; \ddot{\varphi}_0]$ and $X_f = [\varphi_f \; \dot{\varphi}_f \; \ddot{\varphi}_f]$. Provided that these conditions are achieved for a given time interval t_f, the desired polynomial has the form:

$$\hat{\varphi}(t) = \sum_{j=0}^{r} a_j t^j, \tag{3}$$

where t is an independent variable (time), $\varphi(t)$ is a dependent variable (rotation angle), a_j are the desired coefficients of a polynomial of degree r.

We consider an approach to the construction of a terminal control [11]. Let us construct a polynomial that will describe the change in the angle of rotation in time in such a way that the values of the polynomial at the initial and final moments will completely coincide with the given boundary conditions, and these conditions will be achieved in a given time interval t_f. This approach is valid for solving the problem because restrictions on the trajectory are imposed only at the initial and final stages, and the intermediate trajectory should be similar to the experimental one, without leaving the workspace. In general, the trajectory can be described by relations of the form:

$$\varphi(t) = \sum_{i=0}^{5} c_i t^i,$$

$$\dot{\varphi}(t) = \sum_{i=1}^{5} i c_i t^{i-1}, \tag{4}$$

$$\ddot{\varphi}(t) = \sum_{i=2}^{5} \frac{i!}{(i-2)!} c_i t^{i-2}$$

where the coefficients c_i are determined based on the boundary conditions imposed on the starting and ending points of the designated motion path and the given transition time to the terminal state, r is the size of the vector of initial conditions (in our case $r = 3$), n is the size of the vector of final conditions ($n = 3$).

The coefficients c_i in (4) can be found as a solution to the system of algebraic equations constructed based on the polynomial representation and its derivatives, as well as based on the specified boundary conditions determined by the vectors $x(t_0)$ and $x(t_f)$. In general, this system has the form:

$$\left.\begin{array}{l}
x(t_0) = c_0 + c_1 t_0 + c_2 t_0^2 + \ldots + c_n t_0^n \\
x^{(1)}(t_0) = c_1 + 2c_2 t_0 + \ldots + n c_n t_0^{n-1} \\
x^{(n)}(t_0) = n! c_n \\
x(t_f) = c_0 + c_1 t_f + c_2 t_f^2 + \ldots + c_n t_f^n \\
x^{(1)}(t_f) = c_1 + 2c_2 t_f + \ldots + n c_n t_f^{n-1} \\
x^{(n)}(t_f) = n! c_n.
\end{array}\right\} \tag{5}$$

For the considered time series, the constructed polynomial will have the form:

$$\varphi(t) = 68.466t^5 - 256.747t^4 + 256.747t^3 + 57.436. \tag{6}$$

The graphic dependence corresponding to this polynomial is shown in Fig. 16. We note that the calculated curve obtained using a polynomial (6) completely coincides with the experimental data only at the ends of the time interval – at points t_0 and t_f. Nevertheless, the main requirement is fulfilled – the error between the experimental data and the polynomial dependence at the start and endpoints of the interval is zero, and the time to reach the final interval is equal to the specified. The trajectory corresponding to these conditions is called a «terminal» trajectory [12] (Fig. 15).

4.2 Generation of Assigned Motion Based on the Neural Network Approach

As an alternative, we consider the application of the common approach of finding a polynomial representation based on a regression model using neural network training. The polynomial $\hat{\varphi}(t)$ should minimize the relation:

$$S = \sum_{i=0}^{n} (\varphi(t_i) - \hat{\varphi}(t_i))^2 \to \min, \tag{7}$$

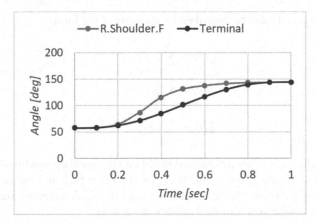

Fig. 15. Experimental data and polynomial terminal trajectory.

where $\varphi(t_i)$ is the experimental data, $\hat{\varphi}(t_i)$ is the calculated data.

As a training sample, we will use the initial time series from the constructed knowledge base.

To solve this regression problem, we use the Accord.NET Framework library of numerical methods. This library contains a description of the class implementation of the PolynomialLeastSquares class, which uses the least-squares method to build the best system model in terms of minimizing errors. When creating an instance of the class, the desired degree of the resulting polynomial representation is indicated. (Unlike the previous terminal method, the degree of the polynomial is determined by the number of initial and final conditions and cannot be changed arbitrarily).

In the example, by analogy, we create an instance of a class with a polynomial of the 5th degree. A training sample is transferred to the class instance, which consists of a set of values of an independent variable (time samples act as an independent variable) and a corresponding set of attributes (for a given problem, a set of attributes is the value of the angle of rotation of the motor of the CRS manipulator node).

As a result of calculations, a 5th order polynomial is obtained, which has the form:

$$\varphi(t) = -470.87t^5 + 2119.627t^4 - 3149.54t^3 + \ldots \\ \ldots + 1789.2t^2 - 202.48t + 58.65. \tag{8}$$

The graphic dependence corresponding to this polynomial is shown in Fig. 16.

From Fig. 16 it can be seen that despite the high degree of correspondence between the initial experimental trajectory and the trajectories constructed for the regression model, the error between the experimental and calculated values at the ends of the interval is not zero. Significant deviations are also visible in the initial and final sections of the trajectory caused by the so-called retraining of the model.

The number of nonzero elements of the constructed polynomial is higher when applying a regression model using neural network training (which is worse from the point of view of using the memory of a computing device). In addition, it should be noted that from the point of view of computing costs, the first method is much less resource-intensive and takes 50–60 times less in time. The time it took to calculate the terminal trajectory was 0.384 ms. The time of the regression model calculation was 23.448 ms. This fact can be decisive when choosing an algorithm when constructing real-time systems.

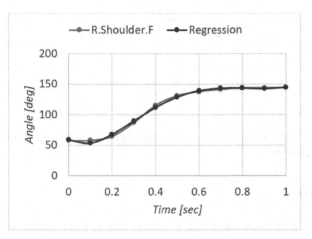

Fig. 16. Experimental data and the trajectory obtained using the regression model with a degree of polynomial equal to 5.

An attempt to reduce the degree of the polynomial when applying the regression model by training the neural network does not give a significant increase in time, the estimated time was 20.185 ms, while the standard error increased from 5.76 to 39.5. For example, a 3rd order polynomial has the form:

$$\varphi(t) = -236.5t^3 + 249.209t^2 + 77.43t + 51.3 \qquad (9)$$

As can be seen from Fig. 17 the use of a regression model with a polynomial of degree 3 yielded results unacceptable in terms of accuracy because boundary conditions at the ends of the trajectory are practically not observed.

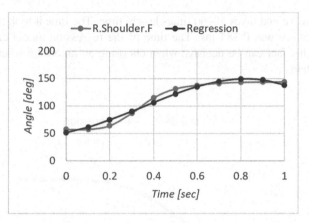

Fig. 17. Experimental data and the trajectory obtained using the regression model with a degree of polynomial equal to 3.

5 Conclusion

The possibility of applying the teaching-teacher approach to build control of the anthropomorphic manipulator CRS SAR-400 is considered. The principle of creating a knowledge base based on signals received from the sensors of the copying suit is considered. An approach is proposed based on the construction of the knowledge base of the MS SQL Server database, which is structured and allows you to store data in an optimized way, allowing you to solve the "target" task of manipulation. Based on data from the knowledge base, it is proposed to build a terminal control of the RTK manipulator, which determines the dynamics of changes in the control parameters in time, in terms of achieving the specified boundary values for a given time interval, which will help to solve the "manipulator motion path" problem. The proposed approach for reproducing the designated movements of the CRS manipulator allows storing, in the knowledge base, not the entire time series of the experimental trajectory but only the coefficients of the polynomial terminal trajectory. Further, it will be sufficient only to calculate the values of the angles using the known polynomial at predetermined time intervals in real-time and transmit the corresponding signals to the CRS actuators.

The study is accomplished within the framework of the state order of the Ministry of Science and Higher Education of the Russian Federation: "Fundamental principles and development of new methods of analysis and synthesis of information and control systems of autonomous marine robots of various types and purposes".

References

1. Zhidenko, I.G., Kutlubayev, I.M., Bogdanov, A.A., Sychkov, V.B.: Basis of structural scheme selection of space application robots. Reshetnev's Readings **17**, 278–280 (2017)
2. Peters, J., Lee, D., Kober, J., Nguyen-Tuong, D., Bagnell, A., Schaal, S.: Robot learning. In: Siciliano, B., Khatib, O. (eds.) Springer Handbook of Robotics, pp. 357–398. Springer International Publishing, Cham (2016). https://doi.org/10.1007/978-3-319-32552-1_15

3. Münch, S., Kreuziger, J., Kaiser, M., Dillmann, R.: Robot programming by demonstration (RPD) – using machine learning and user interaction methods for the development of easy and comfortable robot programming systems. In: Proceedings of the 25th International Symposium on Industrial Robots, pp. 685–693. Hannover Messe, Flexible Production, Flexible Automation (1994)
4. Siciliano, B., Khatib, O.: Robot Programming by Demonstration, Handbook of Robotics. Springer-Verlag, Heidelberg (2008). https://doi.org/10.1007/978-3-540-30301-5_60
5. Alchakov, V., Kramar, V., Larionenko, A.: Basic approach to programming by demonstration for an anthropomorphic robot. IOP Conf. Ser. Mater. Sci. Eng. **709**, 022092 (2020)
6. Skoglund, A.: Programming by Demonstration of Robot Manipulators. Orebro University, Sweden (2009)
7. Zhu, Z., Hu, H.: Robot learning from demonstration in robotic assembly: a survey. Robotics **7**(17), 1–25 (2018)
8. Sarka, D., Radivojevic, M., Durkin, W.: SQL Server 2017 Developer's Guide. Pacts Publishing Ltd, Birmingham (2018)
9. Bottou, O., Chapelle, D., DeCoste, J.: Large-Scale Kernel Machines. MIT, Cambridge (2007)
10. Attaway, S.: Matlab: A Practical Introduction to Programming and Problem Solving. Elsevier Inc., Amsterdam (2009)
11. Batenko, A.P.: Linear models in terminal-state control systems. Electron. Model. **3**(6), 1290–1299 (1984)
12. Batenko, A.P.: Optimization of terminal controls by the method of gradual improvement. Eng. Cybern. **18**(5), 134–140 (1980)

Developing a Microprocessor-Based Equipment Control Panel for Rifle Sports Complexes

Ishembek Kadyrov[1](✉) ⓘ, Nurzat Karaeva[1], Zheenbek Andarbekov[1],
and Khusein Kasmanbetov[2]

[1] Skryabin Kyrgyz National Agrarian University, Mederov Street 68,
720005 Bishkek, Kyrgyz Republic
[2] Razzakov Kyrgyz State Technical University, Ch. Aitmatov Avenue 66,
720044 Bishkek, Kyrgyz Republic

Abstract. The article is dedicated to problems in development of microprocessor-enabled range equipment control panels. Such a panel is intended to control firing range equipment consisting of stationary and movable popup targets in target shooting sports centers, as well as auxiliary equipment, alarms and communication with other facilities. The solution is intended to be used in rifle sports complexes. A short explanation is given on the philosophy of signal receiving and transferring by means of radio communication links, as well as by power cable from the control panel located at the command observation post and receiving radio station located at a switchgear. Separation of control and information signals takes place at the reception module of the switchgear by means of seven filters in parallel arrangement set to one lead frequency and six command frequencies. The switchgear identifies two command sequences: one of them provides energizing the input unit relay corresponding to the object's address; the other sequence is related to the duration of the command execution. The active relay supplies power to the controlled object through its closed contacts. Advantages of microprocessor-based range equipment control panels have been identified that provide flexible control of equipment, acquisition of reliable information on status of all the relevant objects, step-by-step querying and information display on the screen.

Keywords: Rifle sport · Range equipment control · Microprocessor-based control · Switchgear · Range safety

1 Introduction

From times immemorial, people have been doing sports in order to develop such physical attributes as strength, speed, dexterity, endurance, flexibility, while systematic and methodical training allows perfecting these attributes, which is especially true of such a sport as target shooting. Target shooting is a sport that requires creating special conditions for training, i.e., specially equipped training grounds for continuous training that facilitates development of skills: situational control, endurance training, will power, strength of character that allows momentarily reacting to an existing situation, quickly finding a

V. Jordan et al. (Eds.): HPCST 2021, CCIS 1526, pp. 314–324, 2022.
https://doi.org/10.1007/978-3-030-94141-3_25

correct solution and above all else having everything under control. Most notably, it is true of beginning sportsmen, methodically developing innate physical qualities by continuous training. Even for middle-aged people, target shooting is a fascinating leisure pursuit, aimed at strengthening one's health, stimulating self-actualization and bringing joy. For many people who became fascinated with this sport in their youth, it has been creating a purpose in their life ever since [1].

In modern target shooting centers, there are shooting ranges for rifle and pistol shooting and artificial landscapes are created to imitate natural conditions encountered during amateur hunting. Training of sportsmen in target shooting usually involves preparing shooting sites for three main athletic disciplines:

- practical shooting (pistol, carbine);
- trap shooting (clay target shooting);
- precision engagement (100 and 800 m).

2 Problem of Firing Range Automation

Training grounds for precision engagement training shall be equipped with specialized shooting range equipment that includes popup targets intended for raising and lowering targets used during the training; moving targets (animal cutouts) for training hunters in rifle and pistol shooting. The range safety officer controls the range equipment by means of control panels, which may be either portable or installed in specially equipped locations. Besides, the control panel shall control the operation of additional equipment, activate alarms, communication equipment and other components of the range equipment.

2.1 Functions of Control Panel

The control panel for shooting range equipment shall perform the following operations [2]:

- provide manual as well as programmable control of popup and moving target actions, the latter usually includes two or three variants of target activation;
- record target hits and time of exercise completion;
- unblock previously hit targets for subsequent exercises;
- provide continuous monitoring of moving target locations;
- monitor the situation in the fire area and inform on presence of a target or a group of targets, as well as operation of electric drives, etc.;
- during the shooting, *ATTENTION*, *FIRE* and *ALL CLEAR* signals shall be clearly displayed by visual signaling devices, selection of initial positions, opening and ceasing fire, main firing direction boundaries and dangerous directions shall be implemented with bright lighting devices;
- communication between range safety officer and students (selector or over-the-radio) shall be continuous.

Thus, in order to form control inputs for range equipment meeting the above requirements, a range equipment control panel shall be either implemented in hardware where each requirements is implemented with the help of ICs of medium and large-scale integration brought together into a digital system, or by means of microprocessor technology.

The digital system allows implementing a shooting range equipment control panel that performs some or most of the listed tasks, depending on the system's complexity. At that, implementation of individual functions may use separate elements or groups of elements.

2.2 Design Constraints

During the development of hardware-based range control equipment it shall include a possibility for time settings to be applied to a single popup, groups of popups in a given direction, or all popups in all directions. At that, transmission of information on a target being hit to the control panel requires laying a control cable and installing an indicator on the control panel to display the resulting hits in the decimal numeric form. To that end, the control board shall include binary-decimal counter, decoder of binary-decimal code to the seven-segment code used to transform the number of target hits into the numeric code with subsequent indication.

The control panel shall include an integrated digital stopwatch for setting up delays for raising and lowering the targets and controlling the time of completion of the exercises, at that the timer information shall be displayed on the front panel in the form of second count and in the minutes and seconds format.

Shooting control panels are usually fixed in a special location and are usually called a command post. In this case, within the firing range there are usually special sites for installation of popup targets at various distances from the shooter location, while information on hit targets comes over the control cables. However, it is possible to set up the popup targets arbitrarily through the fire range, in accordance with the wish of the range safety officer. In this case, the most convenient variant for control over the range equipment is wireless communication with the control panel.

Shooting control panel has functional capabilities to provide radio communication and control of equipment over the radio. To that end, there are remote control command blocks provided for both individual targets and groups of targets. The principle of frequency-division multiplexing used in the control panel allows forming the lead frequency and six additional fixed command frequencies, which are usually lower than the lead frequency [3–6]. Figure 1 shows a functional diagram illustrating the operation principle of the remote control system.

2.3 Operational Concept

When a command received to *RAISE* or *LOWER*, the RC-generator and encoder are activated and for 1.5 s provide leading frequency at the modulator input of the control panel radio transmitter. From these commands, the remote control system automatically readjusts the generator to producing one of six operating frequencies, while the encoder

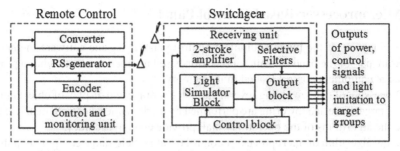

Fig. 1. Functional diagram of the remote control system.

supplies the necessary command frequency for no more than 0.4 s, after that the encoder disconnects the transmitter modulator input from generator output.

Remote control transmitter set to the same frequency as the receiver located near the switchboard, receives the remote control signal and amplifies it in the receiving section of the switchboard. Having being amplified by a push-pull amplifier, the signal is supplied to seven parallel filters, set to the leading frequency and six command frequencies. Command distinction is performed by means of current resonance appearing in the filter set to the lead frequency, which results in actuation of a device that supplies power to all the devices related to command frequency selection filters for 0.5 s. The relevant output relay will be activated if during this time one of command frequencies arrive, resonating with the selective filter tuned to the same frequency. The relay will be energized and its closed contacts will supply the service power to the executive circuit.

To exclude false execution of commands, the receiving unit relays are disconnected after 0.5 s if there are not command frequencies following the lead frequency.

The above example of signal transmission over radio channels demonstrates that in digital range control panel it is possible to make provisions for transmission and reception of commands and telemetry not only by radio but by a two-wire line as well. At that, there is no need to lay a separate control cable, as it is possible to use power cables for command transmission and reception.

In this variant of facility control, two sequences of radiofrequency signals are transmitted through the power cable or over the radio. Of them, one contains the address of the controlled object, and the other contains the information about duration of the command execution.

In order to continue the training cycle, previously hit targets may be unblocked by ceasing power supply to the popup target in the local control mode, or by disconnecting supply of power to the range equipment control panel for a short time in the remote mode.

The digital system that allows for hardware implementation of the range control panel is highly reliable, provides smooth operation of all the facilities and does not require additional operational expenses [2].

Its main drawback is that its boards include a large number of discrete electronic components, thus they are cumbersome and expensive. Due to that, there is a need to switch to development of range control panels using the software implementation of necessary control algorithms.

3   Microprocessor-Based Control Panel

In development of the range equipment control panel using the software method, the hardware part of the panel is a microprocessor-based microcomputer that has a program for range equipment control loaded in its memory.

Processing of data involving several variables, storage and display of object number, time of target raise and lowering are performed by modern microcontrollers in real-time, while the algorithms of the operations shall provide enough accuracy.

In the algorithm of microprocessor control of target field range equipment, unblocking signals are formed for individual addresses of the targets hit and recorded in the microprocessor memory. Simultaneously, the number of unblocking signals shall correspond to the number of hit targets if there are several of them in the direction of shooting.

3.1   Control Logic

The algorithm of the microprocessor-based range control panel is usually composed as a result of studying functional capabilities included in typical range control panels and covering the same sequences of operation during shooting trainings [2]. In order to ensure enough flexibility to microprocessor control of range equipment, the performed tasks may be expanded, thus the developer is given a possibility to introduce additional function to maximally use capabilities of the microprocessor systems.

Range objects controlled by microprocessor control panel get the executive commands from special output ports of the microcontroller, which are used to arrange energizing the contact switches of actuators. It gives foundations to select a microprocessor time, at that, productivity of control signal formation depends on the number of units of equipment controlled from the panel. Development of microprocessor-based shooting range control panels shall be based on typical control panels that operate 12 popup targets and 2 movable frames for moving targets. Such control panels provide actuation of visual alarms to signal a change in the situation: *ATTENTION* during the preparatory period, *FIRE* when there is an ongoing shooting training, *ALL CLEAR*, signaling the end of the exercise; the signals shall be actuated with three switches; there are four switches for shooting position lighting, opening and ceasing fire, emphasizing the main direction of shooting as well as boundaries of dangerous directions.

In total, the number of switches installed in typical range control panels in order to provide control of appearing and moving targets, visual alarms and lighting amounts to 21. Thus, the microcontroller-based control panel shall have the same number of inputs.

Taking into account organization of communication between the range safety officer and students, as well as with neighboring areas, it would require at least 3 switches. It increases the minimum number of output ports to 24, at that, the number of inputs shall be at least 40, taking into account the number of incoming data signals.

Transition to microprocessor-based system for range equipment control system is justified by provision of flexible control, graphic display of information on the status of all the controlled objects on screen. The microprocessor-based control of range equipment allows quickly and reliably conducting stage-by-stage query, at that, the most convenient fact is that the information is reflected in the textual form, which is difficult to accomplish in the hardware-based variant.

Due to that, the following objectives may be stated for development of the microprocessor-based variant for range equipment control in the context of this paper:

- determining the hardware component for the microprocessor-based range equipment control panel;
- development of software that allows meeting all the above stated requirements to range equipment control schemes.

Figure 2 shows functional diagrams for popup targets PT1 – PTN, provided by means of the microprocessor-based range equipment control panel (MRECP) under development. Figure 2a shows a layout diagram for the principal range equipment control over the radio, where transmission and reception of control signals and telemetry is covered by the use of additional radio communication elements. Figure 2b shows the same diagram but in the variant for two-wire communication with the range equipment [2, 7–9].

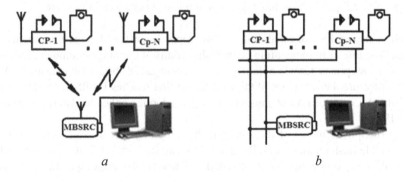

a b

Fig. 2. Two variants for range equipment control.

In order to organize control of range equipment with a radio-controlled MRECP (Fig. 2a) it is necessary to provide each popup target (PT) with their own independent power source (accumulator battery). At that, the radio frequency used for PT control shall be 450 MHz.

As for the second layout, that is, control of PTs over power cable, as shown in Fig. 2b, raise or lowering of all the popup targets is performed simultaneously by supplying or suspending power voltage, at that, control signals and telemetry are transmitted through the power cable with the radiofrequency component.

3.2 Hardware Design

As stated above, selection of the microcontroller, type depends on the number of objects controlled from the panel. This number determines the number of output ports necessary to arrange switching of final elements. It was suggested to base the development of the microprocessor-based range equipment control panel the layout of the most typical panel that operates 12 popup targets and 2 moving targets. At that, both variants outlined above use the same method for signal transmission and reception. The method is frequency modulation with time division channeling to control various range equipment.

Due to that, let us identify the principal elements of the microprocessor-based range equipment control panel shown in Fig. 2:

1. Microprocessor-based range equipment control panel that controls the range equipment and alarms within the target field.
2. Power cable providing electric power supply to equipment and communication between the microprocessor-based range equipment control panel and a personal computer.
3. Communication means providing radio communications between the MRECP and popup targets.
4. MRECP software, tasked to provide reliable control of range equipment in both manual and programmed modes. In addition to that, the software shall be provided with an algorithm for reception, storage and display of telemetry signals, tracking the state of targets appearing within the target field. This algorithm keeps score of target hits, keeps track of time taken to complete shooting exercises, etc.

Preliminary analysis of capabilities of a microprocessor-based range equipment control panel capable of implementing control algorithms of the range equipment led us to selecting a low-power CMOS microcontroller Atmega128, based on extended AVR-RISC architecture. Performance of this microcontroller reaches 1 million operations per second at a clock rate of 1 MHz, thus warranting its adoption as key hardware component of the MRECP [4, 10–12].

The principal elements of the Atmega128 microcontroller are: 128 kB of system programmable flash memory with Read While Write support; 4 kB of reprogrammable ROM with electric erasing; 4 kB of RAM; 53 universal input/output lines; 32 universal workspace registers; real-time counter (RTC); 4 flexible time counters allowing implementing comparison modes and PWM; 2 universal synchronous-asynchronous transceivers; two-wire serial user interface oriented to single byte information transmission; 10-bit ADCs with 8 input channels and optional differential programmable gain coefficient; programmable watchdog relay with integrated generator; SPI serial port. Additionally, the microcontroller includes a JTAG testing interface, compatible with the IEEE 1149.1 standard, used to access in-built debugging and programming system; six program-selectable power reduction modes.

Let us consider a simplified basic circuit arrangement of the microprocessor-based range equipment control panel shown in Fig. 3 and intended to control 12 popup targets in two directions and 2 moving targets. The layout of the panel is similar to a commonly used panels.

From Fig. 3 it is evident that the microprocessor-based range equipment control panel (MRECP) provides a serial input/output interface intended for connection to a radio channel or a radiofrequency cable transmission unit. Control of the radiofrequency signal transmission is by the PB0 output signal, the value of which affects reception

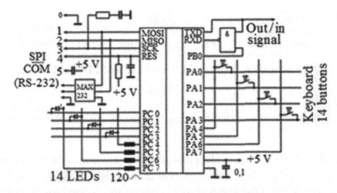

Fig. 3. Basic circuit arrangement of the microprocessor-based range equipment control panel.

and transmission of control and data signals in the controller. At that, PB0 = 0 means transmission of control signals and PB0 = 1 means reception of data signals (telemetry).

Manual control mode of the range equipment including stationary and movable targets is provided by means of a matrix of 14 switches connected to the controller's input, while dynamic querying is provided by means of a matrix of 14 LEDs connected to the controller's output.

SPI connector (shown in Fig. 3) is used for program input to the microcontroller, in this case it is integrated with the PC interface over RS-232. Interface connection over RS-232 is provided by means of IC MAX-232.

Provision of two-way simplex communication between popup targets and the MRECP is by means of ATMEL microcontroller type AT90S2313. This microcontroller is produced as a basic communication element and ensures reliable and continuous communication between the MRECP and all the range equipment units [13].

Independent of the data transmission method used (over the radio or by power cable), the common communication interface developed for this system uses time domain distribution of communication between the MRECP and popup targets following the cycle detailed below.

From the Start of Interval, as per time diagram (Fig. 4), transmission of the first byte W0 starts, consisting of consecutive 10 bits.

The first byte W0 contains information on the address of the popup target for which the subsequent control information is intended. The second byte W1 contains information about the command itself, (raise or lower), at that, the number of possible commands may reach 255. The third byte W2 ends the information transmission and contains a checksum $W2 = 256 - W0 - W1$.

Then there is a hold interval, during which all 12 popup targets are analyzing the received address and subsequently only one unit with the address corresponding to W0 starts answering with a R0 byte. This byte contains information on the status of the target (raised, lowered or hit). The next byte $R1$ contains the checksum, similar to the command transmission part: $R1 = 256 - R0$. After that, one time interval ends, having been spent to command and data exchange between the control panel and one of the popup targets.

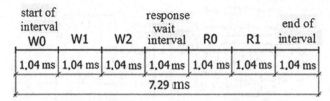

Fig. 4. Time diagram of information exchange between the control panel and a popup target.

From the time diagram, it is evident that after transmission of three information bytes of W0, W1 and W2 there is a waiting period at the MRECP output equal to 1.04 ms, which is required to form the status signal at one of the popup targets. Following that, in order to avoid breaking the common time balance in microcontroller operation, the MRECP continues with transmission of the address of the next popup target 7.29 ms later, etc.; this process continues until all the popup targets are queried. At that, transmission and reception of information through the assigned interface has the bit rate of 9600 bps.

Thus, the total time of querying only 12 stationary popup targets is 87.5 ms; this time is the maximum response time for controlling actions of the panel being developed.

3.3 Software Design

Microprocessor program is a sequence of commands that controls data processing in the microprocessor in order to provide control over all the connected targets. The command sequence may be represented graphically as a flowchart developed on the basis of existing functional or line diagram of the control circuit [14, 15].

It should be noted that the notation system, mathematical and logical operations are true only for the diagram shown in Fig. 4. This system of composing, debugging and compiling the program in Imagecraft version 7.0 may partially or differ completely from those encountered in other development programs.

Blocks shown in Fig. 5 are intended for performance of the following operations:

- UART is a universal synchronous-asynchronous transceiver.
- Bit PB0 = 1 corresponds to transmission of control signals.
- Setting timer interrupts to TIMER0 – 1ms, TIMER1 – 7.29 ms;
- SEI is permission of global interrupts;
- Exchange with blocks is data exchange between the MRECP and a PT;
- UDR is a UART data register;
- ADR0 is a transmission data register in PT no. 1;
- ADRN is a transmission data register in PT no. N;
- UDRE = 1 corresponds to the end of *UART* transmission;
- COM0 is the command register for transmission in PT no. 1;
- UDR = 256–COM0–ADR0 represents the checksum for transmission in PT no. 1;
- PORTA = 0x0F, DDRA = 0xF0 where half of the port is 1, and another half is 0, meaning that a half of the port operates as output and another operates as input (intended for analysis of button presses);
- PORTS1 is a register containing information on the state of port A;

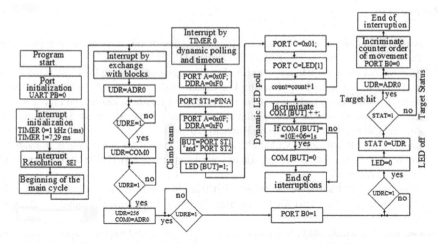

Fig. 5. Flowchart reflecting the control algorithm of the MRECP.

- PINA is an input data register of the port A;
- BUT is a register containing the number of the button pressed;
- BUT = PORT ST1 |PORT ST2;
- LED is a register containing information on energized LED (data array in RAM with the addresses of corresponding 14 energized LEDS);
- CSM is the checksum data register;
- COUNT is the time counter for the moment of command transmission to the PT no. 1.

4 Conclusions

During development of the microprocessor-based range equipment control panel, a typical control panel (based on medium and large IC) was taken as a basis for determining the number of control commands and telemetry lines.

The main drawback of the existing digital range control systems is that the boards contain a large number of discrete electronic component, making them bulky and expensive. Due to that, there is a need to switch to development of range control panels using the software implementation of necessary control algorithms.

The main advantage of the microprocessor-based range equipment control panel is that its software may be provided with functions providing flexible control, acquisition of reliable information on status of all the controlled objects, systematic querying and reflection of obtained information on screen.

In the radio-enabled variant, the range equipment units (popup targets) are provided with portable autonomous power sources and control of all the PTs is conducted through a 450 MHz radio channel.

In the variant of control over power cable, the power cables are connected to the range electrical system, while control and information signals from and to MRECP pass through the same cables as a high-frequency component.

References

1. Jasim, A.-S.H., Faisal, S.F.: Design and Implementation of O/C relay using microprocessor. Tikrit J. Eng. Sci. **19**(1) (2012). https://doi.org/10.2312/tjes.v19i1.10
2. Akulova, A.I., Korolev, P.I., Ivanova O.A.: Developing coordination in 13–15 years old shooters during technical training (Razvitie koordinacionnyh sposobnostej strelkov 13–15 let v processe tehnicheskoj podgotovki). In: Proceedings of Russia Scientific and Practical Conference with International Participation at the premises of the All-Russia State Institute of Physical Culture. Elist, Voronezh (in Russian) (2018)
3. Kadyrov, I.S., Bochkarev, I.V.: Developing a control system for popup targets (Razrabotka sistemy upravlenija ustanovki dlja podema i opuskanija mishenej). Herald KRSU **8**(1), 89–93 (in Russian) (2008)
4. Sadomskii, A.S.: Radiotechnical Information Transmission Systems (Radiotehnicheskie sistemy peredachi informacii). Ulyanvosk State Technical University, Ulyanovsk (in Russian) (2014)
5. Lukman, A., Mikail, O.O., Kolo, J.G., Ajao, A.: Project-based microcontroller system laboratory using BK300 development board with PIC16F887 chip. Int. J. Embed. Syst. Appl. **5**(3), 15–28 (2015). https://doi.org/10.5121/ijesa.2015.5302
6. Karimov, B.T., Bakytov, R.B., Karmyshakov, A.K.: Modern Wireless Communication Systems (Sovremennye Sistemy Besprovodnoj Svjazi). Kalem, Bishkek (in Russian) (2018)
7. Baskakov, S.I.: Radiotechnical Circuits and Signals (Radiotehnicheskie Cepi i Signaly). Vysshaia Shkola, Moscow (in Russian) (1983)
8. Borisov, V.A.: Radiotechnical Information Transmission Systems (Radiotehnicheskie Sistemy Peredachi Informacii). Radio and Communication, Moscow (in Russian) (1990)
9. Kliuchev, V.I., Terekhov, I.M.: Electric Drive and Automation of Common Industrial Mechanisms (Jelektroprivod i Avtomatizacija Obshhepromyshlennyh Mehanizmov). Energia, Moscow (In Russian) (2000)
10. Danilov, P.E., Baryshnikov, V.A., Razhkov, V.V.: Electric Drive Theory (Teorija Jelektroprivoda). Direct-Media, Berlin (in Russian) (2018)
11. Kadyrov, I.S.: Designing Electromechanical Systems for Automated Machines (Proektirovanie Jelektromehanicheskih Sistem dlja Mashin Avtomaticheskogo Dejstvija). Tekhnik, Bishkek (in Russian) (2006)
12. Rudenko, V.S., Sen'ko, V.I., Chizhenko, I.M.: Foundations of Converting Devices (Osnovy Preobrazovatel'noj Tehniki). Vysshaia Shkola, Moscow (in Russian) (1980)
13. Kadyrov, I.S.: Principles, Methods and Algorithms in Construction of Microprocessor-Based Control Systems for Electromechanical Machinery (Principy, Metody ш Algoritmy Postroenija Mikroprocessornyh Sistem Upravlenija Jelektromehanicheskimi Mashinnymi Agregatami). Tekhnik, Bishkek (in Russian) (2007)
14. Alekseev, K.B., Palaguta, K.A.: Microcontrollers in Electric Drives (Mikrokontrollernoe Upravlenie Jelektroprivodom). Moscow State Industrial University, Moscow (in Russian) (2008)
15. Lukman, A., Abisoye, O., Agajo, J., Ajao, A., Femi Salami, A., Mu'Azu, M.: Automated multiple water tanks control system using ATMEGA and FPGA technology. In: 2019 IEEE 1st International Conference on Mechatronics, Automation and Cyber-Physical Computer System, 18–20 March 2019, Ilmenau, Germany, pp. 346–353 (2019)
16. AVR Microcontrollers: Atmel AVR Instruction Set Manual. http://ww1.microchip.com/downloads/en/devicedoc/atmel-0856-avr-instruction-set-manual.pdf. Accessed 18 Feb 2021

Methods for Domain Adaptation of Automated Systems for Aspect Annotation of Customer Review Texts

Elena Kryuchkova⬤ and Alena Korney(✉) ⬤

AltSTU – Polzunov Altai State Technical University, Lenin Avenue 46, Barnaul 656038, Russia

Abstract. Today, social media and instant messengers are a widely used information channel that has a powerful impact on a public opinion. Therefore, the rapid identification of the main topics and generalized content of a set of texts becomes an important task. In fact, the problem arises of the aspect-based annotation of texts, interrelated on some of the topics presented in them. A set of texts can contain data for a variety of semantic categories. Therefore, it is of interest to obtain annotations for categories automatically extracted from texts. This task essentially depends on specific subject areas. Therefore, the issue of quick and effective adaptation of existing models to new domains is highly relevant. This paper proposes a hybrid method of aspect-oriented analysis and text annotation based on data extracted from both common dictionaries and domain-oriented unstructured texts. The introduced characteristic functions and numerical metrics make it possible to assess the significance of individual terms within the entire domain. An algorithm for the categorization of texts is proposed, based on the selection of semantic clusters in a domain semantic graph. A method for highlighting the most significant text fragments included in the annotation, based on statistical data, is proposed. The results of experiments are presented, which makes it possible to evaluate the quality of the algorithms.

Keywords: Text annotation · Text categorization · Semantic graph · Semantic-statistical algorithm

1 Introduction

Social networks and instant messengers have become a tool for illegal content distribution, including the propaganda of terrorism, child suicide, drug trafficking, etc. Moreover, this area is characterized by constantly changing terminology, new techniques, and methods of material presentation. There is an urgent need to quickly and efficiently modernize systems for detecting volatile inappropriate content. And this means the need to develop such models and algorithms that allow us to quickly adapt the existing system to a new application area without a huge investment of working resources. The appropriate toolkit should provide not only information search but mainly its classification, systematization, and annotation, which allows you to get access to exactly the information that the user needs.

© Springer Nature Switzerland AG 2022
V. Jordan et al. (Eds.): HPCST 2021, CCIS 1526, pp. 325–337, 2022.
https://doi.org/10.1007/978-3-030-94141-3_26

Information retrieval (IR) is based on many individual tasks of automatic text processing [1, 2]. The main goal of information retrieval is to provide the most relevant information in response to a user request, both in the form of full-text documents and in the form of some text fragments. Classical information retrieval methods are based, for example, on the frequency of individual terms [3, 4], or the similarity of individual phrases [5], or on the correspondence between the lexicon of the query and the document [6], etc. In recent years, there has been an increased interest in neural network models [7].

Classification/Categorization, Clustering [8–10] are broad classes of problems related to the extraction and analysis of main topics of documents. The basis of the system designed for topic analysis is the semantic model of the subject area. Topic modeling is one of the modern actively developing areas of natural language processing and, to some degree, simulates human understanding of the text [11]. The task of a topic model building can be considered as the task of clustering documents or their fragments over a set of clusters that represent topics. Topic models can be used in various tasks of information retrieval, document classification and categorization, spam detection, news trending, image, and video analysis.

For an effective application, the methods and principles of automatic natural language texts annotation should be related to the general topic of the domain area to which the annotated text belongs. Constructions in the text should be distinguished by their contribution to the content of the text, depending on the different domain structures. This is especially important when processing both destructive propaganda information and consumer feedback on goods and services. The texts of such documents are usually short, contain concentrated information, from which it is necessary to extract the most significant domain-specific data. The presence of a large number of such documents leads to the need to select concentrated information from their entire set. Therefore, as one of the main tasks in this work, the task of adequately identifying and interpreting the text fragments significance degree is considered. The characteristics of the significance of analyzed text components should depend on the text belonging to a particular domain. The language system complexity primarily lies in its multi-layered nature, reflecting our ideas about a diverse world. As a result, at the formal level, the model of the language system should consist of many subsystems with different semantics, defined based on domain areas. These subsystems form semantic subsets of the language with their aspects, categories, and dependencies between them. Only with the help of the concept of lexical and semantic dependence of the level on the specifics of the domain can we talk about professional annotation. Neither a person who is not familiar with the specifics of the area nor a system without special data can build a high-quality annotation. Thus, aspect analysis of a domain can be considered as the basis for building an annotation system.

In this work, the authors take into account the fact that many of the corresponding domain terms are not always clearly present not only in the analyzed text fragments, but even in training samples (or are present in them in small numbers), but they can appear in our minds as a result of established associative links.

2 Aspect-Based Summarization and Annotation

Summarization and annotating text are ways to reduce the amount of text to obtain a summary while maintaining the main content of the processed text. Summaries and annotations help to establish the main content of the document, allow the user to speed up the search in documents, and determine the need to refer to the source.

Writing an abstract is a full-fledged selection of key fragments of the text, main ideas, and conclusions. Compared to summarizing, annotation is the construction of less detailed content and is aimed at extracting a shortlist of issues considered in the text, creating a shortlist of key topics of the text.

Both automatic summarization and annotation are based on the selection of the most significant sentences of the processed document based on the statistics of words and phrases [12, 13].

There are two types of annotation: general and thematic-oriented [14]. With a general approach, almost no assumptions are made about the genre or subject area of the annotated material. The importance of the information is determined solely concerning the content of the text without regard to the specifics of the domain. It is assumed that the information is intended for the reader to quickly determine the main idea of the text without reading the entire document. Thematic annotations, on the other hand, are intended to highlight information in source texts that is relevant to a specific user request or associated with a specific domain area. To draw up such an annotation, it is necessary to take into account both the document itself and the specifics of the domain.

Automatic annotation methods are usually divided into two types: extractive and generative [15]. Generative methods are based on connecting separate fragments of the source text by some logical connectives. For example, in [16] the link is built based on logical-semantic relations between text fragments.

Extractive methods build the annotation from the source text sentences. For these methods, extracting sentences containing the most important information is a major challenge. A large number of different methods have been developed to solve this problem. Known extraction methods can be based on lexical chains [17], Latent Semantic Analysis (LSA) [18], Latent Dirichlet Allocation (LDA) [19], etc.

In this paper, we will consider methods for annotating texts of a special type: consumer reviews about events, goods, and services. Based on such reviews, people often make purchasing decisions, choosing a restaurant, a movie theater, etc. For businesses, consumer feedback expressed in reviews and ratings is very important. Automated processing of such reviews can be considered in the following areas:

1. Sentiment analysis of one specific consumer review (individual sentiment analysis).
2. Extracting the predominant sentiment of a group of reviews (generalized sentiment analysis).
3. Extracting characteristics for a separate category (individual aspect analysis).
4. Extracting the predominant sentiment of a group of reviews by separate categories (generalized aspect analysis).

The last two problems are the most interesting ones. Their solution will allow automatically extracting key categories from a specific domain, and then generating an annotation from customer reviews for individual categories. The constructed annotations can be further processed, for example, to determine the sentiment of the selected category. Both the category listing and aspect terms are highly domain-dependent, so the system must be adaptable and transparent.

3 Semantic Graph Model

For effective aspect annotation, the problem arises of combining in a single semantic core general information about the world and highly specialized knowledge related to a specific application area. In this work, such core includes two structural elements:

1. Semantic graph G_0 built based on commonly used dictionaries of the Russian language. In this work, a dictionary of synonyms [20] and an explanatory dictionary [21] are selected as the basic source. Such a graph can be viewed as a semantic web - a reliable and proven way of representing knowledge.
2. Weighted graph G_{domain}, built based on processing the graph G_0 and large texts related to a specialized area. The presence of domain-oriented data ensures the simultaneous existence of both general and domain-dependent information in the system.

3.1 Basic Semantic Graph

Natural language dictionaries can be viewed as a source of generalized knowledge about the world around us. Therefore, the knowledge extracted from them can be used as basic domain-independent semantic information. Knowledge extracted from explanatory dictionaries, dictionaries of synonyms, and other general linguistic dictionaries describe interrelated objects, events, phenomena of the world around us. Therefore, the authors of this article believe that the corresponding semantics of relationships should adequately represent the semantic graph of the base level. This semantic graph was implemented by the authors based on general linguistic dictionaries of the Russian language. The structure of the oriented semantic graph $G = (V, U)$ is presented in detail in [22]. Within the framework of this article, it is enough to understand the following:

1. The vertices of the set V are represented by the concepts of the Russian language
2. Vertices are connected by oriented arcs of the set U. In this case, each edge has labels of types of relations between concepts: $L = \{l_a, l_s, l_d\}$, where l_a is an association relation, l_s is a synonymy relation, l_d is a definition relation.
3. The farther from each other the vertices are in the graph, the less they are semantically connected.
4. The base graph is weighted, that is, the edges have a weight initially equal to the weight of the relationship type from L. Each type of relationship will initially be assigned a certain weight that does not depend on the words at the vertices and is determined only by the type of connection between them.

All further calculations were carried out based on data on the initial weights of the relations. Our goal was to build a domain model that would combine domain specificity with common semantics. Experiments have shown that, with fixed weights of synonymy and definition, the main contribution to the expansion of the domain vocabulary is made by association relations. With the weights l_a close to zero, the l_s and l_d weights do not lead to a significant expansion of the domain dictionary based on common knowledge. Good results were obtained with the initial l_a values in the range [0.45; 0.65], allowing to expand the domain dictionary on average from 30% to 45% at the expense of commonly used terms. For example, when using the set of restaurant reviews published as part of SemEval-2016 (Task 5, Aspect based sentiment analysis) [23] as a training sample, 0.48% of words from the basic vocabulary were added to the Restaurant cluster, including such rare for the simplified vocabulary of reviews, words like "head waiter" or "cabaret".

3.2 Building a Domain-Oriented Graph

Consider the process of constructing a domain-oriented graph G_{domain}. As an example, we will use the previously mentioned set of restaurant reviews [23]. The set includes 312 documents of 41205 words, which correspond to 4114 unique canonical word forms of the Russian language. The G_{domain} graph construction algorithm consists of two phases:

- the phase of associative links strengthening;
- the phase of vertex weights calculation.

Both phases are based on processing the statistics of the training set of texts. Consider the first stage - the phase of associative links strengthening.

In addition to the frequency of the individual words, data on the word co-occurrence frequency are important too (for example, frequency of word pairs - bigrams and, in the general case, N-grams). Following Zipf's law [24], for the word list of a text, the frequency of any word is inversely proportional to its rank in the frequency table. The inverse dependence of the frequency $f_N(i)$ on the serial number i is typical not only for unigrams, but in the general case for N-grams, and with increasing N, the absolute value of the derivative of the function $f_N(i)$ increases. The use of this fact allows one not only to extract the sets of significant N-grams by the threshold, but also to establish a correspondence between the thresholds for different N. Figure 1 shows the corresponding graph for unigrams.

Knowing the frequency of N-grams in the text, we can obtain information about not only the lexical but also the semantic features of the texts. The collocations, speech patterns, and idioms that are most commonly used in a domain can be used to reveal a strong semantic relationship between corresponding words.

The algorithm for strengthening connections based on the training sample uses the frequencies of the bigrams selected from the complete set as the most significant, using the cutoff threshold. Words from the training sample are reduced to their canonical forms, then stop words are removed from the sample, and then the frequency of bigrams is counted. It is necessary to select the most significant bigrams from the entire obtained set. Using the specified threshold T_2, rare bigrams with a low frequency are cut off.

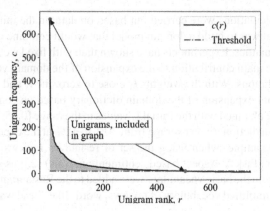

Fig. 1. The dependence of the frequency of unigrams on their ranks and the cut-off threshold for the "Restaurants" domain.

According to the construction of both the base graph G_0 and the domain-oriented graph G_{domain}, each edge corresponds to the presence of a semantic connection between the corresponding words. The higher the edge weight, the more semantically related the words are. If two words x and y are connected in a graph by an edge $u(x, y) \in U$ with weight $p(x, y)$, then this weight can be considered as the probability of a semantic connection between words x and y. Then the presence of a path between any two words x and y can be considered as a joint event of the appearance of these words in one text. This means that the presence of a path between objects can be considered as a measure of the semantic proximity between them, that is, as a joint event of the appearance in the text of all words along this path. Then the maximum probability of a joint event corresponds to the path $R_j(x, y)$ with the maximum corresponding value of the path weight between x and y:

$$d(x, y) = max_{r_j}\left(\prod_{(w_{k-1}, w_k) \in R_j} p(w_{k-1}, w_k)\right). \tag{1}$$

For each bigram $b = (w_1, w_2)$ from the set of significant bigrams, it is necessary to find the shortest path $d(w_1, w_2)$ between the vertices w_1 and w_2 according to formula (1). We modify the edges of the found path by multiplying the weight of each by $(1 + \beta)$, where the weight gain β is equal to the ratio of the frequency $H_2(b)$ of the considered bigram b to the maximum frequency of bigrams in the processed text:

$$\beta = H_2(b) \max_i \{H_2(b_i)\} \tag{2}$$

If there is no path in the graph between the vertices w_1 and w_2, it is necessary to add a new associative edge (w_1, w_2) with a weight equal to the relative frequency β in accordance with formula (2). As a result, the modification of the weights of the edges strengthened the associative links between meaningful word combinations of the subject area.

Let us normalize the calculated edge weights, as a result of which all weights will be in the range [0; 1]. We note that the edge weights depend both on the initial data taken from the dictionaries and on the domain data obtained as a result of the analysis of word combinations in the training text. Thus, after the phase of strengthening the weights of arcs for each word x, one can find a semantic neighborhood $O(x, \varepsilon)$ of object x, in which distance (1) as a measure of proximity between x and any vertex of this neighborhood from the set V does not exceed some given threshold ε.

The vertex weights propagation algorithm works after the edge weights are recalculated and are designed to define meaningful terminology in the domain. The concept of a semantic neighborhood O (x, ε) leads to an obvious definition of the radius of the subgraph corresponding to this neighborhood. Considering the eccentricity of all vertices x (the distance in $O(x, \varepsilon)$ from x to the most distant vertex), we obtain the value of the graph radius as the minimum eccentricity among all the graph vertices. And vice versa, using the selected value of the graph radius, for each vertex, it is possible to find its semantic neighborhood corresponding to this radius. Then from all the vertices, you can choose the central vertices – the vertices, the eccentricity of which is equal to the radius of the graph. To select cluster centers from all central vertices, we apply the vertex weight distribution algorithm. The constructed graph $G_{domain} = (V_{domain}, U_{domain})$ with the obtained weights of the vertices will be the basis for the selection of aspects and further annotation. And for a given radius, the centers of the clusters will be the central vertices of such subgraphs that are formed around the vertices of the G_{domain} graph with the maximum weight and are at a distance from the center that does not exceed a given radius.

The algorithm for spreading the frequency of unigrams along neighboring vertices works taking into account the attenuation along with the distance from the original vertex. We preliminarily set the weights of all vertices of the graph G_{domain} to zero, and then, as in the analysis of bigrams, we will cut off the set of unigrams of the training sample at a given threshold, as a result of which we will select the most significant unigrams. It should be noted that the cut-off thresholds for significant unigrams and bigrams must be agreed upon. The probability of occurrence of the bigram $b = (w_1, w_2)$ in the domain can be considered as the probability of a joint event of the occurrence of the words w_1 and w_2: $p(b) = p(w_1) * p(w_2) \leq p_{max}^2$. If the relative frequency of a word is considered as the probability of the appearance of this word in the text, then the values of the cut-off thresholds for unigrams T_1 and bigrams T_2 must satisfy the equality $T_2 = \sqrt{T_1}$.

Let M be a set of significant unigrams, each unigram $w_i \in M$ has frequency $H_1(w_i)$. For each vertex w_i, we add its frequency $H_1(w_i)$ to the weight of the vertex, and then distribute its weight to the surrounding vertices in radius R. The vertices adjacent to w_i receive some part of the frequency $H_1(w_i)$. In this case, the farther from w_i the modified vertex is, the less influence the value of the frequency $H_1(w_i)$ should have on it. However, the higher the weight of the connection between the vertices, the greater the influence should be from the frequency $H_1(w_i)$. Experiments have shown a good quality of constructing weights when using the recursive formula for calculating the additional weight for the vertex w_k depending on the current source vertex w_i:

$$D(w_k) = H_2(w_i, w_k) * H_1(w_i) * \delta, \qquad (3)$$

where $D(w_k)$ is the additional weight for the vertex w_k, $H_2(w_i, w_k)$ – weight of the edge between w_i and w_k, $H_1(w_i)$ – distributed weight of the vertex w_i adjacent to w_k; δ is the attenuation coefficient.

Thus, the transmitted weight at a distance r from the original vertex is multiplied by δ^r and decreases rapidly.

3.3 Cluster Selection

In the constructed graph G_{domain}, sets of vertices with high weight are formed. It is these vertices that are contenders for the centers of clusters. We will choose the centers of the clusters as vertices with the value of the function $f_{focus}(v)$ exceeding a certain threshold, where $v \in V_{domain}$. Depending on the form of the function $f_{focus}(v)$, vertices with the maximum value of weights can become the centers of the clusters (when choosing the function $f_{focus}(v) = H(v)$, where $H(v)$ is the weight of the vertex v) and (with the choice of the corresponding functions) the centers of the neighborhoods of the vertices with a high total weight. For example, as the function $f_{focus}(v)$, you can use the sum $H(v_i)$ of the immediate neighbors of the vertex v. The vertices that got into the top by the value of the $f_{focus}(v)$ function will be considered the centers of the clusters, and the set of the surrounding vertices at a distance not more than a given cluster radius – as aspect terms of this cluster.

The analysis of the proposed method application on the marked-up domain "Restaurants" showed a coincidence of 70% with the markup, and the remaining 30%, which were not selected, fall, as a rule, to the low-frequency region and are quite rare in the text (Table 1).

Table 1. Clusters with maximal weight.

No.	Central vertex	Central vertex weight	Cluster weight
1	Restaurant (Ресторан)	913.392	913.392
2	Dish (Блюдо)	442.380	498.491
3	Waiter (Официант)	330.585	460.942
4	Table (Столик)	319.381	437.395
5	Cuisine (Кухня)	400.136	436.965
6	Interior (Интерьер)	380.292	396.511
7	Food (Еда)	252.974	394.116
8	Service (Обслуживание)	366.732	366.733
9	Menu (Меню)	322.253	334.826
...	...		
25	Ambience (Атмосфера)	134.404	152.655

4 Cluster Annotation Method

4.1 Justification of the Algorithm

Let the centers of the clusters be built and the list of the most significant terms in the cluster be selected using the described method. We will consider the annotation process as the process of extracting phrases from the text that are most significant for the cluster. Let $T = \{t_1, t_2, \ldots, t_n\}$ be cluster centers. According to Shannon's formula, the amount of information in the message $\varphi = w_1 w_2 \ldots w_k$ is determined as:

$$I(\varphi) = -\sum_{j=1}^{k} p(w_j) * log_2 p(w_j), \tag{4}$$

where $p(w_j)$ is the probability of the word w_j appearing in the message. The relative weight of a vertex in the resulting graph G_{domain} can be considered as a relative frequency. The relative frequency, in fact, is the probability of the word w_j appearing in the text belonging to the domain: $p(w_j) = H(w_j)/l$, where $H(w_j)$ is the weight of the vertex w_j in the graph G_{domain}, l is the total weight of all vertices of this graph. Thus, formula (4) makes it possible to estimate the information content of a message within the entire domain. To estimate the information content of a message for a certain cluster, we will use the cluster radius R. All vertices w located no further than R steps from the cluster center have the weight $H_i(w) \leq H_r(w)$. Introducing the attenuation coefficient $0 < \gamma < 1$ we will take into account the decrease in the significance of the term for the category with distance from the center of the cluster. Taking into account the attenuation coefficient, the weight of the term in the cluster is calculated as:

$$H_i(w) = \gamma^k H_r(w), \text{где } 0 \leq k \leq R. \tag{5}$$

Then, for the set of words $A(t_i, R) = \{a_1, a_2, \ldots, a_m\}$, contained in a given sentence 0 we can calculate the probabilities $p(a_j, t_i)$ of the appearance of the term a_j for $j \in \{0, 1, \ldots, m\}$ in a cluster with center t_i:$p(a_j, t_i) = H_i(a_j)/N_i$, where $N_i = \sum_{w \in A(t_i, R)} H_i(w)$ is the total weight of all vertices in $A(t_i, R)$.

The quantitative characteristic of φ belonging to the cluster t_i is determined by the formula (4) as the amount of information contained in φ and corresponding to the cluster t_i:

$$I(\varphi, t_i) = -\sum_{j=1}^{k} p(w_j, t_i) * log_2 p(w_j, t_i). \tag{6}$$

Taking into account the definition of the value of the probability $p(a_j, t_i)$ and due to the relation $H_i(a, t_i) \ll N_i$ the upper bound of expression (5) can be used as the characteristic function:

$$F(\varphi, t_i) = \frac{1}{N_i} \sum_{w_j = a \& a \in A(t_i, R)} H_i(a, t_i) * log_2 N_i.$$

Moreover, the value of the function $F(\varphi, t_i)$ does not depend on the total number of words in the sentence, but is determined only by the aspect terms of the cluster.

Let's return to the previously selected sets of clusters $T = \{t_1, t_2, \ldots, t_n\}$, each of which corresponds to a certain semantic category. For any sentence φ, an n-dimensional vector of characteristics can be calculated:

$$\overline{F}(\varphi, T) = \{F(\varphi, t_1), F(\varphi, t_2), \ldots, F(\varphi, t_n)\}. \tag{7}$$

This vector allows assessing the degree of belonging of the proposal to each of the selected clusters.

The list of clusters with the most significant content is a list of contenders for an annotated list of categories. Now it is enough to choose for each such category the proposals with the maximum values of the function from a vector (7).

4.2 Automatic Adjustment of the Annotation Algorithm

The proposed algorithm allows you to quickly tune the system to a specific application area. Once the semantic graph G_0 and is built based on commonly used dictionaries, we do not need to rebuild it. We can use unstructured domain-dependent texts to build the graph G_{domain}, select the clusters, and the system will be ready for the aspect-based annotation of arbitrary text. However, both in the construction of the G_{domain} graph and in the selection of clusters, the problem of an adequate choice of thresholds arises. While testing the algorithm on the Restaurants domain, we selected these thresholds manually. The thresholds were selected in such a way that the domain graph was not too large and at the same time important vocabulary for the domain was not lost. Taking into account the collected statistics for one domain, we would like to unify the calculation of thresholds for others. The more diverse the lexicon of a domain, the higher the relative threshold for frequency should be used. The word diversity factor introduced by us allows you to choose thresholds for different domains with the same frequency characteristics. Let l be the total number of words in the text, m is the number of unique canonical forms, then $d = l/m$ is the coefficient of constancy of the corpus of words. The value d characterizes the number of words on average per one canonical form, and the higher this value, the less lexically diverse the texts are. Using the value of the constancy of the text corpus and the empirical laws of Hips and Zipf, the following criteria were formulated. They relate the cutoff thresholds for significant N-grams at $N > 0$ to different domains: $T(N)_1/T(N)_2 = \sqrt[n]{t_1/t_2}$, where $T(N)_1/T(N)_2$ is the ratio of the N-gram thresholds for the selected domains. t_1/t_2 is the ratio of the cut-off thresholds for significant unigrams, determined by the internal statistics of the selected domains: $t_1/t_2 = f_1/f_2 \sqrt[n]{d_1/d_2}$, where f_1/f_2 is the ratio of the maximum word frequencies in the domains. The experiments carried out by the authors [25] of applying these ratios when switching from the Restaurants domain to the Movies domain have shown the applicability of this ratio in the automatic selection of thresholds. The structure of the system is shown in Fig. 2.

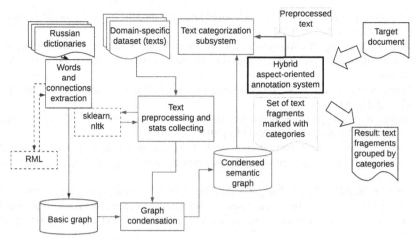

Fig. 2. Automated annotation system scheme.

5 Conclusions

A combined semantic-statistical algorithm for determining aspect terms, suitable for solving problems of extracting the most significant sentences from the text, is proposed and implemented. The semantic graph helps to partially remove the problem of adaptation to domains, and the proposed algorithms allow you to move to a new subject area with minimal cost. The most expensive phase of the work is text preprocessing and statistical data extraction. Building a domain-oriented graph based on ready-made statistics takes on average 10 to 20 s. The categorization of 282 offers of the Restaurants domain is performed in 720 ms, which indicates a low computational complexity of the algorithm. The accuracy of categorization ranges from 65 to 72. The combination of the described characteristics makes it possible to use the proposed algorithm for the problems of aspectual annotation.

References

1. Mitra, B., Craswell, N.: An introduction to neural information retrieval. Found. Trends® Inf. Ret. **13**(1), 1–126 (2018)
2. Grossman, D.A., Frieder, O.: Information retrieval: Algorithms and Heuristics. Springer, Heidelberg (2012). https://doi.org/10.1007/978-1-4615-5539-1
3. Robertson, S., Zaragoza, H.: The probabilistic relevance framework: BM25 and beyond. Found. Trends® Inf. Retr. **3**(4), 333–389 (2009). https://doi.org/10.1561/1500000019
4. Ponte, J. M., Croft, W.B.: A language modeling approach to information retrieval. In: Proceedings of the 21st Annual International ACM SIGIR Conference on Research and Development in Information Retrieval August 1998, Melbourne, Australia, pp. 275–281 (1998)
5. Gao, J., Nie, J.Y., Wu, G., Cao, G.: Dependence language model for information retrieval. In: Proceedings of the 27th Annual International ACM SIGIR Conference on Research and Development in Information Retrieval, July 2004, pp. 170–177. The University of Sheffield, UK (2004)

6. Lavrenko, V., Croft, W.B.: Relevance-based language models. In: ACM SIGIR Forum, vol. 51, No. 2, pp. 260–267. ACM, New York (2017)

7. Onal, K.D., Zhang, Y., Altingovde, I.S., Rahman, M.M., Karagoz, P., Braylan, A., et al.: Neural information retrieval: at the end of the early years. Inf. Retr. J. **21**(2–3), 111–182 (2018)

8. Korde, V., Mahender, C.N.: Text classification and classifiers: a survey. Int. J. Artif. Intell. Appl. **3**(2), 85 (2012)

9. Altinel, B., Ganiz, M.C.: Semantic text classification: a survey of past and recent advances. Inf. Process. Manag. **54**(6), 1129–1153 (2018)

10. Patra, A., Singh, D.: A survey report on text classification with different term weighing methods and comparison between classification algorithms. Int. J. Comput. Appl. **75**(7), 14–18 (2013)

11. Chang J., Boyd-Graber, J., Wang, C., Gerrish, S., Blei, D.: Reading tea leaves: how humans interpret topic models. In: Proceedings of 23rd Annual Conference on Neural Information Processing Systems, Vancouver, British Columbia, Canada, 7–10 December 2009, pp. 288–296 (2009)

12. Dyachenko, P., Iomdin, L., Lazursky, A., Mityushin, L., Podlesskaya, O., Sizov, S., et al.: Modern state of the deeply annotated corpus of Russian texts (Syn-TagRus) (Sovremennoye sostoyaniye gluboko annotirovannogo korpusa tekstov russkogo yazyka (Syn-TagRus)). Trudy Instituta Russkogo Yazyka imeniV.V. Vinogradova, **6**, 272–299 (2015). (in Russian)

13. Droganova, K., Medyankin, N.: NLP pipeline for Russian: an easy-to-use web application for morphological and syntactic annotation. In: Proceedings of the International Conference "Dialogue", Mocsow, June 2016 (2016)

14. Nenkova, A., McKeown, K.: Automatic summarization. Found. Trends Inf. Retr. **5**(2–3), 103–233 (2011)

15. Osminin, P.G.: Modern approaches to automatic abstracting and annotation. Bull. South Ural State Univ. Ser. Linguist. **25**, 134–135 (2012)

16. Shi W., Yung F., Rubino R., Demberg V.: Using explicit discourse connectives in translation for implicit discourse relation classification. In: Proceedings of the 8th International Joint Conference on Natural Language Processing, Taipei, pp. 484–495 (2017)

17. Barzilay, R., Elhadad, M.: Using lexical chains for text summarization. In: Mani, I., Maybury, M.T. (eds.) Advances in Automatic Text Summarization, pp. 111–121. MIT Press, Cambridge (1999)

18. Hoffman, T.: Probabilistic latent semantic analysis. In: Proceedings of the Fifteenth Conference on Uncertainty Iin Artificial Intelligence (UAI'99), pp. 289–296. Morgan Kaufmann Publishers, San Francisco (2013)

19. Blei, D., Ng, A., Jordan, M.: Latent Dirichlet allocation. J. Mach. Learn. Res. **3**, 993–1022 (2003)

20. Abramov, N.: Dictionary Russian Synonyms (2007). Russkie Slovary, Moscow (1999). (in Russian)

21. Ozhegov, S.I., Shvedova, N.: Explanatory Dictionary of the Russian Language (1992). Az, Moscow (1992). (in Russian)

22. Korney, A., Kryuchkova, E., Savchenko, V.: Information retrieval approach using semiotic models based on multi-layered semantic graphs. In: Jordan, V., Filimonov, N., Tarasov, I., Faerman, V. (eds.) HPCST 2020. CCIS, vol. 1304, pp. 162–177. Springer, Cham (2020). https://doi.org/10.1007/978-3-030-66895-2_11

23. Pontiki, M., Galanis, D., Papageorgiou, H., Androutsopoulos, I., Manandhar, S., Al-Smadi, M., et al.: SemEval-2016 task 5: aspect based sentiment analysis. In: Proceedings of the 10th International Workshop on Semantic Evaluation (SemEval-2016), pp. 19–30. Association for Computational Linguistics, San Diego (2016)

24. Maslov, B.P.: Refinement of Zipf's law for frequency dictionaries. Doklady Mathematics. 72(3) 924–945 (2005)
25. Korney, A.O., Kryuchkova, E.N.: Text categorization based on the condensed graph. Inf. Technol. **27**(3), 138–146 (2021). (in Russian)

Neuro-Computer Interface Control of Cyber-Physical Systems

Yaroslav Turovskiy ⓘ, Daniyar Volf ⓘ, Anastasia Iskhakova$^{(\boxtimes)}$ ⓘ,
and Andrey Iskhakov ⓘ

V. A. Trapeznikov Institute of Control Sciences of the Russian Academy of Sciences,
Profsoyuznaya Street 65, 117997 Moscow, Russia

Abstract. The paper proposes an approach to and solves the problem of controlling a robot by using neural interface technology, describes the general scheme and working principle of the main idea of non-invasive neural interface control of a robot using the original convolutional neural network. The authors describe the principles of an original convolutional neural network and an approach to the modern network design, present a model of a one-dimensional convolutional network based on the principles of a human inner ear. The structure of a software package is proposed. The results of a comparison of algorithms for the analysis of human brain evoked potentials used in the design of brain-computer interfaces are presented. The authors used the Fourier transform algorithm and the multidimensional synchronization index (MSI) algorithm in various modifications to perform the experiment. Analysis of the initial signal, the accumulated evoked potential, in addition to the accumulated evoked potential spectrum were proposed as variations. Linear correlation was also evaluated with analysis using a user-derived reference signal sample and various variations of wavelet filtering. In addition, model signals, which were a combination of white noise and a harmonic oscillation simulating a stable visual evoked potential, were used. The best results (error rate <10%) with an analysis time of 3 s were obtained for the MSI of the original signal, MSI with the Fourier transform. Also in this list, there is a MSI where the wavelet filtering result of coherent accumulation was used as an etalon, a linear correlation coefficient. In a MSI the evoked potential, recovered after the wavelet transform, was used as an etalon.

Keywords: Robot · Neural interface · Steady state · Visually evoked potential · Electroencephalography · Convolutional neural network

1 Introduction

The development of modern interdisciplinary approaches at the interface between information technology and physiology has led in recent decades to the appearance of a large number of human-computer communication devices. It is planned to use them to solve a wide range of tasks related to the rehabilitation of patients with neurological and trauma problems, to improve the control of various devices: from a personal computer

V. Jordan et al. (Eds.): HPCST 2021, CCIS 1526, pp. 338–353, 2022.
https://doi.org/10.1007/978-3-030-94141-3_27

to aviation systems. The most common problems currently being solved are improving their hardware, developing new algorithms for processing the received signals and transforming them into commands for the effector devices, searching for new physiological phenomena that can be used as a basis for commands transmitted through new interfaces. The development of human-machine interfaces, including brain-computer interfaces, is traditionally based on the paradigm of arbitrary control [1, 2]. Applied research and development aimed at creating products and technologies of intelligent robotics represent a promising direction in cyberphysics. Among them is the creation of original artificial neural networks for generating control signals in intelligent control systems and solving control problems of dynamic objects of robotics. There are also developing projects on creation of heterogeneous intelligent systems of human-machine interaction by brain neurons for the neural communication interface [3, 4]. Works on creation of methods and software based on neural interface systems - devices of data exchange between the brain and an external device, the Internet of Things [5], represent also a perspective direction in cyberphysics [6–8].

One of the directions of digital signal processing development in neuroscience is the creation of new methods of processing brain signals and improvement of existing ones obtained by different methods. Traditionally, due to a fairly widespread and high informative value, methods that use algorithms for processing electroencephalograms (EEG) – records of brain electrical activity – are of considerable interest. Along with clinical solutions aimed largely at assessing and predicting the patient's seizure states, and fundamental research, the development and research of new algorithms are aimed at brain-computer interface systems (neurocomputer interfaces). There, the signals registered in the brain are transformed into commands replacing external input devices: a keyboard, a joystick, or a mouse. There are two main trends in the development of brain-computer interfaces: synchronous and asynchronous interfaces. Synchronous interfaces use external stimulation of the user, for example, in the form of light flashes or illumination of certain icons on the monitor screen. In response to such stimuli, so-called "evoked" (event-related) potentials (EPs) appear in the EEG structure, usually related to visual or cognitive EPs. Their amplitude-frequency parameters can be used in forming commands for performing certain actions.

There is a significant number of algorithms for the extraction and processing of evoked potentials; however, in most cases, the comparison is made exclusively at the level of ready-made interfaces, the efficiency of which can be affected by a wide range of conditions, being far from that always related to the stability, resource intensity, or accuracy of the algorithm. Such conditions may include the state of the user (activity, fatigue, preceding meals), the quality of sensors (for example, in the case of EEG), their location relative to certain parts of the brain, hardware characteristics of the brain activity recording device, etc. Thus, it is relevant to compare the algorithms for processing electroencephalograms containing evoked potentials in their structure.

In this article, based on the hardware components available on the market, the authors consider the possibility of creating a prototype software product for neuropiloting and controlling a robot in the "brain-computer interface" mode, based on the extraction and decoding of a steady state visually evoked potentials (SSVEP) by retinal excitation systems, electroencephalography and convolutional neural networks (CNN).

The development of such a software package would allow controlling a robot or a drone by means of the SSVEP received by smart glasses and a neural headset. SSVEP refers to visually evoked steady state potentials which are signals that the brain generates in response to visual stimulation (Fig. 1 and 2). When the retina is excited by flashes with a frequency from 3.5 to 75 Hz, the occipital lobe of the brain generates electrical activity at the flashing frequency. The extraction and deciphering of the SSVEP are proposed to be performed with the help of EEG and CNN. In the practice, the expected result can be obtained using a software package for smart glasses like EPSON smart glasses Moverio bt-350 and an electroencephalograph-analyzer such as EEG-21/26-"Encephalan-131-03", "Neuron-Spektr-4", or a wireless mobile system for recording human EEG with dry, gel-free electrodes, such as NeuroPlay-8C (neural headsets). According to this obvious approach, the user should consciously set goals and at the training stage learn to consciously change his or her activity, for example, to influence the amplitude of certain EEG rhythms.

2 Non-invasive Neural Interface for Robot Control

2.1 Use of Evoked Potentials

Steady state visual evoked potentials (SSVEP) and the P300 potential (or component) are the most common evoked potentials in synchronous human-computer interface systems [9, 10]. Although a number of other EEG phenomena associated with certain external or internal events and evoked potentials are of interest for use as signals to create commands, they are nevertheless significantly inferior to the above two phenomena in their sensitivity to human state characteristics. Of the two above-mentioned phenomena, the SSVEP potential is considered to be the main one for application in the fastest interfaces. Thus, the operator controls a robot or a drone, focusing his or her attention on the appropriate stimulus displayed in the smart glasses. The operator can select one of the five actions available in the control. For example, this can correspond to six stimuli that flicker with different frequencies:

- forward (9 Hz);
- backward (10 Hz);
- to the left (11 Hz);
- to the right (12 Hz);
- down (13 Hz);
- up (14 Hz).

The EEG signals act as input, and the assigned tasks are the labels for the supervised deep learning system. An 8-electrode EEG helmet is supposed to be used, which corresponds to 8 channels of input data. The output data and temporal signals are converted to a frequency spectrum with a fast Fourier transform.

A model of an SSVEP classifier based on a convolutional neural network can be built using CNN-1 technology [11] (Fig. 3). Such a model contains two hidden layers with a kernel size of 1 by 8 and 11 by 1, respectively. With them, there is an output layer with 6 parts, which corresponds to 6 possible actions to control a robot or an unmanned vehicle. To build a supervised deep learning classifier, first, it is necessary to collect the training and test data and to perform the tenfold cross-validation with training data (at least 13500) and test data (at least 1500).

Other neural networks and signal processing techniques can also be used, such as:

- CNN-1 architecture with an additional full-link layer and with three parts in front of the output layer (CNN-2).
- Direct propagation neural network: a simple three-layer full-link neural network with direct connectivity.
- Canonical correlation analysis (CCA) for the SSVEP classification.
- Multivariate index synchronization (MIS) with the estimation of synchronization between two signals as a coefficient for decoding the stimulus frequency.
- Canonical k-Nearest Neighbor Correlation Analysis (k-NN).

2.2 Experimental Setting

Figure 1 shows a block diagram with the flow of information based on the hardware products available on the market and the implementation of a software product for neuropiloting.

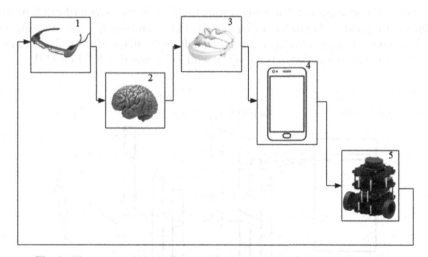

Fig. 1. The proposed block diagram of robot control using a neural interface.

The block diagram includes the following blocks:

1. Smart glasses or a smart helmet act as a visual stimulus for the SSVEP.
2. A human brain to produce EEG signals in the occipital area.
3. A neuro-headset for reading EEG signals.
4. A system for collecting and processing EEG signals, generating control signals by the robot based on the decision making with the help of the CNN.
5. A robot.

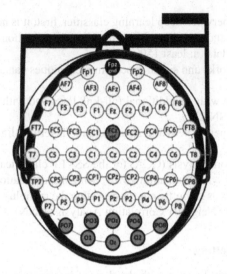

Fig. 2. EEG channels, 8 channels to acquire SSVEP from the back of the human head (with the neural interface on).

In the primary experiment, it was necessary to choose 8 electrodes on the EEG helmet, which correspond to 8 channels of input data (Fig. 2). It also allowed an accelerated Fourier transform to convert the temporal signals to the frequency signals. The result was 120 samples of input data, i.e., a signal with a dimension of 120 by 8 [12].

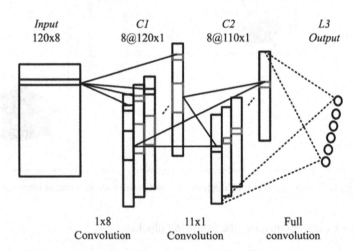

Fig. 3. CNN-1 architecture consists of two convolutional layers and an output layer.

- The problem with CNN-1 technology is that the architecture of such CNNs uses two-dimensional cores (2D), which is very costly for capability-limited systems. Therefore, for such purposes, an original one-dimensional CNN based on the principle of a human inner ear was developed at the Trapeznikov Institute of Control Problems of the Russian Academy of Sciences (Fig. 4) [13, 14]. A basic hypothesis was that the emotional characteristic in the speech signal is also stored in an averaged vector of frequency characteristics and its derivatives, such as the fine-frequency cepstral coefficients of the acoustic signal (MFCC) [14].

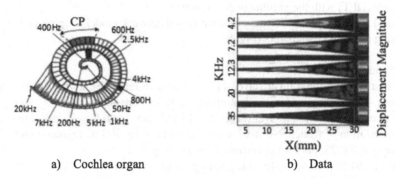

a)   Cochlea organ   b)   Data

Fig. 4. Human inner ear cochlea: a) frequency distribution of the acoustic wave following the principle of frequency masking (CP - critical band); b) training data – mean magnitude along the basilar membrane length (averaged vector of frequency characteristics).

Human hearing organs have the property of frequency masking. The notion closely related to this concept is that of the critical band, another characteristic of speech along with the frequency. Unlike frequency, critical bands are determined according to auditory perception. Therefore, in practice, frequency components outside this range are discarded and, accordingly, do not carry any meaningful information. Studies in the area of psychophysical perception have demonstrated that the basic relevant information is located in the actual frequency spectrum. That is why after the Fourier transform is performed, only the actual signal spectrum is picked out for further analysis, and the phase information is not taken into account. The biorhythm command can be represented as a discrete Fourier decomposition function (1):

$$x_n = \sum_{k=0}^{\frac{N}{2}-1} C_k e^{i\omega_k n}, \quad \omega_k = \frac{2\pi k}{N}, \quad C_k = A_k e^{\varphi_k}, \quad n = 0, \ldots, N-1, \tag{1}$$

where ω_k – radial frequency of the k-th harmonic;
A_k – amplitude of the k-th harmonic;
e^{φ_k} – phase of the k-th harmonic;
N – number of counts (for continuous function (1) - period T);
n – number of counts (for continuous function (1) - time t).

By solving the inverse problem for (1), we parametrically estimate the spectrum in which the entire admissible frequency range ω_k (ω) is scanned within volume N (period T) (2):

$$C_k = \frac{1}{N} \sum_{n=0}^{N-1} x_n e^{-i\omega_k n}, \quad k = 0, \ldots, \frac{N}{2} - 1. \tag{2}$$

The result of the solution of (2) is a frequency spectrum of the discrete Fourier transform (DFT) with the volume of $N/2$ counts.

Based on this approach, a convolutional neural network model is developed with the following technical parameters (Fig. 5):

- the input layer – vector – 64;
- the first convolutional layer (layer 1) – 128 same filters (SF), kernel size (KS) – 4, strides – 1, padding – same, activation by the ReLu function;
- the second convolutional layer (layer 2) – 128 SF, KS 4, strides – 1, padding – same, normalization – (Batch Normalization), activation by ReLu, regularization factor (Dropout) – 0.25, pooling operation (Max pooling) – 2;
- layer 3 – 64 SF, KS 4, strides – 1, padding – same, ReLu;
- layer 4 – 64 SF, KS 4, strides – 1, padding – same, ReLu;
- layer 5 – 64 SF, KS 4, strides – 1, padding – same, ReLu;
- layer 6 – 64 SF, KS 4, strides – 1, padding – same, Batch Normalization, ReLu, Dropout – 0.25, Max pooling – 2;
- layer 7 – 32 SF, KS 2, strides – 1, padding – same, ReLu;
- layer 8 – 32 SF, KS 4, strides – 1, padding – same, ReLu;
- layer 9 (full-connected layer), flatten – 512 neurons; output full-connected layer (Dense) – 10 neurons, Softmax activation.

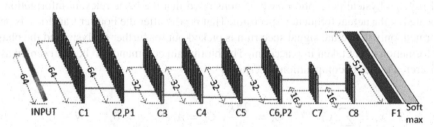

Fig. 5. Block diagram of the proposed CNN: 1D-Cochlea-organ-cnn developed by Trapeznikov Institute of Control Problems of the Russian Academy of Sciences.

The block diagram in Fig. 5 of the developed CNN consists in the combination of 11 functional levels (so-called layers) to transform EEG signals transmitted through them. Each unit in the layer receives input from a set of the units adjacent to the previous layer. Each output of a convolutional layer is supported by the layer activation function; the output result of the convolutional operation calculated by each kernel is collected into matrices which are called feature maps and represent the actual output data of the convolutional layers. The last CNN layer is the layer that performs the target prediction of the neural network. Unlike the previous convolutional layers, it consists of fully connected neurons (fully connected layer), so that each of them receives data from the entire previous layer at once. The problem of finding the optimal values of synaptic coefficients for each core and neurons of the fully connected layer(s) in the deep learning mode of CNN is reduced to the optimization problem. It is known that certain architecture of CNN, including the problem of classification of biological signals, affects the solution of this class of problems.

2.3 Software Complex

The complex must operate in two modes: a training mode and a robot control mode. In the training mode, the program complex must be able to collect spectrograms of EEG signals (training samples) for further deep learning. The following modules are proposed to be included in the software package, which provides the neuro interface.

1. Software module for known platforms like OS Android (based on Flutter):

    a. Software module for receiving and processing EEG signals coming from the neuro-headset:

        1) Receiving EEG signals from the neuro-headset.
        2) Cleaning received signals.
        3) Obtaining spectrograms with the possibility of setting time intervals.
        4) The function of saving spectrograms into separate files for further training samples and the possibility of transferring them to the hard drive of a personal computer.

    b. A software module for generating control signals to control the robot.

2. Development of the CNN for the Android OS (based on Flutter):

    a. Brain signal decoding and interpretation.
    b. A model of the original CNN capable of performing the classification of SSVEP.
    c. Integration of the developed CNN model into CP.

3. Development of developer and user documentation for the CP.

This approach has proven to be very promising, but it has several drawbacks primarily related to the incomplete reproduction of human behavioral patterns. Indeed, there is a large layer of reactions to certain unconscious stimuli. It can be assumed that such phenomena can serve as a basis for a new class of human-computer interfaces (including brain-computer interfaces) based on involuntary control of effector devices. This approach should not be considered as competing with the approaches on the paradigm of arbitrary control, but as one complementing them, forming, for example, elements of artificial emotional intelligence [15]. The search for and evaluation of brain activity phenomena, first of all, EEG activity, which can serve as input signals into systems of human-computer interfaces, seem promising [16, 17]. Similar attempts have been made, for example, in estimating changes in the amplitudes of EEG rhythms. However, this direction has not been sufficiently developed. At the same time, the EEG amplitude analysis has several drawbacks related both to the change of resistance under the electrodes during the prolonged registration, and to the necessity for the brain to maintain a certain level of EEG wave amplitude at given frequencies. In this aspect, it may be more promising to analyze the connections between certain parts of the brain assessed by EEG pattern correlations.

3 Training Sample for Deep Machine Learning

3.1 Multichannel SSVEP Potential Detection

As it has been shown [18–21], the SSVEP potential has the form of a periodic oscillation with the frequency equal to the frequency of the conducted stimulation; and the waveform resembles a harmonic oscillation. Therefore, a sinusoid additively augmented with white noise which simulated not only the EEG signal but also artifacts associated with the movement of electrodes on the skin and with the electrical activity of pericranial muscles was used as a model of the evoked potential. It has been taken into account that the amplitude of the SSVEP potential can vary from $0.5\,\mu V$ to $\approx 10\,\mu V$, while the background EEG signal in the same areas reaches values of 80–$100\,\mu V$. During modeling, the signal-to-noise ratio varied in the range from the complete absence of noise (the initial variant) to a value of $1/300$. A model was considered in which one of six possible frequencies in the range from 7.5 Hz to 20 Hz was chosen as the EEG frequency range where the SSVEP amplitude is expressed as a maximum. A standard approach based on coherent signal accumulation was used for the extraction of evoked potentials, if the conditions of the numerical experiment required it, with a signal registration time of 1 s or 4 s for all considered cases, and an accumulated evoked potential time of 0.5 s or 3 s. The results of 100 cycles of signal recognition were analyzed.

The algorithms for multichannel SSVEP potential detection were chosen as follows:

1. Fourier transform of the accumulated signal as a part of the evoked potential extraction in the same time window for all frequencies. Also, the power spectral density (PSD) was calculated, both at the corresponding SSVEP frequency and in its vicinity, defined as the average distance between frequencies at which the desired signal could appear. According to the results of PSD estimation, the solution was obtained by three options: choosing the highest value of PSD; choosing the biggest sum of PSD obtained from different channels; "voting" of channels when each of the EEG channels determined its own frequency, and the obtained estimation results were summed up. Thus, the frequency was chosen that was selected by the largest number of channels.

2. Fourier transform performed, unlike the previous case, not in a constant time window but in a window containing the same number of oscillations of each of the sought frequencies. Otherwise, the same sequence of operations was performed as in step 1.

3. Multivariate Synchronization Index (MSI) algorithm [22] is essentially a further development of canonical correlation analysis methods. According to [22], the values obtained using the MSI algorithm for the native model signal were evaluated in comparison with the reference signal which was represented by the harmonics of the desired frequencies. At the same time, similarly to the approaches used in the Fourier transform, the selections of the largest value of the synchronization index, as well as the selection of the largest sum of the synchronization indices from different channels and "voting" of channels, were used in the search for the desired frequency.

4. The MSI algorithm applied not to the native signal, but to the accumulated evoked potential. In this case, while reducing the analysis epoch (which negatively affects the signal recognition) due to the coherent accumulation, the signal to noise ratio improves, which theoretically may lead to more successful recognition results. The desired frequency selection based on the results of this transformation was carried out in the same way as in steps 1 and 2.

5. MSI algorithm applied to the Fourier spectrum of the accumulated signal only in the investigated frequency range. This limitation is caused by the necessity to exclude the influence of those spectral components which are outside the investigated frequency range but, according to the calculation algorithm, can significantly influence the result of frequency selection. The selection of the desired frequency according to the results of the transform was carried out in the same way as in steps 1, 3.

6. Calculation of the linear correlation coefficient between the accumulated evoked potential and the sample obtained during interface training on a particular user or test signal generator.

7. Calculation by the MSI algorithm using as a reference sample signal obtained by spatial (from different channels) coherent accumulation. This approach simulates the consideration of possible differences in the potential of different users.

8. Calculation by the MSI algorithm using the EP signal sample as a reference, obtained by filtering the original signal known to contain the desired evoked potential. This approach considers the possibility of using different filters obtained, for example, based on genetic algorithms [23]. Thus, filters created this way, as well as the filters received analytically, can be specialized on the extraction of certain features of the investigated signal. Taking into account the fact that a sinusoidal function was used in the model as an SSVEP simulator, the Morlet wavelet, which is an amplitude-modulated harmonic function whose frequency was calculated based on the "stimulation" frequency equal to the SSVEP frequency, was chosen as the filter. At the given sampling frequency of the model signal of 5 kHz, the frequency resolution in the studied area was higher than 0.08 Hz for the upper limit of the studied range.

9. Calculation by the MSI algorithm using the EP signal sample as a reference obtained by direct and inverse wavelet transforms, accumulated EP known to contain the desired evoked potential. At the same time, the recovery was not performed over the entire matrix of the wavelet transform coefficients. According to [24], the frequency range of the signal recovery was determined as the difference between two neighboring local minima of the matrix of squares of the wavelet transform coefficients between which the analyzed frequency was located. Thus, we analyzed an algorithm for signal reconstruction based on its original structure of chains of local maxima

and minima of the squares matrix of the wavelet transform coefficients [24]. This approach allows us to reconstruct signal fragments based on the signal's existing frequency-time features, rather than on a priori assumptions about their existence.

3.2 Experimental Results

Thirty-three people (26 men and 7 women) took part in the study; they were between 19 and 27 years of age and gave informed consent to participate in the experiment, and had no color perception pathology [25]. The study included two types of observation: with the feedback and the control one (without feedback). The subjects were not informed which experiment was the control one and which one was with the feedback. Before the EEG recording, three preferred ("favorite") and three avoided ("hated") colors were determined in a ranking order. The test subject, following the instruction, independently chose the colors from a full-color palette (224 colors). Further studies were conducted on the same computer, which made it possible to avoid the need for color correction. The EEG data were recorded for 3 min for the control one and 3 min – for the feedback experiment. The order of the experiments in the series was determined randomly. The break between the experiments was 3 min. The subjects were positioned in a chair at a distance of 0.75 to 1.50 m from the 22-inch monitor, determining the most comfortable distance for themselves. The EEG was recorded monopolarly in symmetrical leads PO7, PO3, POz, PO4, PO8, O1, Oz, O2 using Neuron-Spektr-4 electroencephalograph (Neurosoft, OOO) with the turned-off filter on and low- and high-pass filters off. The API presented by the manufacturers made it possible to implement a biofeedback system in which correlation coefficients calculated in pairs of symmetrical leads PO7, PO8, PO3-PO4, O1-O2 were transformed into RGB color space coordinates in the course of the experiment according to the formulas (3):

$$
\begin{cases}
x_R = \left\lfloor \dfrac{d-1}{2} * \max(MinR, \min(MaxR, k_R)) \right\rfloor; \\[2mm]
x_G = \left\lfloor \dfrac{d-1}{2} * \max(MinG, \min(MaxG, k_G)) \right\rfloor; \\[2mm]
x_B = \left\lfloor \dfrac{d-1}{2} * \max(MinB, \min(MaxB, k_B)) \right\rfloor;
\end{cases}
\tag{3}
$$

where $d = 256$ is the number of gradations of each of the three primary colors in the standard RG palette; $[MinR, MaxR]$ is the range of red-color representation and similarly – for green $[MinG, MaxG]$ and blue colors $[MinB, MaxB]$.

3.3 Interpretation and Discussion

In the experiment with the feedback, the analysis epoch was 1 s, while in the case of the control study, the colors changed with the same period but randomly, so that the probabilities of their appearance were the same. After EEG recording in the control experiment, the data were processed using the same algorithm as for the experiment with feedback. Two trajectories were obtained in the RGB space: the one formed with the feedback, of which the subject was not informed, and the one formed without the feedback between colors on the monitor screen and EEG correlations in symmetric leads. Since the preferred and avoided colors are known for each person involved in the study, each of the above color groups contains four elements: the colors declared by the test person and the Torricelli point, or, more strictly, the first Torricelli point.

In the statistical analysis, given the number of subjects and multidimensional results, we decided to use exploratory statistical approaches based on Correspondence analysis. The resulting coordinates in the n-dimensional space actually reflect the degree of "similarity" of the distribution of variable values. In our case, these would be, on the one hand, the frequencies of occurrence of different variants of point mutations and, on the other hand, the parameters of successful mastering of human-computer interfaces. At the same time, the obtained coordinates in the multidimensional space are quite complicated for interpretation, since it is necessary to analyze a large number of two- and three-dimensional projections. In this case, an approach based on hierarchical cluster analysis procedures was applied. The far-neighbor method, weighted and unweighted centroid methods and pairwise average methods were used as clustering algorithms. Different clustering methods and approaches to estimating the distance between the studied variables (Euclidean, Chebyshev, Manhattan) provided an assessment of the reproducibility of the identified phenomena. Processing was performed both in the Statistica 8.0 software package and with the original software. The specific version of Statistica 8.0 was verified using the test samples with known processing results.

The results of the computational experiments are shown in Fig. 6. In Fig. 6, the following notations for the algorithms are used:

- "MSI" – native signal processing with the MSI algorithm (item 3);
- "MSI accumulation" – the application of the MSI algorithm for the accumulated evoked potential (item 4);
- "MSI-FFT" – the application of MSI for Fourier spectrum analysis (item 5);
- "FFT" – the analysis based on the Fourier spectrum of equal length analysis epochs (item 1);
- "FFT-C" – the application of Fourier spectrum calculated by an equal number of oscillations of the sought frequencies (item 2);
- "Linear correlation" – the calculation based on the results of signal correlation with the sample obtained from the "user" (test signal generator) during the interface training (item 6);
- "MSI (filter)" – the benchmark for this algorithm is obtained by filtering the accumulated signal by Morlet wavelet, the central frequency of which coincides with the frequency sought in the signal (item 8);
- "MSI (by sample)" – (item 7);
- "MSI (restored)" – the benchmark is the signal restored based on the approaches of analysis of the chains of local maxima and minima.

In general, the methods demonstrated a high level of recognition of the useful signal up to a signal-to-noise ratio of 1 to 40, which, taking into account the SSVEP amplitude, would give from 20 to ~ 400 µV of "noise" – i.e. the background EEG. Taking into account the fact that the amplitude of the background EEG in the occipital regions decreases significantly during mental load, the existing recognition accuracy should be considered quite sufficient for stable detection of the required potential. Besides, in the presence of α-rhythm depression during the photostimulation, it gives a high quality of recognition of a useful signal. Although the recognition with a signal-to-noise ratio of 1/100 or more is possible for a number of algorithms, in general, the algorithms show the accuracy that does not allow using them for controlling a drone, self-propelled chassis, typing. In other words, it is difficult to apply the functions for which the brain-computer interface is created. At a signal-to-noise ratio of 1/300, it turns out to be practically impossible to ensure the functioning of the brain-computer interface at an acceptable speed, even despite the coherent accumulation of the evoked potential.

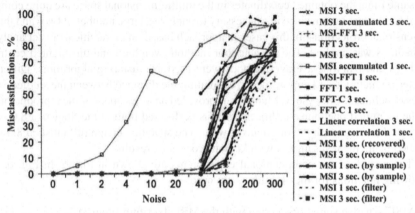

Fig. 6. Results of computational experiments. The dependence of misclassifications zhigher than the amplitude of the useful signal. The amplitude of the useful signal is taken as a unit.

At the signal/noise level of 1/100, the following algorithms have proved to be the best: MSI (3 s) for raw signals, MSI (3 s) for Fourier transform results, MSI (3 s) with coherent accumulation wavelet filtering as a reference, linear correlation coefficient (3 s) and MSI (3 s) with EP reconstructed after wavelet transform as a reference. At the same time, two algorithms have advantages over the other investigated algorithms due to their significantly lower resource intensity: the MSI algorithm and the linear correlation algorithm, which, in fact, is a convolution of the accumulated evoked potential using only one function. The algorithm for pre-filtering coherent accumulation by wavelets in a known frequency range (which is, in fact, a variant of linear correlation) is somewhat less resource-intensive. However, this resource-intensiveness problem is easily solved if we consider that the generation of the benchmark is performed once after training the software-hardware part of the brain-computer interface and immediately before the user's work. When the analysis epoch is reduced to 1 s, almost all of the considered algorithms still select the desired components with a sufficiently high accuracy. The only exception is the MSI algorithm, which analyzes the accumulated signal [26].

4 Conclusions

The results of the development, improvement and testing of ergatic systems are presented, the hardware and software part of which is a computer or device under its control. Such devices include self-propelled chassis, flying platforms, and the PC itself. The work is based on modeling and design of an ergatic system, using bionic approaches at the following stages: processing of received signals, modeling of decision-making system architecture, modeling of system functioning, system-user feedback. We proposed the original approach to control and solved the problem of control of a robot using the neural interface technology. And we described the general scheme and working principle of the basic idea of non-invasive neural interface control of the robot using the original CNN. A structure of the software package is proposed. The correlation patterns of EEG implemented in the biofeedback system through the change of colors on the monitor screen were analyzed. It was shown that the subjects maintained the trend of dynamics during the experiment: if in the presence of the feedback the distance to the preferred colors decreased, then in the control experiment (without the presence of the feedback) the distance decreased similarly. The effect of the feedback was multidirectional. The distance from the first to the fourth quantile increased for the experiments with the feedback, the values were smaller than those in the control experiment. Conversely, when the distance decreased, the values for the control experiment were smaller than those for the experiment. The decrease in the standard deviation by the end of the experiment was found. Thus, the range of variation of EEG correlations was decreasing. Differences were also revealed between the two groups under study in the experiments with the presence of the feedback. The group that demonstrated approach to the target (the preferred color) had initially a greater distance to it, but lower standard deviation values. It was shown that the greatest response of the EEG correlation pattern was the characteristic of the first 45 s of the feedback formation. This paper presents the results of the comparison of the algorithms for analyzing evoked brain potentials used to construct brain-computer interfaces. For computational experiments, the Fourier transform algorithm and the MSI algorithm were taken, which is a development of canonical correlation analysis methods in different modifications: analysis of the initial signal; analysis of the accumulated evoked potential; analysis of the spectrum of the accumulated evoked potential. For the study, model signals were used, which were a summation of white noise and a harmonic, imitating a stable visual evoked potential. The signal-to-noise ratio varied in the range from the complete absence of noise to 1/300. The results showed that when the signal-to-noise ratio ranged from the complete absence of noise to 1/40, none of the considered algorithms had an advantage in the accuracy of evoked potential recognition. When the signal-to-noise ratio is 1/300, none of the considered algorithms provided the necessary accuracy of the evoked potential recognition. In the intermediate range of such ratios, the most stable results for the 3-s analysis epoch were demonstrated by the initial signal MSI, Fourier transform MSI, MSI where the benchmark was the result of coherent accumulation wavelet filtering, linear correlation coefficient, and MSI where the benchmark was the EP recovered after the wavelet transform. They also proved to be the best for short 1-s segments, which allows us to consider these algorithms as promising for creating high-speed synchronous brain-computer interfaces. However, the use of traditional ergative paradigms based on the experience of creating and operating control systems is not always justified in this case. First of all, we are talking about psycho-physiological features of mastering certain technologies. At the same time, these features can be both acquired and genetically determined.

Acknowledgements. The reported study was partially funded by RFBR, project number 19-29-01156.

References

1. Lebedev, M.A., Nicolelis, M.A.: Brain-machine interfaces: from basic science to neuroprostheses and neurorehabilitation. Physiol. Rev. **97**(2), 767–837 (2017). https://doi.org/10.1152/physrev.00027.2016
2. Wolpaw, J.R., Birbaumer, N., McFarland, D.J., Pfurtscheller, G., Vaughan, T.M.: Brain-computer interfaces for communication and control. Clin Neurophysiol. **113**(6), 767–791 (2002). https://doi.org/10.1016/s1388-2457(02)00057-3
3. Galin, R.R., Meshcheryakov, R.V.: Human-robot interaction efficiency and human-robot collaboration. In: Kravets, A.G. (ed.) Robotics: Industry 4.0 Issues & New Intelligent Control Paradigms. SSDC, vol. 272, pp. 55–63. Springer, Cham (2020). https://doi.org/10.1007/978-3-030-37841-7_5
4. Galin, R., Meshcheryakov, R.: Review on human–robot interaction during collaboration in a shared workspace. In: Ronzhin, A., Rigoll, G., Meshcheryakov, R. (eds.) ICR 2019. LNCS (LNAI), vol. 11659, pp. 63–74. Springer, Cham (2019). https://doi.org/10.1007/978-3-030-26118-4_7
5. Meshcheryakov, R.V., Iskhakov, A.Y., Evsutin, O.O.: Analysis of modern methods to ensure data integrity in cyber-physical system management protocols. Inf. Autom. **19**(5), 1089–1122 (2020). https://doi.org/10.15622/ia.2020.19.5.7
6. Kharchenko, S., Meshcheryakov, R., Turovsky, Y., Volf, D.: Implementation of robot–human control bio-interface when highlighting visual-evoked potentials based on multivariate synchronization index. In: Ronzhin, A., Shishlakov, V. (eds.) Proceedings of 15th International Conference on Electromechanics and Robotics "Zavalishin's Readings." SIST, vol. 187, pp. 225–236. Springer, Singapore (2021). https://doi.org/10.1007/978-981-15-5580-0_18
7. Kharchenko, S., Turovsky, Y., Meshcheryakov, R., Iskhakova, A.: Restrictions of the measurement system and a patient when using visually evoked potentials. In: Proceedings of the 12th International Conference on Developments in eSystems Engineering (DeSE), pp. 15–19. IEEE, Kazan (2019). https://doi.org/10.1109/DeSE.2019.00013
8. Fatih, D.A.: Bio-inspired filter banks for SSVEP-based brain-computer interfaces. In: 2016 IEEE International Conference on Biomedical and Health Informatics (BHI), pp. 144–147. IEEE, Las Vegas (2016). https://doi.org/10.1109/BHI.2016.7455855
9. Zhu, D., Bieger, J., Molina, G., Aarts, R.M.: A Survey of stimulation methods used in SSVEP-based BCIs. Comput. Intell. Neurosci. **2010**, 1–12 (2010). https://doi.org/10.1155/2010/702357
10. Farwell, L.A., Donchin, E.: Talking off the top of your head: towards mental prosthesis utilizing event-related brain potentials. Electroencephalogr. Clin. Neurophysiol. **70**(6), 510–523 (1988). https://doi.org/10.1016/0013-4694(88)90149-6
11. Kwak, N.-S., Muller, K.-R., Lee, S.-W.: A convolutional neural network for steady state visual evoked potential classification under ambulatory environment. PLoS ONE **12**(2), 1–20 (2017). https://doi.org/10.1371/journal.pone.0172578

12. Middendorf, M., McMillan, G., Calhoun, G., Jones, K.: Brain-computer interfaces based on the steady-state visual-evoked response. IEEE Trans. Rehabil. Eng. **8**(2), 211–214 (2000). https://doi.org/10.1109/86.847819
13. Haq S., Jackson, P.J.: Multimodal emotion recognition. In: Machine Audition: Principles, Algorithms and Systems, pp. 398–423. IGI Global (2011). https://doi.org/10.4018/978-1-61520-919-4.ch017
14. Han, K., Yu, D., Tashev, I.: Speech emotion recognition using deep neural network and extreme learning machine. In: INTERSPEECH, Singapore, Malaysia, pp. 223–227 (2014)
15. Minsky, M.: The Emotion Machine: Commonsense Thinking, Artificial Intelligence, and the Future of the Human Mind. Simon and Schuster, New York (2007)
16. Yan, J., Chen, S., Deng, S.: A EEG-based emotion recognition model with rhythm and time characteristics. Brain Inf. **6**(1), 1–8 (2019). https://doi.org/10.1186/s40708-019-0100-y
17. Yue, K., Wang, D.: EEG-based 3D visual fatigue evaluation using CNN. Electronics **8**(11), 1208 (2019). https://doi.org/10.3390/electronics8111208
18. Wang, Y., Wang, Y., Cheng, C., Jung, T.: Developing stimulus presentation on mobile devices for a truly portable SSVEP-based BCI. In: 2013 35th Annual International Conference of the IEEE Engineering in Medicine and Biology Society (EMBC), Osaka, Japan, pp. 5271–5274 (2013). https://doi.org/10.1109/EMBC.2013.6610738
19. Volosyak, I.: SSVEP based Bremen-BCI boosting information transfer rates. J. Neural Eng. **8**(3), 036020 (2011). https://doi.org/10.1088/1741-2560/8/3/036020
20. Resalat, S.N., Setarehdan, S.K.: An Improved SSVEP based BCI system using frequency domain feature classification. Am. J. Biomed. Eng. **3**(1), 1–8 (2013). https://doi.org/10.5923/j.ajbe.20130301.01
21. Iskhakova, A., Alekhin, M., Bogomolov, A.: Time-frequency transforms in analysis of non-stationary quasi-periodic biomedical signal patterns for acoustic anomaly detection. Inf. Control Syst. **1**, 15–23 (2020). https://doi.org/10.31799/1684-8853-2020-1-15-23
22. Zhang, Y., Peng, X., Cheng, K., Yao, D.: Multivariate synchronization index for frequency recognition of SSVEP-based brain–computer interface. J. Neurosci. Methods **221**, 32–40 (2014). https://doi.org/10.1016/j.jneumeth.2013.07.018
23. Belobrodsky, V.A., Kurgalin, S.D., Turovsky, Y., Vahtin, A.A.: Developing a genetic algorithm for digital filters design to classify biomedical signals and testing the algorithm on known property signals. Biomed. Radioelectron. **2**, 56–64 (2015). (In Russ.)
24. Turovsky, Y., Kurgalin, S.D., Vahtin, A.A., Borzunov, S.V., Belobrodsky, V.A.: Event-related brain potential investigation using the adaptive wavelet recovery method. Biophysics **60**(3), 443–448 (2015). https://doi.org/10.1134/S0006350915030203
25. Turovsky, Y.A., Borzunov, S.V., Danilova, A.V., Glagoleva, E.P.: Dynamics of involuntary formation of EEG correlation patterns by biofeedback mechanism. Ulyanovsk Med. Biol. J. **2**, 90–99 (2020). https://doi.org/10.34014/2227-1848-2020-2-90-99
26. Turovsky, Y.A.: Comparative characteristics of the algorithms of detection steady state visually evoked potentials of the brain on an electroencephalogram. Cifrovaya Obrabotka Signalov **1**, 51–55 (2018)

Software Development for Agricultural Tillage Robot Based on Technologies of Machine Intelligence

Roman N. Panarin$^{(\boxtimes)}$ ⓘ and Lubov A. Khvorova

Altai State University, Lenin Avenue 61, 656049 Barnaul, Russia

Abstract. The article is devoted to the development of software for robots designed for spot mechanical tillage. The need to develop software for the digital twin of the agro-robot with the use of artificial intelligence technologies is dictated by the need of farmers in its practical use. The article describes four high-level nodes of an agricultural robot: the control unit, which is an NVIDIA Jetson NANO computing module; the executive mechanism, which is a 6-axis desktop robotic arm; the machine vision unit, consisting of an Intel RealSense camera; the chassis unit, represented as crawler tracks and drivers for their control. The implementation of the software is carried out independently of the manufacture of the robot, so for the developer there is a task to minimize the risk of its implementation in the manufactured robot. The developed software fully meets the requirements imposed by the customer. For instance, the digital robot twin takes into account the environmental conditions, as well as the terrain in which the prototype robot will work, and then the serial device. Second, the use of ROS (Robot Operating System) in software development will allow one with minimal effort to transfer the digital model to the physical one (prototype and serial robot), without changing the source code. Third, taking into account the physical environment conditions when programming the digital robot twin allowed one to build mathematical models of device control that are close to reality, as well as to debug and test them.

Keywords: Agrorobot · Software · Artificial intelligence · Algorithm · Robot movement control

1 Introduction

The National Strategy of the Russian Federation includes the Artificial Intelligence (AI) development in the 21st century, measures to use it for the implementation of the strategic national prioritiesas well as for the scientific and technological development. Artificial Intelligence is defined as a technology solution complex (TSC) that allows imitating human cognitive functions and receiving the results comparable to the results of the human intellectual activity in fulfilling specific practical tasks. The TSC includes an information and communication infrastructure, software where the Machine Learning methods, processes, and services are used for data processing and finding solutions. We

© Springer Nature Switzerland AG 2022
V. Jordan et al. (Eds.): HPCST 2021, CCIS 1526, pp. 354–367, 2022.
https://doi.org/10.1007/978-3-030-94141-3_28

are seeing the usage of AI technologies in the fields of automaking, robotics technology, unmanned vehicle control, IoT, and big data analysis.

The rural sector relates to the high-priority areas of the AI technology development and usage. The agricultural machinery manufacturers throughout the world are increasingly engaging more scientific employees and software developers on the AI basis to fulfill the needs of the agricultural sector of the economy. At the request of agricultural holdings, robots and systems with AI elements are developed. They are used for employees' labor automation and saving, and sometimes for full substitution of manual labor with machinery. Robotic systems are expected to be able to scatter fields with seeds, evenly distribute fertilizers and herbicides, and perform highly accurate, autonomous weeding out which in turn accelerates the development of the precision agriculture field.

Widespread introduction of robots in the agrarian sector will lead to the optimization of food production, yield enhancement, and reduction of chemical load on soil and underground waters.

The technologies used nowadays such as large agricultural equipment and manned aviation have some disadvantages:

- high cost of usage and consequently – increase of the final product cost;
- unselective approach to the fertilizers distribution that leads to local ecological disasters;
- loss in final product quality that leads to the fall in demand on the manufacturers' production in the context of rising popularity of healthful lifestyle.

The defined disadvantages determine the necessity of a new area development – small robots intended for spot mechanical tillage. The control of such robots is done by the software that scientific employees and engineers are developing and implementing.

The topicality of this work lies in the necessity of software development using AI technology for controlling a robotic crawler and the introduction of this software for a practical use in one of the agrarian holdings in Altai Krai.

Object of the research – autonomous unmanned robots and systems with artificial intelligence.

Subject of the research – the robot crawler software responsible for controlling in the external uncertain environment.

The purpose of the research – software development for the digital twin of an agro-robot. The software makes it possible to take technological decisions based on Artificial Intelligence and fulfills the following requirements:

- Autonomous control of the rolling stock and the actuating mechanism (manipulator);
- The robot's software should be developed in the simulated environment so that the robot will be able to perform the tasks without extra settings after the software installation;
- The robot should be able to work on various types of ground and in any weather conditions.

At the same time, maximum robot performance should be achieved that, in this case, includes savings in the resources used – fertilizers and herbicides, minimal time of the plant treatment and the absence of human inference in the treatment process.

The following research and practice tasks are at the fore:

1. Decomposing the basic task, finding and synthesizing solutions.
2. The development and implementation of the algorithms for motion control.
3. The development and implementation of the algorithms for controlling the actuating mechanism.
4. Computer-based testing of the algorithms.
5. The software implementation.
6. The assurance of the quality and the efficiency of the results.

2 Agrorobot Concept

2.1 Software Modules

Describe the basic worker nodes of the agrarian robot. The whole system can be represented as four high-level nodes:

1. The control panel includes a computer module NVIDIA Jetson NANO.
2. The actuating mechanism includes a 6-axis desk robotic arm.
3. Computer Vision block includes the IntelRealSense camera.
4. The chassis block includes chain tracks and drivers for controlling them.

Fig. 1. Agricultural land with ridges and seedlings of crops.

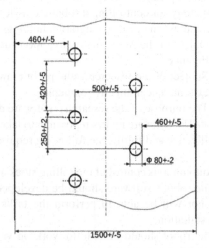

Fig. 2. The scheme of the film perforation.

The environment where the robot will work is an agricultural holding with a complex landscape where the ridges with seedlings are located (Fig. 1). The ridges are covered with perforated plastic film of black color. The scheme of perforation is provided in Fig. 2.

For the description of the environment, it will be sufficient to define the locations of ridges, the obstacles encountered at the time of working, and the particular seedlings to be treated if we formalize the environment. We decided to use parallelepipeds and the related speed of the presumed objects as an all-in-one approach to describe the obstacles and define separate seedlings. The speed of the parallelepipeds that describe the seedlings is equal to zero.

Form the mathematical point of view this representation is the following vector:

$$\left(x_j^i, y_j^i, z_j^i, v^i\right),\qquad(1)$$

where $x, y, z \in R$, $i \in [0; 65535]$ is the number of the object being tracked. The interval is resulted from the limitation of the commuter module's resources; $j \in [0; 7]$ stands for the number of a point in the parallelepiped; $v \in [0; \infty)$ – object's speed.

A ridge is a set of 3D check points that describe its boundaries. The distance that is being described in a specific point in time is 5 m ahead with respect to the position of the robot's camera. The scheme of the formalized environment is provided in Fig. 3.

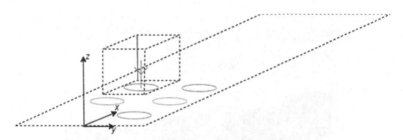

Fig. 3. The scheme of the formalized environment.

The system of coordinates XYZ is a center of the agrarian robot's camera. All the coordinates are set relatively to it.

The movable part of the robot is a tracked chassis with a frame to which the executive mechanism, the camera, and the control module are attached. Off-road capability is the advantage of the tracked locomotor. Due to a larger contact area with the ground if compared with wheeled platform, tracked locomotor attains low ground pressure.

2.2 Control Module

The control module is based on a dynamic model, on the basis of which the software was developed [1–3].

$$
\begin{cases}
m\frac{d^2x}{dt^2} = F_1 + F_2 - F_{\text{center}} \sin\alpha - R_1 - R_2 \\
m\frac{d^2y}{dt^2} = F_{\text{center}} \cos\alpha - g\mu_l, \; I_z\frac{d\omega}{dt} = M_c - M_r \\
M_c = \frac{b}{2}[(F_1 - R_1) - (F_2 - R_2)], M_r = \frac{mgl\mu_l}{3} \\
R_1 = \left(\frac{w}{2} - \frac{HmV_1^2x}{bR}\right)\mu_r, R_2 = \left(\frac{w}{2} - \frac{HmV_2^2x}{bR}\right)\mu_r \\
\alpha = \text{arctg}\frac{\omega^2 l}{4g\mu_l}
\end{cases}
\tag{2}
$$

where m – robot's mass; x, y – robot's coordinates on the x-axis and y-axis respectively; F_1, F_2 – pull on the right and on the left track respectively; F_{center} – centrifugal pull that influences the object in case of turning; α – gliding angle; R_1, R_2 – longitudinal resistant forces; g – free fall acceleration; μ_l – coefficient of the side resistance; I_z – inertia moment with respect to vertical axis Z; ω – turning rate with respect to axis of mass; M_C – moment with respect to axis of mass; M_r – moment of the resistance to turning; W – robot's weight; H – height of the inertia center; b – width of the wheel track; V_1, V_2 – speed of the right and the left track respectively; μ_r – coefficient of the longitudinal resistance; l – length of the track.

Fig. 4. The manipulator's photo.

2.3 Actuator Module

A manipulator is used as an executive mechanism (Fig. 4). The manipulator meets the following limits: only rotational and linear joints, all the joints have motors. The used manipulator consists of 5 motors (joints) and 6 links where the 1st link is fixed.

To describe the condition of the manipulator it is necessary to define the generalized coordinate vector $q = [q_1, q_2, q_3, q_4, q_5, q_6]$, each component of which defines a turn in the corresponding joint (Fig. 5), and the vector of generalized forces $Q = [Q_1, Q_2, Q_3, Q_4, Q_5]$ that defines the force or the moment in the corresponding joint.

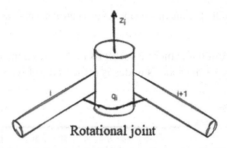

Fig. 5. Rotational joints and the corresponding generalized coordinates.

2.4 Machine Vision Module

The camera (Figs. 6 and 7) is a separate USB device that is connected to the control panel. The main peculiarity of this device is the ability of presenting data not only in RGB channels but also in a depth channel that allows defining the distance to a specific point.

Fig. 6. The camera Intel RealSense D435.

The considered device version uses the following configuration: resolution is 1280 × 720 (in the Depth mode), frame rate is 90 FPS (in the Depth mode). The minimum depth distance in case of maximum resolution is 28 cm.

Computer vision system
Intel RealSence

Computing unit
Nvidia Jetson Xavier NX

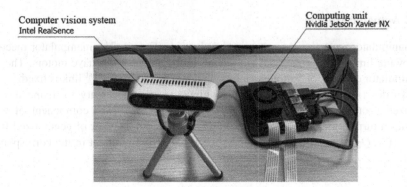

Fig. 7. RGB-D camera – on the left, a control panel – on the right.

The output data from the camera is an RGB image and a data cloud (a depth map). The functional scheme of the robot's nodes is presented in Fig. 8.

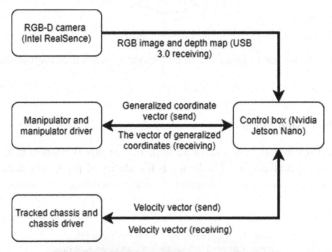

Fig. 8. The functional scheme of the robot's nodes.

Based on the analysis of the robot's nodes interconnection, the software functional scheme is developed (see Fig. 9). As the software implementation is carried out independently of the manufacture of the robot, there are tasks to minimize the risk of its implementation in the manufactured robot.

Taking into account this requirement there is a necessity to develop a robot's digital twin that will allow creating the software independent from the used executive mechanisms. Based on the analysis of the software functional scheme, let us consider microservice architecture as the main one that is implemented with the help of ROS (Robot Operating System) in some extent. The main advantage of ROS is a standard in the field and the availability of enormous number of modules necessary for the robot creation.

This approach allows carrying out continuous software development with debugging of complex scenarios. The usage of the designed nodes of the digital twin allows running the software on the robot prototype.

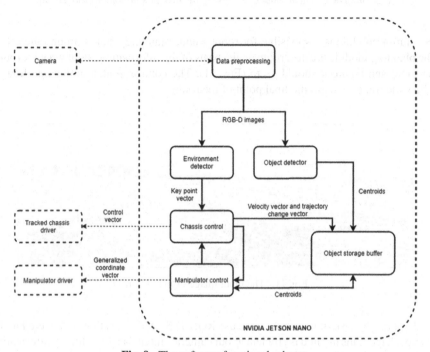

Fig. 9. The software functional scheme.

We use Copellia Sim (previously V-REP) as a simulation modelling environment, it has ROS integration. This simulator has some advantages: a broad library of models, the ability to communicate with the real world for a user during the process of modelling, and, most importantly, the control of the net and optimization. Besides, Coppelia Sim produces new threads on several kernels of a CPU automatically and, consequently, uses total capacity of a CPU when it is necessary.

To work with the manipulator and the movable system in ROS, it is necessary to create their URDF model [4]. The model is required for controlling the robo-arm with the means of Move IT package.

3   Rolling Stock and Actuator Control

The basic tasks being solved are the control of the moving element and the actuating mechanism. The task of controlling the moving element is being solved according to the classical theory of the robotics [5] (Fig. 10).

Let us divide our task of autonomous movement of the robot into four modules. The localization module is responsible for robot's understanding where it is located. The

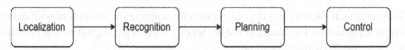

Fig. 10. The classical scheme of solving the task of autonomous movement.

recognition module is responsible for robot's understanding what is around the robot. The planning module create a route on the basis of the information about what is around the robot and where it should go to (Fig. 11). The control module points out how to follow the route to get to the final point of the route.

Fig. 11. The input image of the camera.

To solve the task of localization we use RGB-D SLAM [6–8] that is delivered in the ROS package. This method is efficient as our camera's input data form highly informative 3D images.

The task of the recognition is being solved with the use of two networks. The first one is YOLO4 [9] that is used for objects detection. We can define the distance to them using Distance Map[i][j] (Fig. 12) – depth map that defines the distance to the object with coordinates (i, j).

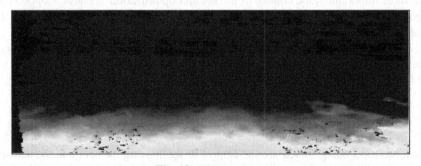

Fig. 12. Distance map.

The second neural network is Detectron2 [10], it solves the task of semantic segmentation of the visual environment (see Fig. 13). It is necessary for the extraction of the landscape of a ridge, ground, and other surfaces.

The task of planning is a classical task of correcting the trajectory that is about holding the robot's size in the frames of a ridge. In the case of deviation from a ridge we use the correcting of the trajectory that is a turn to the necessary direction. In the case of correcting the trajectory, we perform the recomputation of the centroids that are in the objects queue in the new coordinates. The movement planning is performed at the distance of 5 m.

Fig. 13. The output of the semantic segmentation model of the visual environment.

The task of controlling is solved by means of classical toolkit based on fuzzy logic [11], as the robot's trajectory is a right line and slightly deviates. For U-turns and other manoeuvrable actions, the corresponding subprograms are written. The examples of such subprograms can be a U-turn between ridges, getting to the first ridge, getting off the ridge in reverse if there is an obstacle that is difficult to pass without changing the trajectory.

We use the classical task of the inverse kinematic [12, 13] to control the executive mechanism – a manipulator. Let us review the scheme below (Fig. 14) and introduce the notations that we will use to solve the task of controlling the manipulator.

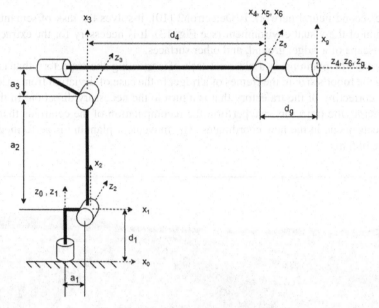

Fig. 14. The scheme of the manipulator.

Let us define α_{i-1} as the angle between axis z_{i-1} and axis z_i that is measured about axis x_{i-1}; α_i is the distance from axis z_{i-1} to axis x_i that is measured along axis z_i; θ_i– the angle between axis x_{i-1} and axis x_i that is measured along axis z_i (Table 1)

Table 1. Parameter table.

i	α_{i-1}	α_i, m	d_i, m	θ_i
1	0	0	$5.507 \cdot 10^{-2}$	q_1
2	$-\pi/2$	$3.69 \cdot 10^{-2}$	0	$q_2 - \pi/2$
3	0	$9.55 \cdot 10^{-2}$	0	q_3
4	$-\pi/2$	$1.991 \cdot 10^{-2}$	$3.68 \cdot 10^{-1}$	q_4
5	$\pi/2$	0	0	q_5
6	$-\pi/2$	0	0	q_6
g	0	0	$1.675 \cdot 10^{-2}$	0

With the use of the scheme below and the introduced notations, we can make a table of the Denavit-Hartenberg parameters [14, 15] – these are four parameters that are connected with a certain agreement of adding report systems to the links of the spatial kinematic chain or a robot-manipulator. Aspects related to program implementation and outputs of matrices of transitions from Cartesian coordinates to generalized coordinates are not considered in this article.

4   Trials and Discussion

To debug the manipulator, a graphical interface has been developed (Fig. 15 and 16) with debugging information and a control interface.

Fig. 15. Screenshot of the module for setting the parameters of the three links of the manipulator and a point in space.

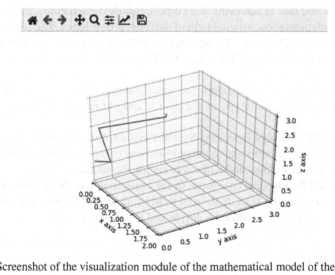

Fig. 16. Screenshot of the visualization module of the mathematical model of the manipulator.

To collect information, we used a tripod, an Intel RealSence camera and a laptop with the specialized Intel RealSenceViewer software installed.

The main data collected were: RGB images, depth maps and point clouds. The photographing of the ridges took place directly in the fields where the robot is to work. Specialized software CVAT (Computer Vision Annotation Tool) was used as a means of marking. The Polygon tool was used to mark the areas containing the ridges, and the Cuboid tool was used to annotate the seedlings. The marking results are shown in Fig. 17.

Fig. 17. Screenshot of the CVAT screen. Marking holes with seedlings.

The basic purpose of the research work is the software development for the digital twin of an agrorobot. The software can take technological decisions using Artificial Intelligence. The stated task of achieving this purpose is fully implemented. In the process of the project implementation, a digital twin of the robot is developed. The created software fulfills the stated requirements. In the process of the project implementation, a digital twin of the robot is developed. The created software fulfills the stated requirements:

- the robot's digital twin considers the environmental conditions and the ground landscape where the prototype of the device and the production device will work in;
- the usage of ROS (Robot Operating System) in the software development will allow us to transfer the digital model to the physical one (the prototype and the production robot) with minimal effort and without changing the source code;
- we considered the physical conditions of the environment in the process of programming the robot's digital twin. It allowed us to build, test, and debug the mathematical models that are used to control the device and are closest to reality.

5   Conclusion

In conclusion, it should be mentioned that this project is implemented during cooperation with Integra Sources Company and the Support Program for scientific and pedagogical workers of the Altai State University. Integra Sources is a company that provides services of embedded systems and software development that are used by numerous interested companies from all over the world for solutions for customers' business-tasks. As a test polygon for the agrorobot approbation, we will use the agriculturally used areas of Company "Altai Gardens", which deals with cultivation of crops in remote areas of Altai Krai.

References

1. Yatsun, S.F., Kyaw, P.W., Malchikov, A.V., Tarasova, E.S.: Mathematical modeling of full-track robot (Matematicheskoe modelirovanie mobilnogo gusenichnogo robota). Mod. Prob. Sci. Educ. **6**, 11005 (2013). (in Russ.)
2. Sidi, M.H.A., Hudha, K., Kadir, Z.A., Amer, N.H.: Modeling and path tracking control of a tracked mobile robot. In: IEEE 14th International Colloquium on Signal Processing & Its Applications (CSPA) , Penang, Malaysia, 9–10 March 2018, pp. 72–76 (2018). https://doi.org/10.1109/CSPA.2018.8368688
3. Ramesh, A., Archana, R.: Mathematical modelling and control of a mobile robot for path tracking. Int. J. Sci. Res. **5**(9), 1328–1330 (2016)
4. Lentin, J.: Mastering ROS for Robotics Programming. Packt, Birmingham-Mumbai (2015)
5. Szikora, P., Madarász, N.: Self-driving cars – the human side. In: IEEE 14th International Scientific Conference on Informatics, Poprad, Slovakia, 14–16 November 2017, pp. 383–387 (2017)
6. Kim, P., Coltin, B., Kim, H.J.: Linear RGB-D SLAM for planar environments. In: Ferrari, V., Hebert, M., Sminchisescu, C., Weiss, Y. (eds.) ECCV 2018. LNCS, vol. 11208, pp. 350–366. Springer, Cham (2018). https://doi.org/10.1007/978-3-030-01225-0_21
7. Civera, J., Lee, S.H.: RGB-D odometry and SLAM. In: Rosin, P.L., Lai, Y.-K., Shao, L., Liu, Y. (eds.) RGB-D Image Analysis and Processing. ACVPR, pp. 117–144. Springer, Cham (2019). https://doi.org/10.1007/978-3-030-28603-3_6
8. da Silva, B.M.F., Xavier, R.S., do Nascimento T.P., Gonçalves L.M.G.: Experimental Evaluation of ROS Compatible SLAM Algorithms for RGB-D Sensors. In: Proceedings of the European Conference on Computer Vision (ECCV) , Munich, Germany, 8–14 September 2018, pp. 333–348 (2018)
9. Bochkovskiy, A., Wang, C.-L., Liao, H.-Yu.M.: YOLOv4: optimal speed and accuracy of object detection (2020). https://arxiv.org/abs/2004.10934
10. Chen, Y., et al.: SimpleDet: a simple and versatile distributed framework for object detection and instance recognition. J. Mach. Learn. Res. **20**(156), 1–8 (2019)
11. Beloglazov, D.A., Kosenko, E.Yu., Soloviev, V.V., Titov, A.E., Shapovalov, I.O.: Development of a method for planning the trajectory of movement of a mobile autonomous robot in a three-dimensional environment based on the fuzzy logic apparatus (Razrabotka metoda planirovaniia traektorii peremeshcheniia mobilnogo avtonomnogo robota v trekhmernoi srede na osnove apparata nechetkoi logiki). Inzhenernyi Vestnik Dona **4**(1), 1–14 (2015). (in Russ.)
12. Song, W., Hu, G.: A fast inverse kinematics algorithm for joint animation. In: In-ternational Conference on Advances in Engineering, Nanjing, China, 24–25 December 2011 (2012)
13. Rokbani, N., Casals, A., Alimi, A.M.: IK-FA, a new heuristic inverse kinematics solver using firefly algorithm. In: Azar, A.T., Vaidyanathan, S. (eds.) Computational Intelligence Applications in Modeling and Control. SCI, vol. 575, pp. 369–395. Springer, Cham (2015). https://doi.org/10.1007/978-3-319-11017-2_15
14. Spong, M.W., Hutchinson, S., Vidyasagar, M.: Robot Dynamics and Control, 2nd ed. (2004). https://www.academia.edu/34800428
15. Denavit, J., Hartenberg, R.S.: A kinematic notation for lower pair mechanisms based on matrices. ASME J. Appl. Mech. **6**, 215–221 (1955)

Computing Technologies in Information Security Applications

Implementing Open Source Biometric Face Authentication for Multi-factor Authentication Procedures

Natalya Minakova[ID] and Alexander Mansurov[(⊠)] [ID]

Altai State University, Lenin Avenue 61, Barnaul 656049, Russia
minakova@asu.ru

Abstract. This study proposes a solution that extends the capabilities of web information systems with single-factor authentication by introducing an additional authentication factor based on biometric face recognition. The proposed solution design and its main operation steps are presented and discussed. The solution utilizes the standard multimedia functionality of popular web browsers and supports available or built-in image capturing devices (photo and web cameras). Robust program algorithms from the open source computer vision library are used for face image processing and analysis. Experimental testing and validation of the algorithms for face localization and recognition are conducted with image sets produced with consideration of reality. Experimental results demonstrate high effectiveness with a success rate of 80% ... 93% for the solution based on the local binary pattern face localization algorithm with the local binary pattern histogram face recognition algorithm.

Keywords: Biometrics · Face authentication · Face recognition · Computer vision · Local binary pattern

1 Introduction

Modern web applications and web information systems are complex and sophisticated solutions that typically process information with different levels of confidentiality. Such solutions often become targets of various hacker attacks when the attackers try to obtain the data circulated in web information systems by exploiting the weaknesses of web solution algorithms or bugs in software. According to sources [1–3], faults related to the authentication stage (or "Broken Authentication" in [1]) are rated as the second among the top 10 web application security risks, with up to 45% of similar vulnerabilities found during the conducted analysis [2]. Besides, there are several essential moments mentioned in [1] as crucial, like usage of well-known passwords, weak password database protection, susceptibility to brute-force attacks, and (what is important) missing or non-effective multi-factor authentication.

Using multi-factor authentication and adopting additional authentication factors can indeed increase the efficiency of the identification and authentication stage of web applications and web information systems [4, 5]. The research report "The State of Strong

Authentication 2019" produced by Javelin Strategy and Research [3] states that there are many widely used supplementary authentication factors (that follow the first traditional password factor), such as pre-generated one-time passwords, SMS passwords, hardware cryptographic keys, and security questions. At the same time, biometric information inextricably linked with the web system user should also be considered the reliable authentication factor. Nowadays, fingerprint scanning (44%) and face recognition (10%) are actively used due to the widely spread mobile platforms already equipped with the necessary scanners [3, 6].

Biometric authentication requires certain cooperation on the user side and hardware and software support to acquire the user's biometric data. However, modern smartphones, laptops, tablet computers, and workstations are capable of obtaining various biometric data easily with minimal cooperation of the user. For example, behaviometric data can be collected silently, and the voice and face image of a user can be acquired with a built-in microphone or camera and simple instructions. The latter (face image, in particular) appears to have the potential for being used in biometric solutions and systems.

Not all current biometric face identification and recognition solutions can be considered open source and free to use [7]. It is also noted that their functionalities differ significantly. Some solutions are inclined to deprecated methods of utilizing multimedia devices and require additional supporting software components to be downloaded or installed on the user side.

Therefore, it is of importance to propose a solution for web information systems with single-factor authentication. The solution should introduce an additional authentication factor based on the biometric face recognition and be open source. Several requirements should also be considered, such as the capability to be incorporated into the existing web system authentication procedure, support of the standard web browser multimedia functionality, and usage of available (or built-in) image capturing devices (photo and web cameras).

2   Solution Design and Software Implementation

2.1   Concept of the Solution

The proposed solution includes all the necessary steps and modifications for the user side and server side of the web information system. The overall design is shown in Fig. 1.

The solution can be incorporated into the web information system algorithms right after the first authentication step. The starting point of the proposed solution, in general, does not require any specific parameters for its operation. However, the solution should comply with the already implemented web information system application program interface (API). If several parameters inherited from the previous step have to pass through to the web system operation step after authentication, then they should be collected and passed at the exit point of the solution. Thus, compatibility with the web system API is achieved.

The proposed solution starts the pre-arranged HTML code on the user side to initiate the biometric authentication step. The HTML code contains verbal instructions for users and program instructions to activate available multimedia devices on the user side for face image capturing (typically, a web camera or frontal photo camera). The web browser on

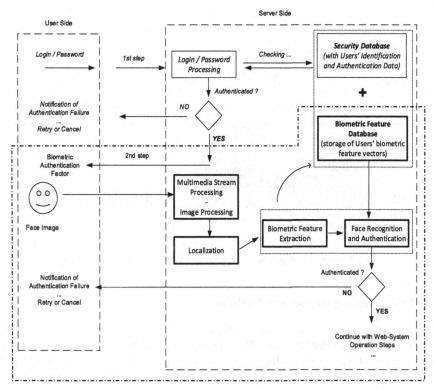

Fig. 1. The proposed solution overall design and its structure elements.

the user side fully handles all operations with the multimedia devices. The introduction of the HTML5 standard enhanced web browser multimedia capabilities significantly [8, 9]. Support of video streaming, capturing images from video streams, and operating the built-in multimedia devices on mobile platforms are of particular interest. WebRTC (Web Real-Time Communication) is a technology that enables Web applications and sites to capture and optionally stream audio and/or video media, as well as to exchange arbitrary data between browsers without requiring an intermediary [9]. Access to the data from photo and web cameras is provided by the *getUserMedia()* function that is supported by almost all latest web browsers on a variety of platforms running various operating systems [10] (Fig. 2).

Parameters of the *getUserMedia()* function can specify the data source and the desired format and quality of the video stream data. The JavaScript language is used to handle the operations. Program instructions necessary for engaging the camera and transmitting the acquired face image to the server side are incorporated into the web page designed for the biometric authentication step on the user side.

The captured face image is transmitted to the server side for processing and analysis. The server side algorithms can be developed separately and assembled into a complete project later [11]. Source codes of the algorithms can be produced independently or taken from the appropriate software library.

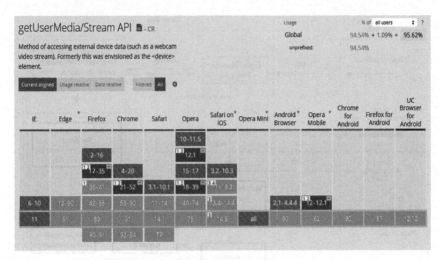

Fig. 2. Support of getUserMedia/Stream API by web browsers [10].

2.2 Processing Algorithms and Methods

Comprehensive studies [7, 12] suggest that the open source computer vision library OpenCV [13] and its PHP frontend PHP-OpenCV seem to be among the most effective open source software libraries for video and image processing and analysis. OpenCV includes several hundreds of computer vision algorithms, and there are many adaptive (trainable) algorithms based on artificial neural networks (ANN). These algorithms are highly effective for processing images, calculating specific features (feature vectors), localizing and detecting objects in images. Therefore, it seems prospective to utilize the algorithms included in the OpenCV software library.

In this study, the performance of several face localization methods is tested and evaluated to select the best performing method for its further implementation as the main one. The following face localization algorithms available in the OpenCV library are utilized: linear binary patterns (LBP) [14], FacemarkLBF [15], Haar cascades [16]. This part is necessary due to the importance of successful face localization. Once the face is localized in an image, it is possible to continue with face recognition. Otherwise, appropriate actions should be taken to acquire a new face image.

Face recognition is conducted using the trainable classifier based on the local binary pattern histograms (LBPH) [14, 17–19]. The LBP operator [14] is applied to the localized face image to calculate feature histograms representing local texture and shapes over the processed areas. The localized face image is divided into small regions from which LBP histograms are extracted to produce the resulting feature histogram vector (feature vector) (Fig. 3) [19]. Calculated feature vectors for successful classifications are stored in the Biometric feature database (when the user face image is processed for the first time) for further accumulation and enrichment of the training dataset.

The transmitted image undergoes normalization of brightness and contrast before being passed to the localization step. Unsuccessful localization of a face in the image or localization of the facial profile leads to disqualification of the image under processing.

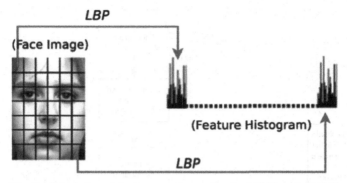

Fig. 3. Calculation of the feature vector using the LBPH method [19].

In this case, all operations start from the beginning, and the user side should provide another face image. The overall flowchart of face image processing and analysis is shown in Fig. 4.

3   Testing and Evaluation

Several available algorithms are taken for testing and evaluation of their performance to select the most efficient ones. These algorithms provide face localization and detection in processed images which can be acquired in various environments and be of different quality.

Testing and performance evaluation of face localization algorithms is conducted using the assembled set of 514 images of various faces. The assembled set contains images from several groups, and each group has almost the same number of images. These groups are named according to the specific 'trait' that all images within the group possess. The assembled set includes images from the following groups:

- ideal images with a proper light balance and faces positioned at the center ("*Ideal*");
- images with faces out of focus or images contain parts of faces only ("*Part-Face*");
- images with partially covered faces ("*Hidden*");
- images with excessive darkness or images with shadows on faces ("*Dark*");
- images with excessive light ("*Light*").

Experimental results are shown in Table 1 with percentages that represent successful face localization for each group.

"*Haarcascade alt*" and "*Haarcascade alt2*" algorithms demonstrate good results with clear tendencies to localize small faces or embossed objects. These algorithms provide the best results when processing images with excessive light or images from the "*Part-Face*" group. The algorithms are suitable for processing images acquired using mobile platforms. The "*Haar cascade alt tree*" algorithm shows good performance when dealing with images with partially covered faces or with faces out of focus.

The "*LBF*" algorithm is able to detect facial key points and fit for detailed localization. However, "*LBP*" and "*LBP improved*" algorithms demonstrate accurate and stable

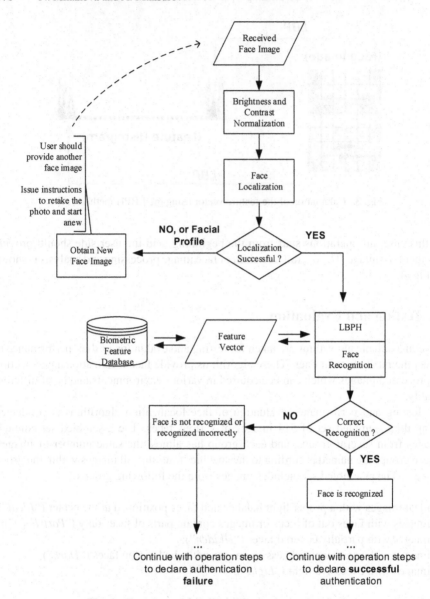

Fig. 4. Flowchart of face image processing and analysis.

Table 1. Experimental results of face localization for several groups of face images.

Algorithm\Image group	Dark	Hidden	Ideal	Light	Part-Face
Haarcascadealt	0.44	0.48	0.97	0.94	0.84
Haarcascade alt2	0.59	0.43	0.93	0.93	0.75
Haarcascadealttree	0.14	0.93	0.29	0.24	0.96
Haarcascadedefault	0.39	0.29	0.82	0.80	0.74
LBF	0.59	0.59	0.90	0.68	0.66
LBP	0.46	0.61	0.84	0.70	0.73
LBP improved	0.74	0.53	0.94	0.94	0.64

results for all groups of images in the assembled set. Thus, the *"LBP improved"* algorithm is selected as the best performing algorithm for its implementation as the main localization algorithm of the proposed solution.

The LBPH-based trainable classifier is used further to perform face recognition. In this study, the LBPH based classifier produces two possible outputs – "affirmative" (recognition is done, even if the face is matched incorrectly) and "negative" (face is not recognized / no match found).

There are two experimental samples prepared to train and evaluate the LBPH based classifier. Test sample "A" contains 58 various face images of the same person taken under various conditions. These conditions are equivalent to the ones for the image groups of the previously discussed assembled image set for localization testing. The training sample includes 20 images from the sample "A" and 100 images of other (different) persons.

Test sample "B" contains 50 various high-quality face images of the same person. There are no images with partially covered faces or images with faces out of focus in this test sample. However, images with excessive light or darkness are included in the test sample "B". The training sample for this case includes 20 images from the sample "B" and 100 images of other (different) persons. All images comply with the conditions mentioned earlier.

Table 2 demonstrates the performance results (in percentage) of the trainable LBPH-based classifier with the two experimental samples.

Table 2. Performance results of the LBPH-based classifier.

Results\Samples	Test sample "A"	Test sample "B"
Correct recognition	0.7	0.87
1st type error	0.1	0.06
2nd type error	0.2	0.07

Here, the "*1st type error*" stands for erroneous recognition of face images belonging to one user as belonging to another. The "*2nd type error*" stands for unsuccessful recognition when the face is not matched with the face of any user.

Results of the experiment demonstrate a high rate of correct face recognition. It can be seen that the most optimal case would be direct utilization of two output classes and adoption of the "1st type error" results as successful face recognition. However, the biometric authentication factor, in this case, should be interpreted as a very soft authentication step with only two outcomes:

1. the face is matched, and so the user is known to the web information system;
2. the face is not matched, and so the user is unknown to the web information system.

The rate of correct face recognition can be increased by using more robust adaptive algorithms and models [17]. Also, the proposed biometric authentication step can be improved by utilizing additional biometric data and processing algorithms. For example, face recognition can be supplemented by iris scanning [20] or any other biometric technique.

After the biometric authentication step is acknowledged as successful, the control returns to the web information system algorithms at the point located right after the initial authentication procedure of the web information system.

4   Conclusion

This paper presents the solution that extends the capabilities of web information systems with single-factor authentication by introducing an additional authentication factor based on biometric face recognition. The proposed solution is based on algorithms from the open source software library. It uses the standard web browser multimedia functionality and available (or built-in) image capturing devices (photo and web cameras).

The proposed solution can be easily integrated into existing authentication procedures of web information systems. Face localization and recognition algorithms are based on adaptive ANN techniques and demonstrate a high success rate. They can be replaced during further operation by more robust and prospective ones to fully satisfy the specific requirements of a particular web information system and incorporate all achievements in the area of biometric data analysis and face recognition.

References

1. The OWASP: OWASP Top Ten Web Application Security Risks. https://owasp.org/www-pro ject-top-ten/, Accessed 14 May 2021
2. Positive Technologies: Web Applications Vulnerabilities and Threats: Statistics for 2019. https://www.ptsecurity.com/ww-en/analytics/web-vulnerabilities-2020/, Accessed 14 May 2021
3. Pascual, A., Maarchini, K.: The State of strong authentication 2019. Adoption Rises under New Threats and Regulations. Report, Javelin Strategy & Research (GA Javelin LLC), Pleasanton, CA, USA (2019)

4. Shah, Y., Choyi, V., Subramanian, L.: Multi-factor authentication as a service. In: IEEE International Conference on Mobile Cloud Computing, Services, and Engineering (MobileCloud 2015), San-Francisco, USA, pp. 144–150. (2015). https://doi.org/10.1109/MobileCloud.2015.35

5. Jacomme, C., Kremer, S.: An extensive formal analysis of multi-factor authentication protocols. In: 2018 IEEE 31st Computer Security Foundations Symposium (CSF) 2018, Oxford, UK, 2018, pp. 1–15. (2018). https://doi.org/10.1109/CSF.2018.00008

6. Ometov, A., Bezzateev, S., Mäkitalo, N., Andreev, S., Mikkonen, T., Koucheryavy, Y.: Authentication: a survey. Cryptography 2 (2018). https://doi.org/10.3390/cryptography2010001

7. Masek, P., Thulin, M.: Evaluation of face recognition APIs and libraries. https://gupea.ub.gu.se/bitstream/2077/38856/1/gupea_2077_38856_1.pdf, Accessed 14 May 2021

8. The W3C: HTML Media Capture. https://www.w3.org/TR/html-media-capture/, Accessed 14 May 2021

9. MDN Web Docs: WebRTC API. https://developer.mozilla.org/en-US/docs/Web/API/WebRTC_API, Accessed 14 May 2021

10. The "Can I use" Project: "getusermedia". https://caniuse.com/?search=getusermedia, Accessed 14 May 2021

11. Minakova, N., Petrov, I.: Modeling and prototyping of biometric systems using dataflow programming. J. Phys. Conf. Ser. 944(1), 012080 (2018). https://doi.org/10.1088/1742-6596/944/1/012080

12. Ranjan, R., Bansai, A., Zheng, J., Xu, H., Gleason, J., Lu, B., et al.: A fast and accurate system for face detection, identification, and verification. IEEE Trans. Biometrics, Behav. Identity Sci. 1(2), 82–96 (2019). https://doi.org/10.1109/TBIOM.2019.2908436

13. OpenCV: OpenCV Modules. https://docs.opencv.org, Accessed 14 May 2021

14. Ahonen, T., Hadid, A., Pietikäinen, M.: Face recognition with local binary patterns. In: Pajdla, T., Matas, J. (eds.) ECCV 2004. LNCS, vol. 3021, pp. 469–481. Springer, Heidelberg (2004). https://doi.org/10.1007/978-3-540-24670-1_36

15. Ren, S., Cao, X., Wei, Y., Sun, J.: Face alignment via regressing local binary features. IEEE Trans. Image Process. 25(3), 1233–1245 (2016). https://doi.org/10.1109/TIP.2016.2518867

16. Hapsari, D.T.P., Berliana, C.G., Winda, P., Soeleman, M.A.: Face detection using haar cascade in difference illumination. In: 2018 International Seminar on Application for Technology of Information and Communication, Semarang, Indonesia, 2018, pp. 555–559 (2018). https://doi.org/10.1109/ISEMANTIC.2018.8549752

17. Goncharov, V.: Tutorial for computer vision and machine learning in PHP 7/8 by opencv (installation + examples + documentation). https://github.com/php-opencv/php-opencv-examples, Accessed 14 May 2021

18. Deeba, F., Memon, H., Dharejo, F., Ahmed, A., Ghaffar, A.: LBPH-based enhanced real-time face recognition. Int. J Adv. Comput. Sci. Appl. 10(5), 274–280 (2019). https://doi.org/10.14569/IJACSA.2019.0100535

19. Shan, C., Gong, S., McOwan, P.W.: Facial expression recognition based on local binary patterns: a comprehensive study. Image Vis. Comput. 27(6), 803–816 (2009)

20. Minacova, N., Petrov, I.: Method of preliminary localization of the iris in biometric access control systems. IOP Conf. Ser. Mater. Sci. Eng. 93, 012056 (2015). https://doi.org/10.1088/1757-899X/93/1/012056

Application of Recurrent Networks to Develop Models for Hard Disk State Classification

Anton Filatov[(✉)] [iD] and Liliya Demidova[(✉)] [iD]

MIREA – Russian Technological University, Vernadsky Avenue 78, 119454 Moscow, Russia

Abstract. This article discusses the possibilities of using machine learning technologies to solve the problem of classifying the state of hard disks. The use of machine learning algorithms is implemented with the use of recurrent neural networks, specifically, the SimpleRNN and LSTM (Long Short-Term Memory) architectures. Classification models are developed using a data set formed based on the values of SMART (Self-Monitoring, Analysis and Reporting Technology) technology indicators. The analysis of aspects of the formation of a representative data set based on SMART-sensor indicators containing relevant information for the development of the classification model is carried out. The nature of recording changes in SMART sensor indicators suggests their use in the format of multidimensional time series. Binary and multiclass classification models are proposed, which contain two LSTM layers, as well as a Dropout layer and a Dense layer. The parameters of the implemented classification models are given. The proposed classification models are tested on the basis of the publicly available data set of the BackBlaze cloud storage company. Graphical dependencies for training and validation losses are provided. The main classification quality indicators are evaluated to confirm the feasibility of further development of the implemented models.

Keywords: Recurrent neural networks · Simple RUN · LSTM · Hard drives · SMART · Binary classification · Multiclass classification

1 Introduction

In an era of constant technological development and the use of a huge number of different devices, the question arises about the safety and performance of almost everything that surrounds us. The task of monitoring and diagnosing the state of objects of various complexity is one of the primary tasks in any field of activity.

The task of monitoring, diagnosing and identifying malfunctions in complex devices is often solved through the use of non-destructive testing (NDT) methods. In the last century, this concept was understood mainly as methods for monitoring the state of various industrial facilities and used together with the concept of technical diagnostics. These concepts often overlap in various fields. In the modern world, NDT and technical diagnostics are used not only in relation to industrial facilities, but also to all kinds of technical devices that fill our modern life.

Every day, a huge amount of information is used and generated in the world, which is why one of the main tasks is the need to regularly solve the issue of storing and

V. Jordan et al. (Eds.): HPCST 2021, CCIS 1526, pp. 380–390, 2022.
https://doi.org/10.1007/978-3-030-94141-3_30

operating large amounts of data (Big Data). The loss of data can disrupt the operation of enterprises, deprive them of the ability to provide services, lead to the loss of reputation, or even cease to exist due to the loss of data necessary for further operation. NDT and technical diagnostic can be effectively used to solve this problem.

The main devices for storing information at the moment are hard disk drives (HDD) and solid-state drives (SSD). They allow storing large amounts of data, which makes it possible to timely access them with subsequent operation.

Along with the increase in the volume of stored information, the risks associated with their loss also increase. Modern hard drives used in various enterprises can have a volume of up to 16 terabytes (TB) of data and the loss of this amount of information will be extremely serious. According to the Backblaze cloud storage service for 2020, the percentage of the company's failed disks is about 1%. Given that they use more than 100 thousand disk drives with a large amount of memory, the losses if the failure was detected late could be catastrophic.

Most hard drives fail not because of a destructive external impact, but because of quite obvious internal breakdowns due to active operation. Such breakdowns are often impossible to notice without analyzing the drive or the appearance of serious problems in its performance. To prevent this, it is much more effective to monitor the disk status in real time.

In recent decades, one of the main technologies used to monitor the health and storage of hard disk statistics in real time is the SMART technology (Self-Monitoring, Analysis and Reporting Technology). This technology is used in most modern hard drives and allows data to be received almost instantly. The technology assumes monitoring the state of the device from its very first start and displays data on a compiled list of sensors responsible for various parameters, ranging from the number of disk starts and ending with the temperature of the device. Although most parameters are recorded by sensors in the same way for different manufacturers, some sensors can still record values in different ways, which is often prescribed in the manufacturer's specification [1]. The purpose of the SMART technology is to display changes in the operation of the device and in most cases does not allow finding out the cause of a potential failure of the device. But it makes it possible to track the main parameters of its operation, which will allow you to see an impending problem and warn the user about it.

In the modern world, there is an active development and application of machine learning (ML) technologies. The approaches and methods used in this technology are used to develop new and improve existing approaches to solving a variety of applied problems. Working with Big Data is also one of the main areas of ML application, since training neural network models on existing data allows programs to see such relationships between data that it will be extremely difficult for a person to reproduce. Tasks such as the described ones are well suited for solving using machine learning technologies [2, 3].

The use of machine learning technologies in general and in recurrent neural networks in particular is a promising method for solving the problem of classifying the state of hard drives, and in recent years a number of studies have been carried out on this topic [4–6].

The research described in this article is devoted to the development of models for classifying the state of hard drives using recurrent neural networks. In particular, the work of the LSTM-model (Long Short-Term Memory), which implements the solution to the problem, is considered, the specifics of preparing data for further work are analyzed, a comparison is made with the results of the model on the SimpleRNN architecture, the results obtained and conclusions based on the results of the study are shown.

2   Approaches and Technologies

To solve this problem, it is necessary to clearly define the main goal of the study, namely, to classify the state of the hard disk based on the indicators of SMART sensors. In the case of a binary classification, the result will be presented in the form of one of two possible classes, and in the case of a multiclass classification, one of three.

There are a number of software solutions that allow you to monitor the health of your disk drive, and many of them use SMART technology. Most disk drive manufacturers use this technology in their products. The problem in saving and using data on the functioning of disk drives is the proprietary specifications of manufacturers, which may not use some of the SMART parameters (attributes) or have their own format for recording them. Models implemented on the basis of recurrent neural network architectures will be able to more clearly trace the dependencies between the available data and make a more accurate assessment of the state of the device.

In this paper, to solve the problem of classifying the state of disk drives, it is proposed to use a number of architectures of recurrent neural networks: Simple RNN and LSTM (Fig. 1), which are actively used for solving non-destructive testing problems, including when working with Big Data.

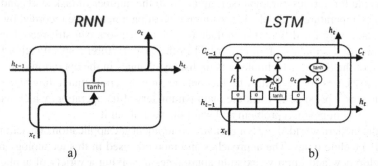

Fig. 1. RNN and LSTM network cell architecture: a) x_t – input vector, h_t – hidden layer vector, o_t – output vector, tanh–activation function g; b) C_t – hidden layer vector, f_t – forget gate, i_t – input gate, o_t – output gate, σ – activation function, "×" – pointwise multiplication operation, "+" – pointwise addition operation.

The classification model being developed should record changes in the indicators over a long time interval, as well as determine the dependencies between the indicators of the sensors. Both architectures are used when working with time series, but LSTM has a characteristic feature that is particularly suitable for solving this problem, namely the ability to preserve long-term dependencies.

The peculiarities of the LSTM architecture are the presence of various gates (f_t, i_t, etc), through the use of which it is possible to improve the quality of the classification model. This architecture is actively used to work with multidimensional time series, in particular, in the development of classification models [7].

First of all, models are developed to solve the problem of the binary classification. To solve it, the selected SMART sensor indicators are used, as well as two new indicators calculated using existing data:

- RUL – the indicator that determines the number of days until the moment when the failure (disk failure) indicator does not take the value equal to 1;
- Label1 – the indicator that takes the value 1 if RUL indicator is less than or equal to 30. This indicator is the target variable for binary classification.

In addition, another indicator has been added to the dataset - Label2. It copies the values of the Label1 metric, but at the same time replaces the value with 2 if the RUL metric is equal to or less than 15. Thus, the Label2 metric will take integer values from {0, 1, 2}, which will determine the model class. The multiclass classification will be carried out only into 3 classes, since the specifics of the data used in this study and the indicators of SMART sensors do not predispose to division into a larger number of classes. Based on this indicator, an initial check of the capabilities of the models for multiclass classification will be carried out.

The neural network model for binary classification was implemented as follows.

- The model contains two layers of the neural network the first one has 50 neurons, the second one has 25 neurons.
- The model applies a Dropout layer with a neuron exclusion parameter of 0.2 after each layer of the neural network.
- The last layer of the model contains a Dense layer with a sigmoid activation function.
- Adam method as an optimization method.
- The binary cross entropy function (formula 1) as the loss function.

$$-\frac{1}{n} \cdot \sum_{i=1}^{n} (y_i \cdot \log(p_i) + (1 - y_i)) \cdot (\log(1 - p_i)), \tag{1}$$

where y_i – true value, p_i – predicted value, n – number of examples in the training sample.

- The model uses the Accuracy indicator as the main indicator of classification quality (formula 2).

$$Accuracy = \frac{TP + TN}{TP + TN + FP + FN}, \tag{2}$$

where *TP* (*True Positive*) – number of true positive outcomes;
TN (*True Negative*) – number of true-negative outcomes;
FP (*False Positive*) – number of false-positive outcomes;
FN (*False Negative*) – the number of false-negative outcomes.

The neural network model for multiclass classification was implemented on the basis of the binary classification model, but some fundamental parameters that are necessary to solve the problem have been changed. In particular, the neural network model for multiclass classification uses:

- *Dense layer* with soft max activation function;
- The categorical cross-entropy function as a loss function:

$$-\frac{1}{n}\sum_{i=1}^{n}\log p_{\text{model}}[y_i \in C_{y_i}] \tag{3}$$

where p_{model} – predicted probability of observation, C – class, n – number of examples in the training sample.

The value of the Accuracy indicator is key, but when developing a classification model, it is necessary to control the values of training and validation losses. The values of training and validation losses must be minimized and, in addition, must be made so that their values are close to each other.

In the case of binary classification models, the quality of the model will be additionally assessed using the following classification quality indicators on the test sample as: precision, recall, f-score. These indicators will make it possible to verify the feasibility of the study [8].

The research was carried out in the Google Colab environment in Python 3.9 using the GPU (Graphics Processing Unit).

3 Empirical Validation of the Proposed Approach

3.1 Data Preparation

The dataset for testing the proposed approach is freely available on the Internet. This set was obtained from the official website of the cloud storage company BackBlaze (https://www.backblaze.com). The data set contains all the data about the company's hard drives, collected using SMART technology, and stored as csv files. The data archive contained 365 csv files – one for each day of 2015. The existing files were combined into one, after which the common file was checked for the presence of NaN elements in the cells.

After checking and receiving statistics on the fullness of the data set, the available cells were evaluated and analyzed for the information stored in them and its significance, as well as the form of filling. For example, the indicators of one of the SMART attributes began to be filled with non-NaN elements only towards the end of the data set. In this regard, the use of this sensor data would have a negative impact on training, so it was decided to remove it from the data set. It is worth noting that the sensor was originally filled with NaN elements due to the lack of fixing its indicators on the part of the creator of the data set, and not in connection with the specification of the sensor itself. The list of indicators stored in the processed dataset is presented in Table 1.

The key elements in the processed dataset are hard drives that have failed during the period monitored by the dataset. In such disks, you can most clearly track the change

Table 1. Indicators (attributes) used in the processed dataset.

Indicator (attribute)	Description of the indicator (attribute)
date	Hard disk working date
serial_number	Hard disk serial number
Failure	A value of "1" indicates that the disk failed on the day corresponding to the date of operation of the hard disk
Smart_1	Raw Read Error Rate
Smart_5	Reallocated Sector Count
Smart_7	Seek Error Rate
Smart_187	Reported UNC Errors
Smart_188	Command Timeout
Smart_189	High Fly Rites
Smart_197	Current Pending Sector Count
Smart_198	Uncorrectable Sector Count
RUL	Remaining lifetime
Label1	Target variable
Label2	Second target variable

in the indicators of SMART attributes throughout their life cycle and determine the characteristic values for a particular class.

The indicators of some SMART attributes may have a rather large scatter in values, so for effective training of the model, their indicators were normalized. After normalization, new indicators were added to the dataset for each element: RUL, Label1 and Label2.

The key parameters for solving the classification problem are the indicators of the remaining SMART attributes. In order for the neural network to use them for training, a large tensor with features was compiled. To do this, the data was processed in such a way that the final version contained large time series for each disk, sorted by the selected features.

The content of the available SMART sensors was presented in a graphical format, which will allow you to more clearly demonstrate the distribution of sensor values and analyze their distribution pattern. After analyzing some of the disks from the data set, you can find that the data distribution for each of them is significantly different. Figure 2 shows the data distribution of two devices belonging to the same model, and the graphical dependencies show that even in this case, the distribution of values is different. In the case of disks belonging to different models or manufacturers, the values of their sensors on the timeline are even more dissimilar.

After analyzing the available data, it was decided to create a new one from the processed data set, which will contain data on broken disks, the period of which is more than 50 days. After that, this set was divided into a ratio of 75 to 25 into training and test sets.

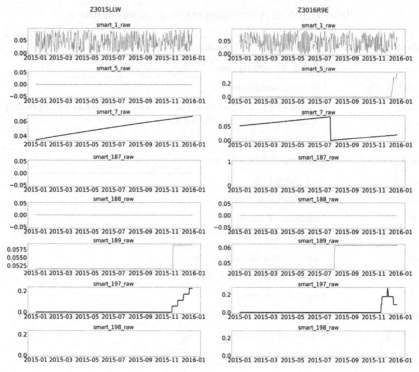

Fig. 2. Graphs of SMART attributes on a timeline.

3.2 Training Without Early Stopping

After completing all the necessary preparatory procedures and preparing the data, you can start training neural networks. The binary classification models were trained for 100 epochs, and the training sample data was converted to the required format at the data preparation stage. It is worth noting that part of the stored data, namely 5%, was used for validation. This was done using the *validation_split* training parameter.

The results of training binary classification models (see Fig. 3) allow us to conclude that the values of losses during validation stop decreasing and begin to increase at a certain moment on all architectures at 100 epochs. This indicates the retraining of the neural network and the need to interrupt training at an earlier date for each of the presented models.

It can also be seen that the model with the SimpleRNN architecture needs 2 times more time to achieve the minimum value of validation losses and the time spent on training is higher (Table 2).

To minimize validation losses, the condition for early stopping of training was set: at each epoch, the value of the validation loss is compared with the value at the previous epoch, and in case of deterioration (increase), training is stopped. At the same time, in order not to interrupt the training at the moment of a small and short-term deterioration in the value of the loss of validation, the tolerance condition was added.

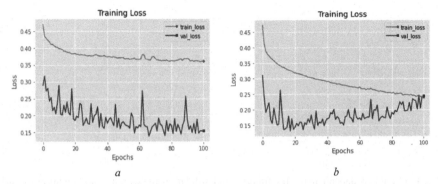

Fig. 3. Graphical dependencies for training and validation losses when implementing the training of a binary classification model over 100 epochs (train_loss – training losses, val_loss – validation losses): a – *RNN*, b – *LSTM*.

3.3   Training with Early Stopping

A fragment of the program code that implements the training of the model and contains the above elements is shown below.

```
hist = model.fit(seq_array, label_array, epochs =
EPOCHS, batch_size = 200, validation_split =
0.05, verbose = 1,
        callbacks = [keras.callbacks.EarlyStopping(monitor
= 'val_loss', min_delta = 0, patience=10, verbose =
0, mode = 'auto')])
```

The results shown in Fig. 4 allow us to confirm the hypothesis about the higher efficiency of the LSTM architecture compared to SimpleRNN for solving the binary classification problem.

In the next step, we get the error matrix obtained as a result of training the model. On its basis, additional indicators for evaluating binary classification models are calculated: accuracy, recall, f1-score. All calculations are performed on a test sample.

Indicators of evaluation indicators for Simple RNN are

```
Confusion matrix
- x-axis is true labels.
- y-axis is predicted labels
array([[112873,    3248],
       [ 16824,   16138]])
precision =  0.82818
 recall =   0.48959
 f1 =   0.61539
```

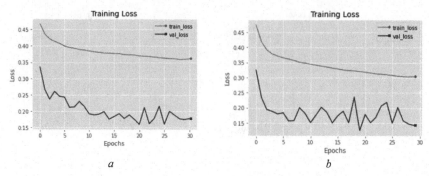

Fig. 4. Graphical dependencies for training and validation losses with the condition of early stopping of binary classification models (train_loss – training losses, val_loss – validation losses): *a – RNN, b – LSTM.*

Indicators of the evaluation indicators for LSTM are

```
Confusion matrix
- x-axis is true labels.
- y-axis is predicted labels
array([[114270,    1951],
       [ 12083,   20879]])
precision =  0.91454
 recall =   0.63342
   f1 =   0.74845
```

3.4 Multiclass Classification

Multiclass classification models were also implemented. The models were developed based on the Label2 parameter, so the model can be classified into 3 classes. Training was also conducted over 100 epochs and 5% of the data was allocated for validation. The results of training models of multiclass classification are shown in Fig. 5.

3.5 Comparison of Training Results

For a more complete assessment of the results obtained, Table 2 shows the training time and the accuracy of the trained models in the course of this study.

Based on the results obtained, we can conclude that the problem of binary classification of disk drives using machine learning technologies is effectively solved when interacting with recurrent neural network architectures. The LSTM architecture shows itself from the better side, in comparison with SimpleRNN, which leads to the conclusion that its further development is advisable. The training and validation losses in the LSTM model reach their best value much earlier, and the shorter training time and higher accuracy confirm its effectiveness.

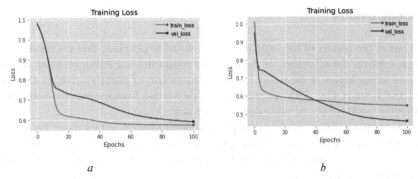

Fig. 5. Graphical dependencies for losses during training and validation of multiclass classification models during 100 epochs (train_loss – training losses, val_loss – validation losses): *a – RNN*, *b – LSTM*.

Table 2. Time spent on training and model accuracy at 100 epochs.

Model type	Architecture	Training time, hours:minutes:seconds	Training condition	Accuracy
Binary	*SimpleRNN*	1:23:24	100epochs	0,8648
Binary	*LSTM*	0:32:12	100epochs	0,9094
Binary	*SimpleRNN*	0:25:06	Early stop	0,8502
Binary	*LSTM*	0:09:48	Early stop	0,8867
Multiclass	*Simple RNN*	1:31:23	100epochs	0,8168
Multiclass	*LSTM*	0:34:52	100epochs	0,8261

Multiclass classification models show results lower than binary classification models, but at the same time, less time is spent on their development at this stage, since the primary ideas for development are aimed at binary classification models.

SimpleRNN and LSTM multiclass models showed approximately equal results in all parameters. The LSTM architecture still comes out ahead in all respects, but in this study, the work was performed on the Google Colab resource and, depending on the access time, machines of different performance could be issued. The difference between these two models has so far been accepted as a statistical error, and in the future it is planned to continue the study of both architectures, but giving priority to LSTMs. It is worth noting that the increase in the Accuracy indicator in these models stopped rather quickly, therefore, to obtain a more accurate result, it is necessary to select more effective model hyperparameters and to increase the number of tools used for classification. For the stated reason, as well as due to a decrease in the rates of learning and validation losses, at this stage, the condition of early stopping was not introduced for multiclass classification models.

4   Conclusions

Analysis of the results of the experiments allows us to conclude that the results of the models confirm the relevance of the task and reflect the feasibility of using machine learning technologies in the future to solve the problem of classifying the state of hard disks. In this study, the LSTM architecture has shown its advantage over the SimpleRNN architecture and will be the main one in future work.

Binary classification models already show decent results at this stage, but it is still necessary to conduct research on the selection of the most suitable hypermarameters, experiments with different model structures, expansion of the tools used in the models and expansion of the dataset.

The multiclass classification models show the general feasibility of using machine learning technologies to solve the problem, but they lag behind the model indicators in terms of results. In addition to conducting studies similar to binary models, it is especially important to test the effectiveness of the model on other datasets, for example, on data from other time periods of the Backblaze company, and then think about combining them into one large dataset.

References

1. Li, Q., Li, H., Zhang, K.: A survey of SSD lifecycle prediction. In: 10th IEEE International Conference on Software Engineering and Service Science (ICSESS), Beijing, China, 18–20 October 2019 (2019)
2. Demidova, L.A., Ivkina, M.S., Marchev, D.V.: Application of the machine learning tools in the problem of classifying failures in the work of the complex technical systems. In: 1st International Conference on Control Systems, Mathematical Modelling, Automation and Energy Efficiency (SUMMA), Lipetsk, Russia, 20–22 November 2019 (2019)
3. Demidova, L.A., Marchev, D.V.: Application of recurrent neural networks in the problem of classification of failures of complex technical systems in the framework of proactive maintenance. Bull. Ryazan State Radio Eng. Univ. **69**, 135–148 (2019). https://doi.org/10.21667/1995-4565-2019-69-135-148. (in Russian)
4. Pereira, F.L.F., Teixeira, D.N., Gomes, J.P.P., Machado, J.C.: Evaluating one-class classifiers for fault detection in hard disk drives. In: 8th Brazilian Conference of Intelligent Systems (BRACIS), Salvador, Brazil, 15–18 October 2019. IEEE (2019)
5. Quieroz, L.P., Rodrigues, F.C.M., Gomes, J.P.P., Brito, F.T., Chaves, L.C., Paula, M.R.P., et al.: A fault detection method for hard disk drives based on mixture of Gaussian and non-parametric statistics. IEEE Trans. Ind. Inform. **13**(2), 542–550 (2017)
6. Ragmania, A., Elomria, A., Abghoura, N., Moussaida, K., Ridaa, M., Badidib, E.: Adaptive fault-tolerant model for improving cloud computing performance using artificial neural network. Procedia Comput. Sci. **170**, 929–934 (2020)
7. Andrianova, E.G., Golovin, S.A., Zykov, S.V., Les'ko, S.A., Chukalina, E.R.: Review of modern models and methods for analyzing time series of dynamics of processes in social, economic and socio-technical systems. Russ. Technol. J. **8**(4), 7–45 (2020)
8. Tatbul, N., Lee, T.J., Zdonik, S., Alam, M., Gottschlich, J.: Precision and recall for time series. In: 32nd Conference on Neural Information Processing Systems (NeurIPS 2018), Montreal, Canada, 2–8 December 2018 (2019)

Software Implementation of Neural Recurrent Model to Predict Remaining Useful Life of Data Storage Devices

Liliya Demidova[iD] and Ilya Fursov[(✉)] [iD]

MIREA – Russian Technological University, Vernadsky Avenue 78, 119454 Moscow, Russia

Abstract. This article explores the problem of predicting the remaining useful life, which often arises when working with disk drives. The approaches to effectively solving this problem using recurrent neural networks, in particular, SimpleRNN, GRU (Gated Recurrent Unit), and LSTM (Long Short-Term Memory) are considered. At the same time, for the development of predicting models, the dataset of the BackBlaze service is used, which is publicly available. The data are presented as multidimensional time series, which were formed according to the readings of SMART (Self-Monitoring, Analysis and Reporting Technology) sensors of the data accumulators. Approaches to improving predicting accuracy are considered. The software implementation of the predicting models was performed in Python 3.8. The models were trained over 20 epochs. The results of predicting the remaining service life of disk drives from the BackBlaze database, as well as graphical dependences of the loss function and comparative tables with neural networks used in the study are presented.

Keywords: Multidimensional time series · Disk storage · RUL · RNN · GRU · LSTM

1 Introduction

Today it is impossible to imagine a computer without a data storage device. Nowadays, all information is stored most often either on hard or solid-state drives. In data centers, the number of such storage devices can reach thousands, so it is important to diagnose them automatically and without errors.

Storage vendors equip their products with special self-monitoring, analysis and reporting technology (SMART, Self-Monitoring, Analysis and Reporting Technology). This technology relies on the use of a set of sensors, each of which monitors a certain parameter of the drive during its operation (e.g., temperature, number of write operations, number of errors during writing or reading, etc.).

This technology allows you to collect data on disk performance for further diagnostics. To diagnose the health of a disk and predict its useful life, several indicators are usually used that seem to have the most impact on its remaining useful life. These metrics are used in a final calculation formula that calculates Remaining Useful Life (RUL) [5].

V. Jordan et al. (Eds.): HPCST 2021, CCIS 1526, pp. 391–400, 2022.
https://doi.org/10.1007/978-3-030-94141-3_31

However, this approach has several disadvantages.

Firstly, the limited number of sensors under consideration is not always indicative, because a small number of them give us a less objective picture, so you can lose some of the subtle nuances.

Secondly, despite the fact that each sensor is independent and does not depend on others, the readings of some that are not so important at first glance may have an indirect effect, both on other sensors and on the disk device as a whole.

Thirdly, it is more difficult to combine a larger number of sensor indicators into a single formula, since the logic of operation of one sensor can be very different from the logic of operation of the second sensor. For example, you can take the number of written bytes and divide by the number of worked days, however, if you add the disk temperature to two parameters, it becomes more difficult to combine these three characteristics into one calculation formula.

At present, when solving problems of predicting the RUL of data storage devices, various machine learning algorithms are successfully applied, for example, RNN, LSTM, GRU [2, 3], CNN [8] algorithms, as well as algorithms that implement decision trees and forest of decision trees [4]. Depending on how the problem is posed, these algorithms can be used to solve both classification problems and regression problems. At the same time, technologies based on deep learning are increasingly being used in solving such problems [6, 7].

Recently, Recurrent Neural Networks (RNN) have been actively used to work with multidimensional time series [10, 12]. At the same time, modifications of models of RNN, such as the Long Short-Term Memory network (LSTM) and the Gated Recurrent Unit network (GRU), allow solving the problem of vanishing gradient, which enables the network to effectively learn and solve regression and classification problems [9].

This article discusses the solution of the RUL forecasting problem of data storage devices, such as hard and solid-state disks. Recurrent neural networks, as well as their modifications, in particular, LSTM and GRU, are used when solving this problem. At the same time, forecasting models are being developed using data sets based on multidimensional time series [11], formed based on the results of the readings of the corresponding sensors.

2 Recurrent Neural Networks

A recurrent network, in a general sense, consists of one layer, through which a direct pass is performed, training the neural network. For simplicity, it can be represented in the form of a sweep shown in Fig. 1.

Each "layer" of such a sweep consists of an input vector x, an output vector y at time t. Between them is a hidden block h, which is the current state of the network memory. U, V, W are network parameters, where U and V are used to calculate the current state of the memory h and predict the output vector y, respectively. W is passed to the next learning iteration, on which the state of memory h also depends.

The fundamental difference between a conventional recurrent network, LSTM and GRU lies in the structure of their blocks, where the current state of the cell is calculated.

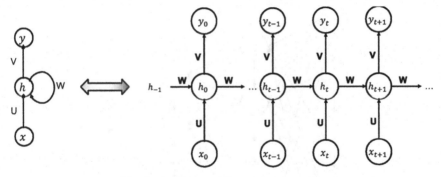

Fig. 1. Architecture of recurrent networks.

GRU block has two gates – the first remembers important information, and the second forgets unnecessary information.

Three gates are used in the LSTM network block - the first controls the flow of incoming information, the second controls the amount of information from the previous state of the memory, and the third controls the flow of outgoing information.

3   Approaches to Model Development

Prediction of the RUL of the data stores can be performed using a prediction model based on recurrent neural networks. The main task of the model is to predict the time that the data storage device can still work before it is out of order. The remaining life estimator model can be developed using a dataset based on multivariate time series generated from the results of SMART sensor readings.

To solve the optimization problem on the training sample, a choice is made in favor of the Mean Square Error (MSE) indicator, which should be minimized. As an additional indicator, it is advisable to take the Root Mean Squared Error (RMSE), which will ensure the visibility of the results of model development.

The mathematical expressions for the indicator (metrics) designated MSE and RMSE are shown below.

$$MSE = \sum_{i=1}^{n} (y_{true} - y_{pred})^2,$$

$$RMSE = \sqrt{\sum_{i=1}^{n} (y_{true} - y_{pred})^2}.$$

The architectures of the constructed models are shown in Fig. 2. On each odd layer there are blocks corresponding to a specific network.

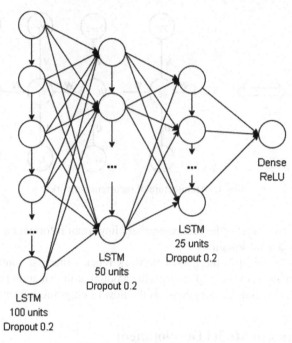

Fig. 2. Model architecture.

The approaches to effectively solving this problem using recurrent neural networks, in particular, SimpleRNN, GRU (Gated Recurrent Unit), and LSTM (Long Short-Term Memory) are considered.

Figure 3 shows the structures of these specific models. In the process of predicting the remaining life for data drives, you should rely on the readings of SMART sensors, each of which monitors a specific characteristic of the disk (Fig. 4).

Layer (type)	Output Shape	Param #
simple_rnn (SimpleRNN)	(None, 10, 100)	10600
dropout_3 (Dropout)	(None, 10, 100)	0
simple_rnn_1 (SimpleRNN)	(None, 10, 50)	7550
dropout_4 (Dropout)	(None, 10, 50)	0
simple_rnn_2 (SimpleRNN)	(None, 25)	1900
dropout_5 (Dropout)	(None, 25)	0
dense_1 (Dense)	(None, 1)	26

Total params: 20,076
Trainable params: 20,076
Non-trainable params: 0

a)

Layer (type)	Output Shape	Param #
lstm (LSTM)	(None, 10, 100)	42400
dropout (Dropout)	(None, 10, 100)	0
lstm_1 (LSTM)	(None, 10, 50)	30200
dropout_1 (Dropout)	(None, 10, 50)	0
lstm_2 (LSTM)	(None, 25)	7600
dropout_2 (Dropout)	(None, 25)	0
dense (Dense)	(None, 1)	26

Total params: 80,226
Trainable params: 80,226
Non-trainable params: 0

b)

Layer (type)	Output Shape	Param #
gru (GRU)	(None, 10, 100)	32100
dropout_6 (Dropout)	(None, 10, 100)	0
gru_1 (GRU)	(None, 10, 50)	22800
dropout_7 (Dropout)	(None, 10, 50)	0
gru_2 (GRU)	(None, 25)	5775
dropout_8 (Dropout)	(None, 25)	0
dense_2 (Dense)	(None, 1)	26

Total params: 60,701
Trainable params: 60,701
Non-trainable params: 0

c)

Fig. 3. Model structures. *a* - SimpleRNN, *b* - LSTM, *c* – GRU.

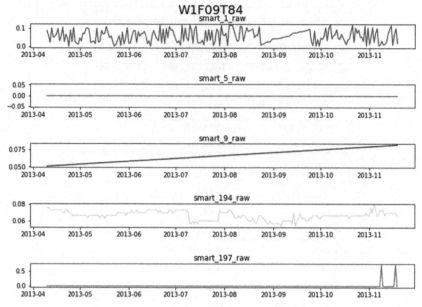

Fig. 4. Readings of SMART sensors of the disk W1F09T84.

In this case, the data of each disk is processed as follows. Taking a certain number of days, considered a kind of window, will scan the time series for each disk. The step of such a window will be single. Thus, this window will go through the entire history for each disk and get many [N, M] matrices, where N is the window length, M is the number of features.

Each matrix will be associated with a corresponding calculated remaining life value, which will be used for training and predicting.

4   Software Implementation and Testing of Predicting Models

Approbation of approaches to the development of predicting models was carried out using the example of the BackBlaze dataset for 2013 for data drives [1]. The dataset is a large number of csv tables that contain the history of measurements of almost 30,000 disks over 8 months.

The RUL is not contained in the databases, so it was calculated independently and quite simply. Since one measurement of the readings of the disk sensors corresponds to one day, the RUL can be calculated based on the number of records for each disk.

The software implementation of the forecasting models was performed in Python 3.8. The training was carried out over 20 eras.

Since the dataset was represented by a large number of csv tables, in which it turned out that the data of one disk could appear in two tables at once, so they had to combine them into one large table, with which further work was already carried out.

In the BackBlaze dataset, only a few sensors have non-trivial readings. The names of such sensors and the indicators described by them are given in Table 1.

Table 1. Sensors and indicators described by them.

Sensor	Description
smart_1_raw	Read error rate
smart_5_raw	Reallocated sector count
smart_9_raw	Power on hours count (power-on time)
smart_194_raw	Temperature
smart_197_raw	Current pending sector count

In order to reduce the chance of overfitting the model, the normalization technique from the sklearn library with the L2 norm parameter was applied. This means that the data is projected onto a multidimensional sphere and located on it in such a way as to be equidistant from its center [13].

At the same time, data for each disk was taken from the entire table, brought to a digestible form and fed to the input of the model during training.

Fragment of the program code that prepares data for training each of the disks.

```
def get_normalize_drive_data(serial_number):
    temp = df.query(f'serial_number=="{serial_number}"')
    temp['date'] = pd.to_datetime(temp['date'])
    temp.sort_values(by='date', inplace=True)
    temp['smart_1_raw'] = normalize(temp['smart_1_raw'][:,
np.newaxis], axis=0).ravel()
    temp['smart_5_raw'] = normalize(temp['smart_5_raw'][:,
np.newaxis], axis=0).ravel()
    temp['smart_9_raw'] = normalize(temp['smart_9_raw'][:,
np.newaxis], axis=0).ravel()
    temp['smart_194_raw'] = normal-
ize(temp['smart_194_raw'][:, np.newaxis], axis=0).ravel()
    temp['smart_197_raw'] = normal-
ize(temp['smart_197_raw'][:, np.newaxis], axis=0).ravel()
    temp = temp.reset_index().drop(['index', 'Unnamed: 0',
'model', 'capacity_bytes'], axis=1)
    total_rul = temp.shape[0] - 1
    list_ruls = [i for i in range(total_rul, -1, -1)]
    temp['RUL'] = list_ruls
    return temp
```

During training of the models, the loss function was calculated by the MSE formula. With each new era, its indicator sometimes decreased more than two times.

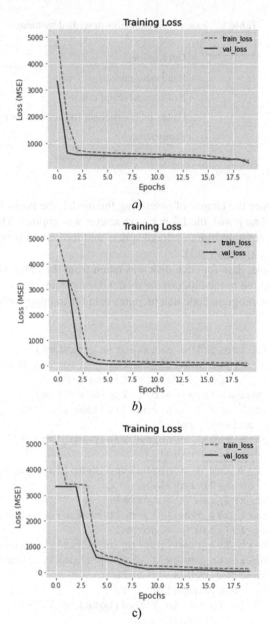

Fig. 5. Graphical dependences of the learning loss functions: a – SimpleRNN, b – GRU, c – LSTM.

Each model has been trained over 20 epochs. The graphs in Fig. 5 show that the loss curve after 4–8 epochs begins to change slightly, so it is advisable to use the early stopping technique, which allows you to stop training the model after several upward jumps of the error function value. In TensorFlow, this is handled by the EarlyStopping tool with the patience parameter, which tells how many jumps during training can be ignored. It has been empirically calculated that the patience parameter can be set equal to 3.

Table 2 presents comparative data on the learning rate of the models. It can be seen that the usual recurrent network took much longer to train at all epochs. The training was carried out on NVIDIA TESLA T4 16 GB graphics accelerators with CUDA cores version 11.2.

Table 2. Comparison of the learning rate of models in minutes.

Models	SimpleRNN	GRU	LSTM
Learning time	53.33	13.33	15.08

The data for training were divided into two samples: training and test in a ratio of 80/20, respectively. From the training data, a validation subsample was additionally distinguished, the size of which was 10% of the training one. This subsample is needed to cross-validate data during training. The analysis of the results of the development of the model is presented in Table 3.

Table 3. Comparison of model metrics.

Model/Indicator	MSE	RMSE
SimpleRNN	485.38	22.03
GRU	44.45	6.66
LSTM	60.05	7.74

5 Conclusion

Analyzing the results obtained, we can conclude that the considered approaches to the development of systems for predicting the remaining service life of disk drives using neural networks are justified and it is necessary to improve the accuracy, as well as expand the above approaches. It is planned to add feature generation, automatic selection of hyperparameters, as well as apply new algorithms so that they can be compared with those obtained in this article.

References

1. BackBlaze dataset. https://www.backblaze.com/b2/hard-drive-test-data.html. Accessed 15 May 2021
2. Xu, C., Wang, G., Liu, X., Guo, D., Liu, T.-Y.: Health status assessment and failure prediction for hard drives with recurrent neural networks. IEEE Trans. Comput. **65**(11), 3502–3508. https://doi.org/10.1109/TC.2016.2538237
3. Lu, S., Luo, B., Patel, T., Yao, Y., Tiwari, D., Shi, W.: Making disk failure predictions SMARTer!. In: 18th USENIX Conference on File and Storage Technologies (FAST 20), Santa Clara, CA, USA, 24–27 February, pp. 151–167 (2020)
4. Anantharaman, P., Qiao, M., Jadav, D.: Large scale predictive analytics for hard disk remaining useful life estimation. In: 2018 IEEE International Congress on Big Data, San Francisco, CA, USA, 2–7 July 2018, pp. 251–254 (2018). https://doi.org/10.1109/BigDataCongress.2018. 00044
5. Bagul, Y.G.: Assessment of current health and remaining useful life of hard disk drives. Master thesis, Northeastern University, Boston, MA, USA (2009). https://doi.org/10.17760/ d10016971
6. Aussel, N., Jaulin, S., Gandon, G., Petetin, Y., Fazli, E., Chabridon, S.: Predictive models of hard drive failures based on operational data. In: 16th IEEE International Conference on Machine Learning and Applications (ICMLA), 18–21 December 2017, pp. 619–625 (2017). https://doi.org/10.1109/ICMLA.2017.00-92
7. Basak, S., Sengupta, S., Dubey, A.: Mechanisms for integrated feature normalization and remaining useful life estimation using LSTMs applied to hard-disks. In: 2019 IEEE International Conference on Smart Computing (SMARTCOMP), Washington, DC, USA, 12–15 June 2019, pp. 208–216 (2019). https://doi.org/10.1109/SMARTCOMP.2019.00055
8. Sateesh Babu, G., Zhao, P., Li, X.-L.: Deep convolutional neural network based regression approach for estimation of remaining useful life. In: Navathe, S.B., Wu, W., Shekhar, S., Du, X., Wang, X.S., Xiong, H. (eds.) DASFAA 2016. LNCS, vol. 9642, pp. 214–228. Springer, Cham (2016). https://doi.org/10.1007/978-3-319-32025-0_14
9. Wang, Q., Zheng, S., Farahat, A., Serita, S., Gupta, C.: Remaining useful life estimation using functional data analysis. ArXiv preprint on Machine Learning (2019). https://arxiv.org/pdf/ 1904.06442.pdf. Accessed 30 Aug 2021
10. Demidova, L.A., Ivkina, M.S., Marchev, D.V.: Application of the machine learning tools in the problem of classifying failures in the work of the complex technical systems. In: Proceedings of 1st International Conference on Control Systems, Mathematical Modelling, Automation and Energy Efficiency (SUMMA), Lipetsk, Russia, 20–22 November 2019, pp. 540–545 (2020). https://doi.org/10.1109/SUMMA48161.2019.8947561
11. Andrianova E.G., Golovin S.A., Zykov S.V., Lesko S.A., Chukalina E.R.: Review of modern models and methods of analysis of time series of dynamics of processes in social, economic and socio-technical systems. Russ. Technol. J. **8**(4), 7–45 (2020). https://doi.org/10.32362/ 2500-316X-2020-8-4-7-45. (in Russian)
12. Demidova, L.A., Marchev, D.V.: Application of recurrent neural networks in the classification problem of failures in the complex technical systems within the framework of proactive maintenance. Bull. Ryazan State Radio Eng. Univ. **69**, 135–148 (2019). https://doi.org/10. 21667/1995-4565-2019-69-135-148
13. Serneels, S., De Nolf, E., van Espen, P.J.: Spatial sign preprocessing: a simple way to impart moderate robustness to multivariate estimators. J. Chem. Inf. Model. **46**(3), 1402–1409 (2006). https://doi.org/10.1021/ci050498u

Testing Methods for Blockchain Applications

Sergey Staroletov[1]([✉]) [iD] and Roman Galkin[1,2]

[1] Polzunov Altai State Technical University, Barnaul 656038, Russia
[2] WinteX Solutions LLC, wintex.pro, Barnaul 656049, Russia

Abstract. A blockchain application is a form of modern software that runs in its ecosystem and interacts with other application instances. Such applications run decentralized on a large number of nodes and process requests from a large number of users. Thus, they are high-performance applications that are prone to specific errors due to difficult-to-predict network behavior. In addition, they are predisposed to errors inherent in all software systems. Since bugs can potentially lead to losing an immense amount of funds in cryptocurrencies, learning how to test such applications is an important task. In this paper, we explore the internal quality assurance methods of the Bitcoin and Ethereum platforms at their various levels of logical organization. Next, we describe our test bench designed for functional testing of cryptocurrency payment gateways. The solution provides a software abstraction for making API calls to virtualized nodes of various platforms using emulators of real blockchain networks.

Keywords: Software testing · Ethereum · Bitcoin · RPC

1 Introduction

The testing process is currently the primary means of ensuring the quality of software systems. Since the proof of program correctness is directly related to the halting problem [1] (which is undecidable, in general, in existing theory of algorithms [2]), therefore, we can state that such a process cannot guarantee 100% quality. Consequently, the current strategy in the field is "methodological diversity" [3], conducting testing and program analysis at different levels of software abstraction. For example, it can comprise working on code coverage with tests, implementing static analysis, fuzzing and formal verification methods. All this leads to greater confidence in the correct functioning of the developed software.

These methods, however, can significantly increase the cost and slow down the production of software. Therefore, at the start of any project, some managerial decisions should be made with the justification of the use of each checking method in the development process.

Typically, a large number of verification methods in one project are used simultaneously for applications that are responsible for critical areas of human activity [4] and control related workflows. However, financial applications that operate with a large number of users can also be attributed to this class [5], because the loss of funds from incorrect functioning here can be immense.

© Springer Nature Switzerland AG 2022
V. Jordan et al. (Eds.): HPCST 2021, CCIS 1526, pp. 401–418, 2022.
https://doi.org/10.1007/978-3-030-94141-3_32

After a colossal injection of money into the economy, the virtual coins market again is gaining tremendous popularity. At the same time, it is regularly experiencing drops due to the inevitable downfall of speculative expectations and unresolved problems with the transactions speed [6]. While some analysts predict the quickest death of cryptocurrencies, others see the great opportunity to provide people with a very realistic way to handle reliable payment transactions in next-generation information systems.

In the software market, novel information systems are beginning to be designed in the form of multitier applications with decentralized [7] parts internally based on blockchain or ledger technologies. To attract more users, innovative Internet companies are now trying to keep their data inside a blockchain, develop trusted and verifiable software and embed cryptocurrency funds processing in their corporate payment systems.

Blockchain applications are such modern applications that store their states in own blockchain instance, which is identical to the chain of blocks of all other network participants and is synchronized with them using a consensus algorithm [8]. They are also called as decentralized applications and represent the next evolution step of distributive applications.

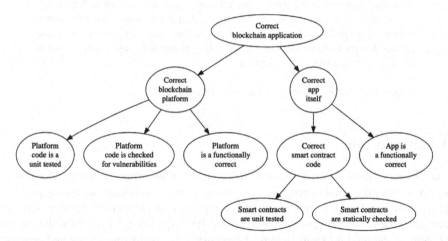

Fig. 1. Towards a correct blockchain application.

Since the original Bitcoin blockchain has been launched, developers have an opportunity to implement extensions in the forms of *smart contracts* (code that works in a blockchain environment) [9]. However, the code is not directly accessible from the graphical interface and not Turing-complete unlike the next step of blockchain systems as Ethereum [10], which became blockchain platforms.

In Fig. 1, we describe approaches to design a correct blockchain application. Such an application can be checked both at the lower logical level (by unit testing [11]) and at the upper level (by functional testing). Smart contracts need to be tested and verified for specific vulnerabilities. In addition, we should take care of checking the correctness of the blockchain platform itself, for which the same methods should also be applied.

Although there are known attempts to ensure total quality at all levels with formal proof of properties of software systems and protocols (in particular, a project from the University of Innopolis [12]), however, such attempts are laborious. It is not clear when they will be completed; in addition, the relationship between the models and the actual source code remains questionable. Therefore, we believe that the developers and communities of the platform should examine the correctness of their platform. In the same time, the layer of a working blockchain application should be checked by third-party authors during the development with the addition of checks for invariants concerning the expected operation of the system.

The paper deals with methods of automatic testing blockchain platforms and applications for them. We proceed to browse main problems in this area, study current methods of quality assurance and abilities which popular blockchain platforms propose to developers to ensure the testing process inside the blockchain. We then describe our high-performance solution to test information systems with cryptocurrency gateways. In the present work, we are targeting in testing Bitcoin and Ethereum applications. These decentralized platforms are the most popular and the most interesting for us at present. Accordingly, everything that relates to the code also applies to such forks as Ethereum Classic, Bitcoin Hash, Litecoin and DOGE.

Our research is entirely based on a personal study of the open-source code repositories of blockchain platforms, as well as the original Internet resources produced by the community. Nowadays, the forums like *bitcointalk* are the primary source on the exchange of ideas and suggestions for new opportunities in the blockchain development. Therefore, we provide links to such forums in order to clarify the terms. Preliminary parts of this work were defended in the form of a master's thesis [13], discussed at local conferences in Altai STU [14], and the final version was presented at the "International Conference on High-performance computing systems and technologies in scientific research, automation of control and production".

The rest of the paper is organized as follows. In Sect. 2, we declare major problems related to the testing process of blockchain applications based on our experience of outsourcing work in this sphere. In Sect. 3, we conduct a survey based on browsing original source code repositories of Bitcoin and Ethereum, including their internal tests frameworks, unit and functional tests as well as other relevant parts. In Sect. 4, we present our solution to test cryptocurrency gateway software, moreover, we discuss real types of errors that were found with the help of our technique. Finally, in Conclusion section, we summarize the efforts and discuss future work.

2 Challenges of Testing Blockchain Applications Using Real Networks

Modern managers need to understand that the integration of a blockchain component into an enterprise information system is unthinkable without some proper testing. As the destiny of digital funds in a blockchain-enabled platform directly depends on the correct operations of distributed consensus-based algorithms, testing should be the main focus while developing such systems. However, the process of ensuring the quality of such classes of software is quite complicated, which is objectively caused by several blockchain-related issues.

Based on our expertise in implementing and testing blockchain applications including cryptocurrency gateways [14], we can emphasize here some typical problems related to testing blockchain applications on live networks.

1. *Average rate of new blocks in the blockchain.* Speed of committing transactions in the blockchain is a crucial factor for accompanying automated functional tests in different ecosystems. In addition to the troubles in the delay in transfers of cryptocurrency payments, the low speed of block appearance significantly slows down testing. In a blockchain-based system, furthermore, after waiting for the next transaction block, it is also necessary to expect related confirmation blocks in order to use Proof-of-Stake [15] algorithms with confidence. Although many public blockchain are still waiting 20–30 min (and even more during busy networks) for the new block, we cannot spend an hour or two to perform a single test script. Moreover, the rate is also influenced by a mining fee determined by a transaction sender, so faster time can turn golden.

2. *Cost.* In addition to paying for transactions themselves, testers must also provide some means in virtual currencies to be able to confirm the transfers by paying a miner fee. Observing all this, the testing process on a live blockchain can be expensive and inconvenient. Also, there are certain risks of funds losing during the testing if any error occurs in assembling the transaction using series of software API calls.

   A possible solution is to use so-called test networks (*testnets*). However, their condition is often offensive (we can state here an insufficient number of miners and frequent attempts to perform "*51% attack*" [16]), moreover, not every blockchain provides a working public test network.

3. *Infrastructure investments.* To assemble correct transactions, different block-chains utilized in a project need to be synchronized. This process may take a substantial amount of time; additionally, it requires a sufficiently large amount of physical memory, so the process must run on powerful servers. Hence, we need to pay an enormous cost for server hardware in order to host working instances of blockchain applications.

4. *Security.* During the testing, it is necessary to ensure sufficient security for wallets access. Therefore, we should provide controlled admittance for developers, testers, customers and other participants.

To address these issues and make the development and testing more easily, two popular ecosystems present some out-of-the-box solutions.

- Bitcoin offers the so-called *regtest mode* [17]. It is intended for checking the Bitcoin protocol itself, for example, regressive testing and running new changes in *bitcoind* daemon, and we are interested in it as a complete implementation of the Bitcoin protocol (including its forks) capable of performing transactions.
- For Ethereum applications testing, the developers propose to adopt some kind of real network emulator written in Javascript (*testrpc* tool or *ganache* [18]) which is now becoming a de-facto standard tool widely used by the Ethereum smart contract developers. Remarkably, the tool was initially developed with the purpose of testing the operation of smart contracts. However, as it turned out, with a proper configuration,

it is entirely feasible to use this tool as a system for testing transaction-related activities in Ethereum. In this case, the tool provides the developers with virtual accounts with private/public keys, wallets, raw information about blocks, transaction data, gas usage statistics and other Ethereum-related things.

However, as we will see later, testing of applications for the listed platforms is not limited to these solutions. In addition, it is possible to build an abstraction over them.

3   Methods of Quality Assurance for Blockchain Platforms

As we are interested in quality assurance of blockchain applications, we decided first to check internal methods that Bitcoin and Ethereum creators currently use to satisfy the quality of blockchain system code. It can be useful to develop methods of testing of blockchain applications correlate with their platforms in the future. A general survey on blockchain languages and related techniques can be read in [19], in the further subsections we are targeted only on testing. We use original source code repositories as source data for the analysis.

3.1   Bitcoin Tests Overview

Bitcoin tests repository contains integration tests that check bitcoind and its utilities in their entirety. Unit tests were included in the source tree (/src/test, /src/wallet/ test, etc.).
    Bitcoin developers produced the following sets of tests:

- *functional* used to test the functionality of *bitcoind* and *bitcoin-qt* by interacting with them through the RPC and P2P interfaces;
- *util* used to test Bitcoin utilities, currently only *bitcoin-tx*;
- *lint* used to perform various static analysis checks.

The util tests are run as a part of the build target. The functional tests and lint scripts are run by the *travis* continuous integration build process whenever a pull request is opened [20].
    Let us consider the internal framework for functional testing of Bitcoin. It is implemented in Python3 and provides high-level programming interfaces to prepare custom network and run behaviour tests. In Fig. 2, we decompose some central parts of this framework based on its source code as well as internal helper classes. We propose to draw such diagrams for any interesting open-source software based on test code to make the tests understandable.
    Bitcoin functional tests are quite interesting. They model specific behavior of the blockchain system driven by features in code using the functional testing framework. These tests can be good documentation of how related features work. For example, based on source code and comments, we constructed a map of the SegWit protocol upgrade [21] testing on a local P2P network (this feature has been introduced and activated over working Bitcoin network with amounts of users). In Fig. 3, we show the corresponding

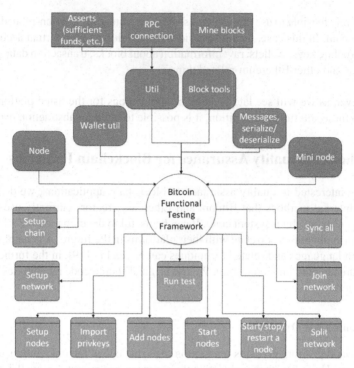

Fig. 2. Bitcoin functional testing framework.

test in action, while in Fig. 4, we depict an overview of the test in a graphical representation. The Bitcoin test developers distinguished the following four states: {*defined, started, locked_in, active*}, then they created some blocks and transactions that satisfied or declined rules on these states. Some checks are executed on different states to test the regression. Using such tests one can study how to write a code to interact with the network to make correct transactions.

According to Bitcoin unit tests, they are written using the Boost test framework and seems to cover all internal classes. The most complicated test (by the length) is a test for Bitcoin Script [22], a stack-based internal language for manipulating transactions. Consider an interesting test of coin view caching: the caching facilities for unspent transaction dataset view. The test is executed by randomized transitions in a loop; depending on random occasions, values are inserted, removed from a stack that is emulating a cache. There are nine control variables and the test asserts that they all were set during the transitions. Of course, this test can fail because not all the states can be visited based on that random walk, but the Bitcoin developers use special sequential iteration-based random and big count of iterations (40000), so the test started to be more deterministic. We think that for such types of tests, some formal methods like Model-Based Testing [23] and Model-Based Checking [24] can be applied because they can ensure the behavior of real non-deterministic automata models.

```
sergey@orangepipc2:~/bitcoin/test/functional$ python3 ./p2p_segwit.py
2021-07-06T06:09:08.810000Z TestFramework (INFO): Initializing test directory /tmp/bitcoin_func_test_275m7x12
2021-07-06T06:09:11.378000Z TestFramework (INFO): Subtest: test_non_witness_transaction (Segwit status = defined)
2021-07-06T06:09:14.604000Z TestFramework (INFO): Subtest: test_unnecessary_witness_before_segwit_activation (Segwit status
= defined)
2021-07-06T06:09:14.758000Z TestFramework (INFO): Subtest: test_v0_outputs_arent_spendable (Segwit status = defined)
2021-07-06T06:09:15.336000Z TestFramework (INFO): Subtest: test_block_relay (Segwit status = defined)
2021-07-06T06:09:16.907000Z TestFramework (INFO): Subtest: advance_to_segwit_started (Segwit status = defined)
2021-07-06T06:09:17.769000Z TestFramework (INFO): Subtest: test_getblocktemplate_before_lockin (Segwit status = started)
2021-07-06T06:09:18.415000Z TestFramework (INFO): Subtest: advance_to_segwit_lockin (Segwit status = started)
2021-07-06T06:09:22.162000Z TestFramework (INFO): Subtest: test_unnecessary_witness_before_segwit_activation (Segwit status
= locked_in)
2021-07-06T06:09:22.319000Z TestFramework (INFO): Subtest: test_witness_tx_relay_before_segwit_activation (Segwit status =
locked_in)
2021-07-06T06:09:24.699000Z TestFramework (INFO): Subtest: test_block_relay (Segwit status = locked_in)
2021-07-06T06:09:26.273000Z TestFramework (INFO): Subtest: test_standardness_v0 (Segwit status = locked_in)
2021-07-06T06:09:26.826000Z TestFramework (INFO): Subtest: advance_to_segwit_active (Segwit status = locked_in)
2021-07-06T06:09:31.199000Z TestFramework (INFO): Subtest: test_p2sh_witness (Segwit status = active)
2021-07-06T06:09:31.630000Z TestFramework (INFO): Subtest: test_witness_commitments (Segwit status = active)
2021-07-06T06:09:32.018000Z TestFramework (INFO): Subtest: test_block_malleability (Segwit status = active)
2021-07-06T06:09:38.610000Z TestFramework (INFO): Subtest: test_witness_block_size (Segwit status = active)
2021-07-06T06:09:58.227000Z TestFramework (INFO): Subtest: test_submit_block (Segwit status = active)
2021-07-06T06:09:58.373000Z TestFramework (INFO): Subtest: test_extra_witness_data (Segwit status = active)
2021-07-06T06:09:58.744000Z TestFramework (INFO): Subtest: test_max_witness_push_length (Segwit status = active)
2021-07-06T06:09:58.922000Z TestFramework (INFO): Subtest: test_max_witness_program_length (Segwit status = active)
2021-07-06T06:09:59.139000Z TestFramework (INFO): Subtest: test_witness_input_length (Segwit status = active)
2021-07-06T06:09:59.522000Z TestFramework (INFO): Subtest: test_block_relay (Segwit status = active)
2021-07-06T06:10:00.220000Z TestFramework (INFO): Subtest: test_tx_relay_after_segwit_activation (Segwit status = active)
2021-07-06T06:10:01.665000Z TestFramework (INFO): Subtest: test_standardness_v0 (Segwit status = active)
2021-07-06T06:10:02.123000Z TestFramework (INFO): Subtest: test_segwit_versions (Segwit status = active)
2021-07-06T06:10:04.614000Z TestFramework (INFO): Subtest: test_premature_coinbase_witness_spend (Segwit status = active)
2021-07-06T06:10:12.297000Z TestFramework (INFO): Subtest: test_uncompressed_pubkey (Segwit status = active)
2021-07-06T06:10:12.972000Z TestFramework (INFO): Subtest: test_signature_version_1 (Segwit status = active)
2021-07-06T06:13:08.194000Z TestFramework (INFO): Subtest: test_non_standard_witness_blinding (Segwit status = active)
2021-07-06T06:13:08.721000Z TestFramework (INFO): Subtest: test_non_standard_witness (Segwit status = active)
2021-07-06T06:13:12.233000Z TestFramework (INFO): Subtest: test_upgrade_after_activation (Segwit status = active)
2021-07-06T06:13:38.313000Z TestFramework (INFO): Subtest: test_witness_sigops (Segwit status = active)
2021-07-06T06:13:42.239000Z TestFramework (INFO): Stopping nodes
2021-07-06T06:13:42.560000Z TestFramework (INFO): Cleaning up /tmp/bitcoin_func_test_275m7x12 on exit
2021-07-06T06:13:42.560000Z TestFramework (INFO): Tests successful
```

Fig. 3. SegWit P2P test in action.

It is interesting that for Bitcoin Script [25] (which is a stack machine) the developers do not use such testing techniques like random stack population, they use bunches of pre-defined test-cases, which can lead to some wrong untested behavior and possible vulnerabilities.

3.2 Ethereum Tests Overview

Ethereum ecosystem tests are divided into modules by their functionality [26]:

– *Blockchain Tests.* The blockchain tests aim to do the fundamental testing of a blockchain. Tests are based on the notion of executing lists of single blocks.
– *General State Tests.* The state tests aim to test the basic workings of the state in isolation.
– *RLP Tests.* The purpose of RLP (Recursive Length Prefix) is to encode arbitrarily nested arrays of binary data, and RLP is the main encoding method used to serialize objects in Ethereum.
– *Difficulty Tests.* These tests are designed to check the difficulty formula of blocks.
– *Transaction Tests.* Check complete transactions and their RLP representations using pre-defined.json files.
– *VM Tests.* The VM tests aim to test the basic functioning of the VM in isolation. This is specifically not intended to cover transactions, creation or call processing, or management of the state trie [27].
– *General Consensus Tests.* Consensus tests are test cases for all Ethereum implementations. The test cases are distributed in the "filled" form, which may contain an expected state root hash after transactions. The filled test cases are usually not written by hand, but generated from "test filler" files.

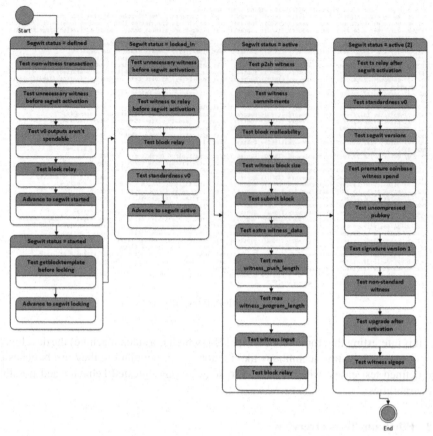

Fig. 4. Map of testing SegWit transactions and blocks on a P2P network using the Bitcoin functional testing framework.

Also, there are some tests in additional components repositories. For example, *ethash* implements Ethereum hashing function and it is known that unit tests for it can be used as a reference source for construction of implementations of Proof-of-Work mining algorithms, optimized for special devices (in this case, usually GPU devices [28, 29]).

Solidity repository comes with tests for the smart contracts language. Solidity developers apply continuous fuzzing at every upstream commit using *oss-fuzz* [30] by Google and LLVM *libFuzzer*. Input programs (currently in the *Yul* intermediate language) are generated by describing the language grammar using a *protobuf* structure [31], visiting language nodes and populating them from a given dictionary with tokens then fuzzing the compiler and optimizer. Moreover, *libSolidity* has an interface to use formal methods like SMT checkers, and there is a sample unit test case (*SMTchecker*) contains some static code that checks "division by zero", so in future, using this interface, the community can build sets of axioms for SMT solver (like *Z3* [32]) and implement special and complex checks of contracts for possible vulnerabilities.

3.3 Methods Related to Blockchain Applications

In Sect. 2, we described primarily tools for testing applications that provide some emulation of Ethereum and Bitcoin ecosystems. Now we proceed to give a more detailed description of each.

```
eth_sendTransaction

 Transaction: 0x0284332b78ae1a07c57ab3aa85ba4b2b1f77caa62195c8cb995319
78e11f3c5b
 Contract created: 0x602db993eb285d7b77597800e31b157e2d259dc8
 Gas usage: 1853564
 Block Number: 1
```

Fig. 5. Testrpc/ganache tool in action: we see the just executed transaction to create a smart contract in the local test environment.

First we consider the *testrpc* tool for working with Ethereum (currently known as ganache, ganache-cli). The main purpose of this tool is still primarily focused on testing of smart contracts. Ganache is essentially an emulation of the Ethereum blockchain. Blocks are made instantly as transactions arrive (see Fig. 5), although it is possible to set a specific time interval between blocks in seconds. The tool supports all commands from the Ethereum RPC specification [33], but there are also some useful commands [18] to work directly with EVM (Ethereum Virtual Machine):

- *evm_snapshot*: snapshot the blockchain state at the current block.
- *evm_revert*: revert the blockchain state to a previous snapshot.
- *evm_increaseTime*: jump forward in time.
- *evm_mine*: force a block to be mined. Mines a block independent of whether or not mining is started or stopped.

If we talk about blockchain applications testing, we note that using this tool one cannot create a private test blockchain network of the Ethereum ecosystem. This does not allow, for example, to test the behavior of an application when blocks are dropped due to the selection of the longest chain, which may be important, considering that on average 700 blocks are discarded per day. Thus, the tool is useful for testing the behavior of smart contracts in the blockchain but is not sufficiently functional for testing applications with the different behavior of the network, therefore for these purposes, it is necessary to up a full Ethereum network. Again, even using this method to test an application with different network behavior will still be quite tricky.

Moving to Bitcoin applications, for circumstances when interaction with random peers and blocks is unnecessary or unwanted, Bitcoin Core's regression test mode (regtest mode) allows developers to create a private blockchain with the same basic rules as testnet, but with one significant variation: they can choose to create new blocks, so they have complete control over the Bitcoin environment. Many developers consider using regtest as the preferred way to develop new applications. The mode supports all RPC commands; furthermore the state of the blockchain, the wallets of nodes and blocks will be stored in a separate directory, which allows developers to use specific states in testing. Nodes that run in the regtest mode can be combined into full-fledged bitcoin

P2P networks, which enable emulating various network interactions and behaviors of network participants.

3.4   A Web IDE for Smart Contracts Testing

Let us consider an approach to testing smart contracts in the Ethereum ecosystem that is in line with current trends in software engineering, such as code writing in a browser, service-oriented paradigm, unit testing, web-based debugging, and vulnerability testing. Today, these ideas are implemented in the Remix IDE [34] (see Fig. 6). Typically, this tool is the basic one used by smart contract developers, who usually do not take into account the other methods we have discussed. Nevertheless, the shell provides all the basic mechanisms for quality assurance when writing smart contracts. It does not require a running Ethereum node, and also allows the developers to take into account the distinctiveness of various versions of the Solidity smart contract language.

Separately, we should mention the mechanisms for static code checking for correctness, including vulnerabilities. Currently, a large number of research works are concentrated in this area [35–37]. The methods used in the field are theorem provers, SMT solvers, symbolic execution, and others. As for the codebase for verification, the

Fig. 6. Remix IDE.

researchers use datasets of ever developed smart contracts, including open repositories with already proven contracts [38]. Tools such as Remix concede the developers to validate code with the one-button approach while complex code analysis and proofing methods are run internally.

4 Cryptocurrency Gateways Testing Technology

A payment using cryptocurrency funds between two virtual sides happens without unnecessary intermediaries using a receiving address that can be created just for one transaction. The transfer is truly immutable: there is no way for cancelling an already confirmed operation (including the cases when the payment was sent to an erroneous or non-existent address by mistake, or when the transaction was signed with a compromised private key). Also, no one can block (arrest) cryptocurrency funds, even temporarily, except the owner of the private key (or a person to whom it has become known). However, there exists a multi-signature technology that allows attracting a third party (an arbiter) and implement special *"reversible transactions"* [39].

Cryptocurrency payment processing for buying some assets (real or virtual) through digital platforms is carried out with special software called payment gateways (we suggest naming them here as *cryptocurrency gateways*), and further, we discuss the specifics of its testing.

4.1 Cryptocurrency Payment Gateways Market Analysis

Currently, there are a large number of online tools that provide a cryptocurrency payment gateway as a service. The most popular and multifunctional ones are *Coinpayments, Blockchain.info* and *Coingate*. These services offer a fairly functional REST API and some HTTP webhooks for building various interactions with them. A large number of other gateways are in fact analogous to the Blockchain.info service, which can work with only one cryptocurrency, particularly Bitcoin. That makes them less functional with respect to other two previously indicated.

Coinpayments and Coingate provide the ability to accept more than 50 cryptocurrencies, though these services are focused on stores (or online stores), which have become necessary to also accept cryptocurrencies in the essence of payment. These services do not allow owners to fully control money, it is convenient to accumulate cryptocurrency on user's accounts external to the service (cold wallets). Both services also take a large commission, a percentage of the transaction, the future percentage for withdrawing funds. Given the disadvantages listed above, owners of online stores, exchange points and cryptocurrency exchanges prefer to order custom implementations of their own cryptocurrency payment gateways, which can provide them with complete control over the cryptocurrency flows, as well as the ability to accept only the cryptocurrency that interests them, without overpaying the service fee for conducting transactions.

So, the further subsections can be useful for gateway service developers, because the construction of such a service is a matter of time, and in this case, it is necessary to allocate it to the processes of ensuring the quality of development.

4.2   A Containerization-Oriented High-Performance Solution

Docker-containerization of blockchain nodes and the creation of virtual private control-lable networks with functionality similar to real blockchains are quite capable of solving principal problems of testing applications that process cryptocurrencies.

Docker is system software for running, deploying and managing applications in a virtualized environment with necessary dependencies at the level of operating system. It allows to "pack" an application with all its data into a self-unfolding container that can be transferred to any Linux system with the support for the *cgroups* mechanism in the kernel, as well as it provides a container management environment [40]. Containers can be prepared by enthusiasts, shared over the Internet and easily replicated on one or many machines.

Today, virtual machines are actively used to run applications inside the guest oper-ating system, perfectly suited to completely isolate the process for the application. Con-tainers supply a level of isolation similar to virtual machines, but due to the proper use of low-level mechanisms of the host operating system, they do it with several times less load. Docker provides a standard programming interface that greatly simplified the creation and use of containers, and allows the community to work together on container libraries.

RabbitMQ is a multi-protocol message broker that allows organizing a failover cluster with full data replication to several nodes where each node can serve read and write requests. It is written in Erlang and uses the AMQP protocol [41]. We consider the interaction scheme of objects in AMQP, presented in Fig. 7. The queue stores and provides all incoming messages to consumers. The exchange is engaged in routing messages (but does not store them) based on the created links (binding) between it and the queues (or other exchangers).

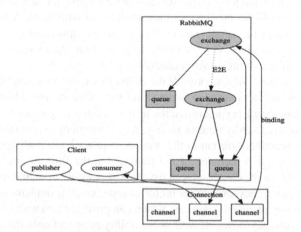

Fig. 7. Infrastructure scheme of the RabbitMQ usage.

From the point of view of RabbitMQ, a queue is an Erlang process [42] with a state (where the messages themselves can be cached), and the exchange is a "link" to a module with a code that contains routing logic. That is, for example, 10 thousand exchanges will consume about 12 MB of memory, when 10 thousand queues are already about 800 MB [43].

In cluster mode, meta-information is copied to all nodes. That is, each node contains a complete list of exchanges, queues, their connections, consumers and other objects. The processes with queues themselves are located by default on only one node, but with the help of policies, one can enable replication (mirrored queues), and the data will be automatically distributed over the desired number of nodes.

The tools we have mentioned in the section require a lot of preliminary setups before using them as executable models of real decentralized networks on a test bench. So, it is necessary to prepare configuration files and then make Docker containers with nodes of the necessary blockchain ecosystems. For convenient interaction with clients' remote procedure calls (RPC) in prepared containers and aggregation of their calls, we have implemented a separate microservice [44].

In Fig. 8, we propose a test infrastructure for cryptocurrency gateways. Here, the application under test interacts with the infrastructure through a dedicated input (*Control App* in the figure) via HTTP. This access point is a REST API application that controls pre-created containers with blockchain nodes. The main idea of this API is to make a single transparent interface (a wrapper) to use by the blockchain developer who is interested in working with accounts, completing transactions, obtaining information about them, generating blocks and performing other actions related to cryptocurrencies. For example, the names of methods and parameters of transaction assembling calls in the two ecosystems under consideration are significantly different, so the API abstracts from them and provides a generalized interface. At the same time, all calls are monitored and logged.

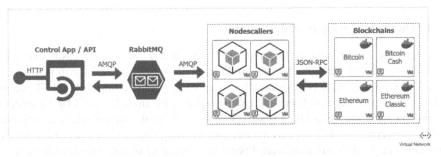

Fig. 8. Infrastructure scheme for the cryptocurrency payment gateways test bench [14].

The REST API is the only entry point that, in addition to making calls, also stores an editable set of scripts (a set of Linux shell commands).

Partial restriction of access is implemented as follows:

– access via the SSH protocol using a password is disabled on the controlled machines, and access is enabled only by the RSA key;

– a private key is generated for the REST API of the application (in fact, this is the private key of the virtual machine on which this service is deployed), which is added to the allowed keys on the controlled machines.

Thus, infrastructure clients do not have the ability to directly connect to infrastructure machines, but they can run predefined sets of scripts using this service.

The following two elements of the system are implemented in order to increase the fault tolerance of the testing stand. In practice, we found that if 4–5 threads are simultaneously using the JSON-RPC protocol to interact with an Ethereum node, then in 90% of cases, the node crashes, which leads, respectively, to the failure of all remaining tests.

So, we came to the use of server queues (implemented with the help of the RabbitMQ message broker) as well as a limited number of consumers. In other words, we created a pool that artificially restricts the threads that operate contemporaneously with blockchain nodes to the number we need. These solutions minimize the risk of system failure and retests.

Elements of the *Nodes callers'* level are simple working server scripts implemented in Javascript. This infrastructure fulfils the classic RPC interaction model using a queue server, described, for example, in tutorial [45]. In our scheme, the workers receive a message, as well as a unique identifier of the queue, to which the response must be returned after interacting with the blockchain on the basis of JSON-RPC.

The last level in the scheme consists of prepared Docker containers with emulated blockchain nodes. For the Ethereum ecosystem, the actual running service there can be a containerized *testrpc* (*ganache-cli*) or a *geth* running with the *dev* parameter. For the Bitcoin ecosystem, the core is a fully independent application (*bitcoind*, *bitcoinabc*, *litecoin*) launched in the discussed *regtest* mode.

4.3   On the Extensibility of the Solution

We can note here that the architecture of our test bench can be quite easily expanded and upgraded. For example, we are thinking about the creation of a web interface at the *Control App* point to provide monitoring and web-configuration abilities. The queue server is not a changeless thing and can be replaced by any other used by a particular development team. Certainly, it is also possible to integrate other blockchains (by providing pre-configured Docker containers and the wrapping API) or even entire private networks of blockchains with several peers for simulating different network behaviors.

We also found out that the presented architecture is quite flexible and can be used not just only in cryptocurrency gateways testing. For example, the Ethereum node access point can be utilized as an HTTP provider for the *web3* library, followed by automatic testing of Ethereum smart contracts using the ideas implemented in [9].

It will also be convenient to assist in developing applications that use the concept of atomic transactions and the *Lightning Network protocol* [46]. The ephemeral nature of containers accomplishes unambiguous testing, which actually was our goal. On the opposite, if there is a need to test some series of historical data, then it is only necessary to mount the container storage into the host OS.

Thanks to the Docker concept, the presented architecture can be deployed using a single server script or the *docker-compose* tool, which makes it possible to very quickly expanding such a test bench to remote server machines or even to cloud infrastructures. Also, within the framework of the resulting architecture, it is relatively easy to practice the continuous integration/continuous deployment (CI/CD) approach [47]. For example, *gitlab-runner* (a Docker container option) can run all containers with their copies and then perform auto-tests, we just need to organize the internal network properly.

4.4   Test Results Using the Bench

At first, we were able to test some real smart contracts. We found out that they had two main weak points: contracts logic could be vulnerable to attacks, or the internal states were broken due to a wrong sequence of client calls.

Next, we tested cryptocurrency gateways and found some specific errors with incorrectly assembling raw Bitcoin transactions (for creating a correct transaction, it is necessary to specify all the previous inputs, outputs, calculate the change, etc., and if we are talking about multisig-addresses [48] here, we should also sign the inputs and outputs correctly).

Also, we found some errors related to asynchronous operations timings, for example, synchronization with mined blocks, so fixes were here to wait for the mining before continue to work further.

In a gateway to the EOS platform, we detected some errors on calculating necessary RAM and CPU prices (it is needed to buy the resources for carrying out transactions, and the price is changeable [49]).

And finally, the testing stand helped us to understand a behavior when a part of a chain is becoming known to *no longer be the longest* [50]. It was necessary to debug how transaction monitors work.

5   Conclusion

In this paper, we browsed existing methods of blockchain platforms testing. We state that automated testing methods of Bitcoin and Ethereum are very advanced and not much different from other applications of such a class. We created graphical representations of a test that can be used in the training or technology understanding process.

The presented wrapper-based and Docker-oriented architecture of the test stand for cryptocurrency gateways testing successfully showed itself in some real blockchain applications related to assembling the transactions. It can be applied not only for testing payment gateways but also for testing callback functions of various services and for assistance in developing new applications. The bench made it possible to detect and eliminate some serious errors in blockchain applications, as well as to reveal vulnerabilities caused by unpredictable blockchain network behavior. That sort of errors is not possible to detect by manual testing.

For further work, we plan to continue to analyze testing techniques in this field, develop a quality improvement plan, apply DevOps techniques and integrate formal verification and model-based methods into the development process of enterprise blockchain applications.

References

1. Staroletov, S.: Basics of Software Testing and Verification (Osnovy testirovanija i verifikacii programmnogo obespechenija). Lanbook, St. Petersburg, Russia (2018). (in Russian). https://e.lanbook.com/book/138181. Accessed 03 Sep 2021
2. Turing, A.M.: On computable numbers, with an application to the Entscheidungsproblem. Proc. London Math. Soc. **2**(1), 230–265 (1937)
3. Finkelsteiin, A., Kramer, J.: Software engineering: a roadmap. In: Proceedings of the Conference on the Future of Software Engineering ICSE 2000, pp. 3–22. Association for Computing Machinery, New York (2000)
4. Shan, L., Sangchoolie, B., Folkesson, P., Vinter, J., Schoitsch, E., Loiseaux, C.: A survey on the applicability of safety, security and privacy standards in developing dependable systems. In: Romanovsky, A., Troubitsyna, E., Gashi, I., Schoitsch, E., Bitsch, F. (eds.) SAFECOMP 2019. LNCS, vol. 11699, pp. 74–86. Springer, Cham (2019). https://doi.org/10.1007/978-3-030-26250-1_6
5. Zakeriyan, A., Khosravi, R., Safari, H., Khamespanah, E.: Towards automatic test case generation for industrial software systems based on functional specifications. In: Hojjat, H., Massink, M. (eds.) Fundamentals of Software Engineering, pp. 142–156. IPM, Tehran (2021). https://cs.rit.edu/~hh/fsen.pdf. Accessed 21 Aug 2021
6. Peck, M.E.: Blockchain world-do you need a blockchain? This chart will tell you if the technology can solve your problem. IEEE Spectr. **54**(10), 38–60 (2017)
7. Raval, S.: Decentralized Applications: Harnessing Bitcoin's Blockchain Technology. O'Reilly Media, Sebastopol (2016)
8. Wang, W., Hoang, D.T., Hu, P., Xiong, Z., Niyato, D., Wang, P., et al.: A survey on consensus mechanisms and mining strategy management in blockchain networks. IEEE Access **7**, 22328–22370 (2019)
9. Medium.com: Smart Contract Testing & Ethereum Simulator (2017). https://medium.com/etherereum-salon/eth-testing-472c2f73b4c3. Accessed 21 Aug 2021
10. Wood, G.: Ethereum: A secure decentralized generalized transaction ledger. Ethereum project yellow paper (2017). https://gavwood.com/paper.pdf. Accessed 21 Aug 2021
11. Beck, K., Gamma, E.: Test infected: programmers love writing tests. Java Rep. **3**(7), 37–50 (1998)
12. Kukharenko, V.A., Ziborov, K.V., Sadykov, R.F., Naumchev, A.V., Rezin, R.M., Merkin-Janson, L.A.: Innochain: a distributed ledger for industry with formal verification on all implementation levels. Model. Anal. Inf. Syst. **27**(4), 454–471 (2020)
13. Galkin, R.: Blockchain applications testing and verification technology. Master's thesis, Altai State Technical University, Barnaul, Russia (2018). (in Russian). http://elib.altstu.ru/diploma/download_vkr/id/127409. Accessed 21 Aug 2021
14. Galkin, R., Staroletov, S.: Cryptocurrency gateway testing technology (Tehnologija testirovanija kriptovaljutnyh shljuzov). In: All-Russian Scientific and Practical Youth Conference "Software and Hardware for Automated Systems". Altai State Technical University, Barnaul, Russia (2018). (in Russian). https://www.elibrary.ru/item.asp?id=37414945. Accessed 21 Aug 2021
15. Bitcointalk.org: Proof of stake instead of proof of work. https://bitcointalk.org/index.php?topic=27787.0. Accessed 21 Aug 2021
16. Bastiaan, M.: Preventing the 51%-attack: a stochastic analysis of two phase proof of work in Bitcoin. In: Proceedings of 22nd Twente Student Conference on IT, 23 January 2015, Enschede, The Netherlands (2015). https://fmt.ewi.utwente.nl/media/175.pdf. Accessed 21 Aug 2021

17. Bitcoin.org: Bitcoin Developer Examples. https://bitcoin.org/en/developer-examples. Accessed 21 Aug 2021
18. Trufflesuite: Fast Ethereum RPC client for testing and development. https://github.com/truffl esuite/ganache-cli. Accessed 21 Aug 2021
19. Tyurin, A.V., Tyulyandin, I.V., Maltsev, V.S., Kirilenko, I.A., Berezun, D.A.: Overview of the languages for safe smart contract programming. Proc. ISP RAS **31**(3), 157–176 (2019)
20. Bitcoin.org: Bitcoin Test. https://github.com/bitcoin/bitcoin/tree/master/test. Accessed 21 Aug 2021
21. Bitcoin.it: Segregated Witness. https://en.bitcoin.it/wiki/Segregated_Witness. Accessed 21 Aug 2021
22. Brakmic, H.: Bitcoin script. In: Bitcoin and Lightning Network on Raspberry Pi, pp. 201–224. Apress, Troisdorf (2019)
23. Veanes, M., Campbell, C., Grieskamp, W., Schulte, W., Tillmann, N., Nachmanson, L.: Model-based testing of object-oriented reactive systems with Spec Explorer. In: Hierons, R.M., Bowen, J.P., Harman, M. (eds.) Formal Methods and Testing. LNCS, vol. 4949, pp. 39–76. Springer, Heidelberg (2008). https://doi.org/10.1007/978-3-540-78917-8_2
24. Baier, C., Katoen, J.P.: Principles of Model Checking. MIT Press, Cambridge (2008)
25. Bitcoin.it: Script. https://en.bitcoin.it/wiki/Script. Accessed 21 Aug 2021
26. Community: Ethereum Tests. https://ethereum-tests.readthedocs.io/en/latest/test_types/blo ckchain_tests.html. Accessed 21 Aug 2021
27. Brickwood, D.: Understanding Trie Databases in Ethereum. https://medium.com/shyft-network-media/understanding-trie-databases-in-ethereum-9f03d2c3325d. Accessed 21 Aug 2021
28. Ethereum: ethash. https://github.com/ethereum/ethash/blob/master/test/c/test.cpp. Accessed 21 Aug 2021
29. Ethereum-mining: Ethminer is an Ethash GPU mining worker (2019). https://github.com/eth ereum-mining/ethminer. Accessed 21 Aug 2021
30. Serebryany, K.: OSS-Fuzz-Google's Continuous Fuzzing service for open source software. USENIX, Vancouver, BC, Canada (2017)
31. Ethereum: Ethereum/solidity. yulProto.proto. https://github.com/ethereum/solidity/blob/dev elop/test/tools/ossfuzz/yulProto.proto. Accessed 21 Aug 2021
32. de Moura, L., Bjørner, N.: Z3: an efficient SMT solver. In: Ramakrishnan, C.R., Rehof, J. (eds.) TACAS 2008. LNCS, vol. 4963, pp. 337–340. Springer, Heidelberg (2008). https://doi. org/10.1007/978-3-540-78800-3_24
33. Ethereum.org: JSON RPC. Ethereum/wiki (2020). https://github.com/ethereum/wiki/wiki/ JSON-RPC. Accessed 21 Aug 2021
34. Ethereum.org: Remix, an Ethereum IDE. http://remix.ethereum.org. Accessed 21 Aug 2021
35. Shishkin, E.: Debugging smart contract's business logic using symbolic model checking. Program. Comput. Softw. **45**(8), 590–599 (2019)
36. Luu, L., Chu, D.H., Olickel, H., Saxena, P., Hobor, A.: Making smart contracts smarter. In: Proceedings of the 2016 ACM SIGSAC Conference on Computer and Communications Security, pp. 254–269. ACM, New York (2016)
37. Hirai, Y.: Defining the Ethereum virtual machine for interactive theorem provers. In: Brenner, M., et al. (eds.) FC 2017. LNCS, vol. 10323, pp. 520–535. Springer, Cham (2017). https:// doi.org/10.1007/978-3-319-70278-0_33
38. Etherscan.io: Contracts with verified source codes only. https://etherscan.io/contractsVerified. Accessed 21 Aug 2021
39. Nakamoto, S.: Bitcoin: A peer-to-peer electronic cash system. https://bitcoin.org/bitcoin.pdf. Accessed 21 Aug 2021
40. Mouat, A.: Using Docker: Developing and Deploying Software with Containers. O'Reilly Media, Sebastopol (2015)

41. Vinoski, S.: Advanced message queuing protocol. IEEE Internet Comput. **10**(6), 87–89 (2006)
42. Armstrong, J.: Erlang. Commun. ACM **53**(9), 68–75 (2010)
43. Rostanski, M., Seman, A.: Evaluation of highly available and fault-tolerant middleware clustered architectures using RabbitMQ. In: 2014 Federated Conference on Computer Science and Information Systems, Warsaw, Poland, 7–10 2014, pp. 879–884 (2014)
44. Fowler, M., Lewis, J.: Microservices. http://martinfowler.com/articles/microservices.html. Accessed 21 Aug 2021
45. RabbitMQ: Remote procedure call (RPC) (using the amqp.node client). https://www.rabbitmq.com/tutorials/tutorial-six-javascript.html. Accessed 21 Aug 2021
46. Poon, J., Dryja, T.: The Bitcoin Lightning network: Scalable off-chain instant payments. https://www.bitcoinlightning.com/wp-content/uploads/2018/03/lightning-network-paper.pdf. Accessed 21 Aug 2021
47. Humble, J., Farley, D.: Continuous Delivery: Reliable Software Releases Through Build, Test, and Deployment Automation. Pearson Education, Crawfordsville (2010)
48. Buterin, V.: Bitcoin Multisig Wallet: The Future of Bitcoin. Bitcoin Magazine (2014). https://bitcoinmagazine.com/articles/multisig-future-bitcoin-1394686504. Accessed 21 Aug 2021
49. Xu, B., Luthta, D., Cole, Z., Blakey, N.: EOS: An Architectural, Performance, and Economic Analysis. https://blog.bitmex.com/wp-content/uploads/2018/11/eos-test-report.pdf. Accessed 21 Aug 2021
50. Bitcoin.it: Bitcoin Wiki. Orphan Block. https://en.bitcoin.it/wiki/Orphan_Block. Accessed 21 Aug 2021

Author Index

Printed in the United States
by Baker & Taylor Publisher Services